Beginning iPhone 4 Development

Exploring the iOS SDK

Dave Mark
Jack Nutting
Jeff LaMarche

Apress®

Beginning iPhone 4 Development: Exploring the iOS SDK

ISBN-13 (pbk): 978-1-4302-3024-3

ISBN-13 (electronic): 978-1-4302-3025-0

Printed and bound in the United States of America 9 8 7 6 5 4 3 2 1

Trademarked names may appear in this book. Rather than use a trademark symbol with every occurrence of a trademarked name, we use the names only in an editorial fashion and to the benefit of the trademark owner, with no intention of infringement of the trademark.

President and Publisher: Paul Manning
Lead Editor: Steve Anglin
Developmental Editor: Tom Welsh
Technical Reviewer: Mark Dalrymple
Editorial Board: Steve Anglin, Mark Beckner, Ewan Buckingham, Gary Cornell, Jonathan Gennick, Jonathan Hassell, Michelle Lowman, Matthew Moodie, Jeffrey Pepper, Douglas Pundick, Ben Renow-Clarke, Dominic Shakeshaft, Matt Wade, Tom Welsh
Coordinating Editor: Kelly Moritz
Copy Editors: Marilyn Smith and Kim Wimpsett
Compositor: MacPS, LLC
Indexer: Brenda Miller
Artist: April Milne
Cover Designer: Anna Ishchenko

Distributed to the book trade worldwide by Springer Science+Business Media, LLC., 233 Spring Street, 6th Floor, New York, NY 10013. Phone 1-800-SPRINGER, fax 201-348-4505, e-mail orders-ny@springer-sbm.com, or visit www.springeronline.com.

For information on translations, please e-mail rights@apress.com, or visit www.apress.com.

Apress and friends of ED books may be purchased in bulk for academic, corporate, or promotional use. eBook versions and licenses are also available for most titles. For more information, reference our Special Bulk Sales–eBook Licensing web page at www.apress.com/info/bulksales.

The information in this book is distributed on an "as is" basis, without warranty. Although every precaution has been taken in the preparation of this work, neither the author(s) nor Apress shall have any liability to any person or entity with respect to any loss or damage caused or alleged to be caused directly or indirectly by the information contained in this work.

The source code for this book is available to readers at www.apress.com.

To Deneen, Daniel, Kelley, and Ryan, LFU4FRNMWWA…
—Dave

To Weronica, Henrietta, and Dorotea.
—Jack

To the most important people in my life, my wife and kids.
—Jeff

Contents at a Glance

Contents

About the Authors

 **Dave Mark** is a longtime Mac developer and author, who has written a number of books on Mac and iOS development, including *Beginning iPhone 3 Development* (Apress, 2009), *More iPhone 3 Development* (Apress, 2010), *Learn C on the Mac* (Apress, 2008), *The Macintosh Programming Primer* series (Addison-Wesley, 1992), and *Ultimate Mac Programming* (Wiley, 1995). Dave is a principal at MartianCraft, an iOS and Android development house. Dave loves the water and spends as much time as possible on it, in it, or near it. He lives with his wife and three children in Virginia.

 **Jack Nutting** has been using Cocoa since the olden days, long before it was even called Cocoa. He has used Cocoa and its predecessors to develop software for a wide range of industries and applications, including gaming, graphic design, online digital distribution, telecommunications, finance, publishing, and travel. When he is not working on Mac or iOS projects, he is developing web applications with Ruby on Rails. Jack is a passionate proponent of Objective-C and the Cocoa frameworks. At the drop of a hat, he will speak at length on the virtues of dynamic dispatch and runtime class manipulations to anyone who will listen (and even to some who won't). Jack is the primary author of *Learn Cocoa on the Mac* (Apress, 2010) and *Beginning iPad Development for iPhone Developers (*Apress, 2010). He blogs from time to time at http://www.nuthole.com.

 **Jeff LaMarche** is a Mac and iOS developer with more than 20 years of programming experience. Jeff has written a number of iOS and Mac development books, including *Beginning iPhone 3 Development* (Apress, 2009), *More iPhone 3 Development* (Apress, 2010), and *Learn Cocoa on the Mac* (Apress, 2010). Jeff is a principal at MartianCraft, an iOS and Android development house. He has written about Cocoa and Objective-C for *MacTech Magazine*, as well as articles for Apple's developer web site. Jeff also writes about iOS development for his widely read blog at http://iphonedevelopment.blogspot.com.

About the Technical Reviewer

 **Mark Dalrymple** is a longtime Mac and Unix programmer, working on cross-platform toolkits, Internet publishing tools, high-performance web servers, and end-user desktop applications. He is also the principal author of *Advanced Mac OS X Programming* (Big Nerd Ranch, 2005) and *Learn Objective-C on the Mac* (Apress, 2009). In his spare time, Mark plays trombone and bassoon, and makes balloon animals.

Acknowledgments

This book could not have been written without our mighty, kind, and clever families, friends, and cohorts. First and foremost, eternal thanks to Terry, Weronica, and Deneen for putting up with us, and for keeping the rest of the universe at bay while we toiled away on this book. This project saw us tucked away in our writers' cubby for many long hours, and somehow, you didn't complain once. We are lucky men.

This book could not have been written without the fine folks at Apress. Clay Andres brought us to Apress in the first place and carried this book on his back. Dominic Shakeshaft was the gracious mastermind who dealt with all of our complaints with a smile on his face, and somehow found solutions that made sense and made this book better. Kelly Moritz, our wonderful and gracious coordinating editor, was the irresistible force to our slowly movable object. Tom Welsh, our developmental editor, helped us with some terrific feedback along the way. They kept the book on the right track and always pointed in the right direction. Marilyn Smith and Kim Wimpsett, copy editors *extraordinaire*, you were both such a pleasure to work with! Jeffrey Pepper, Frank McGuckin, Brigid Duffy, and the Apress production team took all these pieces and somehow made them whole. Leo Cuellar, Dylan Wooters, and Jeff Stonefield assembled the marketing message and got it out to the world. To all the folks at Apress, thank you, thank you, thank you!

A very special shout-out to our incredibly talented technical reviewer, Mark Dalrymple. In addition to providing insightful feedback, Mark tested all the code in this book, and he helped keep us on the straight and narrow. Thanks, Mark!

Finally, thanks to our children for their patience while their dads were working so hard. This book is for you, Maddie, Gwynnie, Ian, Kai, Henrietta, Dorotea, Daniel, Kelley, and Ryan.

Preface

The preface to the previous edition of this book, *Beginning iPhone 3 Development*, started with the phrase, "What an amazing journey!" Well, it's true. We're having a blast, making a lot of new friends, and above all, learning, learning, learning. The iOS SDK continues to evolve, and with each new release, it brings new concepts to explore and new design patterns to master.

So, what's new with this edition? A lot! For starters, we've gone through every single line of code and made whatever changes were necessary to bring each project into line with the latest version of iOS and the latest released SDK. All the projects were created with Xcode 3.2.5, the newest release version of Xcode. As you would expect, we've gone through the text, too, so the explanations are all up to date.

Is it worth buying this book if you already own an earlier edition? That is an excellent question. We've made a lot of minor tweaks throughout the book, but we've also made many major changes. We've added two new chapters: one on programming for iPad, and a second on threading and background processing. Both of these chapters feature all new code and are designed with iOS 4 in mind.

In short, we've definitely made the book a lot better. If you've already been through the previous edition and feel very comfortable with all the material, go ahead and move on to *More iPhone 4 Development*, which we're working on as this book goes to press.

If you haven't made it through the entire first or second edition yet, if you feel a bit fuzzy still, or if you just want to help us out as authors, then by all means, pick up this third edition. We do appreciate your support. Be sure to check out `http://iphonedevbook.com`, and drop us a line to let us know about your amazing new apps. We look forward to seeing you on the forum. Happy coding!

Dave, Jack, and Jeff

Chapter 1

Welcome to the Jungle

So, you want to write iPhone, iPod touch, and iPad applications? Well, we can't say that we blame you. iOS, the core software of all of these devices, might just be the most interesting new platform to come around in a long time. Certainly, it is the most interesting mobile platform to date, especially now that Apple has provided a set of elegant, well-documented tools for developing iOS applications. And with the release of version 4 of the iOS software development kit (SDK), things have only gotten better.

What This Book Is

This book is a guide to help you get started down the path to creating your own iOS applications. Our goal is to get you past the initial learning curve to help you understand the way iOS applications work and how they are built. As you work your way through this book, you will create a number of small applications, each designed to highlight specific iOS features and show you how to control or interact with those features. If you combine the foundation you'll gain by making your way through this book with your own creativity and determination, and then add in the extensive and well-written documentation provided by Apple, you'll have everything you need to build your own professional iPhone and iPad applications.

> **TIP:** Dave, Jack, and Jeff have a forum set up for this book. It's a great place to meet like-minded folks, get your questions answered, and even answer other people's questions. It's at `http://iphonedevbook.com/forum`. Be sure to check it out!

What You Need

Before you can begin writing software for iOS, you'll need a few things. For starters, you'll need an Intel-based Macintosh running Snow Leopard (OS X 10.6.5 or later). Any recent Intel-based Macintosh computer—laptop or desktop—should work just fine.

You'll also need to sign up to become a registered iOS developer. Apple requires this step before you're allowed to download the iOS SDK.

To sign up, navigate to `http://developer.apple.com/ios/`, which will bring you to a page similar to the one shown in Figure 1–1.

Figure 1–1. *Apple's iOS Dev Center web site*

First, click the button labeled *Log in*. You'll be prompted for your *Apple ID*. If you don't have an Apple ID, click the *Create Apple ID* button, create one, and then log in. Once you are logged in, you'll be taken to the main iOS development page. Not only will you see a link to the SDK download, but you'll also find links to a wealth of documentation, videos, sample code, and the like—all dedicated to teaching you the finer points of iOS application development.

One of the most important downloads on this page is **Xcode**, Apple's integrated development environment (IDE). Xcode includes tools for creating and debugging source code, compiling applications, and performance tuning the applications you've written. By the time you are finished with this book, you will become an Xcode aficionado!

SDK VERSIONS AND SOURCE CODE FOR THE EXAMPLES

As the versions of the SDK and Xcode evolve, the mechanism for downloading them will also change. Sometimes the SDK and Xcode are featured as separate downloads; other times, they will be merged as a single download. Bottom line: you want to download the latest released (nonbeta) version of the SDK and Xcode.

This book has been written to work with the latest version of the SDK. In some places, we have chosen to use new functions or methods introduced with version 4 that may prove incompatible with earlier versions of the SDK. We'll be sure to point those situations out as they arise in this book.

Be sure to download the latest and greatest source code archives from the book's web site at `http://iphonedevbook.com`.

We'll update the code as new versions of the SDK are released, so be sure to check the site periodically.

Developer Options

The free SDK download option includes a simulator that will allow you to build and run iPhone and iPad apps on your Mac. This is perfect for learning how to program for iOS. However, the simulator does *not* support hardware-dependent features, such as the iPhone's accelerometer or camera. Also, the free option will not allow you to download your applications onto your actual iPhone or other device. And it does not give you the ability to distribute your applications on Apple's App Store. For those capabilities, you'll need to sign up for one of the other options, which aren't free:

> The Standard program costs $99/year. It provides a host of development tools and resources, technical support, distribution of your application via Apple's App Store, and, most important, the ability to test and debug your code on an iOS device, rather than just in the simulator.

> The Enterprise program costs $299/year. It is designed for companies developing proprietary, in-house iOS applications and for those developing applications for the Apple's App Store, and with more than one developer working on the project.

For more details on these programs, visit `http://developer.apple.com/programs/ios` and `http://developer.apple.com/programs/ios/enterprise` to compare the two.

Because iOS supports an always-connected mobile device that uses other companies' wireless infrastructure, Apple has needed to place far more restrictions on iOS developers than it ever has on Mac developers (who are able—at least as of this writing—to write and distribute programs with absolutely no oversight or approval from Apple). Even though the iPod touch and the Wi-Fi–only versions of the iPad don't use anyone else's infrastructure, they're still subject to these same restrictions.

Apple has not added restrictions to be mean, but rather as an attempt to minimize the chances of malicious or poorly written programs being distributed that could degrade performance on the shared network. Developing for iOS may seem like it presents a lot of hoops to jump through, but Apple has expended quite an effort to make the process as painless as possible. And also consider that $99 is still considerably less than buying, for example, Visual Studio, which is Microsoft's software development IDE.

This may seem obvious, but you'll also need an iPhone, iPod touch, or iPad. While much of your code can be tested using the iOS simulator, not all programs can be. And even those that can run on the simulator really need to be thoroughly tested on an actual device before you ever consider releasing your application to the public.

> **NOTE:** If you are going to sign up for the Standard or Enterprise program, you should go do it right now. The approval process can take a while, and you'll need that approval to be able to run your applications on an actual device. Don't worry, though, because all the projects in the first several chapters and the majority of the applications in this book will run just fine on the iOS simulator.

What You Need to Know

This book assumes that you already have some programming knowledge. It assumes that you understand the fundamentals of object-oriented programming (you know what objects, loops, and variables are, for example). It also assumes you are familiar with the Objective-C programming language. Cocoa Touch, the part of the SDK that you will be using through most of this book, uses Objective-C 2.0. But don't worry if you're not familiar with the more recent additions to the Objective-C language. We highlight any of the 2.0 language features we take advantage of, and explain how they work and why we are using them.

You should also be familiar with iOS itself, as a user. Just as you would with any platform for which you wanted to write an application, get to know the iPhone, iPad, or iPod touch's nuances and quirks. Take the time to get familiar with the iOS interface and with the way Apple's iPhone and/or iPad applications look and feel.

NEW TO OBJECTIVE-C?

If you have not programmed in Objective-C before, here are a few resources to help you get started:

Check out *Learn Objective-C on the Mac*, an excellent and approachable introduction to Objective-C by Mac programming experts Mark Dalrymple and Scott Knaster (Apress, 2009):

`http://www.apress.com/book/view/9781430218159`

See Apple's introduction to the language, *Learning Objective-C: A Primer*:

`http://developer.apple.com/library/ios/#referencelibrary/`
`GettingStarted/Learning_Objective-C_A_Primer`

Take a look at *The Objective-C Programming Language*, a very detailed and extensive description of the language and a great reference guide:

`http://developer.apple.com/library/ios/#documentation/Cocoa/`
`Conceptual/ObjectiveC`

That last one is also available as a free download from iBooks on your iPhone, iPod touch, or iPad. Perfect for reading on the go! Apple has released several developer titles in this format, and we hope that more are on the way. Search for "apple developer publications" in iBooks to find them.

What's Different About Coding for iOS?

If you have never used Cocoa or its predecessors NeXTSTEP and OpenStep, you may find Cocoa Touch, the application framework you'll be using to write iOS applications, a little alien. It has some fundamental differences from other common application frameworks, such as those used when building .NET or Java applications. Don't worry too much if you feel a little lost at first. Just keep plugging away at the exercises, and it will all start to fall into place after a while.

If you have written programs using Cocoa or NeXTSTEP, a lot in the iOS SDK will be familiar to you. A great many classes are unchanged from the versions that are used to develop for Mac OS X. Even those that are different tend to follow the same basic principles and use design patterns similar to the ones in the previous version. However, several differences exist between Cocoa and Cocoa Touch.

Regardless of your background, you need to keep in mind some key differences between iOS development and desktop application development.

Only One Active Application

On iOS, only one application can be active and displayed on the screen at any given time. Starting with iOS 4, applications can sometimes continue to run in the background after the user presses the home button, but even that is limited to particular usages and situations.

When your application isn't active or running in the background, it doesn't receive any attention from the CPU whatsoever, which will wreak havoc with open network connections and the like. iOS 4 makes great strides forward in allowing background processing, but making your apps play nicely in this situation will require some effort on your part.

Only One Window

Desktop and laptop operating systems allow many running programs to coexist, each with the ability to create and control multiple windows. However, iOS gives your application just one "window" to work with. All of your application's interaction with the user takes place inside this one window, and its size is fixed at the size of the screen.

Limited Access

Programs on a computer pretty much have access to everything the user who launched them does. However, iOS seriously restricts what your application can get to.

You can read and write files only from the part of iOS's file system that was created for your application. This area is called your application's **sandbox**. Your sandbox is where your application will store documents, preferences, and every other kind of data it may need to store.

Your application is also constrained in some other ways. You will not be able to access low-number network ports on iOS, for example, or do anything else that would typically require root or administrative access on a desktop computer.

Limited Response Time

Because of the way it is used, iOS needs to be snappy, and it expects the same of your application. When your program is launched, you need to get your application open, preferences and data loaded, and the main view shown on the screen as fast as possible—in no more than a few seconds.

At any time when your program is running, it may have the rug pulled out from under it. If the user presses the home button, iOS goes home, and you must quickly save everything and quit. If you take longer than five seconds to save and give up control, your application process will be killed, regardless of whether you are finished saving.

Note that in iOS 4, this situation is ameliorated somewhat by the existence of a new API that allows your app to ask for additional time to work when it's about to go dark.

Limited Screen Size

The iPhone's screen is really nice. When introduced, it was the highest-resolution screen available on a consumer device, by far.

But the iPhone display just isn't all that big, and as a result, you have a lot less room to work with than on modern computers. The screen is just 640 × 960 on the latest Retina display devices (iPhone 4, and fourth-generation iPod touch) and 320 × 480 pixels on older devices. And that 640 × 960 Retina display is crammed into the same old form factor, so you can't count on fitting more controls or anything like that—they will all just be higher resolution than before.

The iPad increases things a bit by offering a 1024 × 768 display, but even today, that's not so terribly large. To give an interesting contrast, at the time of this writing, Apple's least expensive iMac supports 1920 × 1080 pixels, and its least expensive notebook computer, the MacBook, supports 1280 × 800 pixels. On the other end of the spectrum, Apple's largest current monitor, the 27-inch LED Cinema Display, offers a whopping 2560 × 1440 pixels.

Limited System Resources

Any old-time programmers who are reading this are likely laughing at the idea of a machine with at least 256MB of RAM and 8GB of storage being in any way resource-constrained, but it is true. Developing for iOS is not, perhaps, in exactly the same league as trying to write a complex spreadsheet application on a machine with 48KB of memory. But given the graphical nature of iOS and all the things it is capable of doing, running out of memory is very, very easy.

The iOS devices available right now all have either 256MB or 512MB of physical RAM, though that will likely increase over time. Some of that memory is used for the screen buffer and by other system processes. Usually, no more than half of that memory is left for your application to use, and the amount can be considerably less.

Although that may sound like it leaves a pretty decent amount of memory for such a small computer, there is another factor to consider when it comes to memory on iOS. Modern computer operating systems like Mac OS X will take chunks of memory that aren't being used and write them out to disk in something called a **swap file**. The swap file allows applications to keep running, even when they have requested more memory than is actually available on the computer. iOS, however, will not write volatile memory, such as application data, out to a swap file. As a result, the amount of memory available to your application is constrained by the amount of unused physical memory in the iOS device.

Cocoa Touch has built-in mechanisms for letting your application know that memory is getting low. When that happens, your application must free up unneeded memory or risk being forced to quit.

No Garbage Collection

We mentioned earlier that Cocoa Touch uses Objective-C 2.0, but one of the key new features of that language is not available with iOS: Cocoa Touch does not support garbage collection.

Some New Stuff

Since we've mentioned that Cocoa Touch is missing some features that Cocoa has, it seems only fair to mention that the iOS SDK contains some functionality that is not currently present in Cocoa or, at least, is not available on every Mac:

> The iOS SDK provides a way for your application to determine the iOS device's current geographic coordinates using Core Location.

> Most iOS devices have built-in cameras and photo libraries, and the SDK provides mechanisms that allow your application to access both.

> iOS devices have a built-in accelerometer (and, in the latest iPhone and iPod touch, a gyroscope) that lets you detect how your device is being held and moved.

A Different Approach

Two things iOS devices don't have are a physical keyboard and a mouse, which means you have a fundamentally different way of interacting with the user than you do when programming for a general-purpose computer. Fortunately, most of that interaction is handled for you. For example, if you add a text field to your application, iOS knows to bring up a keyboard when the user clicks in that field, without you needing to write any extra code.

> **NOTE:** Current devices do allow you to connect an external keyboard via Bluetooth, which gives you a nice keyboard experience and saves some screen real estate, but this is still a fairly rare usage. Connecting a mouse is still not an option at all.

What's in This Book

Here is a very brief overview of the remaining chapters in this book:

In Chapter 2, you'll learn how to use Xcode's partner in crime, Interface Builder, to create a simple interface, placing some text on the screen.

In Chapter 3, you'll start interacting with the user, building a simple application that dynamically updates displayed text at runtime based on buttons the user presses.

Chapter 4 will build on Chapter 3 by introducing you to several more of iOS's standard user interface controls. We'll also look at how to use alerts and action sheets to prompt users to make a decision or to inform them that something out of the ordinary has occurred.

In Chapter 5, we'll look at handling autorotation and autosize attributes, the mechanisms that allow iOS applications to be used in both portrait and landscape modes.

In Chapter 6, we'll move into more advanced user interfaces and look at creating applications that support multiple views. We'll show you how to change which view is being shown to the user at runtime, which will greatly enhance the potential of your apps.

Tab bars and pickers are part of the standard iOS user interface. In Chapter 7, we'll look at how to implement these interface elements.

In Chapter 8, we'll look at table views, the primary way of providing lists of data to the user and the foundation of hierarchical navigation-based applications. We'll also see how to let the user search in your application data.

One of the most common iOS application interfaces is the hierarchical list that lets you drill down to see more data or more details. In Chapter 9, you'll learn what's involved in implementing this standard type of interface.

The iPad, with its different form factor from the other iOS devices, requires a different approach to displaying a GUI and provides some components to help make that happen. In Chapter 10, we'll show you how to use the iPad-specific parts of the SDK.

In Chapter 11, we'll look at implementing application settings, which is iOS's mechanism for letting users set their application-level preferences.

Chapter 12 looks at data management on iOS. We'll talk about creating objects to hold application data and see how that data can be persisted to iOS's file system. We'll also cover the basics of using Core Data, which allows you to save and retrieve data easily.

Starting with iOS 4, developers have access to a new approach to multithreaded development using Grand Central Dispatch, and also have the ability to make their apps run in the background in certain circumstances. In Chapter 13, we'll show you how it's done.

Everyone loves to draw, so we'll look at doing some custom drawing in Chapter 14. We'll use basic drawing functions in Quartz 2D and OpenGL ES.

The multitouch screen common to all iOS devices can accept a wide variety of gestural inputs from the user. In Chapter 15, you'll learn all about detecting basic gestures, such as the pinch and swipe. We'll also look at the process of defining new gestures and talk about when new gestures are appropriate.

iOS is capable of determining its latitude and longitude thanks to Core Location. In Chapter 16, we'll build some code that makes use of Core Location to figure out where in the world your device is and use that information in our quest for world dominance.

In Chapter 17, we'll look at interfacing with iOS's accelerometer and gyroscope, which is how your device knows which way it's being held and the speed and direction in which it is moving. We'll look at some of the fun things your application can do with that information.

Nearly every iOS device has a camera and a library of pictures, both of which are available to your application, if you ask nicely! In Chapter 18, we'll show you how to ask nicely.

iOS devices are currently available in more than 90 countries. In Chapter 19, we'll show you how to write your applications in such a way that all parts can be easily translated into other languages. This helps expand the potential audience for your applications.

By the end of this book, you'll have mastered the fundamental building blocks for creating iPhone and iPad applications. But where do you go from here? In Chapter 20, we'll explore the logical next steps for you to take on your journey to master the iOS SDK.

What's New in This Update?

Since the first edition of this book hit the bookstores, the growth of the iOS development community has been phenomenal. The SDK has continually evolved, with Apple releasing a steady stream of SDK updates.

Well, we've been busy, too! The second we found out about iOS SDK 4, we immediately went to work, updating every single project to ensure not only that the code for each one compiles using the latest release versions of Xcode and the SDK, but also that each one takes advantage of the latest and greatest features offered by Cocoa Touch. We made a ton of subtle changes throughout the book, and added a good amount of substantive changes as well, both to the code and to the explanations. We added a new chapter on threading and multitasking, and another on programming for iPad. And, of course, we reshot every single screen shown in the book.

Are You Ready?

iOS is an incredible computing platform and an exciting new frontier for your development pleasure. Programming for iOS is going to be a new experience—different from working on any other platform. For everything that looks familiar, there will be something alien, but as you work through the book's code, the concepts should all come together and start to make sense.

Keep in mind that the exercises in this book are not simply a checklist that, when completed, magically grants you iOS developer guru status. Make sure you understand what you did and why before moving on to the next project. Don't be afraid to make changes to the code. Observing the results of your experimentation is one of the best ways you can wrap your head around the complexities of coding in an environment like Cocoa Touch.

That said, if you have your iOS SDK installed, turn the page. If not, get to it! Got it? Good. Then let's go!

Appeasing the Tiki Gods

As you're probably well aware, it has become something of a tradition to call the first project in any book on programming "Hello, World!" We considered breaking this tradition but were scared that the tiki gods would inflict some painful retribution on us for such a gross breach of etiquette. So, let's do it by the book, shall we?

In this chapter, we're going use Xcode and Interface Builder to create a small iOS application to display the text "Hello, World!" on the screen of a simulated iOS device. We'll look at what's involved in creating an iOS application project in Xcode, work through the specifics of using Interface Builder to design our application's user interface, and then run our application on the iOS simulator. After that, we'll give our application an icon and a unique identifier to make it feel more like a real iOS application.

We've got a lot to do here, so let's get going.

Setting Up Your Project in Xcode

By now, you should have Xcode and the iOS SDK installed on your machine. You should also download the book projects archive from the book web site. Here's a link:

```
http://www.iphonedevbook.com/forum/
```

The book forums are a great place to download the latest book source code, get your questions answered, and meet up with like-minded people. Of course, you can also find the source code on the Apress web site:

```
http://www.apress.com
```

NOTE: Even though you have the complete set of project files at your disposal in the book project archive, we think you'll get more out of the book if you create each project by hand, rather than simply running the version you downloaded. That way, you'll gain familiarity and expertise working with the various tools as you roll your own projects. There's just no substitute for actually clicking and dragging out interface elements and scrolling through source code to make changes as we move from one version of a program to another.

Our first project is in the *02 - Hello World* folder. If you'll be creating your own projects, create a new folder to hold all of your book projects. As you follow along in the book, save all your new projects in that master folder.

Now launch Xcode, which is located in */Developer/Applications*. Put more plainly, you'll find a folder named *Developer* at the top level of your hard drive. Within that folder is a folder named *Applications*, and within that folder is an application named *Xcode.app*. Before you launch Xcode, consider dragging its icon to the dock. In the same folder, you'll find a program named *Interface Builder.app*. Drag its icon to the dock as well. You'll be using both of these programs throughout the book.

If this is your first time using Xcode, don't worry; we'll walk you through the process of creating a new project. If you're already an old hand, just skim ahead.

When you first launch Xcode, you'll be presented with a welcome window like the one shown in Figure 2–1. From here, you can choose to create a new project, dig into a *Getting started with Xcode* tutorial, and jump to the Apple Developer Connection web site. You can also jump directly to any recent projects you may have created from the list shown on the right side of the window. If this is your first project, that list will be empty.

TIP: Consider taking a moment to click over to the Apple Developer Connection web site and taking a look at the iOS developer program. If you plan on building apps and selling them on the App Store, you'll definitely need to join this program. Since membership in this program can take some time to get approved, it might be worth your while applying now. Hopefully, by the time you finish this book, your membership will be approved.

If you'd rather not see the welcome window each time Xcode launches, just uncheck the *Show this window when Xcode launches* checkbox before closing it. If you feel like poking through the information here for a few minutes, by all means, go right ahead. When you're done, close the window, and we'll proceed.

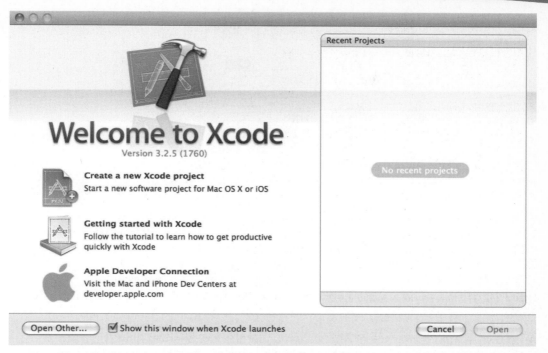

Figure 2–1. *The Xcode welcome window. Note that if this is the first time you are running Xcode, there will be no recent projects. This will change as you make your way through the book.*

NOTE: If you have an iOS device connected to your machine, you might see a message when you first launch Xcode asking whether you want to use that device for development. Alternatively, a window titled *Organizer,* designed to list the devices you'll be working with, might appear. For now, click the *Ignore* button or, in the case of the *Organizer* window, close the window. If you choose to join the paid iOS Developer Program, you will gain access to a program portal that will tell you how to use your iOS device for development and testing.

Create a new project by selecting **File ➤ New Project...**, or by pressing ⇧⌘**N**, which will bring up the New Project assistant (see Figure 2–2). The pane on the left side of the sheet is divided into two main sections: *iOS* and *Mac OS X*.

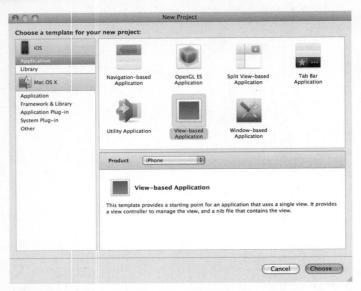

Figure 2–2. *The New Project assistant, which lets you select from various file templates when creating a new project*

As shown in Figure 2–2, select *Application* under the iOS heading, and you'll see a number of icons in the upper-right pane, each of which represents a separate **project template** that can be used as a starting point for your iOS applications. The icon labeled *View-based Application* is the simplest template and the one we'll be using for the first several chapters. The others provide additional code and/or resources needed to create common iOS application interfaces, as you'll see in later chapters.

Click the *View-based Application* icon (as in Figure 2–2), and then select *iPhone* from the *Product* popup menu in the middle of the window. This tells Xcode that we'll be targeting this particular app at the iPhone and its particular sized screen. As of this writing, the iPhone and iPad are the only iOS devices supported by this template. For now, we'll stick with the iPhone. No worries, we'll get to the iPad later in the book.

To continue, click the *Choose...* button. You'll be asked to save your new project using the standard save sheet (see Figure 2–3). Type *Hello World* for the project name, and save it wherever you want it stored. The *Document* folder is not a bad place, but you might want to create a dedicated folder for your Xcode projects.

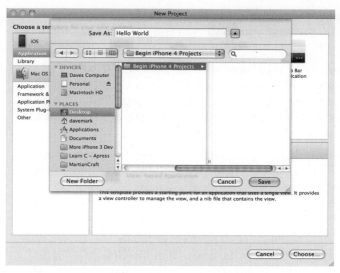

Figure 2–3. *Selecting the name and location for your project*

The Xcode Project Window

After you click *Save*, Xcode will create and then open your project, and a new **project window** will appear that looks like Figure 2–4. We find that the project window, when first created, is a little small for our tastes, so we usually expand the window to take up more of the screen. There's a lot of information crammed into this window, and it's where you will be spending a lot of your iOS development time.

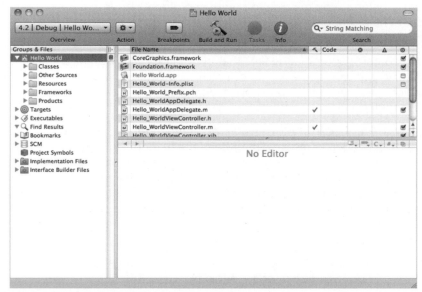

Figure 2–4. *The Hello World project in Xcode*

Your project window features a toolbar across the top, which gives you ready access to a lot of commonly used commands. Below the toolbar, the window is divided into three main sections, or panes.

The pane that runs down the left side of the window is called the *Groups & Files* pane. All of the resources that make up your project are grouped here, as are a number of relevant project settings. Just as in the Finder, clicking the little triangle to the left of an item expands that item to show available subitems. Click the triangle again to hide the subitems.

The top-right pane is called the *Detail View* (or just *Detail* pane) and shows you detailed information about items selected in the *Groups & Files* pane. The lower-right pane is called the *Editor* pane. If you select a single file in either the *Groups & Files* or *Detail* pane and Xcode knows how to display that kind of file, the contents of the file will be displayed in the *Editor* pane. Editable files, such as source code, can also be edited here. In fact, this is where you will be writing and editing your application's source code.

Now that we have the terminology out of the way, take a look at the *Groups & Files* pane. The first item in the list should bear the same name as your project, in this case, *Hello World*. This item is the gathering point for the source code and the other resources specific to your project. For the time being, don't worry about the items in the *Groups & Files* pane except those under *Hello World*.

Take a look at Figure 2–4. Note that the disclosure triangle to the left of *Hello World* is open, and there are five subfolders: *Classes, Other Sources, Resources, Frameworks,* and *Products*. Let's briefly talk about what each subfolder is used for:

- *Classes* is where you will spend much of your time. This is where most of the code that you write will go, since this is where all Objective-C classes rightfully belong. You are free to create subfolders under the *Classes* folder to help organize your code. We'll be using this folder starting in the next chapter.

- *Other Sources* contains source code files that aren't Objective-C classes. Typically, you won't spend a lot of time in the *Other Sources* folder. When you create a new iPhone application project, there are two files in this folder:

  - *Hello_World_Prefix.pch*: The extension *.pch* stands for "precompiled header." This is a list of header files from external frameworks that are used by our project. Xcode will precompile the headers contained in this file, which will reduce the amount of time it takes to compile your project whenever you select **Build** or **Build and Go**. It will be a while before you have to worry about this, because the most commonly used header files are already included for you.

  - *main.m*: This is where your application's main() function is. You normally won't need to edit or change this file.

- *Resources* contains noncode files that will be included as part of your application. This is where you will include files such as your application's icon image and other images, sound files, movie files, text files, or property lists that your program may need while it's running. Remember, since your application runs in its own sandbox, you will have to include any files you need here, because you won't be able to access files located elsewhere on the iPhone except through sanctioned APIs, such as the ones that provide access to the iPhone's photo library and address book. There should be three items in this folder:

  - *Hello_WorldViewController.xib*: This file contains information used by the program Interface Builder, which we'll take for a spin a bit later in this chapter.

  - *MainWindow.xib*: This is your application's main Interface Builder (or "nib") file. In a simple application like the one we're building in this chapter, there's often no need to touch this file. In later chapters, when we design more complex interfaces, we will work with this file and look at it in more depth.

  - *Hello_World-Info.plist*: This is a property list that contains information about our application. We'll look at this file a little bit later in the chapter too.

- *Frameworks* are a special kind of library that can contain code as well as resources such as image and sound files. Any framework or library that you add to this folder will be linked in to your application, and your code will be able to use objects, functions, and resources contained in that framework or library. The most commonly needed frameworks and libraries are linked in to our project by default, so most of the time, we will not need to do anything with this folder. Less commonly used libraries and frameworks, however, are not included by default, and you will see how to link to them into an application later in this book.

- *Products* contains the application that this project produces when it is compiled. If you expand *Products*, you'll see an item called *Hello World.app*. This is the application that this particular project creates. *Hello World.app* is this project's only product. Right now, *Hello World.app* is listed in red, which means that the file cannot be found, which makes sense, since we haven't compiled our project yet! Highlighting a file's name in red is Xcode's way of telling us that it can't find the underlying physical file.

NOTE: The "folders" in the *Groups & Files* pane do not necessarily correspond to folders in your Mac's file system. These are logical groupings within Xcode to help you keep everything organized and to make it faster and easier to find what you're looking for while working on your application. If you look into your project's folder on your hard drive, you'll notice that while there is a *Classes* folder, there is no folder called *Other Sources* or *Resources*. Often, the items contained in those two project folders are stored right in the project's root directory, but you can store them anywhere, even outside of your project folder if you want. The hierarchy inside Xcode is completely independent of the file system hierarchy. Moving a file out of the *Classes* folder in Xcode, for example, will not change the file's location on your hard drive.

Introducing Interface Builder

Now that you're familiar with the basics of Xcode, let's take a look at the other half of the dynamic duo used in iPhone software development: Interface Builder, commonly referred to as IB.

In your project window's *Groups & Files* list, expand the *Resources* group, and then double-click the file *Hello_WorldViewController.xib*. This will open that file in Interface Builder. If this is your first time using Interface Builder, a window grouping similar to that shown in Figure 2–5 should appear. If you've used Interface Builder before, the windows will be where you left them the last time you used it.

Figure 2–5. *Hello_WorldViewController.xib in Interface Builder*

NOTE: Interface Builder has a long history; it has been around since 1988 and has been used to develop applications for NeXtSTEP, OpenSTEP, Mac OS X, and now iPhone. Interface Builder supports two file types: an older format that uses the extension *.nib* and a newer format that utilizes the extension *.xib*. The iPhone project templates all use *.xib* files by default, but until very recently, all Interface Builder files had the extension *.nib*, and as a result, most developers took to calling Interface Builder files nib files. Interface Builder files are commonly called nib files regardless of whether the extension actually used for the file is *.xib* or *.nib*. In fact, Apple actually uses the terms nib and nib file throughout its documentation.

The window labeled *Hello_WorldViewController.xib* (the left-most window in Figure 2–5) is the nib's main window. It is your home base and starting point in this particular nib file. With the exception of the first two icons (*File's Owner* and *First Responder*), every icon in this window represents a single instance of an Objective-C class that will be created automatically for you when this nib file is loaded. Our nib file has one additional icon beyond the required *File's Owner* and *First Responder*. That third icon represents a view object.

Want to create an instance of a button? You could, of course, create the button by writing code. But more commonly, you will use Interface Builder to create the button and specify its attributes (shape, size, label, etc.).

The *Hello_WorldViewController.xib* file we are looking at right now gets loaded automatically when your application launches—for the moment, don't worry about how—so it is an excellent place to create the objects that make up your user interface.

For example, to add a button to your application, you'll need to instantiate an object of type UIButton. You can do this in code by typing a line like this:

```
UIButton *myButton = [[UIButton alloc] initWithFrame:aRect];
```

In Interface Builder, you can accomplish the same exact thing by dragging a button from a palette of interface objects onto your application's main window. Interface Builder makes it easy to set the button's attributes, and since the button will be saved in the nib file, the button will be automatically instantiated when your application starts up. You'll see how this works in a minute.

What's in the Nib File?

Take a look at Figure 2–5. As we mentioned earlier, the window labeled *Hello_WorldViewController.xib* (the upper-left window) is the nib file's main window. Every nib file starts off with the same two icons, *File's Owner* and *First Responder*. They are created automatically and cannot be deleted. From that, you can probably guess that they are important, and they are.

File's Owner will always be the first icon in any nib file and represents the object that loaded the nib file from disk. In other words, *File's Owner* is the object that "owns" this copy of the nib file. If this is a bit confusing, don't worry; it's not important at the moment. When it does become important later, we'll go over it again.

The second icon in this and any other nib file is called *First Responder*. We'll talk more about responders later in the book, but in very basic terms, the first responder is the object with which the user is currently interacting. If, for example, the user is currently entering data into a text field, that field is the current first responder. The first responder changes as the user interacts with the interface, and the *First Responder* icon gives you a convenient way to communicate with whatever control or view is the current first responder without having to write code to determine which control or view that might be. Again, we'll talk about this much more later, so don't worry if this concept is a bit fuzzy right now.

Every other icon in this window, other than these first two special cases, represents an object instance that will be created when the nib file loads. In our case, as you can see in Figure 2–5, there is a third icon called *View*.

The *View* icon represents an instance of the UIView class. A UIView object is an area that a user can see and interact with. In this application, we will have only one view, so this icon represents everything that the user can see in our application. Later, we'll build more complex applications that have more than one view, but for now, just think of this as what the users can see when they're using your application.

> **NOTE:** Technically speaking, our application will actually have more than one view. All user interface elements that can be displayed on the screen, including buttons, text fields, and labels, are all subclasses of UIView. When you see the term view used in this book, however, we will generally be referring only to actual instances of UIView, and this application has only one of those.

If you go back to Figure 2–5, you'll notice two other windows open besides the main window. Look at the window that has the word *View* in the title bar. That window is the graphical representation of that third icon in the nib's main window. If you close this window and then double-click the *View* icon in the nib file's main window, this window will open again. This is where you can design your user interface graphically. Let's do that now.

Adding a Label to the View

The rightmost window shown in Figure 2–5 is the **library**, which you can see in more detail in Figure 2–6. This is where you will find all the stock Cocoa Touch objects that Interface Builder supports. Dragging an item from the library to a nib file window will add an instance of that class to your application. If you close the library window, you can get it to reappear by selecting **Tools ➤ Library** or by pressing ⇧⌘L. The items on this palette are primarily from the iOS UIKit, which is a framework of objects used to create an application's user interface.

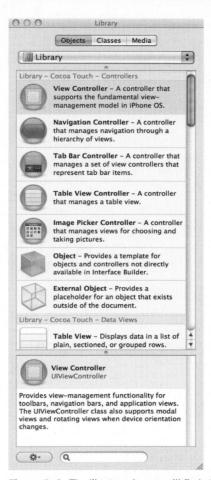

Figure 2–6. *The library, where you'll find stock objects from the UIKit that are available for use in Interface Builder*

UIKit fulfills the same role in Cocoa Touch as AppKit does in Cocoa. The two frameworks are similar conceptually, but because of differences in the platforms, there are obviously many differences between them. On the other hand, the Foundation framework classes, such as NSString and NSArray, are shared between Cocoa and Cocoa Touch.

Scroll through the list of objects in the library until you find one called *Label* (see Figure 2–7).

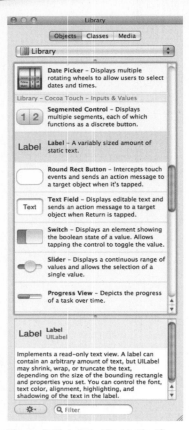

Figure 2–7. *Label object in the library*

A label represents a bit of text that can be displayed on an iOS device's screen but can't be directly edited by the user. In a moment, we're going to add a label to our view.

Because user interface objects are hierarchical, we'll be adding our label as a **subview** to our main view (the view named *View*). Interface Builder is smart. If an object does not accept subviews, you will not be able to drag other objects onto it.

Dragging a label from the library to the view called *View* will add an instance of `UILabel` as a subview of our application's main view. Got that?

> **TIP:** Having trouble finding the Label in that long list of library objects? No problem! Click in the search field at the bottom of the library (or, as a shortcut, press ⇧⌘**L** to get there), and type the word *label*. As you type, the list of objects is reduced to match your search term. Be sure to empty the search window when you are done so you can see the full list again.

Drag a *Label* from the library into the *View* window. The view should look something like Figure 2–8 when you're done.

Figure 2–8. *Adding a label to your application's View window*

Let's edit the label so it says something profound. Double-click the label you just created, and type the text *Hello, World!*. Next, drag the label to wherever you want it to appear on the screen.

Guess what? Once we save, we're finished. Select **File ➤ Save**, and go back to Xcode so we can build and run our application.

In Xcode, select **Build ➤ Build and Run** (or press ⌘R). Xcode will compile our application and launch it in the iPhone simulator, as shown in Figure 2.9.

Figure 2–9. *Here's the Hello World program in its full iPhone glory!*

When you are finished admiring your handiwork, be sure to quit the simulator. Xcode, Interface Builder, and the simulator are all separate applications.

CAUTION: If your iOS device is connected to your Mac when you build and run, things might not go quite as planned. In a nutshell, in order to be able to build and run your applications on your iPhone, you have to sign up and pay for one of Apple's iOS developer programs and then go through the process of configuring Xcode appropriately. When you join the program, Apple will send you the information you'll need to get this done. In the meantime, most of the programs in this book will run just fine using the iOS simulator. If your device is plugged in, before you select Build and Run, select Project ➤ Set Active SDK ➤ Simulator.

Wait a second! That's it? But, we didn't write any code.

That's right. Pretty neat, huh?

But what if we had wanted to change some of the properties of the label, like the text size or color? We'd have to write code to do that, right?

Nope.

Changing Attributes

Head back to Interface Builder and single-click the Hello World label so that it is selected. Now press ⌘1 or select Tools ➤ Inspector. This will open a window called the **inspector**, where you can set the attributes of the currently selected item (see Figure 2–10).

From the inspector, you can change things like the font size, color, and drop shadow— just lots of stuff. The inspector is context sensitive. If you select a text field, you will be shown the editable attributes of a text field. If you select a button, you will be shown the editable attributes of a button, and so on.

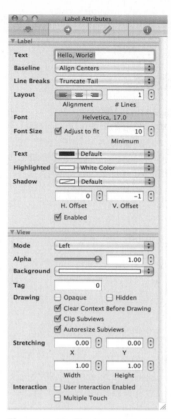

Figure 2–10. *The inspector showing our label's attributes*

Go ahead and change the label's appearance to your heart's delight, and then save, go back to Xcode, and select **Build and Run** again. The changes you made should show up in your application, once again without writing any code. By letting you design your interface graphically, Interface Builder frees you up to spend time writing the code that is specific to your application instead of spending time writing tedious code to construct your user interface.

> **NOTE:** Don't worry too much about what all the fields in the object attributes mean or fret if you can't get one of your changes to show up. As you make your way through the book, you'll learn a lot about the attributes inspector and what each of the fields do.

Most modern application development environments have some tool that lets you build your user interface graphically. One distinction between Interface Builder and many of these other tools is that Interface Builder does not generate any code that has to be maintained. Instead, Interface Builder creates Objective-C objects, just as you would do in code, and then serializes those objects into the nib file so that they can be loaded directly into memory at runtime. This avoids many of the problems associated with code generation and is, overall, a more powerful approach.

Some iPhone Polish—Finishing Touches

Before we leave this chapter, let's just put a last little bit of spit and polish on our application to make it feel a little more like an authentic iOS application. First, run your project. When the simulator window appears, click the iPhone simulator's home button, the black button with the white square at the very bottom of the window. That will bring you back to the iPhone home screen (see Figure 2–11). Notice anything a bit, well, boring?

Figure 2–11. *Our Hello World application icon is just plain boring.*

Take a look at the Hello World icon at the top of the screen. Yeah, that icon will never do, will it? To fix it, you need to create an icon and save it as a portable network graphic (*.png*) file. It needs to be 57 × 57 pixels in size. Do not try to match the style of the buttons that are already on the phone; your iPhone will automatically round the edges and give it that nice glassy appearance. Just create a normal flat, square image. We have provided an icon image in the project's archive (within the *02 Hello World* folder) that you can use if you don't want to create your own.

> **NOTE:** For your application's icon, you have to use a *.png* image, but you should actually use the *.png* format for all images you add to your iOS projects. Even though most common image formats will display correctly, you should use *.png* files unless you have a compelling reason to use another format. Xcode automatically optimizes *.png* images at build time to make them the fastest and most efficient image type for use in iOS applications.

After you've designed your application icon, drag the *.png* file from the Finder to the *Resources* folder in Xcode, as shown in Figure 2–12, or select the *Resources* folder in Xcode, choose **Project ➤ Add to Project...**, and navigate to your icon image file.

If you'd rather not design your own icon, you can navigate to the book's project archive, then into the folder *02 – Hello World*, where you'll find an icon we created just for you to add to your project. The file name is *icon.png*. Find that file and drag it onto the *Resources* folder in your project.

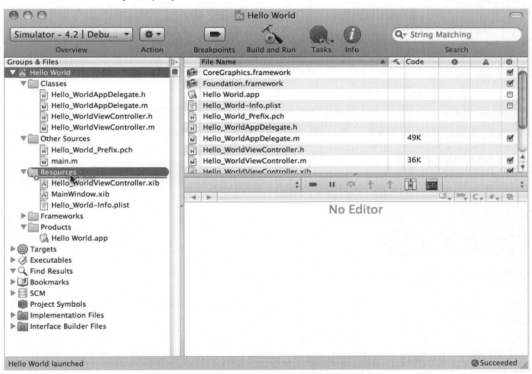

Figure 2–12. *Dragging an icon file into the Resources folder of your Xcode project*

Once you've done this, Xcode will prompt you for some specifics (see Figure 2–13). You can choose to have Xcode copy the file into your project directory, or you can just add it to your project as a reference to the original file. Generally, it's a good idea to copy resources into your Xcode project unless the file is shared with other projects.

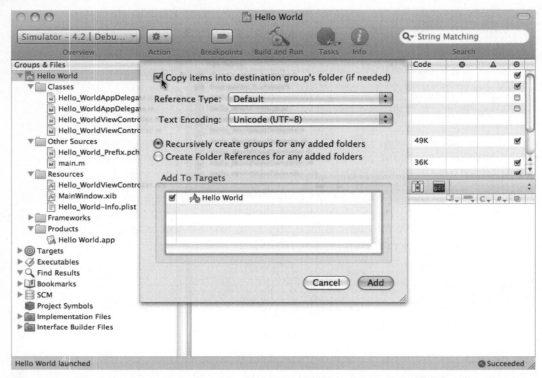

Figure 2–13. *Selecting how to add the file to the project. It's a good idea to copy the added item into the project.*

When you add any common kind of file to your project, Xcode knows what to do with it, and as a result, this image file will now get compiled into our application automatically without requiring you to do anything further.

What we've done so far is incorporate the *icon.png* image into the project, which will result in the image getting built into our application bundle. The next thing we need to do is to specify that this particular image should be used as our application's icon.

In your Xcode project window's *Groups & Files* pane, expand the *Resources* folder, if it isn't already, and then single-click the *Hello_World-Info.plist* file. This is a **property list** file that contains some general information about our application including, among other things, the name of the icon file.

When you select *Hello_World-Info.plist*, the property list will appear in the editing pane (see Figure 2–14). Within the property list, find a row with the label *Icon file* in the left column. The corresponding right column in that same row should be empty. Double-click the empty cell, and type in the name of the *.png* file you just added to your project.

NOTE: If you ignored the *Icon file* entry in the plist, your icon will likely show up anyway. Huh? Why's that? By default, if no icon file name is provided, the SDK looks for a resource named *icon.png* and uses that. Just thought you'd like to know!

Key	Value
▼ Information Property List	(12 items)
Localization native development re	English
Bundle display name	${PRODUCT_NAME}
Executable file	${EXECUTABLE_NAME}
Icon file ⇕	icon.png ⊕
Bundle identifier	com.yourcompany.${PRODUCT_NAME:rfc1034identifier}
InfoDictionary version	6.0
Bundle name	${PRODUCT_NAME}
Bundle OS Type code	APPL
Bundle creator OS Type code	????
Bundle version	1.0
Application requires iPhone enviror	☑
Main nib file base name	MainWindow

Figure 2–14. *Specifying the icon file*

Ready to Compile and Run

Before we compile and run, take a look at the other rows in *Hello_World-Info.plist*. While most of these settings are fine as they are, one in particular requires our attention, the setting named *Bundle identifier*. This is a unique identifier for your application and should always be set. If you're just going to run your application on the iOS simulator, the standard naming convention for bundle identifiers is to use one of the top-level Internet domains such as com or org followed by a period, then the name of your company or organization followed by another period, and finally the name of your application. If you want to run your application on an actual iOS device, creating your application's bundle identifier is a little more involved process that you can read about in the iPhone Program Portal if you choose to pay to join the iPhone SDK Program. Since we're here, why don't we double-click the word *yourcompany* in the existing bundle identifier and change that to *apress*. The value at the end of the string is a special code that will get replaced with your application's name when your application is built. This allows you to tie your application's bundle identifier to its name.

Once that change is made, compile and run. When the simulator has finished launching, press the button with the white square to go home, and check out your snazzy new icon. Ours is shown in Figure 2–15.

Figure 2–15. *Your application now has a snazzy icon!*

You may have noticed that Figure 2–15 shows two different Hello World applications, one with a generic icon and one with a shiny new icon. What gives? As it turns out, the Bundle Identifier that you just changed is what uniquely identifies a specific application. When you changed *yourcompany* to *apress*, you told iOS that this was a brand new, different application.

> **Note.** When you want to clear out old applications from the iPhone simulator's home screen, you can simply delete the folder called *iPhone Simulator* from the *Application Support* folder contained in your home directory's *Library* folder. You can also reset the simulator by selecting iOS Simulator ➤ Reset Content and Settings…

Bring It on Home

Pat yourself on the back. Although it may not seem like you accomplished all that much in this chapter, we actually covered a lot of ground. You learned about the iOS project templates, created an application, saw how to use Interface Builder, and learned how to set your application icon and bundle identifier.

Hello World, however, is a strictly one-way application: we show some information to the user, but we never get any input from them. When you're ready to see how we go about getting input from the user of an iOS device and taking actions based on that input, take a deep breath and turn the page.

Chapter 3

Handling Basic Interaction

Our Hello World application was a good introduction to iOS development using Cocoa Touch, but it was missing a crucial capability: the ability to interact with the user. Without that, our application is severely limited in terms of what it can accomplish.

In this chapter, we're going to write a slightly more complex application, which will have two buttons as well as a label, as shown in Figure 3–1. When the user taps either of the buttons, the label's text changes. This may seem like a rather simplistic example, but it demonstrates the key concepts of implementing user interaction in your iOS applications.

Figure 3–1. *The simple two-button application we will build in this chapter*

The Model-View-Controller Paradigm

Before diving in, a bit of theory is in order. The designers of Cocoa Touch were guided by a concept called **Model-View-Controller** (MVC), which is a very logical way of dividing the code that makes up a GUI-based application. These days, almost all object-oriented frameworks pay a certain amount of homage to MVC, but few are as true to the MVC model as Cocoa Touch.

The MVC pattern divides all functionality into three distinct categories:

- **Model**: The classes that hold your application's data

- **View**: Made up of the windows, controls, and other elements that the user can see and interact with

- **Controller**: Binds the model and view together and is the application logic that decides how to handle the user's inputs

The goal in MVC is to make the objects that implement these three types of code as distinct from one another as possible. Any object you create should be readily identifiable as belonging in one of the three categories, with little or no functionality that could be classified within either of the other two. An object that implements a button, for example, shouldn't contain code to process data when that button is tapped, and an implementation of a bank account shouldn't contain code to draw a table to display its transactions.

MVC helps ensure maximum reusability. A class that implements a generic button can be used in any application. A class that implements a button that does some particular calculation when it is clicked can be used only in the application for which it was originally written.

When you write Cocoa Touch applications, you will primarily create your view components using Interface Builder, although you will sometimes also modify your interface from code, or you might subclass existing views and controls.

Your model will be created by crafting Objective-C classes designed to hold your application's data or by building a data model using Core Data, which you'll learn about in Chapter 12. We won't be creating any model objects in this chapter's application, because we do not need to store or preserve data, but we will introduce model objects as our applications get more complex in future chapters.

Your controller component will typically be composed of classes that you create and that are specific to your application. Controllers can be completely custom classes (NSObject subclasses), but more often, they will be subclasses of one of several existing generic controller classes from the UIKit framework, such as UIViewController, which you'll see in the next section. By subclassing one of these existing classes, you will get a lot of functionality for free and won't need to spend time recoding the wheel, so to speak.

As we get deeper into Cocoa Touch, you will quickly start to see how the classes of the UIKit framework follow the principles of MVC. If you keep this concept in the back of your head as you develop, you will end up creating cleaner, more easily maintained code.

Creating Our Project

It's time to create our next Xcode project. We're going to use the same template that we used in the previous chapter: *View-based Application*. By starting with this simple template again, it will be easier for you to see how the view and controller objects work together in an iOS application. We'll use some of the other templates in later chapters.

Go ahead and create your project, setting the *Product* popup to *iPhone*, and saving it under the name *Button Fun*. If you have any trouble creating your project, refer to the preceding chapter for the proper steps.

You probably remember that the project template created some classes for us. You'll find those same classes in your new project, although the names will be a little different because some class names are based on the project name.

Creating the View Controller

A little later in this chapter, we'll design a view (or user interface) for our application using Interface Builder, just as we did in the previous chapter. Before we do that, we're going to look at and make some changes to the source code files that were created for us. Yes, Virginia, we're actually going to write some code in this chapter.

Before we make any changes, let's look at the files that were created for us. In the Groups & Files pane, expand the *Classes* folder to reveal the four files it contains, as shown in Figure 3–2.

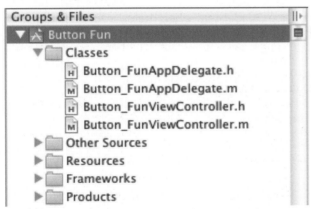

Figure 3–2. *The Groups & Files pane, showing the class files that were created for us by the project template. Note that the project name was incorporated into the class file names.*

These four files implement two classes, each of which contains a *.m* and *.h* file. The application we are creating in this chapter has only one view, and the controller class that is responsible for managing that one view is called `Button_FunViewController`. The `Button_Fun` part of the name comes from our project name, and the `ViewController` part of the name means this class is, well, a view controller. Click *Button_FunView Controller.h* in the *Groups & Files* pane, and take a look at the contents of the file:

```
#import <UIKit/UIKit.h>

@interface Button_FunViewController : UIViewController {
}

@end
```

Not much to it, is there? `Button_FunViewController` is a subclass of `UIViewController`, which is one of those generic controller classes we mentioned earlier. It is part of the UIKit and gives us a bunch of functionality for free. Xcode doesn't know what our application-specific functionality is going to be, but it does know we're going to have some, so it has created this class to hold that functionality.

Take a look back at Figure 3–1. Our program consists of two buttons and a text label that reflects which button was tapped. We'll create all three of these elements in Interface Builder. Since we're also going to be writing code, there must be some way for our code to interact with the elements we create in Interface Builder, right?

Absolutely right. Our controller class can refer to objects in the nib file by using a special kind of instance variable called an **outlet**. Think of an outlet as a pointer that points to an object within the nib. For example, suppose you created a text label in Interface Builder and wanted to change the label's text from within your code. By declaring an outlet and connecting that outlet to the label object, you could use the outlet from within your code to change the text displayed by the label. You'll see how to do just that in this chapter.

Going in the opposite direction, interface objects in our nib file can be set up to trigger special methods in our controller class. These special methods are known as **action** methods. For example, you can tell Interface Builder that when the user touches up (pulls a finger off the screen) within a button, a specific action method within your code should be called.

In our code, we'll create an outlet that points to the label, and this outlet will allow us to change the text of that label. We'll also create a method named `buttonPressed:` that will fire whenever one of the two buttons is tapped. `buttonPressed:` will set the label's text to let the user know which button was tapped.

We'll use Interface Builder to create the buttons and label, and then we'll do some clicking and dragging to connect the label to our label outlet and our buttons to our `buttonPressed:` action.

But before we get to our code, here's a bit more detail on outlets and actions.

Outlets

Outlets are instance variables that are declared using the keyword IBOutlet. A declaration of an outlet in your controller's header file might look like this:

```
@property (nonatomic, retain) IBOutlet UIButton *myButton;
```

The IBOutlet keyword is defined like this:

```
#ifndef IBOutlet
#define IBOutlet
#endif
```

Confused? IBOutlet does absolutely nothing as far as the compiler is concerned. Its sole purpose is to act as a hint to tell Interface Builder that this is an instance variable that we're going to connect to an object in a nib file. Any instance variable that you create and want to connect to an object in a nib file must be preceded by the IBOutlet keyword. When you open a nib file from the Groups & Files pane, Interface Builder will scan your project header files for occurrences of this keyword and will allow you to make connections from your code to the nib based on these (and only these) variables. In the "Connecting Outlets" section later in this chapter, you'll see how to actually make the connection between an outlet and a user interface object in Interface Builder.

OUTLET CHANGES

In the first version of the book, we placed the IBOutlet keyword before the instance variable declaration, like this:

```
IBOutlet UIButton *myButton;
```

Since that time, Apple's sample code has been moving toward placing the IBOutlet keyword in the property declaration, like this:

```
@property (nonatomic, retain) IBOutlet UIButton *myButton;
```

Both mechanisms are supported, and for the most part, there is no difference in the way things work based on where you put the keyword. There is one exception to that, however. If you declare a property with a different name than its underlying instance variable (which can be done in the @synthesize directive), then you must put the IBOutlet keyword in the property declaration, rather than before the instance variable declaration, in order for it to work correctly. If you are a bit fuzzy on the property concept, we'll talk you through it in just a bit.

Although both approaches work, we've followed Apple's lead and have moved the IBOutlet keyword to the property declaration in all of our code.

You can read more about the new Objective-C properties in the book *Learn Objective-C on the Mac* by Mark Dalrymple and Scott Knaster (Apress, 2009), and in the document *Introduction to The Objective-C Programming Language* available from Apple's developer web site at http://developer.apple.com/documentation/Cocoa/Conceptual/ObjectiveC.

Actions

Actions are methods that are part of your controller class. They are also declared with a special keyword, `IBAction`, which tells Interface Builder that this method is an action and can be triggered by a control. Typically, the declaration for an action method will look like this:

```
- (IBAction)doSomething:(id)sender;
```

The actual name of the method can be anything you want, but it must have a return type of `IBAction`, which is the same as declaring a return type of `void`. This is another way of saying that action methods do not return a value. Usually, the action method will take one argument, and it's typically defined as `id` and given a name of `sender`. The control that triggers your action will use the `sender` argument to pass a reference to itself. So, for example, if your action method was called as the result of a button tap, the argument `sender` would contain a reference to the specific button that was tapped.

As you'll see in the next section, our program will use that `sender` argument to set the label to the text "left" or "right," depending on which button was tapped. If you don't need to know which control called your method, you can also define action methods without a `sender` parameter. This would look like so:

```
- (IBAction)doSomething;
```

It won't hurt anything if you declare an action method with a `sender` argument and then ignore `sender`. You will likely see a lot of sample code that does just that, because historically, action methods in Cocoa had to accept `sender` whether they used it or not.

Adding Actions and Outlets to the View Controller

Now that you know what outlets and actions are, let's go ahead and add one of each to our controller class. We need an outlet so we can change the label's text. Since we won't be changing the buttons, we don't need an outlet for them.

We'll also declare a single action method that will be called by both buttons. While many action methods are specific to a single control, it's possible to use a single action to handle input from multiple controls, which is what we're going to do here. Our action will grab the button's name from its `sender` argument and use the label outlet to embed that button name in the label's text. You'll see how this is done in a few pages, when we review the `buttonPressed:` method.

> **NOTE:** Because Xcode creates files for us to use that already contain some of the code we need, we will often be inserting code into an existing file. When you see code listings like the one for *Button_FunViewController.h*, any code that is in a `normal typeface` is existing code that should already be in the file. Code that is listed in **bold** is new code that you need to type.

Go ahead and add the following code to *Button_FunViewController.h*:

```
#import <UIKit/UIKit.h>

@interface Button_FunViewController : UIViewController {
    UILabel     *statusText;
}
@property (nonatomic, retain) IBOutlet UILabel *statusText;
- (IBAction)buttonPressed:(id)sender;
@end
```

If you have worked with Objective-C 2.0, you're probably familiar with the @property declaration, but if you aren't, that line of code might look a little intimidating. Fear not— Objective-C properties are really quite simple. Let's take a quick detour to talk about them, since they are used extensively in this book. Even if you are already a master of the property, please do read on, because there is a bit of information specific to Cocoa Touch that you'll definitely find useful.

Objective-C Properties

Before the property was added to Objective-C, programmers traditionally defined pairs of methods to set and retrieve the values for each of a class's instance variables. These methods are called **accessors** and **mutators** (or, if you prefer, **getters** and **setters**), and might look something like this:

```
- (id)foo {
    return foo;
}

- (void)setFoo:(id)aFoo {
    if (aFoo != foo) {
        [aFoo retain];
        [foo release];
        foo = aFoo;
    }
}
```

Although this approach is still perfectly valid, the @property declaration allows you to say good-bye to the tedious process of creating accessor and mutator methods, if you want. The @property declarations we just typed, combined with another declaration in the implementation file (@synthesize, which you'll see when we make changes to the *Button_FunViewController.m* file), will tell the compiler to create the getter and setter methods at compile time. You'll normally declare the underlying instance variables as we did here, but you do not need to define the accessor or mutator.

> **NOTE:** You may have noticed that in that previous paragraph, we said that you will "normally" declare instance variables to match properties, which seems to imply that there are "abnormal" cases where you can skip them. This is, in fact, the case. Objective-C 2.0 lets you omit instance variable declaration any time the instance variable and property have the same name, leaving just the property declaration in place. However, this functionality is limited to the newest runtime environments that Apple provides, which include both iOS as well as 64-bit applications in Mac OS X 10.6 or later, but does *not* include 32-bit applications on Mac OS X. Up until the summer of 2010, this limitation also included software running in the iPhone simulator. Since every developer uses the simulator to some extent, using a code base that omitted instance variables would be kind of a pain in the neck, which means that almost all software written for iOS up to this point includes the instance variables. Even now, tool support for omitting instance variables seems a bit spotty. For example, Xcode's debugger has difficulty presenting information about a property if the instance variable wasn't declared. In this book, we're going to include the instance variables most of the time, but you should be aware that at some point in your iOS development career, the tools will catch up, and those instance variables will feel like a thing of the past.

In our declaration, the @property keyword is followed by some optional attributes, wrapped in parentheses. These define how the accessors and mutators will be created by the compiler, and also provide programmers reading the code some context, since they describe how the object will treat its instance variable. The two you see here will be used often when defining properties in iPhone applications:

```
@property (retain, nonatomic) IBOutlet UILabel *statusText;
```

The first of these attributes, retain, tells the compiler to send a retain message to any object that we assign to this property. This will keep the instance variable underlying our property from being flushed from memory while we're still using it. This is necessary because the default behavior (assign) is intended for use with either low-level C datatypes or with garbage collection, a feature of Objective-C 2.0 that isn't currently available under any version of iOS. As a result, if you define a property that is an object (as opposed to a raw datatype like int), you should generally specify retain in the optional attributes. When declaring a property for an int, float, or other raw datatype, you do not need to specify any optional attributes. In fact, specifying retain in a property declaration for a low-level datatype will end up causing errors, since anything that isn't an Objective-C object can't receive any messages at all, not even retain or release.

The second of our optional attributes, nonatomic, changes the way that the accessor and mutator methods are generated. Without getting too technical, let's just say that, by default, these methods are created with some additional code that is helpful when writing multithreaded programs. That additional overhead, though small, is unnecessary when declaring a pointer to a user interface object, so we declare nonatomic to save a bit of overhead. There will be times when you don't want to specify nonatomic for a property, but as a general rule, usually you will specify `nonatomic` when writing iOS applications.

Objective-C 2.0 has another nice feature that we'll be using along with properties. It introduced the use of **dot notation** to the language. Traditionally, to use an accessor method, you would send a message to the object, like this:

```
myVar = [someObject foo];
```

This approach still works just fine. But when you've defined a property, you also have the option of using dot notation, similar to that used in Java, C++, and C#, like so:

```
myVar = someObject.foo;
```

Those two statements are identical as far as the compiler is concerned; use whichever one makes you happy. Dot notation also works with mutators. The statement shown here:

```
someObject.foo = myVar;
```

is functionally identical to the following:

```
[someObject setFoo:myVar];
```

> **NOTE:** For this book, we've decided on a rather strict policy for dealing with properties. Any time we're accessing an instance variable that is also a property, we're going to do it by invoking the property getters and setters, either by calling the methods directly or by using dot notation. We could have skipped this for references to properties within the same object, thereby leaving out the `self.` piece of a reference like `self.propertyName`, but for the sake of consistency (other objects must access our instance variables with properties anyway) and program correctness (a getter or setter may have desirable side effects that we don't want to short-circuit), we're using properties everywhere. The only exceptions to this are inside `init` and `dealloc` methods, where we access the instance variables directly. This is because when those methods are called, the receiver is necessarily in a state of transition (either having just been created or just about to be destroyed), so the potential side effects of calling a getter or setter would probably be undesirable at that time. Be aware also that some of Apple's code, generated by Xcode from a template, does not follow these guidelines, but the code we add always will.

Declaring the Action Method

After the property declaration, we added another line of code:

```
- (IBAction)buttonPressed:(id)sender;
```

This is our action method declaration. By placing this declaration here, we are informing other classes, and Interface Builder, that our class has an action method called `buttonPressed:`.

Adding Actions and Outlets to the Implementation File

We are finished with our controller class header file for the time being, so save it and single-click the class's implementation file, *Button_FunViewController.m*. The file should look like something like this:

```objectivec
#import "Button_FunViewController.h"

@implementation Button_FunViewController
/*
// The designated initializer. Override to perform setup
// that is required before the view is loaded.
- (id)initWithNibName:(NSString *)nibNameOrNil bundle:
        (NSBundle *)nibBundleOrNil {
    if (self=[super initWithNibName:nibNameOrNil bundle:nibBundleOrNil]) {
        // Custom initialization
    }
    return self;
}
*/

/*
// Implement loadView to create a view hierarchy programmatically,
// without using a nib.
- (void)loadView {
}
*/

/*
// Implement viewDidLoad to do additional setup after loading the view,
// typically from a nib.
- (void)viewDidLoad {
    [super viewDidLoad];
}
*/

/*
// Override to allow orientations other than the default portrait
// orientation.
- (BOOL)shouldAutorotateToInterfaceOrientation:
        (UIInterfaceOrientation)interfaceOrientation {
    // Return YES for supported orientations
    return (interfaceOrientation == UIInterfaceOrientationPortrait);
}
*/

- (void)didReceiveMemoryWarning {
    // Releases the view if it doesn't have a superview.
    [super didReceiveMemoryWarning];

    // Release any cached data, images, etc that aren't in use.
}

- (void)viewDidUnload {
    // Release any retained subviews of the main view.
    // e.g. self.myOutlet = nil;
}
```

```
- (void)dealloc {
    [super dealloc];
}
```

```
@end
```

Apple has anticipated some of the methods that we are likely to override and has included method stubs in the implementation file. Some of them are commented out and can be either uncommented or deleted as appropriate. The ones that aren't commented out are either used by the template or are so commonly used that they were included to save us time. We won't need any of the commented-out methods for this application, so go ahead and delete them, which will shorten the code and make it easier to follow as we insert new code into this file.

Once you've deleted the commented-out methods, add the following code. When you're finished, meet us back here, and we'll talk about what we did.

```
#import "Button_FunViewController.h"

@implementation Button_FunViewController
@synthesize statusText;

- (IBAction)buttonPressed:(id)sender {
    NSString *title = [sender titleForState:UIControlStateNormal];
    NSString *newText = [[NSString alloc] initWithFormat:
                            @"%@ button pressed.", title];
    statusText.text = newText;
    [newText release];
}

- (void)didReceiveMemoryWarning {
    [super didReceiveMemoryWarning]; // Releases the view if it
    // doesn't have a superview
    // Release anything that's not essential, such as cached data
}

- (void)viewDidUnload {
    // Release any retained subviews of the main view.
    // e.g. self.myOutlet = nil;
    self.statusText = nil;
}

- (void)dealloc {
    [statusText release];
    [super dealloc];
}

@end
```

OK, let's look at the newly added code. First, we added this:

```
@synthesize statusText;
```

This is how we tell the compiler to automatically create the accessor and mutator methods for us. By virtue of this line of code, there are now two "invisible" methods in our class: statusText and setStatusText:. We didn't write them, but they are there nonetheless, waiting for us to use them.

The next bit of newly added code is the implementation of our action method that will be called when either button is tapped:

```
-(IBAction)buttonPressed: (id)sender {
    NSString *title = [sender titleForState:UIControlStateNormal];
    NSString *newText = [[NSString alloc] initWithFormat:
                        @"%@ button pressed.", title];
    statusText.text = newText;
    [newText release];
}
```

Remember that the parameter passed into an action method is the control or object that invoked it. So, in our application, sender will always point to the button that was tapped. This is a very handy mechanism, because it allows us to have one action method handle the input from multiple controls, which is exactly what we're doing here. Both buttons call this method, and we tell them apart by looking at sender. The first line of code in this method grabs the tapped button's title from sender.

```
NSString *title = [sender titleForState:UIControlStateNormal];
```

> **NOTE:** We needed to provide a **control state** when we requested the button's title. The four possible states are **normal**, which represents the control when it's active but not currently being used; **highlighted**, which represents the control when it is in the process of being tapped or otherwise used; **disabled**, which is the state of a button that is not enabled and can't be used; and **selected**, which is a state that only certain controls have and which indicates that the control is currently selected. UIControlStateNormal represents a control's normal state and is the one you will use the vast majority of the time. If values for the other states are not specified, those states will have the same value as the normal state.

The next thing we do is create a new string based on that title:

```
NSString *newText = [[NSString alloc] initWithFormat:
                    @"%@ button pressed.", title];
```

This new string will append the text "button pressed." to the name of the button. So if we tapped a button with a title of "Left," this new string would equal "Left button pressed."

Then we set the text of our label to this new string:

```
statusText.text = newText;
```

We're using dot notation here to set the label's text, but we could have also used [statusText setText:newText]; instead.

Finally, we release the string:

```
[newText release];
```

The importance of releasing objects when you're finished with them cannot be overstated. The iPhone, iPad, and other iOS devices are very resource-constrained, and even a small number of memory leaks can cause your program to crash. It's also worth pointing out that we *didn't* do this:

```
NSString *newText = [NSString stringWithFormat:
                     @"%@ button pressed.", title];
```

This code would work exactly the same as the code we used. Class methods like this one are called **convenience** or **factory** methods, and they return an autoreleased object. Following the general memory rule that "if you didn't allocate it or retain it, don't release it," these autoreleased objects don't need to be released unless you specifically retain them, and using them often results in code that's a little shorter and more readable.

But there is a cost associated with these convenience methods because they use the autorelease pool. The memory allocated for an autoreleased object will stay allocated for some period of time after we're finished with it. On Mac OS X, with swap files and relatively large amounts of physical memory, the cost of using autoreleased objects is nominal, but on iPhone, these objects can have a detrimental effect on your application's memory footprint. It is OK to use autorelease, but try to use it only when you really need to, not just to save typing a line or two of code.

Next, we added a single line of code to the existing viewDidUnload: method:

```
self.statusText = nil;
```

Don't worry too much about this line of code for now; we'll explain why we need it in the next chapter. For now, just remember that you need to set any outlets your class has to nil in viewDidUnload.

> **TIP:** If you're a bit fuzzy on Objective-C memory management, you really should review the memory management "contract" at http://developer.apple.com/documentation/Cocoa/Conceptual/MemoryMgmt. Even a small number of memory leaks can wreak havoc in an iOS application.

The last thing we did was to release the outlet in our dealloc method:

```
[statusText release];
```

Releasing this item might seem strange. You might be thinking, since we didn't instantiate it, we shouldn't be responsible for releasing it. If you have worked with older versions of Cocoa and Objective-C, you're probably thinking this is just plain wrong. However, because we implemented properties for each of these outlets and specified retain in that property's attributes, releasing it is correct and necessary. Interface Builder will use our generated mutator method when assigning the outlets, and that mutator will retain the object that is assigned to it, so it's important to release the outlet here to avoid leaking memory.

> **NOTE:** You may have noticed that after releasing `statusText` by calling its `release` method (as opposed to calling `[self setStatusText:nil]`), our object is actually left in an invalid state for a brief period of time, since the `statusText` variable still contains a pointer to the object we just released, which may very well not exist anymore. If our object's parent class (or any other ancestor, all the way up the hierarchy) should happen to call a method that accesses our object's `statusText` property, this is likely to cause a crash. Also, in a multithreaded application, you might have a bug where an object that is being `dealloced` in one thread is simultaneously being accessed by another, which could also lead to crashes, deadlocks, or other kinds of misbehavior. We could work around this by setting the pointer to `nil` in the `dealloc` method, but that approach has potential problems of its own. If some of your code is causing the sort of misbehavior we just described—either accidentally accessing properties from a subclass during `dealloc` or using an object across multiple threads and not properly managing its retain count—you would rather find and fix those bugs than have them lurking in your applications! Setting all instance variables to `nil` in the `dealloc` method might make it easier for those bugs to hide, instead of being found during development. This topic is a subject of lively debate and discussion among Objective-C programmers from time to time, and Jeff LaMarche's blog contains a detailed description of all the various positions at `http://iphonedevelopment.blogspot.com/2010/09/dealloc.html`. If you're interested in further discussion of such matters, including how keeping those invalid pointers around can actually help debug memory management errors, you might also want to read up on "zombie objects" at `http://www.cocoadev.com/index.pl?NSZombieEnabled`.

Before moving on, make sure you've saved this file, and then go ahead and build the project by pressing ⌘**B** to make sure you didn't make any mistakes while typing. If it doesn't compile, go back and compare your code to the code in this book.

MESSAGE NESTING

Objective-C messages are often nested by some developers. You may come across code like this in your travels:

```
statusText.text = [NSString stringWithFormat:@"%@ button pressed.",
    [sender titleForState:UIControlStateNormal]];
```

This one line of code will function exactly the same as the four lines of code that make up our `buttonPressed:` method. For the sake of clarity, we won't generally nest Objective-C messages in the code examples in this book, with the exception of calls to `alloc` and `init`, which, by long-standing convention, are almost always nested.

Using the Application Delegate

The other two files in the *Classes* folder implement our **application delegate**. Cocoa Touch makes extensive use of **delegates**, which are classes that take responsibility for doing certain tasks on behalf of another object. The application delegate lets us do things at certain predefined times on behalf of the UIApplication class. Every iPhone application has one and only one instance of UIApplication, which is responsible for the application's run loop and handles application-level functionality such as routing input to the appropriate controller class.

UIApplication is a standard part of the UIKit, and it does its job mostly behind the scenes, so you don't need to worry about it for the most part. At certain well-defined times during an application's execution, however, UIApplication will call specific delegate methods, if there is a delegate and if it implements that method. For example, if you have code that needs to fire just before your program quits, you would implement the method applicationWillTerminate: in your application delegate and put your termination code there. This type of delegation allows your application to implement common application-wide behavior without needing to subclass UIApplication or, indeed, to even know anything about its inner workings.

Click *Button_FunAppDelegate.h* in the *Groups & Files* Pane to see the application delegate's header file. It should look similar to this:

```
#import <UIKit/UIKit.h>

@class Button_FunViewController;

@interface Button_FunAppDelegate : NSObject <UIApplicationDelegate> {
    UIWindow *window;
    Button_FunViewController *viewController;
}
@property (nonatomic, retain) IBOutlet UIWindow *window;
@property (nonatomic, retain) IBOutlet Button_FunViewController
    *viewController;

@end
```

We don't need to make any changes to this file, and after implementing our controller class, most of its contents should look familiar to you. One thing worth pointing out is this line of code:

```
@interface Button_FunAppDelegate : NSObject <UIApplicationDelegate> {
```

Do you see that value between the angle brackets? This indicates that this class conforms to a protocol called UIApplicationDelegate. Hold down the option key, and move your cursor so that it is over the word UIApplicationDelegate. Your cursor should turn into crosshairs; when it does, double-click. This will open a small window showing a brief overview of the UIApplicationDelegate protocol, as shown in Figure 3–3.

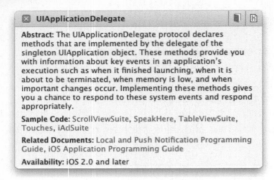

Figure 3–3. *We option-double-clicked <UIApplicationDelegate> from within our source code, and Xcode popped up this window, called the Quick Help panel, which describes the protocol.*

Notice the two icons in the upper-right corner of the floating documentation window. Click the left icon to view the full documentation for this symbol, or click the right icon to view the symbol's definition in a header file. This same trick works with class, protocol, and category names, as well as method names displayed in the editor pane. Just option-double-click a word, and it will search for that word in the documentation browser.

Knowing how to quickly look up things in the documentation is definitely worthwhile, but looking at the definition of this protocol is perhaps more important. Here's where you'll find which methods the application delegate can implement and when those methods will be called. It's probably worth your time to read over the descriptions of these methods.

> **NOTE:** If you've worked with Objective-C before but not with Objective-C 2.0, you should be aware that protocols can now specify optional methods. UIApplicationDelegate contains many optional methods. You do not need to implement any of the optional methods in your application delegate unless you have a reason to do so.

In the project's *Groups & Files* pane, click *Button_FunAppDelegate.m* to see the implementation of the application delegate. It should look something like this:

```
#import "Button_FunAppDelegate.h"
#import "Button_FunViewController.h"

@implementation Button_FunAppDelegate

@synthesize window;
@synthesize viewController;

- (BOOL)application:(UIApplication *)application
        didFinishLaunchingWithOptions:(NSDictionary *)launchOptions {

    // Override point for customization after application launch
```

```objc
    [window addSubview:viewController.view];
    [window makeKeyAndVisible];
    return YES;
}

- (void)applicationWillTerminate:(UIApplication *)application {
    // Save data if appropriate.
}

- (void)dealloc {
    [window release];
    [viewController release];
    [super dealloc];
}

@end
```

In the middle of the file, you can see that our application delegate has implemented one of the protocol's methods, `application:didFinishLaunchingWithOptions:` which, as you can probably guess, fires as soon as the application has finished all the setup work and is ready to start interacting with the user.

Our delegate version of `application:didFinishLaunchingWithOptions:` adds our view controller's view as a subview to the application's main window and makes the window visible, which is how the view we are going to design gets shown to the user. You don't need to do anything to make this happen; it's all part of the code generated by the template we used to build this project.

We just wanted to give you a bit of background on application delegates and show how this all ties together.

Editing MainWindow.xib

So far, we've looked at the four files in our project's *Classes* tab (two `.m` files, two `.h` files). In previous chapters, we've had experience with two of the three files in our project's `Resources` tab. We looked at the equivalent of *Button_Fun-Info.plist* when we added our icon to the project, and we looked at the equivalent of `Button_FunViewController.xib` when we added our "Hello, World!" label.

There's one other file in the *Resources* tab that we want to talk about. The file *MainWindow.xib* is what causes your application's delegate, main window, and view controller instances to get created at runtime. Remember, this file is provided as part of the project template. You don't need to change or do anything here. This is just a chance to see what's going on behind the scenes, to get a glimpse of the big picture.

Figure 3–4. *Our application's MainWindow.xib as it appears in Interface Builder*

Expand the *Resources* folder in Xcode's *Groups & Files* pane, and double-click *MainWindow.xib*. Once Interface Builder opens, take a look at the nib's main window — the one labeled *MainWindow.xib*, which should look like Figure 3–4.

You should recognize the first two icons in this window from Chapter 2. As a reminder, every icon in a nib window after the first two represents an object that will get instantiated when the nib file loads. Let's take a look at the third, fourth, and fifth icons.

> **NOTE:** Long names get truncated in the nib file's main window in the default view, as you can see in Figure 3–4. If you hold your cursor over one of these icons for a few seconds, a tooltip will pop up to show you the full name of the item. Note also that the names shown in the main window do not necessarily indicate the underlying class of the object. The default name for a new instance usually will clue you in to the underlying class, but these names can be, and often are, changed.

The third icon is an instance of `Button_FunAppDelegate`. The fourth icon is an instance of `Button_FunViewController`. And, finally, the fifth icon is our application's one and only window (an instance of `UIWindow`). These three icons indicate that once the nib file is loaded, our application will have one instance of the application delegate, `Button_FunAppDelegate`; one instance of our view controller, `Button_FunViewController`; and one instance of `UIWindow` (the class that represents the application's one and only window). As you can see, Interface Builder can do much more than just create interface elements. It allows you to create instances of other classes as well. This is an incredibly powerful feature. Every line of code that you don't write is a line of code you don't have to debug or maintain. Right here, we're creating three object instances at launch time without having to write a single line of code.

OK, that's all there is to see here, folks; move along. Be sure to close this nib file on the way out. And if you are prompted to save, just say "no," because you shouldn't have changed anything.

Editing Button_FunViewController.xib

Now that you have a handle on the files that make up our project and the concepts that bring them all together, let's go ahead and construct our interface.

Creating the View in Interface Builder

In Xcode, double-click *Button_FunViewController.xib* in the *Groups & Files* pane. The nib file should open in Interface Builder. Make sure the library is visible. If it's not, you can show it by selecting **Library** from the **Tools** menu. You also need to make sure that the nib's *View* window is open. If it's not, double-click the icon called *View* in the nib's main window (see Figure 3–5).

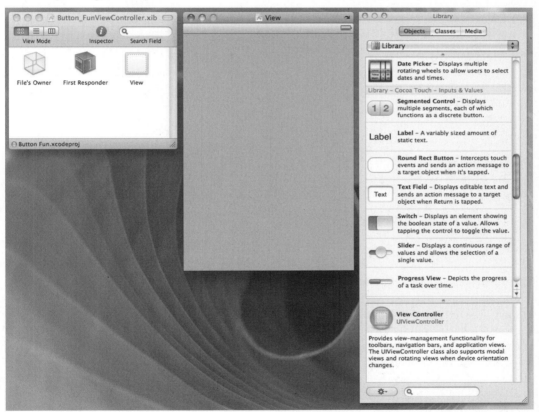

Figure 3–5. *Button_FunViewController.xib open in Interface Builder*

Now we're ready to design our interface. Drag a label from the library over to the view window, just as you did in the previous chapter. Place the label toward the bottom of the view, so the label lines up with the left and bottom blue guidelines (see Figure 3–6). Next, expand the label so the right side lines up with the guideline on the right side of the window.

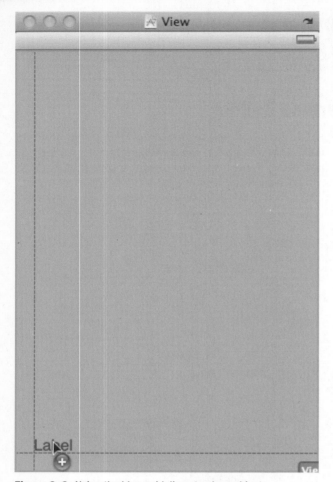

Figure 3–6. *Using the blue guidelines to place objects*

NOTE: The little blue guidelines are there to help you stick to the *Apple Human Interface Guidelines* (usually referred to as "the HIG"). Yep, just like it does for Mac OS X, Apple provides the *iPhone Human Interface Guidelines* for designing iPhone applications. The HIG tells you how you should—and shouldn't—design your user interface. You really should read it, because it contains valuable information that every iPhone developer needs to know. You'll find it at http://developer.apple.com/iphone/library/documentation/UserExperience/Conceptual/MobileHIG/.

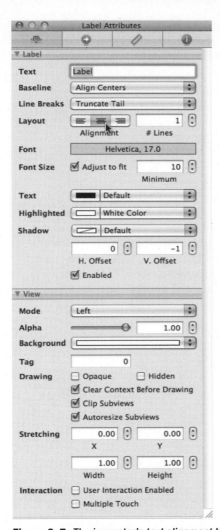

Figure 3–7. *The inspector's text alignment buttons*

After you've placed the label at the bottom of the view, click it to select it, and press ⌘1 to bring up the inspector. Change the text alignment to centered by using the text alignment buttons on the inspector (see Figure 3–7).

Now, double-click the label, and delete the existing text. We don't want any text to display until a button has been tapped.

Next, we're going to drag two *Round Rect Buttons* from the library (see Figure 3–8) to our view.

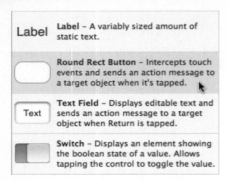

Label	**Label** – A variably sized amount of static text.
	Round Rect Button – Intercepts touch events and sends an action message to a target object when it's tapped.
Text	**Text Field** – Displays editable text and sends an action message to a target object when Return is tapped.
	Switch – Displays an element showing the boolean state of a value. Allows tapping the control to toggle the value.

Figure 3–8. *The Round Rect Button as it appears in the library*

Place the two buttons next to each other, roughly in the middle of the view. The exact placement doesn't matter. Double-click the button that you placed on the left. Doing this will allow the button's title to be edited, so go ahead and change its text to read "Left." Next, double-click the button on the right, and change its text to read "Right." When you're done, your view should look something like the one shown in Figure 3–9.

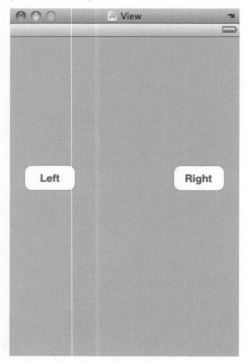

Figure 3–9. *The finished view*

Connecting Everything

We now have all the pieces of our interface. All that's left is to make the various connections that will allow these pieces to work together.

The first step is to make a connection from *File's Owner* to the label in the *View* window. Why *File's Owner*?

When an instance of `UIViewController` or one of its subclasses is instantiated, it can be told to initialize itself from a nib. In the template we've used, the `Button_FunViewController` class will be loaded from the nib file *Button_FunViewController.xib*. We don't have to do anything to make that happen; it's part of the project template we chose. In future chapters, you'll see exactly how that process works. Since the *MainWindow.xib* file contains an icon that represents *Button_FunViewController*, an instance of `Button_FunViewController` will get created automagically when our application launches. When that happens, that instance will automatically load *Button_FunViewController.xib* into memory and become its file's owner.

Earlier in the chapter, we added an outlet to `Button_FunViewController`, which is this nib's owner. We can now make a connection between that outlet and the label using the *File's Owner* icon. Let's look at how we do that.

> **NOTE:** It's OK if you don't fully understand the nib loading process yet. It's complicated, and we'll be talking about it and seeing it in action in several of the later chapters. For now, just remember that your controller class is the file's owner for the nib file of the same name.

Connecting Outlets

Hold down the control key; click the *File's Owner* icon in the main nib window; and keep the mouse button down. Drag away from the *File's Owner* icon toward the *View window*. A blue guideline should appear. Keep dragging until your cursor is over the label in the *View* window. Even though you won't be able to see the label, it will magically appear once you are over it (see Figure 3–10).

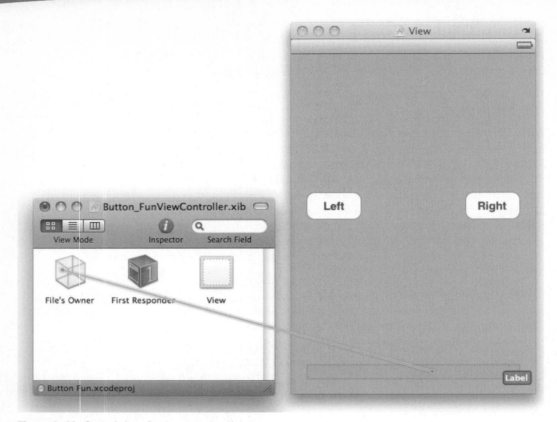

Figure 3–10. *Control-dragging to connect outlets*

With the cursor still over the label, let go of the mouse button, and a small gray menu like the one shown in Figure 3–11 should pop up.

Select *statusText* from the gray menu.

By control-dragging from *File's Owner* to an interface object, you are telling Interface Builder that you want to connect one of the *File's Owner's* outlets to this object when the nib file is loaded. In this case, the file's owner is the class Button_FunViewController, and the Button_FunViewController outlet we are interested in is statusText. When we control-dragged from *File's Owner* to the label object and selected statusText from the pop-up menu that appeared, we told Interface Builder to have Button_FunViewController's statusText outlet point to the label, so any time we refer to statusText in our code, we will be dealing with this label. Cool, eh?

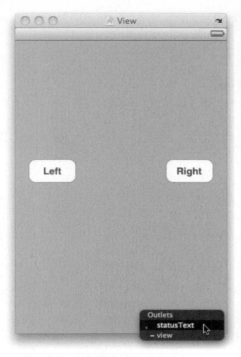

Figure 3–11. *Outlet selection menu*

Specifying Actions

The only thing left to do is to identify which actions these buttons trigger and under what circumstances they trigger them. If you're familiar with Cocoa programming for Mac OS X, you're probably getting ready to control-drag from the buttons over to the *File's Owner* icon. And, to be honest, that will work, but it's not the best way to do it.

iPhone is different from Mac OS X, and here's one of the places where that difference becomes apparent. On the Mac, a control can be associated with just one action, and that action is typically triggered when that control is used. There are some exceptions to this, but by and large, a control triggers its corresponding action method when the mouse button is released if the cursor is still inside the bounds of that control.

Figure 3–12. *The connections inspector showing our button's available events*

Controls in Cocoa Touch offer a lot more possibilities, so instead of click-dragging from the control, it's best to get in the habit of using the connections inspector, which we can get to by pressing ⌘2 or selecting **Connection Inspector** from the **Tools** menu. Click the *Left* button, and then bring up the connections inspector. It should look like Figure 3–12.

Under the heading *Events*, you'll see a whole list of events that can potentially trigger an action. If you like, you can associate different actions with different events. For example, you might use *Touch Up Inside* to trigger one action, while *Touch Drag Inside* triggers a different action. Our situation is relatively simple and straightforward. When the user taps our button, we want it to call our `buttonPressed:` method. The first question is, which of the events in Figure 3–12 do we use?

The answer, which may not be obvious at first, is *Touch Up Inside*. When the user's finger lifts up from the screen, if the last place it touched before lifting was inside the button, the user triggers a touch up inside. Think about what happens in most of your iPhone applications if you touch the screen and change your mind. You move your finger off the button before lifting up, right? We should give our users the same ability. If our user's finger is still on the button when it's lifted off the screen, then we can safely assume that the button tap is intended.

Now that we know the event we want to trigger our action, how do we associate the event with a specific action method?

See that little circle in the inspector to the right of *Touch Up Inside*? Click in that circle and drag away with the mouse button still pressed; there's no need to hold down the control key this time. You should get a gray connection line, just as you did when we were connecting outlets earlier. Drag this line over to the *File's Owner* icon, and when the little gray menu pops up, select button Pressed:. Remember, the *File's Owner* icon represents the class whose nib we are editing. In this case, *File's Owner* represents our application's sole instance of the `Button_FunView Controller` class. When we drag from the button's event to the *File's Owner* icon, we are telling Interface Builder to call the selected method when the specified event occurs. So when the user touches up inside the button, the `Button_FunViewController` class's `buttonPressed:` method will be called.

Do this same sequence with the other button and then save. Now, any time the user taps one of these buttons, our `buttonPressed:` method will get called.

Trying It Out

Save the nib file; then head back to Xcode and take your application for a spin. Select **Build and Run** from the **Build** menu. Your code should compile, and your application should come up in the iPhone Simulator. When you tap the left button, the text "Left button pressed." should appear, as it does in Figure 3–1. If you then tap the right button, the label will change to say "Right button pressed."

Bring It on Home

This chapter's simple application introduced you to MVC, creating and connecting outlets and actions, implementing view controllers, and using application delegates. You learned how to trigger action methods when a button is tapped and saw how to change the text of a label at runtime. Although we built a simple application, the basic concepts we used are the same as those that underlie the use of all controls under iOS, not just buttons. In fact, the way we used buttons and labels in this chapter is pretty much the way that we will implement and interact with most of the standard controls under iOS.

It's critical that you understand everything we did in this chapter and why we did it. If you don't, go back and redo the parts that you don't fully understand. This is important stuff! If you don't make sure you understand everything now, you will only get more confused as we get into creating more complex interfaces later on in this book.

In the next chapter, we'll take a look at some of the other standard iOS controls. You'll also learn how to use alerts to notify the user of important happenings and how to use action sheets to indicate that the user needs to make a choice before proceeding. When you feel you're ready to proceed, give yourself a pat on the back for being such an awesome student, and head on over to the next chapter.

Chapter **4**

More User Interface Fun

In Chapter 3, we discussed the MVC concept and built an application that brought that idea to life. You learned about outlets and actions, and used them to tie a button control to a text label. In this chapter, we're going to build an application that will take your knowledge of controls to a whole new level.

We'll implement an image view, a slider, two different text fields, a segmented control, a couple of switches, and an iOS button that looks more like, well, an iOS button. You'll learn how to use the view hierarchy to group multiple items under a common parent view and make manipulating the interface at runtime easier. You'll see how to set and retrieve the values of various controls, both by using outlets and by using the sender argument of our action methods. After that, we'll look at using action sheets to force the user to make a choice and alerts to give the user important feedback. You'll also learn about control states and the use of stretchable images to make buttons look the way they should.

Because this chapter's application uses so many different user interface items, we're going to work a little differently than we did in the previous two chapters. We'll break our application into pieces, implementing one piece at a time and bouncing back and forth between Xcode and the iOS simulator, testing each piece before we move on to the next. Dividing the process of building a complex interface into smaller chunks makes it much less intimidating, as well as more like the actual process you'll go through when building your own applications. This code-compile-debug cycle makes up a large part of a software developer's typical day.

A Screen Full of Controls

As we mentioned, the application we're going to build in this chapter is a bit more complex than the one we created in Chapter 3. We're still going to use only a single view and controller, but as you can see in Figure 4–1, there's quite a bit more going on in this one view.

Figure 4–1. *The Control Fun application, featuring text fields, labels, a slider, and several other stock iOS controls*

The logo at the top of the iPhone screen is an **image view**, and in this application, it does nothing more than display a static image. Below the logo are two **text fields**: one that allows the entry of alphanumeric text and one that allows only numbers. Below the text fields is a **slider**. As the user moves the slider, the value of the label next to it will change so that it always reflects the slider's value.

Below the slider are a **segmented control** and two **switches**. The segmented control will toggle between two different types of controls in the space below it. When the application first launches, two switches will appear below the segmented control. Changing the value of either switch will cause the other one to change its value to match. Now, this isn't something you would likely do in a real application, but it does demonstrate how to change the value of a control programmatically and how Cocoa Touch animates certain actions without you needing to do any work.

Figure 4–2 shows what happens when the user taps the segmented control. The switches disappear and are replaced by a button. When the *Do Something* button is pressed, an action sheet pops up, asking users if they really meant to tap the button (see Figure 4–3). This is the standard way of responding to input that is potentially dangerous or that could have significant repercussions, and gives users a chance to stop potential badness from happening. If *Yes, I'm Sure!* is selected, the application will put up an alert, letting the user know that everything is OK (see Figure 4–4).

Figure 4–2. *Tapping the segmented controller on the left side cause a pair of switches to be displayed. Tapping the right side causes a button to be displayed.*

Figure 4–3. *Our application uses an action sheet to solicit a response from the user.*

Figure 4–4. *Alerts are used to notify the user when important things happen. We use one here to confirm that everything went OK.*

Active, and Passive Controls

User interface controls come in three basic forms: active and passive. The buttons that we used in the previous chapter are classic examples of active controls. You push them, and something happens—usually, a piece of code fires.

Some controls can work in a passive manner, simply holding on to a value that the user has entered until you're ready for it. These controls don't trigger action methods, but the user can interact with them and change their values. A classic example of a passive control is a text field on a web page. Although there can be validation code that fires when you tab out of a field, the vast majority of web page text fields are simply containers for data that's submitted to the server when you click the submit button. The text fields themselves don't actually trigger any code to fire, but when the submit button is clicked, the text field's data goes along for the ride.

On an iOS device, many of the available controls can be used in all both ways, depending on your needs. All iOS controls are subclasses of UIControl and, because of that, are capable of triggering action methods. Most controls can also be used passively. However, some controls, such as buttons, really don't serve much purpose unless they are used in an active manner to trigger code.

As you might expect, there are some behavioral differences between controls on iOS and those on your Mac. Here are a few examples:

- Because of the multitouch interface, all iOS controls can trigger multiple actions depending on how they are touched. The user might trigger a different action with a finger swipe across the control than with just a touch.

- You could have one action fire when the user presses down on a button and a separate action fire when the finger is lifted off the button.

- You could have a single control call multiple action methods on a single event. You could have two different action methods fire on the touch up inside event, meaning that both methods would be called when the user's finger is lifted after touching that button.

NOTE: Having a control call multiple action methods would be a bit of a deviation from the MVC architecture, and you're probably better off implementing a single action method that does all you need for that particular button press instead. But it's good to bear in mind when working in Interface Builder that connecting an event to an action doesn't necessarily disconnect a previously connected action from the same event! This can lead to surprising misbehaviors in your app, so keep an eye open when retargeting an event in Interface Builder.

Another major difference between iOS and the Mac stems from the fact that, normally, iOS devices have no physical keyboard (unless, of course, you attach an external keyboard). The standard iOS keyboard is actually just a view filled with a series of button controls. Your code will likely never directly interact with the iOS keyboard, but as you'll see later in the chapter, sometimes you need to write code to make the keyboard behave in exactly the manner you want.

Creating the Application

Fire up Xcode if it's not already open, and create a new project called *Control Fun*. We're going to use the View-based Application template again, so create your project just as you did in the previous two chapters.

Now that you've created your project, let's get the image we'll use in our image view. The image must be imported into Xcode before it will be available for use inside Interface Builder, so we'll import it now. You can find a suitable *.png* image in the project archives in the *04 Control Fun* folder, or you can use an image of your own choosing. If you use your own image, make sure that it is a *.png* image sized correctly for the space available. It should be fewer than 100 pixels tall and a maximum of 300 pixels wide so that it can comfortably fit at the top of the view without being resized.

Add the image to the *Resources* folder of your project, just as we did in Chapter 2, by dragging the image from the Finder to the *Resources* folder.

Implementing the Image View and Text Fields

With the image added to your project, your next step is to implement the five interface elements at the top of the application's screen: the image view, the two text fields, and the two labels (see Figure 4–5).

Figure 4–5. *The image view, labels, and text fields we will implement first*

Determining Outlets

Before we start building this GUI, we need to figure out which of these objects requires an outlet. Remember that outlets must be defined in your controller class's header file before you can connect them to anything in the nib editor.

The image view is just a static image. We're going to designate the image to be displayed directly in Interface Builder, and that image won't change while our application is running. As a result, it does not require an outlet. If we *did* want to change the image or any of its characteristics at runtime, we *would* need an outlet. That is not the case here.

The same is true for the two labels. They are there to display text, but won't be changed at runtime, and the user won't interact with them. So, we don't need outlets for them either.

On the other hand, the two text fields are not really much use if we can't get to the data they contain. The way to access the data held by a passive control is to use an outlet, so we need to define an outlet for each of these text fields. This is old hat for you by now, so why don't you add two outlets and their corresponding properties to your *Control_FunViewController.h* class file using the names `nameField` and `numberField`? When you're finished, *Control_FunViewController.h* should look something like this:

```
#import <UIKit/UIKit.h>

@interface Control_FunViewController : UIViewController {
    UITextField *nameField;
    UITextField *numberField;
}
@property (nonatomic, retain) IBOutlet UITextField *nameField;
@property (nonatomic, retain) IBOutlet UITextField *numberField;
@end
```

Before we move on to the nib file, let's also add our @synthesize directives to
Control_FunViewController.m:

```
#import "Control_FunViewController.h"

@implementation Control_FunViewController
@synthesize nameField;
@synthesize numberField;
...
```

> **NOTE:** See the ellipsis (**...**) at the end of that code listing? We'll use that symbol to indicate that
> there is existing code beyond what we've shown in the listing that does not require any changes.
> In this chapter, we'll add all of our code to the top of the implementation file, so by using the
> ellipsis, we can avoid needing to show the whole file every time we have you add a line or two of
> code.

We also need to make sure that we're careful about memory. Since we declared the
`nameField` and `numberField` properties with the `retain` keyword, we need to release
them both in our `dealloc` method. Scroll down to the bottom of the file, and add the
following two lines to the existing `dealloc` method:

```
- (void)dealloc {
    [nameField release];
    [numberField release];
    [super dealloc];
}
```

Determining Actions

Take a look at the five objects in Figure 4–5 again. Do you see the need to declare any
actions? Since we won't be allowing our user to interact with the labels or image view,
there's no reason to create actions for them, right? Right.

What about the two text fields? Text fields are the classic passive control. The vast
majority of the time, all they do is hold onto values until you're ready for them. We're not
doing any validation on these fields, other than limiting the input of the number field by
showing only the number pad instead of the full keyboard (which we can do entirely in
Interface Builder), so we don't need an action for these either, right? Well, hold that
thought. Let's build and test the first part of our user interface.

Building the Interface

Make sure both of those files are saved, expand the *Resources* folder in the *Groups &
Files* pane, and double-click *Control_FunViewController.xib* to launch Interface Builder. If
the window titled *View* is not open, double-click the *View* icon in the nib file's main
window.

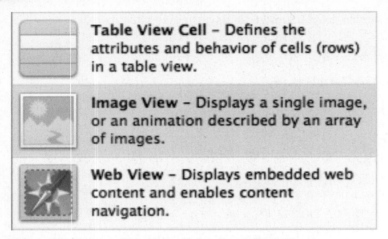

Figure 4–6. *The Image View element in Interface Builder's library*

Now, turn your attention to the library. If it's not open, select **Library** from the **Tools** menu. Scroll about one-fourth of the way through the list until you find *Image View* (see Figure 4–6).

Adding the Image View

Drag an image view onto the window called *View*. Because this is the first item you're putting on your view, Interface Builder is going to automatically resize the image view so that it's the same size as the view. Since we don't want our image view to take the entire space, use the drag handles to resize the image view to the approximate size of the image you imported into Xcode. Don't worry about getting it exactly right yet. It'll be easier to do that in a moment.

By the way, sometimes an object will get deselected and can be very hard to select again because it is behind another object, takes up the entire view, or has no drawn border. In those cases, don't despair! There is a way to select the object again. In the nib's main window, you'll see three buttons labeled *View Mode*. Click the middle one, and you'll get a hierarchical view of the nib, which will let you drill down into subviews, as shown in Figure 4–7. Double-clicking any item in this view will also cause the same item to become selected in the *View* window.

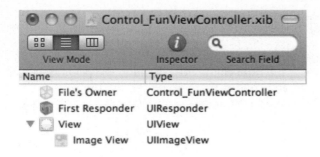

Figure 4–7. *Putting the nib's main window in hierarchical view and drilling down to subviews*

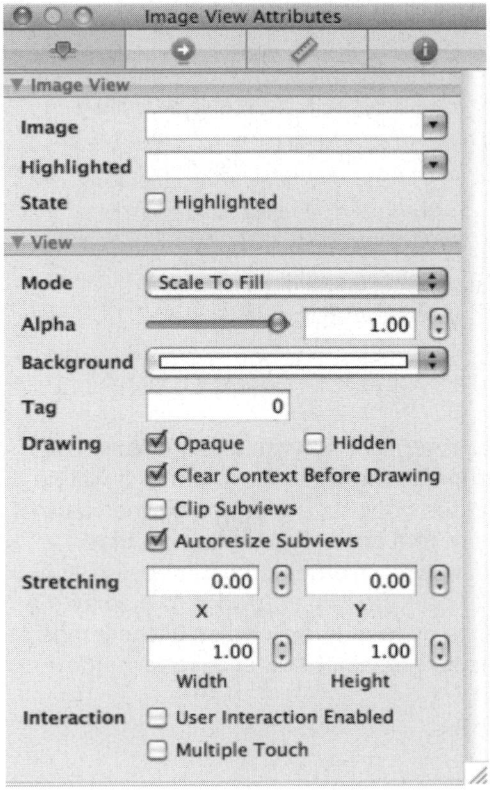

Figure 4–8. *The image view attributes inspector*

With the image view selected, bring up the inspector by pressing ⌘1, and you should see the editable options of the UIImageView class, as shown in Figure 4–8.

The most important setting for our image view is the topmost item in the inspector, labeled *Image*. If you click the little arrow to the right of the field, a menu will pop up with the available images, which should include any images that you added to your Xcode project. Select the image you added a minute ago. Your image should now appear in your image view.

Resize the Image View

Now, resize your image view so that it is exactly the same size as your image. We'll talk about why in a moment. An easy way to resize the view so that it's the same size as the selected image is to press ⌘= or to select **Size to Fit** from the **Layout** menu, which will automatically resize any view to the exact size needed to contain its contents. You'll also want to move the resized image so that it's centered and the top is aligned with the blue guidelines. You can easily center an item in the view by choosing **Align Horizontal Center in Container** from the **Layout** menu's **Alignment** submenu.

> **TIP:** Dragging and resizing views in Interface Builder can be tricky. Don't forget about the hierarchical *View Mode* button in the main nib window. It will help you find and select (double-click) the image view. When it comes to resizing, hold down the option key. Interface Builder will draw some helpful red lines on the screen that make it much easier to get a sense of the image view's size. This trick won't work for dragging, but if you select **Show Bounds Rectangles** from the **Layout** Menu, it will draw a line around all of your interface items, making them easier to see. You can turn those lines off by selecting **Show Bounds Rectangles** a second time.

The Mode Attribute

The next option down in the image view inspector is a pop-up menu labeled **Mode**. The **Mode** menu defines how the image will be aligned inside the view and whether it will be scaled to fit. You can feel free to play with the various options, but choosing the value of *Center* is probably best for our needs. Keep in mind that choosing any option that causes the image to scale will potentially add processing overhead, so it's best to avoid those and size your images correctly before you import them. If you want to display the same image at multiple sizes, generally it's better to have multiple copies of the image at different sizes in your project rather than force the iOS device to do scaling at runtime.

The Alpha Slider

The next item in the inspector is *Alpha*, and this is one you need to be very careful with. Alpha defines how transparent your image is: how much of what's beneath it shows through. If you have any value less than 1.0, your iPhone will draw this view as transparent so that any objects underneath it show through. With a value less than 1.0, even if there's nothing actually underneath your image, you will cause your application to spend processor cycles calculating transparency, so don't set this to anything other than 1.0 unless you have a very good reason for doing so.

Ignore the Background

You can ignore the next item down, called *Background*. This is a property inherited from UIView, but it doesn't impact the appearance of an image view.

The Tag Attribute

The next item down—*Tag*—is worth mentioning, though we won't be using it in this chapter. All subclasses of UIView, including all views and controls, have a property called *tag*, which is just a numeric value that you can set that will tag along with your image view. The tag is designed for your use; the system will never set or change its value. If you assign a tag value to a control or view, you can be sure that the tag will always have that value unless you change it.

Tags provide an easy, language-independent way of identifying objects on your interface. Let's say you had five different buttons, each with a different label, and you wanted to use a single action method to handle all five buttons. In that case, you would probably need some way to differentiate among the buttons when your action method was called. Sure, you could look at the button's title, but code that does that probably won't work when your application is translated into Swahili or Sanskrit. Unlike labels, tags will never change, so if you set a tag value here in Interface Builder, you can then use that as a fast and reliable way to check which control was passed into an action method in the sender argument.

The Drawing Checkboxes

Below *Tag* are a series of *Drawing* checkboxes. The first one is labeled *Opaque*. Make sure it is checked. This tells the iOS that nothing behind your view should be drawn and allows the iOS drawing methods to do some optimizations that speed up drawing.

You might be wondering why we need to select the Opaque checkbox, when we've already set the value of *Alpha* to 1.0 to indicate no transparency. The reason is that the alpha value applies to the parts of the image to be drawn, but if an image doesn't completely fill the image view, or there are holes in the image thanks to an alpha channel or clipping path, the objects below will still show through regardless of the value set in *Alpha*. By selecting *Opaque*, we are telling iOS that nothing below this view ever needs to be drawn no matter what, so it needn't waste processing time with anything below our object. We can safely select the Opaque checkbox, because we earlier selected *Size to Fit*, which caused the image view to match the size of the image it contains.

The *Hidden* checkbox does exactly what you think it does. If it's checked, the user can't see this control. Hiding the control can be useful at times, including later in this chapter when we hide the switches and button, but the vast majority of the time you want this to remain unchecked. We can leave this at the default value.

The next checkbox, called *Clear Context Before Drawing*, will rarely need to be checked. When it is checked, iOS will draw the entire area covered by the control in transparent black before it actually draws the control. Again, it is turned off for the sake of performance and because it's rarely needed. Make sure this check box is unchecked.

Clip Subviews is an interesting option. If your view has subviews, and those subviews are not completely contained within the bounds of its parent view, this checkbox determines how the subviews will be drawn. If *Clip Subviews* is checked, only the portions of subviews that lie within the bounds of the parent will be drawn. If *Clip Subviews* is unchecked, subviews will be drawn completely even if they lie outside of the bounds of the parent.

It might seem that the default behavior should be the opposite of what it actually is: that *Clip Subviews* should be enabled by default. As with many other things on the iPhone, this has to do with performance. Calculating the clipping area and displaying only part of the subviews is a somewhat costly operation, mathematically speaking, and most of the time, a subview won't lay outside the bounds of the superview. You can turn on *Clip Subviews* if you really need it for some reason, but it is off by default for the sake of performance.

The final checkbox in this section, *Autoresize Subviews*, tells iOS to resize any subviews if this view is resized. Leave this checked. Since we don't allow the view to be resized, this setting does not really matter.

The Interaction Checkboxes

The last two checkboxes have to do with user interaction. The first checkbox, *User Interaction Enabled*, specifies whether the user can do anything at all with this object. For most controls, this box will be checked, because if it's not, the control will never be able to trigger action methods. However, labels and image views default to unchecked, because they are very often used just for the display of static information. Since all we're doing here is displaying a picture on the screen, there is no need to turn this on.

The last checkbox is *Multiple Touch*, and it determines whether this control is capable of receiving multitouch events. Multitouch events allows complex gestures like the pinch gesture used to zoom in many iOS applications. We'll talk more about gestures and multitouch events in Chapter 15. Since this image view doesn't accept user interaction at all, there's no reason to turn on multitouch events, so leave it unchecked.

Adding the Text Fields

Once you have your image view all finished, grab a text field from the library, and drag it over to the *View* window. Place it underneath the image view, using the blue guides to align it with the right margin (see Figure 4–9). A horizontal blue guideline will appear just above the text field when you move it very close to the bottom of your image. That guideline tells you when you are as close as you should possibly be to another object. You can leave your text field there for now, but to give it a balanced appearance, consider moving the text field just a little further down. Remember, you can always come back to Interface Builder and change the position and size of interface elements without having to change code or reestablish connections.

After you drop the text field, grab a label from the library, and drag that over so it is aligned with the left margin of the view and aligned vertically with the text field you placed earlier. Note that multiple blue guidelines will pop up as you move the label around, making it easy to align the label to the text field using the top, bottom, middle, or text baseline. We're going to align the label and the text field using the text baseline guide, which will draw a line from the bottom of the label's text going through the text field, as shown in Figure 4–10. If the blue guideline is being drawn through the middle of the label's text, you're on the center guideline, not the text baseline guide. Using the text baseline guide will cause the label's text label and the text that the user will type into the text field to be at the same vertical position on the screen.

Figure 4–9. *Placing the text field. Notice the blue guideline just above the text field that tells you not to move the text field any closer to the image.*

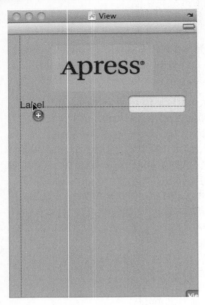

Figure 4–10. *Aligning the label and text field using the baseline guide*

Double-click the label you just dropped, change it to read *Name*: instead of *Label*, and press the return key to commit your changes. Next, drag another text field from the library to the view, and use the guidelines to place it below the first text field (see Figure 4–11).

Once you've placed the second text field, grab another label from the library, and place it on the left side, below the existing label. Use the blue text baseline guide again to align it with the second text field. Double-click the new label, and change it to read *Number:*.

Now, let's expand the size of the bottom text field to the left. Single-click the bottom text field, and drag the left resize dot to the left until a blue guideline appears to tell you that you are as close as you should ever be to the label (see Figure 4–12).

Now expand the top text field the same way so that it matches the bottom one in size. Note that we did the bottom one first because the bottom label is the larger of the two labels.

We're basically done with the text fields except for one small detail. Look back at Figure 4–5. See how the *Name*: and *Number*: are right-aligned? Right now, ours are both against the left margin. To align the right sides of the two labels, click the *Name*: label, hold down the shift key, and click the *Number*: label so both labels are selected. From the **Alignment** submenu of the **Layout** menu, select **Align Right Edges**.

Figure 4–11. *Adding the second text field*

Figure 4–12. *Expanding the size of the bottom text field*

Figure 4–13. *The inspector for a text field showing the default values*

When you are done, the interface should look very much like the one shown in Figure 4–5. The only difference is the light gray text in each text field. We'll add that now.

Click somewhere where there's no control to deselect the two labels, then select the top text field and press ⌘**1** to bring up the inspector (see Figure 4–13).

The Text Field Inspector Settings

Text fields are one of the most complex controls on iOS as well as being one of the most commonly used. Let's look at the topmost section of the inspector first. In the first field, *Text*, you can set a default value for this field. Whatever you type in this field will show up in the text field when your application launches.

The second field, *Placeholder*, allows you to specify a bit of text that will be displayed in gray inside the text field, but only when the field has no value. You can use a placeholder instead of a label if space is tight, or you can use it to clarify what the user should type into this field.

Type in the text *Type in a name* as the placeholder for this text field.

The next two fields are used only if you need to customize the appearance of your text field, which is completely unnecessary and actually ill-advised the vast majority of the time. Users expect text fields to look a certain way. As a result, we're going to skip right over the *Background* and *Disabled* fields and leave them blank.

Below these fields are three buttons for controlling the alignment of the text displayed in the field. We'll leave this field at the default value of left-aligned (the leftmost button).

Next are four buttons labeled *Border*. These allow you to change the way the text field's edge will be drawn. You can feel free to try all four different styles, but the default value is the rightmost button, and it creates the text field style that users are most accustomed to seeing for normal text fields in an iOS application, so when you're done playing, set it back to that one.

The *Clear When Editing Begins* checkbox specifies what happens when the user touches this field. If this box is checked, any value that was previously in this field will get deleted, and the user will start with an empty field. If this box is unchecked, the previous value will stay in the field, and the user will be able to edit it. Make sure this checkbox is unchecked.

The *Text Color* field is a combination of a color well (if you click on the left side) and a popup menu. We'll leave *Text Color* at its default setting of black.

The *Adjust to Fit* checkbox specifies whether the size of the text should shrink if the text field is reduced in size. Adjusting to fit will keep the entire text visible in the view even if the text would normally be too big to fit in the allotted space. To the right of the checkbox is a text field that allows you to specify a minimum text size. No matter the size of the field, the text will not be resized below that minimum size. Specifying a minimum size will allow you to make sure that the text doesn't get too small to be readable.

Text Input Traits

The next section defines how the keyboard will look and behave when this text field is being used. Since we're expecting a name, let's change the *Capitalize* drop-down to *Words*, which will cause every word to be automatically capitalized, which is what you typically want with names. Let's also change the value of the *Return Key* pop-up to *Done* and leave all the other text input traits at their default values. The *Return Key* is the key on the lower right of the keyboard, and its label changes based on what you're doing. If you are entering text into Safari's search field, for example, then it says *Google*. In an application like this, where there text fields share the screen with other controls, *Done* is the right choice. We'll leave the other three popups at their default values.

If the *Auto-enable Return Key* checkbox is checked, the return key is disabled until at least one character is typed into the text field. Leave this unchecked because we want to allow the text field to remain empty if the user so chooses.

The *Secure* checkbox specifies whether the characters being typed are displayed in the text field. You'd check this checkbox if this text field was being used as a password field. Leave it unchecked.

And the Rest . . .

The next section allows you to set general control attributes inherited from UIControl, but these generally don't apply to text fields and, with the exception of the *Enabled* checkbox, won't affect the field's appearance. We want to leave these text fields enabled so that the user can interact with them, so just leave everything here as is.

The last section on the inspector should look familiar to you. It's identical to the section of the same name on the image view inspector we looked at a few minutes ago. These are attributes inherited from the UIView class, and since all controls are subclasses of UIView, they all share this section of attributes. Note that for a text field, you do not want to check Opaque, because doing so will make the entered text unreadable. In fact, you can leave all the values in this section exactly as they are.

Set the Attributes for the Second Text Field

Next, single-click the second text field in the *View* window, and return to the inspector. In the *Placeholder* field, type *Type in a number*. In the section called *Text Input Traits*, click the *Keyboard Type* pop-up menu. Since we want the user to enter numbers only, not letters, go ahead and select *Number Pad*. By doing this, the users will be presented with a keyboard containing only numbers, meaning they won't be able to enter alphabetical characters, symbols, or anything besides numbers. We don't have to set the *Return Key* value for the numeric keypad, because that style of keyboard doesn't have a return key, so everything else on the inspector can stay at the default values.

Connecting Outlets

OK, for this first part of the interface, all that's left is hooking up our outlets. Control-drag from *File's Owner* to each of the text fields, and connect them to their corresponding outlets. Save the nib file once you've connected both text fields to their corresponding outlets, and then go back to Xcode.

Closing the Keyboard

Let's see how our app works, shall we? Select **Build and Run** from Xcode's **Build** menu. Your application should come up in the iOS simulator. Click the *Name* text field. The traditional keyboard should appear. Type in a name. Now, tap the *Number* field. The numeric keypad should appear (see Figure 4–14). Cocoa Touch gives us all this functionality for free just by adding text fields to our interface.

Figure 4–14. *The keyboard comes up automatically when you touch either the text field or the number field.*

Woo-hoo! But there's a little problem. How do you get the keyboard to go away? Go ahead and try. We'll wait right here while you do that.

Closing the Keyboard When Done Is Tapped

Because the keyboard is software-based, rather than a physical keyboard, we need to take a few extra steps to make sure the keyboard goes away when the user is finished with it. When the user taps the *Done* button on the text keyboard, a *Did End On Exit* event will be generated, and at that time, we need to tell the text field to give up control so that the keyboard will go away. In order to do that, we need to add an action method to our controller class, so add the following line of code to *Control_FunViewController.h*:

```
#import <UIKit/UIKit.h>

@interface Control_FunViewController : UIViewController {
    UITextField     *nameField;
    UITextField     *numberField;
}
@property (nonatomic, retain) IBOutlet UITextField *nameField;
@property (nonatomic, retain) IBOutlet UITextField *numberField;
- (IBAction)textFieldDoneEditing:(id)sender;
@end
```

Now switch over to *Control_FunViewController.m*, and we'll implement this method. Only one line of code is needed in this new action method to make it work. Add the following method to *Control_FunViewController.m*:

```
- (IBAction)textFieldDoneEditing:(id)sender {
    [sender resignFirstResponder];
}
```

As you've learned in Chapter 2, the first responder is the control with which the user is currently interacting. In our new method, we tell our control to resign as a first responder, giving up that role to the previous control the user worked with. When a text field yields first responder status, the keyboard associated with it goes away.

Save both of the files you just edited. Double-click *Control_FunViewController.xib* to hop back over to Interface Builder and trigger this action from both of our text fields.

Once you're back in Interface Builder, single-click the *Name* text field, and press ⌘2 to bring up the connections inspector. This time, we don't want the *Touch Up Inside* event that we used in the previous chapter. Instead, we want *Did End On Exit* since that is the event that will fire when the user taps the *Done* button on the keyboard. Drag from the circle next to *Did End On Exit* to the *File's Owner* icon, and connect it to the `textFieldDoneEditing:` action. Repeat with the other text field, and save. Let's go back to Xcode to build and run again.

> **TIP:** If you drag from *Did End On Exit* but the *File's Owner* icon does not highlight, signifying you can complete the drag, chances are that you did not save your source code before you switched over to editing the nib file. Select the controller's header file, save, and try again. That should do the trick!

When the simulator appears, click the *Name* field, type in something, and then tap the *Done* button. Sure enough, the keyboard drops away, just as you expected. All right! What about the *Number* field, though? Um, where's the *Done* button on that one (see Figure 4–14)?

Well, crud! Not all keyboard layouts feature a *Done* button. We could force the user to tap the *Name* field and then tap *Done*, but that's not very user-friendly, is it? And we most definitely want our application to be user-friendly. Let's see how to handle this situation.

Touching the Background to Close the Keyboard

Can you recall what Apple's iOS applications do in this situation? Well, in most places where there are text fields, tapping anywhere in the view where there's no active control will cause the keyboard to go away. How do we implement that?

The answer is probably going to surprise you because of its simplicity. Our view controller has a property called view that it inherited from UIViewController. This view property corresponds to the *View* icon in the nib file. This property points to an instance of UIView in the nib that acts as a container for all the items in our user interface. It has no appearance in the user interface, but it covers the entire iPhone window, sitting "below" all of the other user interface objects. It is sometimes referred to as a nib's **container view** because its main purpose is to simply hold other views and controls. For all intents and purposes, the container view is the background of our user interface.

Using Interface Builder, we can change the class of the object that view points to so that its underlying class is UIControl instead of UIView. Because UIControl is a subclass of UIView, it is perfectly appropriate for us to connect our view property to an instance of UIControl. Remember that when a class subclasses another object, it is just a more specific version of that class, so a UIControl *is* a UIView. If we simply change the instance that is created from UIView to UIControl, we gain the ability to trigger action methods. Before we do that, though, we need to create an action method that will be called when the background is tapped.

We need to add one more action to our controller class. Add the following line to your *Control_FunViewController.h* file:

```
#import <UIKit/UIKit.h>

@interface Control_FunViewController : UIViewController {
    UITextField *nameField;
    UITextField *numberField;
}
@property (nonatomic, retain) IBOutlet UITextField *nameField;
@property (nonatomic, retain) IBOutlet UITextField *numberField;
- (IBAction)textFieldDoneEditing:(id)sender;
- (IBAction)backgroundTap:(id)sender;
@end
```

Save the header file.

Now, switch over to the implementation file and add the following code, which simply tells both text fields to yield first responder status if they have it. It is perfectly safe to call resignFirstResponder on a control that is not the first responder, so we can call it on both text fields without needing to check whether either is the first responder.

```
- (IBAction)backgroundTap:(id)sender {
    [nameField resignFirstResponder];
    [numberField resignFirstResponder];
}
```

> **TIP:** You'll be switching between header and implementation files a lot as you code. Fortunately, in addition to the convenience provided by the assistant, Xcode also has a key combination that will switch you between counterparts quickly. The default key combination is ⌥⌘↑ (option-command-up arrow), although you can change it to anything you want using Xcode's preferences.

Save this file, and go back to Interface Builder. We now need to change the underlying class of our nib's view. If you look at the nib's main window in icon view mode (Figure 4–15), you'll see that there are three icons in that view. The third icon, View, is our nib's main view that holds all the other controls and views as subviews.

Figure 4–15. *The nib's main window has three icons. The third one, labeled View, is our nib's content view.*

Single-click the *View* icon and press ⌘**4** to bring up the **identity inspector** (Figure 4–16). This is where we can change the underlying class of any object instance in Interface Builder.

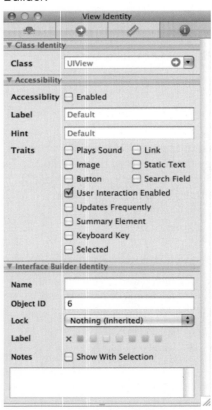

Figure 4–16. *The identity inspector allows you to change the underlying class of any object instance in a nib.*

The field labeled *Class* currently says *UIView*. Change it to read *UIControl*. All controls that are capable of triggering action methods are subclasses of UIControl, so by changing the underlying class, we have just given this view the ability to trigger action methods. You can verify this by pressing ⌘**2** to bring up the connections inspector (Figure 4–17). You should now see all the events that you saw before when you were connecting buttons to actions in the previous chapter.

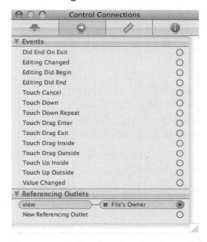

Figure 4–17. *By changing the class of our view from UIView to UIControl, we gain the ability to trigger action methods on any of the standard events.*

Drag from the *Touch Down* event to the *File's Owner* icon, and choose the backgroundTap: action. Now, touches anywhere in the view without an active control will trigger our new action method, which will cause the keyboard to retract.

> **NOTE:** You might be wondering why we selected Touch Down instead of Touch Up Inside, like we did in the previous chapter. The answer is that the background isn't a button. It's not a control in the eyes of the user, so it wouldn't occur to most users to try to drag their finger somewhere to cancel the action.

Save the nib, and let's go back and try it. Compile and run your application again. This time, the keyboard should disappear not only when the *Done* button is tapped but also when you click anywhere that's not an active control, which is the behavior that your user will expect.

Excellent! Now that we have this section all squared away, are you ready to move onto the next group of controls?

Implementing the Slider and Label

Now that we have the text fields complete, let's implement the slider. We'll also add a label that will change to reflect the slider's value.

Determining Outlets and Actions

Want to take a stab at figuring out how many outlets we'll need for our slider and label? Well, the label will need to be changed programmatically when the slider changes, so we'll need an outlet for it. What about the slider?

The slider will trigger an action, and when it does, that action method will receive a pointer to the slider in the sender argument. We'll be able to retrieve the slider's value from sender, so we won't need an outlet to get the slider's value. So, do we need an outlet for the slider at all? In other words, do we need access to the slider's value outside the action method it will call?

In a real application, you will often need access to a slider's value. For instance, you might be presenting a view controller that needs to display an existing value in the slider. Without an outlet, you would have no way to set it. Here, since we have another control that will have the same value as the slider and already has an outlet, there's no reason to have one for the slider itself.

Remember that you want to get in the habit of being cautious with memory when programming for iOS devices. Even though a pointer is a minimal amount of memory, why use it if you don't need it, and why clutter up your code with extra stuff you aren't going to use?

Figuring out the actions for this pair of controls is straightforward. We need one for the slider to call when it is changed. The label is static, and the user can't do anything with it directly, so it won't need to trigger any actions.

Adding Outlets and Actions

Let's declare one more outlet and one more action in our *Control_FunViewController.h* file, like so:

```
#import <UIKit/UIKit.h>

@interface Control_FunViewController : UIViewController {
    UITextField *nameField;
    UITextField *numberField;
    UILabel     *sliderLabel;
}
@property (nonatomic, retain) IBOutlet UITextField *nameField;
@property (nonatomic, retain) IBOutlet UITextField *numberField;
@property (nonatomic, retain) IBOutlet UILabel *sliderLabel;
- (IBAction)textFieldDoneEditing:(id)sender;
- (IBAction)backgroundTap:(id)sender;
- (IBAction)sliderChanged:(id)sender;
@end
```

Since we know exactly what our method needs to do, let's switch to *Control_FunViewController.m* to add our property synthesizer and write our sliderChanged: method:

```
#import "Control_FunViewController.h"

@implementation Control_FunViewController
@synthesize nameField;
@synthesize numberField;
@synthesize sliderLabel;

- (IBAction)sliderChanged:(id)sender {
    UISlider *slider = (UISlider *)sender;
    int progressAsInt = (int)(slider.value + 0.5f);
    NSString *newText = [[NSString alloc] initWithFormat:@"%d",
    progressAsInt];
    sliderLabel.text = newText;
    [newText release];
}

- (IBAction)backgroundTap:(id)sender {
...
```

Let's talk about what's going on in the sliderChanged: method. The first thing we do is cast sender to a UISlider *. This simply makes our code more readable and lets us avoid needing to typecast sender every time we use it. After that, we get the value of the slider as an int, add 0.5 in order to round it to the nearest integer, and use that integer to create a new string that we use to set the label's text. Since we allocated newText, we are responsible for releasing it, so we do that in the last line of code in the method. Simple enough, right?

Speaking of being responsible for memory, since we added the sliderLabel property with the retain keyword, we need to make sure we release it. To do that, add the following line of code to the dealloc method:

```
- (void)dealloc {
    [nameField release];
    [numberField release];
    [sliderLabel release];
    [super dealloc];
}
```

We're finished here, so save your changes. Next, we'll add the objects to our interface.

Adding the Slider and Label

You know the routine by now. Double-click *Control_FunViewController.xib*, or if it's already open, just go back to Interface Builder.

Before we add the slider, let's add a little bit of breathing room to our design. The blue guidelines we used to determine the spacing between the top text field and the image above it are really suggestions for minimum proximity. In other words, the blue guidelines tell you, "don't get any closer than this." Drag the two text fields and their labels down a bit, using Figure 4–1 as a guide. Now let's add the slider.

From the library, bring over a slider and arrange it below the number text field taking up most but not all of the horizontal space. Leave a little room to the left for the label. Again, use Figure 4–1 as a guide. Single-click the newly added slider to select it, and then press ⌘1 to go back to the inspector if it's not already visible. The inspector should look similar to the one shown in Figure 4–18.

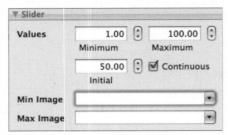

Figure 4–18. *The inspector showing attributes for a slider*

A slider lets you choose a number in a given range, and here, we can set the range and the initial value in Interface Builder. Put in a minimum value of *1*, a maximum value of *100*, and an initial value of *50*. That's all we need to worry about for now.

Bring over a label and place it next to the slider, using the blue guidelines to align it vertically with the slider and to align its left edge with the left margin of the view (see Figure 4–19).

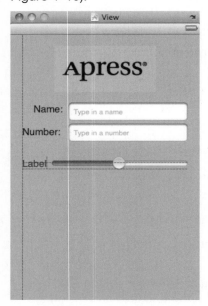

Figure 4–19. *Placing the slider and label*

Double-click the newly placed label, and change its text from *Label* to *100*. This is the largest value that the slider can hold, and we can use that to determine the correct width of the slider. Since "100" is shorter than "Label," you should resize the label by grabbing the right-middle resize dot and dragging to the left. Make sure you stop resizing before the text starts to get smaller. If it does start to get smaller, bring the resize dot back to the right until it returns to its original size. You can also use the size-to-fit option we discussed earlier by pressing ⌘= or selecting **Size to Fit** from the **Layout** Menu. Next, resize the slider by single-clicking the slider to select it and dragging the left resize dot to the left until the blue guides indicate that you should stop.

Now double-click the label again, and change its value to *50*. That is the starting value of the slider, and we need to change it back to make sure that the interface looks correct at launch time; once the slider is used, the code we just wrote will make sure the label continues to show the correct value.

Connecting the Actions and Outlets

All that's left to do with these two controls is to connect the outlet and action. Well, what are you waiting for? You know how to do that. Well, in case you've forgotten, control-drag from the *File's Owner* icon to the label you just added, and select `sliderLabel`. Next, single-click the slider, press ⌘2 to bring up the connections inspector, and drag from—hmm, we don't want *Touch Up Inside*, this time, do we? How about *Value Changed*? That sounds like a good one, huh? Yep, go ahead and drag from that one to *File's Owner*, and select `sliderChanged`.

Save the nib; go back to Xcode; and try out the slider. As you move it, you should see the label's text change in real time. Another piece falls into place. Now, let's look at implementing the switches.

Implementing the Switches, Button, and Segmented Control

Back to Xcode we go once again. Getting dizzy yet? This back and forth may seem a bit strange, but it's fairly common to bounce around, editing source code in Xcode, tweaking your interface in Interface Builder, with the occasional stop to test your app in the appropriate iOS simulator while you're developing.

Our application will have two switches, which are small controls that can have only two states: on and off. We'll also add a segmented control to hide and show the switches. Along with that control, we'll add a button that is revealed when the segmented control's right side is tapped. Let's implement those next.

Adding Outlets and Actions

We won't need an outlet for the segmented control, since we won't be changing its attributes from code. We will need some outlets for the switches, however, since changing the value of one switch will trigger a change in the value of the other switch. We'll have access to the selected switch via sender. To get at the other switch, we'll need an outlet. We'll also need an outlet for the button we'll be adding.

The segmented control will need to trigger an action method that will hide or show the switches. We're also going to need an action that will fire when either switch is tapped. We'll have both switches call the same action method, just as we did with the two buttons in Chapter 3. In *Control_FunViewController.h*, add three outlets and two actions, like so:

```
#import <UIKit/UIKit.h>

#define kSwitchesSegmentIndex    0

@interface Control_FunViewController : UIViewController {
    UITextField    *nameField;
    UITextField    *numberField;
    UILabel        *sliderLabel;
    UISwitch       *leftSwitch;
    UISwitch       *rightSwitch;
    UIButton       *doSomethingButton;
}
@property (nonatomic, retain) IBOutlet UITextField *nameField;
@property (nonatomic, retain) IBOutlet UITextField *numberField;
@property (nonatomic, retain) IBOutlet UILabel *sliderLabel;
@property (nonatomic, retain) IBOutlet UISwitch *leftSwitch;
@property (nonatomic, retain) IBOutlet UISwitch *rightSwitch;
@property (nonatomic, retain) IBOutlet UIButton *doSomethingButton;
- (IBAction)textFieldDoneEditing:(id)sender;
- (IBAction)backgroundTap:(id)sender;
- (IBAction)sliderChanged:(id)sender;
- (IBAction)toggleControls:(id)sender;
- (IBAction)switchChanged:(id)sender;
- (IBAction)buttonPressed;
@end
```

In the code we'll be writing soon, we're going to refer to a UISegmentedControl property named selectedSegmentIndex, which tells us which segment is currently selected. That property is an integer number. The *Switches* segment will have an index of 0. Rather than stick that 0 in our code, the meaning of which we might not remember a few months from now, we define the constant kSwitchesSegmentIndex to use instead, which will make our code more readable.

Switch over to *Control_FunViewController.m*, and add the following code:

```
#import "Control_FunViewController.h"

@implementation Control_FunViewController
@synthesize nameField;
@synthesize numberField;
@synthesize sliderLabel;
```

```
@synthesize leftSwitch;
@synthesize rightSwitch;
@synthesize doSomethingButton;

- (IBAction)toggleControls:(id)sender {
    if ([sender selectedSegmentIndex] == kSwitchesSegmentIndex)
    {
        leftSwitch.hidden = NO;
        rightSwitch.hidden = NO;
        doSomethingButton.hidden = YES;
    }
    else
    {
        leftSwitch.hidden = YES;
        rightSwitch.hidden = YES;
        doSomethingButton.hidden = NO;
    }
}

- (IBAction)switchChanged:(id)sender {
    UISwitch *whichSwitch = (UISwitch *)sender;
    BOOL setting = whichSwitch.isOn;
    [leftSwitch setOn:setting animated:YES];
    [rightSwitch setOn:setting animated:YES];
}

- (IBAction)buttonPressed {
    // TODO: Implement Action Sheet and Alert
}

- (IBAction)sliderChanged:(id)sender {
...
```

The first method we added here, toggleControls:, is called whenever the segmented control is tapped. In this method, we look at the selected segment and either hide the switches and show the button or show the switches and hide the button, as appropriate.

The second method we added, switchChanged:, is called whenever one of the two switches is tapped. In this method, we simply grab the value of sender, which represents the switch that was pressed, and use that value to set both switches. Now, sender is always going to be either leftSwitch or rightSwitch, so you might be wondering why we're setting them both. It's less work to just set the value of both switches every time than to determine which switch made the call and set only the other one. Whichever switch called this method will already be set to the correct value, and setting it again to that same value won't have any effect.

Notice that when we change the value of the switch, we call the setOn:animated: method, which takes two BOOL values as parameters. The first parameter determines whether the switch should be on or off. The second parameter lets us specify whether the button should slide over slowly, just as if someone had pressed it, or it should just be moved instantly to the new position. For the first parameter, we send the new on/off value that we determined based on the current state. For the second parameter, we specified YES because having the switches slide over looks cool, and iOS device users have come to expect that kind of visual feedback. You can try specifying NO if you want to see the difference, but unless you have a good reason, it's generally a good idea to animate changes made programmatically to the user interface so the user is aware of them.

The third new method, buttonPressed, is called when the button is pressed. We're not going to implement this method quite yet, but we stubbed it out as a reminder.

Since we declared three new outlets, we need to release those outlets in our dealloc method. Add the following three lines to the existing dealloc method in *Control_FunViewController.m*:

```
- (void)dealloc {
    [nameField release];
    [numberField release];
    [sliderLabel release];
    [leftSwitch release];
    [rightSwitch release];
    [doSomethingButton release];
    [super dealloc];
}
```

Adding the Switches, Button, and Segmented Control

Next, we're going to tackle the segmented control and the switches and button that it toggles between. Back in Interface Builder, drag a segmented control from the library (see Figure 4–20) and place it on the *View* window, a little below the slider.

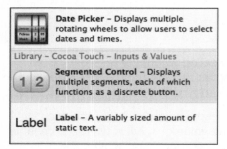

Figure 4–20. *The Segmented Control option in the library*

Expand the width of the segmented control so that it stretches from the view's left blue guideline to its right right blue guideline, as it does in Figure 4–21. Place your cursor over the word *First* on the segmented control and double-click. This should cause the segment's title to become editable, so change it from *First* to *Switches*, as shown in Figure 4–21. After doing that, repeat the process with the *Second* segment; rename it *Button*.

Figure 4–21. *Renaming the segments*

Adding Two Labeled Switches

Grab a switch from the library, and place it on the view. Place it below the segmented control, against the left margin (Figure 4–22). Drag a second switch and place it against the right margin, aligned vertically with the first switch.

TIP: Holding down the option key and dragging an object in Interface Builder will create a copy of that item. When you have many instances of the same object to create, it can be faster to drag only one object from the library and then option-drag as many copies as you need.

Figure 4–22. *Adding the switches to the view*

Connecting the Switch Outlets and Actions

Before we add the button, we're going to connect the switches to the leftSwitch and rightSwitch outlets. The button that we'll be adding in a moment will actually sit on top of the switches, making it harder to control-drag to and from them, so we want to do the switches' connections before we add the button. Since the button and the switches will never be visible at the same time, having them in the same physical location won't be a problem.

Control-drag from *File's Owner* to each of the switches, and connect them to the appropriate leftSwitch or rightSwitch outlet.

Now select the left switch again by single-clicking it, and press ⌘2 to bring up the connections inspector. Drag from the *Value Changed* event to the *File's Owner* icon, and select the switchChanged: action. Repeat with the other switch.

Single-click the segmented control, and look for the *Value Changed* event on the connections inspector. Drag from the circle next to it to the *File's Owner* icon, and select the toggleControls: action method.

Adding the Button

Next, drag a Round Rect Button from the library to your view. Add this one right on top of the left-most button, aligning it with the left margin and vertically aligning its center with the two switches (Figure 4–23).

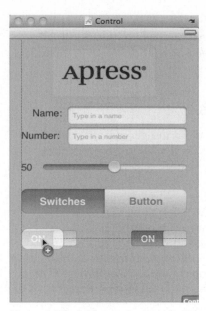

Figure 4–23. *Adding a round rect button on top of the existing switches*

Now grab the right center resize handle and drag all the way to the right until you reach the blue guideline that indicates the right margin. The button should completely cover the two switches (Figure 4–24).

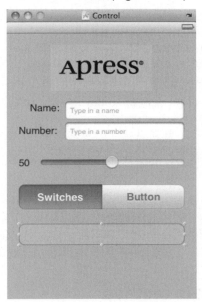

Figure 4–24. *The round rect button, once placed and resized, will completely obscure the two switches.*

Double-click the button and give it a label of *Do Something*. Because the segmented control will start with the *Switches* segment selected, we need to hide this button. Press ⌘1 to bring up the attribute inspector and click the *Hidden* checkbox down in the bottommost section.

Connecting the Buttons Outlets and Actions

Control-drag from *File's Owner* to the new button, and select the *doSomethingButton* outlet. Then, press ⌘2 to go back to the connections inspector. Drag from the circle next to the *Touch Up Inside* event to *File's Owner*, and select the *buttonPressed* action. Now your button is all wired up.

Save your work.

Go back to Xcode, and take the application for a test drive. The segmented control should now be live. When you tap the *Switches* segment, the pair of switches should appear. Tap one of the switches, and both switches should toggle. Tap the *Button* segment, and the switches should be be hidden, replaced by the *Do Something* button. Tapping the button doesn't do anything yet, because we haven't implemented that particular method. Let's do that now.

Implementing the Action Sheet and Alert

Action sheets and **alerts** are both used to provide the user with feedback.

Action sheets are used to force the user to make a choice between two or more items. The action sheet comes up from the bottom of the screen and displays a series of buttons for the user to select from (Figure 4–3). The user is unable to continue using the application until they have tapped one of the buttons. Action sheets are often used to confirm a potentially dangerous or irreversible action such as deleting an object.

Alerts appear as a blue rounded rectangle in the middle of the screen (Figure 4–4). Just like action sheets, alerts force users to respond before they are allowed to continue using their application. Alerts are used more to inform the user that something important or out of the ordinary has occurred and, unlike action sheets, alerts may be presented with only a single button, though you have the option of presenting multiple buttons if more than one response is appropriate.

> **NOTE:** A view that forces users to make a choice before they are allowed to continue using their application is known as a **modal view**.

Conforming to the Action Sheet Delegate Method

Remember back in Chapter 3 when we talked about the application delegate? Well, UIApplication is not the only class in Cocoa Touch that uses delegates. In fact, delegation is a common design pattern in Cocoa Touch. Action sheets and alerts both use delegates so that they know which object to notify when they're dismissed. In our application, we'll need to be notified when the action sheet is dismissed. We don't need to know when the alert is dismissed, because we're just using it to notify the user of something, not to actually solicit a choice.

In order for our controller class to act as the delegate for an action sheet, it needs to conform to a protocol called UIActionSheetDelegate. We do that by adding the name of the protocol in angle brackets after the superclass in our class declaration.

Add the following code to *Control_FunViewController.h*:

```
#import <UIKit/UIKit.h>

#define kSwitchesSegmentIndex    0

@interface Control_FunViewController : UIViewController
      <UIActionSheetDelegate> {
    UITextField *nameField;
    UITextField *numberField;
    UILabel     *sliderLabel;
...
```

Showing the Action Sheet

Let's switch over to *Control_FunViewController.m* and implement the button's action method. We actually need to implement another method in addition to our existing action method: the UIActionSheetDelegate method that the action sheet will use to notify us that it has been dismissed.

Here are the changes you need to make to the buttonPressed method in *Control_FunViewController.m*:

```
- (IBAction)buttonPressed {
    // TODO: Implement Action Sheet and Alert
    UIActionSheet *actionSheet = [[UIActionSheet alloc]
                                initWithTitle:@"Are you sure?"
                                delegate:self
                                cancelButtonTitle:@"No Way!"
                                destructiveButtonTitle:@"Yes, I'm Sure!"
                                otherButtonTitles:nil];
    [actionSheet showInView:self.view];
    [actionSheet release];
}
```

Next, add this method to *Control_FunViewController.m*, just below the buttonPressed method:

```
- (void)actionSheet:(UIActionSheet *)actionSheet
    didDismissWithButtonIndex:(NSInteger)buttonIndex
{
    if (buttonIndex != [actionSheet cancelButtonIndex])
    {
        NSString *msg = nil;
```

```
        if (nameField.text.length > 0)
            msg = [[NSString alloc] initWithFormat:
                    @"You can breathe easy, %@, everything went OK.",
                    nameField.text];
        else
            msg = @"You can breathe easy, everything went OK.";
        UIAlertView *alert = [[UIAlertView alloc]
                                initWithTitle:@"Something was done"
                                message:msg
                                delegate:self
                                cancelButtonTitle:@"Phew!"
                                otherButtonTitles:nil];
        [alert show];
        [alert release];
        [msg release];
    }
}
```

What exactly did we do there? Well, first, in the buttonPressed action method, we allocated and initialized a UIActionSheet object, which is the object that represents an action sheet (in case you couldn't puzzle that one out for yourself):

```
    UIActionSheet *actionSheet = [[UIActionSheet alloc]
            initWithTitle:@"Are you sure?"
            delegate:self
            cancelButtonTitle:@"No Way!"
            destructiveButtonTitle:@"Yes, I'm Sure!"
            otherButtonTitles:nil];
```

The initializer method takes a number of parameters. Let's look at each of them in turn. The first parameter is the title to be displayed. Refer back to Figure 4–3 to see how the title we're supplying will be displayed at the top of the action sheet.

The next argument is the delegate for the action sheet. The action sheet's delegate will be notified when a button on that sheet has been tapped. More specifically, the delegate's actionSheet:didDismissWithButtonIndex: method will be called. By passing self as the delegate parameter, we ensure that our version of actionSheet:didDismissWithButtonIndex: will be called.

Next, we pass in the title for the button that users will tap to indicate they do not want to proceed. All action sheets should have a cancel button, though you can give it any title that is appropriate to your situation. You do not want to use an action sheet if there is no choice to be made. In situations where you want to notify the user without giving a choice of options, an alert view is more appropriate.

The next parameter is the destructive button, and you can think of this as the "yes, please go ahead" button, though once again, you can assign it any title.

The last parameter allows you to specify any number of other buttons that you may want shown on the sheet. This final argument can take a variable number of values, which is one of the nice features of the Objective-C language. If we had wanted two more buttons on our action sheet, we could have done it like this:

```
UIActionSheet *actionSheet = [[UIActionSheet alloc]
    initWithTitle:@"Are you sure?"
    delegate:self
    cancelButtonTitle:@"No Way!"
    destructiveButtonTitle:@"Yes, I'm Sure!"
    otherButtonTitles:@"Foo", @"Bar", nil];
```

This code would have resulted in an action sheet with four buttons. You can pass as many arguments as you want in the otherButtonTitles parameter, as long as you pass nil as the last one. Of course, there is a practical limitation on how many buttons you can have, based on the amount of screen space available.

After we create the action sheet, we tell it to show itself:

```
[actionSheet showInView:self.view];
```

Action sheets always have a parent, which must be a view that is currently visible to the user. In our case, we want the view that we designed in Interface Builder to be the parent, so we use self.view. Note the use of Objective-C dot notation. self.view is equivalent to saying [self view], using the accessor to return the value of our view property.

Why didn't we just use view, instead of self.view? view is a private instance variable of the UIViewController class and must be accessed via the accessor.

Finally, when we're finished, we release the action sheet. Don't worry—it will stick around until the user has tapped a button.

Using the Action Sheet Delegate

Well, that wasn't so hard, was it? In just a few lines of code, we showed an action sheet and required the user to make a decision. iOS will even animate the sheet for us without requiring us to do any additional work. Now, we just need to find out which button the user tapped. The other method that we just implemented, actionSheet:didDismissWithButtonIndex, is one of the UIActionSheetDelegate methods, and since we specified self as our action sheet's delegate, this method will automatically be called by the action sheet when a button is tapped.

The argument buttonIndex will tell us which button was actually tapped. But how do we know which button index refers to the cancel button and which one refers to the destructive button? Fortunately, the delegate method receives a pointer to the UIActionSheet object that represents the sheet, and that action sheet object knows which button is the cancel button. We just need look at one of its properties, cancelButtonIndex:

```
if (buttonIndex != [actionSheet cancelButtonIndex])
```

This line of code makes sure the user didn't tap the cancel button. Since we gave the user only two options, we know that if the cancel button wasn't tapped, the destructive button must have been tapped, and it's OK to proceed. Once we know the user didn't cancel, the first thing we do is create a new string that will be displayed to the user. In a real application, here you would do whatever processing the user requested. We're just going to pretend we did something, and notify the user using an alert.

If the user has entered a name in the top text field, we'll grab that, and we'll use it in the message that we'll display in the alert. Otherwise, we'll just craft a generic message to show:

```
NSString *msg = nil;

if (nameField.text.length > 0)
    msg = [[NSString alloc] initWithFormat:
        @"You can breathe easy, %@, everything went OK.",
        nameField.text];
else
    msg = @"You can breathe easy, everything went OK.";
```

The next lines of code are going to look kind of familiar. Alert views and action sheets are created and used in a very similar manner:

```
UIAlertView *alert = [[UIAlertView alloc]
        initWithTitle:@"Something was done"
        message:msg
        delegate:nil
        cancelButtonTitle:@"Phew!"
        otherButtonTitles:nil];
```

Again, we pass a title to be displayed. We also pass a more detailed message, which is that string we just created. Alert views have delegates, too, and if we needed to know when the user had dismissed the alert view or which button was tapped, we could specify self as the delegate here, just as we did with the action sheet. If we had done that, we would now need to conform our class to the UIAlertViewDelegate protocol also, and implement one or more of the methods from that protocol. In this case, we're just informing the user of something and giving the user only one button. We don't really care when the button is tapped, and we already know which button will be tapped, so we just specify nil here to indicate that we don't need to be pinged when the user is finished with the alert view.

Alert views, unlike action sheets, are not tied to a particular view, so we just tell the alert view to show itself without specifying a parent view. After that, it's just a matter of some memory cleanup, and we're finished. Save the file, and then build, run, and try out the completed application.

Spiffing Up the Button

If you compare your running application to Figure 4–2, you might notice an interesting difference. Your *Do Something* button doesn't look like the one in the figure, and it doesn't look like the button on the action sheet or those in other iOS applications, does it? The default round rect button doesn't really look that spiffy, so let's take care of that before we finish up the app.

Most of the buttons you see on your iOS device are drawn using images. Don't worry; you don't need to create images in an image editor for every button. All you need to do is specify a kind of template image that iOS will use when drawing your buttons.

It's important to keep in mind that your application is sandboxed. You can't get to the template images that are used in other applications on your iOS device or the ones used by iOS itself, so you must make sure that any images you need are in your application's bundle. So, where can you get these image templates?

Fortunately, Apple has provided a bunch for you. You can get them from the iOS sample application called UICatalog, available from the iOS Reference Library:

```
http://developer.apple.com/library/ios/#samplecode/➥
UICatalog/Introduction/Intro.html
```

Alternatively, you can simply copy the images out of the *04 - Control Fun* folder from this book's project archive. Yes, it is OK to use these images in your own applications, because Apple's sample code license specifically allows you to use and distribute them.

Add the two images named *blueButton.png* and *whiteButton.png* to your Xcode project, grabbing them from either the *04 - Control Fun* folder or the *Images* subfolder of the UICatalog project's folder.

If you open one of these two images in *Preview.app* or in an image editing program, you'll see that there's not very much to them, and there's a trick to using them for your buttons.

Go back to Interface Builder, single-click the *Do Something* button, and press ⌘1 to open the attributes inspector. In the inspector, use the first pop-up menu to change the type from *Rounded Rect to Custom*. You'll see in the inspector that you can specify an image for your button, but we're not going to do that, because these image templates need to be handled a little differently. Save the nib, and go back to Xcode.

Using the viewDidLoad Method

UIViewController, our controller's superclass, has a method called viewDidLoad that we can override if we need to modify any of the objects that were created from our nib. Because we can't do what we want completely in Interface Builder, we're going to take advantage of viewDidLoad. Go ahead and add the following method to your *Control_FunViewController.m* file. When you're finished, we'll talk about what the method does.

```
- (void)viewDidLoad
{
    UIImage *buttonImageNormal = [UIImage imageNamed:@"whiteButton.png"];
    UIImage *stretchableButtonImageNormal = [buttonImageNormal
        stretchableImageWithLeftCapWidth:12 topCapHeight:0];
    [doSomethingButton setBackgroundImage:stretchableButtonImageNormal
        forState:UIControlStateNormal];

    UIImage *buttonImagePressed = [UIImage imageNamed:@"blueButton.png"];
    UIImage *stretchableButtonImagePressed = [buttonImagePressed
        stretchableImageWithLeftCapWidth:12 topCapHeight:0];
        [doSomethingButton setBackgroundImage:stretchableButtonImagePressed
        forState:UIControlStateHighlighted];
}
```

NOTE: The project template we used actually created a stub implementation of `viewDidLoad`, but it's commented out in the file. You can place the preceding code inside that stub, or simply retype the method from scratch and delete the commented-out stub—whichever you prefer.

This code sets the background image for the button based on those template images we added to our project. It specifies that, while being touched, the button should change from using the white image to the blue image. This short method introduces two new concepts: **control states**, and **stretchable images**. Let's look at each of them in turn.

Control States

Every iOS control has four possible control states and is always in one and only one of these states at any given moment:

- **Normal**: The most common state is the normal control state, which is the default state. It's the state that controls are in when not in any of the other states.

- **Highlighted**: The highlighted state is the state a control is in when it's currently being used. For a button, this would be while the user has a finger on the button.

- **Disabled**: Controls are in the disabled state when they've been turned off, which can be done by unchecking the *Enabled* check box in Interface Builder or setting the control's `enabled` property to `NO`.

- **Selected**: Only some controls support the selected state. It is usually used to indicate that the control is turned on or selected. Selected is similar to highlighted, but a control can continue to be selected when the user is no longer directly using that control.

Certain iOS controls have attributes that can take on different values depending on their state. For example, by specifying one image for `UIControlStateNormal` and a different image for `UIControlStateHighlighted`, we are telling iOS to use one image when the user has a finger on the button and a different image the rest of the time.

Stretchable Images

Stretchable images are an interesting concept. A stretchable image is a resizable image that knows how to resize itself intelligently so that it maintains the correct appearance. For these button templates, we don't want the edges to stretch evenly with the rest of the image. **End caps** are the parts of an image, measured in pixels, that should not be resized. We want the bevel around the edges to stay the same, no matter what size we make the button, so we specify a left end cap size of 12.

Because we pass in the new stretchable image to our button rather than the image template, iOS knows how to draw the button properly at any size. We could now go in and change the size of the button in the nib file, and it would still be drawn correctly. If we had specified the button image right in the nib file, it would resize the entire image evenly, and our button would look weird at most sizes.

TIP: How did we know what value to use for the end caps? It's simple really: we copied them from Apple's sample code.

Being a Good Memory Citizen

Before we take our new button for a spin, there's one more topic we would like to discuss. In every version of iOS since 3.0, the UIViewController class includes a method to help our apps maintain a low memory footprint. UIViewController is the class from which all view controllers in Cocoa Touch descend, including Control_FunViewController. This new method is called viewDidUnload, and it's an important method in terms of keeping down memory overhead

In Chapter 6, we'll start talking about applications with multiple views. We don't want you to worry too much about multiple views yet, but we do want to show you the correct way of implementing a view controller class.

When you have multiple views, iOS will load and unload nib files to preserve memory. When a view is unloaded, any object that your controller class has an outlet to can't be flushed from memory, because you have retained that object by specifying the retain keyword in the outlet's property. Therefore, when your controller is notified that its view has been unloaded, it is important to set all the controller's outlet properties to nil so that memory can be freed. Cocoa Touch will automatically reconnect your outlets when the nib file is reloaded, so there's no danger here. Using this approach makes you a good memory citizen who does not hog memory you don't need.

Our Control Fun application is a single-view application, so viewDidUnload will never be called while the program is running. But just because an application starts as a single-view application doesn't mean it will always be one, so you should be a good memory citizen even when you know you can get away with not being one. Let's be good memory citizens by replacing the stub of the following method in *Control_FunViewController.m* to free up our outlets when our view is unloaded:

```
- (void)viewDidUnload {
    self.nameField = nil;
    self.numberField = nil;
    self.sliderLabel = nil;
    self.leftSwitch = nil;
    self.rightSwitch = nil;
    self.doSomethingButton = nil;

    [super viewDidUnload];
```

```
}
```

Note the use of Objective-C dot notation once again. This time, since it is used as the left side of an assignment, the dot notation is equivalent to calling our mutator. For example, this line of code:

```
self.nameField = nil;
```

is equivalent to this line of code:

```
[self setNameField:nil];
```

Think about what happens when our mutator does its thing. Remember that we synthesized our mutators using the `retain` keyword. First, our mutator retains the new object, then it releases the old object, and then it assigns the new object to its instance variable. In this case, the mutator retains `nil`, which doesn't do anything. Next, the old object is released, which is exactly what we want to do, since that old object was retained when it was originally connected. And, finally, `nil` is assigned to `nameField`. Pretty cool, eh?

Once you've added that method, why don't you save the file and try out our app? Everything should work exactly as it did earlier, but that button should look a lot more iPhone-like. You won't see any difference in the way the application behaves as a result of adding the `viewDidUnload` method, but you can sleep soundly at night knowing you did the right thing. Good job, citizen!

Crossing the Finish Line

This was a big chapter. Conceptually, we didn't hit you with too much new stuff, but we took you through the use of a good number of controls and showed you a lot of different implementation details. You got a lot more practice with outlets and actions, and saw how to use the hierarchical nature of views to your advantage. You learned about control states and stretchable images, and you also learned to use both action sheets and alerts.

There's a lot going on in this little application. Feel free to go back and play with it. Change values, experiment by adding and modifying code, and see what different settings in Interface Builder do. There's no way we could take you through every permutation of every control available in iOS, but the application you just put together is a good starting point and covers a lot of the basics.

In the next chapter, we're going to look at what happens when the user rotates an iOS device from portrait to landscape orientation or vice versa. You're probably well aware that many apps change their displays based on the way the user is holding the device, and we're going to show you how to do that in your own applications.

Chapter 5

Autorotation and Autosizing

The iPhone, iPad, and other iOS devices are all amazing pieces of engineering. Apple engineers found all kinds of ways to squeeze maximum functionality into a pretty darn small package. One example is the mechanism that allows applications to be used in either portrait (tall and skinny) or landscape (short and wide) mode, and to change that orientation at runtime if the phone is rotated. A prime example of this behavior, which is called **autorotation**, can be seen in iOS's web browser, Mobile Safari (see Figure 5–1).

Figure 5–1. *Like many iOS applications, Mobile Safari changes its display based on how it is held, making the most of the available screen space.*

In this chapter, we'll cover autorotation in detail. We'll start with an overview of the ins and outs of autorotation.

The Mechanics of Autorotation

Autorotation might not be right for every application. Several of Apple's iPhone applications support only a single orientation. Movies can be watched only in landscape mode, for example, and contacts can be edited only in portrait mode. However, that's not true for the iPad, for which Apple recommends that essentially all applications (with the possible exception of games that are designed around a particular layout) should support every orientation.

In fact, all of Apple's own iPad apps work fine in both orientations. Many of them use the different orientations to show you different views of your data. For example, the Mail and Notes apps use landscape orientation to show a list of items (folders, messages, or notes) on the left and the selected item on the right, and portrait orientation to let you focus on the details of just the selected item.

The bottom line is that if autorotation enhances the user experience, add it to your application. Fortunately, Apple did a great job of hiding the complexities of autorotation in iOS and in the UIKit, so implementing this behavior in your own iOS applications is actually quite easy.

Autorotation is specified in the view controller, so if the user rotates the device, the active view controller will be asked if it's OK to rotate to the new orientation (which you'll see how to do in this chapter). If the view controller responds in the affirmative, the application's window and views will be rotated, and the window and view will be resized to fit the new orientation.

On the iPhone and iPod touch, a view that starts in portrait mode will be 320 pixels wide and 480 pixels tall. On the iPad, portrait mode means 768 pixels wide and 1024 pixels tall. The amount of screen real estate available for your app will be decreased by 20 pixels vertically if your app is showing the **status bar**. The status bar is the 20-pixel strip at the top of the screen (see Figure 5–1) that shows things like signal strength, time, and battery charge.

When the phone is switched to landscape mode, the view rotates, along with the application's window, and is resized to fit the new orientation, so that it is 480 pixels wide by 320 pixels tall (iPhone and iPod touch) or 1024 pixels wide by 768 pixels tall (iPad). As before, the vertical space actually available to your app is reduced by 20 pixels if you're showing the status bar, which most apps do.

TIP: At this point, you may be wondering where the iPhone 4 and iPod touch's **retina display** fits into this scenario. The retina display is Apple's marketing term for the high-resolution screen on the iPhone 4 and iPod touch, which doubles the screen resolution to 640 by 960 pixels. Thanks to Apple's smart handling of the graphics, you typically won't need to think about that extra resolution (unless you really want to). The retina display screen has twice the physical resolution in both directions, but when you're building Cocoa Touch apps, you'll typically be dealing with the normal iPhone and iPod touch resolution of 320 by 480 pixels. Think of it as a "virtual resolution," which iOS automatically maps to the physical screen resolution. We'll talk more about this in Chapter 14.

Most of the work in actually moving the pixels around the screen is managed by iOS. Your application's main job in all this is making sure everything fits nicely and looks proper in the resized window.

Your application can take three general approaches when managing rotation. Which one you use depends on the complexity of your interface. We'll look at all three approaches in this chapter.

With simpler interfaces, you can simply specify the correct **autosize** attributes for all of the objects that make up your interface. Autosize attributes tell the iOS device how your controls should behave when their enclosing view is resized. If you've worked with Cocoa on Mac OS X, you're already familiar with the basic process, because it is the same one used to specify how Cocoa controls behave when the user resizes the window in which they are contained.

Autosize is quick and easy, but not appropriate for all applications. More complex interfaces must handle autorotation in a different manner. For more complex views, you have two additional approaches. One approach is to manually reposition the objects in your view when notified that your view is rotating. The second approach is to actually design two different versions of your view in Interface Builder—one view for portrait mode and a separate view for landscape mode. In both cases, you will need to override methods from `UIViewController` in your view's controller class.

Let's get started, shall we? We'll look at autosizing first.

Handling Rotation Using Autosize Attributes

Start a new project in Xcode, and call it *Autosize*. We're going to stick with the same View-based Application template for this application, and once again choose iPhone as the target device. Before we lay out our GUI in Interface Builder, we need to tell iOS that our view supports autorotation. We do that by modifying the view controller class.

Specifying Rotation Support

Once your project is open in Xcode, expand the *Classes* folder, and single-click *AutoSizeViewController.m*. In the code that's already there, you'll see a method called shouldAutorotateToInterfaceOrientation: provided for you, courtesy of the template, but it's commented out. That's fine, as we'll be replacing this commented out version in just a minute.

```
...
/*
// Override to allow orientations other than the default portrait
// orientation.
- (BOOL)shouldAutorotateToInterfaceOrientation:(UIInterfaceOrientation)
        interfaceOrientation {
    // Return YES for supported orientations
    return (interfaceOrientation == UIInterfaceOrientationPortrait);
}
*/
...
```

This method is the system's way of asking your view controller if it's OK to rotate to a specific orientation. Four defined orientations correspond to the four general ways that an iOS device can be held:

- UIInterfaceOrientationPortrait

- UIInterfaceOrientationPortraitUpsideDown

- UIInterfaceOrientationLandscapeLeft

- UIInterfaceOrientationLandscapeRight

In the case of the iPhone, the template defaults to supporting a single autorotate orientation, UIInterfaceOrientationPortrait. If we had instead created an iPad project here, the default version of the shouldAutorotateToInterfaceOrientation: method created by the template would be different. In that case, the method would just return YES, since Apple's recommendation to iPad app developers is to allow the device to be rotated to any of the four defined orientations.

When the iOS device is changed to a new orientation, this method is called on the active view controller. The parameter interfaceOrientation will contain one of the four values in the preceding list, and this method needs to return either YES or NO to signify whether the application's window should be rotated to match the new orientation. Because every view controller subclass can implement this differently, it is possible for one application to support autorotation with some of its views but not with others.

CODE SENSE

Have you noticed that the defined system constants on iPhone are always designed so that values that work together start with the same letters? One reason why `UIInterfaceOrientationPortrait`, `UIInterfaceOrientationPortraitUpsideDown`, `UIInterfaceOrientationLandscapeLeft`, and `UIInterfaceOrientationLandscapeRight` all begin with `UIInterfaceOrientation` is to let you take advantage of Xcode's **Code Sense** feature.

You've probably noticed that as you type, Xcode frequently tries to complete the word you are typing. That's Code Sense in action. Developers cannot possibly remember all the various defined constants in the system, but you can remember the common beginning for the groups you use frequently. When you need to specify an orientation, simply type *UIInterfaceOrientation* (or even *UIInterf*), and then press the escape key to bring up a list of all matches. (In Xcode's preferences, you can change that matching key from escape to something else.) You can use the arrow keys to navigate the list that appears and make a selection by pressing the tab or return key. This is much faster than needing to go look up the values in the documentation or header files.

The default implementation of this method looks at `interfaceOrientation` and returns YES only if it is equal to `UIInterfaceOrientationPortrait`, which limits this application to one orientation, effectively disabling autorotation.

To enable rotation to any orientation, simply change the method to return YES for any value passed in, like so:

```
- (BOOL)shouldAutorotateToInterfaceOrientation:
    (UIInterfaceOrientation)interfaceOrientation {
    return YES;
}
```

In fact, as we mentioned earlier, that's precisely the way the method looks when you create an iPad project instead of an iPhone project.

In order to support some but not all orientations, we need to look at the value of `interfaceOrientation` and return YES for those that we want to support and NO for those we don't. For example, to support portrait mode and landscape mode in both directions but not rotation to the upside-down portrait mode, we use the following code:

```
- (BOOL)shouldAutorotateToInterfaceOrientation:
    (UIInterfaceOrientation)interfaceOrientation {
    return (interfaceOrientation !=
        UIInterfaceOrientationPortraitUpsideDown);
}
```

Go ahead and change the commented out `shouldAutorotateToInterfaceOrientation:` method to match the preceding version. As a general rule, `UIInterfaceOrientationPortraitUpsideDown` is discouraged by Apple on the iPhone, because if the phone rings while it is being held upside down, the phone is likely to remain upside down when it's answered. This doesn't apply to the iPad, where the meaning of "upside down" isn't so clear, and the device is meant to be turned around as much as you like.

Save your project. Now, let's look at setting autosize attributes in a nib file using Interface Builder.

Designing an Interface with Autosize Attributes

In Xcode, expand the *Resources* folder, and double-click *AutosizeViewController.xib* to open the file in Interface Builder. One nice thing about using autosize attributes is that they require very little code. We do need to specify which orientations we support, as we just did in our view controller code, but the rest of the autoresize implementation can be done right here in Interface Builder.

To see how this works, drag six *Round Rect Buttons* from the library over to your view, and place them as shown in Figure 5–2. Double-click each button, and assign a title to each one so you can tell them apart later. We've numbered ours from 1 to 6.

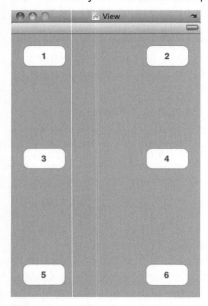

Figure 5–2. *Adding six numbered buttons to the interface*

Let's see what happens now that we've specified that we support autorotation but haven't set any autosize attributes.

First, save your nib file. Then return to Xcode and build and run the app. Once the iPhone simulator comes up, select **Hardware ➤ Rotate Left**, which will simulate turning the iPhone to landscape mode. Take a look at Figure 5–3. Oh, dear.

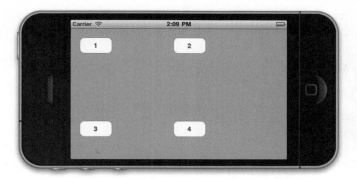

Figure 5–3. *Well, that's not very useful, is it? Where are buttons 5 and 6?*

Most controls default to a setting that has them stay where they are in relation to the left side and top of the screen. For some controls this would be appropriate. The top-left button, number 1, for example, is probably right where we want it. The rest of them, however, do not fare as well.

Quit the simulator and go back to Interface Builder. Let's get to work fixing the GUI so that it adapts to the screen size in a sensible way.

Using the Size Inspector's Autosize Attributes

Single-click the top-left button on your view, and then press ⌘**3** to bring up the size inspector, which should look like Figure 5–4.

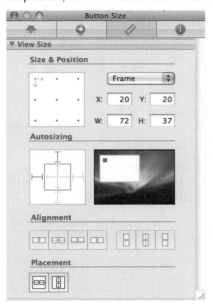

Figure 5–4. *The size inspector allows you to set an object's autosize attributes.*

The **size inspector** allows you to set an object's **autosize attributes**. Figure 5–5 shows the part of the size inspector that controls an object's autosize attributes.

Figure 5–5. *The Autosizing section of the size inspector*

The box on the left in Figure 5–5 is where we actually set the attributes; the box on the right is a little animation that will show us how the object will behave during a resize. Note that the animation only plays when your cursor moves over the animation area. In the box on the left, the inner square represents the current object. If a button is selected, the inner square represents that button.

The red arrows inside the inner square represent the horizontal and vertical space inside the selected object. Clicking either arrow will change it from solid to dashed or from dashed back to solid. If the horizontal arrow is solid, the width of the object is free to change as the window resizes; if the horizontal arrow is dashed, the iPhone will try to keep the width of the object at its original value if possible. The same is true for the height of the object and the vertical arrow.

The four red "I" shapes outside the inner box represent the distance between the edge of the selected object and the same edge of the view that contains it. If the "I" is dashed, the space is flexible, and if it's solid red, the amount of space should be kept constant if possible.

Huh?

Perhaps this concept will make a little more sense if you actually see it in action. Take a look back at Figure 5–5, which represents the default autosize settings. These default settings specify that the object's size will remain constant as its superview is resized and that the distance from the left and top edges should also stay constant.

Move your cursor over the animation next to the autosize control, so you can see how it will behave during a resize. Notice that the inner box stays in the same place relative to the left and top edges of the parent view as the parent view changes in size.

Try this experiment. Click both of the solid red "I" shapes (to the top and left of the inner box) so they become dashed and look like the ones shown in Figure 5–6.

Figure 5–6. *With all dashed lines, your control floats in the parent and keeps its size.*

With all the lines set to dashed, the size of the object will be kept the same, and it will float in the middle of the superview as the superview is resized.

Now, click the vertical arrow inside the box and the "I" shape both above and below the box so that your autosize attributes look like the ones shown in Figure 5–7.

Figure 5–7. *This configuration allows the vertical size of our object to change.*

Here, we are indicating that the vertical size of our object can change and that the distance from the top of our object to the top of the window and the distance from the bottom of our object to the bottom of the window should stay constant. With this configuration, the width of the object wouldn't change, but its height would. Change the autosize attributes a few more times and watch the animation until you grok how different settings will impact the behavior when the view is rotated and resized.

Setting the Buttons' Autosize Attributes

Now, let's set the autosize attributes for our six buttons. Go ahead and see if you can figure them out. If you get stumped, take a look at Figure 5–8, which shows the autosize attributes needed for each button in order to keep them on the screen when the phone is rotated.

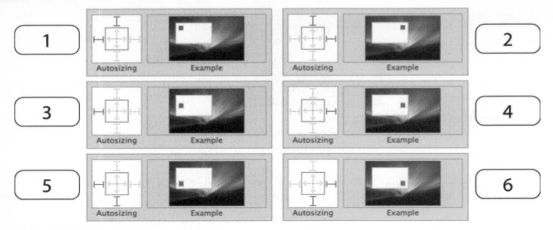

Figure 5–8. *Autosize attributes for all six buttons*

Once you have the attributes set the same as Figure 5–8, save the nib, go back to Xcode, and build and run. This time, when the iPhone simulator comes up, you should be able to select **Hardware ➤ Rotate Left** or **Rotate Right** and have all the buttons stay on the screen (see Figure 5–9). If you rotate back, they should return to their original position. This technique will work for a great many applications.

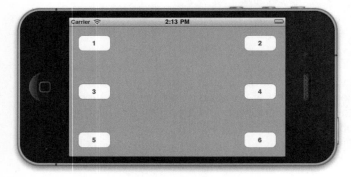

Figure 5–9. *The buttons in their new positions after rotating*

In this example, we kept our buttons the same size, so now all of our buttons are visible and usable, but there is an awful lot of unused space on the screen. Perhaps it would be better if we allowed the width or height of our buttons to change so that there will be less empty space on the interface? Feel free to experiment with the autosize attributes of these six buttons, and add some other buttons if you want. Play around until you feel comfortable with the way autosize works.

In the course of your experimentation, you're bound to notice that, sometimes, no combination of autosize attributes will give you exactly what you want. Sometimes, you are going to need to rearrange your interface more drastically than can be handled with this technique. For those situations, a little more code is in order. Let's take a look at that, shall we?

Restructuring a View When Rotated

In Interface Builder, single-click each of the buttons, and use the size inspector to change the *W* (for width) and *H* (for height) fields to *125*, which will set the width and height of the buttons to 125 pixels. When you are finished, rearrange your buttons using the blue guidelines so that your view looks like Figure 5–10.

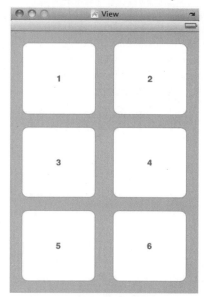

Figure 5–10. *View after resizing all the buttons*

Save your nib file and go back to Xcode and run your project again. Can you guess what's going to happen now when we rotate the screen? Well, assuming that you kept the buttons' autosize attributes to the settings shown in Figure 5–8, you probably won't be pleased. The buttons will overlap and look like Figure 5–11, because there simply isn't enough height on the screen in landscape mode to accommodate three buttons that are 125 pixels tall.

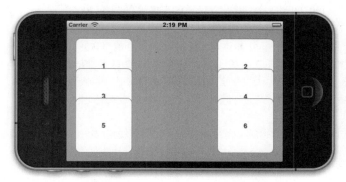

Figure 5–11. *Not exactly what we want. Too much overlap. We need another solution.*

We could accommodate this scenario using the autosize attributes by allowing the height of the buttons to change, but that's wouldn't make the best use of our screen real estate, because it would leave a large gap in the middle of the screen. If there was room for six square buttons in portrait mode, there should still be room for six square buttons in landscape mode—we just need to shuffle them around a bit. One way we can handle this is to specify new positions for each of the buttons when the view is rotated.

Declaring and Connecting Outlets

To change a control's attributes, we need an outlet that points to the object we want to change. This means that we need to declare an outlet for each of the six buttons in order to rearrange them. Add the following code to *AutosizeViewController.h:*

```
#import <UIKit/UIKit.h>

@interface AutosizeViewController : UIViewController {
    UIButton *button1;
    UIButton *button2;
    UIButton *button3;
    UIButton *button4;
    UIButton *button5;
    UIButton *button6;
}
@property (nonatomic, retain) IBOutlet UIButton *button1;
@property (nonatomic, retain) IBOutlet UIButton *button2;
@property (nonatomic, retain) IBOutlet UIButton *button3;
@property (nonatomic, retain) IBOutlet UIButton *button4;
@property (nonatomic, retain) IBOutlet UIButton *button5;
@property (nonatomic, retain) IBOutlet UIButton *button6;
@end
```

Save this file, and go back to Interface Builder. Control-drag from the *File's Owner* icon to each of the six buttons, and connect them to the corresponding outlet. Once you've connected all six, save the nib, and pop back over to Xcode

> **TIP:** Notice our working pattern here. We add our outlet declarations to our header file and then save, so Interface Builder is aware of the outlets. We then edit the nib file to connect those outlets. We'll do this a lot. One of the biggest problems that new iOS developers run into is forgetting to save their header file before they switch back to Interface Builder to connect their outlets. If you forget to save before you select your nib file and switch to Interface Builder, when you control-drag from *File's Owner* to your interface object, Interface Builder won't include your unsaved outlets in the list it presents. The bottom line is that you should always save after you add your outlets. Make it a habit.

Moving the Buttons on Rotation

To move these buttons to make the best use of space, we need to override the method willAnimateRotationToInterfaceOrientation:duration: in *AutosizeViewController.m*. This method is called automatically after a rotation has occurred but before the final rotation animations have occurred.

Add the following code, and then we'll talk about what it's doing.

```
#import "AutosizeViewController.h"

@implementation AutosizeViewController
@synthesize button1;
@synthesize button2;
@synthesize button3;
@synthesize button4;
@synthesize button5;
@synthesize button6;

- (void)willAnimateRotationToInterfaceOrientation:(UIInterfaceOrientation)
    interfaceOrientation duration:(NSTimeInterval)duration {
    if (interfaceOrientation == UIInterfaceOrientationPortrait
            || interfaceOrientation ==
            UIInterfaceOrientationPortraitUpsideDown)
    {
        button1.frame = CGRectMake(20, 20, 125, 125);
        button2.frame = CGRectMake(175, 20, 125, 125);
        button3.frame = CGRectMake(20, 168, 125, 125);
        button4.frame = CGRectMake(175, 168, 125, 125);
        button5.frame = CGRectMake(20, 315, 125, 125);
        button6.frame = CGRectMake(175, 315, 125, 125);
    }
    else
    {
        button1.frame = CGRectMake(20, 20, 125, 125);
        button2.frame = CGRectMake(20, 155, 125, 125);
        button3.frame = CGRectMake(177, 20, 125, 125);
        button4.frame = CGRectMake(177, 155, 125, 125);
        button5.frame = CGRectMake(328, 20, 125, 125);
        button6.frame = CGRectMake(328, 155, 125, 125);
    }
}

- (BOOL)shouldAutorotateToInterfaceOrientation:
    (UIInterfaceOrientation)interfaceOrientation {
    return (interfaceOrientation !=
        UIInterfaceOrientationPortraitUpsideDown);
}

- (void)didReceiveMemoryWarning {
    [super didReceiveMemoryWarning];
    // Releases the view if it doesn't have a superview
    // Release anything that's not essential, such as cached data
}
```

```
- (void)viewDidUnload {
    // Release any retained subviews of the main view.
    // e.g. self.myOutlet = nil;
    self.button1 = nil;
    self.button2 = nil;
    self.button3 = nil;
    self.button4 = nil;
    self.button5 = nil;
    self.button6 = nil;
    [super viewDidUnload];
}

- (void)dealloc {
    [button1 release];
    [button2 release];
    [button3 release];
    [button4 release];
    [button5 release];
    [button6 release];
    [super dealloc];
}
```

The size and position of all views, including controls such as buttons, are specified in a property called frame, which is a struct of type CGRect. CGRectMake() is a function provided by Apple that lets you easily create a CGRect by specifying the x and y positions along with the width and height.

> **NOTE:** The function CGRect() begins with the letters CG, indicating that it comes from the Core Graphics framework. As its name implies, the Core Graphics framework contains code related to graphics and drawing. In earlier versions of the iOS SDK, the Core Graphics framework was not included in Xcode project templates and needed to be added manually. That step is no longer necessary, since the Core Graphics framework is automatically included when you use any of the Xcode templates to create an iPhone or iPad application.

Save this code. Now build and run to see it in action. Try rotating, and watch how the buttons end up in their new positions.

Swapping Views

Moving controls to different locations, as we did in the previous section, can be a very tedious process, especially with a complex interface. Wouldn't it be nice if we could just design the landscape and portrait views separately, and then swap them out when the phone is rotated?

Well, we can. But it's a moderately complicated option, which you'll likely use only in the case of very complex interfaces.

While controls on both views can trigger the same actions, we will need to have two completely distinct sets of outlets—one for each of the views—and that will add a certain complexity to our code. It is by no means an insurmountable degree of complexity, and there are times when this option is the best one. Let's try it out.

To demonstrate, we'll build an app with separate views for portrait and landscape orientation. Although the interface we'll build is not complex enough to justify the technique we're using, keeping the interface simple will help clarify the process.

Create a new project in Xcode using the View-based Application template again (we'll start working with other templates in the next chapter). Call this project *Swap*. The application will start up in portrait mode, with two buttons, one on top of the other (see Figure 5–12).

Figure 5–12. *The Swap application at launch. This is the portrait view and its two buttons.*

Rotating the phone swaps in a completely different view, specifically designed for landscape orientation. The landscape view will also feature two buttons with the exact same labels (see Figure 5–13), so the user won't know they're looking at two different views.

Figure 5–13. *Similar but not the same. This is the landscape view, with two different buttons.*

When a button is tapped, it will become hidden. In a real application, there may be times when you want to hide or disable a button like this. As an example, you might create a button that kicks off a lengthy process and you don't want the user tapping the same button again until that process has finished.

Determining Outlets and Actions

Because each view has two buttons, and because an outlet can't point to more than one object, we need to declare four outlets: two for the landscape view buttons and two for the portrait view buttons. When using this technique, it becomes very important to put some thought into your outlet names to keep your code from becoming confusing.

But, oho! Is that someone in the back saying, "Do we really need outlets for all these buttons? Since we're deactivating the button that was tapped, can't we just use sender instead?" And in a single-view scenario, that would be exactly the right way to go about it.

Think about this. What if the user taps the *Foo* button and then rotates the phone? The *Foo* button on the other view is a completely different button, and it will still be visible, which isn't the behavior we want. We don't really want to advertise to the users that the object they're dealing with now isn't the same one they were dealing with a moment ago.

In addition to the outlets for the buttons, we need two more outlets to point to the two different versions of our view. When working with a single view only, our parent class's view property was all we needed. But since we're going to be changing the value of view at runtime, we need to make sure that we have a way to get to both views, hence the need for two UIView outlets.

Our buttons need to trigger an action, so we're definitely going to need at least one action method. We're going to design a single action method to handle the pressing of any of the buttons, so we'll just declare a single buttonPressed: action in our view controller class.

Declaring Actions and Outlets

Add the following code to *SwapViewController.h* to create the outlets we'll need when we go to Interface Builder.

```
#import <UIKit/UIKit.h>

#define degreesToRadians(x) (M_PI * (x) / 180.0)

@interface SwapViewController : UIViewController {
    UIView *landscape;
    UIView *portrait;

    // Foo
    UIButton *landscapeFooButton;
    UIButton *portraitFooButton;

    // Bar
    UIButton *landscapeBarButton;
    UIButton *portraitBarButton;
}
@property (nonatomic, retain) IBOutlet UIView *landscape;
@property (nonatomic, retain) IBOutlet UIView *portrait;
@property (nonatomic, retain) IBOutlet UIButton *landscapeFooButton;
@property (nonatomic, retain) IBOutlet UIButton *portraitFooButton;
@property (nonatomic, retain) IBOutlet UIButton *landscapeBarButton;
@property (nonatomic, retain) IBOutlet UIButton *portraitBarButton;
- (IBAction)buttonPressed:(id)sender;
@end
```

The following line of code is simply a macro to convert between degrees and radians:

```
#define degreesToRadians(x) (M_PI * (x) / 180.0)
```

We'll use this when calling a function that requires radians as an input. Most people don't think in radians, so this macro will make our code much more readable by letting us specify angles in degrees instead of radians. Everything else in this header should be familiar to you.

Now that we have our outlets implemented, let's go to Interface Builder and build the two views we need. Double click *SwapViewController.xib* in the *Resources* folder to open the file in Interface Builder.

Designing the Two Views

Ideally, what you're seeing in Interface Builder right now should feel very familiar to you. We'll need two views in our nib. We don't want to use the existing view that was provided as part of the template because its size can't be changed. Instead, we'll delete the default view and create two new ones.

In the main window, single-click the *View* icon, and press the *Delete* key. Next, drag two *Views* from the library over to the main window. After doing that, you'll have two icons labeled *View*. That might get a little confusing, so let's rename them to make it obvious what each one does.

To rename an icon in the nib's main window, you have to single-click the view to select it, wait a second or two, and then click the name of the icon. After another second, the name will become editable, and you can type the new name. Note that this trick works only in the icon view mode. Name one view *Portrait* and the other *Landscape*.

Now Control-drag from the *File's Owner* icon to the *Portrait* icon, and when the gray menu pops up, select the *portrait* outlet. Then, control-drag from *File's Owner* to the *Landscape* icon, and select the landscape outlet. Now control-drag a third time from *File's Owner* to *Portrait*, and select the *view* outlet to indicate which view should be shown at launch time.

Double-click the icon called *Landscape*, and press ⌘3 to bring up the size inspector. Right now, the size of this view should be 320 pixels wide by 460 pixels tall. Change the values so that it is 480 pixels wide by 300 pixels tall, or you can press the little arrow icon in the right side of the view's title bar, which will automatically change the view's proportions to landscape. Now drag two *Round Rect Buttons* over from the library onto the *Landscape* view. The exact size and placement doesn't matter, but we made them nice and big at 125 pixels wide and 125 pixels tall. Double-click the left button, and give it a title of *Foo*; then double-click the right one, and give it a title of *Bar*.

Control-drag from the *File's Owner* icon to the *Foo* button, and assign it to the landscapeFooButton outlet; then do the same thing to assign the *Bar* button to the landscapeBarButton outlet.

Now, single-click the *Foo* button, and switch to the connections inspector by pressing ⌘2. Drag from the circle that represents the *Touch Up Inside* event to the *File's Owner* icon, and select the *buttonPressed*: action. Repeat with the *Bar* button so that both buttons trigger the buttonPressed: action method. You can now close the *Landscape* window.

Double-click the *Portrait* icon to open that view for editing. Drag two more *Round Rect Buttons* from the library, placing them one above the other this time. Again, make the size of each button 125 pixels wide and 125 pixels tall. Double-click the top button, and give it a title of *Foo*. Then, double-click the bottom button, and assign it a title of *Bar*.

Control-drag from the *File's Owner* icon to the Foo button, and assign it to the portraitFooButton outlet. Control-drag from the File's Owner icon once again to the *Bar* button, and assign it to the portraitBarButton outlet.

Click the *Foo* button, and drag from the *Touch Up Inside* event on the connections inspector over to the *File's Owner* icon, and select the buttonPressed: action. Repeat this connection with the *Bar* button.

Save the nib, and go back to Xcode.

Implementing the Swap and the Action

We're almost finished with our app. We just need to put the code in place to handle the swap and the button taps. Add the code that follows to your *SwapViewController.m* file.

> **NOTE:** This code listing does not show commented-out methods provided by the stub. Feel free to delete the commented-out methods that were already in your controller class.

```objc
#import "SwapViewController.h"

@implementation SwapViewController
@synthesize landscape;
@synthesize portrait;
@synthesize landscapeFooButton;
@synthesize portraitFooButton;
@synthesize landscapeBarButton;
@synthesize portraitBarButton;

- (void)willAnimateRotationToInterfaceOrientation:(UIInterfaceOrientation)
      interfaceOrientation duration:(NSTimeInterval)duration {
    if (interfaceOrientation == UIInterfaceOrientationPortrait) {
        self.view = self.portrait;
        self.view.transform = CGAffineTransformIdentity;
        self.view.transform =
            CGAffineTransformMakeRotation(degreesToRadians(0));
        self.view.bounds = CGRectMake(0.0, 0.0, 320.0, 460.0);
    }
    else if (interfaceOrientation == UIInterfaceOrientationLandscapeLeft) {
        self.view = self.landscape;
        self.view.transform = CGAffineTransformIdentity;
        self.view.transform =
        CGAffineTransformMakeRotation(degreesToRadians(-90));
        self.view.bounds = CGRectMake(0.0, 0.0, 480.0, 300.0);
    }
    else if (interfaceOrientation ==
            UIInterfaceOrientationPortraitUpsideDown) {
        self.view = self.portrait;
        self.view.transform = CGAffineTransformIdentity;
        self.view.transform =
            CGAffineTransformMakeRotation(degreesToRadians(180));
        self.view.bounds = CGRectMake(0.0, 0.0, 320.0, 460.0);
    }
    else if (interfaceOrientation ==
            UIInterfaceOrientationLandscapeRight) {
        self.view = self.landscape;
        self.view.transform = CGAffineTransformIdentity;
        self.view.transform =
          CGAffineTransformMakeRotation(degreesToRadians(90));
        self.view.bounds = CGRectMake(0.0, 0.0, 480.0, 300.0);
    }
```

```
    }

    - (IBAction)buttonPressed:(id)sender {
        if (sender == portraitFooButton || sender == landscapeFooButton) {
            portraitFooButton.hidden = YES;
            landscapeFooButton.hidden = YES;
        } else {
            portraitBarButton.hidden = YES;
            landscapeBarButton.hidden = YES;
        }
    }

    - (BOOL)shouldAutorotateToInterfaceOrientation:(UIInterfaceOrientation)
        interfaceOrientation {
        return YES;
    }

    - (void)didReceiveMemoryWarning {
        // Releases the view if it doesn't have a superview
        [super didReceiveMemoryWarning];

        // Release anything that's not essential, such as cached data
    }

    - (void)viewDidUnload {
        // Release any retained subviews of the main view.
        // e.g. self.myOutlet = nil;
        self.landscape = nil;
        self.portrait = nil;
        self.landscapeFooButton = nil;
        self.portraitFooButton = nil;
        self.landscapeBarButton = nil;
        self.portraitBarButton = nil;
        [super viewDidUnload];
    }

    - (void)dealloc {
        [landscape release];
        [portrait release];
        [landscapeFooButton release];
        [portraitFooButton release];
        [landscapeBarButton release];
        [portraitBarButton release];

        [super dealloc];
    }
    @end
```

The first method in our new code is called
willAnimateRotationToInterfaceOrientation:duration:. This is a method from our
superclass that we've overridden that is called as the rotation begins but before the
rotation actually happens. Actions that we take in this method will be animated as part
of the first half of the rotation animation.

In this method, we look at the orientation that we're rotating to and set the `view` property to either `landscape` or `portrait`, as appropriate for the new orientation. We then call `CGAffineTransformMakeRotation`, part of the Core Graphics framework, to create a **rotation transformation**. A **transformation** is a mathematical description of changes to an object's size, position, or angle. Ordinarily, iOS takes care of setting the transform value automatically when the device is rotated. However, when we swap in our new view here, we need to make sure that we give it the correct value so as not to confuse the operating system. That's what `willAnimateRotationToInterfaceOrientation:duration:` is doing each time it sets the view's `transform` property. Once the view has been rotated, we adjust its frame so that it fits snugly into the window at the current orientation.

Next up is our `buttonPressed:` method, and there shouldn't be anything too surprising there. We look at the button that was tapped, hide it, and then hide the corresponding button on the other view.

You should be comfortable with everything else we wrote in this class. The new `shouldAutorotateToInterfaceOrientation:` method returns `YES` to tell the iPhone that we support rotation to any orientation, and the code added to the `dealloc` method is simple memory cleanup.

Now, compile and give it a run.

> **NOTE:** If you accidentally click both buttons, the only way to bring them back is to quit the simulator and rerun the project. Don't use this approach in your own applications.

Rotating Out of Here

In this chapter, you tried out three completely different approaches to supporting autorotation in your applications. You learned about autosize attributes and how to restructure your views, in code, when the iOS device rotates. You saw how to swap between two completely different views when the device rotates, and you learned how to link new frameworks into your project.

In this chapter, you also got your first taste of using multiple views in an application by swapping between two views from the same nib. In the next chapter, we're going to start looking at true multiview applications. Every application we've written so far has used a single view controller, and all except the last used a single content view. A lot of complex iOS applications such as Mail and Contacts, however, are only made possible by the use of multiple views and view controllers, and we're going to look at exactly how that works in Chapter 6.

Chapter 6

Multiview Applications

Up until this point, we've written applications with a single view controller. While there certainly is a lot you can do with a single view, the real power of the iOS platform emerges when you can switch out views based on user input. Multiview applications come in several different flavors, but the underlying mechanism is the same, regardless of how it may appear on the screen.

In this chapter, we're going to focus on the structure of multiview applications and the basics of swapping content views by building our own multiview application from scratch. We will write our own custom controller class that switches between two different content views, which will give you a strong foundation for taking advantage of the various multiview controllers that Apple provides.

But before we start building our application, let's see how multiple-view applications can be useful.

Common Types of Multiview Apps

Strictly speaking, we have worked with multiple views in our previous applications, since buttons, labels, and other controls are all subclasses of UIView and can all go into the view hierarchy. But when Apple uses the term "view" in documentation, it is generally referring to a UIView or one of its subclasses that has a corresponding view controller. These types of views are also sometimes referred to as **content views**, because they are the primary container for the content of your application.

The simplest example of a multiview application is a utility application. A utility application focuses primarily on a single view but offers a second view that can be used to configure the application or to provide more detail than the primary view. The Stocks application that ships with iPhone is a good example (see Figure 6–1). If you click the little *i* icon in the lower-right corner, the view flips over to let you configure the list of stocks tracked by the application.

Figure 6–1. *The Stocks application that ships with iPhone has two views: one to display the data and another to configure the stock list.*

There are also several **tab bar applications** that ship with the iPhone, such as the Phone application (see Figure 6–2) and the Clock application. A tab bar application is a multiview application that displays a row of buttons, called the **tab bar**, at the bottom of the screen. Tapping one of the buttons causes a new view controller to become active and a new view to be shown. In the Phone application, for example, tapping *Contacts* shows a different view than the one shown when you tap *Keypad*.

Figure 6–2. *The Phone application is an example of a multiview application using a tab bar*

Another common kind of multiview iPhone application is the navigation-based application, which features a navigation controller that uses a **navigation bar** to control a hierarchical series of views. The Settings application is a good example. In Settings, the first view you get is a series of rows, each row corresponding to a cluster of settings or a specific app. Touching one of those rows takes you to a new view where you can customize one particular set of settings. Some views present a list that allows you to dive even deeper. The navigation controller keeps track of how deep you go and gives you a control to let you make your way back out to the previous view.

For example, if you select the *Sounds* preference, you'll be presented a view with a list of sound-related options. At the top of that view is a navigation bar with a left arrow that takes you back to the previous view if you tap it. Within the sound options is a row labeled *Ringtone*. Tap *Ringtone*, and you're taken to a new view (see Figure 6–3) featuring a list of ring tones and a navigation bar that takes you back to the main *Sounds* preference view. A navigation-based application is useful when you want to present a hierarchy of views.

Figure 6–3. *The iPhone Settings application is an example of a multiview application using a navigation bar.*

On the iPad, most navigation-based applications, such as Mail, are implemented using a **split view**, where the navigation elements appear on the left side of the screen, and the item you select to view or edit appears on the right. You'll learn more about split views and other iPad-specific GUI elements in Chapter 10.

Because views are themselves hierarchical in nature, it's even possible to combine different mechanisms for swapping views within a single application. For example, the iPhone's iPod application uses a tab bar to switch between different methods of organizing your music, and a navigation controller and its associated navigation bar to allow you to browse your music based on that selection. In Figure 6–4, the tab bar is at the bottom of the screen, and the navigation bar is at the top of the screen.

Figure 6–4. *The iPod application uses both a navigation bar and a tab bar.*

Some applications make use of a **toolbar**, which is often confused with a tab bar. A tab bar is used for selecting one and only one option from among two or more. A toolbar can hold buttons and certain other controls, but those items are not mutually exclusive. A perfect example of a toolbar is at the bottom of the main Safari view (see Figure 6–5). If you compare the toolbar at the bottom of the Safari view with the tab bar at the bottom of the Phone or iPod application, you'll find the two pretty easy to tell apart. The tab bar is divided into clearly defined segments, while the toolbar, typically, is not.

Figure 6–5. *Mobile Safari features a toolbar at the bottom. The toolbar is like a free-form bar that allows you to include a variety of controls.*

Each of these types of multiview application uses a specific controller class from the UIKit. Tab bar interfaces are implemented using the class `UITabBarController`, and navigation interfaces are implemented using `UINavigationController`.

The Architecture of a Multiview Application

The application we're going to build in this chapter, View Switcher, is fairly simple in appearance, but in terms of the code we're going to write, it's by far the most complex application we've yet tackled. View Switcher will consist of three different controllers, three nibs, and an application delegate.

When first launched, View Switcher will look like Figure 6–6, with a toolbar at the bottom containing a single button. The rest of the view will contain a blue background and a button yearning to be pressed.

Figure 6–6. *When we first launch the application, we'll see a blue view with a button and a toolbar with its own button.*

When the *Switch Views* button is pressed, the background will turn yellow, and the button's title will change (see Figure 6–7).

Figure 6–7. *When we press the Switch Views button, the blue view flips over to reveal the yellow view.*

If either the *Press Me* or *Press Me, Too* button is pressed, an alert will pop up indicating which view's button was pressed (see Figure 6–8).

Figure 6–8. *When the Press Me or Press Me, Too button is pressed, an alert is displayed.*

Although we could achieve this same functionality by writing a single-view application, we're taking this more complex approach to demonstrate the mechanics of a multiview application. There are actually three view controllers interacting in this simple application: one that controls the blue view, one that controls the yellow view, and a third special controller that swaps the other two in and out when the *Switch Views* button is pressed.

Before we start building our application, let's talk a little bit about the way iPhone multiview applications are put together. Most multiview applications use the same basic pattern.

The Root Controller

The nib file is a key player here. For our View Switcher application, you'll find the file *MainWindow.xib* in your project window's *Resources* folder. That file contains the application delegate and the application's main window, along with the *File's Owner* and *First Responder* icons. We'll add an instance of a controller class that is responsible for managing which other view is currently being shown to the user. We call this controller the **root controller** (as in "the root of the tree" or "the root of all evil") because it is the first controller the user sees and the controller that is loaded when the application loads.

This root controller is often an instance of `UINavigationController` or `UITabBarController`, though it can also be a custom subclass of `UIViewController`.

In a multiview application, the job of the root controller is to take two or more other views and present them to the user as appropriate, based on the user's input. A tab bar controller, for example, will swap in different views and view controllers based on which tab bar item was last tapped. A navigation controller will do the same thing as the user drills down and backs up through hierarchical data.

> **NOTE:** The root controller is the primary view controller for the application and, as such, is the view that specifies whether it is OK to automatically rotate to a new orientation. However, the root controller can pass responsibility for things like that to the currently active controller.

In multiview applications, most of the screen will be taken up by a content view, and each content view will have its own controller with its own outlets and actions. In a tab bar application, for example, taps on the tab bar will go to the tab bar controller, but taps anywhere else on the screen will go to the controller that corresponds to the content view currently being displayed.

Anatomy of a Content View

In a multiview application, each view controller controls a content view, and these content views are where the bulk of your application's user interface is built. Each content view generally consists of up to three pieces: the view controller, the nib, and a subclass of `UIView`. Unless you are doing something really unusual, your content view will always have an associated view controller, will usually have a nib, and will sometimes subclass `UIView`. Although you can create your interface in code rather than using a nib file, few people choose that route because it is more time-consuming and difficult to maintain. In this chapter, we'll be creating only a nib and a controller class for each content view.

In the *View Switcher* project, our root controller controls a content view that consists of a toolbar that occupies the bottom of the screen. The root controller then loads a blue view controller, placing the blue content view as a subview to the root controller view. When the root controller's switch views button is pressed (the button is in the toolbar), the root controller swaps out the blue view controller and swaps in a yellow view controller, instantiating that controller if it needs to do so. Confused? Don't worry, because this will become clearer as we walk through the code.

Building View Switcher

Enough theory! Let's go ahead and build our project. Select **File ➤ New Project...** or press ⇧⌘**N**. When the assistant opens, select *Window-based Application* (see Figure 6–9), and make sure the check box labeled *Use Core Data for storage* is unchecked and the *Product* popup button is set to *iPhone*. Type in a product name of *View Switcher*.

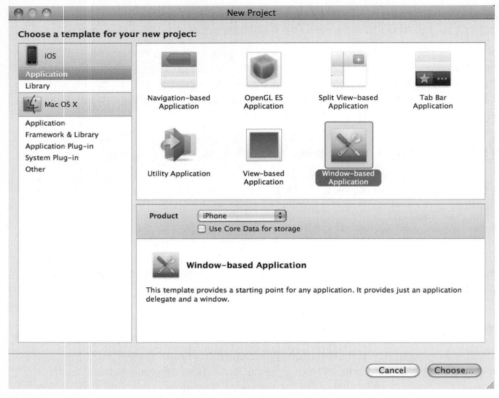

Figure 6–9. *Creating a new project using the Window-based Application project template*

The template we just selected is actually even simpler than the *View-based Application* template we've been using up to now. This template will give us a **window**, an application delegate, and nothing else—no views, no controllers, no nothing.

> **Note:** The window is the most basic container in iOS. Each app has exactly one window that belongs to it, though it is possible to see more than one window on the screen at a time. For example, if your app is running and a Short Message Service (SMS) message comes in, you'll see the SMS message displayed in its window. Your app can't access that overlaid window. It belongs to the SMS app.

You won't use the *Window-based Application* template very often when you're creating applications, but by starting from nothing, you'll really get a feel for the way multiview applications are put together.

Take a second to expand the *Resources* and *Classes* folders in the *Groups & Files* pane and look at what's there. You'll find a single nib file, *MainWindow.xib;* the *View_Switcher-Info.plist* file; and the two files in the *Classes* folder that implement the application delegate. Everything else we need for our application, we must create.

Creating Our View Controller and Nib Files

One of the more daunting aspects of building a multiview application from scratch is that we need to create several interconnected objects. We're going to create all the files that will make up our application before we do anything in Interface Builder and before we write any code. By creating all the files first, we'll be able to use Xcode's Code Sense to write our code faster. If a class hasn't been declared, Code Sense has no way to know about it, so we would need to type its name in full every time, which takes longer and is more error-prone.

Fortunately, in addition to project templates, Xcode also provides file templates for many standard file types, which helps simplify the process of creating the basic skeleton of our application.

Single-click the *Classes* folder in the project navigator, and then press ⌘N or select File ➤ New File.... Take a look at the window that opens (see Figure 6–10).

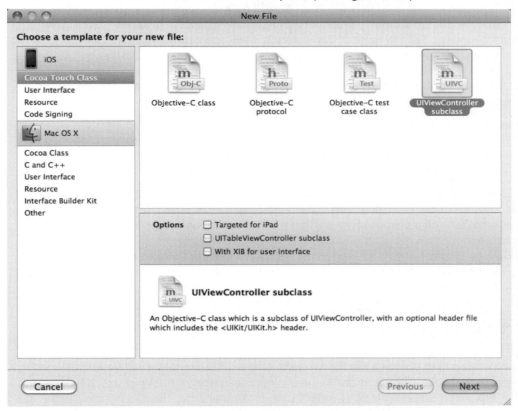

Figure 6–10. *The template we'll use to create a new view controller subclass*

If you select *Cocoa Touch Class* from the left pane, you will be given templates for a number of common Cocoa Touch classes. Select *UIViewController subclass*. In the middle-right pane, you'll see three check boxes:

- The first is labeled *Targeted for iPad*, and should be unchecked (since we're not making an iPad GUI right now).

- The second is labeled *UITableViewController subclass*, and would be helpful if we were going to create a table-based layout, but we're not, so make sure that's unchecked, too.

- The third is labeled *With XIB for user interface*. If that box is checked, click it to uncheck it. If you select that option, Xcode will also create a nib file that corresponds to this controller class. We will start using that option in the next chapter, but for now, we want you to see how the different parts of the puzzle fit together by creating them all individually.

Click *Next*. A window appears that lets you name your file, specify if you'd like the *.h* file created to go along with the *.m* file, choose a particular directory in which to save the files, and pick a project and target for your files.

the usual file-saving window, which lets you choose where to save the file and what it should be called. For the sake of consistency, navigate into the *Classes* directory, which Xcode set up when you created this project; it should already contain the `View_SwitcherAppDelegate` class. That's where Xcode puts all of the Objective-C classes that are created as part of the project, and it's as good a place as any for you to put your own classes.

Name your new file *SwitchViewController.m* and make sure that *Also create "SwitchViewController.h"* is checked. Next, click the *Choose...* button and choose the project's *Classes* folder. Leave the project and target selections at their default settings and click the *Finish* button.

Xcode should add two files to your *Classes* folder. `SwitchViewController` will be your root controller—the controller that swaps the other views in and out. Now we need to create the controllers for the two content views that will be swapped in and out. Repeat the same steps two more times to create *BlueViewController.m*, *YellowViewController.m*, and their *.h* counterparts, adding them to the *Classes* group and saving them in the *Classes* folder in your project folder as well.

> **Caution:** Make sure you check your spelling, as a typo here will create classes that don't match the source code later in the chapter.

Our next step is to create a nib file for each of the two content views we just created. Single-click the *Resources* folder in the project navigator, and then press ⌘N or select **File ➤ New File...** again. This time, select *User Interface* under the *iOS* heading in the left pane (see Figure 6–11). Next, select the icon for the *View XIB* template, which will create a nib with a content view. Then select *iPhone* from the *Product* popup, and click the *Next button*.

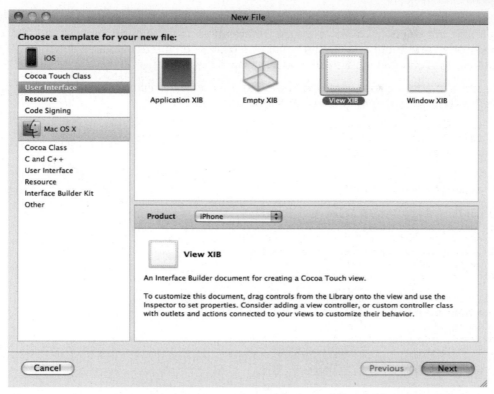

Figure 6–11. We're creating a new nib file, using the View XIB template in the User Interface section.

When prompted for a file name, type *BlueView.xib*.

Now repeat the steps to create a second nib file called *YellowView.xib*. Once you've done that, you have all the files you need. It's time to start hooking everything together.

Modifying the App Delegate

Our first stop on the multiview express is the application delegate. Single-click the file *View_SwitcherAppDelegate.h* in the Groups & Files pane (make sure it's the app delegate and not *SwitchViewcontroller.h*), and make the following changes to that file:

```
#import <UIKit/UIKit.h>
@class SwitchViewController;
@interface View_SwitcherAppDelegate : NSObject <UIApplicationDelegate> {
    UIWindow *window;
    SwitchViewController *switchViewController;
}

@property (nonatomic, retain) IBOutlet UIWindow *window;
@property (nonatomic, retain) IBOutlet SwitchViewController
    *switchViewController;
@end
```

The IBOutlet declaration you just typed is an outlet that will point to our application's root controller. We need this outlet because we are about to write code that will add the root controller's view to our application's main window when the application launches. We'll hook up that outlet when we edit *MainWindow.xib*.

Now, we need to add the root controller's view to our application's main window. Click *View_SwitcherAppDelegate.m*, and add the following code:

```
#import "View_SwitcherAppDelegate.h"
#import "SwitchViewController.h"
@implementation View_SwitcherAppDelegate

@synthesize window;
@synthesize switchViewController;

- (void) application:(UIApplication *)application
didFinishLaunchingWithOptions:(NSDictionary *)launchOptions{
    // Override point for customization after application launch
    [self.window addSubview:switchViewController.view];
    [self.window makeKeyAndVisible];
    return YES;
}

- (void)dealloc {
    [window release];
    [switchViewController release];
    [super dealloc];
}

@end
```

Besides implementing the switchViewController outlet, we are adding the root controller's view to the window. Remember that the window is the only gateway to the user, so anything that needs to be displayed to the user must be added as a subview of the application's window.

If you go back to Chapter 5's *Swap* project and examine the code in *SwapAppDelegate.m*, you'll see that the template added the view controller's view to the application window for you. Since we're using a much simpler template for this project, we need to take care of that wiring together business ourselves.

SwitchViewController.h

Because we're going to be adding an instance of SwitchViewController to *MainWindow.xib*, now is the time to add any needed outlets or actions to the *SwitchViewController.h* header file.

We'll need one action method to toggle between the yellow and blue views. We won't need any outlets, but we will need two other pointers, one to each of the view controllers that we're going to be swapping in and out. These don't need to be outlets, because we're going to create them in code rather than in a nib. Add the following code to *SwitchViewController.h*:

```
#import <UIKit/UIKit.h>

@class YellowViewController;
@class BlueViewController;

@interface SwitchViewController : UIViewController {
    YellowViewController *yellowViewController;
    BlueViewController *blueViewController;
}
@property (retain, nonatomic) YellowViewController *yellowViewController;
@property (retain, nonatomic) BlueViewController *blueViewController;

- (IBAction)switchViews:(id)sender;
@end
```

Now that we've declared the action we need, we can add an instance of this class to *MainWindow.xib*.

Adding a View Controller

Save your source code, and double-click *MainWindow.xib* to open it in Interface Builder. Four icons should appear in the nib's main window: *File's Owner, First Responder, View_SwitcherAppDelegate,* and *Window* (see Figure 6–12). We need to add one more icon that will represent an instance of our root controller. Since Interface Builder's library doesn't have a SwitchViewController, we'll need to add a view controller and change its class to SwitchViewController.

Figure 6–12. *MainWindow.xib, showing File's Owner, First Responder, View_SwitcherAppDelegate, and Window*

Since the class we need to add is a subclass of UIViewController, look in the library for a *View Controller (see Figure 6–13)*, and drag one to the nib's main window (the window with the icons and the title *MainWindow.xib*).

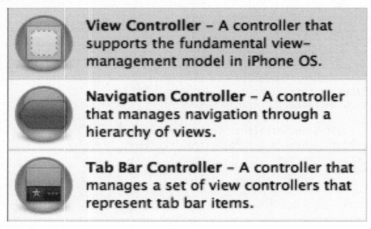

Figure 6–13. *View Controller in the Library*

Once you do this, your nib's main window will now have five icons, and a new window containing a dashed, gray, rounded rectangle labeled View should appear (see Figure 6–14).

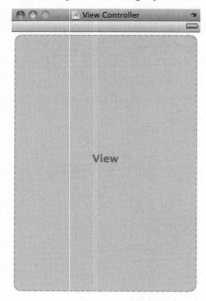

Figure 6–14. *The window representing your view controller in Interface Builder*

We just added an instance of UIViewController to our nib, but we actually need an instance of SwitchViewController, so let's change our view controller's class to SwitchViewController. Single-click the *View Controller* icon in the nib's main window, and press ⌘4 to open the identity inspector (see Figure 6–15).

Figure 6–15. *Notice that the class is currently set to UIViewController in the identity inspector. We're about to change that.*

The identity inspector allows you to specify the class of the currently selected object. Our view controller is currently specified as a UIViewController, and it has no actions defined. Click inside the combo box labeled *Class*, the one at the top of the inspector that currently reads *UIViewController*. Change the *Class* to *SwitchViewController*.

Once you make that change, you should notice that in the nib's main window, the name of our newly added *View Controller* has changed to *Switch View Controller*. Hold down the control key and click on the *Switch View Controller* icon in the main nib window. A summary popup window will appear (see Figure 6–16) giving a little detail about the clicked on object. Notice that the *Received Actions* section now lists the action switchViews:. This is your clue that the class of your view controller has indeed been changed to *SwitchViewController*. You'll see how we make use of this action in the next section.

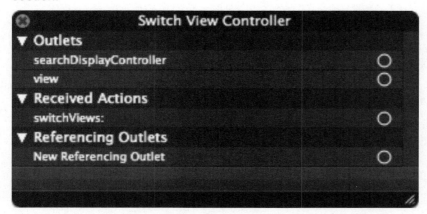

Figure 6–16. *A control-click on the SwitchViewController brings up this popup window which shows a bit of detail about the clicked-on object.*

CAUTION: If you don't see the `switchViews:` action in the popup window shown in Figure 6–16, check the spelling of your class file names. If you don't get the name exactly right, things won't match up. Watch your spelling!

Save your nib file and move to the next step.

Building a View with a Toolbar

We now need to build a view to add to `SwitchViewController`. As a reminder, this new view controller will be our root view controller—the controller that is in play when our application is launched. `SwitchViewController`'s content view will consist of a toolbar that occupies the bottom of the screen. Its job is to switch between the blue view and the yellow view, so it will need a way for the user to change the views. For that, we're going to use a toolbar with a button. Let's build the toolbar view now.

Take a look back at the view controller shown in Figure 6–14. Notice the rounded gray rectangle with a dashed outline inside the view controller window. Find that same gray rectangle in Interface Builder. This gray rectangle represents the view controlled by that view controller. We're going to drag in a view to replace that gray rectangle. If you can't find that window, double-click on the *Switch View Controller* icon in the main nib window.

Drag a *View* from the library onto the gray rounded rect. The gray background should be replaced by this new view. As your cursor enters the gray rectangle, it will highlight, showing that it is receiving the drag (see Figure 6–17). Release the mouse button, and your new view will be in place.

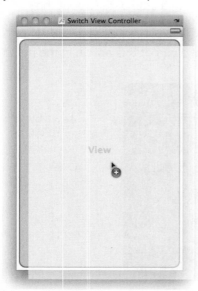

Figure 6–17. *Dragging a View onto the SwitchViewController's view, replacing the default view*

Now, let's add a toolbar to the bottom of the view. Grab a *Toolbar* from the library, drag it onto your view, and place it at the bottom, so that it looks like Figure 6–18.

Figure 6–18. *We dragged a Toolbar onto our new view. Notice that the Toolbar features a single button labeled Item.*

The toolbar features a single button. We'll use that button to let the user switch between the different content views. Double-click the button, and change its title to *Switch Views*. Press the return key to commit your change.

Now, we can link the toolbar button to our action method. Before doing that, though, we should warn you: toolbar buttons aren't like other iOS controls. They support only a single target action, and they trigger that action only at one well-defined moment—the equivalent of a *Touch Up Inside* event on other iOS controls.

Selecting a toolbar button in Interface Builder can be tricky. Click the view so we are all starting in the same place. Now single-click the toolbar button. Notice that this selects the toolbar, and not the button. Now, click the button a second time. This should select the button itself. You can confirm you have the button selected by switching to the attributes inspector (⌘1) and making sure it says *Bar Button Item*.

Once you have the *Switch Views* button selected, control-drag from it over to the *Switch View Controller* icon, and select the **switchViews:** action. If the switchViews: action doesn't pop up and instead you see an outlet called **delegate**, you've most likely control-dragged from the toolbar rather than the button. To fix it, just make sure you have the button and not the toolbar selected, and then redo your control-drag.

Tip. Remember, you can always view the main nib window in list mode and use the disclosure triangles to drill down through the hierarchy to get to any element in the view hierarchy.

Earlier, we created an outlet in *View_SwitcherAppDelegate.h* so our application could get to our instance of SwitchViewController and add its view to the main application window. Now, we need to connect the instance of SwitchViewController in our nib to that outlet. Control-drag from the *View Switcher App Delegate* icon to the *Switch View Controller* icon, and select the **switchViewController** outlet. You may see a second outlet called **viewController**. If you do, make sure you connect to **switchViewController** and not **viewController**.

That's all we need to do here, so save your nib file. Next, let's get started implementing SwitchViewController.

Writing the Root View Controller

It's time to write our root view controller. Its job is to switch between the yellow view and the blue view whenever the user clicks the *Switch Views* button.

Making the following changes to *SwitchViewController.m*. You can delete the commented-out methods provided by the template if you want to shorten the code.

```
#import "SwitchViewController.h"
#import "YellowViewController.h"
#import "BlueViewController.h"

@implementation SwitchViewController
@synthesize yellowViewController;
@synthesize blueViewController;

- (void)viewDidLoad
{
    BlueViewController *blueController = [[BlueViewController alloc]
            initWithNibName:@"BlueView" bundle:nil];
    self.blueViewController = blueController;
    [self.view insertSubview:blueController.view atIndex:0];
    [blueController release];
    [super viewDidLoad];
}

- (IBAction)switchViews:(id)sender
{
    if (self.yellowViewController.view.superview == nil)
    {
        if (self.yellowViewController == nil)
        {
            YellowViewController *yellowController =
            [[YellowViewController alloc] initWithNibName:@"YellowView"
                                                    bundle:nil];
            self.yellowViewController = yellowController;
```

```
                [yellowController release];
            }
        [blueViewController.view removeFromSuperview];
        [self.view insertSubview:yellowViewController.view atIndex:0];
    }
    else
    {
        if (self.blueViewController == nil)
        {
            BlueViewController *blueController =
            [[BlueViewController alloc] initWithNibName:@"BlueView"
                                            bundle:nil];
            self.blueViewController = blueController;
            [blueController release];
        }
        [yellowViewController.view removeFromSuperview];
        [self.view insertSubview:blueViewController.view atIndex:0];
    }
}
...
```

Also, add the following code to the existing didReceiveMemoryWarning method:

```
- (void)didReceiveMemoryWarning {
    // Releases the view if it doesn't have a superview
    [super didReceiveMemoryWarning];

    // Release any cached data, images, etc, that aren't in use
    if (self.blueViewController.view.superview == nil)
        self.blueViewController = nil;
    else
        self.yellowViewController = nil;
}
```

Then add the following two statements to the dealloc method:

```
- (void)dealloc {
    [yellowViewController release];
    [blueViewController release];
    [super dealloc];
}
@end
```

The first method we added, viewDidLoad, overrides a UIViewController method that is called when the nib is loaded. How could we tell? Option-double-click the method name, and take a look at the documentation window that appears (see Figure 6–19). The method is defined in our superclass and is intended to be overridden by classes that need to be notified when the view has finished loading.

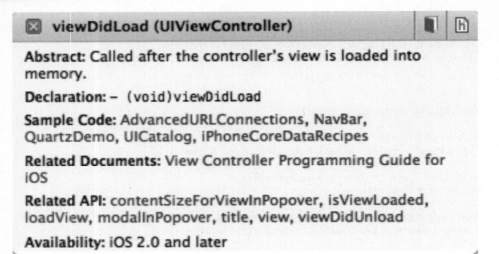

Figure 6–19. *This documentation window appears when you option-double-click the viewDidLoad method. Note the reference to SwitchViewController in the window title.*

This version of viewDidLoad creates an instance of BlueViewController. We use the initWithNibName method to load the BlueViewController instance from the nib file *BlueView.xib*. Note that the file name provided to initWithNibName does not include the *.xib* extension. Once the BlueViewController is created, we assign this new instance to our blueViewController property.

```
BlueViewController *blueController = [[BlueViewController alloc]
    initWithNibName:@"BlueView" bundle:nil];
self.blueViewController = blueController;
```

Next, we insert the blue view as a subview of the root view. We insert it at index 0, which tells iOS to put this view behind everything else. Sending the view to the back ensures that the toolbar we created in Interface Builder a moment ago will always be visible on the screen, since we're inserting the content views behind it.

```
[self.view insertSubview:blueController.view atIndex:0];
```

Now, why didn't we load the yellow view here also? We're going to need to load it at some point, so why not do it now? Good question. The answer is that the user may never tap the *Switch Views* button. The user might just use the view that's visible when the application launches, and then quit. In that case, why use resources to load the yellow view and its controller?

Instead, we'll load the yellow view the first time we actually need it. This is called **lazy loading**, and it's a standard way of keeping memory overhead down. The actual loading of the yellow view happens in the switchViews: method, so let's take a look at that.

switchViews: first checks which view is being swapped in by seeing whether yellowViewController's view's superview is nil. This will return true if one of two things is true:

- If yellowViewController exists but its view is not being shown to the user, that view will have no superview because it's not presently in the view hierarchy, and the expression will evaluate to true.

- If yellowViewController doesn't exist because it hasn't been created yet or was flushed from memory, it will also return true.

We then check to see whether yellowViewController is nil.

```
if (self.yellowViewController.view.superview == nil)
{
```

If it is, that means there is no instance of yellowViewController, and we need to create one. This could happen because it's the first time the button has been pressed or because the system ran low on memory and it was flushed. In this case, we need to create an instance of YellowViewController as we did for the BlueViewController in the viewDidLoad method:

```
if (self.yellowViewController == nil)
{
    YellowViewController *yellowController =
    [[YellowViewController alloc] initWithNibName:@"YellowView"
                                           bundle:nil];
    self.yellowViewController = yellowController;
    [yellowController release];
}
```

At this point, we know that we have a yellowViewController instance, because either we already had one or we just created it. We then remove blueViewController's view from the view hierarchy and add yellowViewController's view:

```
    [blueViewController.view removeFromSuperview];
    [self.view insertSubview:yellowViewController.view atIndex:0];
}
```

If self.yellowViewController.view.superview is not nil, then we need to do the same thing, but for blueViewController. Although we create an instance of BlueViewController in viewDidLoad, it is still possible that the instance has been flushed because memory got low. Now, in this application, the chances of memory running out are slim, but we're still going to be good memory citizens and make sure we have an instance before proceeding:

```
else
{
    if (self.blueViewController == nil)
    {
        BlueViewController *blueController =
        [[BlueViewController alloc] initWithNibName:@"BlueView"
                                             bundle:nil];
        self.blueViewController = blueController;
        [blueController release];
    }
    [yellowViewController.view removeFromSuperview];
    [self.view insertSubview:blueViewController.view atIndex:0];
}
```

In addition to not using resources for the yellow view and controller if the *Switch Views* button is never tapped, lazy loading also gives us the ability to release whichever view is not being shown to free up its memory. iOS will call the UIViewController method didReceiveMemoryWarning, which is inherited by every view controller, when memory drops below a system-determined level.

Since we know that either view will be reloaded the next time it is shown to the user, we can safely release either controller. We do this by adding a few lines to the existing didReceiveMemoryWarning method:

```
- (void)didReceiveMemoryWarning {
    [super didReceiveMemoryWarning]; // Releases the view if it
                                     // doesn't have a superview
    // Release anything that's not essential, such as cached data
    if (self.blueViewController.view.superview == nil)
        self.blueViewController = nil;
    else
        self.yellowViewController = nil;
}
```

This newly added code checks to see which view is currently being shown to the user and releases the controller for the other view by assigning nil to its property. This will cause the controller, along with the view it controls, to be deallocated, freeing up its memory.

> **TIP:** Lazy loading is a key component of resource management on iOS, and you should implement it anywhere you can. In a complex, multiview application, being responsible and flushing unused objects from memory can be the difference between an application that works well and one that crashes periodically because it runs out of memory.

Implementing the Content Views

The two content views that we are creating in this application are extremely simple. They each have one action method that is triggered by a button, and neither one needs any outlets. The two views are also nearly identical. In fact, they are so similar that they could have been represented by the same class. We chose to make them two separate classes because that's how most multiview applications are constructed. Let's declare an action method in each of the header files. First, in *BlueViewController.h*, add the following declaration:

```
#import <UIKit/UIKit.h>
@interface BlueViewController : UIViewController {

}
- (IBAction)blueButtonPressed;
@end
```

Save it, and then add the following line to *YellowViewController.h*:

```
#import <UIKit/UIKit.h>
```

```
@interface YellowViewController : UIViewController {
}
- (IBAction)yellowButtonPressed;
@end
```

Save this file as well, and then double click *BlueView.xib* to open it in Interface Builder so we can make a few changes. First, we need to specify that the class that will load this nib from disk is `BlueViewController`. Single-click the *File's Owner* icon and press ⌘4 to bring up the identity inspector. *File's Owner* defaults to *NSObject*; change it to *BlueViewController*.

Single-click the *View* icon in the dock and then press ⌘**1** to bring up the attribute inspector. In the inspector's *View* section, click the color well that's labeled *Background*, and use the popup color picker to change the background color of this view to a nice shade of blue. Once you are happy with your blue, close the color picker.

Next, we'll change the size of the view in the nib. In the attributes inspector, the top section is labeled *Simulated User Interface Elements*. If we set these drop-downs to reflect which top and bottom elements are used in our application, Interface Builder will automatically calculate the size of the remaining space. The status bar is already specified. If you select the *Bottom Bar* popup, you can select *Toolbar* to indicate that the enclosing view has a toolbar.

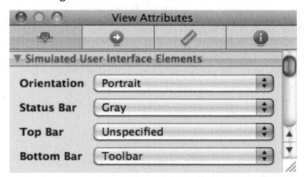

Figure 6–20. The Simulated Metrics section of the View's attributes inspector

Setting this will cause Interface Builder to calculate the correct size for your view automatically, so that you know how much space you have to work with. You can press ⌘**3** to bring up the size inspector to confirm this. After making the change, the height of the window should be 416 pixels, and the width should still be 320 pixels.

Drag a *Round Rect Button* from the library over to the. Double-click the button, and change its title to *Press Me*. You can place the button anywhere that looks good to you. Next, with the button still selected, switch to the connections inspector (by pressing ⌘2), drag from the *Touch Up Inside* event to the *File's Owner* icon, and connect to the `blueButtonPressed` action method.

We have one more thing to do in this nib, which is to connect the `BlueViewController`'s `view` outlet to the view in the nib. The `view` outlet is inherited from the parent class,

UIViewController, and gives the controller access to the view it controls. When we changed the underlying class of the file's owner, the existing outlet connections were broken. So, we need to reestablish the connection from the controller to its view. Control-drag from the *File's Owner* icon to the *View icon*, and select the **view** outlet to do that.

Save the nib, go back to Xcode, and double click *YellowView.xib*. We're going to make almost exactly the same changes to this nib file.

First, click the *File's Owner* icon in the nib window and use the identity inspector to change its class to *YellowViewController*.

Next, select the view and switch to the attributes inspector. In the attributes inspector, click the Background color well and select a bright yellow, and then close the color picker. Also, select *Toolbar* from the *Bottom Bar* popup in the *Simulated User Interface Elements* section.

Next, drag out a *Round Rect Button* from the library and center it on the view, then change its title to *Press Me, Too*. With the button still selected, use the connections inspector to drag from the *Touch Up Inside* event to the *File's Owner* icon, and connect to the *yellowButtonPressed* action method.

Finally, control-drag from the *File's Owner* icon to the *View icon*, and select the *view* outlet.

Once all that is done, save the nib, and get ready to enter some more code.

The two action methods we're going to implement do nothing more than show an alert (as we did in Chapter 4's Control Fun application), so go ahead and add the following code to *BlueViewController.m:*

```
#import "BlueViewController.h"

@implementation BlueViewController

- (IBAction)blueButtonPressed
{
    UIAlertView *alert = [[UIAlertView alloc]
        initWithTitle:@"Blue View Button Pressed"
             message:@"You pressed the button on the blue view"
           delegate:nil
    cancelButtonTitle:@"Yep, I did."
    otherButtonTitles:nil];
    [alert show];
    [alert release];
}
...
```

Save the file. Next, switch over to *YellowViewController.m*, and add this very similar code to that file:

```
#import "YellowViewController.h"

@implementation YellowViewController
```

```
- (IBAction)yellowButtonPressed
{
    UIAlertView *alert = [[UIAlertView alloc]
        initWithTitle:@"Yellow View Button Pressed"
              message:@"You pressed the button on the yellow view"
            delegate:nil
    cancelButtonTitle:@"Yep, I did."
    otherButtonTitles:nil];
    [alert show];
    [alert release];
}
...
```

Save your code, and let's take this bad boy for a spin. When our application launches, it shows the view we built in *BlueView.xib*. When you tap the *Switch Views* button, it will change to show the view that we built in *YellowView.xib*. Tap it again, and it goes back to the view we built in *BlueView.xib*. If you tap the button centered on the blue or yellow view, you'll get an alert view with a message indicating which button was pressed. This alert shows that the correct controller class is being called for the view that is being shown.

The transition between the two views is kind of abrupt, though. Gosh, if only there were some way to make the transition look nicer.

Animating the Transition

Of course, there is a way to make the transition look nicer! We can animate the transition in order to give the user visual feedback of the change. UIView has several class methods we can call to indicate that the transition should be animated, to indicate the type of transition that should be used, and to specify how long the transition should take.

Go back to *SwitchViewController.m*, and replace your switchViews: method with this new version:

```
- (IBAction)switchViews:(id)sender
{
    [UIView beginAnimations:@"View Flip" context:nil];
    [UIView setAnimationDuration:1.25];
    [UIView setAnimationCurve:UIViewAnimationCurveEaseInOut];

    if (self.yellowViewController.view.superview == nil)
    {
        if (self.yellowViewController == nil)
        {
            YellowViewController *yellowController =
            [[YellowViewController alloc] initWithNibName:@"YellowView"
                                                 bundle:nil];
            self.yellowViewController = yellowController;
            [yellowController release];
        }
```

```
            [UIView setAnimationTransition:
             UIViewAnimationTransitionFlipFromRight
                               forView:self.view cache:YES];

            [blueViewController viewWillAppear:YES];
            [yellowViewController viewWillDisappear:YES];

            [blueViewController.view removeFromSuperview];
            [self.view insertSubview:yellowViewController.view atIndex:0];
            [yellowViewController viewDidDisappear:YES];
            [blueViewController viewDidAppear:YES];
        }
    else
    {
        if (self.blueViewController == nil)
        {
            BlueViewController *blueController =
            [[BlueViewController alloc] initWithNibName:@"BlueView"
                                                  bundle:nil];
            self.blueViewController = blueController;
            [blueController release];
        }
            [UIView setAnimationTransition:
             UIViewAnimationTransitionFlipFromLeft
                               forView:self.view cache:YES];

            [yellowViewController viewWillAppear:YES];
            [blueViewController viewWillDisappear:YES];

            [yellowViewController.view removeFromSuperview];
            [self.view insertSubview:blueViewController.view atIndex:0];
            [blueViewController viewDidDisappear:YES];
            [yellowViewController viewDidAppear:YES];
        }
    [UIView commitAnimations];
}
```

Compile this new version, and run your application. When you tap the *Switch Views*
button, instead of the new view just snapping into place, the old view will flip over to
reveal the new view, as shown in Figure 6–21.

Figure 6–21. *One view transitioning to another, using the flip style of animation*

In order to tell iOS that we want a change animated, we need to declare an **animation block** and specify how long the animation should take. Animation blocks are declared by using the UIView class method beginAnimations:context:, like so:

```
[UIView beginAnimations:@"View Flip" context:NULL];
[UIView setAnimationDuration:1.25];
```

beginAnimations:context: takes two parameters. The first is an animation block title. This title comes into play only if you take more direct advantage of Core Animation, the framework behind this animation. For our purposes, we could have used nil. The second parameter is a (void *) that allows you to specify an object (or any other C data type) whose pointer you would like associated with this animation block. We used NULL here, since we don't need to do that.

After that, we set the **animation curve**, which determines the timing of the animation. The default, which is a linear curve, causes the animation to happen at a constant speed. The option we set here, UIViewAnimationCurveEaseInOut, specifies that the animation should start slow but speed up in the middle, slowing down again at the end. This gives the animation a more natural, less mechanical appearance.

```
[UIView setAnimationCurve:UIViewAnimationCurveEaseInOut];
```

Next, we need to specify the transition to use. At the time of this writing, four view transitions are available on iOS:

- UIViewAnimationTransitionFlipFromLeft

- UIViewAnimationTransitionFlipFromRight

- UIViewAnimationTransitionCurlUp

- UIViewAnimationTransitionCurlDown

We chose to use two different effects, depending on which view was being swapped in. Using a left flip for one transition and a right flip for the other makes the view seem to flip back and forth. The cache option speeds up drawing by taking a snapshot of the view when the animation begins and using that image, rather than redrawing the view at each step of the animation. You should always have it cache the animation unless the appearance of the view may need to change during the animation.

```
[UIView setAnimationTransition:UIViewAnimationTransitionFlipFromRight
                forView:self.view cache:YES];
```

After we set the transition, we make two calls, one on each of the views being used in the transition:

```
[self.blueViewController viewWillAppear:YES];
[self.yellowViewController viewWillDisappear:YES];
```

When we're finished swapping the views, we make two more calls on those views:

```
[self.yellowViewController viewDidDisappear:YES];
[self.blueViewController viewDidAppear:YES];
```

The default implementations of these methods in UIViewController do nothing, so our calls to viewDidDisappear: and viewDidAppear: don't do anything, since our controllers didn't override those methods. It's important to make these calls even if you know you're not using them.

Why is it important to make these calls even though they do nothing? Although we're not using those methods now, we might choose to in the future. It's also possible that UIViewController's implementation to those methods won't always be empty, so failing to call these methods could cause our application to behave oddly after a future update of the operating system. The performance hit for making these four calls is meaningless, since they trigger no code, and by putting them in, we can be sure that our application will continue to work. We're future-proofing.

When we're finished specifying the changes to be animated, we call commitAnimations on UIView. Everything between the start of the animation block and the call to commitAnimations will be animated together.

Thanks to Cocoa Touch's use of Core Animation under the hood, we're able to do fairly sophisticated animation with only a handful of code.

Switching Off

Whoo-boy! Creating our own multiview controller was a lot of work, wasn't it? You should have a very good grasp on how multiview applications are put together now that you've built one from scratch. Although Xcode contains project templates for the most common types of multiview applications, you need to understand the overall structure of these types of applications so you can build them yourself from the ground up. The delivered templates are incredible time-savers, but at times, they simply won't meet your needs.

In the next three chapters, we're going to continue building multiview applications to reinforce the concepts from this chapter and to give you a feel for how more complex applications are put together. In the next chapter, we'll construct a tab bar application, and in the two chapters after that, we'll build a navigation-based application.

Chapter 7

Tab Bars and Pickers

In the previous chapter, you built your first multiview application. In this chapter, you're going to build a full tab bar application with five different tabs and five different content views. Building this application will reinforce a lot of what you learned in Chapter 6. Now, you're too smart to spend a whole chapter doing stuff you already sort of know how to do, so we're going to use those five content views to demonstrate a type of iOS control that we have not yet covered. The control is called a **picker view**, or just a **picker.**

You may not be familiar with the name, but you've almost certainly used a picker if you've owned an iPhone or iPod touch for more than, say, 10 minutes. Pickers are the controls with dials that spin. You use them to input dates in the Calendar application or to set a timer in the Clock application (see Figure 7–1). On the iPad, the picker view isn't quite as common, since the larger display lets you present other ways of choosing among multiple items, but even there, it's used in the Calendar application.

Figure 7–1. *A picker in the Clock application*

Pickers are a bit more complex than the iOS controls you've seen so far, and as such, they deserve a little more attention. Pickers can be configured to display one dial or many. By default, pickers display lists of text, but they can also be made to display images.

The Pickers Application

This chapter's application, Pickers, will feature a tab bar. As you build Pickers, you'll change the default tab bar so it has five tabs, add an icon to each of the tab bar items, and then create a series of content views and connect each view to a tab.

The application's content views will feature five different pickers:

- **Date picker**: The first content view we'll build will have a date picker, which is the easiest type of picker to implement (see Figure 7–2). The view will also have a button that, when tapped, will display an alert that shows the date that was picked.

Figure 7–2. *The first tab will show a date picker.*

- **Single-component picker**: The second tab will feature a picker with a single list of values (see Figure 7–3). This picker is a little more work to implement than a date picker. You'll learn how to specify the values to be displayed in the picker by using a delegate and a data source.

Figure 7–3. *A picker displaying a single list of values*

- **Multicomponent picker**: In the third tab, we're going to create a picker with two separate wheels. The technical term for each of these wheels is a **picker component**, so here we are creating a picker with two components. You'll see how to use the data source and delegate to provide two independent lists of data to the picker (see Figure 7–4). Each of this picker's components can be changed without impacting the other one.

Figure 7–4. *A two-component picker, showing an alert that reflects our selection*

- **Picker with dependent components**: In the fourth content view, we'll build another picker with two components. But this time, the values displayed in the component on the right will change based on the value selected in the component on the left. In our example, we're going to display a list of states in the left component and a list of that state's ZIP codes in the right component (see Figure 7–5).

Figure 7–5. *In this picker, one component is dependent on the other. As we select a state in the left component, the right component changes to a list of ZIP codes in that state.*

- **Custom picker with images**: Last, but most certainly not least, we're going to have some fun with the fifth content view. We'll demonstrate how to add image data to a picker, and we're going to do it by writing a little game that uses a picker with five components. In several places in Apple's documentation, the picker's appearance is described as looking a bit like a slot machine. Well, then, what could be more fitting than writing a little slot machine game (see Figure 7–6)? For this picker, the user won't be able to manually change the values of the components, but will be able to select the *Spin* button to make the five wheels spin to a new, randomly selected value. If three copies of the same image appear in a row, the user wins.

Figure 7–6. *Our fifth component picker. Note that we do not condone using your iPhone as a tiny casino.*

Delegates and Data Sources

Before we dive in and start building our application, let's look at what makes pickers more complex than the other controls you've used so far. With the exception of the date picker, you can't use a picker by just grabbing one in the object library, dropping it on your content view, and configuring it. You also need to provide each picker with both a picker **delegate** and a picker **data source**.

By this point, you should be comfortable using delegates. We've already used application delegates and action sheet delegates, and the basic idea is the same here. The picker defers several jobs to its delegate. The most important of these is the task of determining what to actually draw for each of the rows in each of its components. The picker asks the delegate for either a string or a view that will be drawn at a given spot on a given component. The picker gets its data from the delegate.

In addition to the delegate, pickers need to have a data source. In this instance, the name *data source* is a bit of a misnomer. The data source tells the picker how many components it will be working with and how many rows make up each component. The data source works like the delegate, in that its methods are called at certain, prespecified times. Without a data source and a delegate, pickers cannot do their job; in fact, they won't even be drawn.

It's very common for the data source and the delegate to be the same object, and just as common for that object to be the view controller for the picker's enclosing view, which is the approach we'll be using in this application. The view controllers for each of our application's content panes will be the data source and the delegate for their picker.

> **NOTE:** Here's a pop quiz: is the picker data source part of the model, view, or controller portion of the application? It's a trick question. A data source sounds like it must be part of the model, but in fact, it's actually part of the controller. The data source isn't usually an object designed to hold data. In simple applications, the data source might hold data, but its true job is to retrieve data from the model and pass it along to the picker.

Let's fire up Xcode and get to it.

Setting Up the Tab Bar Framework

Although Xcode does provide a template for tab bar applications, we're going to build ours from scratch. It's not much extra work, and it's good practice.

Create a new project, selecting the *Window-based Application* template again. Make sure the check box that says *Use Core Data for storage* is unchecked, and set the *Product* popup to *iPhone*. When prompted for a name, type *Pickers*.

We're going to walk you through the process of building the whole application, but at any step of the way, if you feel like challenging yourself by moving ahead of us, by all means, go ahead. If you get stumped, you can always come back. If you don't feel like skipping ahead, that's just fine. We love the company.

Creating the Files

In the previous chapter, we created a root view controller (root controller for short) to manage the process of swapping our application's other views. We'll be doing that again this time, but we won't need to create our own root view controller class. Apple provides a very good class for managing tab bar views, so we're just going to use an instance of UITabBarController as our root controller.

First, we need to create five new classes in Xcode: the five view controllers that the root controller will swap in and out.

Expand the *Classes* and *Resources* folders in the *Groups & Files* pane. Next, single-click the *Classes* folder, and press ⌘N or select File ➤ New File....

Select *Cocoa Touch Class* in the left pane of the new file assistant, and then select the icon for *UIViewController subclass*. In the middle-right pane named Options, just above the description of the selected template, you should see a check box labeled *With XIB for user interface* (see Figure 7–7). Make sure that's checked (and only that one; the *Targeted for iPad* and *UITableViewController subclass* options should be unchecked) before clicking *Next*.

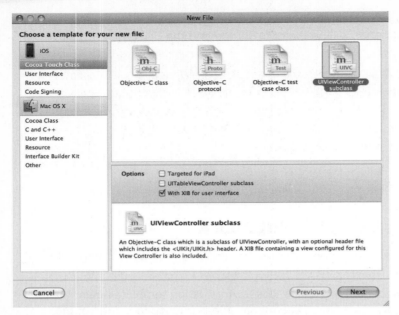

Figure 7–7. *When creating a subclass of UIViewController, Xcode will create the accompanying .xib file for you if you select the With XIB for user interface check box.*

Name the first of your five new classes *DatePickerViewController.m*, making sure to check Also create *"DatePickerViewController.h"*. As always when naming a new class file, carefully check your spelling. A typo here will cause your new class to be named incorrectly.

After you click the *Finish* button, three new files will appear in your *Classes* folder: *DatePickerViewController.h*, *DatePickerViewController.m*, and *DatePickerViewController.xib.* The nib file doesn't belong in the *Classes* folder, so drag *DatePickerViewController.xib* down to the *Resources* folder.

Repeat those steps four more times, using the names *SingleComponentPickerViewController.m*, *DoubleComponentPickerViewController.m*, *DependentComponentPickerViewController.m*, and *CustomPickerViewController.m*.

Adding the Root View Controller

We're going to create our root view controller, which will be an instance of UITabBarController, in Interface Builder. Before we can do that, however, we should declare an outlet for it. Single-click *PickersAppDelegate.h*, and add the following code to it:

```
#import <UIKit/UIKit.h>

@interface PickersAppDelegate : NSObject <UIApplicationDelegate> {
    UIWindow *window;
    UITabBarController *rootController;
}
```

```
@property (nonatomic, retain) IBOutlet UIWindow *window;
@property (nonatomic, retain) IBOutlet UITabBarController *rootController;
@end
```

Before we move to Interface Builder to create our root view controller, let's add the following code to *PickersAppDelegate.m*:

```
#import "PickersAppDelegate.h"

@implementation PickersAppDelegate
@synthesize window;
@synthesize rootController;

- (BOOL)application:(UIApplication *)application
didFinishLaunchingWithOptions:(NSDictionary *)launchOptions {

    // Override point for customization after app launch
    [self.window addSubview:rootController.view];
    [self.window makeKeyAndVisible];

  return YES;

}

- (void)dealloc {
    [rootController release];
    [window release];
    [super dealloc];
}

@end
```

There shouldn't be anything in this code that's a surprise to you. We're doing pretty much the same thing we did in the previous chapter, except that we're using a controller class provided by Apple instead of one we wrote ourselves. Make sure you save both files before continuing.

Tab bars use icons to represent each of the tabs, so we should also add the icons we're going to use before editing the nib file for this class. You can find some suitable icons in the project archive that accompanies this book in the *07 Pickers/Tab Bar Icons/* folder. Add all five of the icons in that folder to the project. You can just drag the folder from the Finder and drop it on the *Resources* folder in the project navigator. When asked, select *Recursively create groups for any added folders*, and Xcode will add a *Tab Bar Icons* subfolder to the *Resources* folder.

The icons you use should be 24-by-24 pixels and saved in *.png* format. The icon file should have a transparent background. Generally, medium-gray icons look the best on a tab bar. Don't worry about trying to match the appearance of the tab bar. Just as it does with the application icon, iOS will take your image and make it look just right.

Editing MainWindow.xib

Now, let's edit *MainWindow.xib* and add in our tab bar controller. Double click *MainWindow.xib* to open the file in Interface Builder. Drag a *Tab Bar Controller* from the object library (see Figure 7–8) over to the nib's main window.

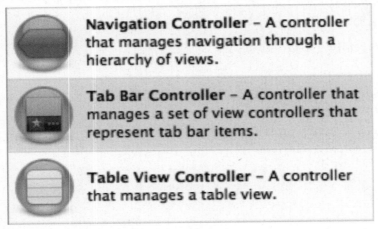

Figure 7–8. *The Tab Bar Controller in the library*

Once you drop the tab bar controller onto your nib's main window, a new window representing the UITabBarController will appear (see Figure 7–9), and you'll see a new icon in the Interface Builder dock. This tab bar controller will be our root controller. As a reminder, the root controller controls the very first view that the user will see when your program runs and is responsible for switching the other views in and out. Since we'll connect each of our views to one of the tab bar tabs, the tab bar controller makes a logical choice as a root controller.

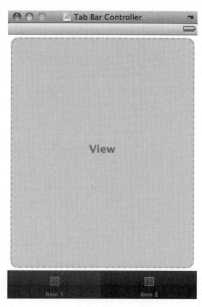

Figure 7–9. *The tab bar controller's window. Notice the tab bar at the bottom of the window, with two individual tabs.*

Our next step is to customize our tab bar to reflect our needs. We'll need five tabs, each representing one of our five pickers.

In Interface Builder, switch the main window over to list view by clicking the middle *View Mode* icon. Open the disclosure triangle to the left of *Tab Bar Controller* to reveal the *Tab Bar* and two *View Controller* entries. Open the disclosure triangles to the left of each *View Controller* to show the *Tab Bar Item* associated with each controller (see Figure 7– 10). By opening everything, you'll have a better understanding of what's happening as we customize this tab bar.

Figure 7–10. *The Tab Bar Controller, opened all the way to show the items nested within*

Let's add three more *Tab Bar Items* to the tab bar. As you'll see, the *View Controllers* will be added automatically when we drag over a new *Tab Bar Item*.

Bring up the library (**Tools ➤ Library**). Locate a *Tab Bar Item* and drag it onto the tab bar (see Figure 7–11). Notice the insertion point. This tells you where on the tab bar your new item will end up. Since we will be customizing all of our tab bar items, it doesn't matter where this one lands.

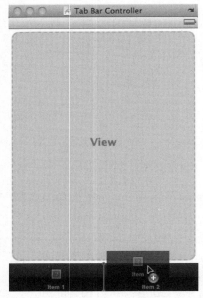

Figure 7–11. *Dragging a Tab Bar Item from the library onto our Tab Bar. Notice the insertion point that shows you where your new item will end up.*

Now drag out two more *Tab Bar Items*, so you have a total of five. If you take a look at your dock, you'll see that your tab bar now consists of five *View Controllers*, each with its own *Tab Bar Item*. Open the disclosure triangle to the left of each *View Controller* so you can see all of them (see Figure 7–12).

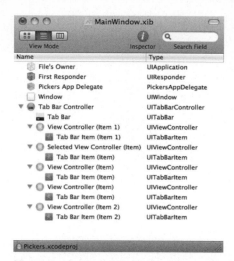

Figure 7–12. *The Tab Bar Controller, opened all the way to show the five View Controllers and their associated Tab Bar Items*

Our next step is to customize each of the five view controllers. In the nib's main window, select the first of the five *View Controllers* (*not* the associated *Tab Bar Item*), and then bring up the attributes inspector (**Tools ➤ Attributes Inspector**). This is where we associate each tab's view controller with the appropriate nib.

In the attributes inspector, leave the *Title* field blank (see Figure 7–13). Tab bar view controllers don't use this title for anything. The check box labeled *Wants Full Screen* can be used to indicate that the view that comes up when you select that tab will overlap and hide the tab bar. If you check this check box, you must provide an alternative mechanism for navigating off that tab. We will leave this value unchecked for all of our tabs. Finally, specify a *NIB Name of DatePickerViewController*. Do not include the *.xib* extension. Leave the *Resize View From NIB* check box checked. This won't apply to our app, since we'll design our views to be the size we want and to not need resizing.

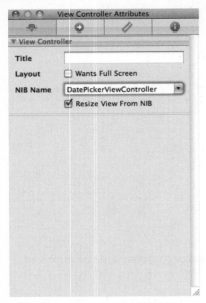

Figure 7–13. *We've selected the first of our five view controllers and associated the nib named DatePickerViewController.xib with the controller. Note that we left off the extension .xib. This is automatically added to the nib name.*

While you're here, press ⌘4. This will bring up the identity inspector for this view controller. Change the class to *DatePickerViewController*, and press return or tab to set it.

Now repeat this same process for the next four view controllers. In the attributes inspector for each, make sure the check boxes are correctly configured, and enter the nib names *SingleComponentPickerViewController*, *DoubleComponentPickerViewController*, *DependentComponentPickerViewController*, and *CustomPickerViewController*, respectively. For each view controller, make sure you also use the identity inspector to change the class to be the same as the name you type in the *NIB Name* field. Be sure you visit the attributes inspector and then the identity inspector for each view controller.

> **Caution:** Be sure you hit return after you enter a name in the *NIB Name* field of an inspector so the class name takes. If you switch inspectors without pressing return, your change may not take effect.

You've just made a lot of changes. Check your work and save it. Let's customize the five *Tab Bar Items* now, so they have the correct icon and label.

In the nib's main window, click the first *Tab Bar Item*. Now press ⌘1 to return to the attributes inspector (see Figure 7–14).

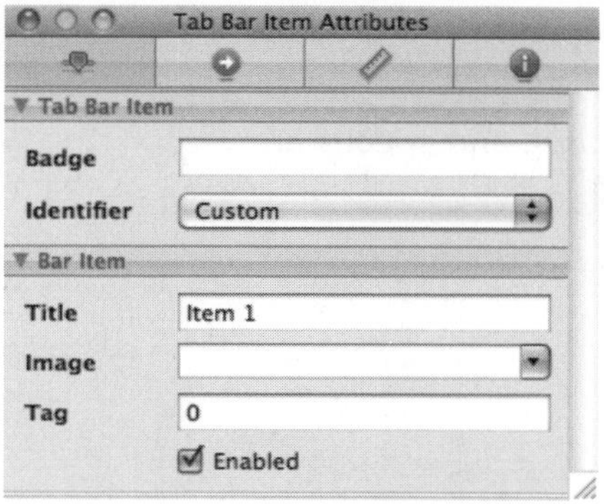

Figure 7–14. *The Tab Bar Item attributes inspector*

The first field in the *Tab Bar Item* section is labeled *Badge.* This can be used to put a red icon onto a tab bar item, similar to the red number placed on the *Mail* icon that tells you how many unread e-mail messages you have. We're not going to use the *Badge* field in this chapter, so you can leave it blank.

Under that, there's a popup button called *Identifier*. This field allows you to select from a set of commonly used tab bar item names and icons such as *Favorites* and *Search*. If you select one of these, the tab bar will provide the name and icon for the item based on your selection. We're not using standard items, so leave this set to *Custom*.

The next two fields down are where we can specify a title and custom tab icon for a tab bar item. Change the *Title* from *Item 1* to *Date*. Next, click the *Image* combo box, and select the *clockicon.png* image. If you are using your own set of icons, select one of the *.png* files you provided instead. For the rest of this chapter, we'll assume you used our resources. Adjust your thinking as necessary.

If you look over at the *Tab Bar Controller* window, you'll see that the leftmost tab bar item now reads *Date* and has a picture of a clock on it (see Figure 7–15). Don't worry about the titles of the other tab items. You're going to change them right now.

Figure 7–15. *Our first tab bar item has changed to a title of Date and an icon of a clock. Cool!*

Repeat this process for the other four tab bar items:

- Change the second *Tab Bar Item* to a *Title* of *Single*, and specify an *Image* of *singleicon.png*.

- Change the third *Tab Bar Item* to a *Title* of *Double*, and specify an *Image* of *doubleicon.png*.

- Change the fourth Tab Bar Item to a Title of Dependent, and specify an Image of *dependenticon.png*.

- Change the fifth *Tab Bar Item* to a *Title* of *Custom*, and specify an *Image* of *toolicon.png*.

Figure 7–16 shows our finished tab bar.

Figure 7–16. *Our finished tab bar, with all five titles and icons in place*

NOTE: Don't worry about the view controller *Title* fields. We don't use them for this application. It doesn't matter whether they are blank or contain text. However, we *do* use the tab bar item *Title* fields. Don't confuse the two.

Before we move on to our next bit of nib editing, save your nib file.

Connect the Outlet, Then Run It

All that we have left to do in this nib file is to control-drag from the *Pickers App Delegate* icon to the *Tab Bar Controller* icon. Select the rootController outlet, and then save the nib file.

At this point, the tab bar and the content views should all be hooked up and working. Return to Xcode, compile and run, and your application should launch with a tab bar that functions. Click each of the tabs in turn. Each tab should be selectable.

There's nothing in the content views now, so the changes won't be very dramatic. But if everything went OK, the basic framework for your multiview application is now set up and working, and we can start designing the individual content views.

TIP: If your simulator bursts into flames when you click one of the tabs, don't panic! Most likely, you've either missed a step or made a typo. Go back and check all the nib file names, make sure the connections are right, and make sure the class names are all set correctly.

If you want to make double sure everything is working, you can add a different label or some other object to each of the content views and then relaunch the application. Then you should see the content of the different views change as you select different tabs.

Implementing the Date Picker

To implement the date picker, we'll need a single outlet and a single action. The outlet will be used to grab the value from the date picker. The action will be triggered by a button and will put up an alert to show the date value pulled from the picker. Single-click *DatePickerViewController.h*, and add the following code:

```
#import <UIKit/UIKit.h>

@interface DatePickerViewController : UIViewController {
    UIDatePicker        *datePicker;
}
@property (nonatomic, retain) IBOutlet UIDatePicker *datePicker;
- (IBAction)buttonPressed;
@end
```

Save this file, and then double click *DatePickerViewController.xib* to edit the content view for our first tab.

The first thing we need to do is size the view so it accounts for the tab bar. Single-click the *View* icon and press ⌘**1** to bring up the attributes inspector. In the *Simulated User Interface Elements* section, set the *Bottom Bar* popup to *Tab Bar*. This will cause Interface Builder to automatically reduce the view's height to 411 pixels and show a simulated tab bar.

Next, find a *Date Picker* in the library, and drag one over to the *View* window. Place the date picker at the top of the view, right up against the bottom of the status bar. It should take up the entire width of your content view and a good portion of the height. Don't use the blue guidelines for the picker; it's designed to fit snugly against the edges of the view (see Figure 7–17).

Figure 7–17. *We dragged a Date Picker from the library. Note that it takes up the entire width of the view and that we placed it at the top of the view, just below the status bar.*

Single-click the date picker if it's not already selected, and go back to the attributes inspector. As you can see in Figure 7–18, a number of attributes can be configured for a date picker. We're going to leave most of the values at their defaults (but feel free to play with the options when we're finished to see what they do). The one thing we will do is limit the range of the picker to reasonable dates. Look for the heading that says *Constraints*, and check the box that reads *Minimum Date.* Leave the value at the default of *1/1/1970*. Also check the box that reads *Maximum Date*, and set that value *to 12/31/2200*.

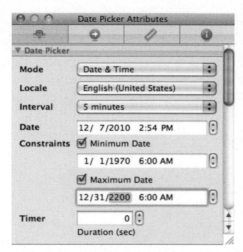

Figure 7–18. *The attributes inspector for a date picker. We'll set the minimum and maximum dates, but leave the rest of the settings at their default values.*

Next, grab a *Round Rect Button* from the library, and place it below the date picker. Double-click the button and give it a title of *Select*.

With the button still selected, press ⌘2 to switch to the connections inspector. Drag from the circle next to the *Touch Up Inside* event over to the *File's Owner* icon, and connect to the buttonPressed action. Then control-drag from the *File's Owner* icon back to the date picker, and select the datePicker outlet. Finally, save your changes to the nib file, since we're finished with this part of the GUI.

Now we just need to implement DatePickerViewController. Return to Xcode and click *DatePickerViewController.m* and start by adding the following code at the top of the file:

```
#import "DatePickerViewController.h"

@implementation DatePickerViewController
@synthesize datePicker;

- (IBAction)buttonPressed {
    NSDate *selected = [datePicker date];
    NSString *message = [[NSString alloc] initWithFormat:
        @"The date and time you selected is: %@", selected];
    UIAlertView *alert = [[UIAlertView alloc]
            initWithTitle:@"Date and Time Selected"
                  message:message
                 delegate:nil
        cancelButtonTitle:@"Yes, I did."
        otherButtonTitles:nil];
    [alert show];
    [alert release];
    [message release];
}

- (void)viewDidLoad {
```

```
    NSDate *now = [[NSDate alloc] init];
    [datePicker setDate:now animated:NO];
    [now release];
}
...
```

Next, add one line to the existing `viewDidUnload:` method:

```
- (void)viewDidUnload {
    [super viewDidUnload];
    // Release any retained subviews of the main view.
    // e.g. self.myOutlet = nil;
    self.datePicker = nil;
}
```

Also add one line to the existing `dealloc` method:

```
- (void)dealloc {
    [datePicker release];
    [super dealloc];
}
```

Here, we first synthesize the accessor and mutator for our `datePicker` outlet, and then we add the implementation of `buttonPressed` and override `viewDidLoad`. In `buttonPressed`, we use our `datePicker` outlet to get the current date value from the date picker, and then we construct a string based on that date and use it to show an alert sheet.

In `viewDidLoad`, we create a new `NSDate` object. An `NSDate` object created this way will hold the current date and time. We then set `datePicker` to that date, which ensures that every time this view is loaded from the nib, the picker will reset to the current date and time.

Go ahead and build and run to make sure your date picker checks out. If everything went OK, your application should look like Figure 7–2 when it runs. If you choose the *Select* button, an alert sheet will pop up, telling you the date and time currently selected in the date picker.

> **NOTE:** The date picker does not allow you to specify seconds or a time zone. The alert displays the time with seconds and in Greenwich Mean Time (GMT). We could have added some code to simplify the string displayed in the alert, but isn't this chapter long enough already? If you're interested in customizing the formatting of the date, take a look at the `NSDateFormatter` class.

Implementing the Single-Component Picker

Our next picker lets the user select from a list of values. In this example, we're going to create an `NSArray` to hold the values we want to display in the picker.

Pickers don't hold any data themselves. Instead, they call methods on their data source and delegate to get the data they need to display. The picker doesn't really care where the underlying data lives. It asks for the data when it needs it, and the data source and delegate (which are often, in practice, the same object) work together to supply that data. As a result, the data could be coming from a static list, as we'll do in this section. It also could be loaded from a file or a URL, or even made up or calculated on the fly.

Declaring Outlets and Actions

As always, we need to make sure our outlets and actions are in place in our controller's header file before we start working on the GUI. In the *Groups & Files* pane, single-click *SingleComponentPickerViewController.h.* This controller class will act as both the data source and the delegate for its picker, so we need to make sure it conforms to the protocols for those two roles. In addition, we need to declare an outlet and an action. Add the following code:

```
#import <UIKit/UIKit.h>

@interface SingleComponentPickerViewController : UIViewController
    <UIPickerViewDelegate, UIPickerViewDataSource> {
        UIPickerView    *singlePicker;
        NSArray         *pickerData;
}
@property (nonatomic, retain) IBOutlet UIPickerView *singlePicker;
@property (nonatomic, retain) NSArray *pickerData;
- (IBAction)buttonPressed;
@end
```

We start by conforming our controller class to two protocols, `UIPickerViewDelegate` and `UIPickerViewDataSource`. After that, we declare an outlet for the picker and a pointer to an `NSArray`, which will be used to hold the list of items that will be displayed in the picker. Finally, we declare the action method for the button, just as we did for the date picker.

Building the View

Save your source code, then double click *SingleComponentPickerViewController.xib* to edit the content view for the second tab in our tab bar. Select the *View* icon and press ⌥⌘3 to bring up the attributes inspector. Set the *Bottom Bar* to *Tab Bar* in the *Simulated User Interface Elements* section. Next, bring over a *Picker View* from the library (see Figure 7–19), and add it to your nib's *View* window, placing it snugly into the top of the view, as you did with the date picker view.

Figure 7–19. *Dragging a Picker View from the library onto our second view*

After placing the picker, control-drag from *File's Owner* to the picker view, and select the **singlePicker** outlet. Next, single-click the picker if it's not already selected, and press ⌘**2** to bring up the connections inspector. If you look at the connections available for the picker view, you'll see that the first two items are *dataSource* and *delegate*. Drag from the circle next to *dataSource* to the *File's Owner* icon. Then drag again from the circle next to *delegate* to the *File's Owner* icon. Now this picker knows that the instance of the `SingleComponentPickerViewController` class in the nib is its data source and delegate, and will ask it to supply the data to be displayed. In other words, when the picker needs information about the data it is going to display, it asks the `SingleComponentPickerViewController` instance that controls this view for that information.

Drag a *Round Rect Button* to the view, double-click it, and give it a title of *Select.* Press return to commit the change. In the connections inspector, drag from the circle next to *Touch Up Inside* to the *File's Owner* icon, selecting the `buttonPressed` action. Now you've finished building the GUI for the second tab. Save the nib file, and let's get back to Xcode for some coding.

Implementing the Controller as Data Source and Delegate

To make our controller work properly as the picker's data source and delegate, we'll start with some code you should feel comfortable with, and then add a few methods that you've never seen before.

Single-click *SingleComponentPickerViewController.m*, and add the following code at the beginning of the file:

```
#import "SingleComponentPickerViewController.h"

@implementation SingleComponentPickerViewController
@synthesize singlePicker;
@synthesize pickerData;

- (IBAction)buttonPressed {
    NSInteger row = [singlePicker selectedRowInComponent:0];
    NSString *selected = [pickerData objectAtIndex:row];
    NSString *title = [[NSString alloc] initWithFormat:
                        @"You selected %@!", selected];
    UIAlertView *alert = [[UIAlertView alloc] initWithTitle:title
                                        message:@"Thank you for choosing."
                                        delegate:nil
                               cancelButtonTitle:@"You're Welcome"
                               otherButtonTitles:nil];
    [alert show];
    [alert release];
    [title release];
}

- (void)viewDidLoad {
    NSArray *array = [[NSArray alloc] initWithObjects:@"Luke", @"Leia",
            @"Han", @"Chewbacca", @"Artoo", @"Threepio", @"Lando", nil];
    self.pickerData = array;
    [array release];
}
...
```

These two methods should be familiar to you by now. The `buttonPressed` method is nearly identical to the one we used with the date picker.

Unlike the date picker, a regular picker can't tell us what data it holds, because it doesn't maintain the data. It hands off that job to the delegate and data source. Instead, we need to ask the picker which row is selected and then grab the corresponding data from our `pickerData` array. Here is how we ask it for the selected row:

```
NSInteger row = [singlePicker selectedRowInComponent:0];
```

Notice that we needed to specify which component we want to know about. We have only one component in this picker, so we simply pass in 0, which is the index of the first component.

NOTE: Did you notice that there is no asterisk between `NSInteger` and `row` in our request for the selected row? Throughout most of the iOS SDK, the prefix NS often indicates an Objective-C class from the Foundation framework, but this is one of the exceptions to that general rule. `NSInteger` is always defined as an integer datatype, either an `int` or a `long`. We use `NSInteger` rather than `int` or `long`, because when we use `NSInteger`, the compiler automatically chooses whichever size is best for the platform for which we are compiling. It will create a 32-bit `int` when compiling for a 32-bit processor and a longer 64-bit `long` when compiling for a 64-bit architecture. Currently, there is no 64-bit iOS device, but who knows? Someday in the future, there likely will be. You might also write classes for your iOS applications that you'll later want to recycle and use in Cocoa applications for Mac OS X, which does run on both 32- and 64-bit machines.

In `viewDidLoad`, we create an array with several objects so that we have data to feed the picker. Usually, your data will come from other sources, like a property list in your project's *Resources* folder. By embedding a list of items in our code the way we've done here, we are making it much harder on ourselves if we need to update this list or if we want to have our application translated into other languages. But this approach is the quickest and easiest way to get data into an array for demonstration purposes. Even though you won't usually create your arrays like this, you will almost always cache the data you are using into an array here in the `viewDidLoad` method, so that you're not constantly going to disk or to the network every time the picker asks you for data.

TIP: If you're not supposed to create arrays from lists of objects in your code as we just did in `viewDidLoad`, how should you do it? Embed the lists in property list files, and add those files to the *Resources* folder of your project. Property list files can be changed without recompiling your source code, which means there is no risk of introducing new bugs when you do so. You can also provide different versions of the list for different languages, as you'll see in Chapter 19. Property lists can be created using the Property List Editor application (*/Developer/Applications/Utilities/Property List Editor.app*) or directly in Xcode, which offers a template for creating a property list in the *Resource* section of the new file assistant, and supports the editing of property lists in the editor pane. Both `NSArray` and `NSDictionary` offer a method called `initWithContentsOfFile:` to allow you to initialize instances from a property list file, as we'll do later in this chapter when we implement the Dependent tab.

Next, insert the following new lines of code into the existing `viewDidUnload` and `dealloc` methods:

```
...
- (void)viewDidUnload {
    [super viewDidUnload];
    // Release any retained subviews of the main view.
    // e.g. self.myOutlet = nil;
```

```
      self.singlePicker = nil;
      self.pickerData = nil;
}

- (void)dealloc {
    [singlePicker release];
    [pickerData release];
    [super dealloc];
}
...
```

Notice that we set both `singlePicker` and `pickerData` to `nil`. In most cases, you'll set only outlets to `nil` and not other instance variables. However, setting `pickerData` to `nil` is appropriate here because the `pickerData` array will be re-created each time the view is reloaded, and we want to free up that memory when the view is unloaded. Anything that is created in the `viewDidLoad` method can be flushed in `viewDidUnload` because `viewDidLoad` will fire again when the view is reloaded.

Finally, insert the following new code at the end of the file:

```
#pragma mark -
#pragma mark Picker Data Source Methods
- (NSInteger)numberOfComponentsInPickerView:(UIPickerView *)pickerView {
    return 1;
}

- (NSInteger)pickerView:(UIPickerView *)pickerView
        numberOfRowsInComponent:(NSInteger)component {
    return [pickerData count];
}

#pragma mark Picker Delegate Methods
- (NSString *)pickerView:(UIPickerView *)pickerView
        titleForRow:(NSInteger)row
        forComponent:(NSInteger)component {
    return [pickerData objectAtIndex:row];
}

@end
```

At the bottom of the file, we get into the new methods required to implement the picker. The first two methods after `dealloc` are from the `UIPickerViewDataSource` protocol, and they are both required for all pickers (except date pickers). Here's the first one:

```
- (NSInteger)numberOfComponentsInPickerView:(UIPickerView *)pickerView {
    return 1;
}
```

Pickers can have more than one spinning wheel, or component, and this is how the picker asks how many components it should display. We want to display only one list this time, so we return a value of 1. Notice that a `UIPickerView` is passed in as a parameter. This parameter points to the picker view that is asking us the question, which makes it possible to have multiple pickers being controlled by the same data source. In our case, we know that we have only one picker, so we can safely ignore this argument because we already know which picker is calling us.

The second data source method is used by the picker to ask how many rows of data there are for a given component:

```
- (NSInteger)pickerView:(UIPickerView *)pickerView
        numberOfRowsInComponent:(NSInteger)component {
    return [pickerData count];
}
```

#PRAGMA WHAT?

Did you notice these lines of code from *SingleComponentPickerViewController.m*?

```
#pragma mark -
#pragma mark Picker Data Source Methods
```

Any line of code that begins with `#pragma` is technically a compiler directive. More specifically, a `#pragma` marks a **pragmatic**, or compiler-specific, directive that won't necessarily work with other compilers or in other environments. If the compiler doesn't recognize the directive, it ignores it, though it may generate a warning. In this case, the `#pragma` directives are actually directives to the IDE, not the compiler, and they tell Xcode's editor to put a break in the popup menu of methods and functions at the top of the editor pane. The first one puts the break in the menu. The second creates a text entry containing whatever the rest of the line holds, which you can use as a sort of descriptive header for groups of methods in your source code.

Some of your classes, especially some of your controller classes, are likely to get rather long, and the methods and functions popup menu makes navigating around your code much easier. Putting in `#pragma` directives and logically organizing your code will make that popup more efficient to use.

Once again, we are told which picker view is asking and which component that picker is asking about. Since we know that we have only one picker and one component, we don't bother with either of the arguments, and simply return the count of objects from our sole data array.

After the two data source methods, we implement one delegate method. Unlike the data source methods, all of the delegate methods are optional. The term *optional* is a bit deceiving, because you do need to implement at least one delegate method. You will usually implement the method that we are implementing here. However, if you want to display something other than text in the picker, you must implement a different method instead, as you'll see when we get to the custom picker.

```
- (NSString *)pickerView:(UIPickerView *)pickerView
        titleForRow:(NSInteger)row
        forComponent:(NSInteger)component {
    return [pickerData objectAtIndex:row];
}
```

In this method, the picker is asking us to provide the data for a specific row in a specific component. We are provided with a pointer to the picker that is asking, along with the component and row that it is asking about. Since our view has one picker with one component, we simply ignore everything except the row argument and use that to return the appropriate item from our data array.

Go ahead and compile and run again. When the simulator comes up, switch to the second tab—the one labeled *Single*—and check out your new custom picker, which should look like Figure 7–3.

When you're done reliving all those *Star Wars* memories, come on back to Xcode and we'll show you how to implement a picker with two components. If you feel up to a challenge, this next content view is actually a good one for you to attempt on your own. You've already seen all the methods you'll need for this picker, so go ahead and take a crack at it. We'll wait here. You might want to start off with a good look at Figure 7–4, just to refresh your memory. When you're finished, read on, and you'll see how we tackled this problem.

Implementing a Multicomponent Picker

The next content pane will have a picker with two components, or wheels, each independent of the other. The left wheel will have a list of sandwich fillings, and the right wheel will have a selection of bread types. We'll write the same data source and delegate methods that we did for the single-component picker. We'll just need to write a little additional code in some of those methods to make sure we're returning the correct value and row count for each component.

Declaring Outlets and Actions

Single-click *DoubleComponentPickerViewController.h*, and add the following code:

```
#import <UIKit/UIKit.h>

#define kFillingComponent 0
#define kBreadComponent   1

@interface DoubleComponentPickerViewController : UIViewController
    <UIPickerViewDelegate, UIPickerViewDataSource>
{

    UIPickerView *doublePicker;
    NSArray *fillingTypes;
    NSArray *breadTypes;
}
@property(nonatomic, retain) IBOutlet UIPickerView *doublePicker;
@property(nonatomic, retain) NSArray *fillingTypes;
@property(nonatomic, retain) NSArray *breadTypes;
-(IBAction)buttonPressed;
@end
```

As you can see, we start out by defining two constants that will represent the two components, which is just to make our code easier to read. Components are assigned numbers, with the leftmost component being assigned zero and increasing by one each move to the right.

Next, we conform our controller class to both the delegate and data source protocols, and we declare an outlet for the picker, as well as for two arrays to hold the data for our two picker components. After declaring properties for each of our instance variables, we declare a single action method for the button, just as we did in the previous two content panes. Save this, and double click *DoubleComponentPickerViewController.xib* to open the nib file for editing.

Building the View

Select the *View* icon, and use the object attributes inspector to set the *Bottom Bar* to *Tab Bar* in the *Simulated User Interface Elements* section.

Add a picker view and a button to the view, change the button label to *Select*, and then make the necessary connections. We're not going to walk you through it this time, but you can refer to the previous section if you need a step-by-step guide, since the two applications are identical in terms of the nib file. Here's a summary of what you need to do:

1. Connect the `doublePicker` outlet on *File's Owner* to the picker.

2. Connect the *DataSource* and *Delegate* connections on the picker view to *File's Owner* (use the connections inspector).

3. Connect the *Touch Up Inside* event of the button to the `buttonPressed` action on *File's Owner* (use the connections inspector).

Make sure you save your nib and close it before you dive back into the code. Oh, and dog-ear this page (or use a bookmark, if you prefer). You'll be referring to it in a bit.

Implementing the Controller

Select *DoubleComponentPickerViewController.m,* and add the following code at the top of the file:

```
#import "DoubleComponentPickerViewController.h"

@implementation DoubleComponentPickerViewController
@synthesize doublePicker;
@synthesize fillingTypes;
@synthesize breadTypes;

-(IBAction)buttonPressed
{
    NSInteger fillingRow = [doublePicker selectedRowInComponent:
                          kFillingComponent];
    NSInteger breadRow = [doublePicker selectedRowInComponent:
                          kBreadComponent];

    NSString *bread = [breadTypes objectAtIndex:breadRow];
    NSString *filling = [fillingTypes objectAtIndex:fillingRow];
```

```objc
        NSString *message = [[NSString alloc] initWithFormat:
                @"Your %@ on %@ bread will be right up.", filling, bread];

        UIAlertView *alert = [[UIAlertView alloc] initWithTitle:
                                            @"Thank you for your order"
                                                      message:message
                                                     delegate:nil
                                            cancelButtonTitle:@"Great!"
                                            otherButtonTitles:nil];
        [alert show];
        [alert release];
        [message release];
}

- (void)viewDidLoad {
    NSArray *fillingArray = [[NSArray alloc] initWithObjects:@"Ham",
                    @"Turkey", @"Peanut Butter", @"Tuna Salad",
                    @"Nutella", @"Roast Beef", @"Vegemite", nil];
    self.fillingTypes = fillingArray;
    [fillingArray release];

    NSArray *breadArray = [[NSArray alloc] initWithObjects:@"White",
            @"Whole Wheat", @"Rye", @"Sourdough", @"Seven Grain",nil];
    self.breadTypes = breadArray;
    [breadArray release];
}
...
```

Also, add the following lines of code to the existing dealloc and viewDidUnload methods:

```objc
...
- (void)viewDidUnload {
    [super viewDidUnload];
    // Release any retained subviews of the main view.
    // e.g. self.myOutlet = nil;
    self.doublePicker = nil;
    self.breadTypes = nil;
    self.fillingTypes = nil;
}

- (void)dealloc {
    [doublePicker release];
    [breadTypes release];
    [fillingTypes release];
    [super dealloc];
}
...
```

And add the delegate and data source methods at the bottom:

```objc
#pragma mark -
#pragma mark Picker Data Source Methods
- (NSInteger)numberOfComponentsInPickerView:(UIPickerView *)pickerView {
    return 2;
```

```
}

- (NSInteger)pickerView:(UIPickerView *)pickerView
    numberOfRowsInComponent:(NSInteger)component {
    if (component == kBreadComponent)
        return [self.breadTypes count];

    return [self.fillingTypes count];
}

#pragma mark Picker Delegate Methods
- (NSString *)pickerView:(UIPickerView *)pickerView
    titleForRow:(NSInteger)row
    forComponent:(NSInteger)component {
    if (component == kBreadComponent)
        return [self.breadTypes objectAtIndex:row];
    return [self.fillingTypes objectAtIndex:row];
}

@end
```

The buttonPressed method is a bit more involved this time, but there's very little there that's new to you. We just need to specify which component we are talking about when we request the selected row using those constants we defined earlier, kBreadComponent and kFillingComponent.

```
NSInteger breadRow = [doublePicker selectedRowInComponent:
        kBreadComponent];
NSInteger fillingRow = [doublePicker selectedRowInComponent:
        kFillingComponent];
```

You can see here that using the two constants instead of 0 and 1 makes our code considerably more readable. From this point on, the buttonPressed method is fundamentally the same as the last one we wrote.

viewDidLoad: is also very similar to the one we wrote for the previous picker. The only difference is that we are loading two arrays with data rather than just one. Again, we're just creating arrays from a hard-coded list of strings—something you generally won't do in your own applications.

When we get down to the data source methods, that's where things start to change a bit. In the first method, we specify that our picker should have two components rather than just one:

```
- (NSInteger)numberOfComponentsInPickerView:(UIPickerView *)pickerView {
    return 2;
}
```

This time, when we are asked for the number of rows, we need to check which component the picker is asking about and return the correct row count for the corresponding array.

```
- (NSInteger)pickerView:(UIPickerView *)pickerView
    numberOfRowsInComponent:(NSInteger)component {
    if (component == kBreadComponent)
```

```
        return [self.breadTypes count];

    return [self.fillingTypes count];
}
```

Then, in our delegate method, we do the same thing. We check the component and use the correct array for the requested component to fetch and return the correct value.

```
- (NSString *)pickerView:(UIPickerView *)pickerView
    titleForRow:(NSInteger)row
        forComponent:(NSInteger)component {
    if (component == kBreadComponent)
        return [self.breadTypes objectAtIndex:row];
    return [self.fillingTypes objectAtIndex:row];
}
```

That wasn't so hard, was it? Compile and run your application, and make sure the *Double* content pane looks like Figure 7–4.

Notice that each wheel is completely independent of the other wheel. Turning one has no effect on the other. That's appropriate in this case. But there will be times when one component is dependent on another. A good example of this is in the date picker. When you change the month, the dial that shows the number of days in the month may need to change, because not all months have the same amount of days. Implementing this isn't really hard once you know how, but it's not the easiest thing to figure out on your own, so let's do that next.

Implementing Dependent Components

We're picking up steam now. For this next section, we're not going to hold your hand quite as much when it comes to material we've already covered. Instead, we'll focus on the new stuff. Our new picker will display a list of US states in the left component and a list of ZIP codes in the right component that correspond to the state currently selected in the left.

We'll need a separate list of ZIP code values for each item in the left-hand component. We'll declare two arrays, one for each component, as we did last time. We'll also need an NSDictionary. In the dictionary, we're going to store an NSArray for each state (see Figure 7–20). Later, we'll implement a delegate method that will notify us when the picker's selection changes. If the value on the left changes, we will grab the correct array out of the dictionary and assign it to the array being used for the right-hand component. Don't worry if you didn't catch all that; we'll talk about it more as we get into the code.

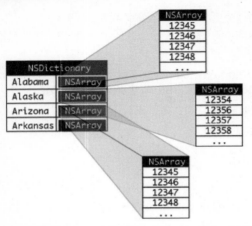

Figure 7-20. *Our application's data. For each state, there will be one entry in a dictionary with the name of the state as the key. Stored under that key will be an NSArray instance containing all the ZIP codes from that state.*

Add the following code to your *DependentComponentPickerViewController.h* file:

```
#import <UIKit/UIKit.h>
#define kStateComponent    0
#define kZipComponent      1

@interface DependentComponentPickerViewController : UIViewController
    <UIPickerViewDelegate, UIPickerViewDataSource> {
    UIPickerView    *picker;

    NSDictionary    *stateZips;
    NSArray         *states;
    NSArray         *zips;
}
@property (retain, nonatomic) IBOutlet UIPickerView *picker;
@property (retain, nonatomic) NSDictionary *stateZips;
@property (retain, nonatomic) NSArray *states;
@property (retain, nonatomic) NSArray *zips;
- (IBAction) buttonPressed;
@end
```

Now it's time to build the content view. That process will be almost identical to the previous two component views we built. If you get lost, flip back to the "Building the View" section for the single-component picker, and follow those step-by-step instructions. Here's a hint: start off by double clicking *DependentComponentPickerViewController.xib*, and then repeat the same basic steps you've done for all the other content views in this chapter. When you're finished, save the nib and return to Xcode.

OK, take a deep breath. Let's implement this controller class. This implementation may seem a little gnarly at first. By making one component dependent on the other, we have added a whole new level of complexity to our controller class. Although the picker displays only two lists at a time, our controller class must know about and manage 51 lists. The technique we're going to use here actually simplifies that process. The data source methods look almost identical to the one we implemented for the *DoublePicker* view. All of the additional complexity is handled elsewhere, between `viewDidLoad` and a new delegate method called `pickerView:didSelectRow:inComponent:`.

Before we write the code, we need some data to display. Up to now, we've created arrays in code by specifying a list of strings. Because we didn't want you to have to type in several thousand values, and because we figured we ought to show you the correct way to do this, we're going to load the data from a property list. As we've mentioned, both `NSArray` and `NSDictionary` objects can be created from property lists. We've included a property list called *statedictionary.plist* in the project archive, under the *07 Pickers* folder.

Copy that file into the *Resources* area in your Xcode project. If you single-click the plist file in the project window, you can see and even edit the data that it contains (see Figure 7–21).

Key	Type	Value
▼ Root	Dictionary ⬍	(50 items)
▶ Alabama	Array	(657 items)
▶ Alaska	Array	(251 items)
▶ Arizona	Array	(376 items)
▶ Arkansas	Array	(618 items)
▶ California	Array	(1757 items)
▶ Colorado	Array	(501 items)
▶ Connecticut	Array	(276 items)
▶ Delaware	Array	(68 items)
▶ Florida	Array	(972 items)
▶ Georgia	Array	(736 items)
▼ Hawaii	Array	(92 items)
Item 0	String	96701
Item 1	String	96703
Item 2	String	96704
Item 3	String	96705
Item 4	String	96706
Item 5	String	96707
Item 6	String	96708
Item 7	String	96710
Item 8	String	96712
Item 9	String	96713
Item 10	String	96714
Item 11	String	96716
Item 12	String	96717
Item 13	String	96718
Item 14	String	96719
Item 15	String	96720

Figure 7–21. *The statedictionary.plist file, showing our list of states. Within Hawaii, you can see the start of a list of ZIP codes.*

Now, let's write some code. Add the following to *DependentComponentPickerViewController.m,* and then we'll break it down into more digestible chunks:

```
#import "DependentComponentPickerViewController.h"

@implementation DependentComponentPickerViewController
@synthesize picker;
```

```objc
@synthesize stateZips;
@synthesize states;
@synthesize zips;

- (IBAction) buttonPressed {
    NSInteger stateRow = [picker selectedRowInComponent:kStateComponent];
    NSInteger zipRow = [picker selectedRowInComponent:kZipComponent];

    NSString *state = [self.states objectAtIndex:stateRow];
    NSString *zip = [self.zips objectAtIndex:zipRow];

    NSString *title = [[NSString alloc] initWithFormat:
                        @"You selected zip code %@.", zip];
    NSString *message = [[NSString alloc] initWithFormat:
                        @"%@ is in %@", zip, state];

    UIAlertView *alert = [[UIAlertView alloc] initWithTitle:title
                                                    message:message
                                                   delegate:nil
                                          cancelButtonTitle:@"OK"
                                          otherButtonTitles:nil];
    [alert show];
    [alert release];
    [title release];
    [message release];
}

- (void)viewDidLoad {

    NSBundle *bundle = [NSBundle mainBundle];
    NSString *plistPath = [bundle pathForResource:
                            @"statedictionary" ofType:@"plist"];

    NSDictionary *dictionary = [[NSDictionary alloc]
                                    initWithContentsOfFile:plistPath];
    self.stateZips = dictionary;
    [dictionary release];

    NSArray *components = [self.stateZips allKeys];
    NSArray *sorted = [components sortedArrayUsingSelector:
                        @selector(compare:)];
    self.states = sorted;

    NSString *selectedState = [self.states objectAtIndex:0];
    NSArray *array = [stateZips objectForKey:selectedState];
    self.zips = array;
}
...
```

Next, add the following lines of code to the existing viewDidUnload and dealloc
methods:

```objc
- (void)viewDidUnload {
    [super viewDidUnload];
    // Release any retained subviews of the main view.
```

```
    // e.g. self.myOutlet = nil;
    self.picker = nil;
    self.stateZips = nil;
    self.states = nil;
    self.zips = nil;
}

- (void)dealloc {
    [picker release];
    [stateZips release];
    [states release];
    [zips release];
    [super dealloc];
}
```

And, finally, add the delegate and data source methods at the bottom of the file:

```
...
#pragma mark -
#pragma mark Picker Data Source Methods
- (NSInteger)numberOfComponentsInPickerView:(UIPickerView *)pickerView {
    return 2;
}

- (NSInteger)pickerView:(UIPickerView *)pickerView
        numberOfRowsInComponent:(NSInteger)component {
    if (component == kStateComponent)
        return [self.states count];
    return [self.zips count];
}

#pragma mark Picker Delegate Methods
- (NSString *)pickerView:(UIPickerView *)pickerView
        titleForRow:(NSInteger)row
        forComponent:(NSInteger)component {
    if (component == kStateComponent)
        return [self.states objectAtIndex:row];
    return [self.zips objectAtIndex:row];
}

- (void)pickerView:(UIPickerView *)pickerView
        didSelectRow:(NSInteger)row
        inComponent:(NSInteger)component {
    if (component == kStateComponent) {
        NSString *selectedState = [self.states objectAtIndex:row];
        NSArray *array = [stateZips objectForKey:selectedState];
        self.zips = array;
        [picker selectRow:0 inComponent:kZipComponent animated:YES];
        [picker reloadComponent:kZipComponent];
    }
}

@end
```

There's no need to talk about the buttonPressed method, since it's fundamentally the same as the previous one. We should talk about the viewDidLoad method, though. There's some stuff going on there that you need to understand, so pull up a chair, and let's chat.

The first thing we do in this new viewDidLoad method is grab a reference to our application's main bundle.

```
NSBundle *bundle = [NSBundle mainBundle];
```

What is a bundle, you ask? Well, a **bundle** is just a special type of folder whose contents follow a specific structure. Applications and frameworks are both bundles, and this call returns a bundle object that represents our application. One of the primary uses of NSBundle is to get to resources that you added to the *Resources* folder of your project. Those files will be copied into your application's bundle when you build your application. We've added resources like images to our projects, but up to now, we've used those only in Interface Builder. If we want to get to those resources in our code, we usually need to use NSBundle. We use the main bundle to retrieve the path of the resource in which we're interested.

```
NSString *plistPath = [bundle pathForResource:@"statedictionary"
    ofType:@"plist"];
```

This will return a string containing the location of the *statedictionary.plist* file. We can then use that path to create an NSDictionary object. Once we do that, the entire contents of that property list will be loaded into the newly created NSDictionary object, which we then assign to stateZips.

```
NSDictionary *dictionary = [[NSDictionary alloc]
    initWithContentsOfFile:plistPath];
self.stateZips = dictionary;
[dictionary release];
```

The dictionary we just loaded uses the names of the states as the keys and contains an NSArray with all the ZIP codes for that state as the values. To populate the array for the left-hand component, we get the list of all keys from our dictionary and assign those to the states array. Before we assign it, though, we sort it alphabetically.

```
NSArray *components = [self.stateZips allKeys];
NSArray *sorted = [components sortedArrayUsingSelector:
    @selector(compare:)];
self.states = sorted;
```

Unless we specifically set the selection to another value, pickers start with the first row (row 0) selected. In order to get the zips array that corresponds to the first row in the states array, we grab the object from the states array that's at index 0. That will return the name of the state that will be selected at launch time. We then use that state name to grab the array of ZIP codes for that state, which we assign to the zips array that will be used to feed data to the right-hand component.

```
NSString *selectedState = [self.states objectAtIndex:0];
NSArray *array = [stateZips objectForKey:selectedState];
self.zips = array;
```

The two data source methods are practically identical to the previous version. We return the number of rows in the appropriate array. The same is true for the first delegate method we implemented. The second delegate method is the new one, and it's where the magic happens.

```
- (void)pickerView:(UIPickerView *)pickerView
      didSelectRow:(NSInteger)row
      inComponent:(NSInteger)component {
    if (component == kStateComponent) {
        NSString *selectedState = [self.states objectAtIndex:row];
        NSArray *array = [stateZips objectForKey:selectedState];
        self.zips = array;
        [picker selectRow:0 inComponent:kZipComponent animated:YES];
        [picker reloadComponent:kZipComponent];
    }
}
```

In this method, which is called any time the picker's selection changes, we look at the component and see whether the left-hand component changed. If it did, we grab the array that corresponds to the new selection and assign it to the zips array. Then we set the right-hand component back to the first row and tell it to reload itself. By swapping the zips array whenever the state changes, the rest of the code remains pretty much the same as it was in the *DoublePicker* example.

We're not quite finished yet. Compile and run your application, and check out the *Dependent* tab (see Figure 7–22). Do you see anything there you don't like?

Figure 7–22. *Do we really want the two components to be equal size? Notice the clipping of a long state name.*

The two components are equal in size. Even though the ZIP code will never be more than five characters long, it has been given equal billing with the state. Since states like Mississippi and Massachusetts won't fit in half of the picker, this seems less than ideal. Fortunately, there's another delegate method we can implement to indicate how wide each component should be. We have about 295 pixels available to the picker components in portrait orientation, but for every additional component we add, we lose a little space to drawing the edges of the new component. You might need to experiment a bit with the values to get it to look right. Add the following method to the delegate section of *DependentComponentPickerViewController.m*:

```
- (CGFloat)pickerView:(UIPickerView *)pickerView
    widthForComponent:(NSInteger)component {
    if (component == kZipComponent)
        return 90;
    return 200;
}
```

In this method, we return a number that represents how many pixels wide each component should be, and the picker will do its best to accommodate this. Save, compile, and run, and the picker on the *Dependent* tab will look more like the one shown in Figure 7–5.

By this point, you should be pretty darn comfortable with both pickers and tab bar applications. We have one more thing to show you about pickers, and we plan to have a little fun while doing it. Let's create a simple slot machine game.

Creating a Simple Game with a Custom Picker

Next up, we're going to create an actual working slot machine. Well, OK, it won't dispense silver dollars, but it does look pretty cool. Take a look back at Figure 7–6 before proceeding so you know what we're building.

Writing the Controller Header File

Add the following code to *CustomPickerViewController.h* for starters:

```
#import <UIKit/UIKit.h>

@interface CustomPickerViewController : UIViewController
        <UIPickerViewDataSource, UIPickerViewDelegate> {
    UIPickerView *picker;
    UILabel *winLabel;

    NSArray *column1;
    NSArray *column2;
    NSArray *column3;
    NSArray *column4;
    NSArray *column5;
}
@property(nonatomic, retain) IBOutlet UIPickerView *picker;
```

```
@property(nonatomic, retain) IBOutlet UILabel *winLabel;
@property(nonatomic, retain) NSArray *column1;
@property(nonatomic, retain) NSArray *column2;
@property(nonatomic, retain) NSArray *column3;
@property(nonatomic, retain) NSArray *column4;
@property(nonatomic, retain) NSArray *column5;
- (IBAction)spin;
@end
```

We're declaring two outlets, one for a picker view and one for a label. The label will be used to tell users when they've won, which happens when they get three of the same symbol in a row.

We also create five pointers to NSArray objects. We'll use these to hold the image views containing the images we want the picker to draw. Even though we're using the same images in all five columns, we need separate arrays for each one with its own set of image views, because each view can be drawn in only one place in the picker at a time. We also declare an action method, this time called spin.

Building the View

Even though the picker in Figure 7–6 looks quite a bit fancier than the other ones we've built, there's actually very little difference in the way we'll design our nib. All the extra work is done in the delegate methods of our controller.

Make sure you've saved your new source code, and then double click *CustomPickerViewController.xib* in the project navigator to edit the GUI. Set the *Simulated User Interface Elements* to simulate a tab bar at the bottom of the view, and then add a picker view, a label below that, and a button below that. Use the blue guideline toward the bottom of your view to place the bottom of your button, and center the label and button. Give the button a title of *Spin*.

Now, move your label so it lines up with the view's left guideline and touches the guideline below the bottom of the picker view. Next, resize the label so it goes all the way to the right guideline and down to the guideline above the top of the button.

With the label selected, bring up the attributes inspector. Set the *Alignment* to centered. Then click the *text* color well to change the text color and set the color to something festive, like a bright fuchsia (we don't actually know what color that is, but it does sound festive).

Next, bring up the font palette (**Font ➤ Show Fonts**). Select your label and use the font palette to change its font size to *48*. Note that you can't use the font palette to change the color of the text. The attribute inspector's text color well rules the day here. After getting the text the way you want it, delete the word *Label* from it, since we don't want any text displayed until the first time the user wins.

After that, make all the connections to outlets and actions. You need to connect the *File's Owner*'s picker outlet to the picker view, the *File's Owner*'s winLabel outlet to the label, and the button's *Touch Up Inside* event to the spin action. After that, just make sure to specify the delegate and data source for the picker.

Oh, and there's one additional thing that you need to do. Select the picker, and bring up the attributes inspector. You need to uncheck the check box labeled *User Interaction Enabled* toward the bottom of the *View* settings so that the user can't manually change the dial and cheat. Once you've done all that, save the changes you've made to the nib file.

Fonts Supported by iOS Devices

Be careful when using the fonts palette in Interface Builder for designing iOS interfaces. Interface Builder will let you assign any font that's on your Mac to the label, but iOS devices have a very limited selection of fonts. You should limit your font selections to one of the font families found on the iOS device you are targeting. This post on Jeff LaMarche's excellent iOS blog shows you how to grab this list programmatically: http://iphonedevelopment.blogspot.com/2010/08/fonts-and-font-families.html:

In a nutshell, create a view-based application and add this code to the method application:didFinishLaunchingWithOptions: in the application delegate:

```
for (NSString *family in [UIFont familyNames]) {
    NSLog(@"%@", family);
    for (NSString *font in [UIFont fontNamesForFamilyName:family]) {
        NSLog(@"\t%@", font);
    }
}
```

Run the project in the appropriate simulator, and your fonts will be displayed in the project's console log.

Adding Image Resources

Now we need to add the images that we'll be using in our game. We've included a set of six image files (*seven.png, bar.png, crown.png, cherry.png, lemon.png, and apple.png*) for you in the project archive under the *07 Pickers/Custom Picker Images* folder. As you did with the tab bar images, add the entire folder of images to the *Resources* folder of your project. It's probably a good idea to copy them into the project folder when prompted to do so.

Implementing the Controller

We have a bunch of new stuff to cover in the implementation of this controller. Add the following code at the beginning of *CustomPickerViewController.m* file:

```
#import "CustomPickerViewController.h"

@implementation CustomPickerViewController
@synthesize picker;
@synthesize winLabel;
```

```objc
@synthesize column1;
@synthesize column2;
@synthesize column3;
@synthesize column4;
@synthesize column5;

- (IBAction)spin {
    BOOL win = NO;
    int numInRow = 1;
    int lastVal = -1;
    for (int i = 0; i < 5; i++) {
        int newValue = random() % [self.column1 count];

        if (newValue == lastVal)
            numInRow++;
        else
            numInRow = 1;

        lastVal = newValue;
        [picker selectRow:newValue inComponent:i animated:YES];
        [picker reloadComponent:i];
        if (numInRow >= 3)
            win = YES;
    }
    if (win)
        winLabel.text = @"WIN!";
    else
      winLabel.text = @"";
}

- (void)viewDidLoad {
    UIImage *seven = [UIImage imageNamed:@"seven.png"];
    UIImage *bar = [UIImage imageNamed:@"bar.png"];
    UIImage *crown = [UIImage imageNamed:@"crown.png"];
    UIImage *cherry = [UIImage imageNamed:@"cherry.png"];
    UIImage *lemon = [UIImage imageNamed:@"lemon.png"];
    UIImage *apple = [UIImage imageNamed:@"apple.png"];

    for (int i = 1; i <= 5; i++) {
        UIImageView *sevenView = [[UIImageView alloc] initWithImage:seven];
        UIImageView *barView = [[UIImageView alloc] initWithImage:bar];
        UIImageView *crownView = [[UIImageView alloc] initWithImage:crown];
        UIImageView *cherryView = [[UIImageView alloc]
                                initWithImage:cherry];
        UIImageView *lemonView = [[UIImageView alloc] initWithImage:lemon];
        UIImageView *appleView = [[UIImageView alloc] initWithImage:apple];
        NSArray *imageViewArray = [[NSArray alloc] initWithObjects:
                    sevenView, barView, crownView, cherryView, lemonView,
                                    appleView, nil];

        NSString *fieldName =
            [[NSString alloc] initWithFormat:@"column%d", i];
        [self setValue:imageViewArray forKey:fieldName];
        [fieldName release];
```

```
        [imageViewArray release];

        [sevenView release];
        [barView release];
        [crownView release];
        [cherryView release];
        [lemonView release];
        [appleView release];
    }

    srandom(time(NULL));
}
...
```

Next, insert the following new lines into the viewDidUnload and dealloc methods:

```
...
- (void)viewDidUnload {
    [super viewDidUnload];
    // Release any retained subviews of the main view.
    // e.g. self.myOutlet = nil;
    self.picker = nil;
    self.winLabel = nil;
    self.column1 = nil;
    self.column2 = nil;
    self.column3 = nil;
    self.column4 = nil;
    self.column5 = nil;
}

- (void)dealloc {
    [picker release];
    [winLabel release];
    [column1 release];
    [column2 release];
    [column3 release];
    [column4 release];
    [column5 release];
    [super dealloc];
}
...
```

Finally, add the following code to the end of the file:

```
...
#pragma mark -
#pragma mark Picker Data Source Methods
- (NSInteger)numberOfComponentsInPickerView:(UIPickerView *)pickerView {
    return 5;
}

- (NSInteger)pickerView:(UIPickerView *)pickerView
    numberOfRowsInComponent:(NSInteger)component {
    return [self.column1 count];
}
```

```
#pragma mark Picker Delegate Methods
- (UIView *)pickerView:(UIPickerView *)pickerView
        viewForRow:(NSInteger)row
            forComponent:(NSInteger)component reusingView:(UIView *)view {
    NSString *arrayName = [[NSString alloc] initWithFormat:@"column%d",
        component+1];
    NSArray *array = [self valueForKey:arrayName];
    [arrayName release];
    return [array objectAtIndex:row];
}
```

```
@end
```

There's a lot going on here, huh? Let's take the new stuff method by method.

The spin Method

The spin method fires when the user touches the *Spin* button. In it, we first declare a few variables that will help us keep track of whether the user has won. We'll use win to keep track of whether we've found three in a row by setting it to YES if we have. We'll use numInRow to keep track of how many of the same value we have in a row so far, and we will keep track of the previous component's value in lastVal so that we have a way to compare the current value to the previous value. We initialize lastVal to -1 because we know that value won't match any of the real values.

```
BOOL win = NO;
int numInRow = 1;
int lastVal = -1;
```

Next, we loop through all five components and set each one to a new, randomly generated row selection. We get the count from the column1 array to do that, which is a shortcut we can use because we know that all five columns have the same number of values.

```
for (int i = 0; i < 5; i++) {
    int newValue = random() % [self.column1 count];
```

We compare the new value to the previous value and increment numInRow if it matches. If the value didn't match, we reset numInRow back to 1. We then assign the new value to lastVal so we'll have it to compare the next time through the loop.

```
if (newValue == lastVal)
    numInRow++;
else
    numInRow = 1;
lastVal = newValue;
```

After that, we set the corresponding component to the new value, telling it to animate the change, and we tell the picker to reload that component.

```
[picker selectRow:newValue inComponent:i animated:YES];
[picker reloadComponent:i];
```

The last thing we do each time through the loop is look to see whether we got three in a row and set win to YES if we have.

```
    if (numInRow >= 3)
        win = YES;
}
```

Once we're finished with the loop, we set the label to say whether the spin was a win.

```
if (win)
    winLabel.text = @"Win!";
else
    winLabel.text = @"";
```

The viewDidLoad Method

The new version of `viewDidLoad` is somewhat scary looking, isn't it? Don't worry—once we break it down, it won't seem quite so much like the monster in your closet. The first thing we do is load six different images. We do this using a convenience method on the `UIImage` class called `imageNamed:`.

```
UIImage *seven = [UIImage imageNamed:@"seven.png"];
UIImage *bar = [UIImage imageNamed:@"bar.png"];
UIImage *crown = [UIImage imageNamed:@"crown.png"];
UIImage *cherry = [UIImage imageNamed:@"cherry.png"];
UIImage *lemon = [UIImage imageNamed:@"lemon.png"];
UIImage *apple = [UIImage imageNamed:@"apple.png"];
```

We've warned you in the past about using convenience class methods to initialize objects because they use the autorelease pool, but we're making an exception here for two reasons. First, this code fires only once, when the application launches. Second, it's just so darn convenient. By using this method, we avoid needing to determine the location of each image on the iPhone, and then use that information to load each image. It's probably saving us a dozen lines of code or more without adding meaningful memory overhead.

Once we have the six images loaded, we then need to create instances of `UIImageView`, one for each image, for each of the five picker components. We do that in a loop.

```
for (int i = 1; i <= 5; i++) {
    UIImageView *sevenView = [[UIImageView alloc] initWithImage:seven];
    UIImageView *barView = [[UIImageView alloc] initWithImage:bar];
    UIImageView *crownView = [[UIImageView alloc] initWithImage:crown];
    UIImageView *cherryView = [[UIImageView alloc]
        initWithImage:cherry];
    UIImageView *lemonView = [[UIImageView alloc] initWithImage:lemon];
    UIImageView *appleView = [[UIImageView alloc] initWithImage:apple];
```

After we have the image views, we put them into an array. This array is the one that will be used to provide data to the picker for one of its five components.

```
NSArray *imageViewArray = [[NSArray alloc] initWithObjects:
    sevenView, barView, crownView, cherryView, lemonView,
    appleView, nil];
```

Now, we just need to assign this array to one of our five arrays. To do that, we create a string that matches the name of one of the arrays. The first time through the loop, this string will be column1, which is the name of the array we'll use to feed the first component in the picker. The second time through, it will equal column2, and so on.

```
NSString *fieldName = [[NSString alloc]
            initWithFormat:@"column%d", i];
```

Once we have the name of one of the five arrays, we can assign this array to that property using a very handy method called setValue:forKey:. This method lets you set a property based on its name. So, if we call this with a value of "column1", it is exactly the same as calling the mutator method setColumn1:.

```
[self setValue:imageViewArray forKey:fieldName];
```

After that, we just do a little memory cleanup.

```
[fieldName release];
[imageViewArray release];
[sevenView release];
[barView release];
[crownView release];
[cherryView release];
[lemonView release];
[appleView release];
}
```

The last thing we do in this method is to seed the random number generator. If we don't do that, the game will play the same way every time you play it, which gets kind of boring.

```
srandom(time(NULL));
}
```

That wasn't so bad, was it? But, um, what do we do with those five arrays now that we've filled them with image views? If you scroll down through the code you just typed, you'll see that two data source methods look pretty much the same as before, but if you look down further into the delegate methods, you'll see that we're using a completely different delegate method to provide data to the picker. The one that we've used up to now returned an NSString *, but this one returns a UIView *.

Using this method instead, we can supply the picker with anything that can be drawn into a UIView. Of course, there are limitations on what will work here and look good at the same time, given the small size of the picker. But this method gives us a lot more freedom in what we display, although it is a bit more work.

```
- (UIView *)pickerView:(UIPickerView *)pickerView
      viewForRow:(NSInteger)row
    forComponent:(NSInteger)component
    reusingView:(UIView *)view {
```

This method returns one of the image views from one of the five arrays. To do that, we once again create an NSString with the name of one of the arrays. Because component is zero-indexed, we add one to it, which gives us a value between column1 and column5 and which will correspond to the component for which the picker is requesting data.

```
NSString *arrayName = [[NSString alloc] initWithFormat:@"column%d",
    component+1];
```

Once we have the name of the array to use, we retrieve that array using a method called valueForKey:, which is the counterpart to the setValue:forKey: method that we used in viewDidLoad. Using it is the same as calling the accessor method for the property you specify. So, calling valueForKey: and specifying "column1" is the same as using the column1 accessor method. Once we have the correct array for the component, we just return the image view from the array that corresponds to the selected row.

```
    NSArray *array = [self valueForKey:arrayName];
    return [array objectAtIndex:row];
}
```

Wow, take a deep breath. You got through all of it in one piece, and now you get to take it for a spin.

Final Details

Our game is rather fun, especially when you think about how little effort it took to build it. Now let's improve it with a couple more tweaks. There are two things about this game right now that really bug us:

- It's so darn quiet. Slot machines aren't quiet!

- It tells us that we've won before the dials have finished spinning, which is a minor thing, but it does tend to eliminate the anticipation. To see this in action, run your application again. It is subtle, but the label really does appear before the wheels finish spinning.

The *07 Pickers/Custom Picker Sounds* folder in the project archive that accompanies the book contains two sound files: *crunch.wav* and *win.wav*. Copy that folder to your project's *Resources* folder. These are the sounds we'll play, respectively, when the users tap the *Spin* button and when they win.

To work with sounds, we'll need access to the iOS Audio Toolbox classes. Next, we need to add an outlet that will point to the button. While the wheels are spinning, we're going to hide the button. We don't want users tapping the button again until the current spin is all done. We'll also need a SystemSoundID to hold the crunchy sound made by the spinner and another to hold the binging sound that occurs when we win. Note that a SystemSoundID is a typedef'ed UInt32 and not an object, so no retain keyword, no asterisk in its declaration.

Add the following code to *CustomPickerViewController.h*:

```
#import <UIKit/UIKit.h>
#import <AudioToolbox/AudioToolbox.h>

@interface CustomPickerViewController : UIViewController
        <UIPickerViewDataSource, UIPickerViewDelegate> {
    UIPickerView *picker;
    UILabel *winLabel;

    NSArray *column1;
    NSArray *column2;
```

```
    NSArray *column3;
    NSArray *column4;
    NSArray *column5;

    UIButton *button;
    SystemSoundID crunchSoundID;
    SystemSoundID winSoundID;
}
@property(nonatomic, retain) IBOutlet UIPickerView *picker;
@property(nonatomic, retain) IBOutlet UILabel *winLabel;
@property(nonatomic, retain) NSArray *column1;
@property(nonatomic, retain) NSArray *column2;
@property(nonatomic, retain) NSArray *column3;
@property(nonatomic, retain) NSArray *column4;
@property(nonatomic, retain) NSArray *column5;
@property(nonatomic, retain) IBOutlet UIButton *button;
@property(nonatomic) SystemSoundID crunchSoundID;
@property(nonatomic) SystemSoundID winSoundID;
- (IBAction)spin;

@end
```

After you type that and save the file, click *CustomPickerViewController.xib* to edit the nib. Once it's open, control-drag from *File's Owner* to the *Spin* button, and connect it to the new button outlet we just created. Save the nib.

Now, we need to do a few things in the implementation of our controller class. First, we need to synthesize the accessor and mutator for our new outlet, so open *CustomPickerViewController.m* and add the following line:

```
@implementation CustomPickerViewController
@synthesize picker;
@synthesize winLabel;
@synthesize column1;
@synthesize column2;
@synthesize column3;
@synthesize column4;
@synthesize column5;
@synthesize button;
@synthesize crunchSoundID;
@synthesize winSoundID;
...
```

We also need a couple of methods added to our controller class. Add the following two methods to *CustomPickerViewController.m* as the first two methods in the class:

```
-(void)showButton {
    button.hidden = NO;
}

-(void)playWinSound {
    AudioServicesPlaySystemSound (winSoundID);
    winLabel.text = @"WIN!";
    [self performSelector:@selector(showButton) withObject:nil
        afterDelay:1.5];
}
```

The first method is used to show the button. We're going to hide the button when the user taps it, because if the wheels are already spinning, there's no point in letting them spin again until they've stopped.

The second method will be called when the user wins. The first line of this method plays our WIN! Sound, which will already have been loaded (you'll see how in a moment). Then we set the label to *WIN!* and call the showButton method, but we call the showButton method in a special way using a method called performSelector:withObject:afterDelay:. This is a very handy method available to all objects. It lets you call the method some time in the future—in this case, one and a half seconds in the future—which will give the dials time to spin to their final locations before telling the user the result.

We also need to make some changes to the spin: method. We will write code to play a sound and to call the playerWon method if the player won. Make the following changes to it now:

```
- (IBAction)spin {
    BOOL win = NO;
    int numInRow = 1;
    int lastVal = -1;
    for (int i = 0; i < 5; i++) {
        int newValue = random() % [self.column1 count];

        if (newValue == lastVal)
            numInRow++;
        else
            numInRow = 1;

        lastVal = newValue;
        [picker selectRow:newValue inComponent:i animated:YES];
        [picker reloadComponent:i];
        if (numInRow >= 3)
            win = YES;
    }

    button.hidden = YES;
    AudioServicesPlaySystemSound(crunchSoundID);

    if (win)
        [self performSelector:@selector(playWinSound)
            withObject:nil
            afterDelay:.5];
    else
        [self performSelector:@selector(showButton)
            withObject:nil
            afterDelay:.5];

    winLabel.text = @"";

    if (win)
        winLabel.text = @"WIN!";
    else
        winLabel.text = @"";
```

```
}
```

The first line of code we added hides the *Spin* button. The next line plays an already loaded sound to let the player know they've spun the wheels. Then, instead of setting the label to *WIN!* as soon as we know the user has won, we do something tricky. We call one of the two methods we just created, but we do it after a delay using `performSelector:afterDelay:`. If the user won, we call our `playerWon` method half a second into the future, which will give time for the dials to spin into place; otherwise, we just wait a half a second and reenable the *Spin* button.

Next, we have to add a bit of code to viewDidLoad to load our two sounds.

```
- (void)viewDidLoad {
    UIImage *seven = [UIImage imageNamed:@"seven.png"];
    UIImage *bar = [UIImage imageNamed:@"bar.png"];
    UIImage *crown = [UIImage imageNamed:@"crown.png"];
    UIImage *cherry = [UIImage imageNamed:@"cherry.png"];
    UIImage *lemon = [UIImage imageNamed:@"lemon.png"];
    UIImage *apple = [UIImage imageNamed:@"apple.png"];

    for (int i = 1; i <= 5; i++) {
        UIImageView *sevenView = [[UIImageView alloc] initWithImage:seven];
        UIImageView *barView = [[UIImageView alloc] initWithImage:bar];
        UIImageView *crownView = [[UIImageView alloc] initWithImage:crown];
        UIImageView *cherryView = [[UIImageView alloc]
                                 initWithImage:cherry];
        UIImageView *lemonView = [[UIImageView alloc] initWithImage:lemon];
        UIImageView *appleView = [[UIImageView alloc] initWithImage:apple];
        NSArray *imageViewArray = [[NSArray alloc] initWithObjects:
            sevenView, barView, crownView, cherryView, lemonView,
                                        appleView, nil];

        NSString *fieldName =
            [[NSString alloc] initWithFormat:@"column%d", i];
        [self setValue:imageViewArray forKey:fieldName];
        [fieldName release];
        [imageViewArray release];

        [sevenView release];
        [barView release];
        [crownView release];
        [cherryView release];
        [lemonView release];
        [appleView release];
    }
    NSString *path = [[NSBundle mainBundle] pathForResource:@"win" ofType:@"wav"];
    AudioServicesCreateSystemSoundID((CFURLRef)[NSURL fileURLWithPath:path],
        &winSoundID);
    path = [[NSBundle mainBundle] pathForResource:@"crunch" ofType:@"wav"];
    AudioServicesCreateSystemSoundID((CFURLRef)[NSURL fileURLWithPath:path],
        &crunchSoundID);

    srandom(time(NULL));
}
```

The only thing left is to make sure we release our button outlet, and unload the sounds we loaded, assuming they are still in memory, so make the following changes to your dealloc and viewDidUnload methods:

```
...
- (void)viewDidUnload {
    [super viewDidUnload];
    // Release any retained subviews of the main view.
    // e.g. self.myOutlet = nil;
    self.picker = nil;
    self.winLabel = nil;
    self.column1 = nil;
    self.column2 = nil;
    self.column3 = nil;
    self.column4 = nil;
    self.column5 = nil;
    self.button = nil;

    if (winSoundID)
        AudioServicesDisposeSystemSoundID(winSoundID), winSoundID = 0;

    if (crunchSoundID)
        AudioServicesDisposeSystemSoundID(crunchSoundID), crunchSoundID = 0;
}

- (void)dealloc {
    [picker release];
    [winLabel release];
    [column1 release];
    [column2 release];
    [column3 release];
    [column4 release];
    [column5 release];
    [button release];

    if (winSoundID)
        AudioServicesDisposeSystemSoundID(winSoundID), winSoundID = 0;

    if (crunchSoundID)
        AudioServicesDisposeSystemSoundID(crunchSoundID), crunchSoundID = 0;

    [super dealloc];
}
...
```

Linking in the Audio Toolbox Framework

If you try to compile now, you'll get a linking error. It turns out that the problem is with those functions we called to load and play sounds. Yeah, they're not in any of the frameworks that are linked in by default. A quick command-double-click on the AudioServicesCreateSystemSoundID function takes us to the header file where it's declared. If we scroll up to the top of that header file, we see this:

```
/*==================================================================
        File: AudioToolbox/AudioServices.h

        Contains: API for general high level audio services.

        Copyright: (c) 2006 - 2008 by Apple Inc., all rights reserved.
...
```

This tells us that the function we're trying to call is part of the Audio Toolbox, so we need to manually link our project to that framework.

Right-click (control-click if you have a single-button mouse) on the *Frameworks* folder in the *Groups & Files* pane in Xcode and select **Existing Frameworks.** . . from the **Add** submenu. Select AudioToolbox.framework from the list, as shown in figure 7–23.

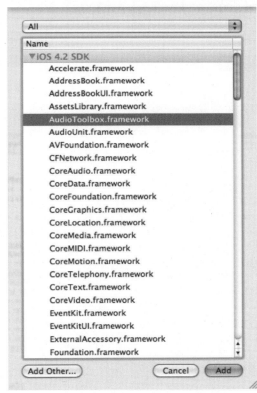

Figure 7–23. *Selecting AudioToolbox.framework from the list of existing frameworks*

Your application should now link properly and, when it runs, the *Spin* button should play one sound and a win should produce a winning sound. Hooray!

Final Spin

By now, you should be comfortable with tab bar applications and pickers. In this chapter, we built a full-fledged tab bar application containing five different content views from scratch. You learned how to use pickers in a number of different configurations, how to create pickers with multiple components, and even how to make the values in one component dependent on the value selected in another component. You also saw how to make the picker display images rather than just text.

Along the way, you learned about picker delegates and data sources, and saw how to load images, play sounds, create dictionaries from property lists, and link your project to additional frameworks. It was a long chapter, so congratulations on making it through! When you're ready to tackle table views, turn the page, and we'll keep going.

Chapter 8

Introduction to Table Views

In the next chapter, we're going to build a hierarchical navigation-based application similar to the Mail application that ships on iOS devices. Our application will allow the user to drill down into nested lists of data and edit that data. But before we can build that application, you need to master the concept of table views. And that's the goal of this chapter.

Table views are the most common mechanism used to display lists of data to the user. They are highly configurable objects that can be made to look practically any way you want them to look. Mail uses table views to show lists of accounts, folders, and messages, but table views are not limited to just the display of textual data. Table views are also used in the YouTube, Settings, and iPod applications, even though these applications have very different appearances (see Figure 8–1).

Figure 8–1. *Though they all look different, the Settings, iPod, and YouTube applications all use table views to display their data.*

Table View Basics

Tables display lists of data. Each item in a table's list is a row. iOS tables can have an unlimited number of rows, constrained only by the amount of available memory. iOS tables can be only one column wide.

Table Views and Table View Cells

A table view is the view object that displays a table's data and is an instance of the class UITableView. Each visible row of the table is implemented by the class UITableViewCell. So, a table view is the object that displays the visible part of a table, and a table view cell is responsible for displaying a single row of the table (see Figure 8–2).

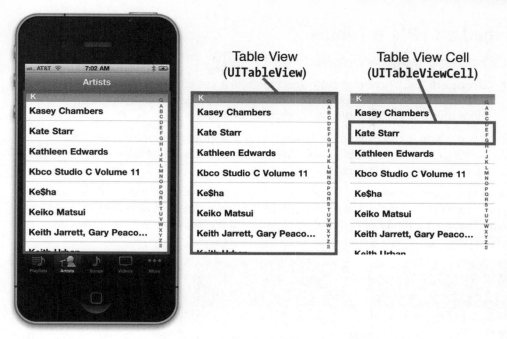

Figure 8–2. *Each table view is an instance of UITableView, and each visible row is an instance of UITableViewCell.*

Table views are not responsible for storing your table's data. They store only enough data to draw the rows that are currently visible. Table views get their configuration data from an object that conforms to the UITableViewDelegate protocol and their row data from an object that conforms to the UITableViewDataSource protocol. You'll see how all this works when we get into our sample programs later in the chapter.

As mentioned, all tables are implemented as a single column. But the YouTube application, shown on the right side of Figure 8–1, does have the appearance of having at least two columns, perhaps even three if you count the icons. But no, each row in the table is represented by a single UITableViewCell. Each UITableViewCell object can be configured with an image, some text, and an optional accessory icon, which is a small icon on the right side (we'll cover accessory icons in detail in the next chapter).

You can put even more data in a cell if you need to by adding subviews to UITableViewCell, using one of two basic techniques: adding subviews programmatically when creating the cell, or loading them from a nib file. You can lay out the table view cell out in any way you like and include any subviews you desire. So, the single-column limitation is far less limiting than it probably sounds at first. If this is confusing, don't worry—we'll show you how to use both of these techniques in this chapter.

Grouped and Plain Tables

Table views come in two basic styles:

- **Grouped**: Each group in a grouped table is a set of rows embedded in a rounded rectangle, as shown in the leftmost picture in Figure 8–3. Note that a grouped table can consist of a single group.

- **Plain**: Plain is the default style. Any table that doesn't feature rounded rectangles is a plain table view. When an index is used, this style is also referred to as **indexed**.

If your data source provides the necessary information, the table view will let the user navigate your list using an index that is displayed down the right side. Figure 8–3 shows a grouped table, a plain table without an index, and a plain table with an index (an indexed table).

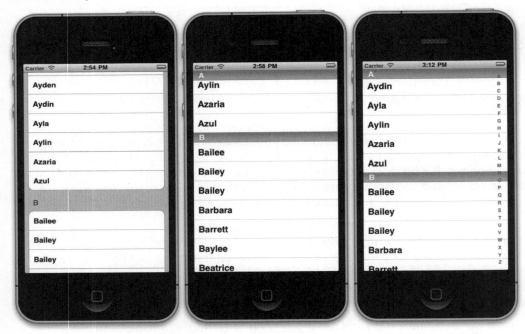

Figure 8–3. *The same table view displayed as a grouped table (left), a plain table without an index (middle), and a plain table with an index, also called an indexed table (right)*

Each division of your table is known to your data source as a **section**. In a grouped table, each group is a section. In an indexed table, each indexed grouping of data is a section. For example, in the indexed table shown in Figure 8–3, all the names beginning with *A* would be one section, those beginning with *B* another, and so on.

Sections have two primary purposes. In a grouped table, each section represents one group. In an indexed table, each section corresponds to one index entry. For example, if you wanted to display a list indexed alphabetically with an index entry for every letter, you would have 26 sections, each containing all the values that begin with a particular letter.

> **CAUTION:** Even though it is technically possible to create a grouped table with an index, you should not do so. The *iPhone Human Interface Guidelines* specifically state that grouped tables should not provide indexes.

Implementing a Simple Table

Let's look at the simplest possible example of a table view to get a feel for how it works. In this example, we're just going to display a list of text values.

Create a new project in Xcode. For this chapter, we're going back to the *View-based Application* template, so select that one. Set the *Product* to *iPhone*, and call your project *Simple Table*.

Designing the View

Expand the *Resources* folder and the *Classes* folder. This is such a simple application that we're not going to need any outlets or actions, so double click *Simple_TableViewController.xib* to edit the GUI. If the *View* window isn't visible, double click its icon in the nib window to open it. Then look in the library for a *Table View* (see Figure 8–4) and drag that over to the *View* window.

Figure 8–4. *Dragging a table view from the library onto our main view. Notice that the table view automatically resizes to the full size of the view.*

The table view should automatically size itself to the height and width of the view. This is exactly what we want. Table views are designed to take up the entire width of the screen and as much of the height as isn't taken up by your application's navigation bars, toolbars, and tab bars.

After dropping the table view onto the *View* window and fitting it just below the status bar, it should still be selected. If it's not, single-click the table view to select it. Then press ⌘**2** to bring up the connections inspector. You'll notice that the first two available connections for the table view are the same as the first two for the picker view: *dataSource* and *delegate*. Drag from the circle next to each of those connections over to the *File's Owner* icon. By doing this, we are making our controller class both the data source and delegate for this table.

After setting the connections, save your nib file and get ready to dig into some UITableView code.

Writing the Controller

The next stop is our controller class's header file. Single-click *Simple_TableViewController.h*, and add the following code:

```
#import <UIKit/UIKit.h>

@interface Simple_TableViewController : UIViewController
    <UITableViewDelegate, UITableViewDataSource>
{
```

```
    NSArray *listData;
}
@property (nonatomic, retain) NSArray *listData;
@end
```

All we're doing here is conforming our class to the two protocols that are needed for it to act as the delegate and data source for the table view, and then declaring an array that will hold the data to be displayed.

Save your changes. Next, switch over to *Simple_TableViewController.m*, and add the following code at the beginning of the file:

```
#import "Simple_TableViewController.h"

@implementation Simple_TableViewController
@synthesize listData;

- (void)viewDidLoad {
    NSArray *array = [[NSArray alloc] initWithObjects:@"Sleepy", @"Sneezy",
        @"Bashful", @"Happy", @"Doc", @"Grumpy", @"Dopey", @"Thorin",
        @"Dorin", @"Nori", @"Ori", @"Balin", @"Dwalin", @"Fili", @"Kili",
        @"Oin", @"Gloin", @"Bifur", @"Bofur", @"Bombur", nil];
    self.listData = array;
    [array release];
    [super viewDidLoad];
}
...
```

Now, add the following lines of code to the existing viewDidUnload and dealloc methods:

```
...
- (void)viewDidUnload {
    // Release any retained subviews of the main view.
    // e.g. self.myOutlet = nil;
    self.listData = nil;
    [super viewDidUnload];
}

- (void)dealloc {
    [listData release];
    [super dealloc];
}
...
```

Finally, add the following code at the end of the file:

```
...
#pragma mark -
#pragma mark Table View Data Source Methods
- (NSInteger)tableView:(UITableView *)tableView
    numberOfRowsInSection:(NSInteger)section {
    return [self.listData count];
}

- (UITableViewCell *)tableView:(UITableView *)tableView
        cellForRowAtIndexPath:(NSIndexPath *)indexPath {
```

```
static NSString *SimpleTableIdentifier = @"SimpleTableIdentifier";

UITableViewCell *cell = [tableView dequeueReusableCellWithIdentifier:
    SimpleTableIdentifier];
if (cell == nil) {
    cell = [[[UITableViewCell alloc]
        initWithStyle:UITableViewCellStyleDefault
        reuseIdentifier:SimpleTableIdentifier] autorelease];
}

NSUInteger row = [indexPath row];
cell.textLabel.text = [listData objectAtIndex:row];
return cell;
}
```

@end

We added three methods to the controller. You should be comfortable with the first one, viewDidLoad, since we've done similar things in the past. We're simply creating an array of data to pass to the table. In a real application, this array would likely come from another source, such as a text file, property list, or URL.

If you scroll down to the end, you can see we added two data source methods. The first one, tableView:numberOfRowsInSection:, is used by the table to ask how many rows are in a particular section. As you might expect, the default number of sections is one, and this method will be called to get the number of rows in the one section that makes up the list. We just return the number of items in our array.

The next method probably requires a little explanation, so let's look at it more closely.

```
- (UITableViewCell *)tableView:(UITableView *)tableView
    cellForRowAtIndexPath:(NSIndexPath *)indexPath {
```

This method is called by the table view when it needs to draw one of its rows. Notice that the second argument to this method is an NSIndexPath instance. This is the mechanism that table views use to wrap the section and row into a single object. To get the row or the section out of an NSIndexPath, you just call either its row method or its section method, both of which return an int.

The first parameter, tableView, is a reference to the table doing the asking. This allows us to create classes that act as a data source for multiple tables.

Next, we declare a static string instance.

```
static NSString *SimpleTableIdentifier = @"SimpleTableIdentifier";
```

This string will be used as a key to represent the type of our table cell. Our table will use only a single type of cell.

A table view can display only a few rows at a time on iPhone's small screen, but the table itself can conceivably hold considerably more. Remember that each row in the table is represented by an instance of UITableViewCell, a subclass of UIView, which means each row can contain subviews. With a large table, this could represent a huge amount of overhead if the table were to try to keep one table view cell instance for every row in the table, regardless of whether that row was currently being displayed. Fortunately, tables don't work that way.

Instead, as table view cells scroll off the screen, they are placed into a queue of cells available to be reused. If the system runs low on memory, the table view will get rid of the cells in the queue. But as long as the system has some available memory for those cells, it will hold on to them in case you want to use them again.

Every time a table view cell rolls off the screen, there's a pretty good chance that another one just rolled onto the screen on the other side. If that new row can just reuse one of the cells that has already rolled off the screen, the system can avoid the overhead associated with constantly creating and releasing those views. To take advantage of this mechanism, we'll ask the table view to give us one of its **dequeued** cells of the specified type. Note that we're making use of the NSString identifier we declared earlier. In effect, we're asking for a reusable cell of type SimpleTableIdentifier.

```
UITableViewCell *cell = [tableView dequeueReusableCellWithIdentifier:
    SimpleTableIdentifier];
```

Now, it's completely possible that the table view won't have any spare cells, so we check cell after the call to see whether it's nil. If it is, we manually create a new table view cell using that identifier string. At some point, we'll inevitably reuse one of the cells we create here, so we need to make sure that we create it using SimpleTableIdentifier.

```
if (cell == nil) {
    cell = [[[UITableViewCell alloc]
        initWithStyle:UITableViewCellStyleDefault
        reuseIdentifier:SimpleTableIdentifier] autorelease];
}
```

Curious about UITableViewCellStyleDefault? Hold that thought. We'll get to it when we look at the table view cell styles.

We now have a table view cell that we can return for the table view to use. So, all we need to do is place whatever information we want displayed in this cell. Displaying text in a row of a table is a very common task, so the table view cell provides a UILabel property called textLabel that we can set in order to display strings. That just requires getting the correct string out of our listData array and using it to set the cell's textLabel.

To get the correct value, however, we need to know which row the table view is asking for. We get that information out of the indexPath variable, like so:

```
NSUInteger row = [indexPath row];
```

We use the row number of the table to get the corresponding string from the array, assign it to the cell's textLabel.text property, and then return the cell.

```
    cell.textLabel.text = [listData objectAtIndex:row];
    return cell;
}
```

That wasn't so bad, was it? Compile and run your application, and you should see the array values displayed in a table view (see Figure 8–5).

Figure 8–5. *The Simple Table application, in all its dwarven glory*

Adding an Image

It would be nice if we could add an image to each row. Guess we would need to create a subclass of UITableViewCell or add subviews in order to do that, huh? Actually, no, not if you can live with the image being on the left side of each row. The default table view cell can handle that situation just fine. Let's check it out.

In the *08 Simple Table folder*, in the project archive, grab the file called *star.png*, and add it to your project's *Resources* folder. *star.png* is a small icon we prepared just for this project.

Next, let's get to the code. In the file *Simple_TableViewController.m*, add the following code to the tableView:cellForRowAtIndexPath: method:

```
- (UITableViewCell *)tableView:(UITableView *)tableView
        cellForRowAtIndexPath:(NSIndexPath *)indexPath {

    static NSString *SimpleTableIdentifier = @" SimpleTableIdentifier ";

    UITableViewCell *cell = [tableView dequeueReusableCellWithIdentifier:
                            SimpleTableIdentifier];
    if (cell == nil) {
        cell = [[[UITableViewCell alloc]
```

```
                initWithStyle:UITableViewCellStyleDefault
                reuseIdentifier:SimpleTableIdentifier] autorelease];
        }

        UIImage *image = [UIImage imageNamed:@"star.png"];
        cell.imageView.image = image;

        NSUInteger row = [indexPath row];
        cell.textLabel.text = [listData objectAtIndex:row];

        return cell;
}
@end
```

Yep, that's it. Each cell has an imageView property. Each imageView has an image property, as well as a highlightedImage property. The image appears to the left of the cell's text and is replaced by the highlightedImage, if one is provided, when the cell is selected. You just set the cell's imageView.image property to whatever image you want to display.

If you compile and run your application now, you should get a list with a bunch of nice little star icons to the left of each row (see Figure 8–6). Of course, we could have included a different image for each row in the table. Or, with very little effort, we could have used one icon for all of Mr. Disney's dwarves and a different one for Mr. Tolkien's.

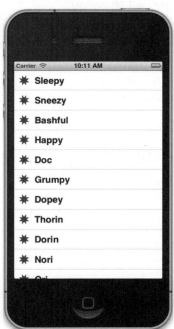

Figure 8–6. *We used the cell's image property to add an image to each of the table view's cells.*

If you like, make a copy of *star.png*, use your favorite graphics application to colorize it a bit, add it to the project, load it with imageNamed:, and use it to set imageView.highlightedImage. Now if you click a cell, your new image will be drawn. If you don't feel like coloring, use the *star2.png* icon we provided in the project archive.

> **NOTE:** UIImage uses a caching mechanism based on the file name, so it won't load a new image property each time imageNamed: is called. Instead, it will use the already cached version.

Using Table View Cell Styles

The work you've done with the table view so far has made use of the default cell style shown in Figure 8–6, represented by the constant UITableViewCellStyleDefault. But the UITableViewCell class includes several other predefined cell styles that let you easily add a bit more variety to your table views. These cell styles make use of three different cell elements:

- **Image**: If an image is part of the specified style, the image is displayed to the left of the cell's text.

- **Text label**: This is the cell's primary text. In the style we used earlier, UITableViewCellStyleDefault, the text label is the only text shown in the cell.

- **Detail text label**: This is the cell's secondary text, usually used as an explanatory note or label.

To see what these new style additions look like, add the following code to tableView:cellForRowAtIndexPath: in *Simple_TableViewController.m*:

```
- (UITableViewCell *)tableView:(UITableView *)tableView
        cellForRowAtIndexPath:(NSIndexPath *)indexPath {

    static NSString *SimpleTableIdentifier = @"SimpleTableIdentifier";

    UITableViewCell *cell = [tableView dequeueReusableCellWithIdentifier:
                            SimpleTableIdentifier];
    if (cell == nil) {
        cell = [[[UITableViewCell alloc]
            initWithStyle:UITableViewCellStyleDefault
            reuseIdentifier: SimpleTableIdentifier] autorelease];
    }

    UIImage *image = [UIImage imageNamed:@"star.png"];
    cell.imageView.image = image;

    NSUInteger row = [indexPath row];
    cell.textLabel.text = [listData objectAtIndex:row];

    if (row < 7)
        cell.detailTextLabel.text = @"Mr. Disney";
    else
        cell.detailTextLabel.text = @"Mr. Tolkien";
```

```
    return cell;
}
```

All we've done here is set the cell's detail text. We use the string @"Mr. Disney" for the first seven rows and @"Mr. Tolkien" for the rest. When you run this code, each cell will look just the same as it did before (see Figure 8–7). That's because we are using the style UITableViewCellStyleDefault, which does not make use of the detail text.

Figure 8–7. *The default cell style shows the image and text label in a straight row.*

Now, change UITableViewCellStyleDefault to UITableViewCellStyleSubtitle and run the app again. With the subtitle style, both text elements are shown, one below the other (see Figure 8–8).

Figure 8–8. *The subtitle style shows the detail text in smaller, gray letters below the text label.*

Change UITableViewCellStyleSubtitle to UITableViewCellStyleValue1, and then build and run. This style places the text label and detail text label on the same line on opposite sides of the cell (see Figure 8–9).

Figure 8–9. *The style value 1 will place the text label on the left side in black letters and the detail text right-justified on the right side in blue letters.*

Finally, change UITableViewCellStyleValue1 to UITableViewCellStyleValue2. This format is often used to display information along with a descriptive label. It doesn't show the cell's icon, but places the detail text label to the left of the text label (see Figure 8–10). In this layout, the detail text label acts as a label describing the type of data held in the text label.

Figure 8–10. *The style value 2 does not display the image and places the detail text label in blue letters to the left of the text label.*

Now that you've seen the cell styles that are available, go ahead and change back to using UITableViewCellStyleDefault before continuing. Later in this chapter, you'll see how to customize the appearance of your table. But before you decide to do that, make sure you consider the available styles to see whether one of them will suit your needs.

You may have noticed that we made our controller both the data source and delegate for this table view, but up to now, we haven't actually implemented any of the methods from UITableViewDelegate. Unlike picker views, simpler table views don't require the use of a delegate in order to do their thing. The data source provides all the data needed to draw the table. The purpose of the delegate is to configure the appearance of the table view and to handle certain user interactions. Let's take a look at a few of the configuration options now. We'll look at a few more in the next chapter.

Setting the Indent Level

The delegate can be used to specify that some rows should be indented. In the file *Simple_TableViewController.m*, add the following method to your code, just above the @end declaration:

```
#pragma mark -
#pragma mark Table Delegate Methods

- (NSInteger)tableView:(UITableView *)tableView
  indentationLevelForRowAtIndexPath:(NSIndexPath *)indexPath {
    NSUInteger row = [indexPath row];
    return row;
}
```

This method sets the **indent level** for each row to its row number, so row 0 will have an indent level of 0, row 1 will have an indent level of 1, and so on. An indent level is simply an integer that tells the table view to move that row a little to the right. The higher the number, the further to the right the row will be indented. You might use this technique, for example, to indicate that one row is subordinate to another row, as Mail does when representing subfolders.

When you run the application again, you can see that each row is now drawn a little further to the right than the last one (see Figure 8–11).

Figure 8–11. *Each row of the table is drawn with an indent level higher than the row before it.*

Handling Row Selection

The table's delegate can use two methods to determine if the user has selected a particular row. One method is called before the row is selected and can be used to prevent the row from being selected, or even change which row gets selected. Let's implement that method and specify that the first row is not selectable. Add the following method to the end of *Simple_TableViewController.m*, just before the @end declaration:

```
-(NSIndexPath *)tableView:(UITableView *)tableView
     willSelectRowAtIndexPath:(NSIndexPath *)indexPath {
   NSUInteger row = [indexPath row];

   if (row == 0)
      return nil;

   return indexPath;
}
```

This method is passed indexPath, which represents the item that's about to be selected. Our code looks at which row is about to be selected. If the row is the first row, which is always index zero, then it returns nil, which indicates that no row should actually be selected. Otherwise, it returns indexPath, which is how we indicate that it's OK for the selection to proceed.

Before you compile and run, let's also implement the delegate method that is called after a row has been selected, which is typically where you'll actually handle the selection. This is where you take whatever action is appropriate when the user selects a row. In the next chapter, we'll use this method to handle the drill-downs, but in this chapter, we'll just put up an alert to show that the row was selected. Add the following method to the bottom of *Simple_TableViewController.m*, just before the @end declaration again:

```
- (void)tableView:(UITableView *)tableView
       didSelectRowAtIndexPath:(NSIndexPath *)indexPath {
   NSUInteger row = [indexPath row];
   NSString *rowValue = [listData objectAtIndex:row];

   NSString *message = [[NSString alloc] initWithFormat:
       @"You selected %@", rowValue];
   UIAlertView *alert = [[UIAlertView alloc]
       initWithTitle:@"Row Selected!"
             message:message
             delegate:nil
    cancelButtonTitle:@"Yes I Did"
    otherButtonTitles:nil];
   [alert show];

   [message release];
   [alert release];
   [tableView deselectRowAtIndexPath:indexPath animated:YES];
}
```

Once you've added this method, compile and run the app, and take it for a spin. See whether you can select the first row (you shouldn't be able to), and then select one of the other rows. The selected row should be highlighted, and then your alert should pop up, telling you which row you selected while the selected row fades in the background (see Figure 8–12).

Figure 8–12. *In this example, the first row is not selectable, and an alert is displayed when any other row is selected. This was done using the delegate methods.*

Note that you can also modify the index path before you pass it back, which would cause a different row and/or section to be selected. You won't do that very often, as you should have a very good reason for changing the user's selection. In the vast majority of cases, when you use this method, you will either return `indexPath` unmodified to allow the selection or return `nil` to or disallow it.

Changing Font Size and Row Height

Let's say that we want to change the size of the font being used in the table view. In most situations, you shouldn't override the default font; it's what users expect to see. But sometimes there are valid reasons to change the font. Add the following line of code to your `tableView:cellForRowAtIndexPath:` method:

```
- (UITableViewCell *)tableView:(UITableView *)tableView
        cellForRowAtIndexPath:(NSIndexPath *)indexPath
{
    static NSString *SimpleTableIdentifier = @"SimpleTableIdentifier";

    UITableViewCell *cell = [tableView dequeueReusableCellWithIdentifier:
                             SimpleTableIdentifier];
    if (cell == nil) {
        cell = [[[UITableViewCell alloc]
            initWithStyle:UITableViewCellStyleDefault
            reuseIdentifier: SimpleTableIdentifier] autorelease];
```

```
    }

    UIImage *image = [UIImage imageNamed:@"star.png"];
    cell.image = image;

    NSUInteger row = [indexPath row];
    cell.textLabel.text = [listData objectAtIndex:row];
    cell.textLabel.font = [UIFont boldSystemFontOfSize:50];

    if (row < 7)
        cell.detailTextLabel.text = @"Mr. Disney";
    else
        cell.detailTextLabel.text = @"Mr. Tolkein";
    return cell;
}
```

When you run the application now, the values in your list are drawn in a really large font size, but they don't exactly fit in the row (see Figure 8–13).

Figure 8–13. *Look how nice and big! But, um, it would be even nicer if we could see everything.*

Well, here comes the table view delegate to the rescue! The table view delegate can specify the height of the table view's rows. In fact, it can specify unique values for each row if you find that necessary. Go ahead and add this method to your controller class, just before @end:

```
- (CGFloat)tableView:(UITableView *)tableView
  heightForRowAtIndexPath:(NSIndexPath *)indexPath {
    return 70;
}
```

We've just told the table view to set the row height for all rows to 70 pixels tall. Compile and run, and your table's rows should be much taller now (see Figure 8–14).

Figure 8–14. *Changing the row size using the delegate*

There are more tasks that the delegate handles, but most of the remaining ones come into play when you start working with hierarchical data, which we'll do in the next chapter. To learn more, use the documentation browser to explore the UITableViewDelegate protocol and see what other methods are available.

Customizing Table View Cells

You can do a lot with table views right out of the box, but often, you will want to format the data for each row in ways that simply aren't supported by UITableViewCell directly. In those cases, there are two basic approaches: one that involves adding subviews to UITableViewCell programmatically when creating the cell, and a second that involves loading a set of subviews from a nib file. Let's look at both techniques.

Adding Subviews to the Table View Cell

To show how to use custom cells, we're going to create a new application with another table view. In each row, we'll display two lines of information along with two labels (see Figure 8–15). Our application will display the name and color of a series of potentially familiar computer models, and we'll show both of those pieces of information in the same table cell by adding subviews to the table view cell.

Figure 8–15. *Adding subviews to the table view cell can give you multiline rows.*

Create a new Xcode project using the *View-based Application* template and *Product* set to *iPhone*. Name the project *Cells*. Double click *CellsViewController.xib* to edit the nib file in Interface Builder.

Add a *Table View* to the main view, and set its delegate and data source to *File's Owner* as we did for the Simple Table application, and then save the nib.

Modifying the Controller Header File

Select *CellsViewController.h*, and add the following code:

```
#import <UIKit/UIKit.h>
#define kNameValueTag    1
#define kColorValueTag   2

@interface CellsViewController : UIViewController
    <UITableViewDataSource, UITableViewDelegate>
{
    NSArray    *computers;
}
@property (nonatomic, retain) NSArray *computers;
@end
```

Notice that we've defined two constants. We're going to use these to assign tags to some of the subviews that we'll be adding to the table view cell. We'll add four subviews to the cell, and two of those need to be changed for every row. In order to do that, we need some mechanism that will allow us to retrieve the two fields from the cell when we go to update that cell with a particular row's data. If we set unique tag values for each label that we'll use again, we'll be able to retrieve them from the table view cell and set their values.

Implementing the Controller's Code

In our controller, we need to set up some data to use, and then implement the table data source methods to feed that data to the table. Switch to *CellsViewController.m*, and add the following code at the beginning of the file:

```
#import "CellsViewController.h"

@implementation CellsViewController
@synthesize computers;

- (void)viewDidLoad {

    NSDictionary *row1 = [[NSDictionary alloc] initWithObjectsAndKeys:
                    @"MacBook", @"Name", @"White", @"Color", nil];
    NSDictionary *row2 = [[NSDictionary alloc] initWithObjectsAndKeys:
                    @"MacBook Pro", @"Name", @"Silver", @"Color", nil];
    NSDictionary *row3 = [[NSDictionary alloc] initWithObjectsAndKeys:
                    @"iMac", @"Name", @"Silver", @"Color", nil];
    NSDictionary *row4 = [[NSDictionary alloc] initWithObjectsAndKeys:
                    @"Mac Mini", @"Name", @"Silver", @"Color", nil];
    NSDictionary *row5 = [[NSDictionary alloc] initWithObjectsAndKeys:
                    @"Mac Pro", @"Name", @"Silver", @"Color", nil];

    NSArray *array = [[NSArray alloc] initWithObjects:row1, row2,
                    row3, row4, row5, nil];
    self.computers = array;

    [row1 release];
    [row2 release];
    [row3 release];
    [row4 release];
    [row5 release];
    [array release];
}
...
```

Of course, we need to be good memory citizens, so make the following changes to the existing `dealloc` and `viewDidUnload` methods:

```
...
- (void)viewDidUnload {
    // Release any retained subviews of the main view.
    // e.g. self.myOutlet = nil;
    self.computers = nil;
    [super viewDidUnload];
}

- (void)dealloc {
```

```
        [computers release];
        [super dealloc];
}
...
```

Then add this code at the end of the file, above the @end declaration:

```
...
#pragma mark -
#pragma mark Table Data Source Methods
- (NSInteger)tableView:(UITableView *)tableView
    numberOfRowsInSection:(NSInteger)section {
    return [self.computers count];
}

-(UITableViewCell *)tableView:(UITableView *)tableView
    cellForRowAtIndexPath:(NSIndexPath *)indexPath {
    static NSString *CellTableIdentifier = @"CellTableIdentifier ";

    UITableViewCell *cell = [tableView dequeueReusableCellWithIdentifier:
        CellTableIdentifier];
    if (cell == nil) {
        cell = [[[UITableViewCell alloc]
            initWithStyle:UITableViewCellStyleDefault
            reuseIdentifier:CellTableIdentifier] autorelease];
        CGRect nameLabelRect = CGRectMake(0, 5, 70, 15);
        UILabel *nameLabel = [[UILabel alloc] initWithFrame:nameLabelRect];
        nameLabel.textAlignment = UITextAlignmentRight;
        nameLabel.text = @"Name:";
        nameLabel.font = [UIFont boldSystemFontOfSize:12];
        [cell.contentView addSubview: nameLabel];
        [nameLabel release];

        CGRect colorLabelRect = CGRectMake(0, 26, 70, 15);
        UILabel *colorLabel = [[UILabel alloc] initWithFrame:colorLabelRect];
        colorLabel.textAlignment = UITextAlignmentRight;
        colorLabel.text = @"Color:";
        colorLabel.font = [UIFont boldSystemFontOfSize:12];
        [cell.contentView addSubview: colorLabel];
        [colorLabel release];
        CGRect nameValueRect = CGRectMake(80, 5, 200, 15);
        UILabel *nameValue = [[UILabel alloc] initWithFrame:
            nameValueRect];
        nameValue.tag = kNameValueTag;
        [cell.contentView addSubview:nameValue];
        [nameValue release];

        CGRect colorValueRect = CGRectMake(80, 25, 200, 15);
        UILabel *colorValue = [[UILabel alloc] initWithFrame:
            colorValueRect];
        colorValue.tag = kColorValueTag;
        [cell.contentView addSubview:colorValue];
        [colorValue release];
    }
```

```
    NSUInteger row = [indexPath row];
    NSDictionary *rowData = [self.computers objectAtIndex:row];
    UILabel *name = (UILabel *)[cell.contentView viewWithTag:
        kNameValueTag];
    name.text = [rowData objectForKey:@"Name"];

    UILabel *color = (UILabel *)[cell.contentView viewWithTag:
        kColorValueTag];
    color.text = [rowData objectForKey:@"Color"];
    return cell;
}
@end
```

This version of `viewDidLoad` creates a series of dictionaries. Each dictionary contains the name and color information for one row in the table. The name for that row is held in the dictionary under the key `Name`, and the color is held under the key `Color`. We stick all the dictionaries into a single array, which is our data for this table.

Let's focus on `tableView:cellForRowWithIndexPath:`, since that's where we're really getting into some new stuff. The first two lines of code are just like our earlier versions. We create an identifier and ask the table to dequeue a table view cell if it has one.

If the table doesn't have any cells available for reuse, we need to create a new cell. When we do this, we also need to create and add the subviews that we'll be using to implement our two-line-per-row table. Let's look at that code a little more closely.

First, we create a cell. This is essentially the same technique as before. We specify the default style, although the style actually won't matter, because we'll be adding our own subviews to display our data, rather than using the provided ones.

```
cell = [[[UITableViewCell alloc]
    initWithStyle:UITableViewCellStyleDefault
    reuseIdentifier:CellTableIdentifier] autorelease];
```

After that, we create four `UILabel`s and add them to the table view cell. The table view cell already has a `UIView` subview called `contentView`, which it uses to group all of its subviews, much the way we grouped those two switches inside a `UIView` back in Chapter 4. As a result, we don't add the labels as subviews directly to the table view cell, but rather to its `contentView`.

```
[cell.contentView addSubview:colorValue];
```

Two of these labels contain static text. The label `nameLabel` contains the text *Name:*, and the label `colorLabel` contains the text *Color:*. Those are just labels that we won't change. The other two labels, however, will be used to display our row-specific data. Remember that we need some way of retrieving these fields later on, so we assign values to both of them. For example, we assign the constant `kNameValueTag` to `nameValue`'s tag field.

```
nameValue.tag = kNameValueTag;
```

In a moment, we'll use that tag to retrieve the correct label from the cell.

Once we're finished creating our new cell, we use the `indexPath` argument that was passed in to determine which row the table is requesting a cell for, and then use that row value to grab the correct dictionary for the requested row. Remember that the dictionary has two key/value pairs, one with name and another with color.

```
NSUInteger row = [indexPath row];
NSDictionary *rowData = [self.computers objectAtIndex:row];
```

Remember those tags we set before? Well, here, we use them to retrieve the label whose value we need to set.

```
UILabel *name = (UILabel *)[cell.contentView viewWithTag:kNameValueTag];
```

Once we have that label, we just set its text to one of the values we pull from the dictionary that represents this row.

```
name.text = [rowData objectForKey:@"Name"];
```

Compile and run your application, and you should see a table of rows, each with two lines of data, as in Figure 8–15.

Being able to add views to the table view provides a lot more flexibility than using the standard table view cell alone, but it can get a little tedious creating, positioning, and adding all the subviews programmatically. Gosh, it sure would be nice if we could design the table view cell graphically, using Xcode's nib editor. Well, we're in luck. As we mentioned earlier, you can use Interface Builder to design your table view cells, and then simply load the views from the nib file when you create a new cell.

Loading a UITableViewCell from a Nib

We're going to re-create that same two-line interface we just built in code using the visual layout capabilities that Xcode provides in Interface Builder. To do this, we'll create a new nib file that will contain the table view cell, and lay out its views using Interface Builder. Then, when we need a table view cell to represent a row, instead of creating a standard table view cell, we'll just load the nib file containing the table view cell and its subviews, and use an outlet connected to the cell to find the labels and set the name and color.

Right-click the *Resources* folder in Xcode, and select **Add ➤ New File...** from the contextual menu. In the left pane of the new file assistant, click *User Interface* (making sure to pick it in the *iOS* section, rather than the *Mac OS X* section). From the upper-right pane, select *Empty XIB*, and leave the *Product* popup set to *iPhone*. Click *Next*. When prompted for a name, type *CustomCell.xib*.

Creating New Outlets

We'll get back to laying out the GUI a bit later, but first let's go ahead and build some infrastructure to support the GUI we're going to create.

By now, you're probably pretty comfortable with the notion that a nib file contains a set of freeze-dried objects that turn into real, live objects in an application when the nib is loaded. Often, we load a nib file in conjunction with a controller, set as file's owner in the nib, either when the controller is created or when it's about to be shown on the screen. You might get the idea from this that a single controller can load a single nib file, but that's not the only usage pattern. You can also have a controller that loads multiple nib files, with the controller set as file's owner in all of them, and have all the outlets and actions connected as configured as the nib as loaded. You can even load the same nib multiple times, and it will create a new set of objects (a fresh copy of all the objects stored in the nib) each time. If the controller has an outlet pointing to an object loaded from a nib, and the nib is loaded yet again, the outlet will simply be changed to point to the most recently loaded copy.

We're going to use an outlet in our controller class to make it easier to set the value that needs to change for each row. As in the previous way of doing things, we'll use tags to locate the specific GUI objects that need to be updated, but this time, we'll set the tag values directly on the objects that we graphically lay out in Interface Builder.

Single-click *CellsViewController.h*, and add the following code:

```
#import <UIKit/UIKit.h>
#define kNameValueTag    1
#define kColorValueTag   2

@interface CellsViewController : UIViewController
    <UITableViewDataSource, UITableViewDelegate>
{
    NSArray     *computers;
    UITableViewCell *tvCell;
}
@property (nonatomic, retain) NSArray *computers;
@property (nonatomic, retain) IBOutlet UITableViewCell *tvCell;
@end
```

That's all we need to do here. Let's switch over to *CellsViewController.m* and add a little more:

```
#import "CellsViewController.h"

@implementation CellsViewController
@synthesize computers;
@synthesize tvCell;
```

Of course, we need to be good memory citizens, so make the following changes to the existing dealloc and viewDidUnload methods:

```
...
- (void)viewDidUnload {
    // Release any retained subviews of the main view.
    // e.g. self.myOutlet = nil;
    self.computers = nil;
    self.tvCell = nil;
    [super viewDidUnload];
}

- (void)dealloc {
```

```
        [computers release];
        [tvCell release];
        [super dealloc];
}
@end
```

Make sure you save both of those files. Now, let's get started with designing the GUI.

Designing the Table View Cell in Interface Builder

Next, double click *CustomCell.xib* in the *Groups & Files pane* to open the file for editing. There are only two icons in this nib's main window: *File's Owner* and *First Responder*. Look in the library for a *Table View Cell* (see Figure 8–16), and drag one of those into the main nib window.

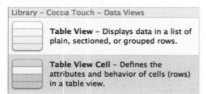

Figure 8–16. *We dragged a Table View Cell from the library and have it selected in the nib editor.*

Make sure the table view cell is selected, press ⌘3 to bring up the size inspector, and change the table view cell's height from *44* to *65*. That will give us a little more room to play with.

Next, press ⌘1 to go to the attributes inspector (Figure 8–17). The first field you'll see there is *Identifier*. That's the reuse identifier that we've been using in our code. If this does not ring a bell, scan back through the chapter and look for `SimpleTableIdentifier`. Set the *Identifier* to *CustomCellIdentifier*.

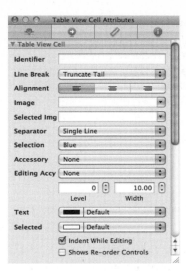

Figure 8–17. *The attributes inspector for a table view cell*

The idea here is that when we retrieve a cell for reuse, perhaps because of scrolling a new cell into view, we want to make sure we get the correct cell type. By setting *Identifier* to *CustomCellIdentifier*, when this particular cell is instantiated from the nib file, you can cause its reuse identifier instance variable to be prepopulated with the NSString you enter in the *Identifier* field. In this case, that NSString is *CustomCellIdentifier*.

Imagine a scenario where you created a table with a header and then a series of "middle" cells. If you scroll a middle cell into view, it's important that you retrieve a middle cell to reuse and not a header cell. The *Identifier* field lets you tag the cells appropriately.

Our next step is to edit our table cell's content view. Double-click the *Table View Cell* in the main nib window. A new window should appear with a rounded gray dashed rectangle with the label *Content View* in the center. As the name states, that's the cell's content view, and that's where we're going to do our editing.

Drag out four labels from the library and place them in the content view, using Figure 8–18 as a guide. Note that the labels will be too close to the top and bottom for those guidelines to be of much help, but the left guideline and the alignment guidelines should serve their purpose.

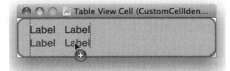

Figure 8–18. *The table view cell's content view, with four labels dragged in*

Next, double-click the upper-left label and change it to *Name:*, and change the lower-left label to *Color:*. Now, select both the *Name:* and *Color:* labels, press ⌘T (or select **Font** ➤ **Show Fonts**) to open the font palette, and then pick *Helvetica* as the font and *Bold* as the typeface. If needed, select the two unchanged label fields on the right and drag them a bit more to the right to give the design a bit of breathing room. Finally, resize the two right-side labels so they stretch all the way to the right guideline. Figure 8–19 should give you a sense of our final cell content view.

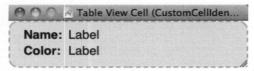

Figure 8–19. *The table view cell's content view with the left label names changed and set to bold, and with the right labels slightly moved and resized*

Now, set the tags for each of the two labels on the right. These tags will be used to identify the correct label in which to store color or name text after the nib file is loaded. It's important that we use the same labels as we do in the code: 1 for the name label and 2 for the color label. To set each, press ⌘1 to bring up the object attributes inspector, and then scroll down to the *View* area and find the *Tag* field. Select the upper-right label and set its tag to *1*. Then select the lower-right label and set its tag to *2*.

At this point, the GUI objects are all set, but there's no connection to the controller class that will be loading the nib. It's time to change that. Select *File's Owner* from nib window, press ⌘4 to bring up the identity inspector, and enter *CellsViewController* in the *Class* field.

Now, control-drag from the *File's Owner* icon to the *Table View Cell* icon in the nib window, assigning it to the outlet *tvCell*. Save the nib, and let's get back to the code.

Using the New Table View Cell

To use the cell we designed, we need to make some pretty drastic changes to the `tableView:cellForRowAtIndexPath:` method in *CellsViewController.m*. Delete the one you currently have, and replace it with this new version:

```
- (UITableViewCell *)tableView:(UITableView *)tableView
        cellForRowAtIndexPath:(NSIndexPath *)indexPath {
    static NSString *CustomCellIdentifier = @"CustomCellIdentifier";

    UITableViewCell *cell = [tableView
        dequeueReusableCellWithIdentifier: CustomCellIdentifier];
    if (cell == nil) {
        NSArray *nib = [[NSBundle mainBundle] loadNibNamed:@"CustomCell"
                                            owner:self options:nil];
        if ([nib count] > 0) {
            cell = self.tvCell;
        } else {
            NSLog(@"failed to load CustomCell nib file!");
        }
```

```
    }
    NSUInteger row = [indexPath row];
    NSDictionary *rowData = [self.computers objectAtIndex:row];

    UILabel *colorLabel = (UILabel *)[cell viewWithTag:kNameValueTag];
    colorLabel.text = [rowData objectForKey:@"Color"];

    UILabel *nameLabel = (UILabel *)[cell viewWithTag:kColorValueTag];
    nameLabel.text = [rowData objectForKey:@"Name"];
    return cell;
}
```

Because we've designed the table view cell in a nib file, if there are no reusable cells, we simply load one from the nib. When we load the nib, we get an outlet connected to the new cell, and then use the tags we defined to access the labels contained within the cell and set their display values.

There's one other addition we need to make. We already changed the height of our table view cell from the default value in *CustomCell.xib*, but that's not quite enough. We also need to inform the table view of that fact; otherwise, it won't leave enough space for the cell to display properly. The simplest way to do that is by editing the nib that contains the table view.

Double click *CellsViewController.xib* in the project navigator to go back to Interface Builder, and then select the table view itself. Be sure to select the table view, not the view (which is the table view's parent). Press ⌘3 to open the size inspector. Look for the *Table View Size* section at the top, where you'll see text fields for directly setting the heights of various parts of the table view's anatomy. Change the value for *Row* to *66.00*.

That's it. Build and run. Now your two-line table cells are based on your mad Interface Builder design skillz.

Grouped and Indexed Sections

Our next project will explore another fundamental aspect of tables. We're still going to use a single table view—no hierarchies yet—but we'll divide data into sections. Create a new Xcode project using the *View-based Application* template again, this time calling it *Sections*.

Building the View

Open the *Classes* and *Resources* folders, and double click *SectionsViewController.xib* to edit the file. Drop a table view onto the *View* window, as we did before. Then press ⌘2, and connect the *dataSource* and *delegate* connections to the *File's Owner* icon.

Next, make sure the table view is selected, and press ⌘1 to bring up the attributes inspector. Change the table view's *Style* from *Plain* to *Grouped* (see Figure 8–20). You should see the change reflected in the sample table shown in the table view. Save your nib, and move along. (We discussed the difference between indexed and grouped styles at the beginning of the chapter.)

Figure 8–20. *The attributes inspector for the table view, showing the Style popup with Grouped selected*

Importing the Data

This project needs a fair amount of data to do its thing. To save you a few hours' worth of typing, we've provided another property list for your tabling pleasure. Grab the file named *sortednames.plist* from the *08 Sections* folder in this book's project archive and add it to your project's *Resources* folder.

Once *sortednames.plist* is added to your project, single-click it just to get a sense of what it looks like (see Figure 8–21). It's a property list that contains a dictionary, with one entry for each letter of the alphabet. Underneath each letter is a list of names that start with that letter.

Key	Type	Value
▼ Root	Dictionary ⬍	(26 items)
▶ A	Array	(245 items)
▶ B	Array	(93 items)
▶ C	Array	(141 items)
▶ D	Array	(117 items)
▶ E	Array	(92 items)
▶ F	Array	(27 items)
▶ G	Array	(64 items)
▼ H	Array	(51 items)
Item 0	String	Haden
Item 1	String	Hadley
Item 2	String	Haiden
Item 3	String	Hailee
Item 4	String	Hailey
Item 5	String	Hailie
Item 6	String	Haleigh
Item 7	String	Haley
Item 8	String	Halle
Item 9	String	Hallie
Item 10	String	Hamza
Item 11	String	Hana
Item 12	String	Hanna
Item 13	String	Hannah
Item 14	String	Harley

Figure 8–21. *The sortednames.plist property list file. We opened the letter H to give you a sense of one of the dictionaries.*

We'll use the data from this property list to feed the table view, creating a section for each letter.

Implementing the Controller

Single-click the *SectionsViewController.h* file, and add both an NSDictionary and an NSArray instance variable and corresponding property declarations. The dictionary will hold all of our data. The array will hold the sections sorted in alphabetical order. We also need to make the class conform to the UITableViewDataSource and UITableViewDelegate protocols:

```
#import <UIKit/UIKit.h>

@interface SectionsViewController : UIViewController
    <UITableViewDataSource, UITableViewDelegate>
{

    NSDictionary *names;
    NSArray      *keys;
}
@property (nonatomic, retain) NSDictionary *names;
@property (nonatomic, retain) NSArray *keys;
@end
```

Now, switch over to *SectionsViewController.m*, and add the following code to the beginning of that file:

```
#import "SectionsViewController.h"

@implementation SectionsViewController
@synthesize names;
@synthesize keys;

- (void)viewDidLoad {
    NSString *path = [[NSBundle mainBundle] pathForResource:@"sortednames"
                                                     ofType:@"plist"];
    NSDictionary *dict = [[NSDictionary alloc]
                          initWithContentsOfFile:path];
    self.names = dict;
    [dict release];

    NSArray *array = [[names allKeys] sortedArrayUsingSelector:
                      @selector(compare:)];
    self.keys = array;
}
...
```

Insert the following lines of code in the existing dealloc and viewDidUnload methods:

```
...
- (void)viewDidUnload {
    // Release any retained subviews of the main view.
    // e.g. self.myOutlet = nil;
    self.names = nil;
    self.keys = nil;
    [super viewDidUnload];
}

- (void)dealloc {
```

```
        [names release];
        [keys release];
        [super dealloc];
}
...
```

Now, add the following code at the end of the file, just above the @end declaration:

```
...
#pragma mark -
#pragma mark Table View Data Source Methods
- (NSInteger)numberOfSectionsInTableView:(UITableView *)tableView {
    return [keys count];
}

- (NSInteger)tableView:(UITableView *)tableView
        numberOfRowsInSection:(NSInteger)section {
    NSString *key = [keys objectAtIndex:section];
    NSArray *nameSection = [names objectForKey:key];
    return [nameSection count];
}

- (UITableViewCell *)tableView:(UITableView *)tableView
    cellForRowAtIndexPath:(NSIndexPath *)indexPath {
    NSUInteger section = [indexPath section];
    NSUInteger row = [indexPath row];

    NSString *key = [keys objectAtIndex:section];
    NSArray *nameSection = [names objectForKey:key];

    static NSString *SectionsTableIdentifier = @"SectionsTableIdentifier";
    UITableViewCell *cell = [tableView dequeueReusableCellWithIdentifier:
        SectionsTableIdentifier];
    if (cell == nil) {
        cell = [[[UITableViewCell alloc]
            initWithStyle:UITableViewCellStyleDefault
            reuseIdentifier:SectionsTableIdentifier] autorelease];
    }

    cell.textLabel.text = [nameSection objectAtIndex:row];
    return cell;
}

- (NSString *)tableView:(UITableView *)tableView
    titleForHeaderInSection:(NSInteger)section {
    NSString *key = [keys objectAtIndex:section];
    return key;
}
@end
```

Most of this isn't too different from what you've seen before. In the viewDidLoad method, we created an NSDictionary instance from the property list we added to our project and assigned it to names. After that, we grabbed all the keys from that dictionary and sorted them to give us an ordered NSArray with all the key values in the dictionary in alphabetical order. Remember that the NSDictionary uses the letters of the alphabet as its keys, so this array will have 26 letters, in order from *A* to *Z*, and we'll use that array to help us keep track of the sections.

Scroll down to the data source methods. The first one we added to our class specifies the number of sections. We didn't implement this method in the earlier example, because we were happy with the default setting of 1. This time, we're telling the table view that we have one section for each key in our dictionary.

```
- (NSInteger)numberOfSectionsInTableView:(UITableView *)tableView {
    return [keys count];
}
```

The next method calculates the number of rows in a specific section. In the previous example, we had only one section, so we just returned the number of rows in our array. This time, we need to break it down by section. We can do that by retrieving the array that corresponds to the section in question and returning the count from that array.

```
- (NSInteger)tableView:(UITableView *)tableView
        numberOfRowsInSection:(NSInteger)section {
    NSString *key = [keys objectAtIndex:section];
    NSArray *nameSection = [names objectForKey:key];
    return [nameSection count];
}
```

In our `tableView:cellForRowAtIndexPath:` method, we need to extract both the section and row from the index path, and use those to determine which value to use. The section will tell us which array to pull out of the names dictionary, and then we can use the row to figure out which value from that array to use. Everything else in that method is basically the same as the version in the Simple Table application we built earlier in the chapter.

The method `tableView:titleForHeaderInSection` allows you to specify an optional header value for each section, and we simply return the letter for this group.

```
- (NSString *)tableView:(UITableView *)tableView
    titleForHeaderInSection:(NSInteger)section {
    NSString *key = [keys objectAtIndex:section];
    return key;
}
```

Compile and run the project, and revel in its grooviness. Remember that we changed the table's *Style* to *Grouped*, so we ended up with a grouped table with 26 sections, which should look like Figure 8–22.

Figure 8–22. *A grouped table with multiple sections*

As a contrast, let's change our table view back to the plain style and see what a plain table view with multiple sections looks like. Double click *SectionViewController.xib* to edit the file in Interface Builder again. Select the table view, and use the attributes inspector to switch the view to *Plain*. Save the project, and then build and run it—same data, different grooviness (see Figure 8–23).

Figure 8–23. *A plain table with sections and no index*

Adding an Index

One problem with our current table is the sheer number of rows. There are 2,000 names in this list. Your finger will get awfully tired looking for Zachariah or Zayne, not to mention Zoie.

One solution to this problem is to add an index down the right side of the table view. Now that we've set our table view style back to *Plain*, that's relatively easy to do. Add the following method to the bottom of *SectionsViewController.m*, just above the @end:

```
- (NSArray *)sectionIndexTitlesForTableView:(UITableView *)tableView {
    return keys;
}
```

Yep, that's it. In this method, the delegate is asking for an array of the values to display in the index. You must have more than one section in your table view to use the index, and the entries in this array must correspond to those sections. The returned array must have the same number of entries as you have sections, and the values must correspond to the appropriate section. In other words, the first item in this array will take the user to the first section, which is section 0.

Compile and run the app again, and you'll have yourself a nice index (see Figure 8–24).

Figure 8–24. *The indexed table view with an index*

Implementing a Search Bar

The index is helpful, but even so, we still have a whole lot of names here. If we want to see whether the name Arabella is in the list, for example, we'll need to scroll for a while even after using the index. It would be nice if we could let the user pare down the list by specifying a search term, wouldn't it? That would be darn user-friendly. Well, it's a bit of extra work, but it's not too bad. We're going to implement a standard iOS search bar, like the one shown in Figure 8–25.

Figure 8–25. *The application with a search bar added to the table*

Rethinking the Design

Before we set about adding a search bar, we need to put some thought into our approach. Currently, we have a dictionary that holds a series of arrays, one for each letter of the alphabet. The dictionary is immutable, which means we can't add or delete values from it, and so are the arrays that it holds. We also need to retain the ability to get back to the original dataset when the user hits cancel or erases the search term.

The solution is to create two dictionaries: an immutable dictionary to hold the full dataset and a mutable copy from which we can remove rows. The delegate and data sources will read from the mutable dictionary, and when the search criteria change or the search is canceled, we can refresh the mutable dictionary from the immutable one. Sounds like a plan. Let's do it.

CAUTION: This next project is a bit advanced and may cause a distinct burning sensation if taken too quickly. If some of these concepts give you a headache, retrieve your copy of *Learn Objective-C on the Mac* by Mark Dalrymple and Scott Knaster (Apress, 2009) and review the bits about categories and mutability.

A Deep Mutable Copy

To use our new approach, there's one problem we'll need to solve. NSDictionary conforms to the NSMutableCopying protocol, which returns an NSMutableDictionary, but that method creates what's called a **shallow** copy. This means that when you call the mutableCopy method, it will create a new NSMutableDictionary object that has all the objects that the original dictionary had. They won't be copies; they will be the same actual objects. This would be fine if, say, we were dealing with a dictionary storing strings, because removing a value from the copy wouldn't do anything to the original. Since we have a dictionary full of arrays, however, if we were to remove objects from the arrays in the copy, we would also be removing them from the arrays in the original, because both the copies and the original point to the same objects. In this particular case, the original arrays are immutable, so you couldn't actually remove objects from them anyway, but our intention is to illustrate the point.

In order to deal with this properly, we need to be able to make a deep mutable copy of a dictionary full of arrays. That's not too hard to do, but where should we put this functionality?

If you said, "in a category," then great, now you're thinking with portals! If you didn't, don't worry, it takes a while to get used to this language. Categories, in case you've forgotten, allow you to add additional methods to existing objects without subclassing them. Categories are frequently overlooked by folks new to Objective-C, because they're a feature most other languages don't have.

With categories, we can add a method to NSDictionary to do a deep copy, returning an NSMutableDictionary with the same data but not containing the same actual objects.

In your project window, select the *Classes* folder, and press ⌘**N** to create a new file. When the assistant comes up, select *Other* from the very bottom of the left side. Unfortunately, there's no file template for categories, so we'll just create a couple of empty files for this purpose. Select the *Empty File* icon, and give this first one a name of *NSDictionary-MutableDeepCopy.h*. Repeat the process, the second time using a name of *NSDictionary-MutableDeepCopy.m*.

TIP: A faster way to create the two files needed for the category is to select the *NSObject subclass* template and then delete the file contents. This option will give you both the header and implementation file, saving you one step.

Put the following code in *NSDictionary-MutableDeepCopy.h*:

```
#import <Foundation/Foundation.h>

@interface NSDictionary(MutableDeepCopy)
- (NSMutableDictionary *)mutableDeepCopy;
@end
```

Flip over to *NSDictionary-MutableDeepCopy.m*, and add the implementation:

```
#import "NSDictionary-MutableDeepCopy.h"

@implementation NSDictionary (MutableDeepCopy)

- (NSMutableDictionary *) mutableDeepCopy {
    NSMutableDictionary *returnDict = [[NSMutableDictionary alloc]
        initWithCapacity:[self count]];
    NSArray *keys = [self allKeys];
    for (id key in keys) {
        id oneValue = [self valueForKey:key];
        id oneCopy = nil;

        if ([oneValue respondsToSelector:@selector(mutableDeepCopy)])
            oneCopy = [oneValue mutableDeepCopy];
        else if ([oneValue respondsToSelector:@selector(mutableCopy)])
            oneCopy = [oneValue mutableCopy];
        if (oneCopy == nil)
            oneCopy = [oneValue copy];
        [returnDict setValue:oneCopy forKey:key];
        [oneCopy release];
    }
    return returnDict;
}
@end
```

This method creates a new mutable dictionary and then loops through all the keys of the original dictionary, making mutable copies of each array it encounters. Since this method will behave just as if it were part of NSDictionary, any reference to self is a reference to the dictionary that this method is being called on. The method first attempts to make a deep mutable copy, and if the object doesn't respond to the mutableDeepCopy message, it tries to make a mutable copy. If the object doesn't respond to the mutableCopy message, it falls back on making a regular copy to ensure that all the objects contained in the dictionary are copied. By doing it this way, if we were to have a dictionary containing dictionaries (or other objects that supported deep mutable copies), the contained ones would also get deep copied.

For a few of you, this might be the first time you've seen this syntax in Objective-C:

```
for (id key in keys)
```

Objective-C 2.0 introduced a feature called fast enumeration. **Fast enumeration** is a language-level replacement for NSEnumerator. It allows you to quickly iterate through a collection, such as an NSArray, without the hassle of creating additional objects or loop variables.

All of the delivered Cocoa collection classes, including NSDictionary, NSArray, and NSSet, support fast enumeration, and you should use this syntax any time you need to iterate over a collection. It will ensure that you get the most efficient loop possible.

You may have noticed that it looks like we have a memory leak here. We allocate and initialize returnDict, but we never release it. That's OK. Because our method has copy in its name, it follows the same memory rules as the copyWithZone: method, which are supposed to return an object with a retain count of 1. On the other hand, you may have noticed that we're releasing every copy we create, and wonder if we are perhaps overreleasing these new objects. In fact, we're releasing each copied object only after adding it to returnDict, which by contract is the one and only object that our method should refrain from releasing.

If we include the *NSDictionary-MutableDeepCopy.h* header file in one of our other classes, we'll be able to call mutableDeepCopy on any NSDictionary object we like. Let's take advantage of that now.

Updating the Controller Header File

Next, we need to add some outlets to our controller class header file. We'll add an outlet for the table view. Up until now, we haven't needed a pointer to the table view outside the data source methods. We need one for our search bar implementation, since we'll tell the table to reload itself based on the result of the search.

We're also going to add an outlet to a search bar, which is a control used for, well, searching.

In addition to those two outlets, we'll add another dictionary. The existing dictionary and array are both immutable objects, and we need to change both of them to the corresponding mutable version, so the NSArray becomes an NSMutableArray and the NSDictionary becomes an NSMutableDictionary.

We won't need any new action methods in our controller, but we will use a couple of new methods. For now, just declare them, and we'll talk about them in detail after you enter the code.

We also must conform our class to the UISearchBarDelegate protocol. We'll need to become the search bar's delegate in addition to being the table view's delegate.

Make the following changes to *SectionsViewController.h*:

```
#import <UIKit/UIKit.h>

@interface SectionsViewController : UIViewController
<UITableViewDataSource, UITableViewDelegate, UISearchBarDelegate>
{
    UITableView *table;
    UISearchBar *search;
    NSDictionary *allNames;
    NSMutableDictionary *names;
    NSMutableArray *keys;
    NSDictionary *names;
}
```

```
    NSArray *keys;
}
@property (nonatomic, retain) NSDictionary *names;
@property (nonatomic, retain) NSArray *keys;
@property (nonatomic, retain) IBOutlet UITableView *table;
@property (nonatomic, retain) IBOutlet UISearchBar *search;
@property (nonatomic, retain) NSDictionary *allNames;
@property (nonatomic, retain) NSMutableDictionary *names;
@property (nonatomic, retain) NSMutableArray *keys;
- (void)resetSearch;
- (void)handleSearchForTerm:(NSString *)searchTerm;
@end
```

Here's what we just did:

- The outlet table will point to our table view.

- The outlet search will point to the search bar.

- The dictionary allNames will hold the full dataset.

- The dictionary names will hold the dataset that matches the current search criteria.

- keys will hold the index values and section names.

If you're clear on everything, let's forge ahead and modify our view.

Modifying the View

Double click *SectionsViewController.xib* to edit the file in Xcode's Interface Builder. Next, grab a *Search Bar* from the library, and add it to the top of the table view.

You're trying to drop the search bar into the table view's header section, a special part of the table view that lies before the first section. The way to do this is to place the search bar at the top of the view. Before you release the mouse button, you should see a rounded, blue rectangle at the top of the view (see Figure 8–26). That's your indication that if you drop the search bar now, it will go into the table header. Let go of the mouse button to drop the search bar once you see that blue rectangle.

Figure 8–26. *Dropping a Search Bar onto the table view. Notice the rounded rectangle that appears at the top of the table view, indicating that the search bar will be added to the table's header.*

Now, control-drag from the *File's Owner* icon to the table view, and select the *table* outlet. Repeat with the search bar, and select the *search* outlet.

Single-click the search bar, and go to the attributes inspector by pressing ⌘**1**. It should look like Figure 8–27.

Figure 8–27. *The attributes inspector for the search bar*

Type *search* in the *Placeholder* field. The word *search* will appear, very lightly, in the search field.

A bit further down you'll find a series of check boxes for adding a search results button or a bookmarks button at the far-right end of the search bar. These buttons don't do anything on their own (except toggle when the user taps them), but you could use them to let the delegate set up some different display content depending on the status of the toggle buttons.

Leave those unchecked, but do check the box that says *Shows Cancel Button*. A *Cancel* button will appear to the right of the search field. The user can tap this button to cancel the search. The final check box is for enabling the scope bar, which is a series of connected buttons, meant to let the user pick from various categories of searchable things (as specified by the series of *Scope Titles* beneath it). We're not going to use the scope functionality, so just leave those parts alone.

Below the check boxes and *Scope Titles*, set the *Correction* popup menu to *No* to indicate that the search bar should not try to correct the user's spelling.

Switch to the connections inspector by pressing ⌘2, and drag from the *delegate* connection to the *File's Owner* icon to tell this search bar that our view controller is also the search bar's delegate.

That should be everything we need here, so make sure to save your work before returning to Xcode. Now, let's dig into some code.

Modifying the Controller Implementation

The changes to accommodate the search bar are fairly drastic. Make the following changes to *SectionsViewController.m*:

```
#import "SectionsViewController.h"
#import "NSDictionary-MutableDeepCopy.h"

@implementation SectionsViewController
@synthesize names;
@synthesize keys;
@synthesize table;
@synthesize search;
@synthesize allNames;

#pragma mark -
#pragma mark Custom Methods
- (void)resetSearch {
    NSMutableDictionary *allNamesCopy = [self.allNames mutableDeepCopy];
    self.names = allNamesCopy;
    [allNamesCopy release];
    NSMutableArray *keyArray = [[NSMutableArray alloc] init];
    [keyArray addObjectsFromArray:[[self.allNames allKeys]
            sortedArrayUsingSelector:@selector(compare:)]];
    self.keys = keyArray;
    [keyArray release];
}

- (void)handleSearchForTerm:(NSString *)searchTerm {
    NSMutableArray *sectionsToRemove = [[NSMutableArray alloc] init];
    [self resetSearch];

    for (NSString *key in self.keys) {
        NSMutableArray *array = [names valueForKey:key];
        NSMutableArray *toRemove = [[NSMutableArray alloc] init];
        for (NSString *name in array) {
            if ([name rangeOfString:searchTerm
                options:NSCaseInsensitiveSearch].location == NSNotFound)
                [toRemove addObject:name];
        }
        if ([array count] == [toRemove count])
            [sectionsToRemove addObject:key];

        [array removeObjectsInArray:toRemove];
        [toRemove release];
    }
    [self.keys removeObjectsInArray:sectionsToRemove];
    [sectionsToRemove release];
    [table reloadData];
}
```

```objc
- (void)viewDidLoad {
    NSString *path = [[NSBundle mainBundle] pathForResource:@"sortednames"
        ofType:@"plist"];
    NSDictionary *dict = [[NSDictionary alloc]
        initWithContentsOfFile:path];
    self.names = dict;
    self.allNames = dict;

    [dict release];

    NSArray *array = [[names allKeys] sortedArrayUsingSelector:
        @selector(compare:)];
    self.keys = array;

    [self resetSearch];
    [table reloadData];
    [table setContentOffset:CGPointMake(0.0, 44.0) animated:NO];
}

- (void)didReceiveMemoryWarning {;
    [super didReceiveMemoryWarning];
    // Releases the view if it doesn't have a superview
    // Release anything that's not essential, such as cached data
}

- (void)viewDidUnload {
    // Release any retained subviews of the main view.
    // e.g. self.myOutlet = nil;
    self.table = nil;
    self.search = nil;
    self.allNames = nil;
    self.names = nil;
    self.keys = nil;
    [super viewDidUnload];
}

- (void)dealloc {
    [table release];
    [search release];
    [allNames release];
    [names release];
    [keys release];

    [super dealloc];
}
#pragma mark -
#pragma mark Table View Data Source Methods
- (NSInteger)numberOfSectionsInTableView:(UITableView *)tableView {
    return [keys count];
    return ([keys count] > 0) ? [keys count] : 1;
}

- (NSInteger)tableView:(UITableView *)aTableView
        numberOfRowsInSection:(NSInteger)section {
    if ([keys count] == 0)
        return 0;
```

```
        NSString *key = [keys objectAtIndex:section];
        NSArray *nameSection = [names objectForKey:key];
        return [nameSection count];
}

- (UITableViewCell *)tableView:(UITableView *)aTableView
        cellForRowAtIndexPath:(NSIndexPath *)indexPath {
    NSUInteger section = [indexPath section];
    NSUInteger row = [indexPath row];

    NSString *key = [keys objectAtIndex:section];
    NSArray *nameSection = [names objectForKey:key];

    static NSString *sectionsTableIdentifier = @"sectionsTableIdentifier";

    UITableViewCell *cell = [aTableView dequeueReusableCellWithIdentifier:
        sectionsTableIdentifier];
    if (cell == nil) {
        cell = [[[UITableViewCell alloc] initWithFrame:CGRectZero
            reuseIdentifier: sectionsTableIdentifier] autorelease];
    }

    cell.text = [nameSection objectAtIndex:row];
    return cell;
}

- (NSString *)tableView:(UITableView *)tableView
    titleForHeaderInSection:(NSInteger)section {
    if ([keys count] == 0)
        return nil;

    NSString *key = [keys objectAtIndex:section];
    return key;
}

- (NSArray *)sectionIndexTitlesForTableView:(UITableView *)tableView {
    return keys;
}

#pragma mark -
#pragma mark Table View Delegate Methods
- (NSIndexPath *)tableView:(UITableView *)tableView
    willSelectRowAtIndexPath:(NSIndexPath *)indexPath {
    [search resignFirstResponder];
    return indexPath;
}

#pragma mark -
#pragma mark Search Bar Delegate Methods
- (void)searchBarSearchButtonClicked:(UISearchBar *)searchBar {
    NSString *searchTerm = [searchBar text];
    [self handleSearchForTerm:searchTerm];
}

- (void)searchBar:(UISearchBar *)searchBar
    textDidChange:(NSString *)searchTerm {
```

```
        if ([searchTerm length] == 0) {
            [self resetSearch];
            [table reloadData];
            return;
        }
        [self handleSearchForTerm:searchTerm];
    }

    - (void)searchBarCancelButtonClicked:(UISearchBar *)searchBar {
        search.text = @"";
        [self resetSearch];
        [table reloadData];
        [searchBar resignFirstResponder];
    }
    @end
```

Wow, are you still with us after all that typing? Let's break it down and see what we just did. We'll start with the first new method we added.

Copying Data from allNames

Our new resetSearch method will be called any time the search is canceled or the search term changes.

```
- (void)resetSearch {
    self.names = [self.allNames mutableDeepCopy];
    NSMutableArray *keyArray = [[NSMutableArray alloc] init];
    [keyArray addObjectsFromArray:[[self.allNames allKeys]
            sortedArrayUsingSelector:@selector(compare:)]];
    self.keys = keyArray;
    [keyArray release];
}
```

All this method does is create a mutable copy of allNames, assign it to names, and then refresh the keys array so it includes all the letters of the alphabet.

We need to refresh the keys array because if a search eliminates all values from a section, we need to get rid of that section, too. Otherwise, the screen would be filled up with headers and empty sections, and it wouldn't look good. We also don't want to provide an index to something that doesn't exist, so as we cull the names based on the search terms, we also cull the empty sections.

Implementing the Search

The other new method we added is the actual search.

```
- (void)handleSearchForTerm:(NSString *)searchTerm {
    NSMutableArray *sectionsToRemove = [[NSMutableArray alloc] init];
    [self resetSearch];

    for (NSString *key in self.keys) {
        NSMutableArray *array = [names valueForKey:key];
        NSMutableArray *toRemove = [[NSMutableArray alloc] init];
```

```
        for (NSString *name in array) {
            if ([name rangeOfString:searchTerm
                options:NSCaseInsensitiveSearch].location == NSNotFound)
                    [toRemove addObject:name];
        }

        if ([array count] == [toRemove count])
            [sectionsToRemove addObject:key];

        [array removeObjectsInArray:toRemove];
        [toRemove release];
    }
    [self.keys removeObjectsInArray:sectionsToRemove];
    [sectionsToRemove release];
    [table reloadData];
}
```

Although we'll kick off the search in the search bar delegate methods, we pulled handleSearchForTerm: into its own method, since we're going to need to use the exact same functionality in two different delegate methods. By embedding the search in the handleSearchForTerm: method, we consolidate the functionality into a single place so it's easier to maintain, and then we just call this new method as required.

Since this is the real meat (or tofu, if you prefer) of this section, let's break this method down into smaller chunks.

First, we create an array that's going to hold the empty sections as we find them. We use this array to remove those empty sections later, because it is not safe to remove objects from a collection while iterating that collection. Since we are using fast enumeration, attempting to do that will raise an exception. So, since we won't be able to remove keys while we're iterating through them, we store the sections to be removed in an array, and after we're finished enumerating, we remove all the objects at once. After allocating the array, we reset the search.

```
NSMutableArray *sectionsToRemove = [[NSMutableArray alloc] init];
[self resetSearch];
```

Next, we enumerate through all the keys in the newly restored keys array.

```
for (NSString *key in self.keys) {
```

Each time through the loop, we grab the array of names that corresponds to the current key and create another array to hold the values we need to remove from the names array. Remember that we're removing names and sections, so we must keep track of which keys are empty as well as which names don't match the search criteria.

```
NSMutableArray *array = [names valueForKey:key];
NSMutableArray *toRemove = [[NSMutableArray alloc] init];
```

Next, we iterate through all the names in the current array. So, if we're currently working through the key of *A*, this loop will enumerate through all the names that begin with *A*.

```
for (NSString *name in array) {
```

Inside this loop, we use one of NSString's methods that returns the location of a substring within a string. We specify an option of NSCaseInsensitiveSearch to tell it we don't care about the search term's case—in other words, *A* is the same as *a*. The value returned by this method is an NSRange struct with two members: location and length. If the search term was not found, the location will be set to NSNotFound, so we just check for that. If the NSRange that is returned contains NSNotFound, we add the name to the array of objects to be removed later.

```
    if ([name rangeOfString:searchTerm
        options:NSCaseInsensitiveSearch].location == NSNotFound)
            [toRemove addObject:name];
}
```

After we've looped through all the names for a given letter, we check to see whether the array of names to be removed is the same length as the array of names. If it is, we know this section is now empty, and we add it to the array of keys to be removed later.

```
    if ([array count] == [toRemove count])
        [sectionsToRemove addObject:key];
```

Next, we actually remove the nonmatching names from this section's arrays, and then release the array we used to keep track of the names. It's important to avoid using convenience methods inside loops like this as much as possible, because they will put something into the autorelease pool every time through the loop. However, the autorelease pool can't be flushed until we're all done with our loop.

```
        [array removeObjectsInArray:toRemove];
        [toRemove release];
}
```

Finally, we remove the empty sections, release the array used to keep track of the empty sections, and tell the table to reload its data.

```
    [self.keys removeObjectsInArray:sectionsToRemove];
    [sectionsToRemove release];
    [table reloadData];
}
```

Changes to viewDidLoad

Down in viewDidLoad, we made a few changes. First, we now load the property list into the allNames dictionary instead of the names dictionary and delete the code that loads the keys array, because that is now done in the resetSearch method. We then call the resetSearch method, which populates the names mutable dictionary and the keys array for us. After that, we call reloadData on our tableView. In the normal flow of the program, reloadData will be called before the user ever sees the table, so most of the time it's not necessary to call it in viewDidLoad:. However, in order for the line after it, setContentOffset:animated:, to work, we need to make sure that the table is all set up before we do that, which we do by calling reloadData on the table.

```
    [table reloadData];
    [table setContentOffset:CGPointMake(0.0, 44.0) animated:NO];
```

So, what does setContentOffset:animated: do? Well, it does exactly what it sounds like. It offsets the contents of the table—in our case, by 44 pixels, the height of the search bar. This causes the search bar to be scrolled off the top when the table first comes up. In effect, we are "hiding" the search bar up there at the top, to be discovered by users the first time they scroll all the way up. This is similar to the way that Mail, Contacts, and other standard iOS applications support searching. Users don't see the search bar at first, but can bring it into view with a simple downward swipe.

Hiding the search bar bears a certain risk that the user might not discover the search functionality at first, or perhaps not at all! However, this is a risk shared among a wide variety of iOS apps, and this usage of the search bar is now so common that there's no real reason to show anything more explicit. We'll talk more about this in the "Adding a Magnifying Glass to the Index" section, coming up soon.

Changes to Data Source Methods

If you skip down to the data source methods, you'll see we made a few minor changes there. Because the names dictionary and keys array are still being used to feed the data source, these methods are basically the same as they were before.

We did need to account for the fact that table views always have a minimum of one section, and yet the search could potentially exclude all names from all sections. So, we added a little code to check for the situation where all sections were removed. In those cases, we feed the table view a single section with no rows and a blank name. This avoids any problems and doesn't give any incorrect feedback to the user.

Adding a Table View Delegate Method

Below the data source methods, we've added a single delegate method. If the user clicks a row while using the search bar, we want the keyboard to go away. We accomplish this by implementing tableView:willSelectRowAtIndexPath: and telling the search bar to resign first responder status, which will cause the keyboard to retract. Next, we return indexPath unchanged.

```
- (NSIndexPath *)tableView:(UITableView *)tableView
    willSelectRowAtIndexPath:(NSIndexPath *)indexPath {
    [search resignFirstResponder];
    return indexPath;
}
```

We could also have done this in tableView:didSelectRowAtIndexPath:, but because we're doing it here, the keyboard retracts a bit sooner.

Adding Search Bar Delegate Methods

The search bar has a number of methods that it calls on its delegate. When the user taps return or the search key on the keyboard, searchBarSearchButtonClicked: will be called. Our version of this method grabs the search term from the search bar and calls our search method, which will remove the nonmatching names from names and the empty sections from keys.

```
- (void)searchBarSearchButtonClicked:(UISearchBar *)searchBar {
    NSString *searchTerm = [searchBar text];
    [self handleSearchForTerm:searchTerm];
}
```

The `searchBarSearchButtonClicked:` method should be implemented any time you use a search bar.

We also implement another search bar delegate method, which requires a bit of caution. This next method implements a live search. Every time the search term changes, regardless of whether the user has selected the search button or tapped return, we redo the search. This behavior is very user-friendly, as the users can see the results change while typing. If users pare the list down far enough on the third character, they can stop typing and select the row they want.

You can easily hamstring the performance of your application implementing live search, especially if you're displaying images or have a complex data model. In this case, with 2,000 strings and no images or accessory icons, things actually work pretty well, even on a first-generation iPhone or iPod touch.

> **CAUTION:** Do not assume that snappy performance in the simulator translates to snappy performance on your device. If you're going to implement a live search like this, you need to test extensively on actual hardware to make sure your application stays responsive. When in doubt, don't use it. Your users will likely be perfectly happy tapping the search button.

To handle a live search, implement the search bar delegate method `searchBar:textDidChange:` like so:

```
- (void)searchBar:(UISearchBar *)searchBar
    textDidChange:(NSString *)searchTerm {
    if ([searchTerm length] == 0) {
        [self resetSearch];
        [table reloadData];
        return;
    }
    [self handleSearchForTerm:searchTerm];
}
```

Notice that we check for an empty string. If the string is empty, we know all names are going to match it, so we simply reset the search and reload the data, without bothering to enumerate over all the names.

Last, we implement a method that allows us to be notified when the user clicks the *Cancel* button on the search bar.

```
- (void)searchBarCancelButtonClicked:(UISearchBar *)searchBar {
    search.text = @"";
    [self resetSearch];
    [table reloadData];
    [searchBar resignFirstResponder];
}
```

When the user clicks *Cancel*, we set the search term to an empty string, reset the search, and reload the data so that all names are showing. We also tell the search bar to yield first responder status, so that the keyboard drops away and the user can resume working with the table view.

If you haven't done so already, fire it up and try out the search functionality. Remember that the search bar is scrolled just off the top of the screen, so drag down to bring it into view. Click in the search field and start typing. The name list should trim to match the text you type. It works, right?

But one thing isn't quite right: the index is overlapping the *Cancel* button (see Figure 8–28).

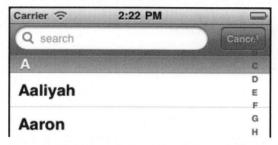

Figure 8–28. *In the current version of our application, the search bar's Cancel button is overlapped by the index.*

It's a subtle thing, but iPhone users often notice subtle things. How do Apple developers deal with this problem in the Contacts application? They make the index disappear when you tap the search bar. We may not be able to duplicate the Contacts approach exactly, but we can come pretty close without too much trouble.

First, let's add an instance variable to keep track of whether the user is currently using the search bar. Add the following to *SectionsViewController.h*:

```
@interface SectionsViewController : UIViewController
<UITableViewDataSource, UITableViewDelegate, UISearchBarDelegate>
{
    UITableView *table;
    UISearchBar *search;
    NSDictionary *allNames;
    NSMutableDictionary *names;
    NSMutableArray *keys;

    BOOL    isSearching;
}
@property (nonatomic, retain) IBOutlet UITableView *table;
@property (nonatomic, retain) IBOutlet UISearchBar *search;
@property (nonatomic, retain) NSDictionary *allNames;
@property (nonatomic, retain) NSMutableDictionary *names;
@property (nonatomic, retain) NSMutableArray *keys;
- (void)resetSearch;
- (void)handleSearchForTerm:(NSString *)searchTerm;
@end
```

Save the file, and let's shift our attention to *SectionsViewController.m*. First, we need to modify the `sectionIndexTitlesForTableView:` method to return `nil` if the user is searching:

```
- (NSArray *)sectionIndexTitlesForTableView:(UITableView *)tableView {
    if (isSearching)
        return nil;
    return keys;
}
```

We need to implement a new delegate method to set `isSearching` to `YES` when searching begins. Add the following method to the search bar delegate methods section of *SectionsViewController.m*:

```
- (void)searchBarTextDidBeginEditing:(UISearchBar *)searchBar {
    isSearching = YES;
    [table reloadData];
}
```

This method is called when the search bar is tapped. In it, we set `isSearching` to `YES`, and then tell the table to reload itself, which causes the index to disappear. We also need to remember to set `isSearching` to `NO` when the user is finished searching. There are two ways that can happen: the user can press the *Cancel* button or tap a row in the table. Therefore, we need to add code to the `searchBarCancelButtonClicked:` method:

```
- (void)searchBarCancelButtonClicked:(UISearchBar *)searchBar {
    isSearching = NO;
    search.text = @"";
    [self resetSearch];
    [table reloadData];
    [searchBar resignFirstResponder];
}
```

We also need to make that change to the `tableView:willSelectRowAtIndexPath:` method:

```
- (NSIndexPath *)tableView:(UITableView *)tableView
  willSelectRowAtIndexPath:(NSIndexPath *)indexPath {
    [search resignFirstResponder];
    isSearching = NO;
    search.text = @"";
    [tableView reloadData];
    return indexPath;
}
```

Now, try it again. You'll see that when you tap the search bar, the index will disappear until you're finished searching.

Adding a Magnifying Glass to the Index

Because we offset the table view's content, the search bar is not visible when the application first launches, but a quick flick down brings the search bar into view so it can be used. It is also acceptable to put a search bar above the table view, rather than in it, so that the bar is always visible, but this eats up valuable screen real estate. Having the search bar scroll with the table uses the iPhone's small screen more efficiently, and the user can always get to the search bar quickly by tapping in the status bar at the top of the screen.

The problem is that not everyone knows that tapping in the status bar takes you to the top of the current table. The ideal solution would be to put a magnifying glass at the top of the index the way that the Contacts application does (see Figure 8–29). And guess what? We can actually do just that. iOS includes the ability to put a magnifying glass in a table index. Let's do that now for our application.

Figure 8–29. *The Contacts application has a magnifying glass icon in the index that takes you to the search bar. Prior to iOS 3, this was not available to other applications, but now it is.*

Only three steps are involved in adding the magnifying glass:

- Add a special value to our keys array to indicate that we want the magnifying glass.

- Prevent iOS from printing a section header in the table for that special value.

- Tell the table to scroll to the top when that item is selected.

Let's tackle these tasks in order.

Adding the Special Value to the Keys Array

To add the special value to our keys array, all we need to do is add one line of code to the resetSearch method:

```
- (void)resetSearch {
    self.names = [self.allNames mutableDeepCopy];
    NSMutableArray *keyArray = [[NSMutableArray alloc] init];
    [keyArray addObject:UITableViewIndexSearch];
    [keyArray addObjectsFromArray:[[self.allNames allKeys]
            sortedArrayUsingSelector:@selector(compare:)]];
    self.keys = keyArray;
    [keyArray release];
}
```

Suppressing the Section Header

Now, we need to suppress that value from coming up as a section title. We do that by adding a check in the existing tableView:titleForHeaderInSection: method, and return nil when it asks for the title for the special search section:

```
- (NSString *)tableView:(UITableView *)tableView
    titleForHeaderInSection:(NSInteger)section {
    if ([keys count] == 0)
        return nil;

    NSString *key = [keys objectAtIndex:section];
    if (key == UITableViewIndexSearch)
        return nil;
    return key;
}
```

Telling the Table View What to Do

Finally, we need to tell the table view what to do when the user taps the magnifying glass in the index. When the user taps the magnifying class, the delegate method tableView:sectionForSectionIndexTitle:atIndex: is called, if it is implemented.

Add this method to the bottom of *SectionsViewController.m*, just above the @end:

```
- (NSInteger)tableView:(UITableView *)tableView
        sectionForSectionIndexTitle:(NSString *)title
        atIndex:(NSInteger)index {
    NSString *key = [keys objectAtIndex:index];
    if (key == UITableViewIndexSearch) {
        [tableView setContentOffset:CGPointZero animated:NO];
        return NSNotFound;
    }
    else return index;
}
```

To tell it to go to the search box, we must do two things. First, we need to get rid of the content offset we added earlier, and then we have to return NSNotFound. When the table view gets this response, it knows to scroll up to the top. So, now that we've removed the offset, it will scroll to the search bar rather than to the top section.

And there you have it—live searching in an iPhone table, with a magnifying glass in the index!

> **TIP:** iOS includes even more cool search stuff. Interested? Go to the documentation browser and do a search for `UISearchDisplay` to read up on `UISearchDisplayController` and `UISearchDisplayDelegate`. You'll likely find this material much easier to understand once you've made your way through Chapter 9.

Putting It All on the Table

Well, how are you doing? This was a pretty hefty chapter, and you've learned a ton! You should have a very solid understanding of the way flat tables work. You should know how to customize tables and table view cells, as well as how to configure table views. You also saw how to implement a search bar, which is a vital tool in any iOS application that presents large volumes of data. Make sure you understand everything we did in this chapter, because we're going to build on it.

We're going to continue working with table views in the next chapter. You'll learn how to use them to present hierarchical data. You'll see how to create content views that allow the user to edit data selected in a table view, as well as how to present checklists in tables, embed controls in table rows, and delete rows.

Chapter 9

Navigation Controllers and Table Views

In the previous chapter, you mastered the basics of working with table views. In this chapter, you'll get a whole lot more practice, because we're going to explore **navigation controllers.**

Table views and navigation controllers work hand in hand. Strictly speaking, a navigation controller doesn't need a table view in order to do its thing. As a practical matter, however, when you implement a navigation controller, you almost always implement at least one table, and usually several, because the strength of the navigation controller lies in the ease with which it handles complex hierarchical data. On the iPhone's small screen, hierarchical data is best presented using a succession of table views.

In this chapter, we're going to build an application progressively, just as we did with the Pickers application back in Chapter 7. We'll get the navigation controller and the first view controller working, and then we'll start adding more controllers and layers to the hierarchy. Each view controller we create will reinforce some aspect of table use or configuration:

- How to drill down from table views into child tables

- How to drill down from table views into content views, where detailed data can be viewed and even edited.

- How to use a table list to allow the user to select from multiple values

- How to use edit mode to allow rows to be deleted from a table view

That's a lot, isn't it? Well, let's get started with an introduction to navigation controllers.

Navigation Controllers

The main tool you'll use to build hierarchical applications is UINavigationController. UINavigationController is similar to UITabBarController in that it manages, and swaps

in and out, multiple content views. The main difference between the two is that
UINavigationController is implemented as a stack, which makes it well suited to
working with hierarchies.

Do you already know everything there is to know about stacks? Scan through the
following subsection, and we'll meet you at the beginning of the next subsection, "A
Stack of Controllers." If you're new to stacks, continue reading. Fortunately, stacks are a
pretty easy concept to grasp.

Stacky Goodness

A **stack** is a commonly used data structure that works on the principle of last in, first out.
Believe it or not, a Pez dispenser is a great example of a stack. Ever try to load one?
According to the little instruction sheet that comes with each and every Pez dispenser,
there are a few easy steps. First, unwrap the pack of Pez candy. Second, open the
dispenser by tipping its head straight back. Third, grab the stack (notice the clever way we
inserted the word "stack" in there!) of candy, holding it firmly between your pointer finger
and thumb, and insert the column into the open dispenser. Fourth, pick up all the little
pieces of candy that flew all over the place because these instructions just never work.

OK, so far this example has not been particularly useful. But what happens next is. As
you pick up the pieces and jam them, one at a time, into the dispenser, you are working
with a stack. Remember that we said a stack was last in, first out? That also means first
in, last out. The first piece of Pez you push into the dispenser will be the last piece that
pops out. The last piece of Pez you push in will be the first piece you pop out. A
computer stack follows the same rules:

- When you add an object to a stack, it's called a **push**. You push an
  object onto the stack.

- The first object you push onto the stack is called the **base** of the
  stack.

- The last object you pushed onto the stack is called the **top** of the
  stack (at least until it is replaced by the next object you push onto the
  stack).

- When you remove an object from the stack, it's called a **pop.** When
  you pop an object off the stack, it's always the last one you pushed
  onto the stack. Conversely, the first object you push onto the stack will
  always be the last one you pop off the stack.

A Stack of Controllers

A navigation controller maintains a stack of view controllers. Any kind of view controller
is fair game for the stack. When you design your navigation controller, you'll need to
specify the very first view the user sees. As we've discussed in previous chapters, that
view is called the **root view controller**, or just **root controller**, and is the base of the

navigation controller's stack of view controllers. As the user selects the next view to display, a new view controller is pushed onto the stack, and the view it controls appears. We refer to these new view controllers as **subcontrollers.** As you'll see, this chapter's application, Nav, is made up of a navigation controller and six subcontrollers.

Take a look at Figure 9–1. Notice the **navigation button** in the upper-left corner of the current view. The navigation button is similar to a web browser's back button. When the user taps that button, the current view controller is popped off the stack, and the previous view becomes the current view.

Navigation Button  Title

Figure 9–1. *The Settings application uses a navigation controller. In the upper left is the navigation button used to pop the current view controller off the stock, returning you to the previous level of the hierarchy. The title of the current content view controller is also displayed.*

We love this design pattern. It allows us to build complex hierarchical applications iteratively. We don't need to know the entire hierarchy to get things up and running. Each controller only needs to know about its child controllers so it can push the appropriate new controller object onto the stack when the user makes a selection. You can build up a large application from many small pieces this way, which is exactly what we're going to do in this chapter.

The navigation controller is really the heart and soul of many iPhone apps, but when it comes to iPad apps, the navigation controller plays a more marginal role. A typical example of this is the Mail app, which features a hierarchical navigation controller to let the user navigate among all their mail servers, folders, and messages. In the iPad version of Mail, the navigation controller never fills the screen, but appears either as a sidebar or a temporary popover window. We'll dig into that usage a little later, when we cover iPad-specific GUI functionality in Chapter 10.

Nav, a Hierarchical Application in Six Parts

The application we're about to build will show you how to do most of the common tasks associated with displaying a hierarchy of data. When the application launches, you'll be presented with a list of options (see Figure 9–2).

Figure 9–2. *This chapter's application's top-level view. Note the accessory icons on the right side of the view. This particular type of accessory icon is called a disclosure indicator. It tells the user that touching that row drills down to another table view.*

Each of the rows in this top-level view represents a different view controller that will be pushed onto the navigation controller's stack when that row is selected. The icons on the right side of each row are called **accessory icons.** This particular accessory icon (the gray arrow) is called a **disclosure indicator**, because it lets the user know that touching that row drills down to another table view.

Meet the Subcontrollers

Before we start building the Nav application, let's take a quick look at each of the views displayed by our six subcontrollers.

The Disclosure Button View

Touching the first row of the table shown in Figure 9–2 will bring up the child view shown in Figure 9–3.

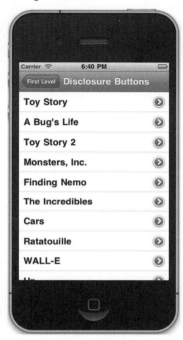

Figure 9–3. *The first of the Nav application's six subcontrollers implement a table in which each row contains a detail disclosure button.*

The accessory icon to the right of each row in Figure 9–3 is a bit different. Each of these icons is known as a **detail disclosure button**. Tapping on the detail disclosure button should allow the user to view, and perhaps edit, more detailed information about the current row.

Unlike the disclosure indicator, the detail disclosure button is not just an icon—it's a control that the user can tap. This means that you can have two different options available for a given row: one action triggered when the user selects the row and another action triggered when the user taps the disclosure button.

A good example of the proper use of the detail disclosure button is found in the iPhone's Phone application. Selecting a person's row from the *Favorites* tab places a call to the person whose row you touched, but selecting the disclosure button next to a name takes you to detailed contact information. The YouTube application offers another great example. Selecting a row plays a video, but tapping the detail disclosure button takes you to more detailed information about the video. In the Contacts application, the list of contacts does not feature detail disclosure buttons, even though selecting a row does take you to a detail view. Since there is only one option available for each row in the Contacts application, no accessory icon is displayed.

Here's a recap of when to use disclosure indicators and detail disclosure buttons:

- If you want to offer a single choice for a row tap, don't use an accessory icon if a row tap will *only* lead to a more detailed view of that row.

- Mark the row with a disclosure indicator (gray arrow) if a row tap will lead to a new view (*not* a detail view).

- If you want to offer two choices for a row, mark the row with a detail disclosure button. This allows the user to tap on the row for a new view or the disclosure button for more details.

The Checklist View

The second of our application's six subcontrollers is shown in Figure 9–4. This is the view that appears when you select *Check One* in Figure 9–2.

Figure 9–4. *The second of the Nav application's six subcontrollers allows you to select one row from many.*

This view comes in handy when you want to present a list from which only one item can be selected. This approach is to iOS what radio buttons are to Mac OS X. These lists use a check mark to mark the currently selected row.

The Rows Control View

The third of our application's six subcontrollers is shown in Figure 9–5. This view features a tappable button in each row's **accessory view.** The accessory view is the far-right part of the table view cell that usually holds the accessory icon, but it can be used for other things. When we get to this part of our application, you'll see how to create controls in the accessory view.

Figure 9–5. *The third of the Nav application's six subcontrollers adds a button to the accessory view of each table view cell.*

The Movable Rows View

The fourth of our application's six subcontrollers is shown in Figure 9–6. In this view, we'll let the user rearrange the order of the rows in a list by having the table enter **edit mode** (more on this when we get to it in code later in this chapter).

Figure 9–6. *The fourth of the Nav application's six subcontrollers lets the user rearrange rows in a list by touching and dragging the move icon.*

The Deletable Rows View

The fifth of our application's six subcontrollers is shown in Figure 9–7. In this view, we're going to demonstrate another use of edit mode by allowing the user to delete rows from our table.

Figure 9–7. *The fifth of the Nav application's six subcontrollers implements edit mode to allow the user to delete items from the table.*

The Editable Detail View

The sixth and last of our application's six subcontrollers is shown in Figure 9–8. It shows an editable detail view using a grouped table. This technique for detail views is used widely by the applications that ship on the iPhone.

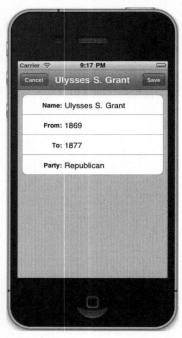

Figure 9–8. *The sixth and last of the Nav application's six subcontrollers implements an editable detail view using a grouped table.*

We have so very much to do. Let's get started!

The Nav Application's Skeleton

Xcode offers a perfectly good template for creating navigation-based applications, and you will likely use it much of the time when you need to create hierarchical applications. However, we're not going to use that template today. Instead, we'll construct our navigation-based application from the ground up so you get a feel for how everything fits together. It's not really much different from the way we built the tab bar controller in Chapter 7, so you shouldn't have any problems keeping up.

In Xcode, press ⌘⇧N to create a new project, and select *Window-based Application* from the iOS *Application* template list, making sure that *Use Core Data for storage* for storage is *not* checked, and that *Product* is set to *iPhone*. Give your new project the name *Nav*.

As you'll see if you click the *Classes* and *Resources* folders, this template gives you an application delegate, a *MainWindow.xib,* and not much else. At this point, there are no view controllers or navigation controllers.

To make this app run, we'll need to add a navigation controller, which includes a navigation bar. We'll also need to add a series of views and view controllers for the navigation bar to show. The first of these views is the top-level view shown in Figure 9–2.

Each row in that top-level view is tied to a child view controller, as shown in Figures 9–3 through 9–8. Don't worry about the specifics. You'll see how those connections work as you make your way through the chapter.

Creating the Top-Level View Controller

In this chapter, we're going to subclass `UITableViewController` instead of `UIViewController` for our table views. When we subclass `UITableViewController`, we inherit some nice functionality from that class that will create a table view with no need for a nib file. We can provide a table view in a nib, as we did in the previous chapter, but if we don't, `UITableViewController` will create a table view automatically. This table view will take up the entire space available and will connect the appropriate outlets in our controller class, making our controller class the delegate and data source for that table. When all you need for a specific controller is a table, subclassing `UITableViewController` is the way to go.

We'll create one class called `FirstLevelViewController` that represents the first level in the navigation hierarchy. That's the table that contains one row for each of the second-level table views. Those second-level table views will each be represented by the `SecondLevelViewController` class. You'll see how all this works as you make your way through the chapter.

In your project window, select the *Classes* folder in the *Groups & Files* pane, and then press ⌘N or select **File ➤ New File…**. When the new file assistant comes up, select *Cocoa Touch Class*, select *Objective-C class,* and then select *NSObject* from the *Subclass of* popup menu. Click *Next*. Give this file a name of *FirstLevelViewController.m*, and make sure that you check *Also create "FirstLevelViewController.h"*. As always, be sure to check your spelling carefully before you click *Finish*.

You may have noticed an entry named *UITableViewController* in the *Subclass of* popup menu. When creating your own applications, feel free to use that template. We didn't use that template so we wouldn't have to spend time sorting through all the unneeded template methods, working out where to insert or delete code. By creating an `NSObject` subclass and, in its declaration, changing the superclass to `UITableViewController`, we get a smaller, more manageable file.

Once the files have been created, single-click *FirstLevelViewController.h,* and make the following change so `FirstLevelViewController` is a subclass of `UITableViewController`:

```
#import <UIKit/UIKit.h>

@interface FirstLevelViewController : NSObject {
```

```objc
@interface FirstLevelViewController : UITableViewController {

}
@end
```

The two files we just created contain the controller class for the top-level view, as shown in Figure 9–2. Our next step is to set up our navigation controller.

Setting Up the Navigation Controller

Our goal here is to edit the application delegate to add our navigation controller's view to the application window.

Let's start by editing *NavAppDelegate.h* to add an outlet, navController, to point to our navigation controller.

```objc
#import <UIKit/UIKit.h>

@interface NavAppDelegate : NSObject <UIApplicationDelegate> {
    UIWindow *window;
    UINavigationController *navController;
}

@property (nonatomic, retain) IBOutlet UIWindow *window;
@property (nonatomic, retain) IBOutlet UINavigationController
    *navController;
@end
```

Next, we need to hop over to the implementation file and add the @synthesize statement for navController. We'll also add navController's view as a subview of our application's window so that it is shown to the user. Single-click *NavAppDelegate.m*, and make the following changes:

```objc
#import "NavAppDelegate.h"

@implementation NavAppDelegate

@synthesize window;
@synthesize navController;

#pragma mark -
#pragma mark Application lifecycle

- (BOOL)application:(UIApplication *)application
        didFinishLaunchingWithOptions:(NSDictionary *)launchOptions {
    // Override point for customization after application launch

    [self.window addSubview:navController.view];
    [self.window makeKeyAndVisible];

    return YES;
}

...
```

```
- (void)dealloc {
    [window release];
    [navController release];
    [super dealloc];
}
@end
```

Save both of these files.

Next, we need to create a navigation controller, connect it to the navController outlet we just declared, and then tell the navigation controller what to use as its root view controller.

Expand the *Resources* folder in the *Groups & Files* pane if necessary, and then double click *MainWindow.xib* to open that file for editing in Interface Builder. If the window titled *Window* (the one associated with the *Window* icon) is open, close it. There should be nothing open but the main nib window.

Look in the object library for a *Navigation Controller* (see Figure 9–9), and drag one over to the main nib window.

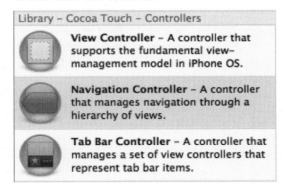

Figure 9–9. *Dragging a Navigation Controller from the library into the nib editing area*

Control-drag from the *Nav App Delegate* icon in the dock to the new *Navigation Controller* icon, and select the *navController* outlet.

We're almost finished, but the next task is a little tricky. We need to tell the navigation controller where to find its root view controller, which will be an instance of the FirstLevelViewController class we created earlier. The easiest way to do that is to change the nib's main window into list mode using the *View Mode* control at the top of the window.

In list mode, click the disclosure triangle to the left of *Navigation Controller* to expand it (see Figure 9–10). Underneath *Navigation Controller*, you'll find two items: *Navigation Bar* and *View Controller (Root View Controller)*.

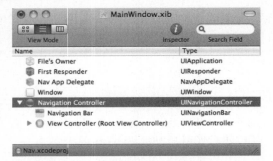

Figure 9–10. *Clicking the disclosure triangle to the left of Navigation Controller reveals Navigation Bar and View Controller items.*

Single-click the *View Controller - Root View Controller* icon, and press ⌘4 to bring up the identity inspector. Change the underlying class to *FirstLevelViewController*, and press return to commit the change. When the nib file loads, the navigation controller will be instantiated, along with a `FirstLevelViewController`.

With the newly renamed *First Level View Controller (Root View Controller)* still selected, switch to the attributes inspector using ⌘1. Notice that the *NIB Name* field is blank. If you specified a nib name here, the `FirstLevelViewController` would load its table view from that nib file. But we'll leave the *NIB Name* field blank, which indicates that the `FirstLevelViewController` will create a UITableView at init time.

Save your changes.

Now, we need a list of rows for our `FirstLevelViewController` to display. In the previous chapter, we used simple arrays of strings to populate our table rows. In this application, the first-level view controller will manage a list of its subcontrollers, which we will be building throughout the chapter.

When we were designing this application, we decided that we wanted our first-level view controller to display an icon to the left of each of its subcontroller names. Instead of adding a `UIImage` property to every subcontroller, we'll create a subclass of `UITableViewController` that has a `UIImage` property to hold the row icon. We will then subclass this new class instead of subclassing `UITableViewController` directly. As a result, all of our subclasses will get that `UIImage` property for free, which will make our code much cleaner.

NOTE: We will never actually create an instance of our new `UITableViewController` subclass. It exists solely to let us add a common item to the rest of the controllers we're going to write. In many languages, we would declare this as an **abstract class,** but Objective-C doesn't include any syntax to support abstract classes. We can make classes that aren't intended to be instantiated, but the Objective-C compiler won't actually prevent us from writing code that creates instances of such a class, the way that the compilers for many other languages might. Objective-C is much more permissive than most other popular languages, and this can be a little hard to get used to.

Single-click the *Classes* folder in Xcode, and then press ⌘**N** to bring up the new file assistant. Select *Cocoa Touch Class* from the left pane, select *Objective-C class,* and select *NSObject* for *Subclass of.* Give the new file the name *SecondLevelViewController.m*. Be sure to create the *.h* file as well. Once the new files are created, select *SecondLevelViewController.h,* and make the following changes:

```
#import <UIKit/UIKit.h>

@interface SecondLevelViewController : NSObject {
@interface SecondLevelViewController : UITableViewController {
    UIImage     *rowImage;
}
@property (nonatomic, retain) UIImage *rowImage;
@end
```

Over in *SecondLevelViewController.m,* add the following line of code:

```
#import "SecondLevelViewController.h"

@implementation SecondLevelViewController
@synthesize rowImage;
@end
```

Any controller class that we want to implement as a second-level controller—in other words, any controller that the user can navigate to directly from the first table shown in our application—should subclass `SecondLevelViewController` instead of `UITableViewController`. Because we're subclassing `SecondLevelViewController`, all of those classes will have a property they can use to store a row image, and we can write our code in `FirstLevelViewController` before we've actually written any concrete second-level controller classes by using `SecondLevelViewController` as a placeholder.

Let's implement our `FirstLevelViewController` class now. Be sure to save the changes you made to `SecondLevelViewController`. Then make these changes to *FirstLevelViewController.h*:

```
#import <UIKit/UIKit.h>

@interface FirstLevelViewController : UITableViewController {
    NSArray *controllers;
}
@property (nonatomic, retain) NSArray *controllers;
@end
```

The array we just added will hold the instances of the second-level view controllers. We'll use it to feed data to our table.

Add the following code to *FirstLevelViewController.m,* and then come on back and gossip with us, 'K?

```objc
#import "FirstLevelViewController.h"
#import "SecondLevelViewController.h"

@implementation FirstLevelViewController
@synthesize controllers;

- (void)viewDidLoad {
    self.title = @"First Level";
    NSMutableArray *array = [[NSMutableArray alloc] init];
    self.controllers = array;
    [array release];
    [super viewDidLoad];
}

- (void)viewDidUnload {
    self.controllers = nil;
    [super viewDidUnload];
}

- (void)dealloc {
    [controllers release];
    [super dealloc];
}

#pragma mark -
#pragma mark Table Data Source Methods
- (NSInteger)tableView:(UITableView *)tableView
 numberOfRowsInSection:(NSInteger)section {
    return [self.controllers count];
}

- (UITableViewCell *)tableView:(UITableView *)tableView
        cellForRowAtIndexPath:(NSIndexPath *)indexPath {

    static NSString *FirstLevelCell= @"FirstLevelCell";
    UITableViewCell *cell = [tableView dequeueReusableCellWithIdentifier:
                        FirstLevelCell];
    if (cell == nil) {
        cell = [[[UITableViewCell alloc]
                initWithStyle:UITableViewCellStyleDefault
                reuseIdentifier: FirstLevelCell] autorelease];
    }
    // Configure the cell
    NSUInteger row = [indexPath row];
    SecondLevelViewController *controller =
        [controllers objectAtIndex:row];
    cell.textLabel.text = controller.title;
    cell.imageView.image = controller.rowImage;
```

```
        cell.accessoryType = UITableViewCellAccessoryDisclosureIndicator;
        return cell;
}

#pragma mark -
#pragma mark Table View Delegate Methods
- (void)tableView:(UITableView *)tableView
        didSelectRowAtIndexPath:(NSIndexPath *)indexPath {
    NSUInteger row = [indexPath row];
    SecondLevelViewController *nextController = [self.controllers
                                                 objectAtIndex:row];
    [self.navigationController pushViewController:nextController
                                        animated:YES];
}

@end
```

First, notice that we've imported that new *SecondLevelViewController.h* header file. Doing that lets us use the SecondLevelViewController class in our code so that the compiler will know about the rowImage property.

Next comes the viewDidLoad method. The first thing we do is set self.title. A navigation controller knows what to display in the title of its navigation bar by asking the currently active controller for its title. Therefore, it's important to set the title for all controller instances in a navigation-based application, so the users know where they are at all times.

We then create a mutable array and assign it to the controllers property we declared earlier. Later, when we're ready to add rows to our table, we will add view controllers to this array, and they will show up in the table automatically. Selecting any row will automatically cause the corresponding controller's view to be presented to the user.

> **TIP:** Did you notice that our controllers property is declared as an NSArray, but that we're creating an NSMutableArray? It's perfectly acceptable to assign a subclass to a property like this. In this case, we use the mutable array in viewDidLoad to make it easier to add new controllers in an iterative fashion, but we leave the property declared as an immutable array as a message to other code that it shouldn't be modifying this array.

The final piece of the viewDidLoad method is the call to [super viewDidLoad]. We do this because we are subclassing UITableViewController. You should always call [super viewDidLoad] when you override the viewDidLoad method, because there's no way to know if your parent class does something important in its own viewDidLoad method.

The tableView:numberOfRowsInSection: method here is identical to ones you've seen in the past. It simply returns the count from our array of controllers. The tableView:cellForRowAtIndexPath: method is also very similar to ones we've written in the past. It gets a dequeued cell, or creates a new one if none exists, and then grabs the controller object from the array corresponding to the row being asked about. It then sets the cell's `textLabel` and `image` properties using the `title` and `rowImage` from that controller.

Notice that we are assuming the object retrieved from the array is an instance of `SecondLevelViewController` and are assigning the controller's `rowImage` property to a `UIImage`. This step will make more sense when we declare and add the first concrete second-level controller to the array, in the next section.

The last method we added is the most important one here, and it's the only functionality that's truly new. You've seen the `tableView:didSelectRowAtIndexPath:` method before—it's the one that is called after a user taps a row. If tapping a row needs to trigger a drill-down, this is how we do it. First, we get the row from `indexPath`.

```
NSUInteger row = [indexPath row];
```

Next, we grab the correct controller from our array that corresponds to that row.

```
SecondLevelViewController *nextController =
    [self.controllers objectAtIndex:row];
```

Then we use our `navigationController` property, which points to our application's navigation controller, to push the next controller—the one we pulled from our array— onto the navigation controller's stack.

```
[self.navigationController pushViewController:nextController
                            animated:YES];
```

That's really all there is to it. Each controller in the hierarchy needs to know only about its children. When a row is selected, the active controller is responsible for getting or creating a new subcontroller, setting its properties if necessary (it's not necessary here), and then pushing that new subcontroller onto the navigation controller's stack. Once you've done that, everything else is handled automatically by the navigation controller.

At this point, the application skeleton is complete. Save all your files, and build and run the app. If all is well, the application should launch, and a navigation bar with the title *First Level* should appear. Since our array is currently empty, no rows will display at this point (see Figure 9–11).

Figure 9–11. *The application skeleton in action*

Now, we're ready to start developing the second-level views. Before we do that, go grab the image icons from the *09 Nav* source code archive directory. A folder called *Images* should have eight *.png* images: six that will act as row images and an additional two that we'll use to make a button look nice later in the chapter. Add the *Images* folder to the *Resources* folder of your Xcode project before proceeding.

First Subcontroller: The Disclosure Button View

Let's implement the first of our second-level view controllers. To do that, we'll need to create a subclass of `SecondLevelViewController`.

Select the *Classes* folder in Xcode, and press ⌘**N** to bring up the new file assistant again. Select *Cocoa Touch Class* in the left pane, and then select *Objective-C class* and *NSObject* for *Subclass of*. Name the file *DisclosureButtonController.m*, and be sure to create the header. This class will manage the table of movie names that will be displayed when the user clicks the *Disclosure Buttons* item from the top-level view (see Figure 9–3).

Creating the Detail View

When the user clicks any movie title, the application will drill down into another view that will report which row was selected. So, we also need to create a detail view for the user to drill down into. Repeat the steps to create another *Objective-C class* file, call it

DisclosureDetailController.m, and be sure to have Xcode create the associated header file.

The detail view will hold just a single label that we can set. It won't be editable; we'll just use it to show how to pass values into a child controller. Because this controller will not be responsible for a table view, we also need a nib file to go along with the controller class. Before we create the nib, let's quickly add the outlet for the label. Make the following changes to *DisclosureDetailController.h*:

```
#import <Foundation/Foundation.h>
#import <UIKit/UIKit.h>

@interface DisclosureDetailController : NSObject {
@interface DisclosureDetailController : UIViewController {
    UILabel    *label;
    NSString   *message;
}
@property (nonatomic, retain) IBOutlet UILabel *label;
@property (nonatomic, copy) NSString *message;
@end
```

First, we replace UIKit with Foundation. This class started out as a subclass of NSObject, which, in theory, could be used in all sorts of programs that need to link against only Foundation, not UIKit (though, in truth, it's hard to imagine an iOS app that doesn't require UIKit). So, we need to change that import.

Why, pray tell, are we adding both a label and a string? Remember the concept of lazy loading? Well, view controllers use lazy loading behind the scenes as well. When we create our controller, it won't load its nib file until it is actually displayed. When the controller is pushed onto the navigation controller's stack, we can't count on there being a label to set. If the nib file has not been loaded, label will just be a pointer set to nil. But it's OK. Instead, we'll set message to the value we want, and in the viewWillAppear: method, we'll set label based on the value in message.

Why are we using viewWillAppear: to do our updating instead of using viewDidLoad, as we've done in the past? The problem is that viewDidLoad is called only the first time the controller's view is loaded. But in our case, we are reusing the DisclosureDetailController's view. No matter which fine Pixar flick you pick, when you tap the disclosure button, the detail message appears in the same DisclosureDetailController view. If we used viewDidLoad to manage our updates, that view would be updated only the very first time the DisclosureDetailController view appeared. When we picked our second fine Pixar flick, we would still see the detail message from the first fine Pixar flick (try saying that ten times fast)—not good. Since viewWillAppear: is called every time a view is about to be drawn, we'll be fine using it for our updating.

Going back to the property declarations, you may notice that the message property is declared using the copy keyword instead of retain. What's up with that? Why should we be copying strings willy-nilly? The reason is the potential existence of mutable strings.

Imagine we had declared the property using `retain`, and an outside piece of code passed in an instance of `NSMutableString` to set the value of the `message` property. If that original caller later decides to change the content of that string, the `DisclosureDetailController` instance will end up in an inconsistent state, where the value of `message` and the value displayed in the text field aren't the same! Using `copy` eliminates that risk, since calling `copy` on any `NSString` (including subclasses that are mutable) always gives us an immutable copy. Also, we don't need to worry about the performance impact too much. As it turns out, sending `copy` to any immutable string instance doesn't actually copy the string. Instead, it returns the same string object, after increasing its reference count. In effect, calling `copy` on an immutable string is the same as calling `retain`, which works out just fine for everyone, since the object can never change.

Add the following code to *DisclosureDetailController.m*:

```
#import "DisclosureDetailController.h"

@implementation DisclosureDetailController
@synthesize label;
@synthesize message;

- (void)viewWillAppear:(BOOL)animated {
    label.text = message;
    [super viewWillAppear:animated];
}

- (void)viewDidUnload {
    self.label = nil;
    self.message = nil;
    [super viewDidUnload];
}

- (void)dealloc {
    [label release];
    [message release];
    [super dealloc];
}

@end
```

That's all pretty straightforward, right? Now, let's create the nib to go along with this source code. Be sure you've saved your source changes.

Select the *Resources* folder in the *Groups & Files* pane, and press ⌘N to create another new file. This time, select *User Interface* from the *iOS* section on the left pane, *View XIB* from the upper right, and a *Product* of *iPhone*. Give this nib file the name *DisclosureDetail.xib*. This file will implement the view seen when the user taps on one of the movie buttons.

Double click *DisclosureDetail.xib* in the *Groups & Files* pane to open the file for editing. Once it's open, single-click *File's Owner*, and press ⌘4 to bring up the identity inspector. Change the underlying class to *DisclosureDetailController*. Now control-drag from the *File's Owner* icon to the *View* icon, and select the *view* outlet to establish a link from the controller to its view.

Double click the *View* icon to open the editor. Drag a *Label* from the library, and place it on the *View* window. Towards the middle of the view is fine. Resize it so that it takes up most of the width of the view, using the blue guidelines to place it correctly, and then use the attributes inspector (⌘1) to change the text alignment to centered. Control-drag from *File's Owner* to the label, and select the *label* outlet. Then save your changes and head on over to Xcode.

Modifying the Disclosure Button Controller

For this example, our table of movies will base its data on rows from an array, so we will declare an NSArray named list to serve that purpose. We also need to declare an instance variable to hold one instance of our child controller, which will point to an instance of the DisclosureDetailController class we just built. We could allocate a new instance of that controller class every time the user taps a detail disclosure button, but it's more efficient to create one and then keep reusing it. Make the following changes to *DisclosureButtonController.h*:

```
#import <Foundation/Foundation.h>
#import <UIKit/UIKit.h>
#import "SecondLevelViewController.h"
@class DisclosureDetailController;

@interface DisclosureButtonController : NSObject {
@interface DisclosureButtonController : SecondLevelViewController {
    NSArray     *list;
    DisclosureDetailController *childController;
}
@property (nonatomic, retain) NSArray *list;
@end
```

Notice that we didn't declare a property for the childController. We are using this instance variable internally in our class and don't want to expose it to others, so we don't advertise its existence by declaring a property.

Now we get to the juicy part. Add the following code to *DisclosureButtonController.m*. We'll talk about what's going on afterward.

```
#import "DisclosureButtonController.h"
#import "NavAppDelegate.h"
#import "DisclosureDetailController.h"

@implementation DisclosureButtonController
@synthesize list;

- (void)viewDidLoad {
    NSArray *array = [[NSArray alloc] initWithObjects:@"Toy Story",
                      @"A Bug's Life", @"Toy Story 2", @"Monsters, Inc.",
                      @"Finding Nemo", @"The Incredibles", @"Cars",
                      @"Ratatouille", @"WALL-E", @"Up", @"Toy Story 3",
```

```objc
                         @"Cars 2", @"Brave", nil];
    self.list = array;
    [array release];
    [super viewDidLoad];
}

- (void)viewDidUnload {
    self.list = nil;
    [childController release], childController = nil;
}

- (void)dealloc {
    [list release];
    [childController release];
    [super dealloc];
}

#pragma mark -
#pragma mark Table Data Source Methods
- (NSInteger)tableView:(UITableView *)tableView
 numberOfRowsInSection:(NSInteger)section {
    return [list count];
}

- (UITableViewCell *)tableView:(UITableView *)tableView
        cellForRowAtIndexPath:(NSIndexPath *)indexPath {

    static NSString * DisclosureButtonCellIdentifier =
        @"DisclosureButtonCellIdentifier";

    UITableViewCell *cell = [tableView dequeueReusableCellWithIdentifier:
                            DisclosureButtonCellIdentifier];
    if (cell == nil) {
        cell = [[[UITableViewCell alloc]
            initWithStyle:UITableViewCellStyleDefault
            reuseIdentifier:DisclosureButtonCellIdentifier] autorelease];
    }
    NSUInteger row = [indexPath row];
    NSString *rowString = [list objectAtIndex:row];
    cell.textLabel.text = rowString;
    cell.accessoryType = UITableViewCellAccessoryDetailDisclosureButton;
    [rowString release];
    return cell;
}

#pragma mark -
#pragma mark Table Delegate Methods
- (void)tableView:(UITableView *)tableView
didSelectRowAtIndexPath:(NSIndexPath *)indexPath {
    UIAlertView *alert = [[UIAlertView alloc] initWithTitle:
            @"Hey, do you see the disclosure button?"
            message:@"If you're trying to drill down, touch that instead"
            delegate:nil
```

```
            cancelButtonTitle:@"Won't happen again"
            otherButtonTitles:nil];
    [alert show];
    [alert release];
}
- (void)tableView:(UITableView *)tableView

        accessoryButtonTappedForRowWithIndexPath:(NSIndexPath *)indexPath {
    if (childController == nil) {
        childController = [[DisclosureDetailController alloc]
                            initWithNibName:@"DisclosureDetail" bundle:nil];
    }
    childController.title = @"Disclosure Button Pressed";
    NSUInteger row = [indexPath row];
    NSString *selectedMovie = [list objectAtIndex:row];
    NSString *detailMessage = [[NSString alloc]
            initWithFormat:@"You pressed the disclosure button for %@.",
            selectedMovie];
    childController.message = detailMessage;
    childController.title = selectedMovie;
    [detailMessage release];
    [self.navigationController pushViewController:childController
                                        animated:YES];

}

@end
```

By now, you should be fairly comfortable with everything up to and including the three data source methods we just added. Let's look at our two new delegate methods.

The first method, `tableView:didSelectRowAtIndexPath:`, is called when the row is selected. It puts up a polite little alert telling the user to tap the disclosure button instead of selecting the row. If the user actually taps the detail disclosure button, the other one of our new delegate methods, `tableView:accessoryButtonTappedForRowWithIndexPath:`, is called.

The first thing we do in `tableView:accessoryButtonTappedForRowWithIndexPath:` is check the `childController` instance variable to see if it's `nil`. If it is, we have not yet allocated and initialized a new instance of `DetailDisclosureController`, so we do that next.

```
    if (childController == nil)
        childController = [[DisclosureDetailController alloc]
                            initWithNibName:@"DisclosureDetail" bundle:nil];
```

This gives us a new controller that we can push onto the navigation stack, just as we did earlier in `FirstLevelViewController`. Before we push it onto the stack, though, we need to give it some text to display.

```
    childController.title = @"Disclosure Button Pressed";
```

In this case, we set `message` to reflect the row whose disclosure button was tapped. We also set the new view's title based on the selected row.

```
    NSUInteger row = [indexPath row];
```

```
NSString *selectedMovie = [list objectAtIndex:row];
NSString *detailMessage = [[NSString alloc]
        initWithFormat:@"You pressed the disclosure button for %@.",
        selectedMovie];
childController.message = detailMessage;
childController.title = selectedMovie;
[detailMessage release];
```

Finally, we push the detail view controller onto the navigation stack.

```
[self.navigationController pushViewController:childController
                              animated:YES];
```

And, with that, our first second-level controller is done, as is our detail controller. The only remaining task is to create an instance of our second-level controller and add it to FirstLevelViewController's controllers.

Adding a Disclosure Button Controller Instance

Single-click *FirstLevelViewController.m*, and insert the following code into the viewDidLoad method:

```
- (void)viewDidLoad {
    self.title = @"First Level";
    NSMutableArray *array = [[NSMutableArray alloc] init];

    // Disclosure Button
    DisclosureButtonController *disclosureButtonController =
        [[DisclosureButtonController alloc]
        initWithStyle:UITableViewStylePlain];
    disclosureButtonController.title = @"Disclosure Buttons";
    disclosureButtonController.rowImage = [UIImage
        imageNamed:@"disclosureButtonControllerIcon.png"];
    [array addObject:disclosureButtonController];
    [disclosureButtonController release];

    self.controllers = array;
    [array release];
    [super viewDidLoad];
}
```

All that we're doing is creating a new instance of DisclosureButtonController. We specify UITableViewStylePlain to indicate that we want an indexed table, not a grouped table. Next, we set the title and the image to one of the *.png* files we added to our project, add the controller to the array, and release the controller. Up at the top of the file, we'll need to add one line of code to import the header class for our new file. Insert this line directly above the @implementation declaration:

```
#import "DisclosureButtonController.h"
```

Save your changes, and try building. If everything went as planned, your project should compile and then launch in the simulator. When it comes up, there should be just a single row (see Figure 9–12).

Figure 9–12. *Our application after adding the first of six second-level controllers*

If you touch the one row, it will take you down to the `DisclosureButtonController` table view we just implemented (see Figure 9–13).

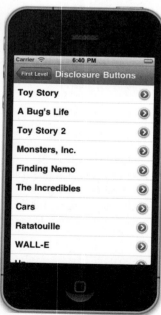

Figure 9–13. *The Disclosure Buttons view*

Notice that the title that we set for our controller is now displayed in the navigation bar, and the title of the view controller we were previously using (*First Level*) is contained in a navigation button. Tapping that button will take you back up to the first level. Select any row in this table, and you will get a gentle reminder that the detail disclosure button is there for drilling down (see Figure 9–14).

Figure 9–14. *Selecting the row does not drill down when there is a detail disclosure button visible.*

If you touch the detail disclosure button itself, you drill down into the DisclosureDetailController view (see Figure 9–15). This view shows information that we passed into it. Even though this is a simple example, the same basic technique is used anytime you show a detail view.

Figure 9–15. *The detail view*

Notice that when you drill down to the detail view, the title again changes, as does the back button, which now takes you to the previous view instead of the root view.

That finishes up the first view controller. Do you see now how the design Apple used here with the navigation controller makes it possible to build your application in small chunks? That's pretty cool, isn't it?

Second Subcontroller: The Checklist

The next second-level view we're going to implement is another table view. But this time, we'll use the accessory icon to let the user select one and only one item from the list. We'll use the accessory icon to place a check mark next to the currently selected row, and we'll change the selection when the user touches another row.

Since this view is a table view and it has no detail view, we don't need a new nib, but we do need to create another subclass of SecondLevelViewController. Select the *Classes* folder in the *Groups & Files* pane in Xcode, and then select **File ➤ New File. . .** or press ⌘**N**. Select *Cocoa Touch Class*, and then select *Objective-C class* and *NSObject* for *Subclass of*. Click the *Next* button, and when prompted for a name, type *CheckListController.m*, and make sure that the header file is created as well.

Creating the Checklist View

To present a checklist, we need a way to keep track of which row is currently selected. We'll declare an NSIndexPath property to track the last row selected. Single-click CheckListController.h, and make the following changes:

```
#import <Foundation/Foundation.h>
#import <UIKit/UIKit.h>
#import "SecondLevelViewController.h"

@interface CheckListController : NSObject {
@interface CheckListController : SecondLevelViewController {
    NSArray         *list;
    NSIndexPath     *lastIndexPath;
}
@property (nonatomic, retain) NSArray *list;
@property (nonatomic, retain) NSIndexPath *lastIndexPath;
@end
```

Then switch over to CheckListController.m, and add the following code:

```
#import "CheckListController.h"

@implementation CheckListController
@synthesize list;
@synthesize lastIndexPath;

- (void)viewDidLoad {

    NSArray *array = [[NSArray alloc] initWithObjects:@"Who Hash",
        @"Bubba Gump Shrimp Étouffée", @"Who Pudding", @"Scooby Snacks",
        @"Everlasting Gobstopper", @"Green Eggs and Ham", @"Soylent Green",
        @"Hard Tack", @"Lembas Bread", @"Roast Beast", @"Blancmange", nil];
    self.list = array;
    [array release];

    [super viewDidLoad];
}

- (void)viewDidUnload {
    self.list = nil;
    self.lastIndexPath = nil;
    [super viewDidUnload];
}

- (void)dealloc {
    [list release];
    [lastIndexPath release];
    [super dealloc];
}

#pragma mark -
#pragma mark Table Data Source Methods
- (NSInteger)tableView:(UITableView *)tableView
 numberOfRowsInSection:(NSInteger)section {
```

```objc
        return [list count];
}

- (UITableViewCell *)tableView:(UITableView *)tableView
            cellForRowAtIndexPath:(NSIndexPath *)indexPath {
    static NSString *CheckMarkCellIdentifier = @"CheckMarkCellIdentifier";

    UITableViewCell *cell = [tableView dequeueReusableCellWithIdentifier:
                                CheckMarkCellIdentifier];
    if (cell == nil) {
        cell = [[[UITableViewCell alloc]
            initWithStyle:UITableViewCellStyleDefault
            reuseIdentifier:CheckMarkCellIdentifier] autorelease];
    }
    NSUInteger row = [indexPath row];
    NSUInteger oldRow = [lastIndexPath row];
    cell.textLabel.text = [list objectAtIndex:row];
    cell.accessoryType = (row == oldRow && lastIndexPath != nil) ?
        UITableViewCellAccessoryCheckmark : UITableViewCellAccessoryNone;

    return cell;
}

#pragma mark -
#pragma mark Table Delegate Methods
- (void)tableView:(UITableView *)tableView
didSelectRowAtIndexPath:(NSIndexPath *)indexPath {
int newRow = [indexPath row];
    int oldRow = (lastIndexPath != nil) ? [lastIndexPath row] : -1;

    if (newRow != oldRow) {
        UITableViewCell *newCell = [tableView cellForRowAtIndexPath:
                                indexPath];
        newCell.accessoryType = UITableViewCellAccessoryCheckmark;

        UITableViewCell *oldCell = [tableView cellForRowAtIndexPath:
                                lastIndexPath];
        oldCell.accessoryType = UITableViewCellAccessoryNone;
        lastIndexPath = indexPath;
    }
    [tableView deselectRowAtIndexPath:indexPath animated:YES];
}

@end
```

Let's start with the tableView:cellForRowAtIndexPath: method, which has a few new things worth noticing. The first several lines should be familiar to you.

```objc
    static NSString *CheckMarkCellIdentifier = @"CheckMarkCellIdentifier";

    UITableViewCell *cell = [tableView dequeueReusableCellWithIdentifier:
        CheckMarkCellIdentifier];
    if (cell == nil) {
        cell = [[[UITableViewCell alloc]
```

```
        initWithStyle:UITableViewCellStyleDefault
        reuseIdentifier:CheckMarkCellIdentifier] autorelease];
}
```

Here's where things get interesting, though. First, we extract the row from this cell and from the current selection.

```
NSUInteger row = [indexPath row];
NSUInteger oldRow = [lastIndexPath row];
```

We grab the value for this row from our array and assign it to the cell's title.

```
cell.textLabel.text = [list objectAtIndex:row];
```

Then we set the accessory to show either a check mark or nothing, depending on whether the two rows are the same. In other words, if the table is requesting a cell for a row that is the currently selected row, we set the accessory icon to be a check mark; otherwise, we set it to be nothing. Notice that we also check lastIndexPath to make sure it's not nil. We do this because a nil lastIndexPath indicates no selection. However, calling the row method on a nil object will return a 0, which is a valid row, but we don't want to put a check mark on row 0 when, in reality, there is no selection.

```
cell.accessoryType = (row == oldRow && lastIndexPath != nil) ?
    UITableViewCellAccessoryCheckmark : UITableViewCellAccessoryNone;
```

After that, we just release the string we declared and return the cell.

```
[rowTitle release];
return cell;
```

Now skip down to the last method. You've seen the tableView:didSelectRowAtIndexPath: method before, but we're doing something new here. We grab not only the row that was just selected, but also the row that was previously selected.

```
int newRow = [indexPath row];
int oldRow = [lastIndexPath row];
```

We do this so if the new row and the old row are the same, we don't bother making any changes.

```
if (newRow != oldRow) {
```

Next, we grab the cell that was just selected and assign a check mark as its accessory icon.

```
UITableViewCell *newCell = [tableView
    cellForRowAtIndexPath:indexPath];
newCell.accessoryType = UITableViewCellAccessoryCheckmark;
```

We then grab the previously selected cell, and we set its accessory icon to none.

```
UITableViewCell *oldCell = [tableView cellForRowAtIndexPath:
    lastIndexPath];
oldCell.accessoryType = UITableViewCellAccessoryNone;
```

After that, we store the index path that was just selected in lastIndexPath, so we'll have it the next time a row is selected.

```
        lastIndexPath = indexPath;
    }
```

When we're finished, we tell the table view to deselect the row that was just selected, because we don't want the row to stay highlighted. We've already marked the row with a check mark, so leaving it blue would just be a distraction.

```
    [tableView deselectRowAtIndexPath:indexPath animated:YES];
}
```

Adding a Checklist Controller Instance

Our next task is to add an instance of this controller to FirstLevelViewController's controllers array. We do that by adding the following code to the viewDidLoad method in *FirstLevelViewController.m*:

```
- (void)viewDidLoad {
    self.title = @"First Level";
    NSMutableArray *array = [[NSMutableArray alloc] init];

    // Disclosure Button
    DisclosureButtonController *disclosureButtonController =
        [[DisclosureButtonController alloc]
        initWithStyle:UITableViewStylePlain];
    disclosureButtonController.title = @"Disclosure Buttons";
    disclosureButtonController.rowImage = [UIImage imageNamed:
        @"disclosureButtonControllerIcon.png"];
    [array addObject:disclosureButtonController];
    [disclosureButtonController release];

    // Checklist
    CheckListController *checkListController = [[CheckListController alloc]
        initWithStyle:UITableViewStylePlain];
    checkListController.title = @"Check One";
    checkListController.rowImage = [UIImage imageNamed:
        @"checkmarkControllerIcon.png"];
    [array addObject:checkListController];
    [checkListController release];

    self.controllers = array;
    [array release];
    [super viewDidLoad];
}
```

Finally, you'll need to import the new header file, so add this line just after all the other #import statements, toward the top of the file:

```
#import "CheckListController.h"
```

Well, what are you waiting for? Save your changes, compile, and run. If everything went smoothly, the application launched again in the simulator, and there was much rejoicing. This time there will be two rows (see Figure 9–16).

Figure 9–16. *Two second-level controllers, two rows. What a coincidence!*

If you touch the *Check One* row, it will take you down to the view controller we just implemented (see Figure 9–17). When it first comes up, no rows will be selected and no check marks will be visible. If you tap a row, a check mark will appear. If you then tap a different row, the check mark will switch to the new row. Huzzah!

Figure 9–17. *The checklist view. Note that only a single item can be checked at a time. Soylent Green, anyone?*

Third Subcontroller: Controls on Table Rows

In the previous chapter, we showed you how to add subviews to a table view cell to customize its appearance. However, we didn't put any active controls into the content view; it had only labels. Now let's see how to add controls to a table view cell.

In our example, we'll add a button to each row, but the same technique will work with most controls. We'll add the control to the accessory view, which is the area on the right side of each row where you found the accessory icons covered earlier in the chapter.

To add another row to our `FirstLevelViewController`'s table, we need another second-level controller. You know the drill: select the *Classes folder* in the *Groups & Files* pane in Xcode, and then press ⌘N or select **File ➤ New File. . ..** Select *Cocoa Touch Class*, select *Objective-C class*, and select *NSObject* for *Subclass of*. When prompted for a name, type *RowControlsController.m*, and don't forget to create the header. Just as with the previous subcontroller, this controller can be completely implemented with a single table view; no nib file is necessary.

Creating the Row Controls View

Single-click *RowControlsController.h*, and make the following changes:

```
#import <Foundation/Foundation.h>
#import <UIKit/UIKit.h>
#import "SecondLevelViewController.h"

@interface RowControlsController : NSObject {
@interface RowControlsController : SecondLevelViewController {
    NSArray *list;
}
@property (nonatomic, retain) NSArray *list;
- (IBAction)buttonTapped:(id)sender;
@end
```

Not much there, huh? We change the parent class and create an array to hold our table data. Then we define a property for that array and declare an action method that will be called when the row buttons are pressed.

> **NOTE:** Strictly speaking, we don't need to declare the `buttonTapped:` method an action method by specifying `IBAction`, since we won't be triggering it from controls in a nib file. Since it is an action method and will be called by a control, however, it's still a good idea to use the `IBAction` keyword, since it signals our intent to future readers of this code.

Switch over to *RowControlsController.m,* and make the following changes:

```
#import "RowControlsController.h"

@implementation RowControlsController
@synthesize list;
```

```objc
- (IBAction)buttonTapped:(id)sender {
    UIButton *senderButton = (UIButton *)sender;
    UITableViewCell *buttonCell =
        (UITableViewCell *)[senderButton superview];
    NSUInteger buttonRow = [[self.tableView
        indexPathForCell:buttonCell] row];
    NSString *buttonTitle = [list objectAtIndex:buttonRow];
    UIAlertView *alert = [[UIAlertView alloc]
                    initWithTitle:@"You tapped the button"
                    message:[NSString stringWithFormat:
                        @"You tapped the button for %@", buttonTitle]
                    delegate:nil
                    cancelButtonTitle:@"OK"
                    otherButtonTitles:nil];
    [alert show];
    [alert release];
}

- (void)viewDidLoad {
    NSArray *array = [[NSArray alloc] initWithObjects:@"R2-D2",
            @"C3PO", @"Tik-Tok", @"Robby", @"Rosie", @"Uniblab",
            @"Bender", @"Marvin", @"Lt. Commander Data",
            @"Evil Brother Lore", @"Optimus Prime", @"Tobor", @"HAL",
            @"Orgasmatron", nil];
    self.list = array;
    [array release];
    [super viewDidLoad];
}

- (void)viewDidUnload {
    self.list = nil;
    [super viewDidUnload];
}

- (void)dealloc {
    [list release];
    [super dealloc];
}

#pragma mark -
#pragma mark Table Data Source Methods
- (NSInteger)tableView:(UITableView *)tableView
 numberOfRowsInSection:(NSInteger)section {
    return [list count];
}

- (UITableViewCell *)tableView:(UITableView *)tableView
        cellForRowAtIndexPath:(NSIndexPath *)indexPath {
    static NSString *ControlRowIdentifier = @"ControlRowIdentifier";

    UITableViewCell *cell = [tableView
        dequeueReusableCellWithIdentifier:ControlRowIdentifier];
    if (cell == nil) {
```

```
            cell = [[[UITableViewCell alloc]
                        initWithStyle:UITableViewCellStyleDefault
                        reuseIdentifier:ControlRowIdentifier] autorelease];
        UIImage *buttonUpImage = [UIImage imageNamed:@"button_up.png"];
        UIImage *buttonDownImage = [UIImage imageNamed:@"button_down.png"];
        UIButton *button = [UIButton buttonWithType:UIButtonTypeCustom];
        button.frame = CGRectMake(0.0, 0.0, buttonUpImage.size.width,
            buttonUpImage.size.height);
        [button setBackgroundImage:buttonUpImage
            forState:UIControlStateNormal];
        [button setBackgroundImage:buttonDownImage
            forState:UIControlStateHighlighted];
        [button setTitle:@"Tap" forState:UIControlStateNormal];
        [button addTarget:self action:@selector(buttonTapped:)
            forControlEvents:UIControlEventTouchUpInside];
        cell.accessoryView = button;
    }
    NSUInteger row = [indexPath row];
    NSString *rowTitle = [list objectAtIndex:row];
    cell.textLabel.text = rowTitle;

    return cell;
}

#pragma mark -
#pragma mark Table Delegate Methods
- (void)tableView:(UITableView *)tableView
    didSelectRowAtIndexPath:(NSIndexPath *)indexPath {
    NSUInteger row = [indexPath row];
    NSString *rowTitle = [list objectAtIndex:row];
    UIAlertView *alert = [[UIAlertView alloc]
                            initWithTitle:@"You tapped the row."
                            message:[NSString
                                stringWithFormat:@"You tapped %@.", rowTitle]
                            delegate:nil
                            cancelButtonTitle:@"OK"
                            otherButtonTitles:nil];
    [alert show];
    [alert release];
    [tableView deselectRowAtIndexPath:indexPath animated:YES];
}

@end
```

Let's begin with our new action method. The first thing we do is declare a new UIButton variable and set it to sender. This is just so we don't need to cast sender multiple times throughout our method.

```
UIButton *senderButton = (UIButton *)sender;
```

Next, we get the button's superview, which is the table view cell for the row it's in, and we use that to determine the row that was pressed and to retrieve the title for that row.

```
UITableViewCell *buttonCell =
    (UITableViewCell *)[senderButton superview];
```

```
NSUInteger buttonRow = [[self.tableView
    indexPathForCell:buttonCell] row];
NSString *buttonTitle = [list objectAtIndex:buttonRow];
```

Then we show an alert, telling the user that they pressed the button.

```
UIAlertView *alert = [[UIAlertView alloc]
                initWithTitle:@"You tapped the button"
                message:[NSString stringWithFormat:
                    @"You tapped the button for %@", buttonTitle]
                delegate:nil
                cancelButtonTitle:@"OK"
                otherButtonTitles:nil];
[alert show];
[alert release];
```

Everything from there to tableView:cellForRowAtIndexPath: should be familiar to you, so skip down to that method, which is where we set up the table view cell with the button. The method starts as usual. We declare an identifier and then use it to request a reusable cell.

```
static NSString *ControlRowIdentifier = @"ControlRowIdentifier";
UITableViewCell *cell = [tableView
    dequeueReusableCellWithIdentifier:ControlRowIdentifier];
```

If there are no reusable cells, we create one.

```
if (cell == nil) {
    cell = [[[UITableViewCell alloc]
                initWithStyle:UITableViewCellStyleDefault
                reuseIdentifier:ControlRowIdentifier] autorelease];
```

To create the button, we load in two of the images that were in the *Images* folder you imported earlier. One will represent the button in the normal state; the other will represent the button in its highlighted state or, in other words, when the button is being tapped.

```
UIImage *buttonUpImage = [UIImage imageNamed:@"button_up.png"];
UIImage *buttonDownImage = [UIImage imageNamed:@"button_down.png"];
```

Next, we create a button. Because the buttonType property of UIButton is declared read-only, we need to create the button using the factory method buttonWithType:. If we created it using alloc and init, we wouldn't be able to change the button's type to UIButtonTypeCustom, which we need to do in order to use the custom button images.

```
UIButton *button = [UIButton buttonWithType:UIButtonTypeCustom];
```

Next, we set the button's size to match the images, assign the images for the two states, and give the button a title.

```
button.frame = CGRectMake(0.0, 0.0, buttonUpImage.size.width,
    buttonUpImage.size.height);
[button setBackgroundImage:buttonUpImage
    forState:UIControlStateNormal];
[button setBackgroundImage:buttonDownImage
    forState:UIControlStateHighlighted];
[button setTitle:@"Tap" forState:UIControlStateNormal];
```

Finally, we tell the button to call our action method on the touch up inside event and assign it to the cell's accessory view.

```
[button addTarget:self action:@selector(buttonTapped:)
    forControlEvents:UIControlEventTouchUpInside];
cell.accessoryView = button;
```

Everything else in the `tableView:cellForRowAtIndexPath:` method is just as we've done it in the past.

The last method we implemented is `tableView:didSelectRowAtIndexPath:`, which is the delegate method that is called after the user selects a row. All we do here is find out which row was selected and grab the appropriate title from our array.

```
NSUInteger row = [indexPath row];
NSString *rowTitle = [list objectAtIndex:row];
```

Then we create another alert to inform the user that they tapped the row, but not the button.

```
UIAlertView *alert = [[UIAlertView alloc]
                        initWithTitle:@"You tapped the row."
                        message:[NSString
                            stringWithFormat:@"You tapped %@.", rowTitle]
                        delegate:nil
                        cancelButtonTitle:@"OK"
                        otherButtonTitles:nil];
[alert show];
[alert release];
[tableView deselectRowAtIndexPath:indexPath animated:YES];
```

Adding a Rows Control Controller Instance

Now, all we need to do is add this controller to the array in `FirstLevelViewController`. Single-click *FirstLevelViewController.m,* and add the following code to `viewDidLoad`:

```
- (void)viewDidLoad {
    self.title = @"Root Level";
    NSMutableArray *array = [[NSMutableArray alloc] init];

    // Disclosure Button
    DisclosureButtonController *disclosureButtonController =
        [[DisclosureButtonController alloc]
            initWithStyle:UITableViewStylePlain];
    disclosureButtonController.title = @"Disclosure Buttons";
    disclosureButtonController.rowImage = [UIImage
        imageNamed:@"disclosureButtonControllerIcon.png"];
    [array addObject:disclosureButtonController];
    [disclosureButtonController release];

    // Checklist
    CheckListController *checkListController = [[CheckListController alloc]
                    initWithStyle:UITableViewStylePlain];
    checkListController.title = @"Check One";
    checkListController.rowImage = [UIImage
        imageNamed:@"checkmarkControllerIcon.png"];
```

```
    [array addObject:checkListController];
    [checkListController release];

    // Table Row Controls
    RowControlsController *rowControlsController =
        [[RowControlsController alloc]
            initWithStyle:UITableViewStylePlain];
    rowControlsController.title = @"Row Controls";
    rowControlsController.rowImage = [UIImage imageNamed:
        @"rowControlsIcon.png"];
    [array addObject:rowControlsController];
    [rowControlsController release];

    self.controllers = array;
    [array release];
    [super viewDidLoad];
}
```

In order for this code to compile, we also must import the header file for the
RowControlsController class, so add the following line of code just before the
@implementation line in the same file:

```
#import "RowControlsController.h"
```

Save everything, and compile it. This time, you should see yet another row when your
application launches (see Figure 9–18).

Figure 9–18. *The Row Controls controller added to the root level controller*

If you tap this new row, it will take you down to a new list where every row has a button control on the right side of the row. Tapping either the button or the row will show an alert telling you which one you tapped (Figure 9–19).

Figure 9–19. *The table with buttons in the accessory view*

Tapping a row anywhere but on its switch will display an alert telling you whether the switch for that row is turned on or off.

At this point, you should be getting pretty comfortable with how this all works, so let's try a slightly more difficult case, shall we? Next, we'll take a look at how to allow the user to reorder the rows in a table.

> **NOTE:** how are you doing? Hanging in there? We know this chapter is a bit of a marathon, with a lot of stuff to absorb. At this point, you've already accomplished a lot. Why not take a break, and grab a Fresca and a pastel de belém? We'll do the same. Come back when you're refreshed and ready to move on.

Fourth Subcontroller: Movable Rows

Moving and deleting rows, as well as inserting rows at a specific spot in the table, are tasks that can be implemented fairly easily. All three are implemented by turning on something called **editing mode**, which is done using the `setEditing:animated:` method on the table view.

The `setEditing:animated:` method takes two Booleans. The first indicates whether you are turning on or off editing mode, and the second indicates whether the table should animate the transition. If you set editing to the mode it's already in (in other words, turning it on when it's already on or off when it's already off), the transition will not be animated, regardless of what you specify in the second parameter.

Once editing mode is turned on, a number of new delegate methods come into play. The table view uses them to ask if a certain row can be moved or edited, and again to notify you if the user actually does move or edit a specific row. It sounds more complex than it is. Let's see it in action in our movable row controller.

Because we don't need to display a detail view, this view controller can be implemented without a nib and with just a single controller class. So, select the *Classes* folder in the *Groups & Files* pane in Xcode, and then press ⌘**N** or select File ➤ New File…. Select *Cocoa Touch Class*, select *Objective-C class* and *NSObject* for *Subclass of*. When prompted for a name, type *MoveMeController.m*. Don't forget that header file!

Creating the Movable Row View

In our header file, we need two things. First, we need a mutable array to hold our data and keep track of the order of the rows. It must be mutable because we need to be able to move items around as we get notified of moves. We also need an action method to toggle edit mode on and off. The action method will be called by a navigation bar button that we will create.

Single-click *MoveMeController.h,* and make the following changes:

```
#import <Foundation/Foundation.h>
#import <UIKit/UIKit.h>
#import "SecondLevelViewController.h"

@interface MoveMeController : NSObject {
@interface MoveMeController : SecondLevelViewController {
    NSMutableArray *list;
}
@property (nonatomic, retain) NSMutableArray *list;
- (IBAction)toggleMove;
@end
```

Now, switch over to *MoveMeController.m*, and add the following code:

```
#import "MoveMeController.h"

@implementation MoveMeController
@synthesize list;

- (IBAction)toggleMove{
    [self.tableView setEditing:!self.tableView.editing animated:YES];

    if (self.tableView.editing)
```

```
            [self.navigationItem.rightBarButtonItem setTitle:@"Done"];
    else
            [self.navigationItem.rightBarButtonItem setTitle:@"Move"];
}


- (void)viewDidLoad {
    if (list == nil) {
        NSMutableArray *array = [[NSMutableArray alloc] initWithObjects:
                        @"Eeny", @"Meeny", @"Miney", @"Moe", @"Catch", @"A",
                        @"Tiger", @"By", @"The", @"Toe", nil];
        self.list = array;
        [array release];
    }

    UIBarButtonItem *moveButton = [[UIBarButtonItem alloc]
                                    initWithTitle:@"Move"
                                    style:UIBarButtonItemStyleBordered
                                    target:self
                                    action:@selector(toggleMove)];
    self.navigationItem.rightBarButtonItem = moveButton;
    [moveButton release];
    [super viewDidLoad];
}

- (void)dealloc {
    [list release];
    [super dealloc];
}

#pragma mark -
#pragma mark Table Data Source Methods
- (NSInteger)tableView:(UITableView *)tableView
 numberOfRowsInSection:(NSInteger)section {
    return [list count];
}

- (UITableViewCell *)tableView:(UITableView *)tableView
        cellForRowAtIndexPath:(NSIndexPath *)indexPath {
static NSString *MoveMeCellIdentifier = @"MoveMeCellIdentifier";
    UITableViewCell *cell = [tableView
        dequeueReusableCellWithIdentifier:MoveMeCellIdentifier];
    if (cell == nil) {
        cell = [[[UITableViewCell alloc]
                initWithStyle:UITableViewCellStyleDefault
                reuseIdentifier:MoveMeCellIdentifier] autorelease];
        cell.showsReorderControl = YES;
    }
    NSUInteger row = [indexPath row];
    cell.textLabel.text = [list objectAtIndex:row];

    return cell;
}
```

```objc
- (UITableViewCellEditingStyle)tableView:(UITableView *)tableView
            editingStyleForRowAtIndexPath:(NSIndexPath *)indexPath {
    return UITableViewCellEditingStyleNone;
}

- (BOOL)tableView:(UITableView *)tableView
    canMoveRowAtIndexPath:(NSIndexPath *)indexPath {
    return YES;
}

- (void)tableView:(UITableView *)tableView
    moveRowAtIndexPath:(NSIndexPath *)fromIndexPath
    toIndexPath:(NSIndexPath *)toIndexPath {
    NSUInteger fromRow = [fromIndexPath row];
    NSUInteger toRow = [toIndexPath row];

    id object = [[list objectAtIndex:fromRow] retain];
    [list removeObjectAtIndex:fromRow];
    [list insertObject:object atIndex:toRow];
    [object release];
}

@end
```

Let's take this one step at a time. The first code we added is the implementation of our action method.

```objc
- (IBAction)toggleMove{
    [self.tableView setEditing:!self.tableView.editing animated:YES];

    if (self.tableView.editing)
        [self.navigationItem.rightBarButtonItem setTitle:@"Done"];
    else
        [self.navigationItem.rightBarButtonItem setTitle:@"Move"];
}
```

All that we're doing here is toggling edit mode and then setting the button's title to an appropriate value. Easy enough, right?

The next method we touched is viewDidLoad. The first part of that method doesn't do anything you haven't seen before. It checks to see if list is nil, and if it is (meaning this is the first time this method has been called), it creates a mutable array filled with values, so our table has some data to show. After that, though, there is something new.

```objc
UIBarButtonItem *moveButton = [[UIBarButtonItem alloc]
            initWithTitle:@"Move"
            style:UIBarButtonItemStyleBordered
            target:self
            action:@selector(toggleMove)];
    self.navigationItem.rightBarButtonItem = moveButton;
    [moveButton release];
```

Here, we're creating a button bar item, which is a button that will sit on the navigation bar. We give it a title of *Move* and specify a constant, UIBarButtonItemStyleBordered, to indicate that we want a standard bordered bar button. The last two arguments, target and action, tell the button what to do when it is tapped. By passing self as the target and giving it a selector to the `toggleMove` method as the action, we are telling the button to call our `toggleMove` method whenever the button is tapped. As a result, any time the user taps this button, editing mode will be toggled. After we create the button, we add it to the right side of the navigation bar, and then release it.

Then we have a standard `dealloc` method, but no `viewDidUnload` method. That's intentional. We have no outlets, and if we were to flush our `list` array, we would lose any reordering that the user had done when the view is flushed, which we don't want to happen. Therefore, since we have nothing to do in the `viewDidUnload` method, we don't bother to override it.

Now, skip down to the `tableView:cellForRowAtIndexPath:` method we just added. Did you notice the following new line of code?

```
cell.showsReorderControl = YES;
```

Standard accessory icons can be specified by setting the `accessoryType` property of the cell. But the reorder control is not a standard accessory icon. It's a special case that's shown only when the table is in edit mode. To enable the reorder control, we need to set a property on the cell itself. Note, though, that setting this property to YES doesn't actually display the reorder control until the table is put into edit mode. Everything else in this method is stuff we've done before.

The next new method is short but important. In our table view, we want to be able to reorder the rows, but we don't want the user to be able to delete or insert rows. As a result, we implement the method `tableView:editingStyleForRowAtIndexPath:`. This method allows the table view to ask if a specific row can be deleted or if a new row can be inserted at a specific spot. By returning `UITableViewCellEditingStyleNone` for each row, we are indicating that we don't support inserts or deletes for any row.

Next comes the method `tableView:canMoveRowAtIndexPath:`. This method is called for each row, and it gives you the chance to disallow the movement of specific rows. If you return `NO` from this method for any row, the reorder control will not be shown for that row, and the user will be unable to move it from its current position. We want to allow full reordering, so we just return `YES` for every row.

The last method, `tableView:moveRowAtIndexPath:fromIndexPath:`, is the one that will actually be called when the user moves a row. The two parameters besides `tableView` are both `NSIndexPath` instances that identify the row that was moved and the row's new position. The table view has already moved the rows in the table so the user is seeing the correct display, but we need to update our data model to keep the two in sync and avoid causing display problems.

First, we retrieve the row that needs to be moved. Then we retrieve the row's new position.

```
NSUInteger fromRow = [fromIndexPath row];
NSUInteger toRow = [toIndexPath row];
```

We now need to remove the specified object from the array and reinsert it at its new location. But before we do that, we retrieve a pointer to the about-to-be-moved object and retain it so that the object isn't released when we remove it from the array. If the array is the only object that has retained the object we're removing (and in our case, it is), removing the selected object from the array will cause its retain count to drop to 0, meaning it will probably disappear on us. By retaining it first, we prevent that from happening.

```
id object = [[list objectAtIndex:fromRow] retain];
[list removeObjectAtIndex:fromRow];
```

After we've removed it, we need to reinsert it into the specified new location.

```
[list insertObject:object atIndex:toRow];
```

And, finally, because we've retained it, we need to release it to avoid leaking memory.

```
[object release];
```

Well, there you have it. We've implemented a table that allows reordering of rows.

Adding a Move Me Controller Instance

Now, we just need to add an instance of this new class to `FirstLevelViewController`'s array of controllers. You're probably comfortable doing this by now, but we'll walk you through it just to keep you company.

In *FirstLevelViewController.m,* import the new view's header file by adding the following line of code just before the @implementation declaration:

```
#import "MoveMeController.h"
```

Now, add the following code to the viewDidLoad method in the same file:

```
- (void)viewDidLoad {
    self.title = @"First Level";
    NSMutableArray *array = [[NSMutableArray alloc] init];

    // Disclosure Button
    DisclosureButtonController *disclosureButtonController =
        [[DisclosureButtonController alloc]
        initWithStyle:UITableViewStylePlain];
    disclosureButtonController.title = @"Disclosure Buttons";
    disclosureButtonController.rowImage = [UIImage
        imageNamed:@"disclosureButtonControllerIcon.png"];
    [array addObject:disclosureButtonController];
    [disclosureButtonController release];

    // Checklist
    CheckListController *checkListController = [[CheckListController alloc]
        initWithStyle:UITableViewStylePlain];
    checkListController.title = @"Check One";
    checkListController.rowImage = [UIImage
        imageNamed:@"checkmarkControllerIcon.png"];
    [array addObject:checkListController];
    [checkListController release];

    // Table Row Controls
    RowControlsController *rowControlsController =
        [[RowControlsController alloc]
```

```
        initWithStyle:UITableViewStylePlain];
    rowControlsController.title = @"Row Controls";
    rowControlsController.rowImage = [UIImage imageNamed:
        @"rowControlsIcon.png"];
    [array addObject:rowControlsController];
    [rowControlsController release];

    // Move Me
    MoveMeController *moveMeController = [[MoveMeController alloc]
        initWithStyle:UITableViewStylePlain];
    moveMeController.title = @"Move Me";
    moveMeController.rowImage = [UIImage imageNamed:@"moveMeIcon.png"];
    [array addObject:moveMeController];
    [moveMeController release];

    self.controllers = array;
    [array release];
    [super viewDidLoad];
}
```

OK, let's go ahead and compile this bad boy and see what shakes out. If everything went smoothly, our application will launch in the simulator with (count 'em) four rows in the root-level table. If you click the new one, called *Move Me*, you'll go to a table whose rows make up a familiar childhood choosing rhyme (see Figure 9–20).

Figure 9–20. *The Move Me view controller when you first drill down to it. Recognize the rhyme?*

To reorder the rows, click the *Move* button in the upper-right corner, and the reorder controls should appear. If you tap in a row's reorder control and then drag, the row should move as you drag, as in Figure 9–6. Once you are happy with the row's new position, release the drag. The row should settle into its new position nicely. You can even navigate back up to the top level and come back down, and your rows will be right where you left them. If you quit and return, they will be restored to their original order, but don't worry; in a few chapters, we'll show you how to save and restore data on a more permanent basis.

> **NOTE:** If you find you have a bit of trouble making contact with the move control, don't panic. This gesture actually requires a little patience. Try holding the mouse button clicked (if you're in the simulator) or your finger pressed on the control (if you're on a device) a bit longer before moving it, in order to make the drag-to-reorder gesture work.

Now let's move on to the fifth subcontroller, which demonstrates another use of edit mode. This time, we'll allow the user to delete our precious rows. Gasp!

Fifth Subcontroller: Deletable Rows

Letting users delete rows isn't really significantly harder than letting them move rows. Let's take a look at that process. Instead of creating an array from a hard-coded list of objects, we're going to load a property list file this time, just to save some typing. You can grab the file called *computers.plist* out of the *09 Nav* folder in the projects archive that accompanies this book and add it to the *Resources* folder of your Xcode project.

Select the *Classes* folder in the *Groups & Files* pane in Xcode, and then press ⌘N or select File ➤ New File…. Select *Cocoa Touch Class*, select *Objective-C class* and *NSObject* for *Subclass of*. When prompted for a name, type *DeleteMeController.m*.

Creating the Deletable Rows View

The changes we're going to make to *DeleteMeController.h* should look familiar, as they're nearly identical to the ones we made in the movable rows view controller we just built. Go ahead and make these changes now:

```
#import <Foundation/Foundation.h>
#import <UIKit/UIKit.h>
#import "SecondLevelViewController.h"

@interface DeleteMeController : NSObject {
@interface DeleteMeController : SecondLevelViewController {
    NSMutableArray *list;
}
@property (nonatomic, retain) NSMutableArray *list;
- (IBAction)toggleEdit:(id)sender;
@end
```

No surprises here, right? We're changing the superclass from NSObject to SecondLevelViewController. After that, we declare a mutable array to hold our data and an action method to toggle edit mode.

In the previous controller, we used edit mode to let the users reorder rows. In this version, edit mode will be used to let them delete rows. You can actually combine both in the same table if you like. We separated them so the concepts would be a bit easier to follow, but the delete and reorder operations do play nicely together.

A row that can be reordered will display the reorder icon anytime that the table is in edit mode. When you tap the red circular icon on the left side of the row (see Figure 9–7), the *Delete* button will pop up, obscuring the reorder icon, but only temporarily.

Switch over to *DeleteMeController.m,* and add the following code:

```objc
#import "DeleteMeController.h"

@implementation DeleteMeController
@synthesize list;

- (IBAction)toggleEdit:(id)sender {
    [self.tableView setEditing:!self.tableView.editing animated:YES];

    if (self.tableView.editing)
        [self.navigationItem.rightBarButtonItem setTitle:@"Done"];
    else
        [self.navigationItem.rightBarButtonItem setTitle:@"Delete"];
}

- (void)viewDidLoad {
    if (list == nil)
    {
        NSString *path = [[NSBundle mainBundle]
            pathForResource:@"computers" ofType:@"plist"];
        NSMutableArray *array = [[NSMutableArray alloc]
                                    initWithContentsOfFile:path];
        self.list = array;
        [array release];
    }
    UIBarButtonItem *editButton = [[UIBarButtonItem alloc]
                                    initWithTitle:@"Delete"
                                    style:UIBarButtonItemStyleBordered
                                    target:self
                                    action:@selector(toggleEdit:)];
    self.navigationItem.rightBarButtonItem = editButton;
    [editButton release];

    [super viewDidLoad];
}

- (void)dealloc {
    [list release];
    [super dealloc];
}
```

```
#pragma mark -
#pragma mark Table Data Source Methods
- (NSInteger)tableView:(UITableView *)tableView
    numberOfRowsInSection:(NSInteger)section {
    return [list count];
}

- (UITableViewCell *)tableView:(UITableView *)tableView
        cellForRowAtIndexPath:(NSIndexPath *)indexPath {
    static NSString *DeleteMeCellIdentifier = @"DeleteMeCellIdentifier";

    UITableViewCell *cell = [tableView dequeueReusableCellWithIdentifier:
                        DeleteMeCellIdentifier];

    if (cell == nil) {
        cell = [[[UITableViewCell alloc]
            initWithStyle:UITableViewCellStyleDefault
            reuseIdentifier:DeleteMeCellIdentifier] autorelease];
    }
    NSInteger row = [indexPath row];
    cell.textLabel.text = [self.list objectAtIndex:row];
    return cell;
}

#pragma mark -
#pragma mark Table View Data Source Methods
- (void)tableView:(UITableView *)tableView
    commitEditingStyle:(UITableViewCellEditingStyle)editingStyle
    forRowAtIndexPath:(NSIndexPath *)indexPath {
    NSUInteger row = [indexPath row];
    [self.list removeObjectAtIndex:row];
    [tableView deleteRowsAtIndexPaths:[NSArray arrayWithObject:indexPath]
                    withRowAnimation:UITableViewRowAnimationFade];
}

@end
```

Here, the new action method, toggleEdit:, is pretty much the same as our previous version. It sets edit mode to on if it's currently off and vice versa, and then sets the button's title as appropriate. The viewDidLoad method is also similar to the one from the previous view controller and, again, we have no viewDidUnload method because we have no outlets and we want to preserve changes made to our mutable array in edit mode. The only difference is that we're loading our array from a property list rather than feeding it a hard-coded list of strings. The property list we're using is a flat array of strings containing a variety of computer model names that might be a bit familiar. We also assign the name *Delete* to the edit button, to make the button's effect obvious to the user.

The two data source methods contain nothing new, but the last method in the class is something you've never seen before, so let's take a closer look at it.

```
- (void)tableView:(UITableView *)tableView
```

```
commitEditingStyle:(UITableViewCellEditingStyle)editingStyle
forRowAtIndexPath:(NSIndexPath *)indexPath {
```

This method is called by the table view when the user has made an edit, which means a delete or an insert. The first argument is the table view on which a row was edited. The second parameter, editingStyle, is a constant that tells us what kind of edit just happened. Currently, three editing styles are defined:

- **UITableViewCellEditingStyleNone**: We used this style in the previous controller to indicate that a row can't be edited. The option UITableViewCellEditingStyleNone will never be passed into this method, because it is used to indicate that editing is not allowed for this row.

- **UITableViewCellEditingStyleDelete**: This is the default option. We ignore this parameter, because the default editing style for rows is the delete style, so we know that every time this method is called, it will be requesting a delete. You can use this parameter to allow both inserts and deletes within a single table.

- **UITableViewCellEditingStyleInsert**: This is generally used when you need to let the user insert rows at a specific spot in a list. In a list whose order is maintained by the system, such as an alphabetical list of names, the user will usually tap a toolbar or navigation bar button to ask the system to create a new object in a detail view. Once the user is finished specifying the new object, the system will place in the appropriate row.

> **NOTE:** We won't be covering the use of inserts, but the insert functionality works in fundamentally the same way as the delete functionality we are about to implement. The only difference is that instead of deleting the specified row from your data model, you need to create a new object and insert it at the specified spot.

The last parameter, indexPath, tells us which row is being edited. For a delete, this index path represents the row to be deleted. For an insert, it represents the index where the new row should be inserted.

In our method, we first retrieve the row that is being edited from indexPath.

```
NSUInteger row = [indexPath row];
```

Then we remove the object from the mutable array we created earlier.

```
[self.list removeObjectAtIndex:row];
```

Finally, we tell the table to delete the row, specifying the constant UITableViewRowAnimationFade, which sets the animation so that the row fades away.

```
[tableView deleteRowsAtIndexPaths:[NSArray arrayWithObject:indexPath]
    withRowAnimation:UITableViewRowAnimationFade];
}
```

> **NOTE:** Several types of animation are available for table views. You can look up
> `UITableViewRowAnimation` in Xcode's document browser to see what other animations are
> available.

And that's all she wrote, folks. That's the whole enchilada for this class.

Adding a Delete Me Controller Instance

Now, let's add an instance of the new controller to our root view controller and try it out.
In *FirstLevelViewController.m,* we first need to import our new controller class's header
file, so add the following line of code directly before the @implementation declaration:

```
#import "DeleteMeController.h"
```

Next, add the following code to the viewDidLoad method:

```
- (void)viewDidLoad {
    self.title = @"First Level";
    NSMutableArray *array = [[NSMutableArray alloc] init];

    // Disclosure Button
    DisclosureButtonController *disclosureButtonController =
        [[DisclosureButtonController alloc]
        initWithStyle:UITableViewStylePlain];
    disclosureButtonController.title = @"Disclosure Buttons";
    disclosureButtonController.rowImage = [UIImage imageNamed:
        @"disclosureButtonControllerIcon.png"];
    [array addObject:disclosureButtonController];
    [disclosureButtonController release];

    // Checklist
    CheckListController *checkListController = [[CheckListController alloc]
        initWithStyle:UITableViewStylePlain];
    checkListController.title = @"Check One";
    checkListController.rowImage = [UIImage imageNamed:
        @"checkmarkControllerIcon.png"];
    [array addObject:checkListController];
    [checkListController release];

    // Table Row Controls
    RowControlsController *rowControlsController =
        [[RowControlsController alloc]
        initWithStyle:UITableViewStylePlain];
    rowControlsController.title = @"Row Controls";
    rowControlsController.rowImage = [UIImage imageNamed:
        @"rowControlsIcon.png"];
    [array addObject:rowControlsController];
    [rowControlsController release];

    // Move Me
    MoveMeController *moveMeController = [[MoveMeController alloc]
        initWithStyle:UITableViewStylePlain];
    moveMeController.title = @"Move Me";
```

```
    moveMeController.rowImage = [UIImage imageNamed:@"moveMeIcon.png"];
    [array addObject:moveMeController];
    [moveMeController release];

    // Delete Me
    DeleteMeController *deleteMeController = [[DeleteMeController alloc]
        initWithStyle:UITableViewStylePlain];
    deleteMeController.title = @"Delete Me";
    deleteMeController.rowImage = [UIImage imageNamed:@"deleteMeIcon.png"];
    [array addObject:deleteMeController];
    [deleteMeController release];

    self.controllers = array;
    [array release];
    [super viewDidLoad];
}
```

Save everything, compile, and let her rip. When the simulator comes up, the root level will now have—can you guess?—five rows. If you select the new *Delete Me* row, you'll be presented with a list of computer models (see Figure 9–21). How many of these have you owned?

Figure 9–21. *The Delete Me view when it first launches. Recognize any of these computers?*

Notice that we again have a button on the right side of the navigation bar, this time labeled *Delete*. If you tap that, the table enters edit mode, which looks like Figure 9–22.

Figure 9–22. *The Delete Me view in edit mode*

Next to each editable row is a little icon that looks a little like a "Do Not Enter" street sign. If you tap the icon, it rotates sideways, and a button labeled *Delete* appears (see Figure 9–7). Tapping that button will cause its row to be deleted, both from the underlying model as well as from the table, using the animation style we specified.

And when you implement edit mode to allow deletions, you get additional functionality for free. Swipe your finger horizontally across a row. Look at that! The *Delete* button comes up for just that row, just as in the Mail application.

We're coming around the bend, now, and the finish line is in sight, albeit still a little ways in the distance. If you're still with us, give yourself a pat on the back, or have someone do it for you. This is a long, tough chapter.

Sixth Subcontroller: An Editable Detail Pane

The next concept we're going to explore is how to implement a reusable editable detail view. You may notice as you look through the various applications that come on your iPhone that many of them, including the Contacts application, implement their detail views as a grouped table (see Figure 9–23).

Figure 9–23. *An example of a grouped table view being used to present an editable table view*

Let's look at how to do this now. Before we begin, we need some data to show, and we need more than just a list of strings. In the previous two chapters, when we needed more complex data, such as with the multiline table in Chapter 8 or the ZIP codes picker in Chapter 7, we used an NSArray to hold a bunch of NSDictionary instances filled with our data. That works fine and is very flexible, but it's a little hard to work with. For this table's data, let's create a custom Objective-C data object to hold the individual instances that will be displayed in the list.

Creating the Data Model Object

The property list we'll be using in this section of the application contains data about the US presidents: each president's name, his party, the year he took office, and the year he left office. Let's create the class to hold that data.

Once again, single-click the *Classes* folder in Xcode to select it, and then press ⌘N to bring up the new file assistant. Select *Cocoa Touch Class* from the left pane, and then select *Objective-C class* and *NSObject* for *Subclass of*. Name this class *President.m* and don't forget the header file.

Click *President.h,* and make the following changes:

```
#import <Foundation/Foundation.h>

#define kPresidentNumberKey        @"President"
#define kPresidentNameKey          @"Name"
```

```
#define kPresidentFromKey          @"FromYear"
#define kPresidentToKey            @"ToYear"
#define kPresidentPartyKey         @"Party"

@interface President : NSObject {
@interface President : NSObject <NSCoding> {
    int         number;
    NSString    *name;
    NSString    *fromYear;
    NSString    *toYear;
    NSString    *party;
}
@property int number;
@property (nonatomic, copy) NSString *name;
@property (nonatomic, copy) NSString *fromYear;
@property (nonatomic, copy) NSString *toYear;
@property (nonatomic, copy) NSString *party;
@end
```

The five constants will be used to identify the fields when they are read from the file system. Conforming this class to the NSCoding protocol is what allows this object to be written to and created from files. The rest of the new stuff we've added to this header file is there to implement the properties needed to hold our data. Switch over to *President.m,* and make these changes:

```
#import "President.h"

@implementation President
@synthesize number;
@synthesize name;
@synthesize fromYear;
@synthesize toYear;
@synthesize party;

- (void)dealloc{
    [name release];
    [fromYear release];
    [toYear release];
    [party release];
    [super dealloc];
}

#pragma mark -
#pragma mark NSCoding
- (void)encodeWithCoder:(NSCoder *)coder {
    [coder encodeInt:self.number forKey:kPresidentNumberKey];
    [coder encodeObject:self.name forKey:kPresidentNameKey];
    [coder encodeObject:self.fromYear forKey:kPresidentFromKey];
    [coder encodeObject:self.toYear forKey:kPresidentToKey];
    [coder encodeObject:self.party forKey:kPresidentPartyKey];
}

- (id)initWithCoder:(NSCoder *)coder {
    if (self = [super init]) {
```

```
        number = [coder decodeIntForKey:kPresidentNumberKey];
        name = [[coder decodeObjectForKey:kPresidentNameKey] retain];
        fromYear = [[coder decodeObjectForKey:kPresidentFromKey] retain];
        toYear = [[coder decodeObjectForKey:kPresidentToKey] retain];
        party = [[coder decodeObjectForKey:kPresidentPartyKey] retain];
    }
    return self;
}

@end
```

Don't worry too much about the encodeWithCoder: and initWithCoder: methods. We'll be covering those in more detail in Chapter 12. All you need to know for now is that these two methods are part of the NSCoding protocol, which can be used to save objects to disk and load them back in. The encodeWithCoder: method encodes our object to be saved. initWithCoder: is used to create new objects from the saved file. These methods will allow us to create President objects from a property list archive file. Everything else in this class should be fairly self-explanatory.

We've provided you with a property list file that contains data for all the US presidents and can be used to create new instances of the President object we just wrote. We will be using this in the next section, so you don't need to type in a whole bunch of data. Grab the *Presidents.plist* file from the *09 Nav* folder in the projects archive, and add it to the *Resources* folder of your project.

Now, we're ready to write our two controller classes.

Creating the Detail View List Controller

For this part of the application, we're going to need two new controllers: one that will show the list to be edited and another to view and edit the details of the item selected in that list. Since both of these view controllers will be based on tables, we won't need to create any nib files, but we will need two separate controller classes. Let's create the files for both classes now and then implement them.

Select the *Classes* folder in the *Groups & Files* pane in Xcode, and then press ⌘**N** or select **File ➤ New File….** Select *Cocoa Touch Class,* select *Objective-C class*, and select *NSObject* for *Subclass of*. For a name, type *PresidentsViewController.m*. Repeat the same process a second time using the name *PresidentDetailController.m*. As always, pay attention to the spelling and remember to create the header files.

> **NOTE:** In case you were wondering, PresidentDetailController is singular (as opposed to PresidentsDetailController) because it deals with the details of a single president. Yes, we actually had a fistfight about that little detail, but one intense paintball session later, we are friends again.

Let's create the view controller that shows the list of presidents first. Single-click *PresidentsViewController.h,* and make the following changes:

```
#import <Foundation/Foundation.h>
#import "SecondLevelViewController.h"

@interface PresidentsViewController : NSObject {
@interface PresidentsViewController : SecondLevelViewController {
    NSMutableArray *list;
}
@property (nonatomic, retain) NSMutableArray *list;
@end
```

Then switch over to *PresidentsViewController.m* and make the following changes:

```
#import "PresidentsViewController.h"
#import "PresidentDetailController.h"
#import "President.h"

@implementation PresidentsViewController
@synthesize list;

- (void)viewDidLoad {
    NSString *path = [[NSBundle mainBundle] pathForResource:@"Presidents"
                                                    ofType:@"plist"];

    NSData *data;
    NSKeyedUnarchiver *unarchiver;

    data = [[NSData alloc] initWithContentsOfFile:path];
    unarchiver = [[NSKeyedUnarchiver alloc] initForReadingWithData:data];
    NSMutableArray *array = [unarchiver decodeObjectForKey:@"Presidents"];
    self.list = array;
    [unarchiver finishDecoding];
    [unarchiver release];
    [data release];

    [super viewDidLoad];
}

- (void)viewWillAppear:(BOOL)animated {
    [self.tableView reloadData];
    [super viewWillAppear:animated];
}

- (void)dealloc {
    [list release];
    [super dealloc];
}

#pragma mark -
#pragma mark Table Data Source Methods
- (NSInteger)tableView:(UITableView *)tableView
 numberOfRowsInSection:(NSInteger)section {
    return [list count];
}

- (UITableViewCell *)tableView:(UITableView *)tableView
        cellForRowAtIndexPath:(NSIndexPath *)indexPath {
```

```objectivec
    static NSString *PresidentListCellIdentifier =
        @"PresidentListCellIdentifier";

    UITableViewCell *cell = [tableView
        dequeueReusableCellWithIdentifier:PresidentListCellIdentifier];
    if (cell == nil) {
        cell = [[[UITableViewCell alloc]
            initWithStyle:UITableViewCellStyleSubtitle
            reuseIdentifier:PresidentListCellIdentifier] autorelease];
    }
    NSUInteger row = [indexPath row];
    President *thePres = [self.list objectAtIndex:row];
    cell.textLabel.text = thePres.name;
    cell.detailTextLabel.text = [NSString stringWithFormat:@"%@ - %@",
        thePres.fromYear, thePres.toYear];
    return cell;
}

#pragma mark -
#pragma mark Table Delegate Methods
- (void)tableView:(UITableView *)tableView
    didSelectRowAtIndexPath:(NSIndexPath *)indexPath {
    NSUInteger row = [indexPath row];
    President *prez = [self.list objectAtIndex:row];

    PresidentDetailController *childController =
    [[PresidentDetailController alloc] initWithStyle:UITableViewStyleGrouped];

    childController.title = prez.name;
    childController.president = prez;

    [self.navigationController pushViewController:childController
        animated:YES];
    [childController release];
}

@end
```

Most of the code you just entered is stuff you've seen before. One new thing is in the viewDidLoad method, where we used an NSKeyedUnarchiver method to create an array full of instances of the President class from our property list file. It's not important that you understand exactly what's going on there, as long as you know that we're loading an array full of Presidents.

First, we get the path for the property file.

```objectivec
    NSString *path = [[NSBundle mainBundle] pathForResource:@"Presidents"
        ofType:@"plist"];
```

Next, we declare a data object that will temporarily hold the encoded archive and an NSKeyedUnarchiver, which we'll use to actually restore the objects from the archive.

```objectivec
    NSData *data;
    NSKeyedUnarchiver *unarchiver;
```

We load the property list into data, and then use data to initialize unarchiver.

```
data = [[NSData alloc] initWithContentsOfFile:path];
unarchiver = [[NSKeyedUnarchiver alloc] initForReadingWithData:data];
```

Now, we decode an array from the archive. The key @"Presidents" is the same value that was used to create this archive.

```
NSMutableArray *array = [unarchiver decodeObjectForKey:@"Presidents"];
```

We then assign this decoded array to our list property, finalize the decoding process, clean up our memory, and make our call to super.

```
self.list = array;
[unarchiver finishDecoding];
[unarchiver release];
[data release];

[super viewDidLoad];
```

We also need to tell our tableView to reload its data in the viewWillAppear: method. If the user changes something in the detail view, we need to make sure that the parent view shows that new data. Rather than testing for a change, we force the parent view to reload its data and redraw each time it appears.

```
- (void)viewWillAppear:(BOOL)animated {
    [self.tableView reloadData];
    [super viewWillAppear:animated];
}
```

There's one other change from the last time we created a detail view. It's in the last method, tableView:didSelectRowAtIndexPath:. When we created the Disclosure Button view, we reused the same child controller every time and just changed its values. That's relatively easy to do when you have a nib with outlets. When you're using a table view to implement your detail view, the methods that fire the first time and the ones that fire subsequent times are different. Also, the table cells that are used to display and change the data are reused. The combination of these two details means your code can get very complex if you're trying to make it behave exactly the same way every time and to make sure that you are able to keep track of all the changes. Therefore, it's well worth the bit of additional overhead from allocating and releasing new controller objects to reduce the complexity of our controller class.

Let's look at the detail controller, because that's where the bulk of the new stuff is this time. This new controller is pushed onto the navigation stack when the user taps one of the rows in the PresidentsViewController table to allow data entry for that president. Let's implement the detail view now.

Creating the Detail View Controller

Please fasten your seatbelts, ladies and gentlemen. We're expecting a little turbulence ahead. Air sickness bags are located in the seat pocket in front of you.

This next controller is just a little on the gnarly side, but we'll get through it safely. Please remain seated. Single-click *PresidentDetailController.h,* and make the following changes:

```objc
#import <Foundation/Foundation.h>
#import <UIKit/UIKit.h>

@class President;
#define kNumberOfEditableRows       4
#define kNameRowIndex               0
#define kFromYearRowIndex           1
#define kToYearRowIndex             2
#define kPartyIndex                 3

#define kLabelTag                   4096

@interface PresidentDetailController : NSObject {
@interface PresidentDetailController : UITableViewController
        <UITextFieldDelegate> {
    President *president;
    NSArray *fieldLabels;
    NSMutableDictionary *tempValues;
    UITextField *textFieldBeingEdited;
}
@property (nonatomic, retain) President *president;
@property (nonatomic, retain) NSArray *fieldLabels;
@property (nonatomic, retain) NSMutableDictionary *tempValues;
@property (nonatomic, retain) UITextField *textFieldBeingEdited;

- (IBAction)cancel:(id)sender;
- (IBAction)save:(id)sender;
- (IBAction)textFieldDone:(id)sender;
@end
```

What the heck is going on here? This is new. In all our previous table view examples, each table row corresponded to a single row in an array. The array provided all the data the table needed. For example, our table of Pixar movies was driven by an array of strings, each string containing the title of a single Pixar movie.

Our presidents example features two different tables. One is a list of president names, and it is driven by an array with one president per row. The second table implements a detail view of a selected president. Since this table has a fixed number of fields, instead of using an array to supply data to this table, we define a series of constants we will use in our table data source methods. These constants define the number of editable fields, along with the index value for the row that will hold each of those properties.

There's also a constant called kLabelTag that we'll use to retrieve the UILabel from the cell so that we can set the label correctly for the row. Shouldn't there be another tag for the UITextField? Normally, yes, but we will need to use the tag property of the text field for another purpose. We'll use another slightly less convenient mechanism to retrieve the text field when we need to set its value. Don't worry if that seems confusing; everything should become clear when we actually write the code.

You should notice that this class conforms to three protocols this time: the table data source and delegate protocols (which this class inherits because it's a subclass of UITableViewController) and a new one, UITextFieldDelegate. By conforming to UITextFieldDelegate, we'll be notified when a user makes a change to a text field so that we can save the field's value. This application doesn't have enough rows for the table to ever need to scroll, but in many applications, a text field could scroll off the screen and, perhaps, be deallocated or reused. If the text field is lost, the value stored in it is lost, so saving the value when the user makes a change is the way to go.

Down a little further, we declare a pointer to a President object. This is the object that we will actually be editing using this view, and it's set in the tableView:didSelectRowAtIndexPath: of our parent controller based on the row selected there. When the user taps the row for Thomas Jefferson, for example, the PresidentsViewController will create an instance of the PresidentDetailController. The PresidentsViewController will then set the president property of that instance to the object that represents Thomas Jefferson, and push the newly created instance of PresidentDetailController onto the navigation stack.

The second instance variable, fieldLabels, is an array that holds a list of labels that correspond to the constants kNameRowIndex, kFromYearRowIndex, kToYearRowIndex, and kPartyIndex. For example, kNameRowIndex is defined as 0. So, the label for the row that shows the president's name is stored at index 0 in the fieldLabels array. You'll see this in action when we get to it in code.

Next, we define a mutable dictionary, tempValues, that will hold values from fields the user changes. We don't want to make the changes directly to the president object because if the user selects the *Cancel* button, we need the original data so we can go back to it. Instead, we will store any value that is changed in our new mutable dictionary, tempValues. For example, if the user edited the *Name:* field and then tapped the *Party:* field to start editing that one, the PresidentDetailController would be notified at that time that the *Name:* field had been edited, because it is the text field's delegate.

When the PresidentDetailController is notified of the change, it stores the new value in the dictionary using the name of the property it represents as the key. In our example, we would store a change to the *Name:* field using the key @"name". That way, regardless of whether users save or cancel, we have the data we need to handle it. If the users cancel, we just discard this dictionary, and if they save, we copy the changed values over to president.

Next up is a pointer to a UITextField, named textFieldBeingEdited. The moment the users click in one of the PresidentDetailController text fields, textFieldBeingEdited is set to point to that text field. Why do we need this text field pointer? We have an interesting timing problem, and textFieldBeingEdited is the solution.

Users can take one of two basic paths to finish editing a text field. First, they can touch another control or text field that becomes first responder. In this case, the text field that was being edited loses first responder status, and the delegate method textFieldDidEndEditing: is called. In this case, textFieldDidEndEditing: takes the new value of the text field and stores it in tempValues.

The second way the users can finish editing a text field by tapping the *Save* or *Cancel* button. When they do this, the save: or cancel: action method is called. In both methods, the PresidentDetailController view must be popped off the stack, since both the save and cancel actions end the editing session. This presents a problem. The save: and cancel: action methods do not have a simple way of finding the just-edited text field to save the data.

The delegate method textFieldDidEndEditing: does have access to the text field, since the text field is passed in as a parameter. That's where textFieldBeingEdited comes in. The cancel: action method ignores textFieldBeingEdited, since the user did not want to save changes, so the changes can be lost with no problem. But the save: method does care about those changes and needs a way to save them.

Since textFieldBeingEdited is maintained as a pointer to the current text field being edited, save: uses that pointer to copy the value in the text field to tempValues. Now, save: can do its job and pop the PresidentDetailController view off the stack, which will bring our list of presidents back to the top of the stack. When the view is popped off the stack, the text field and its value are lost. But since we've saved that sucker already, all is cool.

Single-click *PresidentDetailController.m,* and make the following changes:

```
#import "PresidentDetailController.h"
#import "President.h"

@implementation PresidentDetailController
@synthesize president;
@synthesize fieldLabels;
@synthesize tempValues;
@synthesize textFieldBeingEdited;

- (IBAction)cancel:(id)sender {
    [self.navigationController popViewControllerAnimated:YES];
}

- (IBAction)save:(id)sender {

  if (textFieldBeingEdited != nil) {
      NSNumber *tagAsNum= [[NSNumber alloc]
                          initWithInt:textFieldBeingEdited.tag];
      [tempValues setObject:textFieldBeingEdited.text forKey: tagAsNum];
      [tagAsNum release];
  }
  for (NSNumber *key in [tempValues allKeys]) {
      switch ([key intValue]) {
          case kNameRowIndex:
              president.name = [tempValues objectForKey:key];
              break;
          case kFromYearRowIndex:
              president.fromYear = [tempValues objectForKey:key];
              break;
          case kToYearRowIndex:
              president.toYear = [tempValues objectForKey:key];
```

```
                    break;
            case kPartyIndex:
                president.party = [tempValues objectForKey:key];
            default:
                break;
        }
    }
    [self.navigationController popViewControllerAnimated:YES];

    NSArray *allControllers = self.navigationController.viewControllers;
    UITableViewController *parent = [allControllers lastObject];
    [parent.tableView reloadData];
}

- (IBAction)textFieldDone:(id)sender {
    [sender resignFirstResponder];
}

#pragma mark -
- (void)viewDidLoad {
    NSArray *array = [[NSArray alloc] initWithObjects:@"Name:", @"From:",
                        @"To:", @"Party:", nil];
    self.fieldLabels = array;
    [array release];

    UIBarButtonItem *cancelButton = [[UIBarButtonItem alloc]
                                        initWithTitle:@"Cancel"
                                        style:UIBarButtonItemStylePlain
                                        target:self
                                        action:@selector(cancel:)];
    self.navigationItem.leftBarButtonItem = cancelButton;
    [cancelButton release];

    UIBarButtonItem *saveButton = [[UIBarButtonItem alloc]
                                        initWithTitle:@"Save"
                                        style:UIBarButtonItemStyleDone
                                        target:self
                                        action:@selector(save:)];
    self.navigationItem.rightBarButtonItem = saveButton;
    [saveButton release];

    NSMutableDictionary *dict = [[NSMutableDictionary alloc] init];
    self.tempValues = dict;
    [dict release];
    [super viewDidLoad];
}

- (void)dealloc {
    [president release];
    [fieldLabels release];
    [tempValues release];
    [textFieldBeingEdited release];
    [super dealloc];
}
```

```objc
#pragma mark -
#pragma mark Table Data Source Methods
- (NSInteger)tableView:(UITableView *)tableView
 numberOfRowsInSection:(NSInteger)section {
    return kNumberOfEditableRows;
}

- (UITableViewCell *)tableView:(UITableView *)tableView
        cellForRowAtIndexPath:(NSIndexPath *)indexPath {
    static NSString *PresidentCellIdentifier = @"PresidentCellIdentifier";

    UITableViewCell *cell = [tableView dequeueReusableCellWithIdentifier:
                           PresidentCellIdentifier];
    if (cell == nil) {
cell = [[[UITableViewCell alloc]
            initWithStyle:UITableViewCellStyleDefault
            reuseIdentifier:PresidentCellIdentifier] autorelease];
        UILabel *label = [[UILabel alloc] initWithFrame:
                    CGRectMake(10, 10, 75, 25)];
        label.textAlignment = UITextAlignmentRight;
        label.tag = kLabelTag;
        label.font = [UIFont boldSystemFontOfSize:14];
        [cell.contentView addSubview:label];
        [label release];

        UITextField *textField = [[UITextField alloc] initWithFrame:
                            CGRectMake(90, 12, 200, 25)];
        textField.clearsOnBeginEditing = NO;
        [textField setDelegate:self];
        textField.returnKeyType = UIReturnKeyDone;
        [textField addTarget:self
                    action:@selector(textFieldDone:)
            forControlEvents:UIControlEventEditingDidEndOnExit];
        [cell.contentView addSubview:textField];
    }
    NSUInteger row = [indexPath row];

    UILabel *label = (UILabel *)[cell viewWithTag:kLabelTag];
    UITextField *textField = nil;
    for (UIView *oneView in cell.contentView.subviews) {
        if ([oneView isMemberOfClass:[UITextField class]])
            textField = (UITextField *)oneView;
    }
    label.text = [fieldLabels objectAtIndex:row];
    NSNumber *rowAsNum = [[NSNumber alloc] initWithInt:row];
    switch (row) {
        case kNameRowIndex:
            if ([[tempValues allKeys] containsObject:rowAsNum])
                textField.text = [tempValues objectForKey:rowAsNum];
            else
                textField.text = president.name;
            break;
```

```
        case kFromYearRowIndex:
            if ([[tempValues allKeys] containsObject:rowAsNum])
                textField.text = [tempValues objectForKey:rowAsNum];
            else
                textField.text = president.fromYear;
            break;
        case kToYearRowIndex:
            if ([[tempValues allKeys] containsObject:rowAsNum])
                textField.text = [tempValues objectForKey:rowAsNum];
            else
                textField.text = president.toYear;
            break;
        case kPartyIndex:
        if ([[tempValues allKeys] containsObject:rowAsNum])
            textField.text = [tempValues objectForKey:rowAsNum];
        else
            textField.text = president.party;
        default:
            break;
    }
    if (textFieldBeingEdited == textField) {
        textFieldBeingEdited = nil;
    }
    textField.tag = row;
    [rowAsNum release];
    return cell;
}

#pragma mark -
#pragma mark Table Delegate Methods
- (NSIndexPath *)tableView:(UITableView *)tableView
  willSelectRowAtIndexPath:(NSIndexPath *)indexPath {
    return nil;
}

#pragma mark Text Field Delegate Methods
- (void)textFieldDidBeginEditing:(UITextField *)textField {
    self.textFieldBeingEdited = textField;
}

- (void)textFieldDidEndEditing:(UITextField *)textField {
    NSNumber *tagAsNum = [[NSNumber alloc] initWithInt:textField.tag];
    [tempValues setObject:textField.text forKey:tagAsNum];
    [tagAsNum release];
}

@end
```

The first new method is our cancel: action method. This is called, appropriately enough, when the user taps the *Cancel* button. When the *Cancel* button is tapped, the current view will be popped off the stack, and the previous view will rise to the top of the stack. Ordinarily, that job would be handled by the navigation controller, but a little later in the code, we're going to manually set the left bar button item. This means we're replacing the button that the navigation controller uses for that purpose. We can pop the current view off the stack by getting a reference to the navigation controller and telling it to do just that.

```
- (IBAction)cancel:(id)sender {
    [self.navigationController popViewControllerAnimated:YES];
}
```

The next method is save:, which gets called when the user taps the *Save* button. When the *Save* button is tapped, the values that the user has entered have already been stored in the tempValues dictionary, unless the keyboard is still visible and the cursor is still in one of the text fields. In that case, there may be changes to that text field that have not yet been put into our tempValues dictionary. To account for this, the first thing the save: method does is check to see if there is a text field that is currently being edited. Whenever the user starts editing a text field, we store a pointer to that text field in textFieldBeingEdited. If textFieldBeingEdited is not nil, we grab its value and stick it in tempValues.

```
if (textFieldBeingEdited != nil) {
    NSNumber *tfKey= [[NSNumber alloc] initWithInt:
        textFieldBeingEdited.tag];
    [tempValues setObject:textFieldBeingEdited.text forKey:tfKey];
    [tagAsNum release];
}
```

We then use fast enumeration to step through all the key values in the dictionary, using the row numbers as keys. We can't store raw datatypes like int in an NSDictionary, so we create NSNumber objects based on the row number and use those instead. We use intValue to turn the number represented by key back into an int, and then use a switch on that value using the constants we defined earlier and assign the appropriate value from the tempValues array back to the designated field on our president object.

```
for (NSNumber *key in [tempValues allKeys]) {
    switch ([key intValue]) {
        case kNameRowIndex:
            president.name = [tempValues objectForKey:key];
            break;
        case kFromYearRowIndex:
            president.fromYear = [tempValues objectForKey:key];
            break;
        case kToYearRowIndex:
            president.toYear = [tempValues objectForKey:key];
            break;
        case kPartyIndex:
            president.party = [tempValues objectForKey:key];
        default:
            break;
    }
}
```

Now, our president object has been updated, and we need to move up a level in the view hierarchy. Tapping a *Save* or *Done* button on a detail view should generally bring the user back up to the previous level, so we grab our application delegate and use its navController outlet to pop ourselves off of the navigation stack, sending the user back up to the list of presidents:

```
[self.navigationController popViewControllerAnimated:YES];
```

There's one other thing we need to do here: tell our parent view's table to reload its data. Because one of the fields that the user can edit is the name field, which is displayed in the `PresidentsViewController` table, if we don't have that table reload its data, it will continue to show the old value.

```
UINavigationController *navController = [delegate navController];
NSArray *allControllers = navController.viewControllers;
UITableViewController *parent = [allControllers lastObject];
[parent.tableView reloadData];
```

The third action method will be called when the user taps the *Done* button on the keyboard. Without this method, the keyboard won't retract when the user taps *Done*. This approach isn't strictly necessary in our application, since the four rows that can be edited here fit in the area above the keyboard. That said, you'll need this method if you add a row or in a future application that requires more screen real estate. It's a good idea to keep the behavior consistent from application to application, even if doing so is not critical to your application's functionality.

```
- (IBAction)textFieldDone:(id)sender {
    [sender resignFirstResponder];
}
```

The `viewDidLoad` method doesn't contain anything too surprising. We create the array of field names and assign it the `fieldLabels` property.

```
NSArray *array = [[NSArray alloc] initWithObjects:@"Name:",
        @"From:", @"To:", @"Party:", nil];
self.fieldLabels = array;
[array release];
```

Next, we create two buttons and add them to the navigation bar. We put the *Cancel* button in the left bar button item spot, which supplants the navigation button put there automatically. We put the *Save* button in the right spot and assign it the style `UIBarButtonItemStyleDone`. This style was specifically designed for this occasion—as a button users tap when they are happy with their changes and ready to leave the view. A button with this style will be blue instead of gray, and it usually will carry a label of *Save* or *Done*.

```
UIBarButtonItem *cancelButton = [[UIBarButtonItem alloc]
        initWithTitle:@"Cancel"
        style:UIBarButtonItemStylePlain
        target:self
        action:@selector(cancel:)];
self.navigationItem.leftBarButtonItem = cancelButton;
[cancelButton release];

UIBarButtonItem *saveButton = [[UIBarButtonItem alloc]
        initWithTitle:@"Save"
        style:UIBarButtonItemStyleDone
        target:self
        action:@selector(save:)];
self.navigationItem.rightBarButtonItem = saveButton;
[saveButton release];
```

Finally, we create a new mutable dictionary and assign it to `tempValues` so that we have a place to stick the changed values. If we made the changes directly to the `president` object, we would have no easy way to roll back to the original data if the user tapped *Cancel*.

```
NSMutableDictionary *dict = [[NSMutableDictionary alloc] init];
self.tempValues = dict;
[dict release];
[super viewDidLoad];
```

We can skip over the `dealloc` method and the first data source method, as there is nothing new under the sun there. We do need to stop and chat about `tableView:cellForRowAtIndexPath:`, however, because there are a few gotchas there. The first part of the method is exactly like every other `tableView:cellForRowAtIndexPath:` method we've written.

```
- (UITableViewCell *)tableView:(UITableView *)tableView
    cellForRowAtIndexPath:(NSIndexPath *)indexPath {
    static NSString *PresidentCellIdentifier = @"PresidentCellIdentifier";

    UITableViewCell *cell = [tableView dequeueReusableCellWithIdentifier:
        PresidentCellIdentifier];
    if (cell == nil) {
cell = [[[UITableViewCell alloc] initWithFrame:CGRectZero
                    reuseIdentifier:PresidentCellIdentifier] autorelease];
```

When we create a new cell, we create a label, make it right-aligned and bold, and assign it a tag so that we can retrieve it again later. Next, we add it to the cell's `contentView` and release it.

```
UILabel *label = [[UILabel alloc] initWithFrame:
    CGRectMake(10, 10, 75, 25)];
label.textAlignment = UITextAlignmentRight;
label.tag = kLabelTag;
label.font = [UIFont boldSystemFontOfSize:14];
[cell.contentView addSubview:label];
[label release];
```

After that, we create a new text field. The user actually types in this field. We set it so it does not clear the current value when editing so we don't lose the existing data, and we set `self` as the text field's delegate. By setting the text field's delegate to `self`, we can get notified by the text field when certain events occur by implementing appropriate methods from the `UITextFieldDelegate` protocol. As you'll see soon, we've implemented two text field delegate methods in this class. Those methods will be called by the text fields on all rows when the user begins and ends editing the text they contain. We also set the keyboard's **return key type**, which is how we specify the text for the key in the bottom right of the keyboard. The default value is *Return*, but since we have only single-line fields, we want the key to say *Done* instead, so we pass `UIReturnKeyDone`.

```
UITextField *textField = [[UITextField alloc] initWithFrame:
    CGRectMake(90, 12, 200, 25)];
textField.clearsOnBeginEditing = NO;
[textField setDelegate:self];
textField.returnKeyType = UIReturnKeyDone;
```

After that, we tell the text field to call our `textFieldDone:` method on the *Did End on Exit* event. This is exactly the same thing as dragging from the *Did End on Exit* event in the connections inspector in Interface Builder to *File's Owner* and selecting an action method. Since we don't have a nib file, we must do it programmatically, but the result is the same.

When we're finished configuring the text field, we add it to the cell's content view. Notice, however, that we did not set a tag before we added it to that view.

```
        [textField addTarget:self
                     action:@selector(textFieldDone:)
          forControlEvents:UIControlEventEditingDidEndOnExit];
        [cell.contentView addSubview:textField];
    }
```

At this point, we know that we have either a brand-new cell or a reused cell, but we don't know which. The first thing we do is figure out which row this darn cell is going to represent.

```
    NSUInteger row = [indexPath row];
```

Next, we need to get a reference to the label and the text field from inside this cell. The label is easy; we just use the tag we assigned to it to retrieve it from `cell`.

```
    UILabel *label = (UILabel *)[cell viewWithTag:kLabelTag];
```

The text field, however, isn't going to be quite as easy, because we need the tag in order to tell our text field delegates which text field is calling them. So, we're going to rely on the fact that there's only one text field that is a subview of our cell's `contentView`. We'll use fast enumeration to work through all of its subviews, and when we find a text field, we assign it to the pointer we declared a moment earlier. When the loop is done, the `textField` pointer should be pointing to the one and only text field contained in this cell.

```
    UITextField *textField = nil;

    for (UIView *oneView in cell.contentView.subviews) {
        if ([oneView isMemberOfClass:[UITextField class]])
            textField = (UITextField *)oneView;
    }
```

Now that we have pointers to both the label and the text field, we can assign them the correct values based on which field from the `president` object this row represents. Once again, the label gets its value from the `fieldLabels` array.

```
    label.text = [fieldLabels objectAtIndex:row];
```

To assign the value to the text field, we need to first check to see if there is a value in the `tempValues` dictionary corresponding to this row. If there is, we assign it to the text field. If there isn't any corresponding value in `tempValues`, we know there have been no changes entered for this field, so we assign this field the corresponding value from `president`.

```
    NSNumber *rowAsNum = [[NSNumber alloc] initWithInt:row];
    switch (row) {
```

```
        case kNameRowIndex:
            if ([[tempValues allKeys] containsObject:rowAsNum])
                textField.text = [tempValues objectForKey:rowAsNum];
            else
                textField.text = president.name;
            break;
        case kFromYearRowIndex:
            if ([[tempValues allKeys] containsObject:rowAsNum])
                textField.text = [tempValues objectForKey:rowAsNum];
            else
                textField.text = president.fromYear;
            break;
        case kToYearRowIndex:
            if ([[tempValues allKeys] containsObject:rowAsNum])
                textField.text = [tempValues objectForKey:rowAsNum];
            else
                textField.text = president.toYear;
             break;
        case kPartyIndex:
            if ([[tempValues allKeys] containsObject:rowAsNum])
                textField.text = [tempValues objectForKey:rowAsNum];
            else
                textField.text = president.party;
        default:
            break;
    }
```

If the field we're using is the one that is currently being edited, that's an indication that the value we're holding in `textFieldBeingEdited` is no longer valid, so we set `textFieldBeingEdited` to nil. If the text field did get released or reused, our text field delegate would have been called, and the correct value would already be in the `tempValues` dictionary.

```
    if (textFieldBeingEdited == textField) {
        textFieldBeingEdited = nil;
    }
```

Next, we set the text field's tag to the row it represents, which will allow us to know which field is calling our text field delegate methods.

```
    textField.tag = row;
```

Finally, we release `rowAsNum` to be a good memory citizen and return the `cell`.

```
    [rowAsNum release];
    return cell;
}
```

We do implement one table delegate method this time, which is `tableView:willSelectRowAtIndexPath:`. Remember that this method gets called before a row is selected and gives us a chance to disallow the row selection. In this view, we never want a row to appear selected. We need to know that the user selected a row so we can place a check mark next to it, but we don't want the row to actually be highlighted. Don't worry. A row doesn't need to be selected for a text field on that row to be editable, so this method just keeps the row from staying highlighted after it is touched.

```
- (NSIndexPath *)tableView:(UITableView *)tableView
    willSelectRowAtIndexPath:(NSIndexPath *)indexPath {
    return nil;
}
```

All that's left now are the two text field delegate methods. The first one we implement, textFieldDidBeginEditing:, is called whenever a text field for which we are the delegate becomes first responder. So, if the user taps a field and the keyboard pops up, we get notified. In this method, we store a pointer to the field currently being edited so that we have a way to get to the last changes made before the *Save* button was tapped.

```
- (void)textFieldDidBeginEditing:(UITextField *)textField {
    self.textFieldBeingEdited = textField;
}
```

The last method we wrote is called when the user stops editing a text field by tapping a different text field or pressing the *Done* button, or when another field became the first responder, which will happen, for example, when the user navigates back up to the list of presidents. Here, we save the value from that field in the tempValues dictionary so that we will have the changes if the user taps the *Save* button to confirm the changes.

```
- (void)textFieldDidEndEditing:(UITextField *)textField {
    NSNumber *tagAsNum = [[NSNumber alloc] initWithInt:textField.tag];
    [tempValues setObject:textField.text forKey:tagAsNum];
    [tagAsNum release];
}
```

And that's it. We're finished with these two view controllers.

Adding an Editable Detail View Controller Instance

Now, all we need to do is add an instance of this class to the top-level view controller. You know how to do this by now. Single-click *FirstLevelViewController.m*.

First, import the header from the new second-level view by adding the following line of code directly before the @implementation declaration:

```
#import "PresidentsViewController.h"
```

Then add the following code to the viewDidLoad method:

```
- (void)viewDidLoad {
    self.title = @"Top Level";
    NSMutableArray *array = [[NSMutableArray alloc] init];

    // Disclosure Button
    DisclosureButtonController *disclosureButtonController =
        [[DisclosureButtonController alloc]
            initWithStyle:UITableViewStylePlain];
    disclosureButtonController.title = @"Disclosure Buttons";
    disclosureButtonController.rowImage = [UIImage
        imageNamed:@"disclosureButtonControllerIcon.png"];
    [array addObject:disclosureButtonController];
    [disclosureButtonController release];

    // Checklist
```

```
        CheckListController *checkListController = [[CheckListController alloc]
                initWithStyle:UITableViewStylePlain];
        checkListController.title = @"Check One";
        checkListController.rowImage = [UIImage
            imageNamed:@"checkmarkControllerIcon.png"];
        [array addObject:checkListController];
        [checkListController release];

        // Table Row Controls
        RowControlsController *rowControlsController =
            [[RowControlsController alloc]
            initWithStyle:UITableViewStylePlain];
        rowControlsController.title = @"Row Controls";
        rowControlsController.rowImage =
            [UIImage imageNamed:@"rowControlsIcon.png"];
        [array addObject:rowControlsController];
        [rowControlsController release];

        // Move Me
        MoveMeController *moveMeController = [[MoveMeController alloc]
            initWithStyle:UITableViewStylePlain];
        moveMeController.title = @"Move Me";
        moveMeController.rowImage = [UIImage imageNamed:@"moveMeIcon.png"];
        [array addObject:moveMeController];
        [moveMeController release];

        // Delete Me
        DeleteMeController *deleteMeController = [[DeleteMeController alloc]
                initWithStyle:UITableViewStylePlain];
        deleteMeController.title = @"Delete Me";
        deleteMeController.rowImage = [UIImage imageNamed:@"deleteMeIcon.png"];
        [array addObject:deleteMeController];
        [deleteMeController release];

        // President View/Edit
        PresidentsViewController *presidentsViewController =
            [[PresidentsViewController alloc]
            initWithStyle:UITableViewStylePlain];
        presidentsViewController.title = @"Detail Edit";
        presidentsViewController.rowImage = [UIImage imageNamed:
            @"detailEditIcon.png"];
        [array addObject:presidentsViewController];
        [presidentsViewController release];

        self.controllers = array;
        [array release];
        [super viewDidLoad];
}
```

Save everything, sigh deeply, hold your breath, and then build that sucker. If everything is in order, the simulator will launch, and a sixth and final row will appear, just like the one in Figure 9–2. If you click the new row, you'll be taken to a list of US presidents (see Figure 9–24).

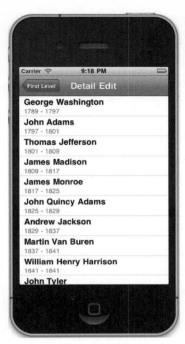

Figure 9–24. *Our sixth and final subcontroller presents a list of US presidents. Tap one of the presidents, and you'll be taken to a detail view (or a secret service agent will wrestle you to the ground).*

Tapping any of the rows will take you down to the detail view that we just built (see Figure 9–8), and you'll be able to edit the values. If you select the *Done* button in the keyboard, the keyboard should retract. Tap one of the editable values, and the keyboard will reappear. Make some changes and tap *Cancel*, and the application will pop back to the list of presidents. If you revisit the president you just canceled out of, your changes will be gone. On the other hand, if you make some changes and tap *Save*, your changes will be reflected in the parent table, and when you come back into the detail view, the new values will still be there.

But There's One More Thing. . .

There's one more bit of polish we need to add to make our application behave the way it should. In the version we just built, the keyboard incorporates a *Done* button that, when tapped, makes the keyboard retract. That behavior is proper if there are other controls on the view that the user might need to access. Since every row on this table view is a text field, however, we need a slightly different solution. The keyboard should feature a *Return* button instead of a *Done* button. When tapped, that button should take the user to the next row's text field.

In order to accomplish this, our first step is to replace the *Done* button with a *Return* button. We can do this by deleting a single line of code from

PresidentDetailController.m. In the `tableView:cellForRowAtIndexPath:` method, delete the following line of code:

```
- (UITableViewCell *)tableView:(UITableView *)tableView
        cellForRowAtIndexPath:(NSIndexPath *)indexPath {
    static NSString *PresidentCellIdentifier = @"PresidentCellIdentifier";
    UITableViewCell *cell = [tableView dequeueReusableCellWithIdentifier:
        PresidentCellIdentifier];
    if (cell == nil) {

        cell = [[[UITableViewCell alloc] initWithFrame:CGRectZero
                        reuseIdentifier:PresidentCellIdentifier] autorelease];
        UILabel *label = [[UILabel alloc] initWithFrame:
            CGRectMake(10, 10, 75, 25)];
        label.textAlignment = UITextAlignmentRight;
        label.tag = kLabelTag;
        label.font = [UIFont boldSystemFontOfSize:14];
        [cell.contentView addSubview:label];
        [label release];

        UITextField *textField = [[UITextField alloc] initWithFrame:
            CGRectMake(90, 12, 200, 25)];
        textField.clearsOnBeginEditing = NO;
        [textField setDelegate:self];
        textField.returnKeyType = UIReturnKeyDone;
        [textField addTarget:self
                    action:@selector(textFieldDone:)
                    forControlEvents:UIControlEventEditingDidEndOnExit];
        [cell.contentView addSubview:textField];
    }
    NSUInteger row = [indexPath row];
    ...
```

The next step isn't quite as straightforward. In our `textFieldDone:` method, instead of simply telling sender to resign first responder status, we need to somehow figure out what the next field should be and tell that field to become the first responder. Replace your current version of `textFieldDone:` with the following new version, and then we'll chat about how it works.

```
- (IBAction)textFieldDone:(id)sender {
    UITableViewCell *cell =
        (UITableViewCell *)[[sender superview] superview];
    UITableView *table = (UITableView *)[cell superview];
    NSIndexPath *textFieldIndexPath = [table indexPathForCell:cell];
    NSUInteger row = [textFieldIndexPath row];
    row++;
    if (row >= kNumberOfEditableRows) {
        row = 0;
    }
    NSIndexPath *newPath = [NSIndexPath indexPathForRow:row inSection:0];
    UITableViewCell *nextCell = [self.tableView
        cellForRowAtIndexPath:newPath];
    UITextField *nextField = nil;
    for (UIView *oneView in nextCell.contentView.subviews) {
        if ([oneView isMemberOfClass:[UITextField class]])
            nextField = (UITextField *)oneView;
```

```
    }
    [nextField becomeFirstResponder];
}
```

Unfortunately, cells don't know which row they represent. The table view, however, does know which row a given cell is currently representing. So, we get a reference to the table view cell. We know that the text field that is triggering this action method is a subview of the table cell view's content view, so we just need to get sender's superview's superview (now say *that* ten times fast).

If that sounded confusing, think of it this way. In this case, sender is the text field being edited. Our sender's superview is the content view that groups the text field and its label. And sender's superview's superview is the cell that encompasses that content view.

```
UITableViewCell *cell = (UITableViewCell *)[[(UIView *)sender
    superview] superview];
```

We also need access to the cell's enclosing table view, which is easy enough, since it's the superview of the cell.

```
UITableView *table = (UITableView *)[cell superview];
```

We then ask the table which row the cell represents. The response is an NSIndexPath, and we get the row from that.

```
NSIndexPath *textFieldIndexPath = [table indexPathForCell:cell];
NSUInteger row = [textFieldIndexPath row];
```

Next, we increment row by one, which represents the next row in the table. If incrementing the row number puts us beyond the last one, we reset row to 0.

```
row++;
if (row >= kNumberOfEditableRows) {
    row = 0;
}
```

Then we build a new NSIndexPath to represent the next row, and use that index path to get a reference to the cell currently representing the next row.

```
NSIndexPath *newPath = [NSIndexPath indexPathForRow:row inSection:0];
UITableViewCell *nextCell = [self.tableView
    cellForRowAtIndexPath:newPath];
```

Note that instead of using alloc and init methods to create the NSIndexPath, we're using a special factory method that exists just for the purpose of creating an index path that points out a row in a UITableView. This deviates somewhat from our policy of avoiding factory methods (which typically end up putting the object they create into an autorelease pool, adding a bit of overhead), but in this case, the benefit to our code is worth it. The normal way of creating an NSIndexPath otherwise involves first creating a C array, and then passing it to the initWithIndexes:length: method along with the length of the array. What we're doing here is much more straightforward.

For the text field, we're already using tag for another purpose, so we need to loop through the subviews of the cell's content view to find the text field rather than using tag to retrieve it.

```
UITextField *nextField = nil;
for (UIView *oneView in nextCell.contentView.subviews) {
    if ([oneView isMemberOfClass:[UITextField class]])
    nextField = (UITextField *)oneView;
}
```

Finally, we can tell that new text field to become the first responder.

```
[nextField becomeFirstResponder];
```

Now, compile and run. This time, when you drill down to the detail view, tapping the *Return* button will take you to the next field in the table, which will make entering data much easier for your users.

Breaking the Tape

This chapter was a marathon, and if you're still standing, you should feel pretty darn good about yourself. Dwelling on these mystical table view and navigation controller objects is important because they are the backbone of a great many iOS applications, and their complexity can definitely get you into trouble if you don't truly understand them.

As you start building your own tables, check back to this chapter and the previous one, and don't be afraid of Apple's documentation, either. Table views are extraordinarily complex, and we could never cover every conceivable permutation, but you should now have a very good set of table view building blocks you can use as you design and build your own applications. As always, feel free to reuse this code in your own applications. It's a gift from us to you. Enjoy!

In the next chapter, we're going to look at some user interface components that are specific to the iPad. In particular, you'll see how to apply the iPhone's navigation style to the iPad without having that whole big screen swishing side to side as you drill down and back out. The next chapter may not be quite the marathon this chapter was, but it's at least a half marathon, so complete your cooldown and drink plenty of fluids before rounding the bend. Oh, and don't forget to stretch.

iPad Considerations

From a technical standpoint, programming for the iPad is pretty much the same as programming for any other iOS device. Apart from the screen size, there's very little that differentiates a 3G iPad from an iPhone, or a Wi-Fi iPad from an iPod touch. In spite of the fundamental similarities between iPhone and iPad, from the user's point of view these devices are really quite different. Fortunately, Apple had the good sense to recognize this fact from the outset and equip the iPad with additional UIKit components that help create applications that better utilize the iPad's screen size and usage patterns. In this chapter, you'll learn how to use these components. Let's get started!

Split Views and Popovers

In Chapter 9, you spent a lot of time dealing with app navigation based on selections in table views, where each selection causes the top-level view, which fills the entire screen, to slide to the left and bring in the next view in the hierarchy, perhaps yet another table view. Plenty of iPhone and iPod touch apps work this way, both among Apple's own apps and third-party apps.

One typical example is Mail, which lets you drill down through servers and folders until you finally make your way to a message. Technically, this approach can work on the iPad as well, but it leads to a user interaction problem. On a screen the size of the iPhone or iPod touch, having a screen-sized view slide away to reveal another screen-sized view works well. On a screen the size of the iPad, however, that same interaction feels a little wrong, a little exaggerated, and even a little overwhelming. In addition, consuming such a large display with a single table view is inefficient in most cases.

As a result, you'll see that the built-in iPad apps do not actually behave that way. Instead, any drill-down navigation functionality, like that used in Mail, is relegated to a narrow column whose contents slide left or right as the user drills down or backs out. With the iPad in landscape mode, the navigation column is in a fixed position on the left, with the content of the selected item displayed on the right. This is what's called, in the iPad world, a split view (see Figure 10–1).

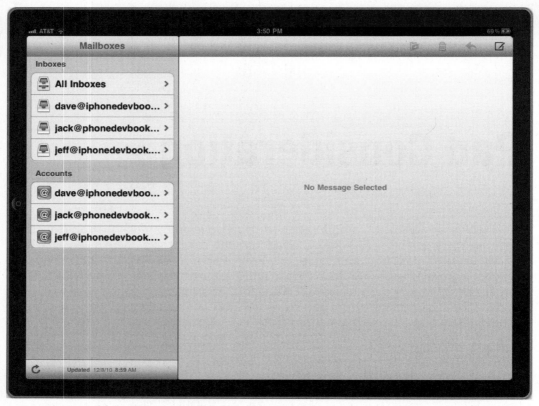

Figure 10–1. *This iPad, in landscape mode, is showing a split view. The navigation column is on the left. Tap an item in the navigation column, in this case a specific mail account, and that item's content is displayed in the area on the right.*

The left side of the split view is always 320 points wide (the same width as an iPhone in its portrait orientation), and the split view itself, with navigation and content side by side, appears only in landscape mode. If you turn the iPad to a portrait orientation, the split view is still in play, but it's no longer visible in the same way. The navigation view loses its permanent location and can be activated only by tapping a toolbar button, which causes the navigation view to pop up in a view that floats in front of everything else on the screen (see Figure 10–2). This is what's called a popover.

Figure 10–2. *This iPad, in portrait mode, does not show the same split view. Instead, the information that made up the left side of the split view in landscape mode is embedded in a popover. Mmmm, popovers.*

In this chapter's example project, you'll see how to create an iPad application that uses both a split view and a popover.

Create a SplitView Project

We're going to start off pretty easily, by taking advantage of one of Xcode's predefined templates to create a split view project. We're going to build an app that presents a slightly different take on Chapter 9's presidential app, listing all the U.S. presidents and showing the Wikipedia entry for whichever one you select.

Go to Xcode and select **File ➤ New Project**…. From the iOS *Application* group, select *Split View-based Application*. Make sure the Core Data check box is off, and name the new project *Presidents*. Xcode will do its usual thing, creating a handful of classes and *.xib* files for you, and then show you the project. Expand the *Classes* and *Resources* folders, and take a look through each one.

From the start, the project contains an app delegate (as usual), a class called `RootViewController`, and a class called `DetailViewController`. Those two view controllers represent, respectively, the views that will appear on the left and right sides of the split view. `RootViewController` defines the top-level of a navigation structure, and

DetailViewController defines what's displayed in the larger area when a navigation element is selected. When the app launches, both of these are contained inside a split view, which as you may recall does a bit of shape-shifting as the device is rotated.

To see what this particular application template gives you in terms of functionality, build and run it in the simulator. Switch between landscape mode (Figure 10–3) and portrait mode (Figure 10–4), and you'll see the split view in action. In landscape mode, the split view works by showing the navigation view on the left and the detail view on the right. In portrait mode, the detail view occupies most of the picture, with the navigation elements confined to the popover, which is brought into view with the tap of the button in the top left of the view.

Figure 10–3. *This screenshot shows the default Split View-based Application template in landscape mode. Note the similarity between this figure and Figure 10–1.*

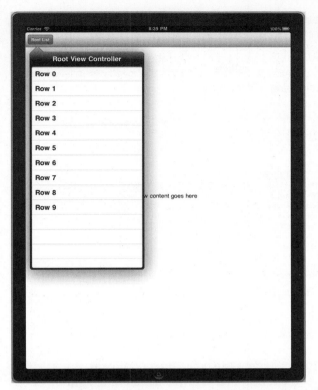

Figure 10–4. *This screenshot shows the default Split View-based Application template in portrait mode with the popover showing. Note the similarity between this figure and Figure 10–2.*

We're going to build on this to make the president-presenting app we want, but first let's dig into what's already there.

The Xib Defines the Structure

Right off the bat, you have a pretty complex set of view controllers in play. There's a split view controller that contains all the elements, a navigation controller to handle the goings-on of the left side of the split, a root view controller inside the navigation controller, and a detail view controller on the right.

In the default Split View-based Application template that we used, these view controllers are set up and interconnected primarily in the main *.xib* file rather than in code. Apart from doing GUI layout, Interface Builder really shines as a way of letting you connect different components without writing a bunch of code just to establish relationships. Let's dig into the project's *.xib* files to see how things are set up.

In the *Resources* folder, double-click *DetailView.xib* to open it in Interface Builder. This *.xib* file is pretty straightforward, containing just a view with a label on it, and the `DetailViewController` class as its file's owner. We'll return to this later and make some changes, but only after we've seen how the other controllers fit together. For now, you can close *DetailView.xib*.

Back in Xcode, double-click *MainWindow.xib* to edit it in Interface Builder. You'll definitely want to switch from icon view to list view in order to get a better sense of the object hierarchy. Figure 10–5 shows all there is to see here.

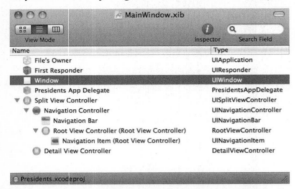

Figure 10–5. *MainWindow.xib open in InterfaceBuilder. This complex object hierarchy is best viewed in list mode, in combination with the connections inspector.*

Open the connections inspector, and spend some time clicking each of the view controllers to get a sense of how they relate to one another. The app delegate contains outlets to each of the other view controllers except the navigation controller. Among the other controllers, you'll see that most of them don't have any outlets pointing at other controllers, but several of them do "contain" one or more of the others, such as the split view, which contains the navigation and detail controllers, and the navigation controller, which contains the root view controller. The exception is the root view controller, which has an outlet to the detail view controller; that lets it update the detail view when the user's selection changes.

Next, open the attributes inspector and spend some time clicking each of the view controllers. Notice that the attributes inspector contains a *View Controller* section, which includes a field labeled *NIB Name*. For most of the view controllers, the *NIB Name* field is empty, but in the case of the detail view controller, it's set to *DetailView*, which you'll recall is the name of the first nib file we looked at. This means that when *MainWindow.xib* is loaded and the detail view controller is created, it won't look for its GUI in the same nib file but will instead load the other nib file that is specified.

This kind of setup gives you a lot of flexibility, since you're free to determine yourself which views belong in the main view and which you want to put in a separate nib. In this case, *MainWindow.xib* really contains one "interesting" view controller, and its view is loaded from an external nib; all the other view controllers are either table view controllers (which create their own table view automatically) or container view controllers (such as `UISplitViewController` and `UINavigationController`), which don't present any editable view at all.

What's left, then, in *MainWindow.xib* is really a definition of how the app's various controllers are interconnected. Like most cases where you're using nib files, this eliminates a lot of code, which is a good thing most of the time. If you're the kind of person who likes to see all such configuration done in code, you're free to do so, but for this example we're going to stick with what Xcode has provided.

The Code Defines the Functionality

One of the main reasons for keeping the view controller interconnections in a nib file is that it doesn't clutter up our source code with configuration information that doesn't need to be there. What's left, therefore, is just the code that defines the actual functionality. So let's start looking at what we have as a starting point. Xcode defined several classes for us when the project was created, and we're going to peek into each of them before we start making any changes.

First up is *PresidentsAppDelegate.h*, which looks something like this:

```
#import <UIKit/UIKit.h>

@class RootViewController;
@class DetailViewController;

@interface PresidentsAppDelegate : NSObject <UIApplicationDelegate> {

    UIWindow *window;

    UISplitViewController *splitViewController;

    RootViewController *rootViewController;
    DetailViewController *detailViewController;
}

@property (nonatomic, retain) IBOutlet UIWindow *window;

@property (nonatomic, retain) IBOutlet UISplitViewController *splitViewController;
@property (nonatomic, retain) IBOutlet RootViewController *rootViewController;
@property (nonatomic, retain) IBOutlet DetailViewController *detailViewController;

@end
```

It's pretty similar to several other application delegates you've seen in this book so far. The biggest difference is that there are outlets for several controllers instead of just one. This lets us use the app delegate as a central point through which all controllers can be accessed. Switch over to the implementation in *PresidentsAppDelegate.m*, which looks something like the following (we've deleted most comments and empty methods here for the sake of brevity):

```
#import "PresidentsAppDelegate.h"
#import "RootViewController.h"
#import "DetailViewController.h"

@implementation PresidentsAppDelegate
```

```
@synthesize window, splitViewController, rootViewController, detailViewController;

- (BOOL)application:(UIApplication *)application
    didFinishLaunchingWithOptions:(NSDictionary *)launchOptions {
    // Override point for customization after app launch.

    // Add the split view controller's view to the window and display.
    [self.window addSubview:splitViewController.view];
    [self.window makeKeyAndVisible];

    return YES;
}

- (void)dealloc {
    [splitViewController release];
    [window release];
    [super dealloc];
}

@end
```

Once again, nothing really is groundbreaking here; this code sets up display of our application's main view (in this case the UISplitViewController that's going to contain everything else), just like you've done many times over the course of this book, and performs some cleanup at the end.

Now let's take a look at RootViewController, which controls the setup of the table view containing the app's navigation. *RootViewController.h* looks like this:

```
#import <UIKit/UIKit.h>

@class DetailViewController;

@interface RootViewController : UITableViewController {
    DetailViewController *detailViewController;
}

@property (nonatomic, retain) IBOutlet DetailViewController *detailViewController;

@end
```

And its corresponding *RootViewController.m* file looks like this (after removing the noncode bits):

```
#import "RootViewController.h"
#import "DetailViewController.h"

@implementation RootViewController

@synthesize detailViewController;

- (void)viewDidLoad {
    [super viewDidLoad];
    self.clearsSelectionOnViewWillAppear = NO;
    self.contentSizeForViewInPopover = CGSizeMake(320.0, 600.0);
}
```

```objc
- (BOOL)shouldAutorotateToInterfaceOrientation:
    (UIInterfaceOrientation)interfaceOrientation {
    return YES;
}

- (NSInteger)numberOfSectionsInTableView:(UITableView *)aTableView {
    return 1;
}

- (NSInteger)tableView:(UITableView *)aTableView
    numberOfRowsInSection:(NSInteger)section {
    return 10;
}

- (UITableViewCell *)tableView:(UITableView *)tableView
    cellForRowAtIndexPath:(NSIndexPath *)indexPath {

    static NSString *CellIdentifier = @"CellIdentifier";

    UITableViewCell *cell = [tableView dequeueReusableCellWithIdentifier:
                                CellIdentifier];
    if (cell == nil) {
        cell = [[[UITableViewCell alloc] initWithStyle:UITableViewCellStyleDefault
            reuseIdentifier:CellIdentifier] autorelease];
        cell.accessoryType = UITableViewCellAccessoryNone;
    }

    // Configure the cell.
    cell.textLabel.text = [NSString stringWithFormat:@"Row %d", indexPath.row];
    return cell;
}

- (void)tableView:(UITableView *)aTableView didSelectRowAtIndexPath:
    (NSIndexPath *)indexPath {
    detailViewController.detailItem = [NSString stringWithFormat:@"Row %d",
        indexPath.row];
}

- (void)dealloc {
    [detailViewController release];
    [super dealloc];
}
```

@end

There's a fair amount of logic there, but, fortunately, Xcode provided it for you as part of the split view template. For the most part, what you are seeing is a standard table view controller. However, there are a few things we want to point out about the code shown previously that are relevant to iPad, which you may not have come across before.

First, the viewDidLoad method includes a line that sets the view's contentSizeForViewInPopover property. Chances are you can guess what this does: It sets the size that will be used if this view controller should happen to be used to provide the display for a popover controller. This rectangle must be at least 320 pixels wide, but apart from that, you can set the size pretty much however you like. We'll get into more popover issues a little later in this chapter.

The second thing worth mentioning is the shouldAutorotateToInterfaceOrientation: method. Typically, in an iPhone app, you'd specify there whether a particular orientation was suitable for your purposes. In an iPad app, however, the recommendation is generally to let your users choose which way is up for themselves. Unless you're making a game, where you want to force the display to a specific orientation, iPad apps nearly always want this method to return YES.

The final point of interest here is the tableView:didSelectRowAtIndexPath: method. In previous chapters, when you implemented table view controllers that respond to a user row selection, at this point you typically created a new view controller and pushed it onto the navigation controller's stack. In this app, however, the view controller we want to show is already in place; it's the instance of DetailViewController contained in the *xib* file. So all we need to do here is tell that DetailViewController instance what to display.

The final class created for us by Xcode is DetailViewController, which takes care of the actual display of the item the user chooses. We've already taken a peek at the *DetailView.xib* nib file. Here's what *DetailViewController.h* looks like:

```
#import <UIKit/UIKit.h>

@interface DetailViewController : UIViewController <UIPopoverControllerDelegate,
    UISplitViewControllerDelegate> {
    UIPopoverController *popoverController;
    UIToolbar *toolbar;
    id detailItem;
    UILabel *detailDescriptionLabel;
}
@property (nonatomic, retain) IBOutlet UIToolbar *toolbar;
@property (nonatomic, retain) id detailItem;
@property (nonatomic, retain) IBOutlet UILabel *detailDescriptionLabel;
@end
```

Apart from the detailItem property that we've seen referenced before (in the RootViewController class), DetailViewController has two outlets for connecting to GUI components in the nib file (toolbar and detailDescriptionLabel) and an instance variable for a popover controller, which we'll describe in a moment.

Switch over to *DetailViewController.m*, where you'll find the following (once again, somewhat abridged):

```
#import "DetailViewController.h"
#import "RootViewController.h"

@interface DetailViewController ()
@property (nonatomic, retain) UIPopoverController *popoverController;
- (void)configureView;
@end

@implementation DetailViewController

@synthesize toolbar, popoverController, detailItem, detailDescriptionLabel;

- (void)setDetailItem:(id)newDetailItem {
    if (detailItem != newDetailItem) {
        [detailItem release];
```

```objc
        detailItem = [newDetailItem retain];

        // Update the view.
        [self configureView];
    }

    if (self.popoverController != nil) {
        [self.popoverController dismissPopoverAnimated:YES];
    }
}


- (void)configureView {
    // Update the user interface for the detail item.
    detailDescriptionLabel.text = [detailItem description];
}

- (void)splitViewController: (UISplitViewController*)svc
    willHideViewController:(UIViewController *)aViewController
    withBarButtonItem:(UIBarButtonItem*)barButtonItem forPopoverController:
    (UIPopoverController*)pc {

    barButtonItem.title = @"Root List";
    NSMutableArray *items = [[toolbar items] mutableCopy];
    [items insertObject:barButtonItem atIndex:0];
    [toolbar setItems:items animated:YES];
    [items release];
    self.popoverController = pc;
}

- (void)splitViewController: (UISplitViewController*)svc
    willShowViewController:(UIViewController *)aViewController
    invalidatingBarButtonItem:(UIBarButtonItem *)barButtonItem {

    NSMutableArray *items = [[toolbar items] mutableCopy];
    [items removeObjectAtIndex:0];
    [toolbar setItems:items animated:YES];
    [items release];
    self.popoverController = nil;
}

- (BOOL)shouldAutorotateToInterfaceOrientation:
    (UIInterfaceOrientation)interfaceOrientation {
    return YES;
}

- (void)viewDidUnload {
    // Release any retained subviews of the main view.
    // e.g. self.myOutlet = nil;
    self.popoverController = nil;
}

- (void)dealloc {
    [popoverController release];
    [toolbar release];
    [detailItem release];
    [detailDescriptionLabel release];
```

```
    [super dealloc];
}
@end
```

Much of this should look familiar to you, but this class contains a few new things worth going over here. The first of these is something called a class extension, declared near the top of the file:

```
@interface DetailViewController ()
@property (nonatomic, retain) UIPopoverController *popoverController;
- (void)configureView;
@end
```

Creating a class extension lets you define some methods and properties that are going to be used within your class but that you don't want to expose to other classes in a header file. Here we've declared a popoverController property, which will make use of the instance variable we declared earlier, and a utility method, which will be called whenever we need to update the display. We still haven't told you what the popoverController property is meant to be used for, but we're getting there!

Just a bit further down, you'll see this method:

```
- (void)setDetailItem:(id)newDetailItem {
    if (detailItem != newDetailItem) {
        [detailItem release];
        detailItem = [newDetailItem retain];

        // Update the view.
        [self configureView];
    }

    if (self.popoverController != nil) {
        [self.popoverController dismissPopoverAnimated:YES];
    }
}
```

The setDetailItem: method may seem surprising to you. We did, after all, define detailItem as a property, and we synthesized it to create the getter and setter for us, so why create a setter in code? In this case, we need to be able to react whenever the user calls the setter so that we can update the display, and this is a good way to do it. The first part of the method seems pretty straightforward, but at the end it diverges into a call to dismiss the current popoverController, if there is one. Where in the world is that hypothetical popupController coming from? The very next method contains the answer:

```
- (void)splitViewController:(UISplitViewController*)svc
        willHideViewController:(UIViewController *)aViewController
        withBarButtonItem:(UIBarButtonItem*)barButtonItem
        forPopoverController:(UIPopoverController*)pc {

    barButtonItem.title = @"Root List";
    NSMutableArray *items = [[toolbar items] mutableCopy];
    [items insertObject:barButtonItem atIndex:0];
    [toolbar setItems:items animated:YES];
    [items release];
    self.popoverController = pc;
}
```

This method is a delegate method for `UISplitViewController`. It's called when the split view controller is no longer going to show the left side of the split view as a permanent fixture (that is, when the iPad is rotated to portrait orientation). The split view controller calls this method in the delegate and passes a couple of interesting items: a `UIPopoverController` and a `UIBarButtonItem`. The `UIPopoverController` is already preconfigured to contain whatever was in the left side of the split view, and the `UIBarButtonItem` is set up to display that very same popover.

What this means is that if our GUI contains a `UIToolbar` (as ours does), we just need to add the button item to our toolbar in order let the user bring up the navigation with a single tap in on the button item. If our GUI didn't contain a `UIToolbar`, we'd still have the popover controller passed in, which we could assign to some other element of our GUI so it could pop open the popover for us. We're also handed the wrapped `UIViewController` itself (`RootViewController`, in this case) in case we'd rather present its contents in some other way entirely.

So, that's where the popover controller comes from. You may not be too surprised to learn that the next method effectively takes it away:

```
- (void)splitViewController: (UISplitViewController*)svc
    willShowViewController:(UIViewController *)aViewController
    invalidatingBarButtonItem:(UIBarButtonItem *)barButtonItem {

    NSMutableArray *items = [[toolbar items] mutableCopy];
    [items removeObjectAtIndex:0];
    [toolbar setItems:items animated:YES];
    [items release];
    self.popoverController = nil;
}
```

That method is called when the user switches back to landscape orientation, at which point the split view controller wants to once again draw the left-side view in a permanent position, so it tells us to get rid of the UIBarButtonItem we were given previously.

That concludes our overview of what Xcode's Split View-based Application template gives you. It might be a lot to absorb at a glance, but ideally, by presenting it a piece at a time, we've helped you understand how all the pieces fit together.

Here Come the Presidents

Now that you've seen the basic layout of this app, it's time to "fill in the blanks" and turn this autogenerated app into something all our own. Start by looking in the book's source code archive, where the folder *10 – Presidents* will contain a file called *PresidentList.plist*. Drag that file into your project's Resources folder in Xcode to add it to the project, making sure that the check box telling Xcode to copy the file itself is in the "on" state. This plist file contains information about all the U.S. presidents so far, consisting of just the name and Wikipedia entry URL for each of them.

Now let's look at the `RootViewController` class and see how we need to modify it to handle the presidential data properly. It's going to be a simple matter of loading the list of presidents, presenting them in the table view, and passing a URL to the detail view for display. In *RootViewController.h*, add the bold lines shown here:

```
@interface RootViewController : UITableViewController {
    DetailViewController *detailViewController;
    NSArray *presidents;
}
@property (nonatomic, retain) IBOutlet DetailViewController *detailViewController;
@property (nonatomic, retain) NSArray *presidents;
@end
```

Then switch to *RootViewController.m*, where the changes are a little more involved (but still not too bad). Start off by synthesizing the presidents property near the top of the file:

```
@implementation RootViewController
@synthesize detailViewController;
@synthesize presidents;
```

Then update the viewDidLoad method, adding a few lines to load the list of presidents:

```
- (void)viewDidLoad {
    [super viewDidLoad];
    self.clearsSelectionOnViewWillAppear = NO;
    self.contentSizeForViewInPopover = CGSizeMake(320.0, 600.0);
    NSString *path = [[NSBundle mainBundle] pathForResource:@"PresidentList"
        ofType:@"plist"];
    NSDictionary *presidentInfo = [NSDictionary dictionaryWithContentsOfFile:path];
    self.presidents = [presidentInfo objectForKey:@"presidents"];
}
```

Complete the "bookkeeping" part of this class by making these changes to the viewDidUnload and dealloc methods further down:

```
- (void)viewDidUnload {
    self.presidents = nil;
}

- (void)dealloc {
    [presidents release];
    [detailViewController release];
    [super dealloc];
}
```

Next, update the method that tells the table view how many rows to display, by deleting the original row that was hardwired to return 10:

```
- (NSInteger)tableView:(UITableView *)tableView numberOfRowsInSection:(NSInteger)section
{
    return 10;
    return [self.presidents count];
}
```

After that, modify the tableView:cellForRowAtIndexPath: method to make each cell display a president's name, by making this change at the end of the method:

```
    // Configure the cell.
    NSDictionary *president = [self.presidents objectAtIndex:indexPath.row];
```

```
    cell.textLabel.text = [president objectForKey:@"name"];
    cell.textLabel.text = [NSString stringWithFormat:@"Row %d", indexPath.row];
    return cell;
```

Finally, it's time to update the behavior of tableView:didSelectRowAtIndexPath: to pass the URL to the detail view controller:

```
- (void)tableView:(UITableView *)aTableView didSelectRowAtIndexPath:(NSIndexPath
*)indexPath {
    detailViewController.detailItem = [NSString stringWithFormat:@"Row %d",
        indexPath.row];
    NSDictionary *president = [self.presidents objectAtIndex:indexPath.row];
    NSString *urlString = [president objectForKey:@"url"];
    detailViewController.detailItem = urlString;
}
```

That's all we need to do for RootViewController. At this point, you can build and run the app again, and you'll see that, in the navigation view, the table of 10 rows the app had from the start has been replaced by a table listing all the presidents. Tapping any one of them will display the URL in the detail view.

Let's finish this section by making that detail view do something a little more useful with that URL. Start with *DetailViewContoller.h*, where we'll add an outlet for a web view to display the Wikipedia page for the selected president. Add the bold lines shown here:

```
@interface DetailViewController : UIViewController <UIPopoverControllerDelegate,
UISplitViewControllerDelegate> {
    UIPopoverController *popoverController;
    UIToolbar *toolbar;
    id detailItem;
    UILabel *detailDescriptionLabel;
    UIWebView *webView;
}
@property (nonatomic, retain) IBOutlet UIToolbar *toolbar;
@property (nonatomic, retain) id detailItem;
@property (nonatomic, retain) IBOutlet UILabel *detailDescriptionLabel;
@property (nonatomic, retain) IBOutlet UIWebView *webView;
@end
```

Then switch to *DetailViewController.m*, where we have a bit more to do (though really, not too much). Start near the top of the class's @implementation block, adding synthesis for the webView property:

```
@synthesize toolbar, popoverController, detailItem, detailDescriptionLabel;
@synthesize webView;
```

Then scroll down to the configureView method, and add the bold methods shown here:

```
- (void)configureView {
    // Update the user interface for the detail item.
    NSURL *url = [NSURL URLWithString:detailItem];
    NSURLRequest *request = [NSURLRequest requestWithURL:url];
    [self.webView loadRequest:request];

    detailDescriptionLabel.text = [detailItem description];
}
```

Those new lines are all that are needed to get our web view to load the requested page. Next, move on down to the splitViewController: willHideViewController:withBarButtonItem:forPopoverController: method, where we're simply going to give the UIBarButtonItem a more relevant title:

```
barButtonItem.title = @"Root List";
barButtonItem.title = @"Presidents";
```

All that's left now is to clean up after ourselves, first in the viewDidUnload method:

```
- (void)viewDidUnload {
    // Release any retained subviews of the main view.
    // e.g. self.myOutlet = nil;
    self.popoverController = nil;
    self.webView = nil;
}
```

and then a bit more in dealloc:

```
- (void)dealloc {
    [popoverController release];
    [toolbar release];
    [detailItem release];
    [detailDescriptionLabel release];
    [webView release];
    [super dealloc];
}
```

Believe it or not, those few edits are all the code we need to write at this point. The final changes we need to make are in *DetailView.xib*. Open it for editing, and start by taking care of the label in the GUI (whose text reads "Detail view content goes here").

Drag the label to the top of the window. Note that the label should run from left to right blue guideline and fit snugly under the toolbar. This label is being repurposed to show us the current URL. But when the application launches, before the user has chosen a president, we want this field to give the user a hint about what to do.

Select the text, and change it to *Select a President*. You should also use the size inspector to make sure that the label's position is anchored to both the left and right sides as well as the top edge and that it allows horizontal resizing so that it can adjust itself between landscape and portrait orientations (see Figure 10–6).

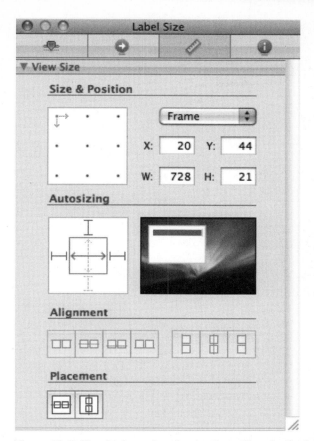

Figure 10–6. *The size inspector, showing the settings for the Select a President label*

Then use the library to find a UIWebView, and drag it into the space below the label you just moved. After dropping it there, use the resize handles to make it fill the rest of the view below the label. Make it go left edge to right edge and from the blue guideline just below the bottom of the label all the way to the very bottom of the window.

Next, use the size inspector to anchor the web view to all four edges, and allow it to resize both horizontally and vertically (Figure 10–7). To hook up the outlet you created, control-drag from the File's Owner icon in the main nib window to our new UIWebView, and connect the webView outlet. Save your changes, and you're done!

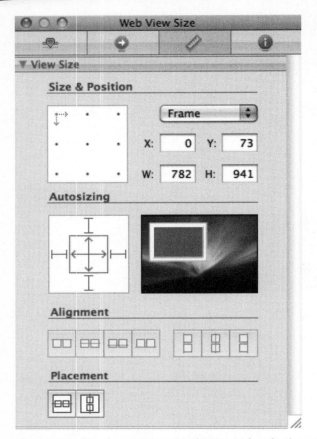

Figure 10–7. *The size inspector, showing the settings for the web view*

Now you can build and run the app, and it will let you see the Wikipedia entries for each of the presidents. Rotate the display between the two orientations, and you'll see how the split view controller handles everything for you, with a little help from the detail view controller for handling the toolbar item required for showing a popover (just like in the original app before we made our changes).

The final change to make in this section is strictly a cosmetic one. When you run this app in landscape orientation, the heading above the navigation view on the left is *Root View Controller*. Switch to portrait orientation, and tap the *Presidents* toolbar button; you see the same.

To fix this, open *MainWindow.xib*, double-click the *Split View Controller* icon in the main nib window, and then double-click the text shown in the upper-left portion of the view, changing it to *Presidents* (Figure 10–8). Save the nib file, return to Xcode, and build and run; you should see your change in place.

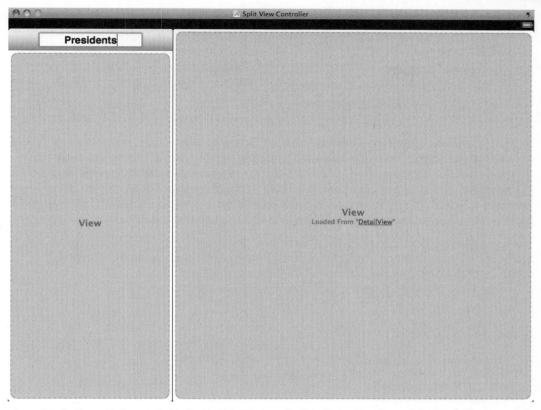

Figure 10–8. *The split view controller inside MainWindow.xib. Note that we've changed the title in the upper-left corner to say Presidents.*

Create Your Own Popover

That's all well and good, but there's still one piece of iPad GUI technology that we haven't dealt with in quite enough detail yet: the creation and display of your own popover. So far, at most we've had a UIPopoverController handed to us from a UISplitView delegate method, which let us keep track of it in an instance variable so we could force it to go away, but popovers really come in handy when you want to present your own view controllers.

To see how this works, we're going to add a popover of our own, to be activated by a permanent toolbar item (unlike the one that the UISplitView delegate method gives us, which is meant to come and go). This popover will display a table view containing a list of languages. If the user picks a language from the list, the web view will load whatever Wikipedia entry was already showing in the new language. This will be a simple enough thing to do, since switching from one language to another in Wikipedia is just a matter of changing a small piece of the URL that contains an embedded country code.

> **NOTE:** Both uses of popovers in this example are in the service of showing a UITableView, but don't let that mislead you; UIPopoverController can be used to handle the display of any view controller content you like! We're sticking with table views for this example because it's a common use case, it's easy to show in a relatively small amount of code, and it's something with which you should already be quite familiar.

Start off by right-clicking the *Classes* folder in Xcode and selecting **Add ➤ New File...** from the contextual menu. When the assistant appears, select *Cocoa Touch Class*, select *UIViewController subclass*, turn on the check boxes next to *Targeted for iPad* and *UITableViewController subclass*, and turn off the check box next to *With XIB for user interface*. Click *Next*, and name the class's source code file *LanguageListController.m*. Be sure the *create header file* check box is checked, and then click *Finish*.

The LanguageListController is going to be a pretty standard table view controller class. It will display a list of items and let the detail view controller know when a choice is made by using a pointer back to the detail view controller. Edit *LanguageListController.h*, adding the bold lines shown here:

```
#import <UIKit/UIKit.h>

@class DetailViewController;

@interface LanguageListController : UITableViewController {
    DetailViewController *detailViewController;
    NSArray *languageNames;
    NSArray *languageCodes;
}

@property (nonatomic, assign) DetailViewController *detailViewController;
@property (nonatomic, retain) NSArray *languageNames;
@property (nonatomic, retain) NSArray *languageCodes;

@end
```

Those additions define a pointer back to the detail view controller (which we'll set from code in the detail view controller itself when we're about to display the language list), as well as a pair of arrays for containing the values that will be displayed ("English," "French," and so on) and the underlying values that will be used to build a URL from the chosen language ("en," "fr," and so on).

If you copy/pasted that code from the book's source archive (or ebook) into your own project or if you typed it yourself a little sloppily, you may not have noticed an important difference in how the detailViewController property was declared earlier. Unlike most properties that reference an object pointer, we declared this one using assign instead of retain. This is something we have to do in order to avoid a retain cycle.

What's a retain cycle? It's a situation where a set of two or more objects have retained one another in a circular fashion. Each object has a retain counter of one or higher and will therefore never release the pointers it contains, so they will never be deallocated either. Most potential retain cycles can be avoided by carefully considering the creation of your objects, often by trying to figure out who "owns" whom. In this sense, an instance of `DetailViewController` "owns" an instance of `LanguageListController` because it's the `DetailViewController` that actually creates the `LanguageListController` in order to get a piece of work done. Whenever you have a pair of objects that each needs to refer to one another, you'll usually want the "owner" object to retain the other, while the other object should specifically not retain its owner.

Now, switch to *LanguageListController.m* to implement the following changes. At the top of the file, start by importing the header for `DetailViewController`, and then synthesize getters and setters for the properties you declared:

```
#import "LanguageListController.h"

#import "DetailViewController.h"

@implementation LanguageListController

@synthesize languageNames;
@synthesize languageCodes;
@synthesize detailViewController;
```

Then scroll down a bit to the `viewDidLoad` method, remove the comment markers around it, and add a bit of setup code:

```
- (void)viewDidLoad {
    [super viewDidLoad];
    self.languageNames = [NSArray arrayWithObjects:@"English", @"French",
        @"German", @"Spanish", nil];
    self.languageCodes = [NSArray arrayWithObjects:@"en", @"fr", @"de", @"es", nil];
    self.clearsSelectionOnViewWillAppear = NO;
    self.contentSizeForViewInPopover = CGSizeMake(320.0,
        [self.languageCodes count] * 44.0);
}
```

That sets up the language arrays and also defines the size that this view will use if shown in a popover (which, as we know, it will be). Without defining that, we'd end up with a popover stretching vertically to fill nearly the whole screen, even with only four entries in it.

Next, we have a couple of methods generated by Xcode's template that don't even contain valid code but instead some placeholder text. Let's replace those with something real:

```
- (NSInteger)numberOfSectionsInTableView:(UITableView *)tableView {
    // Return the number of sections.
    return <#number of sections#>;
    return 1;
}

- (NSInteger)tableView:(UITableView *)tableView numberOfRowsInSection:(NSInteger)section
{
    // Return the number of rows in the section.
    return <#number of rows in section#>;
    return [self.languageCodes count];
```

```
}
```

Then add a line near the end of tableView:cellForRowAtIndexPath: to put a language name into a cell:

```
// Configure the cell.
cell.textLabel.text = [languageNames objectAtIndex:[indexPath row]];
return cell;
```

Next, fix up tableView:didSelectRowAtIndexPath: by eliminating the comment block it contains and adding this new code instead:

```
- (void)tableView:(UITableView *)tableView didSelectRowAtIndexPath:(NSIndexPath *)indexPath {
    detailViewController.languageString = [self.languageCodes objectAtIndex:
        [indexPath row]];
}
```

Note that DetailViewController doesn't actually have a languageString property. We'll take care of that in just a bit. But first, finish LanguageListController by making the following bookkeeping changes:

```
- (void)viewDidUnload {
    self.detailViewController = nil;
    self.languageNames = nil;
    self.languageCodes = nil;
}

- (void)dealloc {
    [detailViewController release];
    [languageNames release];
    [languageCodes release];
    [super dealloc];
}
```

Now it's time to make the changes required for DetailViewController to handle the popover, as well as generate the correct URL whenever the user either changes the display language or picks a different president. Start by making the following changes in *DetailViewController.h*:

```
@interface DetailViewController : UIViewController <UIPopoverControllerDelegate,
UISplitViewControllerDelegate> {

    UIPopoverController *popoverController;
    UIToolbar *toolbar;

    id detailItem;
    UILabel *detailDescriptionLabel;
    UIWebView *webView;
    UIBarButtonItem *languageButton;
    UIPopoverController *languagePopoverController;
    NSString *languageString;
}

@property (nonatomic, retain) IBOutlet UIToolbar *toolbar;

@property (nonatomic, retain) id detailItem;
```

```
@property (nonatomic, retain) IBOutlet UILabel *detailDescriptionLabel;
@property (nonatomic, retain) IBOutlet UIWebView *webView;
@property (nonatomic, retain) IBOutlet UIBarButtonItem *languageButton;
@property (nonatomic, retain) UIPopoverController *languagePopoverController;
@property (nonatomic, copy) NSString *languageString;
- (IBAction)touchLanguageButton;
@end
```

You'll see that one of those properties, `languageButton`, is declared as an `IBOutlet`. Let's go ahead and edit the GUI, creating such a button and hooking it up. Open *DetailView.xib* for editing in Interface Builder.

In the main nib window, double-click the *View* icon so the view window appears. Notice the big, gray, empty toolbar just below the status bar. When you've run the app earlier and rotated to portrait mode, you've seen that the *Presidents* button appears at the left edge of this toolbar. We're going to add a *Choose Language* button so that it appears at the right edge.

Go into the library, and find a *Flexible Space Bar Button Item*. Drag it to the toolbar, and when you drop it there, you'll see that it fills the toolbar with a dashed double-headed arrow (Figure 10–9).

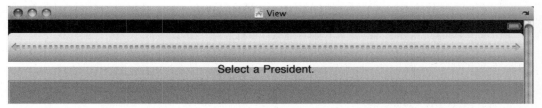

Figure 10–9. *The top of DetailView.xib's view window, showing a Flexible Space Bar Button Item on top of the toolbar. Note that, at this point, the toolbar just shows a dashed double-headed arrow that stretches the length of the toolbar.*

Next, go back to the library, and drag a bar button item to the right edge of the toolbar, and drop it there; it will stay put. Double-click the bar button you just added to edit the text of its label, and change it to say *Choose Language* (Figure 10–10).

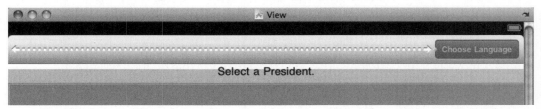

Figure 10–10. *The top of DetailView.xib's view window, this time with a button added to the right of the Flexible Space Bar Button Item*

Now control-drag from the *Choose Language* button to the *File's Owner* in the main nib window, and select the `touchLanguageButton` action method. Then control-drag from *File's Owner* back to the button, and select the `languageButton` outlet. Save your changes, and head back over to Xcode.

All we have to do now is fix up *DetailViewController.m* so that it can handle the language popover and the URL construction. Start off by adding this import somewhere at the top:

```
#import "LanguageListController.h"
```

Then synthesize the new properties just below the @implementation line:

```
@synthesize languageButton, languagePopoverController, languageString;
```

The next thing we're going to add is a function that takes as arguments a URL pointing to a Wikipedia page, as well as a two-letter language code, and returns a URL that combines the two. We'll use this at appropriate spots in our controller code later. You can place this function just about anywhere, including within the class's implementation. The compiler is smart enough to always treat a function as just a function. Why don't you place it just after the last synthesize statement toward the top of the file?

```
static NSString * modifyUrlForLanguage(NSString *url, NSString *lang) {
    if (!lang) {
        return url;
    }

    // We're relying on a particular Wikipedia URL format here. This
    // is a bit fragile!
    NSRange languageCodeRange = NSMakeRange(7, 2);
    if ([[url substringWithRange:languageCodeRange] isEqualToString:lang]) {
        return url;
    } else {
        NSString *newUrl = [url stringByReplacingCharactersInRange:languageCodeRange
            withString:lang];
        return newUrl;
    }
}
```

Why make that a function instead of a method? There are a couple of reasons for this. First, instance methods in a class are typically meant to do something involving one or more instance variables. This function does not make use of any instance variables. It simply performs an operation on two strings and returns another. We could have made it a class method, but even that feels a bit wrong, since what the method does isn't really related specifically to our controller class, either. Sometimes, a function is just what you need.

Our next move is to update the setDetailItem: method. This method will use the function we just defined to combine the URL that's passed in with the chosen languageString to generate the correct URL. It also makes sure that our second popover, if present, disappears just like the first popover (the one that was defined for us) does.

```
- (void)setDetailItem:(id)newDetailItem {
    if (detailItem != newDetailItem) {
        [detailItem release];
        detailItem = [newDetailItem retain];
        detailItem = [modifyUrlForLanguage(newDetailItem, languageString) retain];
```

```
        // Update the view.
        [self configureView];
    }

    if (self.popoverController != nil) {
        [self.popoverController dismissPopoverAnimated:YES];
    }
    if (languagePopoverController != nil) {
        [languagePopoverController dismissPopoverAnimated:YES];
    }
}
```

Next, we implement `setLanguageString:`. This also calls our `modifyUrlForLanguage()` function so that the URL can be regenerated (and the new page loaded) immediately. Add this method to the bottom of the file, just above the `@end`.

```
- (void)setLanguageString:(NSString *)newString {
    if (![newString isEqualToString:languageString]) {
        [languageString release];
        languageString = [newString copy];
        self.detailItem = modifyUrlForLanguage(detailItem, languageString);
    }
}
```

Next, let's define what will happen when the user taps the *Choose Language* button. Simply put, we create a `LanguageListController`, wrap it in a `UIPopoverController`, and display it. Place this method at the bottom of the file, just before the `@end`.

```
- (IBAction)touchLanguageButton {
    LanguageListController *languageListController = [[LanguageListController alloc]
        init];
    languageListController.detailViewController = self;
    UIPopoverController *poc = [[UIPopoverController alloc]
        initWithContentViewController:languageListController];
    [poc presentPopoverFromBarButtonItem:languageButton
                permittedArrowDirections:UIPopoverArrowDirectionAny
                                animated:YES];
    self.languagePopoverController = poc;
    [poc release];
    [languageListController release];
}
```

Then we have to do some additional cleanup in `viewDidUnload`, adding these lines:

```
    self.languageButton = nil;
    self.languagePopoverController = nil;
```

The final change is to add these lines to the `dealloc` method:

```
    [languageButton release];
    [languagePopoverController release];
```

And that's all! You should now be able to run the app in all its glory, switching willy-nilly between presidents and languages. Switching from one language to another should always leave the chosen president intact, and likewise, switching from one president to another should leave the language intact.

iPad Wrap-Up

In this chapter you've learned about the main GUI components—popovers and split views—that are available only on iPad. You've also seen an example of how a complex iPad application with several interconnected view controllers can be configured entirely within Interface Builder. With this hard-won knowledge, you should be well on your way to building your first great iPad app.

Next up, it's time to visit application settings and user defaults.

Chapter 11

Application Settings and User Defaults

All but the simplest computer programs today have a preferences window where the user can set application-specific options. On Mac OS X, the **Preferences…** menu item is usually found in the application menu. Selecting it brings up a window where the user can enter and change various options. The iPhone and other iOS devices have a dedicated application called Settings, which you no doubt have played with any number of times. In this chapter, we'll show you how to add settings for your application to the Settings application, and how to access those settings from within your application.

Getting to Know Your Settings Bundle

The Settings application lets the user enter and change preferences for any application that has a settings bundle. A **settings bundle** is a group of files built in to an application that tells the Settings application which preferences the application wishes to collect from the user.

Pick up your iOS device, and locate your Settings icon. By default, you'll find it on the home screen (see Figure 11–1).

Figure 11–1. *The Settings application icon is in the middle of the last column on this iPhone. It may be in a different spot on your device, but it's always available.*

When you touch the icon, the Settings application will launch. Ours is shown in Figure 11–2.

Figure 11–2. *The Settings application*

The Settings application acts as a common user interface for the iOS User Defaults mechanism. User Defaults is the part of the system that stores and retrieves preferences. In an iOS application, User Defaults is implemented by the NSUserDefaults class. If you've done Cocoa programming on the Mac, you're probably already familiar with NSUserDefaults, because it is the same class that is used to store and read preferences on the Mac. Your applications will use NSUserDefaults to read and store preference data using a key value, just as you would access keyed data from an NSDictionary. The difference is that NSUserDefaults data is persisted to the file system, rather than stored in an object instance in memory.

In this chapter, we're going to create an application, add and configure a settings bundle, and then access and edit those preferences from within our application.

One nice thing about the Settings application is that it provides a solution so that you don't need to design your own user interface for your preferences. You create a property list defining your application's available settings, and the Settings application creates the interface for you.

Immersive applications, such as games, generally should provide their own preferences view so that the user doesn't need to quit in order to make a change. Even utility and productivity applications might, at times, have preferences that a user should be able to change without leaving the application. We'll also show you to how to collect preferences from the user directly in your application, and store those in iOS's User Defaults.

In addition, with the introduction of background processing in iOS 4, the user can actually switch to the Settings app, change a preference, and then switch back to your application. We'll show you how to handle that situation at the end of this chapter.

The AppSettings Application

We're going to build a simple application in this chapter. First, we'll implement a settings bundle so that when the user launches the Settings application, there will be an entry for our application (see Figure 11–3).

Figure 11–3. *The Settings application showing an entry for our application in the simulator*

If the user selects our application, Settings will drill down into a view that shows the preferences relevant to our application. As you can see from Figure 11–4, the Settings application uses text fields, secure text fields, switches, and sliders to coax values out of our intrepid user.

Figure 11–4. *Our application's primary settings view*

Also notice the two items on the view that have disclosure indicators. The first one, *Protocol*, takes the user to another table view that displays the options available for that item. From that table view, the user can select a single value (see Figure 11–5).

Figure 11–5. *Selecting a single preference item from a list*

The *More Settings* disclosure indicator allows the user to drill down to another set of preferences (see Figure 11–6). This child view can have the same kinds of controls as the main settings view, and can even have its own child views. You may have noticed that the Settings application uses a navigation controller, which it needs because it supports the building of hierarchical preference views.

Figure 11–6. *A child settings view in our application*

When users actually launch our application, they will be presented with a list of the preferences gathered in the Settings application (see Figure 11–7).

Figure 11–7. *Our application's main view*

In order to show how to update preferences from within our application, we also provide a little information button in the lower-right corner. This button takes the user to another view showing additional preferences and allowing us to change those preferences directly in our application (see Figure 11–8).

Figure 11–8. *Setting some preferences directly in our application*

Let's get started building AppSettings, shall we?

Creating the Project

In Xcode, press ⌘⇧N or select **File ➤ New Project...** When the new project assistant comes up, select *Application* from under the *iOS* heading in the left pane, click the *Utility Application* icon, and be sure the *Use Core Data* check box is unchecked before clicking the *Choose...* button. Name your new project *AppSettings*.

We haven't used this particular project template before, so let's take a quick look at the project before we proceed. This template creates an application similar to the multiview application we built in Chapter 6. The application has a main view and a secondary view called the **flipside view**. Tapping the information button on the main view takes you to the flipside view, and tapping the *Done* button on the flipside view takes you back to the main view.

It takes several controllers and views to implement this type of application. All of these are provided, as stubs, by the template. Expand the various source code and *Resources* folders, where you'll find the usual application delegate class, as well as two additional controller classes, each with an associated *.xib* file (see Figure 11–9).

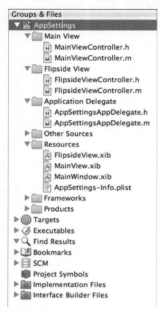

Figure 11–9. *Our project created from the Utility Application template. Notice the application delegate, and the main and flipview controllers, along with their associated nib files.*

Working with the Settings Bundle

The Settings application bases the display of preferences for a given application on the contents of the settings bundle inside that application. Each settings bundle must have a property list, called *Root.plist*, which defines the root-level preferences view. This property list must follow a very precise format, which we'll talk about when we set up the property list for our application.

When the Settings application starts up, it checks each application for a settings bundle and adds a settings group for each application that includes a settings bundle. If we want our preferences to include any subviews, we need to add property lists to the bundle and add an entry to *Root.plist* for each child view. You'll see exactly how to do that in this chapter.

Adding a Settings Bundle to Our Project

In the project navigator, click the root object (the one called *AppSettings*, which should be at the very top of the project navigator's list of files), and then select File ➤ New File… or press ⌘N. In the left pane, select *Resource* under the *iOS* heading, and then select the *Settings Bundle* icon (see Figure 11–10). Click the *Next* button, and choose the default name of *Settings.bundle* by pressing return.

Figure 11–10. *Creating a settings bundle in Xcode*

You should now see a new item in the project window, just beneath the *Products* folder, called *Settings.bundle*. Expand *Settings.bundle*, and you should see two items: an icon named *Root.plist* and a folder named *en.lproj*. We'll discuss *en.lproj* in Chapter 19 when we talk about localizing your application into other languages. Here, we'll concentrate on *Root.plist*.

Setting Up the Property List

Single-click *Root.plist*, and take a look at the editor pane. You're looking at Xcode's property list editor (see Figure 11–11). This editor functions in the same way as the Property List Editor application in */Developer/Applications/Utilities*.

Key	Type	Value
▼ Root	Dictionary ⬍	(2 items)
StringsTable	String	Root
▶ PreferenceSpecifiers	Array	(4 items)

Figure 11–11. *Root.plist in the property list editor pane*

Notice the organization of the items in the plist. Property lists are, essentially, dictionaries, storing item types and values using a key to retrieve them, just as an NSDictionary does.

Several different types of nodes can be put into a property list. The *Boolean, Data, Date, Number, and String* node types are meant to hold individual pieces of data, but you also have a couple of ways to deal with whole collections of nodes as well. In addition to *Dictionary* node types, which allow you to store other nodes under a key, there are *Array* nodes, which store an ordered list of other nodes similar to an NSArray. The *Dictionary* and *Array* types are the only property list node types that can contain other nodes.

> **NOTE:** Although you can use most kinds of objects as keys in an NSDictionary, keys in property list dictionary nodes must be strings. However, you are free to use any node type for the values.

When creating a settings property list, you need to follow a very specific format. Fortunately, *Root.plist*, the plist that came with the settings bundle you just added to your project, follows this format exactly. Let's take a look.

In the *Root.plist* editor pane, the first item under *Root* is a *StringsTable*. A strings table is used in translating your application into another language. We'll cover the strings table in Chapter 19, when we get into localization. Since the strings table is optional, you can delete that entry by clicking it and pressing the delete key. Or you can leave it there if you prefer, since it won't do any harm.

Just below the *StringsTable* is a node named *PreferenceSpecifiers* (see Figure 11–12). *PreferenceSpecifiers* is an array. This array node is designed to hold a set of dictionary nodes, each representing a single preference that the user can enter or a single child view that the user can drill down into.

Key	Type	Value
▼ Root	Dictionary ⇅	(2 items)
StringsTable	String	Root
▼ PreferenceSpecifiers	Array	(4 items)
▶ Item 0	Dictionary	(2 items)
▶ Item 1	Dictionary	(8 items)
▶ Item 2	Dictionary	(4 items)
▶ Item 3	Dictionary	(7 items)

Figure 11–12. *Root.plist in the editor pane, this time with PreferenceSpecifiers expanded*

You'll notice that Xcode's template kindly gave us four nodes. Those nodes aren't likely to reflect our actual preferences, so delete *Item 1, Item 2*, and *Item 3* by single-clicking each of those rows and pressing the delete key, leaving just *Item 0* in place.

Single-click *Item 0* but don't expand it. At the right edge of the row, notice the button with the plus icon (see Figure 11–13). That button is used to add a sibling node after this row. In other words, it will add another node at the same level as this one. If you clicked that icon (but don't do that now), you would get a new row called *Item 1* immediately after *Item 0*.

Key	Type	Value
▼ Root	Dictionary	(1 item)
▼ PreferenceSpecifiers	Array	(1 item)
▸ Item 0	Dictionary ⬍	(2 items) ＋

Figure 11–13. *Item 0 is selected and shows the plus icon at the very right of the row. Click the plus icon to add a new item just below Item 0.*

Now expand *Item 0*, and notice that the button changes to a different icon, which has three horizontal lines (see Figure 11–14). Clicking this new icon will add a child node, as opposed to a sibling node. So if you clicked it (again, don't actually click it now), you would get a new first child row under *Item 0*.

Key	Type	Value
▼ Root	Dictionary	(1 item)
▼ PreferenceSpecifiers	Array	(1 item)
▼ Item 0	Dictionary ⬍	(2 items) ☰
Type	String	PSGroupSpecifier
Title	String	Group

Figure 11–14. *When we expand Item 0, the plus icon changes to an add child icon.*

The first row under *Item 0* has a key of *Type*. Every property list node in the `PreferenceSpecifiers` array must have an entry with this key. The *Type* key is typically the first entry, but order doesn't matter in a dictionary, so the *Type key* doesn't need to be first. The *Type key* tells the Settings application what type of data is associated with this item.

The first child entry under *Item 0* has a *Type* key with a value of *PSGroupSpecifier*. This indicates that the item represents the start of a new group. Each item that follows will be part of this group, until the next item with a *Type* of *PSGroupSpecifier*.

If you look back at Figure 11–4, you'll see that the Settings application presents the application settings in a grouped table. *Item 0* in the *PreferenceSpecifiers* array in a settings bundle property list should always be a *PSGroupSpecifier* so the settings start in a new group, because you need at least one group in every Settings table.

The only other entry in *Item 0* has a key of *Title*, and this is used to set an optional header just above the group that is being started. As shown back in Figure 11–4, we've called our first group *General Info*. Now, double-click the value next to *Title*, and change it from *Group to General Info*.

Adding a Text Field Setting

We now need to add a second item in this array, which will represent the first actual preference field. We're going to start with a simple text field.

If you single-click the *PreferenceSpecifiers* row in the editor pane, and click the button to add a child, the new row will be inserted at the beginning of the list, which is not what we want. We want to add a row at the end of the array. To do this, click the disclosure triangle to the left of *Item 0* to close it, and then select *Item 0* and click the plus button at the end of the row, which will give you a new sibling row after the current row (see Figure 11–15).

Key	Type	Value
▼ Root	Dictionary	(1 item)
▼ PreferenceSpecifiers	Array	(2 items)
▶ Item 0	Dictionary	(2 items)
Item 1	String	

Figure 11–15. *Adding a new sibling row to Item 0*

The new row will default to a *String* node type, which is not what we want. Remember that each item in the *PreferenceSpecifiers* array must be a dictionary, so click the word *String*, and in the popup menu that appears, select the node type *Dictionary*.

Next, click the disclosure triangle next to *Item 1* to expand it. It doesn't actually contain anything yet, so the only differences you'll see are that the disclosure triangle will point down and the button to add sibling nodes will change to let you add child nodes (see Figure 11–16). Click the add child node button (the button to the right with three lines) now to add our first entry to this dictionary.

Key	Type	Value
▼ Root	Dictionary	(1 item)
▼ PreferenceSpecifiers	Array	(2 items)
▶ Item 0	Dictionary	(2 items)
▼ Item 1	Dictionary	(0 items)

Figure 11–16. *Adding a new child to Item 1*

A new row will come up and default to a *String* type, which *is* what we want. The new row's key value will default to *New item*. Change it to *Type*, and then double-click the *Value* column and enter *PSTextFieldSpecifier*. This is the type value used to tell the Settings application that we want the user to edit this setting in a text field.

In this example, *PSTextFieldSpecifier* is a type. More specifically, it is the type of a specific preference field. When you see *Type* in the *Key* column, we're defining the type of field that will be used to edit the preference.

Click the button with the plus icon to the right of the *Type* row to add another item to our dictionary. This new row will specify the label that will be displayed next to the text field. Change the key from *New item* to *Title*.

Now press the tab key. Notice that you are all set to edit the value in the *Value column*. Set it to *Username*.

Next, click the plus button at the end of the *Title* row to add yet another item to our dictionary. Change the key for this new entry to *Key* (no, that's not a misprint; you're really setting the key to *Key*). For a value, type in *username*. Recall that we said that user defaults work like a dictionary? Well, this entry tells the Settings application which key to use when it stores the value entered in this text field.

Recall what we said about NSUserDefaults? It lets you store values using a key, similar to an NSDictionary. Well, the Settings application will do the same thing for each of the preferences it saves on your behalf. If you give it a key value of *foo*, then later in your application, you can request the value for *foo*, and it will give you the value the user entered for that preference. We will use this same key value later to retrieve this setting from the user defaults in our application.

> **NOTE:** Notice that our *Title* has a value of *Username* and our *Key* has a value of *username*. This uppercase/lowercase difference will happen frequently. The *Title* is what appears on the screen, so the capital *U* makes sense. The *Key* is a text string we'll use to retrieve preferences from the user defaults, so all lowercase makes sense there. Could we use all lowercase for a *Title*? You bet. Could we use all capitals for *Key*? Sure! As long as you capitalize it the same way when you save and when you retrieve, it doesn't matter which convention you use for your preference keys.

Add another entry to our *item 1* dictionary, giving this one a key of *AutocapitalizationType* and a value of *None*. This specifies that the text field shouldn't attempt to autocapitalize what the user types in this field.

Create one last new row, and give it a key of *AutocorrectionType* and a value of *No*. This will tell the Settings application not to try to autocorrect values entered into this text field. When you do want the text field to use autocorrection, change the value in this row to *Yes*.

When you're all finished, your property list should look like the one shown in Figure 11–17.

Key	Type	Value
▼ Root	Dictionary	(1 item)
▼ PreferenceSpecifiers	Array	(2 items)
▶ Item 0	Dictionary	(2 items)
▼ Item 1	Dictionary	(5 items)
Type	String	PSTextFieldSpecifier
Title	String	Username
Key	String	username
AutocapitalizationType	String	None
AutocorrectionType	String	No

Figure 11–17. *The finished text field specified in Root.plist*

Adding an Application Icon

Before we try out our new setting, let's add an application icon to the project. You've done this before.

Save the property file. Then make your way into the source code archive and into the *11 – AppSettings* folder. Drag the file *icon.png* into your project's *Resources* folder and, when prompted, have Xcode copy the icon.

Next, still in the *Resources* folder, click the file *AppSettings-info.plist*. When the plist editor appears, select the *Icon file* row and change its value to *icon.png*.

That's it. Now compile and run the application by selecting **Build ➤ Build and Run**. Click the home button, and then click the icon for the Settings application. You will find an entry for our application, which uses the application icon we added earlier (see Figure 11–3). Click the *AppSettings* row, and you will be presented with a simple settings view with a single text field, as shown in Figure 11–18.

Figure 11–18. *Our root view in the Settings application after adding a group and a text field*

Quit the simulator, and go back to Xcode. We're not finished yet, but you should now have a sense of how easy it is to add preferences to your application. Let's add the rest of the fields for our root settings view. The first one we'll add is a secure text field for the user's password.

Adding a Secure Text Field Setting

Click *Root.plist* to return to your setting specifiers. Open *Root*, open *PreferenceSpecifiers*, and then collapse *Item 0* and *Item 1*. Now select *Item 1*. Press ⌘C to copy it to the clipboard, and then press ⌘V to paste it back. This will create a new

Item 2 that is identical to *Item 1*. Expand the new item, and change the *Title* to *Password* and the Key to *password*. (Remember that one has a capital *P* and one a lowercase *p*.)

Next, add one more child to the new item. Remember that the order of items does not matter, so feel free to place it directly below the *Key* item you just edited. To do this, select the *Key/password* row, and then click the plus icon at the end of the row.

Give the new item a *Key* of *IsSecure*, and change the *Type* to *Boolean*. Once you do that, the space where you normally type in a value will change to a check box. Click it to check the box, which tells the Settings application that this field needs to be a password field, rather than just an ordinary text field.

Our finished *Item 2* is shown in Figure 11–19.

Key	Type	Value
▼ Root	Dictionary	(1 item)
▼ PreferenceSpecifiers	Array	(3 items)
▶ Item 0	Dictionary	(2 items)
▶ Item 1	Dictionary	(5 items)
▼ Item 2	Dictionary	(6 items)
Type	String	PSTextFieldSpecifier
Title	String	Password
Key	String	password
isSecure	Boolean	☑
AutocapitalizationType	String	None
AutocorrectionType	String	No

Figure 11–19. *Our finished Item 2, a text field designed to accept a password*

Adding a Multivalue Field

The next item we're going to add is a multivalue field. This type of field will automatically generate a row with a disclosure indicator. Clicking it will take you down to another table where you can select one of several rows.

Collapse *Item 2*, select the row, and then click the plus icon at the end of the row to add *Item 3*. Change *Item 3's Type* to *Dictionary*, and expand *Item 3* by clicking the disclosure triangle.

Click the add child icon to give *Item 3* a child row. Set the key to *Type* and the value to *PSMultiValueSpecifier*. Add a second row with a key of *Title* and value of *Protocol*. Now, create a third row with a key of *Key* and a value of *protocol*. The next part is a little tricky, so let's talk about it before we do it.

We're going to add two more children to *Item 3*, but they will be *Array* type nodes, not *String* type nodes:

- One, called *Titles*, will hold a list of the values from which the user can select.

- The other, called *Values*, will hold a list of the values that actually are stored in the user defaults.

So, if the user selects the first item in the list, which corresponds to the first item in the *Titles* array, the Settings application will actually store the first value from the *Values* array. This pairing of *Titles* and *Values* lets you present user-friendly text to the user but actually store something else, like a number, date, or different string. Both of these arrays are required. If you want them both to be the same, you can create one array, copy it, paste it back in, and change the key so that you have two arrays with the same content but stored under different keys. We'll actually do just that.

Add a new child to *Item 3*. Change its key to *Values* and set its type to *Array*. Expand the array, and add five child nodes. All five nodes should be *String* type nodes and should contain the following values: *HTTP, SMTP, NNTP, IMAP*, and *POP3*.

Once you've entered all five nodes, collapse *Values*, and select it. Then press ⌘C to copy it, and press ⌘V to paste it back. This will create a new item with a key of *Values - 2*. Double-click *Values - 2*, and change it to *Titles*.

We're almost finished with our multivalue field. There's just one more required value in the dictionary, which is the default value. Multivalue fields must have one—and only one—row selected. So, we need to specify the default value to be used if none has yet been selected, and it needs to correspond to one of the items in the *Values* array (not the *Titles* array if they are different). Add another child to *Item 3*. Give it a key of *DefaultValue* and a value of *SMTP*.

Figure 11–20 shows our version of *Item 3*.

Key	Type	Value
▼ Root	Dictionary	(1 item)
▼ PreferenceSpecifiers	Array	(4 items)
▶ Item 0	Dictionary	(2 items)
▶ Item 1	Dictionary	(5 items)
▶ Item 2	Dictionary	(6 items)
▼ Item 3	Dictionary	(6 items)
Type	String	PSMultiValueSpecifier
Title	String	Protocol
Key	String	protocol
▼ Values	Array	(5 items)
Item 0	String	HTTP
Item 1	String	SMTP
Item 2	String	NNTP
Item 3	String	IMAP
Item 4	String	POP3
▶ Titles	Array	(5 items)
DefaultValue	String	SMTP

Figure 11–20. *Our finished Item 3, a multivalue field designed to select from one of five possible values*

Let's check our work. Save the property list, and build and run the application again. When your application starts up, press the home button and launch the Settings application. When you select *AppSettings*, you should see three fields on your root-level view (see Figure 11–21). Go ahead and play with your creation, and then let's move on.

Figure 11–21. *Three fields down. Not too shabby!*

Adding a Toggle Switch Setting

The next item we need to get from the user is a Boolean value that indicates whether our warp engines are turned on. To capture a Boolean value in our preferences, we are going to tell the Settings application to use a UISwitch by adding another item to our *PreferenceSpecifiers* array with a type of *PSToggleSwitchSpecifier*.

Collapse *Item 3* if it's currently expanded, and then single-click it to select it. Click the plus icon at the right side of the row to create *Item 4*. Change its type to *Dictionary*, and then expand *Item 4* and add a child row. Give the child row a key of *Type* and a value of *PSToggleSwitchSpecifier*. Add another child row with a key of *Title* and a value of *Warp Drive*. Next, add a third child row with a key of *Key* and a value of *warp*.

By default, a toggle switch will cause a Boolean YES or NO to be saved into the user defaults. If you would prefer to assign a different value to the on and off positions, you can do that by specifying the optional keys *TrueValue* and *FalseValue*. You can assign strings, dates, or numbers to either the on position (*TrueValue*) or the off position (*FalseValue*), so that the Settings application will store the string you specify instead of just storing YES or NO.

Let's set the on position to save the string Engaged and the off position to store Disabled. Do this by adding two more children to *Item 4*: one with a key of *TrueValue* and a value of *Engaged*, and a second one with a key of *FalseValue* and a value of *Disabled*.

We have one more required item in this dictionary, which is the default value. If we had not supplied the optional *FalseValue* and *TrueValue* items, we would create a new row with a key of *DefaultValue* and change the type from *String* to *Boolean*. However, because we did add those two items, the value we put in *DefaultValue* must match either the value passed in *TrueValue* or the one passed in *FalseValue*.

Let's make our warp engines on by default, so create one last child to *Item 4*. Give it a key of *DefaultValue* and a value of *Engaged*. Note that the string Engaged is what will be stored in the user defaults, not what will appear on the screen. Figure 11–22 shows our completed *Item 4*.

Key	Type	Value
▼ Root	Dictionary	(1 item)
▼ PreferenceSpecifiers	Array	(5 items)
▶ Item 0	Dictionary	(2 items)
▶ Item 1	Dictionary	(5 items)
▶ Item 2	Dictionary	(6 items)
▶ Item 3	Dictionary	(6 items)
▼ Item 4	Dictionary	(6 items)
Type	String	PSToggleSwitchSpecifier
Title	String	Warp
Key	String	warp
TrueValue	String	Engaged
FalseValue	String	Disabled
DefaultValue	String	Engaged

Figure 11–22. *Our finished Item 4, a toggle switch to turn the warp engines on and off. Engage!*

Adding the Slider Setting

The next item we need to implement is a slider. In the Settings application, a slider can have a small image at each end, but it can't have a label. Let's put the slider in its own group with a header so that the user will know what the slider does.

Start by collapsing *Item 4*. Now, single-click *Item 0* under *PreferenceSpecifiers*, and press ⌘C to copy it to the clipboard. Next, select *Item 4*, making sure it's collapsed, and then press ⌘V to paste. Since *Item 0* was a group specifier, the item we just pasted in as the new *Item 5* is also a group specifier and will tell the Settings application to start a new group at this location.

Expand *Item 5*, double-click the value in the row labeled *Title,* and change the value to *Warp Factor*.

Collapse *Item 5* and select it. Then click the button at the end of its row to add a new sibling row. Change the *Type* of the new row, *Item 6*, from *String* to *Dictionary,* and then expand the new row. Add a child row, and give it a key of *Type* and a value of *PSSliderSpecifier*, which indicates to the Settings application that it should use a UISlider to get this information from the user. Add another child with a key of *Key* and a value of *warpFactor* so that the Settings application knows which key to use when storing this value.

We're going to allow the user to enter a value from 1 to 10, and we'll set the default to *warp 5*. Sliders need to have a minimum value, a maximum value, and a starting (or default) value, and all of these need to be stored as numbers, not strings, in your property list. To do this, add three more child rows to *Item 6*, changing the *Type* of all three rows from *String* to *Number*. Give the first one a key of *DefaultValue* and a value of *5*. Give the second one a key of *MinimumValue* and a value of *1*, and give the final one a key of *MaximumValue* and a value of *10*.

If you want to test the slider, go ahead, but hurry back. We're going to do just a bit more customization. As noted, sliders can have images. You can place a small 21 × 21-pixel image at each end of the slider. Let's provide little icons to indicate that moving the slider to the left slows us down, and moving it to the right speeds us up.

Adding Icons to the Settings Bundle

In the *11 - AppSettings* folder in the project archive that accompanies this book, you'll find two icons called *rabbit.png* and *turtle.png*. We need to add both of these to our settings bundle. Because these images need to be used by the Settings application, we can't just put them in our *Resources* folder; we need to put them in the settings bundle so the Settings application can access them. To do that, go to the Finder and navigate to wherever you saved your Xcode project. In that same folder, you'll find an icon named *Settings.bundle*.

Remember that bundles look like files in the Finder, but they are really folders. You can get to their contents by right-clicking (or control-clicking) the bundle's icon and selecting **Show Package Contents** from the contextual menu. This will open the settings bundle in a new Finder window, and you should see the same two items that you see in *Settings.bundle* in Xcode. Copy the two icon files, *rabbit.png* and *turtle.png*, from the *11 - AppSettings* folder into the *Settings.bundle* package contents window.

You can leave this window open in the Finder, as we'll need to copy another file here soon. Now, we'll return to Xcode and tell the slider to use these two images.

Go back to *Root.plist* and add two more child rows under *Item 6*. Give one a key of *MinimumValueImage* and a value of *turtle.png*. Give the other a key of *MaximumValueImage* and a value of *rabbit.png*. Our finished *Item 6* is shown in Figure 11–23.

Key	Type	Value
▼ Root	Dictionary	(1 item)
▼ PreferenceSpecifiers	Array	(7 items)
▶ Item 0	Dictionary	(2 items)
▶ Item 1	Dictionary	(5 items)
▶ Item 2	Dictionary	(6 items)
▶ Item 3	Dictionary	(6 items)
▶ Item 4	Dictionary	(6 items)
▶ Item 5	Dictionary	(2 items)
▼ Item 6	Dictionary	(7 items)
Type	String	PSSliderSpecifier
Key	String	warpFactor
DefaultValue	Number	5
MinimumValue	Number	1
MaximumValue	Number	10
MinimumValueImage	String	turtle.png
MaximumValueImage	String	rabbit.png

Figure 11–23. *Our finished Item 6, a slider with a turtle and a rabbit icon to represent slow and fast*

Save your property list, and let's build and run to make sure everything is still hunky-dory. If everything is, you should be able to navigate to the Settings application and find the slider waiting for you, with the sleepy turtle and the happy rabbit at each end (see Figure 11–24).

Figure 11–24. *We have text fields, multivalue fields, a toggle switch, and a slider. We're almost finished.*

Adding a Child Settings View

We're going to add another preference specifier to tell the Settings application that we want it to display a child settings view. This specifier will present a row with a disclosure indicator that, when tapped, will take the user down to a whole new view full of preferences. Let's get to it.

Since we don't want this new preference to be grouped with the slider, first we'll copy the group specifier in *Item 0* and paste it at the end of the *PreferenceSpecifiers* array to create a new group for our child settings view. In *Root.plist*, collapse all open items, and then single-click *Item 0* to select it and press ⌘C to copy it to the clipboard. Next, select *Item 6*, and then press ⌘V to paste in a new *Item 7*. Expand Item 7, and double-click the *Value* column next to the key *Title*, changing it from *General Info* to *Additional Info*.

Now, collapse *Item 7* again. Select it, and click the add sibling button at the right end of the row to add *Item 8*, which will be our actual child view. Change the new row's type from *String* to *Dictionary*, and expand it by clicking the disclosure triangle. Add a child row, and give it a key of *Type* and a value of *PSChildPaneSpecifier*. Add another child row with a key of *Title* and a value of *More Settings*.

We need to add one final row, which will tell the Settings application which property list to load for the *More Settings* view. Add another child row and give it a key of *File* and a value of *More*. The file extension *.plist* is assumed and must not be included (if it is, the Settings application won't find the property list file).

We are adding a child view to our main preference view. The settings in that child view are specified in the *More.plist file*. We need to copy *More.plist* into the settings bundle. We can't add new files to the bundle in Xcode, and the Property List Editor's Save dialog will not let us save into a bundle. So, we need to create a new property list, save it somewhere else, and then drag it into the *Settings.bundle* window using the Finder.

You've now seen all the different types of preference fields that you can use in a settings bundle property list file. To save yourself some typing, why don't you grab *More.plist* out of the *11 - AppSettings* folder in the project archive that accompanies this book, and drag it into that *Settings.bundle* window we left open earlier.

> **TIP:** When you create your own child settings views, the easiest way is to make a copy of *Root.plist* and give it a new name. Then delete all of the existing preference specifiers except the first one, and add whatever preference specifiers you need for that new file.

We're finished with our settings bundle. Feel free to compile, run, and test the Settings application. You should be able to reach the child view and set values for all the other fields. Go ahead and play with it, and make changes to the property list if you want.

> **TIP:** We've covered almost every configuration option available (at least at the time of this writing). You can find the full documentation of the settings property list format in the document called *Settings Application Schema Reference* in the iOS Dev Center. You can get that document, along with a ton of other useful reference documents, from this page:
>
> http://developer.apple.com/iphone/library/navigation/Reference.html

Before continuing, copy the *rabbit.png* and *turtle.png* icons from the *11 - AppSettings* folder in the project archive into your project's *Resources* folder. We'll use them in our application to show the value of the current settings.

> **NOTE:** You might have noticed that the two icons you just added are exactly the same ones you added to your settings bundle earlier, and you might be wondering why. Remember that iOS applications can't read files out of other applications' sandboxes. The settings bundle doesn't become part of our application's sandbox; it becomes part of the Settings application's sandbox. Since we also want to use those icons in our application, we need to add them separately to our *Resources* folder so they are copied into our application's sandbox as well.

Reading Settings in Our Application

We've now solved half of our problem. The user can get to our preferences, but how do we get to them? As it turns out, that's the easy part.

Retrieving User Settings

We'll take advantage of a class called NSUserDefaults to read in the user's settings. NSUserDefaults is implemented as a singleton, which means there is only one instance of NSUserDefaults running in your application. To get access to that one instance, we call the class method standardUserDefaults, like so:

```
NSUserDefaults *defaults = [NSUserDefaults standardUserDefaults];
```

Once we have a pointer to the standard user defaults, we use it just like an NSDictionary. To get a value out of it, we can call objectForKey: which will return an Objective-C object like an NSString, NSDate, or NSNumber. If we want to retrieve the value as a scalar—like an int, float, or BOOL—we can use other methods, such as intForKey:, floatForKey:, or boolForKey:.

When you were creating the property list for this application, you created an array of *PreferenceSpecifiers*. Some of those specifiers were used to create groups. Others created interface objects that the user used to set the settings. Those are the specifiers we are really interested in, because they hold the real data. Every specifier that was tied to a user setting has a *Key* named *Key*. Take a minute to go back and check. For example, the *Key* for our slider has a value of *warpfactor*. The *Key* for our *Password* field is *password*. We'll use those keys to retrieve the user settings.

So that we have a place to display the settings, let's quickly set up our main view with a bunch of labels. Before going over to Interface Builder, let's create outlets for all the labels we'll need. Single-click *MainViewController.h*, and make the following changes:

```
#import "FlipsideViewController.h"
#define kUsernameKey        @"username"
#define kPasswordKey        @"password"
#define kProtocolKey        @"protocol"
#define kWarpDriveKey       @"warp"
#define kWarpFactorKey      @"warpFactor"
#define kFavoriteTeaKey     @"favoriteTea"
#define kFavoriteCandyKey   @"favoriteCandy"
#define kFavoriteGameKey    @"favoriteGame"
#define kFavoriteExcuseKey  @"favoriteExcuse"
#define kFavoriteSinKey     @"favoriteSin"

@interface MainViewController : UIViewController
        <FlipsideViewControllerDelegate> {
    UILabel *usernameLabel;
    UILabel *passwordLabel;
    UILabel *protocolLabel;
    UILabel *warpDriveLabel;
    UILabel *warpFactorLabel;

    UILabel *favoriteTeaLabel;
    UILabel *favoriteCandyLabel;
    UILabel *favoriteGameLabel;
    UILabel *favoriteExcuseLabel;
    UILabel *favoriteSinLabel;
}
```

```
@property (nonatomic, retain) IBOutlet UILabel *usernameLabel;
@property (nonatomic, retain) IBOutlet UILabel *passwordLabel;
@property (nonatomic, retain) IBOutlet UILabel *protocolLabel;
@property (nonatomic, retain) IBOutlet UILabel *warpDriveLabel;
@property (nonatomic, retain) IBOutlet UILabel *warpFactorLabel;
@property (nonatomic, retain) IBOutlet UILabel *favoriteTeaLabel;
@property (nonatomic, retain) IBOutlet UILabel *favoriteCandyLabel;
@property (nonatomic, retain) IBOutlet UILabel *favoriteGameLabel;
@property (nonatomic, retain) IBOutlet UILabel *favoriteExcuseLabel;
@property (nonatomic, retain) IBOutlet UILabel *favoriteSinLabel;

- (void)refreshFields;
- (IBAction)showInfo;
@end
```

There's nothing new here. We declare a bunch of constants. These are the key values that we used in our property list file for the different preference fields. Then we declare ten outlets, all of them labels, and create properties for each of them. Finally, we declare a method that will read settings out of the user defaults and push those values into the various labels. We put this functionality in its own method, because we need to do this same task in more than one place.

Save your changes. Now that we have our outlets declared, let's head over to the main nib file to create the GUI.

Creating the Main View

Double-click *MainView.xib* to edit it in Interface Builder. When it comes up, you'll notice that the background of the view is dark gray. Let's change it to white. Single-click the *View* icon in the nib's main window, and bring up the attributes inspector. Use the color well labeled *Background* to change the background to white. Note that the color well also functions as a popup menu. If you prefer, use that menu to select *White Color*.

Next, in the nib's main window, click the center *View Mode* icon to put the window in list mode. A disclosure triangle should appear to the left of the *View* icon. Open the disclosure triangle.

Put the layout area's dock in list mode by clicking the small triangle icon, if it's not already in that mode. Next, click the disclosure triangle to the left of the *Main View* icon. This reveals an item called *Light Info Button* (see Figure 11–25).

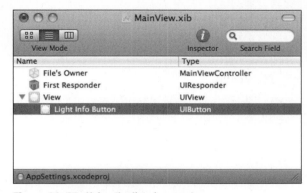

Figure 11–25. *Using the list view mode*

> **TIP:** Got a complex Interface Builder list mode hierarchy that you want to open, all at once? Instead of expanding each of the items individually, you can expand the entire hierarchy by holding down the option key and clicking any of the list's disclosure triangles.

The *Light Info Button*, situated at the lower-right corner of the view, contains an icon that's mostly white, and is therefore hard to see against the white background. We're going to change this icon so it will look good on a white background. Single-click the *Light Info Button* icon to select it, and then bring up the attributes inspector. Change the button's *Type* from *Info Light* to *Info Dark*.

Now we're going to add a bunch of labels to the *View* so it looks like the one shown in Figure 11–26. We'll need a grand total of 20 labels. Half of them will be static labels that are right-aligned and **bold**; the other half will be used to display the actual values retrieved from the user defaults and will have outlets pointing to them.

Use Figure 11–26 as your guide to build this view. You don't need to match the appearance exactly, but you do need to have one label on the view for each of the outlets we declared. Go ahead and design the view. You don't need our help for this. When you're finished and have it looking the way you like, come back, and we'll continue.

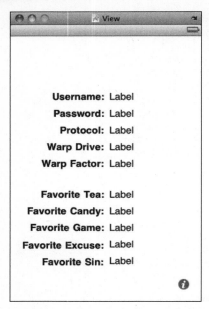

Figure 11–26. *The View window in Interface Builder showing the 20 labels we added*

The next thing we need to do is control-drag from *File's Owner* to each of the labels intended to display a settings value. You will control-drag a total of ten times, setting each label to a different outlet. Once you have all ten outlets connected to labels, save the changes to *MainView.xib* and return to Xcode.

Updating the Main View Controller

In Xcode, select *MainViewController.m*, and add the following code at the beginning of the file:

```
#import "MainViewController.h"


@implementation MainViewController
@synthesize usernameLabel;
@synthesize passwordLabel;
@synthesize protocolLabel;
@synthesize warpDriveLabel;
@synthesize warpFactorLabel;
@synthesize favoriteTeaLabel;
@synthesize favoriteCandyLabel;
@synthesize favoriteGameLabel;
@synthesize favoriteExcuseLabel;
@synthesize favoriteSinLabel;

- (void)refreshFields {
    NSUserDefaults *defaults = [NSUserDefaults standardUserDefaults];
```

```
        usernameLabel.text = [defaults objectForKey:kUsernameKey];
        passwordLabel.text = [defaults objectForKey:kPasswordKey];
        protocolLabel.text = [defaults objectForKey:kProtocolKey];
        warpDriveLabel.text = [defaults objectForKey:kWarpDriveKey];
        warpFactorLabel.text = [[defaults objectForKey:kWarpFactorKey]
                                  stringValue];
        favoriteTeaLabel.text = [defaults objectForKey:kFavoriteTeaKey];
        favoriteCandyLabel.text = [defaults objectForKey:kFavoriteCandyKey];
        favoriteGameLabel.text = [defaults objectForKey:kFavoriteGameKey];
        favoriteExcuseLabel.text = [defaults objectForKey:kFavoriteExcuseKey];
        favoriteSinLabel.text = [defaults objectForKey:kFavoriteSinKey];
}

- (void)viewDidAppear:(BOOL)animated {
        [self refreshFields];
        [super viewDidAppear:animated];
}
...
```

Also, let's be a good memory citizen by inserting the following code into the existing dealloc and viewDidUnload methods:

```
- (void)viewDidUnload {
        // Release any retained subviews of the main view.
        // e.g. self.myOutlet = nil;
        self.usernameLabel = nil;
        self.passwordLabel = nil;
        self.protocolLabel = nil;
        self.warpDriveLabel = nil;
        self.warpFactorLabel = nil;
        self.favoriteTeaLabel = nil;
        self.favoriteCandyLabel = nil;
        self.favoriteGameLabel = nil;
        self.favoriteExcuseLabel = nil;
        self.favoriteSinLabel = nil;
        [super viewDidUnload];
}

- (void)dealloc {
        [usernameLabel release];
        [passwordLabel release];
        [protocolLabel release];
        [warpDriveLabel release];
        [warpFactorLabel release];
        [favoriteTeaLabel release];
        [favoriteCandyLabel release];
        [favoriteGameLabel release];
        [favoriteExcuseLabel release];
        [favoriteSinLabel release];
        [super dealloc];
}
...
```

When the user is finished using the flipside view where some preferences can be changed, our controller will be notified of the fact. When that happens, we need to make sure our labels are updated to show any changes. Add the following line of code to the existing flipsideViewControllerDidFinish: method:

```
- (void)flipsideViewControllerDidFinish:
        (FlipsideViewController *)controller {
    [self refreshFields];
    [self dismissModalViewControllerAnimated:YES];
}
```

There's not really much here that should throw you. The new method, refreshFields, does nothing more than grab the standard user defaults, and sets the text property of all the labels to the appropriate object from the user defaults, using the key values that we put in our properties file. Notice that for warpFactorLabel, we're calling stringValue on the object returned. All of our other preferences are strings, which come back from the user defaults as NSString objects. The preference stored by the slider, however, comes back as an NSNumber, so we call stringValue on it to get a string representation of the value it holds.

After that, we added a viewDidAppear: method, where we call our refreshFields method. We call refreshFields again when we are notified that the flipside controller is being dismissed. This will cause our displayed fields to be set to the appropriate preference values when the view loads, and then to be refreshed when the flipside view is swapped out. Because the flipside view is handled modally, with the main view as its modal parent, the MainViewController's viewDidAppear: method will not be called when the flipside view is dismissed. Fortunately, the Utility Application template we chose has very kindly provided us with a delegate method we can use for exactly that purpose.

This class is complete. You should be able to compile and run your application and have it look something like Figure 11–7, except yours will be showing whatever values you entered in your Settings application, of course. Couldn't be much easier, could it?

Changing Defaults from Our Application

Now that we have the main view up and running, let's build the flipside view.

Creating the Flipside View

As you can see in Figure 11–27, the flipside view features our warp drive switch, as well as the warp factor slider. We'll use the same controls that the Settings application uses for these two items: a switch and a slider. In addition to declaring our outlets, we'll also declare a method called refreshFields, just as we did in MainViewController, and two action methods that will be triggered by the user touching the controls. Select FlipsideViewController.h, and make the following changes:

```
#import <UIKit/UIKit.h>

@protocol FlipsideViewControllerDelegate;

@interface FlipsideViewController : UIViewController {
    id <FlipsideViewControllerDelegate> delegate;
```

```
        UISwitch *engineSwitch;
        UISlider *warpFactorSlider;
}

@property (nonatomic, assign) id <FlipsideViewControllerDelegate> delegate;
@property (nonatomic, retain) IBOutlet UISwitch *engineSwitch;
@property (nonatomic, retain) IBOutlet UISlider *warpFactorSlider;

- (void)refreshFields;
- (IBAction)touchEngineSwitch;
- (IBAction)touchWarpSlider;
- (IBAction)done;
@end

@protocol FlipsideViewControllerDelegate
- (void)flipsideViewControllerDidFinish:
        (FlipsideViewController *)controller;
@end
```

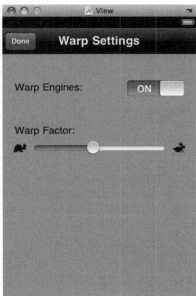

Figure 11–27. *Designing the flipside view in Interface Builder*

NOTE: Don't worry too much about the extra code here. As you saw before, the Utility Application template makes `MainViewController` a delegate of the `FlipsideViewController`. The extra code here that hasn't been in the other file templates we've used implements that delegate relationship.

Now, save your changes and double-click *FlipsideView.xib* to edit the GUI in Interface Builder. First, double-click the title in the title bar and change it to read *Warp Settings*.

Next, select the *View* in the main window, and then bring up the attributes inspector. First, change the background color using the *Background* popup to select *Light Gray Color*. The default flipside view background color is too dark for black text to look good, but light enough that white text is hard to read.

Next, drag two *Labels* from the library and place them on the *View* window. Double-click one of them and change it to read *Warp Engines:*. Double-click the other, and call it *Warp Factor:*. You can use Figure 11–27 as a placement guide.

Next, drag over a *Switch* from the library, and place it against the right side of the view across from the label that reads *Warp Engines*. Control-drag from the *File's Owner* icon to the new switch, and connect it to the *engineSwitch* outlet. Then control-drag from the switch back to the File's Owner icon, and connect it to the *touchEngineSwitch* action.

Now drag over a *Slider* from the library, and place it below the label that reads *Warp Factor:*. Resize the slider so that it stretches from the blue guide line on the left margin to the one on the right, and then control-drag from the *File's Owner* icon to the slider, and connect it to the *warpFactorSlider* outlet. Then control-drag from the slider to *File's Owner*, and select the *touchWarpSlider* action.

Single-click the slider if it's not still selected, and bring up the attributes inspector. Set *Minimum* to *1.00*, *Maximum* to *10.00*, and *Current* to *5.00*. Next, select *turtle.png* for *Min Image* and *rabbit.png* for *Max Image* (you *did* drag them into the project, right?).

Save the nib.

Updating the Flipside View Controller

Now let's head back to Xcode to finish the flipside view controller. Select *FlipsideViewController.m*, and make the following changes:

```
#import "FlipsideViewController.h"
#import "MainViewController.h"

@implementation FlipsideViewController
@synthesize delegate;
@synthesize engineSwitch;
@synthesize warpFactorSlider;

- (void)viewDidLoad {
    [super viewDidLoad];
    [self refreshFields];
    self.view.backgroundColor = [UIColor viewFlipsideBackgroundColor];
}

- (void)refreshFields {
    NSUserDefaults *defaults = [NSUserDefaults standardUserDefaults];
    engineSwitch.on = [[defaults objectForKey:kWarpDriveKey]
        isEqualToString:@"Engaged"] ? YES : NO;
    warpFactorSlider.value = [defaults floatForKey:kWarpFactorKey];

}
```

```
- (IBAction)touchEngineSwitch {
    NSUserDefaults *defaults = [NSUserDefaults standardUserDefaults];
    NSString *prefValue = engineSwitch.on ? @"Engaged" : @"Disabled";
    [defaults setObject:prefValue forKey:kWarpDriveKey];
}

- (IBAction)touchWarpSlider {
    NSUserDefaults *defaults = [NSUserDefaults standardUserDefaults];
    [defaults setFloat:warpFactorSlider.value forKey:kWarpFactorKey];
}
...
```

Add the following lines of code to the existing dealloc and viewDidUnload methods:

```
...
- (void)viewDidUnload {
    // Release any retained subviews of the main view.
    // e.g. self.myOutlet = nil;
    self.engineSwitch = nil;
    self.warpFactorSlider = nil;
    [super viewDidUnload];
}
- (void)dealloc {
    [engineSwitch release];
    [warpFactorSlider release];
    [super dealloc];
}
...
```

In the viewDidLoad method, we deleted one line of code that wasn't really important. Code in the template set the background color of the view using a class method, and that line of code caused the flipside view to have a textured, dark-gray appearance, rather than using the background that was set in Interface Builder. The textured background made it difficult to read the text and to see the slider pictures that we used. We deleted it to let the background color from Interface Builder shine through, so our text and icons can be seen more easily.

Then we added a call to our refreshFields method, whose four lines of code get a reference to the standard user defaults, and then use the outlets for the switch and slider to make them display the values stored in the user defaults. Because we opted to store strings rather than Booleans for the warp drive setting, we need to handle the conversion in our code, because a UISwitch instance is set using a BOOL property.

```
- (void)refreshFields {
    NSUserDefaults *defaults = [NSUserDefaults standardUserDefaults];
    engineSwitch.on = [[defaults objectForKey:kWarpDriveKey]
        isEqualToString:@"Engaged"] ? YES : NO;
    warpFactorSlider.value = [defaults floatForKey:kWarpFactorKey];
}
```

We also implemented the touchEngineSwitch and touchWarpSlider action methods, so that we could stuff the values from our controls back into the user defaults when the user changes them.

Keeping It Real

Now you should be able to run your app, view the settings, and then press the home button and open the Settings app to tweak some values here. Hit the home button again, launch your app again, and you may be in for a surprise. If you're running iOS 4.0 or later on your iOS device or simulator (and we bet you are), then when you go back to your app, you won't see the settings change! They'll remain as they are, showing the old values.

When you're using iOS 4, hitting the home button while an app is running doesn't actually quit the app. Instead, the operating system suspends the app in the background, leaving it ready to be quickly fired up again. This iOS 4 feature is great for switching back and forth between applications, since the amount of time it takes to reawaken a suspended app is much shorter than what it takes to launch it from scratch. However, in our case, we need to do a little more work so that when our app wakes up, it effectively gets a slap in the face, reloads the user preferences, and redisplays the values they contain.

You'll learn more about background applications in Chapter 13, but we'll give you a sneak peek at the basics of how to make your app notice that it has been brought back to life. To do this, we're going to sign up each of our controller classes to receive a notification that is sent by the application when it wakes up from its state of suspended execution.

A **notification** is a lightweight mechanism that objects can use to communicate with each other. Any object can define one or more notifications that it will publish to the application's **notification center**, which is a singleton object that exists only to pass these notifications between objects. Notifications are usually indications that some event occurred, and objects that publish notifications include a list of notifications in their documentation. For example, in Figure 11–28, you can see that the UIApplication class publishes a number of notifications. The purpose of most notifications is usually pretty obvious from their names, but the documentation contains further information if you find one whose purpose is unclear.

```
✓ Notifications
    UIApplicationDidBecomeActiveNotification
    UIApplicationDidChangeStatusBarFrameNotification
    UIApplicationDidChangeStatusBarOrientationNotification
    UIApplicationDidEnterBackgroundNotification
    UIApplicationDidFinishLaunchingNotification
    UIApplicationDidReceiveMemoryWarningNotification
    UIApplicationProtectedDataDidBecomeAvailable
    UIApplicationProtectedDataWillBecomeUnavailable
    UIApplicationSignificantTimeChangeNotification
    UIApplicationWillChangeStatusBarOrientationNotification
    UIApplicationWillChangeStatusBarFrameNotification
    UIApplicationWillEnterForegroundNotification
    UIApplicationWillResignActiveNotification
    UIApplicationWillTerminateNotification
```

Figure 11–28. *The UIApplication documentation lists all the notifications that it publishes.*

Our application needs to refresh its display when the application is about to come to the foreground, so we are interested in the notification called UIApplicationWillEnterForegroundNotification. When we write our viewDidLoad method, we will subscribe to that notification and tell the notification center to call this method when that notification happens. Add this method to both *MainViewController.m* and *FlipsideViewController.m*:

```
- (void)applicationWillEnterForeground:(NSNotification *)notification {
    NSUserDefaults *defaults = [NSUserDefaults standardUserDefaults];
    [defaults synchronize];
    [self refreshFields];
}
```

The method itself is quite simple. First, it gets a reference to the standard user defaults object, and calls its synchronize method, which forces the User Defaults system to save any unsaved changes and also reload any unmodified preferences from storage. In effect, we're forcing it to reread the stored preferences so that we can pick up the changes that were made in the Settings app. Then it calls the refreshFields method, which each class uses to update its display.

Now, we need to make each of our controllers subscribe to the notification we're interested in by adding the following lines to the bottom of the viewDidLoad method in both *MainViewController.m* and *FlipsideViewController.m*. You'll also need to remove the comment markers around the method in *MainViewController.m*, since it has not been used there yet.

```
- (void)viewDidLoad {
    ...
    UIApplication *app = [UIApplication sharedApplication];
    [[NSNotificationCenter defaultCenter] addObserver:self
            selector:@selector(applicationWillEnterForeground:)
            name:UIApplicationWillEnterForegroundNotification
            object:app];
}
```

We start off by getting a reference to our application instance and use that to subscribe to the UIApplicationWillEnterForegroundNotification, using the default NSNotificationCenter instance and a method called addObserver:selector:name:object:. We then pass the following to this method:

- For an observer, we pass self, which means that our controller class (each of them individually, since this code is going into both of them) is the object that needs to be notified.

- For selector, we pass a selector to the applicationWillEnterForeground: method we just wrote, telling the notification center to call that method when the notification is posted.

- The third parameter, name:, is the name of the notification that we're interested in receiving.

■ The final parameter, object:, is the object from which we're interested in getting the notification. If we passed nil for the final parameter, we would get notified any time any method posted the UIApplicationWillEnterForegroundNotification.

That takes care of updating the display, but we also need to consider what happens to the values that are put into the user defaults when the user manipulates the controls in our app. We need to make sure that they are saved to storage before control passes to another app. The easiest way to do that is to call synchronize as soon as the settings are changed, by adding one line to each of our new action methods in *FlipsideViewController.m*:

```
- (IBAction)touchEngineSwitch {
  NSUserDefaults *defaults = [NSUserDefaults standardUserDefaults];
  NSString *prefValue = engineSwitch.on ? @"Engaged" : @"Disabled";
  [defaults setObject:prefValue forKey:kWarpDriveKey];
  [defaults synchronize];
}
```

```
- (IBAction)touchWarpSlider {
  NSUserDefaults *defaults = [NSUserDefaults standardUserDefaults];
  [defaults setFloat:warpFactorSlider.value forKey:kWarpFactorKey];
  [defaults synchronize];
}
```

> **NOTE:** Calling the synchronize method is a potentially expensive operation, since the entire contents of the user defaults in memory must be compared with what's in storage. When you're dealing with a whole lot of user defaults at once and want to make sure everything is in sync, it's best to try to minimize calls to synchronize so that this whole comparison isn't performed over and over again. However, calling it once in response to each user action, as we're doing here, won't cause any noticeable performance problems.

There's one more thing to take care of in order to make this work as cleanly as possible. You already know that you must clean up your memory by releasing variables when they're no longer in use, as well as performing other cleanup tasks. The notification system is another place where you need to clean up after yourself, by telling the default NSNotificationCenter that you don't want to listen to any more notifications. In our case, where we've registered each view controller to observe this notification in its viewDidLoad method, we should unregister in the matching viewDidUnload method. So, in both *MainViewController.m* and *FlipsideViewController.m*, put the following line at the top of the viewDidUnload method:

```
- (void)viewDidUnload {
    [[NSNotificationCenter defaultCenter] removeObserver:self];
    ...
}
```

Note that it's possible to unregister for specific notifications using the removeObserver:name:object: method, by passing in the same values that were used to register your observer in the first place. But the preceding line is a handy way to make sure that the notification center forgets about our observer completely, no matter how many notifications it was registered for.

With that in place, it's time to build and run the app, and see what happens when you switch between your app and the Settings app. Changes you make in the Settings app should now be immediately reflected in your app when you switch back to it.

Beam Me Up, Scotty

At this point, you should have a very solid grasp on both the Settings application and the User Defaults mechanism. You know how to add a settings bundle to your application and how to build a hierarchy of views for your application's preferences. You also learned how to read and write preferences using NSUserDefaults, and how to let the user change preferences from within your application. You even got a chance to use a new project template in Xcode. There really shouldn't be much in the way of application preferences that you are not equipped to handle now.

In the next chapter, we're going to show you how to keep your application's data around after your application quits. Ready? Let's go!

Chapter 12

Basic Data Persistence

So far, we've focused on the controller and view aspects of the MVC paradigm. Although several of our applications have read data out of the application bundle, none of them has saved data to any form of persistent storage—nonvolatile storage that survives a restart of the computer or device. With the exception of Application Settings (in Chapter 11), so far, every sample application either did not store data or used volatile or nonpersistent storage. Every time one of our sample applications launched, it appeared with exactly the same data it had the first time you launched it.

This approach has worked for us up to this point. But in the real world, your applications will need to persist data. When users make changes, they usually like to find those changes when they launch the program again.

A number of different mechanisms are available for persisting data on an iOS device. If you've programmed in Cocoa for Mac OS X, you've likely used some or all of these techniques.

In this chapter, we're going to look at four different mechanisms for persisting data to the iOS file system:

- Property lists
- Object archives (or archiving)
- SQLite3 (iOS's embedded relational database)
- Core Data (Apple's provided persistence tool)

We will write example applications that use all four approaches.

> **NOTE:** Property lists, object archives, SQLite3, and Core Data are not the only ways you can persist data on iOS. They are just the most common and easiest. You always have the option of using traditional C I/O calls like `fopen()` to read and write data. You can also use Cocoa's low-level file management tools. In almost every case, doing so will result in a lot more coding effort and is rarely necessary, but those tools are there if you need them.

Your Application's Sandbox

All four of this chapter's data-persistence mechanisms share an important common element: your application's */Documents* folder. Every application gets its own */Documents* folder, and applications are allowed to read and write from only their own */Documents* directory.

To give you some context, let's take a look at how applications are organized in iOS. Open a Finder window, and navigate to your home directory. Within that, drill down into *Library/Application Support/iPhone Simulator/*. Within that directory, you'll see a subdirectory for each version of iOS supported by your current Xcode installation. For example, you might see one directory named *4.1* and another named *4.2*. Drill down into the directory representing the latest version of iOS supported by your version of Xcode. At this point, you should see four subfolders, including one named *Applications* (see Figure 12–1).

> **NOTE:** If you've installed multiple versions of the SDK, you may see a few additional folders inside the *iPhone Simulator* directory, with names indicating the iOS version number they represent. That's perfectly normal.

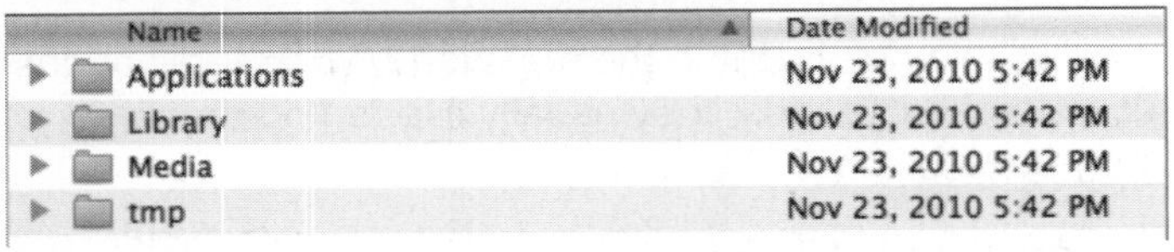

Name	Date Modified
▶ Applications	Nov 23, 2010 5:42 PM
▶ Library	Nov 23, 2010 5:42 PM
▶ Media	Nov 23, 2010 5:42 PM
▶ tmp	Nov 23, 2010 5:42 PM

Figure 12–1. *The layout of one user's Library/Application Support/iPhone Simulator/4.2/ directory showing the Applications folder*

Although this listing represents the simulator, the file structure is similar to what's on the actual device. As is probably obvious, the *Applications* folder is where iOS stores its applications. If you open the *Applications* folder, you'll see a bunch of folders and files with names that are long strings of characters. These names are globally unique identifiers (GUIDs) and are generated automatically by Xcode. Each of these folders contains one application and its supporting folders.

If you open one of the application subdirectories, you should see something that looks familiar. You'll find one of the iOS applications you've built, along with three support folders:

- **Documents**: Your application stores its data in *Documents*, with the exception of NSUserDefaults-based preference settings.

- **Library**: NSUserDefaults-based preference settings are stored in the *Library/Preferences* folder.

■ *tmp*: The *tmp* directory offers a place where your application can store temporary files. Files written into */tmp* will not be backed up by iTunes when your iOS device syncs, but your application does need to take responsibility for deleting the files in */tmp* once they are no longer needed, to avoid filling up the file system.

Getting the Documents Directory

Since our application is in a folder with a seemingly random name, how do we retrieve the full path to the *Documents* directory so that we can read and write our files? It's actually quite easy. The C function NSSearchPathForDirectoriesInDomain() will locate various directories for you. This is a Foundation function, so it is shared with Cocoa for Mac OS X. Many of its available options are designed for Mac OS X and won't return any values on iOS, either because those locations don't exist on iOS (such as the *Downloads* folder) or because your application doesn't have rights to access the location due to iOS's sandboxing mechanism.

Here's some code to retrieve the path to the *Documents* directory:

```
NSArray *paths = NSSearchPathForDirectoriesInDomains(NSDocumentDirectory,
    NSUserDomainMask, YES);
NSString *documentsDirectory = [paths objectAtIndex:0];
```

The constant NSDocumentDirectory says we are looking for the path to the *Documents* directory. The second constant, NSUserDomainMask, indicates that we want to restrict our search to our application's sandbox. In Mac OS X, this same constant is used to indicate that we want the function to look in the user's home directory, which explains its somewhat odd name.

Though an array of matching paths is returned, we can count on our *Documents* directory residing at index 0 in the array. Why? We know that only one directory meets the criteria we've specified, since each application has only one *Documents* directory.

We can create a file name by appending another string onto the end of the path we just retrieved. We'll use an NSString method designed for just that purpose called stringByAppendingPathComponent:.

```
NSString *filename = [documentsDirectory
    stringByAppendingPathComponent:@"theFile.txt"];
```

After this call, filename would contain the full path to a file called *theFile.txt* in our application's *Documents* directory, and we can use filename to create, read, and write from that file.

Getting the tmp Directory

Getting a reference to your application's temporary directory is even easier than getting a reference to the *Documents* directory. The Foundation function called NSTemporaryDirectory() will return a string containing the full path to your application's temporary directory. To create a file name for a file that will be stored in the temporary directory, first find the temporary directory:

```
NSString *tempPath = NSTemporaryDirectory();
```

Then create a path to a file in that directory by appending a file name to that path, like this:

```
NSString *tempFile = [tempPath
    stringByAppendingPathComponent:@"tempFile.txt"];
```

File-Saving Strategies

All four approaches we're going to look at in this chapter make use of the iOS file system.

In the case of SQLite3, you'll create a single SQLite3 database file and let SQLite3 worry about storing and retrieving your data. In its simplest form, Core Data takes care of all the file system management for you. With the other two persistence mechanisms—property lists and archiving—you need to put some thought into whether you are going to store your data in a single file or in multiple files.

Single-File Persistence

Using a single file is the easiest approach, and with many applications, it is a perfectly acceptable one. You start off by creating a root object, usually an NSArray or NSDictionary (your root object can also be based on a custom class when using archiving). Next, you populate your root object with all the program data that needs to be persisted. Whenever you need to save, your code rewrites the entire contents of that root object to a single file. When your application launches, it reads the entire contents of that file into memory; when it quits, it writes out the entire contents. This is the approach we'll use in this chapter.

The downside of using a single file is that you need to load all of your application's data into memory, and you must write all of it to the file system for even the smallest changes. But if your application isn't likely to manage more than a few megabytes of data, this approach is probably fine, and its simplicity will certainly make your life easier.

Multiple-File Persistence

Using multiple files for persistence is an alternative approach. For example, an e-mail application might store each e-mail message in its own file.

There are obvious advantages to this method. It allows the application to load only data that the user has requested (another form of lazy loading), and when the user makes a change, only the files that changed need to be saved. This method also gives you the opportunity to free up memory when you receive a low-memory notification. Any memory that is being used to store data that the user is not currently viewing can be flushed and simply reloaded from the file system the next time it's needed.

The downside of multiple-file persistence is that it adds a fair amount of complexity to your application. For now, we'll stick with single-file persistence.

Next, we'll get into the specifics of each of our persistence methods: property lists, object archives, SQLite3, and Core Data. We'll explore each of these in turn and build an application that uses each mechanism to save some data to the device's file system. We'll start with property lists.

Using Property Lists

Several of our sample applications have made use of property lists, most recently when we used a property list to specify our application preferences. Property lists are convenient. They can be edited manually using Xcode or the Property List Editor application. Also, both NSDictionary and NSArray instances can be written to and created from property lists, as long as the dictionary or array contains only specific serializable objects.

Property List Serialization

A **serialized object** is one that has been converted into a stream of bytes so it can be stored in a file or transferred over a network. Although any object can be made serializable, only certain objects can be placed into a collection class, such as an NSDictionary or NSArray, and then stored to a property list using the collection class's writeToFile:atomically: method. The following Objective-C classes can be serialized this way:

- NSArray
- NSMutableArray
- NSDictionary
- NSMutableDictionary
- NSData
- NSMutableData
- NSString
- NSMutableString
- NSNumber
- NSDate

If you can build your data model from just these objects, you can use property lists to save and load your data.

If you're going to use property lists to persist your application data, you'll use either an NSArray or an NSDictionary to hold the data that needs to be persisted. Assuming that all of the objects that you put into the NSArray or NSDictionary are serializable objects from the preceding list, you can write a property list by calling the writeToFile:atomically: method on the dictionary or array instance, like so:

```
[myArray writeToFile:@"/some/file/location/output.plist" atomically:YES];
```

> **NOTE:** In case you were wondering, the atomically parameter tells the method to write the data to an auxiliary file, not to the specified location. Once it has successfully written the file, it will then copy that auxiliary file to the location specified by the first parameter. This is a safer way to write a file, because if the application crashes during the save, the existing file (if there was one) will not be corrupted. It adds a bit of overhead, but in most situations, it's worth the cost.

One problem with the property list approach is that custom objects cannot be serialized into property lists. You also can't use other delivered classes from Cocoa Touch that aren't specified in the previous list of serializable objects, which means that classes like NSURL, UIImage, and UIColor cannot be used directly.

Apart from the serialization issue, keeping all your model data in the form of property lists means that you can't easily create derived or calculated properties (such as a property that is the sum of two other properties), and some of your code that really should be contained in model classes must be moved to your controller classes. Again, these restrictions are OK for simple data models and simple applications. Most of the time, however, your application will be much easier to maintain if you create dedicated model classes.

Simple property lists can still be useful in complex applications. They are a great way to include static data in your application. For example, when your application has a picker, often the best way to include the list of items for it is to create a property list file and place that file in your project's *Resources* folder, which will cause it to be compiled into your application.

Let's a build a simple application that uses property lists to store its data.

The First Version of the Persistence Application

We're going to build a program that lets you enter data into four text fields, saves those fields to a property list file when the application quits, and then reloads the data back from that property list file the next time the application launches (see Figure 12–2).

Figure 12–2. *The Persistence application*

NOTE: In this chapter's applications, we won't be taking the time to set up all the user interface niceties that we have in the past. Tapping the return key, for example, will neither dismiss the keyboard nor take you to the next field. If you want to add such polish to the application, doing so would be good practice, so we encourage you to do that on your own.

Creating the Persistence Project

In Xcode, create a new project using the View-based Application template, and save the project with the name *Persistence*. This project contains all the files that we'll need to build our application, so we can dive right into things.

Before we build the view with the four text fields, let's create the outlets we need. Expand the *Classes* folder. Then single-click the *PersistenceViewController.h* file, and make the following changes:

```
#import <UIKit/UIKit.h>

#define kFilename        @"data.plist"

@interface PersistenceViewController : UIViewController {
    UITextField *field1;
    UITextField *field2;
```

```
    UITextField *field3;
    UITextField *field4;
}
@property (nonatomic, retain) IBOutlet UITextField *field1;
@property (nonatomic, retain) IBOutlet UITextField *field2;
@property (nonatomic, retain) IBOutlet UITextField *field3;
@property (nonatomic, retain) IBOutlet UITextField *field4;
- (NSString *)dataFilePath;
- (void)applicationWillResignActive:(NSNotification *)notification;
@end
```

In addition to defining four text field outlets, we've also defined a constant for the file name we're going to use, as well as two additional methods. One method, dataFilePath, will create and return the full pathname to our data file by concatenating kFilename onto the path for the *Documents* directory. The other method, applicationWillResignActive: will be called when our application quits and will save data to the property list file. We'll discuss these methods when we edit the persistence classes.

Next, expand the *Resources* folder, and double click *PersistenceViewController.xib* to edit the GUI In Interface Builder.

Designing the Persistence Application View

Once Interface Builder launches, double click the *View* icon to open the *View* window. Drag a *Text Field* from the library, and place it against the top-right blue guide line. Resize it to the left so that it reaches about two-thirds of the way across the window, and then bring up the attributes inspector. Make sure the box labeled *Clear When Editing Begins* is unchecked.

Next, hold down the option key and drag the text box downward, which will create a copy of it. Repeat this step two more times so that you have four text fields. Now, drag four labels to the window, and use Figure 12–3 as a placement and design guide. Notice that we've placed the text fields at the top of our view to leave plenty of room for the keyboard.

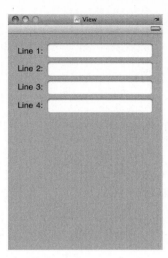

Figure 12–3. *Designing the Persistence application's view*

Once you have all four text fields and labels placed, control-drag from the *File's Owner* icon to each of the four text fields. Connect the topmost text field to the outlet called *field1*, the next one to *field2*, the third to *field3*, and the bottom one to *field4*. When you have all four text fields connected to outlets, save the changes you made to *PersistenceViewController.xib* and return to Xcode.

Editing the Persistence Classes

In the *Groups & Files* pane, select *PersistenceViewController.m*, and add the following code at the beginning of the file:

```
#import "PersistenceViewController.h"

@implementation PersistenceViewController
@synthesize field1;
@synthesize field2;
@synthesize field3;
@synthesize field4;

- (NSString *)dataFilePath {
    NSArray *paths = NSSearchPathForDirectoriesInDomains(
        NSDocumentDirectory, NSUserDomainMask, YES);
    NSString *documentsDirectory = [paths objectAtIndex:0];
    return [documentsDirectory stringByAppendingPathComponent:kFilename];
}

#pragma mark -
- (void)viewDidLoad {
    NSString *filePath = [self dataFilePath];
    if ([[NSFileManager defaultManager] fileExistsAtPath:filePath]) {
        NSArray *array = [[NSArray alloc] initWithContentsOfFile:filePath];
        field1.text = [array objectAtIndex:0];
```

```
            field2.text = [array objectAtIndex:1];
            field3.text = [array objectAtIndex:2];
            field4.text = [array objectAtIndex:3];
            [array release];
        }

        UIApplication *app = [UIApplication sharedApplication];
        [[NSNotificationCenter defaultCenter] addObserver:self
                    selector:@selector(applicationWillResignActive:)
                    name:UIApplicationWillResignActiveNotification
                    object:app];
        [super viewDidLoad];
}
- (void)applicationWillResignActive:(NSNotification *)notification {
        NSMutableArray *array = [[NSMutableArray alloc] init];
        [array addObject:field1.text];
        [array addObject:field2.text];
        [array addObject:field3.text];
        [array addObject:field4.text];
        [array writeToFile:[self dataFilePath] atomically:YES];
        [array release];
}
...
```

Also, insert the following code into the existing dealloc and viewDidUnload methods:

```
...
- (void)viewDidUnload {
        // Release any retained subviews of the main view.
        // e.g. self.myOutlet = nil;
        self.field1 = nil;
        self.field2 = nil;
        self.field3 = nil;
        self.field4 = nil;
        [super viewDidUnload];
}
- (void)dealloc {
        [field1 release];
        [field2 release];
        [field3 release];
        [field4 release];
        [super dealloc];
}
...
```

The first method we added, dataFilePath, returns the full pathname of our data file by finding the *Documents* directory and appending kFilename to it. This method will be called from any code that needs to load or save data.

```
- (NSString *)dataFilePath {
        NSArray *paths = NSSearchPathForDirectoriesInDomains(
            NSDocumentDirectory, NSUserDomainMask, YES);
        NSString *documentsDirectory = [paths objectAtIndex:0];
        return [documentsDirectory stringByAppendingPathComponent:kFilename];
}
```

In the `viewDidLoad` method, we do a few more things. First, we check to see if a data file already exists. If there isn't one, we don't want to bother trying to load it. If the file does exist, we instantiate an array with the contents of that file, and then copy the objects from that array to our four text fields. Because arrays are ordered lists, by copying them in the same order as we saved them, we are always sure to get the correct values in the correct fields.

```
- (void)viewDidLoad {
    NSString *filePath = [self dataFilePath];
    if ([[NSFileManager defaultManager] fileExistsAtPath:filePath]) {
        NSArray *array = [[NSArray alloc] initWithContentsOfFile:filePath];
        field1.text = [array objectAtIndex:0];
        field2.text = [array objectAtIndex:1];
        field3.text = [array objectAtIndex:2];
        field4.text = [array objectAtIndex:3];
        [array release];
    }
}
```

After we load the data from the property list, we get a reference to our application instance and use that to subscribe to the `UIApplicationWillResignActiveNotification`, using the default `NSNotificationCenter` instance and a method called `addObserver:selector:name:object:`. We pass an observer of `self`, specifying that our `PersistenceViewController` should be notified. For `selector`, we pass a selector to the `applicationWillResignActive:` method, telling the notification center to call that method when the notification is posted. The third parameter, `name:`, is the name of the notification that we're interested in receiving. The final parameter, `object:`, is the object we're interested in getting the notification from.

```
UIApplication *app = [UIApplication sharedApplication];
[[NSNotificationCenter defaultCenter] addObserver:self
        selector:@selector(applicationWillResignActive:)
        name:UIApplicationWillResignActiveNotification
        object:app];
```

After subscribing to the notification, we just give our superclass a chance to respond to `viewDidLoad`, and we're finished.

```
    [super viewDidLoad];
}
```

The final new method is called `applicationWillResignActive:`. Notice that it takes a pointer to an `NSNotification` as an argument. You probably recognize this pattern from Chapter 11. `applicationWillResignActive:` is a notification method, and all notifications take a single `NSNotification` instance as their argument.

Our application needs to save its data before the application is terminated or sent to the background, so we are interested in the notification called `UIApplicationWillResignActiveNotification`. This notification is posted whenever an app is no longer the one with which the user is interacting. This includes when the user quits the application and (in iOS 4 and later) when the application is pushed to the background, perhaps to later be brought back to the foreground. Earlier, in the `viewDidLoad` method, we used the notification center to subscribe to that particular notification. This method is called when that notification happens:

```
- (void)applicationWillResignActive:(NSNotification *)notification {
    NSMutableArray *array = [[NSMutableArray alloc] init];
    [array addObject:field1.text];
    [array addObject:field2.text];
    [array addObject:field3.text];
    [array addObject:field4.text];
    [array writeToFile:[self dataFilePath] atomically:YES];
    [array release];
}
```

This method is pretty simple. We create a mutable array, add the text from each of the four fields to the array, and then write the contents of that array out to a property list file. That's all there is to saving our data using property lists.

That wasn't too bad, was it? When our main view is finished loading, we look for a property list file. If it exists, we copy data from it into our text fields. Next, we register to be notified when the application becomes inactive (either by being quit or pushed to the background). When that happens, we gather the values from our four text fields, stick them in a mutable array, and write that mutable array to a property list.

Why don't you compile and run the application? It should build and then launch in the simulator. Once it comes up, you should be able to type into any of the four text fields. When you've typed something in them, press the home button (the circular button with the rounded square in it at the bottom of the simulator window). It's very important that you press the home button. If you just exit the simulator, that's the equivalent of forcibly quitting your application. In that case, you will never receive the notification that the application is terminating, and your data will not be saved.

NOTE: Starting in iOS 4, pressing the home button doesn't typically quit the app—at least not at first. The app is put into a background state, ready to be instantly reactivated in case the user switches back to it. We'll dig into the details of these states and their implications for running and quitting apps in Chapter 13. In the meantime, if you want to verify that the data really was saved, you can quit the iPhone simulator entirely and then restart your app from Xcode. Quitting the simulator is basically the equivalent of rebooting an iPhone, so when it starts up again your app will have a fresh relaunch experience.

Property list serialization is pretty cool and easy to use. However, it's a little limiting, since only a small selection of objects can be stored in property lists. Let's look at a somewhat more robust approach.

Archiving Model Objects

In the last part of Chapter 9, when we built the Presidents data model object, you saw an example of the process of loading archived data using NSCoder. In the Cocoa world, the term **archiving** refers to another form of serialization, but it's a more generic type that any object can implement. Any model object specifically written to hold data should support archiving. The technique of archiving model objects lets you easily write complex objects to a file and then read them back in.

As long as every property you implement in your class is either a scalar, like `int` or `float`, or an instance of a class that conforms to the `NSCoding` protocol, you can archive your objects completely. Since most Foundation and Cocoa Touch classes capable of storing data do conform to `NSCoding` (though there are a few noteworthy exceptions, such as `UIImage`), archiving is actually relatively easy to implement for most classes.

Although not strictly required to make archiving work, another protocol should be implemented along with `NSCoding`: the `NSCopying` protocol, which is a protocol that allows your object to be copied. Being able to copy an object gives you a lot more flexibility when using data model objects. For example, in the Presidents application in Chapter 9, instead of that complex code we wrote to store changes the user made so we could handle both the *Cancel* and *Save* buttons, we could have made a copy of the `president` object and stored the changes in that copy. If the user tapped *Save*, we would just copy the changed version over to replace the original version.

Conforming to NSCoding

The `NSCoding` protocol declares two methods, which are both required. One encodes your object into an archive; the other one creates a new object by decoding an archive. Both methods are passed an instance of `NSCoder`, which you work with in very much the same way as `NSUserDefaults`, introduced in the previous chapter. You can encode and decode both objects and native datatypes like `int` and `float` values using key-value coding.

A method to encode an object might look like this:

```
- (void)encodeWithCoder:(NSCoder *)encoder {
    [encoder encodeObject:foo forKey:kFooKey];
    [encoder encodeObject:bar forKey:kBarKey];
    [encoder encodeInt:someInt forKey:kSomeIntKey];
    [encoder encodeFloat:someFloat forKey:kSomeFloatKey]
}
```

To support archiving in our object, we need to encode each of our instance variables into `encoder` using the appropriate encoding method. We need to implement a method that initializes an object from an `NSCoder`, allowing us to restore an object that was previously archived. If you are subclassing a class that also conforms to `NSCoding`, you need to make sure you call `encodeWithCoder:` on your superclass, meaning your method would look like this instead:

```
- (void)encodeWithCoder:(NSCoder *)encoder {
    [super encodeWithCoder:encoder];
    [encoder encodeObject:foo forKey:kFooKey];
    [encoder encodeObject:bar forKey:kBarKey];
    [encoder encodeInt:someInt forKey:kSomeIntKey];
    [encoder encodeFloat:someFloat forKey:kSomeFloatKey]
}
```

Implementing the initWithCoder: method is slightly more complex than implementing encodeWithcoder:. If you are subclassing NSObject directly, or subclassing some other class that doesn't conform to NSCoding, your method would look something like the following:

```
- (id)initWithCoder:(NSCoder *)decoder {
    if (self = [super init]) {
        foo = [[decoder decodeObjectForKey:kFooKey] retain];
        bar = [[decoder decodeObjectForKey:kBarKey] retain];
        someInt = [decoder decodeIntForKey:kSomeIntKey];
        someFloat = [decoder decodeFloatForKey:kAgeKey];
    }
    return self;
}
```

The method initializes an object instance using [super init]. If that's successful, it sets its properties by decoding values from the passed-in instance of NSCoder. When implementing NSCoding for a class with a superclass that also conforms to NSCoding, the initWithCoder: method needs to look slightly different. Instead of calling init on super, it needs to call initWithCoder:, like so:

```
- (id)initWithCoder:(NSCoder *)decoder {
    if (self = [super initWithCoder:decoder]) {
        foo = [[decoder decodeObjectForKey:kFooKey] retain];
        bar = [[decoder decodeObjectForKey:kBarKey] retain];
        someInt = [decoder decodeIntForKey:kSomeIntKey];
        someFloat = [decoder decodeFloatForKey:kAgeKey];
    }
    return self;
}
```

And that's basically it. As long as you implement these two methods to encode and decode all of your object's properties, your object is archivable and can be written to and read from archives.

Implementing NSCopying

As we mentioned earlier, conforming to NSCopying is a very good idea for any data model objects. NSCopying has one method, called copyWithZone:, and it allows objects to be copied. Implementing NSCopying is very similar to implementing initWithCoder:. You just need to create a new instance of the same class, and then set all of that new instance's properties to the same values as this object's properties. Here's what a copyWithZone: method might look like:

```
- (id)copyWithZone:(NSZone *)zone {
    MyClass *copy = [[[self class] allocWithZone:zone] init];
    copy.foo = [[self.foo copyWithZone:zone] autorelease];
    copy.bar = [[self.bar copyWithZone:zone] autorelease];
    copy.someInt = self.someInt;
    copy.someFloat = self.someFloat;
    return copy;
}
```

Notice that we do not release or autorelease the new object we created. Copied objects are implicitly retained, so they should be released or autoreleased in the code that called copy or `copyWithZone:`.

> **NOTE:** Don't worry too much about the NSZone parameter. This pointer is to a `struct` that is used by the system to manage memory. Only in rare circumstances did developers ever need to worry about zones or create their own, and nowadays, it's almost unheard of to have multiple zones. Calling copy on an object is the same as calling `copyWithZone:` using the default zone, which is almost always what you want.

Archiving and Unarchiving Data Objects

Creating an archive from an object or objects that conforms to NSCoding is relatively easy. First, we create an instance of NSMutableData to hold the encoded data, and then we create an NSKeyedArchiver instance to archive objects into that NSMutableData instance:

```
NSMutableData *data = [[NSMutableData alloc] init];
NSKeyedArchiver *archiver = [[NSKeyedArchiver alloc]
    initForWritingWithMutableData:data];
```

After creating both of those, we then use key-value coding to archive any objects we wish to include in the archive, like this:

```
[archiver encodeObject:myObject forKey:@"keyValueString"];
```

Once we've encoded all the objects we want to include, we just tell the archiver we're finished, write the NSMutableData instance to the file system, and do memory cleanup on our objects:

```
[archiver finishEncoding];
BOOL success = [data writeToFile:@"/path/to/archive" atomically:YES];
[archiver release];
[data release];
```

If anything went wrong while writing the file, success will be set to NO. If success is YES, the data was successfully written to the specified file. Any objects created from this archive will be exact copies of the objects that were last written into the file.

To reconstitute objects from the archive, we go through a similar process. We create an NSData instance from the archive file and create an NSKeyedUnarchiver to decode the data:

```
NSData *data = [[NSData alloc] initWithContentsOfFile:path];
NSKeyedUnarchiver *unarchiver = [[NSKeyedUnarchiver alloc]
    initForReadingWithData:data];
```

After that, we read our objects from the unarchiver using the same key that we used to archive the object:

```
self.object = [unarchiver decodeObjectForKey:@"keyValueString"];
```

> **NOTE:** The object returned by `decodeObjectForKey:` is autoreleased, so if you want to keep it around beyond the current method, you need to retain it. Assigning it to a property declared with the `retain` keyword usually handles this for you. However, if you're not assigning it to a property and need the object to stick around past the end of the current event loop, you need to explicitly send it a `retain` message.

Finally, we tell the archiver we are finished and do our memory cleanup:

```
[unarchiver finishDecoding];
[unarchiver release];
[data release];
```

If you're feeling a little overwhelmed by archiving, don't worry. It's actually fairly straightforward. We're going to retrofit our Persistence application to use archiving, so you'll get to see it in action. Once you've done it a few times, archiving will become second nature, as all you're really doing is storing and retrieving your object's properties using key-value coding.

The Archiving Application

Let's redo the Persistence application so it uses archiving instead of property lists. We're going to be making some fairly significant changes to the Persistence source code, so you might want to make a copy of your project before continuing.

Implementing the FourLines Class

Once you're ready to proceed and have a copy of your *Persistence* project open in Xcode, select the *Classes* folder and press ⌘N or select **File ➤ New File....** When the new file assistant comes up, select *Cocoa Touch Class*, select *Objective-C class* with a *Subclass of NSObject*, and name the file *FourLines.m*. Be sure the header file is created. This class is going to be our data model. It will hold the data that we're currently storing in a dictionary in the property list application. Single-click *FourLines.h*, and make the following changes:

```
#import <UIKit/UIKit.h>x

@interface FourLines : NSObject <NSCoding, NSCopying> {
    NSString *field1;
    NSString *field2;
    NSString *field3;
    NSString *field4;
}
@property (nonatomic, retain) NSString *field1;
@property (nonatomic, retain) NSString *field2;
@property (nonatomic, retain) NSString *field3;
@property (nonatomic, retain) NSString *field4;
@end
```

This is a very straightforward data model class with four string properties. Notice that we've conformed the class to the NSCoding and NSCopying protocols. Now, switch over to *FourLines.m*, and add the following code:

```
#import "FourLines.h"

#define    kField1Key    @"Field1"
#define    kField2Key    @"Field2"
#define    kField3Key    @"Field3"
#define    kField4Key    @"Field4"

@implementation FourLines
@synthesize field1;
@synthesize field2;
@synthesize field3;
@synthesize field4;

#pragma mark NSCoding
- (void)encodeWithCoder:(NSCoder *)encoder {
    [encoder encodeObject:field1 forKey:kField1Key];
    [encoder encodeObject:field2 forKey:kField2Key];
    [encoder encodeObject:field3 forKey:kField3Key];
    [encoder encodeObject:field4 forKey:kField4Key];
}

- (id)initWithCoder:(NSCoder *)decoder {
    if (self = [super init]) {
        field1 = [[decoder decodeObjectForKey:kField1Key] retain];
        field2 = [[decoder decodeObjectForKey:kField2Key] retain];
        field3 = [[decoder decodeObjectForKey:kField3Key] retain];
        field4 = [[decoder decodeObjectForKey:kField4Key] retain];
    }
    return self;
}

#pragma mark -
#pragma mark NSCopying
- (id)copyWithZone:(NSZone *)zone {
    FourLines *copy = [[[self class] allocWithZone: zone] init];
    copy.field1 = [[self.field1 copyWithZone:zone] autorelease];
    copy.field2 = [[self.field2 copyWithZone:zone] autorelease];
    copy.field3 = [[self.field3 copyWithZone:zone] autorelease];
    copy.field4 = [[self.field4 copyWithZone:zone] autorelease];
    return copy;
}
@end
```

We just implemented all the methods necessary to conform to NSCoding and NSCopying. We encode all four of our properties in encodeWithCoder: and decode all four of them using the same four key values in initWithCoder:. In copyWithZone:, we create a new FourLines object and copy all four strings to it. See? It's not hard at all.

Implementing the PersistenceViewController Class

Now that we have an archivable data object, let's use it to persist our application data. Single-click *PersistenceViewController.h*, and make the following changes:

```
#import <UIKit/UIKit.h>

#define kFilename          @"data.plist"
#define kFilename          @"archive"
#define kDataKey           @"Data"

@interface PersistenceViewController : UIViewController {
    UITextField *field1;
    UITextField *field2;
    UITextField *field3;
    UITextField *field4;
}
@property (nonatomic, retain) IBOutlet UITextField *field1;
@property (nonatomic, retain) IBOutlet UITextField *field2;
@property (nonatomic, retain) IBOutlet UITextField *field3;
@property (nonatomic, retain) IBOutlet UITextField *field4;
- (NSString *)dataFilePath;
- (void)applicationWillResignActive:(NSNotification *)notification;
@end
```

All we're doing here is specifying a new file name so that our program doesn't try to load the old property list as an archive. We've also defined a new constant that will be the key value we use to encode and decode our object.

Next, switch over the *PersistenceViewController.m*, and make the following changes:

```
#import "PersistenceViewController.h"
#import "FourLines.h"

@implementation PersistenceViewController
@synthesize field1;
@synthesize field2;
@synthesize field3;
@synthesize field4;

- (NSString *)dataFilePath {
    NSArray *paths = NSSearchPathForDirectoriesInDomains(
        NSDocumentDirectory, NSUserDomainMask, YES);
    NSString *documentsDirectory = [paths objectAtIndex:0];
    return [documentsDirectory stringByAppendingPathComponent:kFilename];
}

#pragma mark -
- (void)viewDidLoad {

    NSString *filePath = [self dataFilePath];
    if ([[NSFileManager defaultManager] fileExistsAtPath:filePath]) {
        NSMutableArray *array =[[NSMutableArray alloc]
            initWithContentsOfFile:filePath];
        field1.text = [array objectAtIndex:0];
        field2.text = [array objectAtIndex:1];
        field3.text = [array objectAtIndex:2];
```

```
        field4.text = [array objectAtIndex:3];
        [array release];

        NSData *data = [[NSMutableData alloc]
            initWithContentsOfFile:[self dataFilePath]];
        NSKeyedUnarchiver *unarchiver = [[NSKeyedUnarchiver alloc]
            initForReadingWithData:data];
        FourLines *fourLines = [unarchiver decodeObjectForKey:kDataKey];
        [unarchiver finishDecoding];

        field1.text = fourLines.field1;
        field2.text = fourLines.field2;
        field3.text = fourLines.field3;
        field4.text = fourLines.field4;

        [unarchiver release];
        [data release];
    }

    UIApplication *app = [UIApplication sharedApplication];
    [[NSNotificationCenter defaultCenter] addObserver:self
            selector:@selector(applicationWillResignActive:)
            name:UIApplicationWillResignActiveNotification
            object:app];
    [super viewDidLoad];
}

- (void)applicationWillResignActive:(NSNotification *)notification {
    NSMutableArray *array = [[NSMutableArray alloc] init];
    [array addObject:field1.text];
    [array addObject:field2.text];
    [array addObject:field3.text];
    [array addObject:field4.text];
    [array writeToFile:[self dataFilePath] atomically:YES];
    [array release];

    FourLines *fourLines = [[FourLines alloc] init];
    fourLines.field1 = field1.text;
    fourLines.field2 = field2.text;
    fourLines.field3 = field3.text;
    fourLines.field4 = field4.text;

    NSMutableData *data = [[NSMutableData alloc] init];
    NSKeyedArchiver *archiver = [[NSKeyedArchiver alloc]
        initForWritingWithMutableData:data];
    [archiver encodeObject:fourLines forKey:kDataKey];
    [archiver finishEncoding];
    [data writeToFile:[self dataFilePath] atomically:YES];
    [fourLines release];
    [archiver release];
    [data release];
}
...
```

Save your changes and take this version of Persistence for a spin.

Not very much has changed, really. The interface is identical to the previous version.

This new version takes several more lines of code to implement than property list serialization, so you might be wondering if there really is an advantage to using archiving over just serializing property lists. For this application, the answer is simple: no, there really isn't any advantage. But think back to the last example in Chapter 9, where we allowed the user to edit a list of presidents, and each president had four different fields that could be edited. To handle archiving that list of presidents with a property list would involve iterating through the list of presidents, creating an NSDictionary instance for each president, copying the value from each of their fields over to the NSDictionary instance, and adding that instance to another array, which could then be written to a property list file. And that's assuming that we restricted ourselves to using only serializable properties. If we didn't, using property list serialization wouldn't even be an option without doing a lot of conversion work.

On the other hand, if we had an array of archivable objects, such as the FourLines class that we just built, we could archive the entire array by archiving the array instance itself. Collection classes like NSArray, when archived, archive all of the objects they contain. As long as every object you put into an array or dictionary conforms to NSCoding, you can archive the array or dictionary and restore it, so that all the objects that were in it when you archived it will be in the restored array or dictionary.

In other words, this approach scales beautifully (in terms of code size, at least). No matter how many objects you add, the work to write those objects to disk (assuming you're using single-file persistence) is exactly the same. With property lists, the amount of work increases with every object you add.

Using iOS's Embedded SQLite3

The third persistence option we're going to discuss is using iOS's embedded SQL database, called SQLite3. SQLite3 is very efficient at storing and retrieving large amounts of data. It's also capable of doing complex aggregations on your data, with much faster results than you would get doing the same thing using objects.

For example, if your application needs to calculate the sum of a particular field across all the objects in your application, or if you need the sum from just the objects that meet certain criteria, SQLite3 allows you to do that without loading every object into memory. Getting aggregations from SQLite3 is several orders of magnitude faster than loading all the objects into memory and summing their values. Being a full-fledged embedded database, SQLite3 contains tools to make it even faster by, for example, creating table indexes that can speed up your queries.

NOTE: There are several schools of thought about the pronunciation of "SQL" and "SQLite." Most official documentation says to pronounce "SQL" as "Ess-Queue-Ell" and "SQLite" as "Ess-Queue-Ell-Light." Many people pronounce them, respectively, as "Sequel" and "Sequel Light." A small cadre of hardened rebels prefer "Squeal" and "Squeal Light." Pick whatever works best for you (and be prepared to be mocked and shunned by the infidels if you choose to join the "Squeal" movement).

SQLite3 uses the Structured Query Language (SQL). SQL is the standard language used to interact with relational databases. Whole books have been written on the syntax of SQL (hundreds of them, in fact), as well as on SQLite itself. So, if you don't already know SQL and you want to use SQLite3 in your application, you have a little work ahead of you. We'll show you how to set up and interact with the SQLite database from your iOS applications, and you'll see some of the basics of the syntax in this chapter. But to really make the most of SQLite3, you'll need to do some additional research and exploration. A couple of good starting points are "An Introduction to the SQLite3 C/C++ Interface" (http://www.sqlite.org/cintro.html) and "SQL As Understood by SQLite" (http://www.sqlite.org/lang.html).

Relational databases, including SQLite3, and object-oriented programming languages use fundamentally different approaches to storing and organizing data. The approaches are different enough that numerous techniques and many libraries and tools for converting between the two have been developed. These different techniques are collectively called **object-relational mapping** (ORM). There are currently several ORM tools available for Cocoa Touch. In fact, we'll look at one ORM solution provided by Apple, called Core Data, later in the chapter.

In this chapter, we're going to focus on the basics, including setting up SQLite3, creating a table to hold your data, and using the database in an application. Obviously, in the real world, such a simple application as the one we're working on wouldn't warrant the investment in SQLite3. But this application's simplicity is exactly what makes it a good learning example.

Creating or Opening the Database

Before you can use SQLite3, you must open the database. The function that's used to do that, sqlite3_open(), will open an existing database, or if none exists at the specified location, it will create a new one. Here's what the code to open a new database might look like:

```
sqlite3 *database;
int result = sqlite3_open("/path/to/database/file", &database);
```

If result is equal to the constant SQLITE_OK, then the database was successfully opened. Note that the path to the database file must be passed in as a C string, not as an NSString. SQLite3 was written in portable C, not Objective-C, and it has no idea what an NSString is. Fortunately, there is an NSString method that generates a C-string from an NSString instance:

```
char *stringPath = [pathString UTF8String];
```

When you're finished with an SQLite3 database, close it:

```
sqlite3_close(database);
```

Databases store all their data in tables. You can create a new table by crafting an SQL CREATE statement and passing it in to an open database using the function sqlite3_exec, like so:

```
char *errorMsg;
const char *createSQL = "CREATE TABLE IF NOT EXISTS PEOPLE ⏎
    (ID INTEGER PRIMARY KEY AUTOINCREMENT, FIELD_DATA TEXT)";
int result = sqlite3_exec(database, createSQL, NULL, NULL, &errorMsg);
```

As you did before, you need to check result for SQLITE_OK to make sure your command ran successfully. If it didn't, errorMsg will contain a description of the problem that occurred.

The function sqlite3_exec is used to run any command against SQLite3 that doesn't return data, including updates, inserts, and deletes. Retrieving data from the database is a little more involved. You first need to prepare the statement by feeding it your SQL SELECT command:

```
NSString *query = @"SELECT ID, FIELD_DATA FROM FIELDS ORDER BY ROW";
sqlite3_stmt *statement;
int result = (sqlite3_prepare_v2(database, [query UTF8String],
    -1, &statement, nil);
```

> **NOTE:** All of the SQLite3 functions that take strings require an old-fashioned C string. In the create example, we created and passed a C string. In this example, we created an NSString and derived a C string by using one of NSString's methods called UTF8String. Either method is acceptable. If you need to do manipulation on the string, using NSString or NSMutableString will be easier, but converting from NSString to a C string incurs a bit of extra overhead.

If result equals SQLITE_OK, your statement was successfully prepared, and you can start stepping through the result set. Here is an example of stepping through a result set and retrieving an int and an NSString from the database:

```
while (sqlite3_step(statement) == SQLITE_ROW) {
    int rowNum = sqlite3_column_int(statement, 0);
    char *rowData = (char *)sqlite3_column_text(statement, 1);
    NSString *fieldValue = [[NSString alloc] initWithUTF8String:rowData];
    // Do something with the data here
    [fieldValue release];
}
sqlite3_finalize(statement);
```

Using Bind Variables

Although it's possible to construct SQL strings to insert values, it is common practice to use something called **bind variables** for this purpose. Handling strings correctly—making sure they don't have invalid characters and that quotes are handled properly—can be quite a chore. With bind variables, those issues are taken care of for us.

To insert a value using a bind variable, you create your SQL statement as normal, but put a question mark (?) into the SQL string. Each question mark represents one variable that must be bound before the statement can be executed. Then you prepare the SQL statement, bind a value to each of the variables, and execute the command.

Here's an example that prepares an SQL statement with two bind variables, binds an int to the first variable and a string to the second variable, and then executes and finalizes the statement:

```
char *sql = "insert into foo values (?, ?);";
sqlite3_stmt *stmt;
if (sqlite3_prepare_v2(database, sql, -1, &stmt, nil) == SQLITE_OK) {
    sqlite3_bind_int(stmt, 1, 235);
    sqlite3_bind_text(stmt, 2, "Bar", -1, NULL);
}
if (sqlite3_step(stmt) != SQLITE_DONE)
    NSLog(@"This should be real error checking!");
sqlite3_finalize(stmt);
```

There are multiple bind statements available depending on the datatype you wish to use. Most bind functions take only three parameters:

■ The first parameter to any bind function, regardless of the datatype, is a pointer to the `sqlite3_stmt` used previously in the `sqlite3_prepare_v2()` call.

■ The second parameter is the index of the variable to which you're binding. This is a one-indexed value, meaning that the first question mark in the SQL statement has index 1, and each one after it is one higher than the one to its left.

■ The third parameter is always the value that should be substituted for the question mark.

■ A few bind functions, such as those for binding text and binary data, have two additional parameters. The first additional parameter is the length of the data being passed in the third parameter. In the case of C strings, you can pass `-1` instead of the string's length, and the function will use the entire string. In all other cases, you need to tell it the length of the data being passed int.

■ The final parameter is an optional function callback in case you need to do any memory cleanup after the statement is executed. Typically, such a function would be used to free memory allocated using `malloc()`.

The syntax that follows the bind statements may seem a little odd, since we're doing an insert. When using bind variables, the same syntax is used for both queries and updates. If the SQL string had an SQL query, rather than an update, we would need to call `sqlite3_step()` multiple times until it returned `SQLITE_DONE`. Since this was an update, we call it only once.

The SQLite3 Application

We've covered the basics, so let's see how this would work in practice. We're going to retrofit our Persistence application again, this time storing its data using SQLite3. We'll use a single table and store the field values in four different rows of that table. We'll give each row a row number that corresponds to its field, so for example, the value from `field1` will get stored in the table with a row number of 1. Let's get started.

Linking to the SQLite3 Library

SQLite 3 is accessed through a procedural API that provides interfaces to a number of C function calls. To use this API, we'll need to link our application to a dynamic library called *libsqlite3.dylib*, located in */usr/lib* on both Mac OS X and iOS.

The process of linking a dynamic library into your project is exactly the same as that of linking in a framework.

Use the Finder to make a copy of your last *Persistence* project directory, then open the new copy's *.xcodeproj* file. Then right click (or control-click) the *Frameworks* folder in your *Files & Groups* pane. Choose **Add ➤ Existing Framework**. Find *libsqlite3.dylib*, select it, and click *Add* (Figure 12–4).

Figure 12–4. *Adding the libsqlite3.dylib framework to the project. Note that there are two frameworks with very similar names. Låt den rätte komma in!*

Note that there may be several other entries in that directory that start with *libsqlite3*. Be sure you select *libsqlite3.dylib*. It is an alias that always points to the latest version of the SQLite3 library.

Modifying the Persistence View Controller

Next, make the following changes to *PersistenceViewController.h*:

```
#import <UIKit/UIKit.h>

#define kFilename     @"dataarchive.plist"
#define kDataKey      @"Data"
#define kFilename     @"data.sqlite3"

@interface PersistenceViewController : UIViewController {
    UITextField *field1;
    UITextField *field2;
    UITextField *field3;
    UITextField *field4;
}
@property (nonatomic, retain) IBOutlet UITextField *field1;
@property (nonatomic, retain) IBOutlet UITextField *field2;
@property (nonatomic, retain) IBOutlet UITextField *field3;
@property (nonatomic, retain) IBOutlet UITextField *field4;

- (NSString *)dataFilePath;
- (void)applicationWillResignActive:(NSNotification *)notification;
@end
```

Once again, we change the file name so that we won't be using the same file that we used in the previous version, and the file name properly reflects the type of the data it holds.

Switch over to *PersistenceViewController.m*, and make the following changes:

```
#import "PersistenceViewController.h"
#import "FourLines.h"
#import <sqlite3.h>

@implementation PersistenceViewController
@synthesize field1;
@synthesize field2;
@synthesize field3;
@synthesize field4;

- (NSString *)dataFilePath {
    NSArray *paths = NSSearchPathForDirectoriesInDomains(
        NSDocumentDirectory, NSUserDomainMask, YES);
    NSString *documentsDirectory = [paths objectAtIndex:0];
    return [documentsDirectory stringByAppendingPathComponent:kFilename];
}

#pragma mark -
- (void)viewDidLoad {
    NSString *filePath = [self dataFilePath];
```

```objc
if ([[NSFileManager defaultManager] fileExistsAtPath:filePath])
{
    NSData *data = [[NSMutableData alloc]
        initWithContentsOfFile:[self dataFilePath]];
    NSKeyedUnarchiver *unarchiver =
        [[NSKeyedUnarchiver alloc] initForReadingWithData:data];
    FourLines *fourLines = [unarchiver decodeObjectForKey:kDataKey];
    [unarchiver finishDecoding];

    field1.text = fourLines.field1;
    field2.text = fourLines.field2;
    field3.text = fourLines.field3;
    field4.text = fourLines.field4;

    [unarchiver release];
    [data release];
}
sqlite3 *database;
if (sqlite3_open([[self dataFilePath] UTF8String], &database)
    != SQLITE_OK) {
    sqlite3_close(database);
    NSAssert(0, @"Failed to open database");
}

char *errorMsg;
    // Note that the continuation char on next line is not part of string...
NSString *createSQL = @"CREATE TABLE IF NOT EXISTS FIELDS ↵
    (ROW INTEGER PRIMARY KEY, FIELD_DATA TEXT);";
if (sqlite3_exec (database, [createSQL UTF8String],
    NULL, NULL, &errorMsg) != SQLITE_OK) {
    sqlite3_close(database);
    NSAssert1(0, @"Error creating table: %s", errorMsg);
}
NSString *query = @"SELECT ROW, FIELD_DATA FROM FIELDS ORDER BY ROW";
sqlite3_stmt *statement;
if (sqlite3_prepare_v2(database, [query UTF8String],
    -1, &statement, nil) == SQLITE_OK) {
    while (sqlite3_step(statement) == SQLITE_ROW) {
        int row = sqlite3_column_int(statement, 0);
        char *rowData = (char *)sqlite3_column_text(statement, 1);

        NSString *fieldName = [[NSString alloc]
            initWithFormat:@"field%d", row];
        NSString *fieldValue = [[NSString alloc]
            initWithUTF8String:rowData];
        UITextField *field = [self valueForKey:fieldName];
        field.text = fieldValue;
        [fieldName release];
        [fieldValue release];
    }
    sqlite3_finalize(statement);
}
sqlite3_close(database);

UIApplication *app = [UIApplication sharedApplication];
```

```
        [[NSNotificationCenter defaultCenter] addObserver:self
                selector:@selector(applicationWillResignActive:)
                name:UIApplicationWillResignActiveNotification
                object:app];
        [super viewDidLoad];
}

- (void)applicationWillResignActive:(NSNotification *)notification {
    FourLines *fourLines = [[FourLines alloc] init];
    fourLines.field1 = field1.text;
    fourLines.field2 = field2.text;
    fourLines.field3 = field3.text;
    fourLines.field4 = field4.text;

    NSMutableData *data = [[NSMutableData alloc] init];
    NSKeyedArchiver *archiver = [[NSKeyedArchiver alloc]
            initForWritingWithMutableData:data];
    [archiver encodeObject:fourLines forKey:kDataKey];
    [archiver finishEncoding];
    [data writeToFile:[self dataFilePath] atomically:YES];
    [fourLines release];
    [archiver release];
    [data release];

    sqlite3 *database;
    if (sqlite3_open([[self dataFilePath] UTF8String], &database)
        != SQLITE_OK) {
        sqlite3_close(database);
        NSAssert(0, @"Failed to open database");
    }
    for (int i = 1; i <= 4; i++) {
        NSString *fieldName = [[NSString alloc]
                            initWithFormat:@"field%d", i];
        UITextField *field = [self valueForKey:fieldName];
        [fieldName release];

        char *errorMsg;
        // Note that the continuation char on next line is not part of string...
        char *update = "INSERT OR REPLACE INTO FIELDS (ROW, FIELD_DATA) ↵
            VALUES (?, ?);";
        sqlite3_stmt *stmt;
        if (sqlite3_prepare_v2(database, update, -1, &stmt, nil)
                == SQLITE_OK) {
            sqlite3_bind_int(stmt, 1, i);
            sqlite3_bind_text(stmt, 2, [field.text UTF8String], -1, NULL);
        }
        if (sqlite3_step(stmt) != SQLITE_DONE)
            NSAssert1(0, @"Error updating table: %s", errorMsg);
        sqlite3_finalize(stmt);
    }

    sqlite3_close(database);
}
...
```

The first new code is in the viewDidLoad method. We begin by opening the database. If we hit a problem with opening the database, we close it and raise an assertion.

```
sqlite3 *database;
if (sqlite3_open([[self dataFilePath] UTF8String], &database)
    != SQLITE_OK) {
    sqlite3_close(database);
    NSAssert(0, @"Failed to open database");
}
```

Next, we need to make sure that we have a table to hold our data. We can use SQL CREATE TABLE to do that. By specifying IF NOT EXISTS, we prevent the database from overwriting existing data. If there is already a table with the same name, this command quietly exits without doing anything, so it's safe to call every time our application launches without explicitly checking to see if a table exists.

```
char *errorMsg;
NSString *createSQL = @"CREATE TABLE IF NOT EXISTS FIELDS ↩
    (ROW INTEGER PRIMARY KEY, FIELD_DATA TEXT);";
if (sqlite3_exec (database, [createSQL UTF8String], NULL, NULL,
    &errorMsg) != SQLITE_OK) {
    sqlite3_close(database);
    NSAssert1(0, @"Error creating table: %s", errorMsg);
}
```

Finally, we need to load our data. We do this using an SQL SELECT statement. In this simple example, we create an SQL SELECT that requests all the rows from the database and ask SQLite3 to prepare our SELECT. We also tell SQLite3 to order the rows by the row number, so that we always get them back in the same order. Absent this, SQLite3 will return the rows in the order in which they are stored internally.

```
NSString *query = @"SELECT ROW, FIELD_DATA FROM FIELDS ORDER BY ROW";
sqlite3_stmt *statement;
if (sqlite3_prepare_v2( database, [query UTF8String],
    -1, &statement, nil) == SQLITE_OK) {
```

Then we step through each of the returned rows:

```
while (sqlite3_step(statement) == SQLITE_ROW) {
```

We grab the row number and store it in an int, and then we grab the field data as a C string.

```
int row = sqlite3_column_int(statement, 0);
char *rowData = (char *)sqlite3_column_text(statement, 1);
```

Next, we create a field name based on the row number (such as field1 for row 1), convert the C string to an NSString, and use that to set the appropriate field with the value retrieved from the database.

```
NSString *fieldName = [[NSString alloc]
    initWithFormat:@"field%d", row];
NSString *fieldValue = [[NSString alloc]
    initWithUTF8String:rowData];
UITextField *field = [self valueForKey:fieldName];
field.text = fieldValue;
```

Finally, we do some memory cleanup, close the database connection, and we're all finished.

```
        [fieldName release];
        [fieldValue release];
    }
    sqlite3_finalize(statement);
}
sqlite3_close(database);
```

Note that we close the database connection as soon as we're finished creating the table and loading any data it contains, rather than keeping it open the entire time the application is running. It's the simplest way of managing the connection, and in this little app, we can just open the connection those few times we need it. In a more database-intensive app, you might want to keep the connection open all the time.

The other changes we made are in the `applicationWillResignActive:` method, where we need to save our application data. Because the data in the database is stored in a table, our application's data will look something like Table 12–1 when stored.

Table 12–1. *Data Stored in the FIELDS Table of the Database*

ROW	FIELD_DATA
1	When in the course of human events,
2	it becomes necessary for one people
3	to dissolve the political bands
4	which have connected them with...

The `applicationWillResignActive:` method starts off by once again opening the database.

```
sqlite3 *database;
if (sqlite3_open([[self dataFilePath] UTF8String], &database)
    != SQLITE_OK) {
    sqlite3_close(database);
    NSAssert(0, @"Failed to open database");
}
```

To save the data, we loop through all four fields and issue a separate command to update each row of the database.

```
for (int i = 1; i <= 4; i++) {
    NSString *fieldName = [[NSString alloc]
        initWithFormat:@"field%d", i];
    UITextField *field = [self valueForKey:fieldName];
```

The first thing we do in the loop is craft a field name so we can retrieve the correct text field outlet. Remember that `valueForKey:` allows you to retrieve a property based on its name. We also declare a pointer to be used for the error message if we encounter an error.

We craft an INSERT OR REPLACE SQL statement with two bind variables. The first represents the row that's being stored; the second is for the actual string value to be stored. By using INSERT OR REPLACE instead of the more standard INSERT, we don't need to worry about whether a row already exists.

```
char *update = "INSERT OR REPLACE INTO FIELDS (ROW, FIELD_DATA) VALUES (?, ?);";
```

Next, we declare a pointer to a statement, prepare our statement with the bind variables, and bind values to both of the bind variables.

```
sqlite3_stmt *stmt;
if (sqlite3_prepare_v2(database, update, -1, &stmt, nil) == SQLITE_OK) {
    sqlite3_bind_int(stmt, 1, i);
    sqlite3_bind_text(stmt, 2, [field.text UTF8String], -1, NULL);
}
```

Then we call sqlite3_step to execute the update, check to make sure it worked, and finalize the statement, ending the loop.

```
    if (sqlite3_step(stmt) != SQLITE_DONE) {
        NSAssert(0, @"Error updating table.");
    }
    sqlite3_finalize(stmt);
}
```

Notice that we used an assertion here to check for an error condition. We use assertions rather than exceptions or manual error checking because this condition should happen only if we, the developers, make a mistake. Using this assertion macro will help us debug our code, and it can be stripped out of our final application. If an error condition is one that a user might reasonably experience, you should probably use some other form of error checking.

> **NOTE:** There is one condition that could cause an error to occur in the preceding SQLite code that is not a programmer error. If the device's storage is completely full, to the extent that SQLite can't save its changes to the database, then an error will occur here as well. However, this condition is fairly rare, and will probably result in deeper problems for the user, outside the scope of our app's data. Probably our app wouldn't even launch successfully if the system were in that state. So we're going to just sidestep the issue entirely.

Once we're finished with the loop, we close the database.

```
sqlite3_close(database);
```

Why don't you compile and run the app? Enter some data, and then press the iPhone simulator's home button. Then relaunch the Persistence application, and that data should be right where you left it. As far as the user is concerned, there's absolutely no difference between the various versions of this application, but each version uses a very different persistence mechanism.

Using Core Data

The final technique we're going to demonstrate in this chapter is how to implement persistence using Apple's Core Data framework. Core Data is a robust, full-featured persistence tool. Here, we will show you how to use Core Data to re-create the same persistence you've seen in our Persistence application so far.

> **NOTE:** For more comprehensive coverage of Core Data, check out *More iPhone 4 Development* by Jack Nutting, Dave Mark, and Jeff LaMarche (Apress, 2011). That book devotes several chapters to Core Data.

In Xcode, create a new project. This time, select the *Window-based Application* template and select *iPhone* from the *Product* popup, but don't click the *Choose...* button just yet. If you look just below the *Product* popup, you should see a check box labeled *Use Core Data for storage* (see Figure 12–5). There's a certain amount of complexity involved in adding Core Data to an existing project, so Apple has kindly provided an option with some application project templates to do much of the work for you.

Figure 12–5. *Some project templates, including Window-based Application, offer the option to use Core Data for persistence.*

Check the *Use Core Data for storage* check box, and then click the *Choose...* button. When prompted, enter a project name of *Core Data Persistence*, and click *Save*.

Before we move on to our code, let's take a look at the project window, which contains some new stuff. Expand both the *Classes* and *Resources* folders (see Figure 12–6).

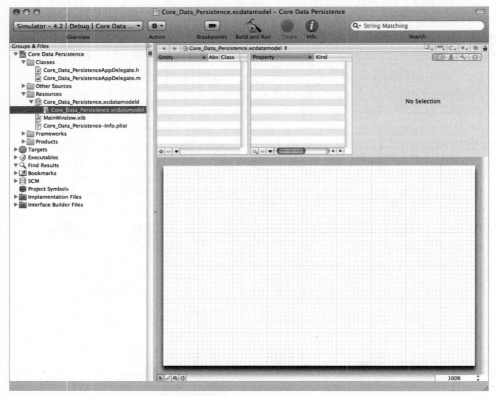

Figure 12–6. *Our project template with the files needed for Core Data. The Core Data model is selected, and the data model editor is shown in the editing pane.*

Entities and Managed Objects

Most of what you see in the *Groups & Files* pane should be familiar: the application delegate, *MainWindow.xib*, and *info.plist* files. In addition, tucked away in the *Resources* folder is a file called *Core_Data_Persistence.xcdatamodeld*. That is a file that contains our data model. You can see our data model file, *Core_Data_Persistence.xcdatamodel* (without the trailing "d") if you expand the disclosure triangle beside *Core_Data_Persistence.xcdatamodeld*. Core Data lets us design our data models visually, without writing code, and stores that data model in the *.xcdatamodel* file.

Expand *Core_Data_Persistence.xcdatamodeld* and single click *Core_Data_Persistence.xcdatamodel* to show the **data model editor**, as shown in Figure 12–6.

Before Core Data, the traditional way to create data models was to create subclasses of NSObject and conform them to NSCoding and NSCopying so that they could be archived, as we did earlier in this chapter. Core Data uses a fundamentally different approach. Instead of classes, you create **entities** here in the data model editor, and then in your code, you create **managed objects** from those entities.

> **NOTE:** The terms *entity* and *managed object* can be a little confusing, since both refer to data model objects. *Entity* refers to the description of an object. *Managed object* refers to actual concrete instances of that entity created at runtime. So, in the data model editor, you create entities, but in your code, you create and retrieve managed objects. The distinction between entities and managed objects is similar to the distinction between a class and instances of that class.

An entity is made up of properties. There are three types of properties:

- **Attributes**: An attribute serves the same function in a Core Data entity as an instance variable does in an Objective-C class. They both hold the data.

- **Relationships**: As the name implies, a relationship defines the relationship between entities. For example, to create a Person entity, you might start by defining a few attributes, like hairColor, eyeColor, height, and weight. You might define address attributes, like state and ZIP code, or you might embed those in a separate, HomeAddress entity. Using the latter approach, you would then create a relationship between a Person and a HomeAddress. Relationships can be **to-one** and **to-many**. The relationship from Person to HomeAddress is probably to-one, since most people have only a single home address. The relationship from HomeAddress to Person might be to-many, since there may be more than one Person living at that HomeAddress.

- **Fetched properties**: A fetched property is an alternative to a relationship. The main difference between them is in the way they affect loading. For example, if a Person has a relationship with a HomeAddress, when the Person is loaded, the HomeAddress will be loaded, too. Alternatively, if a Person references HomeAddress as a fetched property, when the Person is loaded, HomeAddress is not loaded—at least not until HomeAddress is accessed. Can you say "lazy loading"?

Typically, attributes, relationships, and fetched properties are defined using Xcode's data model editor. In our Core Data Persistence application, we'll build a simple entity so you can get a sense of how this all works together.

Key-Value Coding

In your code, instead of using accessors and mutators, you will use **key-value coding** to set properties or retrieve their existing values. Key-value coding may sound intimidating, but you've already used it quite a bit in this book. Every time we used NSDictionary, for example, we were using key-value coding, because every object in a dictionary is stored under a unique key value. The key-value coding used by Core Data is a bit more complex than that used by NSDictionary, but the basic concept is the same.

When working with a managed object, the key you will use to set or retrieve a property's value is the name of the attribute you wish to set. So, here's how to retrieve the value stored in the attribute called name from a managed object:

```
NSString *name = [myManagedObject valueForKey:@"name"];
```

Similarly, to set a new value for a managed object's property, do this:

```
[myManagedObject setValue:@"Gregor Overlander" forKey:@"name"];
```

Putting It All in Context

So, where do these managed objects live? They live in something called a **persistent store**, also referred to as a **backing store**. Persistent stores can take several different forms. By default, a Core Data application implements a backing store as an SQLite database stored in the application's documents directory. Even though your data is stored via SQLite, classes in the Core Data framework do all the work associated with loading and saving your data. If you use Core Data, you don't need to write any SQL statements. You just work with objects, and Core Data figures out what it needs to do behind the scenes.

In addition to as SQLite databases, backing stores can also be implemented as binary flat files. A third option is to create an in-memory store, which you might use if you're writing a caching mechanism, but it doesn't save data beyond the end of the current session. In almost all situations, you should just leave it as the default and use SQLite as your persistent store.

Although most applications will have only one persistent store, it is possible to have multiple persistent stores within the same application. If you're curious about how the backing store is created and configured, take a look at the file Core_Data_PersistenceAppDelegate.m in your Xcode project. The Xcode project template we chose provided us with all the code needed to set up a single persistent store for our application.

Other than creating it (which is handled for you in your application delegate), you generally won't work with your persistent store directly, but rather will use something called a **managed object context**, often referred to as just a **context**. The context manages access to the persistent store and maintains information about which properties have changed since the last time an object was saved. The context also registers all changes with the undo manager, meaning that you always have the ability to undo a single change or roll back all the way to the last time data was saved.

> **NOTE:** You can have multiple contexts pointing to the same persistent store, though most iOS applications will use only one. You can find out more about using multiple contexts and the undo manager in *More iPhone 4 Development*.

Many Core Data calls require an NSManagedObjectContext as a parameter or must be executed against a context. With the exception of very complicated, multithreaded iOS applications, you can just use the managedObjectContext property from your application delegate, which is a default context that is created for you automatically, also courtesy of the Xcode project template.

You may notice that, in addition to a managed object context and a persistent store coordinator, the provided application delegate also contains an instance of NSManagedObjectModel. This class is responsible for loading and representing, at runtime, the data model you will create using the data model editor in Xcode. You generally won't need to interact directly with this class. It's used behind the scenes by the other Core Data classes so they can identify which entities and properties you've defined in your data model. As long as you create your data model using the provided file, there's no need to worry about this class at all.

Creating New Managed Objects

Creating a new instance of a managed object is pretty easy, though not quite as straightforward as creating a normal object instance using alloc and init. Instead, you use the insertNewObjectForEntityForName:inManagedObjectContext: factory method in a class called NSEntityDescription. NSEntityDescription's job is to keep track of all the entities defined in the app's data model. This method returns an instance representing a single entity in memory. It returns either an instance of NSManagedObject that is set up with the correct properties for that particular entity or, if you've configured your entity to be implemented with a specific subclass of NSManagedObject, an instance of that class. Remember that entities are like classes. An entity is a description of an object and defines which properties a particular entity has.

To create a new object, do this:

```
theLine = [NSEntityDescription
    insertNewObjectForEntityForName:@"EntityName"
            inManagedObjectContext:context];
```

The method is called insertNewObjectForEntityForName:inManagedObjectContext: because, in addition to creating the object, it inserts the newly created object into the context and then returns that object. After this call, the object exists in the context but is not yet part of the persistent store. The object will be added to the persistent store the next time the managed object context's save: method is called.

Retrieving Managed Objects

To retrieve managed objects from the persistent store, you'll make use of a **fetch request**, which is Core Data's way of handling a predefined query. For example, you might say, "Give me every Person whose eyeColor is blue."

After first creating a fetch request, you provide it with an NSEntityDescription that specifies the entity of the object or objects you wish to retrieve. Here is an example that creates a fetch request:

```
NSFetchRequest *request = [[NSFetchRequest alloc] init];
NSEntityDescription *entityDescr = [NSEntityDescription
    entityForName:@"EntityName" inManagedObjectContext:context];
[request setEntity:entityDescr];
```

Optionally, you can also specify criteria for a fetch request using the NSPredicate class. A **predicate** is similar to the SQL WHERE clause and allows you to define the criteria used to determine the results of your fetch request.

Here is a simple example of a predicate:

```
NSPredicate *pred = [NSPredicate predicateWithFormat:@"(name = %@)", nameString];
[request setPredicate: pred];
```

The predicate created by the first line of code tells a fetch request that, instead of retrieving all managed objects for the specified entity, retrieve just those where the name property is set to the value currently stored in the nameString variable. So, if nameString is an NSString that holds the value @"Bob", we are telling the fetch request to bring back only managed objects that have a name property set to "Bob". This is a simple example, but predicates can be considerably more complex and can use Boolean logic to specify the precise criteria you might need in most any situation.

> **NOTE:** *Learn Objective-C on the Mac* by Mark Dalrymple and Scott Knaster (Apress, 2009) has an entire chapter devoted to the use of NSPredicate.

After you've created your fetch request, provided it with an entity description, and optionally given it a predicate, you **execute** the fetch request using an instance method on NSManagedObjectContext:

```
NSError *error;
NSArray *objects = [context executeFetchRequest:request error:&error];
if (objects == nil) {
    // handle error
}
```

executeFetchRequest:error: will load the specified objects from the persistent store and return them in an array. If an error is encountered, you will get a nil array, and the error pointer you provided will point to an NSError object that describes the specific problem. Otherwise, you will get a valid array, though it may not have any objects in it, since it is possible that none meet the specified criteria. From this point on, any changes you make to the managed objects returned in that array will be tracked by the managed object context you executed the request against, and saved when you send that context a save: message.

The Core Data Application

Let's take Core Data for a spin now. First, we'll return our attention to Xcode and create our data model.

Designing the Data Model

Single-click *Core_Data_Persistence.xcdatamodel* to open Xcode's data model editor. The upper-left pane of the data model editor is called the **entity pane** because it lists all the entities that are currently in your data model. It's an empty list now, because we haven't created any entities yet (see Figure 12–7).

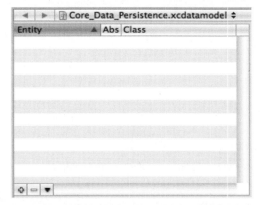

Figure 12–7. *The upper left-pane of the data model editor is the entity pane. Clicking the plus icon in the lower left corner adds an entity*

Remedy that by clicking the plus icon in the lower-left corner of the entity pane, which will create and select an entity titled *Entity*. If you look in the bottom pane of the data model editor, you'll notice that it's no longer empty (see Figure 12–8)!

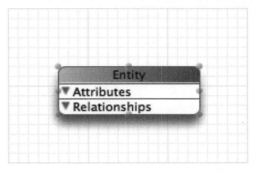

Figure 12–8. *Xcode's data model editor's diagram view shows an editable graphical representation of your data model.*

As you build your data model using the top three panes (collectively called the **browser view**), a graphical representation of your data model is shown in the bottom portion of the screen, which is called the **diagram view**. If you prefer working graphically, you can actually build your entire model in the diagram view. Right-clicking the background of the diagram view will bring up a contextual menu that will allow you to add entities and change the diagram view's appearance. Right-clicking an entity will bring up a menu that allows you to add properties to the selected entity. We're going to stick with the browser view in this chapter because it's easier to explain, but when you're creating your own data models, feel free to work in the diagram view if that approach suits you better.

The upper-right pane of the data model editor is called the **detail pane** (Figure 12–9). The detail pane allows you to edit the currently selected entity or property.

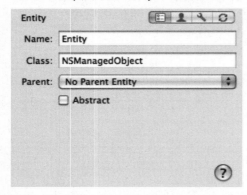

Figure 12–9. *The data model editor's detail pane, which allows you to edit the currently selected entity or property.*

At the moment, the detail pain shows information about the entity we just added. Change the *Name* field from *Entity* to *Line*. You can ignore the other fields in the detail pane for now. Those other fields will come into play when creating more complex data models, like those discussed in *More iPhone 4 Development*.

The data model editor's upper-middle pane is the **property pane** (see Figure 12–10). As its name implies, the property pane allows you to add new properties to your entity.

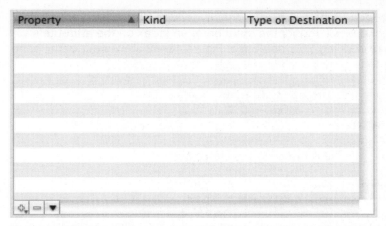

Figure 12–10. *The property pane in Xcode's data model editor. This is where you can add properties to the currently selected entity.*

Notice that plus sign in the lower-left corner of the property pane features a tiny black triangle. This indicates that a click in the plus sign icon will bring up a popup menu, allowing you to add an attribute, fetched property, relationship, or fetch request to your entity (see Figure 12–11).

Figure 12–11. *Clicking the plus icon in the property pane brings up a menu of options.*

Let's add an attribute to our *Line* entity. Make sure the *Line* entity is selected by clicking in it in either the diagram view or the entity pane. Now click the plus sign icon in the lower-left corner of the property pane and select **Add Attribute** from the menu that pops up.

A new attribute named *newAttribute* will appear in the property pane. Make sure that *newAttribute* is selected and then, in the detail pane, change the new attribute's name from *newAttribute* to *lineNum*. Next, change its *Type* from *Undefined* to *Integer 16*, which turns this attribute into one that will hold an integer value. We will be using this attribute to identify which of the four fields the managed object holds data for. Since we only have four options, we selected the smallest integer type available.

There are three checkboxes below the *Name* field. The leftmost one, *Optional*, should currently be selected. Click it to deselect it; we don't want this attribute to be optional. A line that doesn't correspond to a label on our interface is useless. Don't worry about the other two checkboxes for now. The *Transient* checkbox is used to define an attribute that isn't saved in the data store (typically a value that is derived from other attributes). Selecting the *Indexed* checkbox will trigger the creation of an index on the attribute's corresponding field in the underlying SQL database. Figure 12–12 shows our detail pane for the *lineNum* attribute.

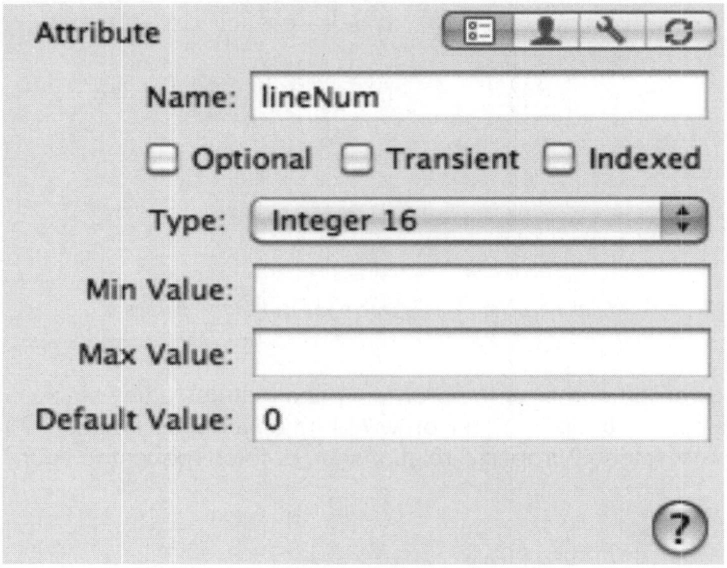

Figure 12–12. *The detail pane showing our settings for the lineNum attribute*

Click the plus-icon, and select *Add Attribute* again, this time creating an attribute with the name *lineText* and changing its *Type* to *String*. This attribute will hold the actual data from the text field. Leave the *Optional* checkbox checked for this one; it is altogether possible that the user won't enter a value for a given field.

When you changed the *Type* to *String*, you'll notice that additional options came up that would let you set a default value or limit the length of the string. We won't be using any of those options for this application, but it's nice to know they're there.

Guess what? Your data model is done. That's all there is to it. Core Data lets you point and click your way to an application data model. Let's finish building the application so we can see how to use our data model from our code.

Creating the Persistence View and Controller

Because we selected the Window-based Application template, we weren't provided with a view controller. Go back to your *Groups & Files* pane, single-click the *Classes* folder, and press ⌘N or select File ➤ New File... to bring up the new file assistant. Select *UIViewController subclass* from the *Cocoa Touch Class* heading, and make sure the boxes labeled *Targeted for iPad* and *UITableViewController subclass* are unchecked. Also make sure to check the box that says *With XIB for user interface* to have Xcode create a nib file for you automatically. Click *Next*, and name the class

PersistenceViewController. When you're finished, *PersistenceViewController.xib* will be placed in your *Classes* folder. Drag it down to the *Resources* folder to keep your project organized.

Select *PersistenceViewController.h*, and make the following changes, which should look very familiar to you:

```
#import <UIKit/UIKit.h>

@interface PersistenceViewController : UIViewController {
    UITextField *line1;
    UITextField *line2;
    UITextField *line3;
    UITextField *line4;
}
@property (nonatomic, retain) IBOutlet UITextField *line1;
@property (nonatomic, retain) IBOutlet UITextField *line2;
@property (nonatomic, retain) IBOutlet UITextField *line3;
@property (nonatomic, retain) IBOutlet UITextField *line4;
@end
```

Save this file. Next, double click *PersistenceViewController.xib* to open Interface Builder. Design the view, and connect the outlets by following the instructions in the "Designing the Persistence Application View" section earlier in this chapter. You might also find it useful to refer back to Figure 12–3. Once you've created the view, save the nib file.

In *PersistenceViewController.m*, insert the following code at the top of the file:

```
#import "PersistenceViewController.h"
#import "Core_Data_PersistenceAppDelegate.h"

@implementation PersistenceViewController
@synthesize line1;
@synthesize line2;
@synthesize line3;
@synthesize line4;

- (void)viewDidLoad {
    Core_Data_PersistenceAppDelegate *appDelegate =
        [[UIApplication sharedApplication] delegate];
    NSManagedObjectContext *context = [appDelegate managedObjectContext];
    NSEntityDescription *entityDescription = [NSEntityDescription
                entityForName:@"Line"
        inManagedObjectContext:context];
    NSFetchRequest *request = [[NSFetchRequest alloc] init];
    [request setEntity:entityDescription];

    NSError *error;
    NSArray *objects = [context executeFetchRequest:request error:&error];
    if (objects == nil) {
        NSLog(@"There was an error!");
        // Do whatever error handling is appropriate
    }

    for (NSManagedObject *oneObject in objects) {
```

```objc
        NSNumber *lineNum = [oneObject valueForKey:@"lineNum"];
        NSString *lineText = [oneObject valueForKey:@"lineText"];

        NSString *fieldName = [NSString
            stringWithFormat:@"line%d", [lineNum integerValue]];
        UITextField *theField = [self valueForKey:fieldName];
        theField.text = lineText;
    }
    [request release];

    UIApplication *app = [UIApplication sharedApplication];
    [[NSNotificationCenter defaultCenter] addObserver:self
        selector:@selector(applicationWillResignActive:)
            name:UIApplicationWillResignActiveNotification
          object:app];
    [super viewDidLoad];
}

- (void)applicationWillResignActive:(NSNotification *)notification {
    Core_Data_PersistenceAppDelegate *appDelegate =
        [[UIApplication sharedApplication] delegate];
    NSManagedObjectContext *context = [appDelegate managedObjectContext];
    NSError *error;
    for (int i = 1; i <= 4; i++) {
        NSString *fieldName = [NSString stringWithFormat:@"line%d", i];
        UITextField *theField = [self valueForKey:fieldName];

        NSFetchRequest *request = [[NSFetchRequest alloc] init];

        NSEntityDescription *entityDescription = [NSEntityDescription
            entityForName:@"Line"
            inManagedObjectContext:context];
        [request setEntity:entityDescription];
        NSPredicate *pred = [NSPredicate
            predicateWithFormat:@"(lineNum = %d)", i];
        [request setPredicate:pred];

        NSManagedObject *theLine = nil;

        NSArray *objects = [context executeFetchRequest:request
            error:&error];

        if (objects == nil) {
            NSLog(@"There was an error!");
            // Do whatever error handling is appropriate
        }
        if ([objects count] > 0)
            theLine = [objects objectAtIndex:0];
        else
            theLine = [NSEntityDescription
                    insertNewObjectForEntityForName:@"Line"
                            inManagedObjectContext:context];

        [theLine setValue:[NSNumber numberWithInt:i] forKey:@"lineNum"];
```

```
        [theLine setValue:theField.text forKey:@"lineText"];

        [request release];
    }
    [context save:&error];
}
...
```

Then, insert the following code into the existing `dealloc` and `viewDidUnload` methods:

```
...
- (void)viewDidUnload {
    // Release any retained subviews of the main view.
    // e.g. self.myOutlet = nil;
    self.line1 = nil;
    self.line2 = nil;
    self.line3 = nil;
    self.line4 = nil;
    [super viewDidUnload];
}

- (void)dealloc {
    [line1 release];
    [line2 release];
    [line3 release];
    [line4 release];
    [super dealloc];
}
...
```

Now, let's look at the `viewDidLoad` method, which needs to check if there is any existing data in the persistent store. If there is, it should load the data and populate the fields with it. The first thing we do in that method is to get a reference to our application delegate, which we then use to get the managed object context that was created for us.

```
Core_Data_PersistenceAppDelegate *appDelegate =
    [[UIApplication sharedApplication] delegate];
NSManagedObjectContext *context = [appDelegate managedObjectContext];
```

Next, we create an entity description that describes our entity.

```
NSEntityDescription *entityDescription = [NSEntityDescription
            entityForName:@"Line"
    inManagedObjectContext:context];
```

The next order of business is to create a fetch request and pass it the entity description so it knows which type of objects to retrieve.

```
NSFetchRequest *request = [[NSFetchRequest alloc] init];
[request setEntity:entityDescription];
```

Since we want to retrieve all `Line` objects in the persistent store, we do not create a predicate. By executing a request without a predicate, we're telling the context to give us every `Line` object in the store.

```
NSError *error;
NSArray *objects = [context executeFetchRequest:request error:&error];
```

We make sure we got back a valid array, and log it if we didn't.

```
if (objects == nil) {
    NSLog(@"There was an error!");
    // Do whatever error handling is appropriate
}
```

Next, we use fast enumeration to loop through the array of retrieved managed objects, pull the lineNum and lineText values from it, and use that information to update one of the text fields on our user interface.

```
for (NSManagedObject *oneObject in objects) {
    NSNumber *lineNum = [oneObject valueForKey:@"lineNum"];
    NSString *lineText = [oneObject valueForKey:@"lineText"];

    NSString *fieldName = [NSString stringWithFormat:@"line%@",
        lineNum];
    UITextField *theField = [self valueForKey:fieldName];
    theField.text = lineText;
}
[request release];
```

Then, just as with all the other applications in this chapter, we register to be notified when the application is about to move out of the active state (either being shuffled to the background or exited completely) so we can save any changes the user has made to the data.

```
UIApplication *app = [UIApplication sharedApplication];
[[NSNotificationCenter defaultCenter] addObserver:self
    selector:@selector(applicationWillResignActive:)
        name:UIApplicationWillResignActiveNotification
      object:app];
[super viewDidLoad];
```

Let's look at applicationWillResignActive: next. We start out the same way as the previous method, by getting a reference to the application delegate and using that to get a pointer to our application's default context.

```
Core_Data_PersistenceAppDelegate *appDelegate =
    [[UIApplication sharedApplication] delegate];
NSManagedObjectContext *context = [appDelegate managedObjectContext];
```

After that, we go into a loop that executes four times, one time for each label.

```
for (int i = 1; i <= 4; i++) {
```

We construct the name of one of the four fields by appending i to the word line and use that to get a reference to the correct field using valueForKey:.

```
NSString *fieldName = [NSString stringWithFormat:@"line%d", i];
UITextField *theField = [self valueForKey:fieldName];
```

Next, we create our fetch request:

```
NSFetchRequest *request = [[NSFetchRequest alloc] init];
```

After that, we create an entity description that describes the *Line* entity we designed earlier in the data model editor and that uses the context we retrieved from the application delegate. Once we create the description, we feed it to the fetch request, so the request knows which type of entity to look for.

```
NSEntityDescription *entityDescription = [NSEntityDescription
            entityForName:@"Line"
    inManagedObjectContext:context];
[request setEntity:entityDescription];
```

Next, we need to find out if there's already a managed object in the persistent store that corresponds to this field, so we create a predicate that identifies the correct object for the field.

```
NSPredicate *pred = [NSPredicate
    predicateWithFormat:@"(lineNum = %d)", i];
[request setPredicate:pred];
```

After that, we declare a pointer to an NSManagedObject and set it to nil. We do this because we don't know yet if we're going to load a managed object from the persistent store or create a new one. We also declare an NSError that the system will use to notify us of the specific nature of the problem if we get back a nil array.

```
NSManagedObject *theLine = nil;
NSError *error;
```

Next, we execute the fetch request against the context.

```
NSArray *objects = [context executeFetchRequest:request
    error:&error];
```

Then we check to make sure that objects is not nil. If it is nil, then there was an error, and we should do whatever error checking is appropriate for our application. For this simple application, we're just logging the error and moving on.

```
if (objects == nil) {
    NSLog(@"There was an error!");
    // Do whatever error handling is appropriate
}
```

After that, we check if an object that matched our criteria was returned. If there is one, we load it. If there isn't one, we create a new managed object to hold this field's text.

```
if ([objects count] > 0)
    theLine = [objects objectAtIndex:0];
else
    theLine = [NSEntityDescription
        insertNewObjectForEntityForName:@"Line"
                inManagedObjectContext:context];
```

Then we use key-value coding to set the line number and text for this managed object.

```
[theLine setValue:[NSNumber numberWithInt:i] forKey:@"lineNum"];
[theLine setValue:theField.text forKey:@"lineText"];
[request release];
}
```

Finally, once we're finished looping, we tell the context to save its changes.

```
[context save:&error];
}
```

Making Persistence View Controller the Application's Root Controller

Because we used the Window-based Application template instead of the View-based Application template, we have one more step to take before our fancy new Core Data application will work. We need to create an instance of `PersistenceViewController` to act as our application's root controller and add its view as a subview of our application's main window. Let's do that now.

First, we need an outlet to the view controller in our application delegate. Single-click *Core_Data_PersistenceAppDelegate.h*, and make the following changes to declare that outlet:

```
#import <UIKit/UIKit.h>
#import <CoreData/CoreData.h>

@class PersistenceViewController;

@interface Core_Data_PersistenceAppDelegate : NSObject
        <UIApplicationDelegate> {
    UIWindow *window;
@private
    NSManagedObjectContext *managedObjectContext_;
    NSManagedObjectModel *managedObjectModel_;
    NSPersistentStoreCoordinator *persistentStoreCoordinator_;

    PersistenceViewController *rootController;
}

@property (nonatomic, retain) IBOutlet UIWindow *window;

@property (nonatomic, retain, readonly) NSManagedObjectContext
    *managedObjectContext;
@property (nonatomic, retain, readonly) NSManagedObjectModel
    *managedObjectModel;
@property (nonatomic, retain, readonly) NSPersistentStoreCoordinator
    *persistentStoreCoordinator;

- (NSURL *)applicationDocumentsDirectory;
- (void)saveContext;

@property (nonatomic, retain) IBOutlet PersistenceViewController
    *rootController;
@end
```

To make the root controller's view a subview of the application's window so that the user can interact with it, single-click *Core_Data_PersistenceAppDelegate.m*, and make the following changes at the top of that file:

```
#import "Core_Data_PersistenceAppDelegate.h"
#import "PersistenceViewController.h"

@implementation Core_Data_PersistenceAppDelegate

@synthesize window;
```

```
@synthesize rootController;

#pragma mark -
#pragma mark Application lifecycle

- (BOOL)application:(UIApplication *)application
    didFinishLaunchingWithOptions:(NSDictionary *)launchOptions {
    // Override point for customization after application launch.
    [self.window addSubview:rootController.view];
    [self.window makeKeyAndVisible];
    return YES;
}
...
```

Finally, we need to use Interface Builder to create the instance of our root controller and connect it to that outlet we just created. Double click *MainWindow.xib* to open it for editing. Drag a *View Controller* from the library, and drop it onto the nib's main window. The new view controller's icon should still be selected (if it's not, just single-click the icon called *View Controller*). Bring up the identity inspector, and change the underlying class from *UIViewController* to *PersistenceViewController*, which should cause the icon label to change from *View Controller* to *Persistence View Controller*.

Next, control-drag from the icon labeled *Core Data Persistence App Delegate* to the icon labeled *Persistence View Controller*, and select the *rootController* outlet.

That's it! Build and run the app to make sure it works. The Core Data version of your application should behave exactly the same as the previous versions.

It may seem that Core Data entails a lot of work and, for a simple application like this, doesn't offer much of an advantage. But in more complex applications, Core Data can substantially decrease the amount of time you spend designing and writing your data model.

Persistence Rewarded

You should now have a solid handle on four different ways of preserving your application data between sessions—five ways if you include the user defaults that you learned how to use in the previous chapter. We built an application that persisted data using property lists and modified the application to save its data using object archives. We then made a change and used the iOS's built-in SQLite3 mechanism to save the application data. Finally, we rebuilt the same application using Core Data. These mechanisms are the basic building blocks for saving and loading data in almost all iOS applications.

Ready for more? It's time to put on your thinking cap, because in the next chapter, you're going to learn how to add concurrency to your application, letting it do things in the background while still presenting a responsive user interface. There will be some tricky new concepts, but also some fun stuff. Let's go!

Chapter 13

Grand Central Dispatch, Background Processing, and You

If you've ever tried your hand at multithreaded programming, in any environment, chances are you've come away from the experience with a feeling of dread, terror, or worse. Fortunately, technology marches on, and lately Apple has come up with a new approach that makes multithreaded programming much easier. This approach is called **Grand Central Dispatch**, and we'll get you started using it in this chapter.

We'll also dig into the new multitasking capabilities in iOS 4, showing you how to adjust your applications to play nicely in this new world, as well as using the new capabilities to make your apps work even better than before.

Grand Central Dispatch

One of the biggest challenges facing developers today is to write software that can perform complex actions in response to user input while remaining responsive so that the user isn't constantly kept waiting while the processor does some behind-the-scenes task. If you think about it, that challenge has been with us all along, and in spite of the advances in computing technology that are always bringing us faster CPUs, the problem persists. If you want evidence, you need look no further than your nearest computer screen. Chances are that the last time you sat down to work at your computer, at some point your workflow was interrupted by a spinning mouse cursor of some kind or another.

So why does this continue to vex us, given all the advances in system architecture? One part of the problem is the way that software is typically written, as a sequence of events to be performed in order. Such software can scale up as CPU speeds increase, but only up to a certain point. As soon as the program gets stuck waiting for an external resource, such as a file or a network connection, the entire sequence of events is effectively paused. All modern OSs now allow the use of multiple threads of execution within a program, so that even if a single thread is stuck waiting for a specific event, the other threads can keep going. Even so, many developers see multithreaded programming as something of a black art and shy away from it.

Fortunately, Apple has some good news for anyone who wants to break up their code into simultaneous chunks without requiring too much hands-on intimacy with the system's threading layer. This good news is called Grand Central Dispatch (GCD for short), and it provides an entirely new API for splitting up the work your application needs to do into smaller chunks that can be spread across multiple threads and, with the right hardware, multiple CPUs. Much of this new API is accessed using blocks, another Apple innovation that adds a sort of anonymous inline function capability to C and Objective-C. Blocks have a lot in common with similar features in languages such as Ruby and Lisp, and they can provide interesting new ways to structure interactions between different objects while keeping related code closer together in your methods.

Introducing SlowWorker

As a platform for demonstrating how GCD works, we'll create a simple application called SlowWorker, which consists of a simple interface driven by a single button and a text view. Click the button, and a synchronous task is immediately started, locking up the app for about ten seconds. Once the task completes, some text appears in the text view (see Figure 13–1).

Figure 13–1. *The SlowWorker application hides its interface behind a single button. Click the button, and the interface hangs for about ten seconds while the application does its work.*

Start by making a new view-based iPhone application in Xcode as you've done many times before, naming this one *SlowWorker*. Make the following additions to *SlowWorkerViewController.h*:

```
#import <UIKit/UIKit.h>

@interface SlowWorkerViewController : UIViewController {
    UIButton *startButton;
    UITextView *resultsTextView;
}

@property (retain, nonatomic) IBOutlet UIButton *startButton;
@property (retain, nonatomic) IBOutlet UITextView *resultsTextView;

- (IBAction)doWork:(id)sender;

@end
```

That simply defines a couple of outlets to the two objects visible in our GUI and an action method to be triggered by the button. Now enter the following code near the top of *SlowWorkerViewController.m*:

```
#import "SlowWorkerViewController.h"

@implementation SlowWorkerViewController

@synthesize startButton, resultsTextView;

- (NSString *)fetchSomethingFromServer {
    [NSThread sleepForTimeInterval:1];
    return @"Hi there";
}

- (NSString *)processData:(NSString *)data {
    [NSThread sleepForTimeInterval:2];
    return [data uppercaseString];
}

- (NSString *)calculateFirstResult:(NSString *)data {
    [NSThread sleepForTimeInterval:3];
    return [NSString stringWithFormat:@"Number of chars: %d",
            [data length]];
}

- (NSString *)calculateSecondResult:(NSString *)data {
    [NSThread sleepForTimeInterval:4];
    return [data stringByReplacingOccurrencesOfString:@"E"
                                           withString:@"e"];
}

- (IBAction)doWork:(id)sender {
    NSDate *startTime = [NSDate date];
    NSString *fetchedData = [self fetchSomethingFromServer];
    NSString *processedData = [self processData:fetchedData];
    NSString *firstResult = [self calculateFirstResult:processedData];
```

```
    NSString *secondResult = [self calculateSecondResult:processedData];
    NSString *resultsSummary = [NSString stringWithFormat:
                               @"First: [%@]\nSecond: [%@]", firstResult,
                               secondResult];
    resultsTextView.text = resultsSummary;
    NSDate *endTime = [NSDate date];
    NSLog(@"Completed in %f seconds",
          [endTime timeIntervalSinceDate:startTime]);
}
```

And, add the usual cleanup code in `viewDidUnload` and `dealloc`:

```
- (void)viewDidUnload {
    // Release any retained subviews of the main view.
    // e.g. self.myOutlet = nil;
    self.startButton = nil;
    self.resultsTextView = nil;
    [super viewDidUnload];
}

- (void)dealloc {
    [startButton release];
    [resultsTextView release];
    [super dealloc];
}
```

As you can see, the "work" of this class (such as it is) is split up into a number of small chunks. This code is just meant to simulate some slow activities, and none of those methods really do anything time-consuming at all. To make things interesting, each method contains a call to the `sleepForTimeInterval:` class method in NSThread, which simply makes the program (specifically, the thread from which the method is called) effectively "pause" and do nothing at all for the given number of seconds. The doWork: method also contains code at the beginning and end to calculate the amount of time it took for all the work to be done.

Now, open *SlowWorkerViewController.xib*, and drag a Round Rect Button and a Text View into the empty view window, laying things out as shown in Figure 13–2. Control-drag from *File's Owner* to connect the view controller's two outlets to the button and the text view. Next, select the button, and go to the connections inspector to connect the button's *Touch Up Inside* event back to the view controller's doWork: method. Finally, select the text view, use the attributes inspector to uncheck the *Editable* check box (it's in the upper-right corner), and delete the default text from the text view.

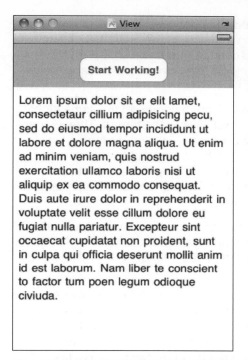

Figure 13–2. *The SlowWorker interface consists of a Round Rect Button and a Text View. Be sure to uncheck the Editable check box for the text view and delete all of its text.*

Now save your work, and hit **Build & Run** in Xcode. Your app should start up, and pressing the button will make it work for about ten seconds (the sum of all those sleep amounts) before showing you the results. During your wait, you'll see that the *Start Working!* button remains dark blue the entire time, never turning back to its normal color until the "work" is done. Also, until the "work" is done, the application's view is unresponsive. Tapping anywhere on the screen has no effect at all. In fact, the only way you can interact with your application at all during this time is by tapping the home button to switch away from it. This is exactly the state of affairs we want to avoid! In this particular case, it's not too bad, since the application appears to be hung for just a few seconds, but if your app regularly "hangs" this way for much longer than that, using your app will be a frustrating experience. In the worst of cases, the OS may actually kill your app if it's unresponsive for too long. In any case, you'll end up with some unhappy users—and maybe even some ex-users!

Threading Basics

Before we start implementing solutions, let's go over some of the basics involved in concurrency. This is far from a complete description of threading in iOS or threading in general. We just want to explain enough for you to understand what we're doing in this chapter.

Most modern OSs (including, of course, iOS) support the notion of threads of execution. Each process can contain multiple threads, which all run concurrently. If there's just one processor core, the OS will switch between all executing threads, much like it switches between all executing processes. If more than one core is available, the threads will be distributed among them just like processes are.

All threads in a process share the same executable program code and the same global data. Each thread can also have some data that is exclusive to the thread. Threads can make use of a special structure called a **mutex** (short for mutual exclusion) or a lock, which can ensure that a particular chunk of code can't be run by multiple threads at once. This is useful for ensuring correct outcomes when multiple threads access the same data simultaneously, by locking out other threads when one thread is updating a value (in what's called a **critical section** of your code).

A common concern when dealing with threads is the idea of code being **thread-safe**. Some software libraries are written with thread concurrency in mind and have all their critical sections properly protected with mutexes. Some code libraries aren't thread-safe.

For example, in Cocoa Touch, the Foundation framework (containing basic classes appropriate for all sorts of Objective-C programming, for example NSString, NSArray, and so on) is generally considered to be thread-safe. However, the UIKit framework (containing the classes specific to building GUI applications, for example UIApplication, UIView and all its subclasses, and so on) is for the most part not thread-safe. This means that in a running iOS application, all method calls that deal with any UIKit objects should be executed from within the same thread, which is commonly known as the **main thread**. If you access UIKit objects from another thread, all bets are off! You are likely to encounter seemingly inexplicable bugs (or, even worse, you won't experience any problems, but some of your users will be affected by them after you ship). By default, the main thread is where all the action of your iOS app (such as dealing with actions triggered by user events) occurs, so for simple applications it's nothing you need to worry about. Action methods triggered by a user are already running in the main thread. Up to this point in the book, our code has been running exclusively on the main thread, but that's about to change.

> **Tip**: There is a lot written about ythread-safety, and it's well worth your time to dig in and try to digest as much of it as you can. One great place to start is in Apple's own documentation. Take a few minutes and read through this page; it'll definitely help:
>
> http://developer.apple.com/library/ios/#documentation/Cocoa/Conceptual/Multithreading/ThreadSafetySummary/ThreadSafetySummary.html

Units of Work

The problem with the threading model described earlier is that for the average programmer, writing error-free, multithreaded code is nearly impossible. This is not meant as a critique of our industry or of the average programmer's abilities; it's simply an observation. The complex interactions you have to account for in your code when synchronizing data and actions across multiple threads are really just too much for most people to tackle. Imagine that 5 percent of all people have the capacity to write software at all. Only a small fraction of those 5 percent are really up to the task of writing heavy-duty multithreaded applications. Even people who have done it successfully will often advise others to not follow their example!

Fortunately, all hope is not lost. It is possible to implement some concurrency without too much low-level thread-twisting. Just as we have the ability to display data on the screen without directly poking bits into video RAM and to read data from disk without interfacing directly with disk controllers, software abstractions exist that let us run our code on multiple threads without requiring us to do much directly with the threads at all. The solutions that Apple encourages us to use are centered around the ideas of splitting up long-running tasks into units of work and putting those units into queues for execution. The system manages the queues for us, executing units of work on multiple threads for us. We don't need to start and manage the background threads directly and are freed from much of the "bookkeeping" that's usually involved in implementing concurrent applications; the system takes care of that for us.

GCD: Low-Level Queueing

This idea of putting units of work into queues that can be executed in the background, with the system managing the threads for you, is really powerful and greatly simplifies many development situations where concurrency is needed. In the 10.6 release of Mac OS X, Grand Central Dispatch made its debut, providing the infrastructure to do just that. With the release of 4.0, the iOS platform has it as well. This technology works not only with Objective-C but also with C and C++. GCD puts some great concepts—units of work, painless background processing, automatic thread management—into a C interface that can be used from all of the C-based languages. To top things off, Apple has made its implementation of GCD open source so that it could be ported to other Unix-like OSs as well.

One of the key concepts of GCD is the queue. The system provides a number of predefined queues, including a queue that's guaranteed to always do its work on the main thread. It's perfect for non-thread-safe UIKit! You can also create your own queues, as many as you like. GCD queues are strictly FIFO (first-in, first-out). Units of work added to a GCD queue will always be started in the order they were placed in the queue. That being said, they may not always finish in the same order, since a GCD queue will automatically distribute its work among multiple threads if possible.

Each queue has access to a pool of threads that are reused throughout the lifetime of the application. GCD will always try to maintain a pool of threads that's appropriate for the machine's architecture, automatically taking advantage of a more powerful machine by utilizing more processor cores when it has work to do. Current iOS devices are all single-core, so this isn't much of an issue today, but when more powerful iOS devices are available, this will really come into play.

Becoming a Blockhead

Along with GCD, Apple has added a bit of new syntax to the C language itself (and, by extension, Objective-C and C++) to implement a language feature called **blocks** (also known as **closures** or **lambdas** in some other languages), which are really important for getting the most out of GCD. The idea behind a block is to let a particular chunk of code be treated like any other C-language type. A block can be assigned to a variable, passed as an argument to a function or method, and (unlike other most other types) executed. In this way, blocks can be used as an alternative to the delegate pattern in Objective-C or to callback functions in C. Much like a method or function, a block can take one or more parameters and specify a return value. To declare a block variable, you make use of the caret (^) symbol along with some additional parenthesized bits to declare parameters and return types. To define the block itself, you do roughly the same but follow it up with the actual code defining the block wrapped in curly braces.

```
// Declare a block variable "loggerBlock" with no parameters and no return value.
void (^loggerBlock)(void);

// Assign a block to the variable declared above.  A block without parameters
// and with no return value, like this one, needs no "decorations" like the use
// of void in the preceeding variable declaration.
loggerBlock = ^{ NSLog(@"I'm just glad they didn't call it a lambda"); };

// Execute the block, just like calling a function.
loggerBlock();  // this produces some output in the console
```

If you've done much C programming, you may recognize that this is similar to the concept of a function pointer in C. However, there are a few critical differences. Perhaps the biggest difference, the one that's the most striking when you first see it, is that blocks can be defined inline in your code; you can define a block right at the point where it's going to be passed to another method or function. Another big difference is that a block can access variables available in the scope where it's created. By default, the block makes a copy of any variable you access this way, leaving the original intact, but you can make an outside variable "read/write" by prepending the storage qualifier __block before its declaration. Note that there are two underscores before block, not just one.

```
// define a variable that can be changed by a block
__block int a = 0;

// define a block that tries to modify a variable in its scope
void (^sillyBlock)(void) = ^{ a = 47; };

// check the value of our variable before calling the block
NSLog(@"a == %d", a); // outputs "a == 0"
```

```
// execute the block
sillyBlock();

// check the values of our variable again, after calling the block
NSLog(@"a == %d", a); // outputs "a == 47"
```

As we mentioned a little while ago, blocks really shine when used with GCD, which lets you take a block and add it to a queue in a single step. When you do this with a block that you define right at that point, rather than a block stored in a variable, then you have the added advantage of being able to see the relevant code right in the context where it's being used.

Improving SlowWorker

To see how this works, let's revisit SlowWorker's doWork: method. It currently looks like this:

```
- (IBAction)doWork:(id)sender {
    NSDate *startTime = [NSDate date];
    NSString *fetchedData = [self fetchSomethingFromServer];
    NSString *processedData = [self processData:fetchedData];
    NSString *firstResult = [self calculateFirstResult:processedData];
    NSString *secondResult = [self calculateSecondResult:processedData];
    NSString *resultsSummary = [NSString stringWithFormat:
                                @"First: [%@]\nSecond: [%@]", firstResult,
                                secondResult];
    resultsTextView.text = resultsSummary;
    NSDate *endTime = [NSDate date];
    NSLog(@"Completed in %f seconds",
        [endTime timeIntervalSinceDate:startTime]);
}
```

We can make that method run entirely in the background by wrapping all the code in a block and passing it to a GCD function called dispatch_async. This function takes two parameters: a GCD queue and a block to assign to the queue. Make this change to your copy of doWork::

```
- (IBAction)doWork:(id)sender {
    NSDate *startTime = [NSDate date];
    dispatch_async(dispatch_get_global_queue(0, 0), ^{
        NSString *fetchedData = [self fetchSomethingFromServer];
        NSString *processedData = [self processData:fetchedData];
        NSString *firstResult = [self calculateFirstResult:processedData];
        NSString *secondResult = [self calculateSecondResult:processedData];
        NSString *resultsSummary = [NSString stringWithFormat:
                                    @"First: [%@]\nSecond: [%@]", firstResult,
                                    secondResult];
        resultsTextView.text = resultsSummary;
        NSDate *endTime = [NSDate date];
        NSLog(@"Completed in %f seconds",
            [endTime timeIntervalSinceDate:startTime]);
    });
}
```

The first line grabs a preexisting global queue that's always available, using the dispatch_get_global_queue() function. That function takes two arguments: the first lets you specify a priority, and the second is currently unused and should always be 0. If you specify a different priority in the first argument, such as DISPATCH_QUEUE_PRIORITY_HIGH or DISPATCH_QUEUE_PRIORITY_LOW (passing a 0 is the same as passing DISPATCH_QUEUE_PRIORITY_DEFAULT), you will actually get a different global queue, which the system will prioritize differently. For now, we'll stick with the default global queue.

The queue is then passed to the dispatch_async() function, along with the block of code that comes after. GCD then takes that entire block and passes it to a background thread, where it will be executed one step at a time, just like when it was running in the main thread.

Don't Forget That Main Thread

There's one problem here: UIKit thread-safety. Remember, messaging any GUI object including our resultsTextView from a background thread is a no-no. Fortunately, GCD provides us with a way to deal with this, too. Inside the block, we can call another dispatching function, passing work back to the main thread! We do this by once again calling dispatch_async(), this time passing in the queue returned by the dispatch_get_main_queue() function, which always gives us the special queue that lives on the main thread, ready to execute blocks that require the use of the main thread. Make one more change to your version of doWork::

```
- (IBAction)doWork:(id)sender {
    NSDate *startTime = [NSDate date];
    dispatch_async(dispatch_get_global_queue(0, 0), ^{
        NSString *fetchedData = [self fetchSomethingFromServer];
        NSString *processedData = [self processData:fetchedData];
        NSString *firstResult = [self calculateFirstResult:processedData];
        NSString *secondResult = [self calculateSecondResult:processedData];
        NSString *resultsSummary = [NSString stringWithFormat:
                                    @"First: [%@]\nSecond: [%@]", firstResult,
                                    secondResult];
        dispatch_async(dispatch_get_main_queue(), ^{
            resultsTextView.text = resultsSummary;
        });
        NSDate *endTime = [NSDate date];
        NSLog(@"Completed in %f seconds",
              [endTime timeIntervalSinceDate:startTime]);
    });
}
```

Giving Some Feedback

If you build and run your app at this point, you'll see that it now seems to work a bit more smoothly, at least in some sense. The button no longer gets stuck in a highlighted position after you touch it, which perhaps leads you to tap again, and again, and so on. If you look in Xcode's console log, you'll see the result of each of these taps, but only the results of the last tap will be shown in the text view. What we really want to do is enhance the GUI so that after the user presses the button, the display is immediately updated in a way that indicates that an action is underway and that the button is disabled while the work is in progress. We'll do this by adding a UIActivitityIndicatorView to our display. This class provides the sort of "spinner" seen in many applications and web sites.

Start by declaring it in file*SlowWorkerViewController.h*:

```
@interface SlowWorkerViewController : UIViewController {
    UIButton *startButton;
    UITextView *resultsTextView;
    UIActivityIndicatorView *spinner;
}

@property (retain, nonatomic) IBOutlet UIButton *startButton;
@property (retain, nonatomic) IBOutlet UITextView *resultsTextView;
@property (retain, nonatomic) IBOutlet UIActivityIndicatorView *spinner;
...
```

Then open file*SlowWorkerViewController.xib*, locate an activity indicator view in the library, and drag it into our view, next to the button (see Figure 13–3).

Figure 13–3. *Dragging an activity indicator view into our main view in Interface Builder*

With the activity indicator spinner selected, use the attributes inspector to check the *Hide When Stopped* check box so that our spinner will appear only when we tell it to start spinning (nobody wants an unspinning spinner in their GUI).

Next, control-drag from the File's Owner icon to the spinner, and connect the *spinner* outlet. Save your changes, and then switch back to Xcode and open

SlowWorkerViewController.m. Here we'll first add the usual code for handling an outlet:

```objc
@implementation SlowWorkerViewController

@synthesize startButton, resultsTextView;
@synthesize spinner;
...
- (void)viewDidUnload {
    // Release any retained subviews of the main view.
    // e.g. self.myOutlet = nil;
    self.startButton = nil;
    self.resultsTextView = nil;
    self.spinner = nil;
    [super viewDidUnload];
}
- (void)dealloc {
    [startButton release];
    [resultsTextView release];
    [spinner release];
    [super dealloc];
}
```

Now let's work on the doWork: method a bit, adding a few lines to manage the appearance of the button and the spinner when the user clicks and when the work is done. We first set the button's enabled property to NO, which prevents it from registering any taps but doesn't give any visual cue. To let the user see that the button is disabled, we'll set its alpha value to 0.5. You can think of the alpha value as a transparency setting, where 0.0 is fully transparent (that is, invisible) and 1.0 is not transparent at all. We'll talk more about alpha values in Chapter 14.

```objc
- (IBAction)doWork:(id)sender {
    startButton.enabled = NO;
    startButton.alpha = 0.5;
    [spinner startAnimating];
    NSDate *startTime = [NSDate date];
    dispatch_async(dispatch_get_global_queue(0, 0), ^{
        NSString *fetchedData = [self fetchSomethingFromServer];
        NSString *processedData = [self processData:fetchedData];
        NSString *firstResult = [self calculateFirstResult:processedData];
        NSString *secondResult = [self calculateSecondResult:processedData];
        NSString *resultsSummary = [NSString stringWithFormat:
                                @"First: [%@]\nSecond: [%@]", firstResult,
                                secondResult];
        dispatch_async(dispatch_get_main_queue(), ^{
            startButton.enabled = YES;
            startButton.alpha = 1.0;
            [spinner stopAnimating];
            resultsTextView.text = resultsSummary;
        });
        NSDate *endTime = [NSDate date];
        NSLog(@"Completed in %f seconds",
            [endTime timeIntervalSinceDate:startTime]);
    });
}
```

Build and run the app, and press the button. That's more like it, eh? Even though the "work" being done takes a few seconds, the user isn't just left hanging; the button is disabled and looks the part as well, and the animated spinner lets the user know that the app hasn't actually hung and can be expected to return to normal at some point.

Concurrent Blocks

So far so good, but we're not quite done yet! The sharp-eyed among you will notice that after going through these motions, we still haven't really changed the basic sequential layout of our algorithm (if you can even call this simple list of steps an algorithm). All that we're doing is moving a chunk of this method to a background thread and then finishing up in the main thread, and the Xcode console output proves it: This "work" takes ten seconds to run, just as it did at the outset. The 900-pound gorilla in the room is that calculateFirstResult: and calculateSecondResult: don't need to be performed in sequence, and doing them concurrently could get us a substantial speedup.

Fortunately, GCD has a way to accomplish this by using what's called a **dispatch group**. All blocks that are dispatched asynchronously within the context of a group, via the dispatch_group_async() function, are set loose to execute as fast as they can, including being distributed to multiple threads for concurrent execution if possible. We can also use dispatch_group_notify() to specify an additional block that will be executed when all the blocks in the group have been run to completion.

Make these changes to your copy of doWork::

```objc
- (IBAction)doWork:(id)sender {
    NSDate *startTime = [NSDate date];
    dispatch_async(dispatch_get_global_queue(0, 0), ^{
        NSString *fetchedData = [self fetchSomethingFromServer];
        NSString *processedData = [self processData:fetchedData];
        NSString *firstResult = [self calculateFirstResult:processedData];
        NSString *secondResult = [self calculateSecondResult:processedData];
        __block NSString *firstResult;
        __block NSString *secondResult;
        dispatch_group_t group = dispatch_group_create();
        dispatch_group_async(group, dispatch_get_global_queue(0, 0), ^{
            firstResult = [[self calculateFirstResult:processedData] retain];
        });
        dispatch_group_async(group, dispatch_get_global_queue(0, 0), ^{
            secondResult = [[self calculateSecondResult:processedData] retain];
        });
        dispatch_group_notify(group, dispatch_get_global_queue(0, 0), ^{
            NSString *resultsSummary = [NSString stringWithFormat:
                                        @"First: [%@]\nSecond: [%@]", firstResult,
                                        secondResult];
            dispatch_async(dispatch_get_main_queue(), ^{
                startButton.enabled = YES;
                startButton.alpha = 1.0;
                [spinner stopAnimating];
                resultsTextView.text = resultsSummary;
            });
            NSDate *endTime = [NSDate date];
```

```
        NSLog(@"Completed in %f seconds",
            [endTime timeIntervalSinceDate:startTime]);
        [firstResult release];
        [secondResult release];
    });
  });
}
```

One complication here is that each of the `calculate` methods returns a value that we want to grab, so we have to first create the variables using the `__block` storage modifier, which ensures the values set inside the blocks are made available to the code that runs later. An additional complication involves memory management. We may not know which block in the group will be completed first, but we can be reasonably sure that they won't be completed at exactly the same time. That means that by the time the final block specified with `dispatch_group_notify()` is called, there's a nearly 100 percent risk that either `firstResult` or `secondResult` will have been released already! The solution is simply to retain each result within the block that does the calculation and then release them in the final block.

With this in place, build and run the app again, and you'll see that your efforts have paid off. What was once a ten-second operation now takes just seven seconds thanks to the fact that we're running both of the calculations simultaneously. Obviously, our contrived example gets the maximum effect because these two "calculations" don't actually do anything but cause the thread they're running on to sleep; in a real application, the speedup would depend on what sort of work is being done and what resources are available. Performing CPU-intensive calculations would be helped only by this technique if multiple CPU cores were available, and at the time of this writing, there are no iOS devices with more than one. Other uses, such as fetching data from multiple network connections at once, would see a speed increase even with just one CPU.

As you can see, GCD is not a panacea. Using GCD won't automatically speed up every application, but by carefully applying these techniques at those points in your app where speed is essential or where you find that your application feels like it's lagging in its responses to the user, you can easily provide a better user experience even in situations where you can't improve the real performance.

Background Processing

Another important addition to iOS 4 is the introduction of background processing, which can allow your apps to run in the background, in some circumstances even after the user has pressed the home button. This functionally should not be confused with the true multitasking that all modern desktop OSs now feature, where all the programs you launch remain resident in the system RAM until you explicitly quit them; iOS devices are still too low on RAM to be able to pull that off very well. Instead, this functionality is meant to allow applications that require specific kinds system functionality to continue to run in a constrained manner. For instance, if you have an app that plays an audio stream from an Internet radio station, iOS 4 will let that app continue to run even if the user switches to another app. Beyond that, it will even provide standard pause and volume controls in the iOS system task bar (the bar that appears at the bottom when you double-tap the home button) while your app is playing audio.

> **NOTE**: The background processing features are available only on devices that meet a certain minimum hardware standard. At the time of this writing, this includes the iPhone 3GS and iPhone 4, the third- and fourth-generation iPod touch, and the iPad. Basically, if you have any iPhone or iPod touch that was available before mid-2009, your device isn't welcome on the multitasking playground. Sorry!

Specifically, if you're creating an app that plays audio, that wants continuous location updates, or that implements VOIP to let users send and receive phone calls on the Internet, you can declare this situation in your app's *Info.plist* file, and the system will treat your app in a special way. This usage, while interesting, is probably not something that most readers of this book will be tackling, so we're not going to delve into it here.

Besides running apps in the background, iOS 4 also includes the ability to put an app into a suspended state after the user presses the home button. This state of suspended execution is conceptually similar to putting your Mac into sleep mode. The entire working memory of the application is held in RAM; it just isn't executed at all while suspended. As a result, switching back to such an application is lightning-fast. This isn't limited to special applications and in fact is the default behavior of any app you compile with the iOS 4 SDK (though this can be disabled by another setting in the *Info.plist* file). To see this in action, open your device's Mail application and drill down into a message; then press the home button, open the Notes application, and select a note. Now double-tap the home button and switch back to Mail. You'll see that there's no perceptible lag; it just slides into place as if it had been running all along.

For most applications, this sort of automatic suspending and resuming is all you're likely to need. However, in some situations, your app may need to know when it's about to be suspended and when it's just been awakened. The system provides ways of notifying an app about changes to its execution state via the UIApplication class, which provides a number of delegate methods and notifications for just this purpose, and we're going to show you how to use them.

When your application is about to be suspended, one thing it can do, regardless of whether it's one of the special backgroundable application types, is request a bit of additional time to run in the background. The idea is to make sure your app has enough time to close any open files, network resources, and so on. We'll give you an example of this in a bit.

Application Life Cycle

Before we get into the specifics of how to deal with changes to your app's execution state, let's talk a bit about what the various states are:

- **Not Running**: This is the state that all apps are in on a freshly rebooted device. In iOS 4, an application will return to this state only if its *Info.plist* includes the UIApplicationExitsOnSuspend key (with its value set to YES), if it was previously Suspended and the system needs to clear out some memory, or if it crashes while running.

- **Active**: This is the normal running state of an application when it's displayed on-screen. It can receive user input and update the display.

- **Background**: In this state, an app is given some time to execute some code but can't directly access the screen or get any user input. All apps enter this state briefly when the user presses the home button; most of them quickly move on to the Suspended state. Apps that want to run in the background stay here until they're made Active again.

- **Suspended**: A Suspended app is frozen. This is what happens to normal apps after their brief stint in the Background state. All the memory the app was using while it was active is held just as it was. If the user brings the app back to the Active state, it will pick up right where it left off. On the other hand, if the system needs more memory for whichever app is currently Active, any Suspended apps may be terminated (and placed back into the Not Running state) and their memory freed for other use.

- **Inactive**: An app enters the Inactive state only as a temporary rest stop between two other states. The only way an app can stay Inactive for any length of time is if the user is dealing with a system prompt (such as those shown for an incoming call or SMS) or if the user has locked the screen. This is a basically a sort of limbo.

State-Change Notifications

To manage changes between these states, UIApplication defines a number of methods that its delegate can implement. In addition to the delegate methods, UIApplication also defines a matching set of notification names (see Table 13–1). This allows other objects besides the app delegate to register for notifications when the application's state changes.

Table 13–1. *Delegate Methods for Tracking Your Application's Execution State and Their Corresponding Notification Names*

Delegate Method	Notification Name
application:didFinishLaunchingWithOptions:	UIApplicationDidFinishLaunchingNotification
applicationWillResignActive:	UIApplicationWillResignActiveNotification
applicationDidBecomeActive:	UIApplicationDidBecomeActiveNotification
applicationDidEnterBackground:	UIApplicationDidEnterBackgroundNotification
applicationWillEnterForeground:	UIApplicationWillEnterForegroundNotification
applicationWillTerminate:	UIApplicationWillTerminateNotification

Note that each of these is directly related to one of the "running" states: Active, Inactive, and Background. Each delegate method is called (and each notification posted) only in one of those states. The most important state transitions are between Active and other states; and some transitions, like from Background to Suspended, occur without any notice whatsoever. Let's go through these methods and discuss how they're meant to be used.

The first of these, `application:didFinishLaunchingWithOptions:`, is one you've already seen many times in this book. It's the primary way of doing application-level coding directly after the app has launched.

The next two methods, `applicationWillResignActive:` and `applicationDidBecomeActive:`, are both used in a number of circumstances. If the user presses the home button, `applicationWillResignActive:` will be called, and if they later bring the app back to the foreground, `applicationDidBecomeActive:` will be called. The same sequence of events occurs if the user receives a phone call. To top it all off, `applicationDidBecomeActive:` is also called when the application launches! In general, this pair of methods bracket the movement of an application from the Active state to the Inactive state and are good places to enable and disable any animations, in-app audio, or other items that deal with the app's presentation to the user. Because of the multiple situations where `applicationDidBecomeActive:` is used, you may want to put some of your app initialization code there instead of in `application:didFinishLaunchingWithOptions:`. Note that you should not assume in `applicationWillResignActive:` that the application is about to be sent to the background, because it may just be a temporary change that ends up with a move back to Active.

After that come two more methods, `applicationDidEnterBackground:` and `GapplicationWillEnterForeground:`, which have a slightly different usage area: dealing with an app that is definitely being sent to the background. `applicationDidEnterBackground:` is where your app should free all resources that can be re-created later, save all user data, close network connections, and so on. This is also the spot where you can request more time to run in the background if you need to, as we'll demonstrate shortly. If you spend too much time doing things in applicationDidEnterBackground:, more than about five seconds, the system will decide that your app is misbehaving and terminate it. You should implement applicationWillEnterForeground: to re-create whatever was torn down in applicationDidEnterBackground:, such as reloading user data, reestablishing network connections, and so on.

Note that when applicationDidEnterBackground: is called, you can safely assume that applicationWillResignActive: has also been recently called; likewise, when applicationWillEnterForeground: is called, you can assume that applicationDidBecomeActive: will soon be called as well.

Last in the list is applicationWillTerminate:, which you'll probably use seldom, if ever. Prior to iOS 4, this was the method you'd implement to save user data and so on, but now that applicationDidEnterBackground: exists, we don't need the old method, which is really called only if our application is already in the background and the system decides to skip suspension for some reason and simply terminate the app.

Now, you should have a basic theoretical understanding of the states an application transitions between. Let's put this knowledge to the test with a simple app that does nothing more than write a message to Xcode's console log each time one of these methods is called. Then we'll manipulate the running app in a variety of ways, just as a user might, and see which transitions occur.

Creating State Lab

In Xcode, create a new project based on the *View-based Application* template, and name it *State Lab*. This app won't display anything but the default gray screen it's born with; all the output it's going to generate will end up in the Xcode console instead. The *State_LabAppDelegate.m* file already contains all the methods we're interested in; all we need to do is add some logging, as shown in bold. Note that we've also removed the comments from these methods, just for the sake of brevity.

```
- (BOOL)application:(UIApplication *)application didFinishLaunchingWithOptions:
    (NSDictionary *)launchOptions {
    NSLog(@"%@", NSStringFromSelector(_cmd));

    [self.window addSubview:viewController.view];
    [self.window makeKeyAndVisible];

    return YES;
}

- (void)applicationWillResignActive:(UIApplication *)application {
    NSLog(@"%@", NSStringFromSelector(_cmd));
}

- (void)applicationDidEnterBackground:(UIApplication *)application {
    NSLog(@"%@", NSStringFromSelector(_cmd));
```

```
}

- (void)applicationWillEnterForeground:(UIApplication *)application {
    NSLog(@"%@", NSStringFromSelector(_cmd));
}

- (void)applicationDidBecomeActive:(UIApplication *)application {
    NSLog(@"%@", NSStringFromSelector(_cmd));
}

- (void)applicationWillTerminate:(UIApplication *)application {
    NSLog(@"%@", NSStringFromSelector(_cmd));
}
```

You may be wondering about that NSLog call we're using in all those methods. Objective-C provides a handy built-in variable called _cmd that always contains the selector of the current method. A selector, in case you need a refresher, is simply Objective-C's way of referring to a method; the NSStringFromSelector() function returns an NSString representation of a given selector. Our usage here simply gives us a shortcut for outputting the current method name without needing to retype it or copy and paste it.

Exploring Execution States

Now, build and run the app. The simulator will appear with its plain gray look. Switch back to Xcode and take a look at the console (**Run ➤ Console**), where you should see something like this:

```
2010-12-28 11:56:52.674 State Lab[3090:207] application:didFinishLaunchingWithOptions:
2010-12-28 11:56:52.677 State Lab[3090:207] applicationDidBecomeActive:
```

Here we can see that the application has successfully launched and been moved into the Active state. Now, go back to the simulator and press the home button, and you should see the following in the console:

```
2010-12-28 11:56:55.874 State Lab[3090:207] applicationWillResignActive:
2010-12-28 11:56:55.875 State Lab[3090:207] applicationDidEnterBackground:
```

Those two lines show the app actually transitioning between two states. It first becomes Inactive and then goes to Background. What you can't see here is that the app also switches to a third state, Suspended. Remember, you get no notification that this has happened; it's completely outside your control. Note that the app is still "live" in some sense, and Xcode is still connected to it, even though it's not actually getting any CPU time. Verify this by tapping the app's icon to relaunch it, which should produce this output:

```
2010-12-28 11:57:00.886 State Lab[3090:207] applicationWillEnterForeground:
2010-12-28 11:57:00.888 State Lab[3090:207] applicationDidBecomeActive:
```

There you are, back in business. The app was previously Suspended, is woken up to Inactive, and then ends up Active again. So, what happens when the app is really terminated? Tap the home button again:

```
2010-12-28 11:57:03.569 State Lab[3090:207] applicationWillResignActive:
2010-12-28 11:57:03.570 State Lab[3090:207] applicationDidEnterBackground:
```

Then double-tap the home button, press and hold the State Lab icon until the little "kill" icon comes up, and kill it. What happens? You may be surprised to see that nothing is printed to the console; all you get is "Debugging terminated" in the status row at the bottom of the console window.

As it turns out, the applicationWillTerminate: method isn't normally called when the system is moving an app from Suspended to Not Running. When an app is Suspended, whether the system decides to dump it to reclaim memory or you manually force-quit it, it simply vanishes and doesn't get a chance to do anything. The applicationWillTerminate: method is called only if the app being terminated is in the Background state. This can occur, for instance, if your app is running in the Background state and is force-quit either by the user or by the system.

Now, there's one more interesting interaction to examine here, and that's what happens when the system shows an alert dialog, temporarily taking over the input stream from the app and putting it into an Inactive state. This state can be readily triggered only when running on a real device instead of the simulator, in particular, an iPhone. If you already have your certificates in order and can build a debug version to run on your phone, do so. Then have someone else send your iPhone an SMS. When your iPhone displays the system alert showing the SMS, this will appear in the Xcode console:

```
2010-12-28 12:05:15.391 State Lab[1069:307] applicationWillResignActive:
```

Note that our app didn't get sent to the background; it's in the Inactive state and can still be seen behind the system alert. If this app were a game or had any video, audio, or animations running, this is where we'd probably want to pause them.

Press the Close button on the alert, and you'll get this:

```
2010-12-28 12:05:24.808 State Lab[1069:307] applicationDidBecomeActive:
```

Now let's see what happens if you decide to reply to the SMS instead. Have someone send you another SMS, generating this:

```
2010-12-28 12:11:04.154 State Lab[1069:307] applicationWillResignActive:
```

This time hit Reply, and you should see the following flurry of activity:

```
2010-12-28 12:11:07.826 State Lab[1069:307] applicationDidBecomeActive:
2010-12-28 12:11:07.966 State Lab[1069:307] applicationWillResignActive:
2010-12-28 12:11:07.984 State Lab[1069:307] applicationDidEnterBackground:
```

Interesting! Our app quickly becomes Active again, becomes then Inactive again, and finally goes to Background (and then, silently, Suspended). Frankly, we're not sure why this particular sequence of transitions occurs. It seems that the extra trip to Active and back to Inactive could be avoided, but this is the way it seems to work, at least in the current version of iOS.

Making Use of Execution State Changes

So, what should we make of all this? Based on what we've just demonstrated, it seems like there's a clear strategy to follow when dealing with these state changes:

Active ➤ Inactive

Use `applicationWillResignActive:`/`UIApplicationWillResignActiveNotification` to "pause" your app's display. If your app is a game, you probably already have the ability to pause the game play in some way. For other kinds of apps, make sure no time-critical demands for user input are in the works, because your app won't be getting any user input for a while.

Inactive ➤ Background

Use `applicationDidEnterBackground:`/`UIApplicationDidEnterBackgroundNotification` to release any resources that don't need to be kept around when the app is backgrounded (such as cached images or other easily reloadable data) or that wouldn't survive backgrounding anyway (such as active network connections). Getting rid of excess memory usage here will make your app's eventual Suspended snapshot smaller, thereby decreasing the risk that your app will be purged from RAM entirely. You should also use this opportunity to save any application data that will help your user pick up where they left off the next time your app is relaunched; if your app comes back to the Active state, normally this won't matter, but in case it's purged and has to be relaunched, your users will appreciate starting off in the same place.

Background ➤ Inactive

Use `applicationWillEnterForeground:`/`UIApplicationWillEnterForeground` to undo anything you did when switching from Inactive to Background. For example, here you can reestablish persistent network connections.

Inactive ➤ Active

Use `applicationDidBecomeActive:`/`UIApplicationDidBecomeActive` to undo anything you did when switching from Active to Inactive. Note that if your app is a game, this probably does not mean dropping out of pause straight to the game; you should let your users do that on their own. Also keep in mind that this method and notification are used when an app is freshly launched, so anything you do here must work in that context as well.

There is one special consideration for the Inactive ➤ Background transition. Not only does it have the longest description in the previous list, but it's also probably the most code- and time-intensive transition in most applications because of the amount of "bookkeeping" you may want your app to do. When this transition is underway, the system won't give you the benefit of an unlimited amount of time to save your changes here; it gives you about five seconds, and if your app takes longer than that to return from the delegate method (and handle any notifications you've registered for), then your app will be summarily purged from memory and pushed into the Not Running state! If this seems unfair, don't worry, because there is a reprieve available. While handling that delegate method or notification, you can ask the system to perform some additional work for you in a background queue, which buys you some extra time. We'll demonstrate that technique in the next section.

Handling the Inactive State

The simplest state change your app is likely to encounter is from Active to Inactive and then back to Active. You may recall that this is what happens if your iPhone receives an SMS while your app is running and displays it for the user. In this section, we're going to make State Lab do something visually interesting so that we can see what happens if we ignore that state change, and then we'll see how to fix it.

What we're going to do here is add a UILabel to our display and make it move using Core Animation, which is a really nice way of animating objects in iOS.

Start by adding a UILabel as an instance variable and property in file*State_LabViewController.h*:

```
@interface State_LabViewController : UIViewController {
    UILabel *label;
}
@property (nonatomic, retain) UILabel *label;
@end
```

Then do the usual memory-management work for this property in file*State_LabViewController.m*:

```
@implementation State_LabViewController
@synthesize label;

...

- (void)viewDidUnload {
    // Release any retained subviews of the main view.
    // e.g. self.myOutlet = nil;
    self.label = nil;
    [super viewDidUnload];
}

- (void)dealloc {
    [label release];
    [super dealloc];
}
```

Now let's set up the label when the view loads. Remove the comment marks around the viewDidLoad method, and add the bold lines shown here:

```
- (void)viewDidLoad {
    [super viewDidLoad];

    CGRect bounds = self.view.bounds;
```

```
CGRect labelFrame = CGRectMake(bounds.origin.x, CGRectGetMidY(bounds) - 50,
                                bounds.size.width, 100);
self.label = [[[UILabel alloc] initWithFrame:labelFrame] autorelease];
label.font = [UIFont fontWithName:@"Helvetica" size:70];
label.text = @"Bazinga!";
label.textAlignment = UITextAlignmentCenter;
label.backgroundColor = [UIColor clearColor];
[self.view addSubview:label];
}
```

Then it's time to set up some animation. We're going to define two methods, one to rotate the label to an upside-down position and one to rotate it back to normal. Let's declare these methods in an class extension at the top of the file, just before the class's @implementation begins:

```
@interface State_LabViewController ()
- (void)rotateLabelUp;
- (void)rotateLabelDown;
@end
```

The method definitions themselves can then be inserted anywhere within the @implementation block:

```
- (void)rotateLabelDown {
    [UIView animateWithDuration:0.5
                     animations:^{
                         label.transform = CGAffineTransformMakeRotation(M_PI);
                     }
                     completion:^(BOOL finished){
                         [self rotateLabelUp];
                     }];
}

- (void)rotateLabelUp {
    [UIView animateWithDuration:0.5
                     animations:^{
                         label.transform = CGAffineTransformMakeRotation(0);
                     }
                     completion:^(BOOL finished){
                         [self rotateLabelDown];
                     }];
}
```

This deserves a bit of explanation. UIView defines a class method called animateWithDuration:animations:completion:, which sets up an animation. Any animatable attributes that we set within the animations block don't have an immediate effect on the receiver. Instead, Core Animation will smoothly transition that attribute from its current value to the new value we specify. This is what's called an **implicit animation** and is one of the main features of Core Animation. This functionality has been present in Core Animation for a while, but this block-based approach to setting it up is new in iOS 4. The final completion block lets us specify what will happen after the animation is complete.

So, each of these methods sets the label's `transform` property to a particular rotation, specified in radians. Each also sets up a completion block to just call the other method, so the text will continue to animate back and forth forever.

Finally, we need to set up a way to kick-start the animation. For now, we'll do this by adding this line at the end of `viewDidLoad` (but we will change this later, for reasons we'll describe at that time):

```
[self rotateLabelDown];
```

Now, build and run the app, and you should see the *Bazinga!* label rotate back and forth (see Figure 13–4).

Figure 13–4. *The State Lab application doing its label rotating magic*

To test the Active ➤ Inactive transition, you really need once again to run this on an actual iPhone and send an SMS to it from elsewhere; unfortunately, there's no way to simulate this behavior in any version of the iOS simulator that Apple has released so far. If you don't yet have the ability to build and install on a device or don't have an iPhone, you won't be able to try this for yourself, but please follow along as best you can!

Build and run the app on an iPhone, and see that the animation is running along. Now send an SMS to the device, and when the system alert comes up to show the SMS, you'll see that the animation keeps on running! That may be slightly comical, but it's probably irritating for a user. We will use transition notifications to stop our animation when this occurs.

Our controller class will need to have some internal state to keep track of whether it should be animating at any given time. For this purpose, let's add an ivar to State_LabViewController.h. Because this is a simple BOOL, not an object (and therefore not a memory-management issue), and since no outside classes will need access to this, we skip the step of making a property.

```
@interface State_LabViewController : UIViewController {
    BOOL animate;
    UILabel *label;
}
```

Since our class isn't the application delegate, we can't just implement the delegate methods and expect them to work; instead, we sign up to receive notifications from the application when the execution state changes. Do this by adding a few lines at the top of the viewDidLoad method in fileState_LabViewController.m:

```
- (void)viewDidLoad {
    [super viewDidLoad];
    [[NSNotificationCenter defaultCenter] addObserver:self
                              selector:@selector(applicationWillResignActive)
                                  name:UIApplicationWillResignActiveNotification
                                object:[UIApplication sharedApplication]];
    [[NSNotificationCenter defaultCenter] addObserver:self
                              selector:@selector(applicationDidBecomeActive)
                                  name:UIApplicationDidBecomeActiveNotification
                                object:[UIApplication sharedApplication]];
    CGRect bounds = self.view.bounds;
    ...
```

That sets up these two notifications to each call a method in our class at the appropriate time. Define these methods anywhere you like inside the @implementation block:

```
- (void)applicationWillResignActive {
    NSLog(@"%@", NSStringFromSelector(_cmd));
    animate = NO;
}

- (void)applicationDidBecomeActive {
    NSLog(@"%@", NSStringFromSelector(_cmd));
    animate = YES;
    [self rotateLabelDown];
}
```

As you can see, we've included the same method logging as before, just so you can see where they occur in the Xcode console. The first of these methods just turns off the animate flag; the second turns the flag back on and then actually starts up the animations again. For that first method to have any effect, we have to add some code to check the animate flag and keep on animating only if it's enabled.

```
- (void)rotateLabelUp {
    [UIView animateWithDuration:0.5
                     animations:^{
                         label.transform = CGAffineTransformMakeRotation(0);
                     }
                     completion:^(BOOL finished){
```

```
        if (animate) {
            [self rotateLabelDown];
        }
    }];
}
```

We added that to the completion block of `rotateLabelUp`, and only there, so that our animation will stop only when the text is right-side up.

Now, build and run again, and see what happens. Chances are, you'll see some flickery madness, with the label rapidly flipping up and down, not even rotating! The reason for this is simple but perhaps not obvious (though we did hint at it earlier). Remember that we started up the animations at the end of `viewDidLoad` by calling `rotateLabelDown`? Well, we're now calling `rotateLabelDown` in `applicationDidBecomeActive` as well, and remember, `applicationDidBecomeActive` will be called not only when we switch from Inactive back to Active but also when the app launches and becomes Active in the first place! That means we're starting our animations twice, and Core Animation doesn't seem to deal well with multiple animations trying to change the same attributes at the same time. The solution is simply to delete the line you previously added at the end of `viewDidLoad`:

```
        [self rotateLabelDown];
```

Now build and run, and you should see that it's animating properly. Once again, send an SMS to your iPhone, and this time when the system alert appears, you'll see that the animation in the background stops as soon as the text is right-side up. Tap the Close button, and the animation starts back up.

Now you've seen what to do for the simple case of switching from Active to Inactive and back. The bigger task, and perhaps the more important one, is dealing with a switch to Background and then back to Foreground.

Handling the Background State

As we mentioned earlier, switching to the background state is pretty important to ensure the best possible user experience. This is the spot where you'll want to discard any resources that can easily be reacquired (or will be lost anyway when your app goes silent) and save info about your app's current state, all without occupying the main thread for more than five seconds.

To demonstrate some of these behaviors, we're going to extend State Lab in a few ways. First, we're going to add an image to the display so that we can later show you how to get rid of the in-memory image. Then, we're going to show you how to save some info about the app's state so we can easily restore it later. Finally, we'll show you how to make sure these activities aren't taking up too much main thread time, by putting all this work into a background queue.

Removing Resources When Entering Background

Start by adding *smiley.png* from the book's source archive to your project's *Resources* folder. You can do this either by dragging it directly from the Finder into the *Resources* folder in the Xcode project window or by right-clicking the Resources folder and selecting **Add ➤ Existing Files…** from the context menu. In either case, be sure to enable the check box that tells Xcode to copy the file to your project directory.

Now, let's add instance variables and properties for both an image and an image view to State_LabViewController.h:

```
@interface State_LabViewController : UIViewController {
    BOOL animate;
    UILabel *label;
    UIImage *smiley;
    UIImageView *smileyView;
}
@property (nonatomic, retain) UILabel *label;
@property (nonatomic, retain) UIImage *smiley;
@property (nonatomic, retain) UIImageView *smileyView;
@end
```

Then switch to the *.m* file again, and add the usual memory-management code:

```
@implementation State_LabViewController

@synthesize label;
@synthesize smiley, smileyView;
...
- (void)viewDidUnload {
    // Release any retained subviews of the main view.
    // e.g. self.myOutlet = nil;
    self.label = nil;
    self.smiley = nil;
    self.smileyView = nil;
    [super viewDidUnload];
}

- (void)dealloc {
    [label release];
    [smiley release];
    [smileyView release];
    [super dealloc];
}
```

Now let's set up the image view and put it on-screen by modifying the viewDidLoad method as shown here:

```
- (void)viewDidLoad {
    [super viewDidLoad];
    [[NSNotificationCenter defaultCenter] addObserver:self
                                   selector:@selector(applicationWillResignActive)
                                       name:UIApplicationWillResignActiveNotification
                                     object:[UIApplication sharedApplication]];
    [[NSNotificationCenter defaultCenter] addObserver:self
                                   selector:@selector(applicationDidBecomeActive)
```

```
                                              name:UIApplicationDidBecomeActiveNotification
                                            object:[UIApplication sharedApplication]];
        CGRect bounds = self.view.bounds;
        CGRect labelFrame = CGRectMake(bounds.origin.x, CGRectGetMidY(bounds) - 50,
                                       bounds.size.width, 100);
        self.label = [[[UILabel alloc] initWithFrame:labelFrame] autorelease];
        label.font = [UIFont fontWithName:@"Helvetica" size:70];
        label.text = @"Bazinga!";
        label.textAlignment = UITextAlignmentCenter;
        label.backgroundColor = [UIColor clearColor];

        // smiley.png is 84 x 84
        CGRect smileyFrame = CGRectMake(CGRectGetMidX(bounds) - 42,
                                        CGRectGetMidY(bounds)/2 - 42,
                                        84, 84);
        self.smileyView = [[[UIImageView alloc] initWithFrame:smileyFrame] autorelease];
        self.smileyView.contentMode = UIViewContentModeCenter;
        NSString *smileyPath = [[NSBundle mainBundle] pathForResource:@"smiley"
                                                               ofType:@"png"];
        self.smiley = [UIImage imageWithContentsOfFile:smileyPath];
        self.smileyView.image = self.smiley;

        [self.view addSubview:smileyView];
        [self.view addSubview:label];
}
```

Now, build and run, and you'll see the incredibly happy-looking smiley face at the top of your screen, above the rotating text (see Figure 13–5).

Figure 13–5. *The State Lab application doing its label-rotating magic with the addition of a smiley icon*

Now, press the home button to switch your app to the background, and then tap its icon to launch it again. Nothing happens, right? Right. Remember that we want to minimize the number of resources our app will use while in the Background state, so we'd really like to free up that image when going to the background and re-create it when coming back from the Background. To do that, we'll need to add two more notification registrations toward the top of viewDidLoad, just after [super viewDidLoad]:

```
[[NSNotificationCenter defaultCenter] addObserver:self
                         selector:@selector(applicationDidEnterBackground)
                             name:UIApplicationDidEnterBackgroundNotification
                           object:[UIApplication sharedApplication]];
[[NSNotificationCenter defaultCenter] addObserver:self
                         selector:@selector(applicationWillEnterForeground)
                             name:UIApplicationWillEnterForegroundNotification
                           object:[UIApplication sharedApplication]];
```

And we want to implement the two new methods:

```
- (void)applicationDidEnterBackground {
    NSLog(@"%@", NSStringFromSelector(_cmd));
    self.smiley = nil;
    self.smileyView.image = nil;
}

- (void)applicationWillEnterForeground {
    NSLog(@"%@", NSStringFromSelector(_cmd));
    NSString *smileyPath = [[NSBundle mainBundle] pathForResource:@"smiley"
                                                           ofType:@"png"];
    self.smiley = [UIImage imageWithContentsOfFile:smileyPath];
    self.smileyView.image = self.smiley;
}
```

Now build and run, and do the same steps of backgrounding your app and switching back to it. You should see that from the user's standpoint, the behavior appears to be about the same. If you want to verify for yourself that this is really happening, comment out the contents of the applicationWillEnterForeground method, and build and run again; you'll see that the image really does disappear.

Saving State When Entering Background

Now that you've seen an example of how to free up some resources when entering the background, it's time to think about saving state. Remember that the idea is to save all info relevant to what the user is doing so that in case your application is later dumped from memory, the next time the user comes back they can still pick up right where they left off. The kind of state we're talking about here is really application-specific. You might want to keep track of which document a user was looking at, their cursor location in a text field, which application view was open, and so on. In our case, we're just going to keep track of the selection in a segmented control.

Start by adding a new instance variable and property in *State_LabViewController.h*:

```
@interface State_LabViewController : UIViewController {
```

```
    BOOL animate;
    UILabel *label;
    UIImage *smiley;
    UIImageView *smileyView;
    UISegmentedControl *segmentedControl;
}
@property (nonatomic, retain) UILabel *label;
@property (nonatomic, retain) UIImage *smiley;
@property (nonatomic, retain) UIImageView *smileyView;
@property (nonatomic, retain) UISegmentedControl *segmentedControl;
@end
```

Then implement the usual boilerplate code for accessors and memory management in m
State_LabViewController.m:

```
@implementation State_LabViewController

@synthesize label;
@synthesize smiley, smileyView;
@synthesize segmentedControl;

...

- (void)viewDidUnload {
    // Release any retained subviews of the main view.
    // e.g. self.myOutlet = nil;
    self.label = nil;
    self.smiley = nil;
    self.smileyView = nil;
    self.segmentedControl = nil;
    [super viewDidUnload];
}

- (void)dealloc {
    [label release];
    [smiley release];
    [smileyView release];
    [segmentedControl release];
    [super dealloc];
}
```

Now move on to the end of the viewDidLoad method, where we'll create the segmented
control and add it to the view:

```
    ...
    self.smileyView.image = self.smiley;

    self.segmentedControl = [[[UISegmentedControl alloc] initWithItems:
                            [NSArray arrayWithObjects:
                                @"One", @"Two", @"Three", @"Four", nil]] autorelease];
    self.segmentedControl.frame = CGRectMake(bounds.origin.x + 20,
                                        CGRectGetMaxY(bounds) - 50,
                                        bounds.size.width - 40, 30);

    [self.view addSubview:segmentedControl];
    [self.view addSubview:smileyView];
    [self.view addSubview:label];
```

```
}
```

If you build and run at this point, you'll see one glaring problem: The segmented control doesn't seem to work! You can tap those segments all you like, and nothing will happen. The problem actually lies with the animation that's going on. By default, the Core Animation method we used to set things up actually prevents any andanduser input from being collected while animations are running. There is an optional way to enable user interation, which requires us to use a longer method name in each of our rotate methods. Modify them as shown here:

```
- (void)rotateLabelDown {
    [UIView animateWithDuration:0.5
                    delay:0
                  options:UIViewAnimationOptionAllowUserInteraction
               animations:^{
                   label.transform = CGAffineTransformMakeRotation(M_PI);
               }
               completion:^(BOOL finished){
                   [self rotateLabelUp]; }];
}

- (void)rotateLabelUp {
    [UIView animateWithDuration:0.5
                    delay:0
                  options:UIViewAnimationOptionAllowUserInteraction
               animations:^{
                   label.transform = CGAffineTransformMakeRotation(0);
               }
               completion:^(BOOL finished){
                   if (animate) {
                       [self rotateLabelDown];
                   }
               }];
}
```

Build and run again, and see what happens. That's more like it, eh? Now, touch any one of the four segments and then down the now-familiar sequence of backgrounding your app and then bringing it back up. You'll see that the segment you chose (I bet it was "Three") is still selected; no surprise there. Background your app again, bring up the task bar and kill your app, and then relaunch it; you'll find yourself back at square one, with no segment selected. That's what we need to fix next.

Saving the selection is simple enough. We just need to add a few lines to the end of the applicationDidEnterBackground method:

```
- (void)applicationDidEnterBackground {
    NSLog(@"%@", NSStringFromSelector(_cmd));
    self.smiley = nil;
    self.smileyView.image = nil;

    NSInteger selectedIndex = self.segmentedControl.selectedSegmentIndex;
    [[NSUserDefaults standardUserDefaults] setInteger:selectedIndex
                                        forKey:@"selectedIndex"];
}
```

But, where should we restore this selection index and use it to configure the segmented control? The inverse of this method, methodapplicationWillEnterForeground, isn't what we want; when that method is called, the app has already been running, and the setting is still intact. Instead, we need to access this when things are being set up after a new launch, which brings us back to the viewDidLoad method. Add the bold lines shown here at the end of the method:

```
...

[self.view addSubview:label];

NSNumber *indexNumber;
if (indexNumber = [[NSUserDefaults standardUserDefaults]
                    objectForKey:@"selectedIndex"]) {
    NSInteger selectedIndex = [indexNumber intValue];
    self.segmentedControl.selectedSegmentIndex = selectedIndex;
}
}
```

We had to include a little sanity check there to see whether there's a value stored for the selectedIndex key at all, to cover cases such as the first app launch, where nothing has been selected.

Now build and run, touch a segment, and then do the full background-kill-restart dance; there it is—your selection is intact! Obviously what we've shown here is pretty minimal, but the concept can be extended to all kinds of application state. It's up to you to decide how far you want to take it in order to maintain the illusion for the user that your app was always there, just waiting for them to come back!

Requesting More Backgrounding Time

Earlier we mentioned the possibility of your app being dumped from memory if moving to the background state takes too much time. To see this in action, just add a single line to the applicationDidEnterBackground method:

```
- (void)applicationDidEnterBackground {
    NSLog(@"%@", NSStringFromSelector(_cmd));
    self.smiley = nil;
    self.smileyView.image = nil;

    NSInteger selectedIndex = self.segmentedControl.selectedSegmentIndex;
    [[NSUserDefaults standardUserDefaults] setInteger:selectedIndex
                                        forKey:@"selectedIndex"];

    // simulate a lengthy procedure
    [NSThread sleepForTimeInterval:10];
}
```

Now build and run, then hit the home button, watch the status line at the bottom of the Xcode console, and wait a few seconds; you'll see the text change to "Debugging terminated." That means that iOS (or the iOS simulator) has decided your app is a bad citizen and kicked you out!

Don't worry, there's a way to avoid this, and it's not too bad. Once again, we'll be using our new acquaintances, GCD and blocks, to make the contents of our applicationDidEnterBackground method run in a separate queue. Modify the method as follows:

```
- (void)applicationDidEnterBackground {
    NSLog(@"%@", NSStringFromSelector(_cmd));
    UIApplication *app = [UIApplication sharedApplication];

    __block UIBackgroundTaskIdentifier taskId;
    taskId = [app beginBackgroundTaskWithExpirationHandler:^{
        NSLog(@"Background task ran out of time and was terminated.");
        [app endBackgroundTask:taskId];
    }];

    if (taskId == UIBackgroundTaskInvalid) {
        NSLog(@"Failed to start background task!");
        return;
    }

    dispatch_async(dispatch_get_global_queue(0, 0), ^{
        NSLog(@"Starting background task with %f seconds remaining",
                app.backgroundTimeRemaining);
        self.smiley = nil;
        self.smileyView.image = nil;

        NSInteger selectedIndex = self.segmentedControl.selectedSegmentIndex;
        [[NSUserDefaults standardUserDefaults] setInteger:selectedIndex
                                          forKey:@"selectedIndex"];
        // simulate a lengthy procedure
        [NSThread sleepForTimeInterval:10];

        NSLog(@"Finishing background task with %f seconds remaining",
                app.backgroundTimeRemaining);
        [app endBackgroundTask:taskId];
    });
}
```

Let's look through that piece by piece. First we grab the shared UIApplication instance since we'll be using it several times in this method. Then comes this:

```
    __block UIBackgroundTaskIdentifier taskId;
    taskId = [app beginBackgroundTaskWithExpirationHandler:^{
        NSLog(@"Background task ran out of time and was terminated.");
        [app endBackgroundTask:taskId];
    }];
```

That call to beginBackgroundTaskWithExpirationHandler: returns an identifier that we'll need to keep track of for later use. We've declared the taskId variable it's stored in with the __block storage qualifier, since we want to be sure the identifier returned by the method is shared among any blocks we create in this method.

With the call to beginBackgroundTaskWithExpirationHandler:, we're basically telling the system that we need more time to accomplish something, and we promise to tell when we're done. The block we give as a parameter may be called if the system decides that we've just been running way too long anyway and decides to stop running.

Note that the block we gave ended with a call to endBackgroundTask:, passing along taskId. That tells the system that we're done with the work for which we previously requested extra time. It's important to balance each call to beginBackgroundTaskWithExpirationHandler: with a matching call to endBackgroundTask: so that the system knows when we're done.

> **NOTE**: Depending on your computing background, the use of the word *task* here may evoke associations with what we usually call a *process*, consisting of a running program that may contain multiple threads, and so on. In this case, try to put that out of your mind. This use of *task* in this context really just means "something that needs to get done." Any "task" you create here is still running within your still-executing app.

Next, we do this:

```
if (taskId == UIBackgroundTaskInvalid) {
    NSLog(@"Failed to start background task!");
    return;
}
```

If our earlier call to beginBackgroundTaskWithExpirationHandler: returned the special value UIBackgroundTaskInvalid, that means the system is refusing to grant us any additional time. In that case, you could try to do the quickest part of whatever needs doing anyway and hope that it completes in five seconds. This is mostly likely to be an issue when running on older devices, such as the iPhone 3G, that let you run iOS 4 but don't support multitasking. In this example, however, we're just letting it slide.

Next comes the interesting part where the work itself is actually done:

```
dispatch_async(dispatch_get_global_queue(0, 0), ^{
    NSLog(@"Starting background task with %f seconds remaining",
        app.backgroundTimeRemaining);
    self.smiley = nil;
    self.smileyView.image = nil;

    NSInteger selectedIndex = self.segmentedControl.selectedSegmentIndex;
    [[NSUserDefaults standardUserDefaults] setInteger:selectedIndex
                                        forKey:@"selectedIndex"];
    // simulate a lengthy procedure
    [NSThread sleepForTimeInterval:10];

    NSLog(@"Finishing background task with %f seconds remaining",
        app.backgroundTimeRemaining);
    [app endBackgroundTask:taskId];
});
```

All this does is take the same work our method was doing in the first place and place it on a background queue. At the end of that block, we call endBackgroundTask: to let the system know that we're done.

With that in place, build and run, and then background your app by pressing the home button; watch the Xcode console as well as the status bar at the bottom of the Xcode window. You'll see that this time, your app stays running (you don't get the "Debugging terminated" message in the status bar), and after ten seconds you will see the final log in your output. A complete run of the app up to this point should give you console output along these lines:

```
2010-12-30 22:35:28.608 State Lab[7449:207] application:didFinishLaunchingWithOptions:
2010-12-30 22:35:28.616 State Lab[7449:207] applicationDidBecomeActive:
2010-12-30 22:35:28.617 State Lab[7449:207] applicationDidBecomeActive
2010-12-30 22:35:31.869 State Lab[7449:207] applicationWillResignActive:
2010-12-30 22:35:31.870 State Lab[7449:207] applicationWillResignActive
2010-12-30 22:35:31.871 State Lab[7449:207] applicationDidEnterBackground:
2010-12-30 22:35:31.873 State Lab[7449:207] applicationDidEnterBackground
2010-12-30 22:35:31.874 State Lab[7449:1903] Starting background task with 599.995069
seconds remaining
2010-12-30 22:35:41.877 State Lab[7449:1903] Finishing background task with 589.993956
seconds remaining
```

As you can see, the system is much more generous with time when doing things in the background than in the main thread of your app, so following this procedure can really help you out if you have any ongoing tasks to deal with.

Note that we asked for a single background task identifier, but in practice you can ask for as many as you need. For example, if you have multiple network transfers happening at Background time and you need to complete them, you can ask for an identifier for each of them and allow each one to continue running in a background queue so you can easily allow multiple operations to run in parallel during the available time. Also consider that the task identifier you receive is a normal C-language value (not an object), and apart from being stored in a local __block variable, it can just as well be stored as an instance variable if that better suits your class design.

Grand Central Dispatch, Over and Out

This has been a pretty heavy chapter, with a lot of new concepts thrown your way. Not only have you learned about a complete new feature set Apple added to the C language, but you've learned about a new conceptual paradigm for dealing with concurrency without worrying about threads and about techniques for making sure your apps play nicely in the multitasking world of iOS 4. Now that we've gotten some of this heavy stuff out of the way, let's move on to the next chapter, which focuses on drawing. Pencils out, let's draw!

Chapter 14

Drawing with Quartz and OpenGL

Every application we've built so far has been constructed from views and controls provided as part of the UIKit framework. You can do a lot with the UIKit stock components, and a great many application interfaces can be constructed using only these objects. Some applications, however, can't be fully realized without looking further.

For instance, at times, an application needs to be able to do custom drawing. Fortunately for us, we have not one but two separate libraries we can call on for our drawing needs:

- Quartz 2D, which is part of the Core Graphics framework
- OpenGL ES,which is a cross-platform graphics library

OpenGL ES is a slimmed-down version of another cross-platform graphic library called OpenGL. OpenGL ES is a subset of OpenGL, designed specifically for embedded systems (hence the letters *ES*) such as the iPhone, iPad, and iPod touch.

In this chapter, we'll explore both of these powerful graphics environments. We'll build sample applications in both, and give you a sense of which environment to use and when.

Two Views of a Graphical World

Although Quartz and OpenGL overlap a lot, distinct differences exist between them.

Quartz is a set of functions, datatypes, and objects designed to let you draw directly into a view or to an image in memory. Quartz treats the view or image that is being drawn into as a virtual canvas. It follows what's called a **painter's model**, which is just a fancy way to say that that drawing commands are applied in much the same way as paint is applied to a canvas.

If a painter paints an entire canvas red, and then paints the bottom half of the canvas blue, the canvas will be half red and half either blue or purple (blue if the paint is opaque; purple if the paint is semitransparent). Quartz's virtual canvas works the same way. If you paint the whole view red, and then paint the bottom half of the view blue, you'll have a view that's half red and half either blue or purple, depending on whether the second drawing action was fully opaque or partially transparent. Each drawing action is applied to the canvas on top of any previous drawing actions.

On the other hand, OpenGL ES is implemented as a **state machine**. This concept is somewhat more difficult to grasp, because it doesn't resolve to a simple metaphor like painting on a virtual canvas. Instead of letting you take actions that directly impact a view, window, or image, OpenGL ES maintains a virtual three-dimensional world. As you add objects to that world, OpenGL keeps track of the state of all objects.

Instead of a virtual canvas, OpenGL ES gives you a virtual window into its world. You add objects to the world and define the location of your virtual window with respect to the world. OpenGL ES then draws what you can see through that window based on the way it is configured and where the various objects are in relation to each other. This concept is a bit abstract, but it will make more sense when we build our OpenGL ES drawing application later in this chapter.

Quartz provides a variety of line, shape, and image drawing functions. Though easy to use, Quartz 2D is limited to two-dimensional drawing. Although many Quartz functions do result in drawing that takes advantage of hardware acceleration, there is no guarantee that any particular action you take in Quartz will be accelerated.

OpenGL, though considerably more complex and conceptually more difficult, offers a lot more power than Quartz. It has tools for both two-dimensional and three-dimensional drawing, and is specifically designed to take full advantage of hardware acceleration. It's also extremely well suited to writing games and other complex, graphically intensive programs.

Now that you have a general idea of the two drawing libraries, let's try them out. We'll start with the basics of how Quartz 2D works, and then build a simple drawing application with it. Then we'll re-create the same application using Open GL ES.

The Quartz Approach to Drawing

When using Quartz, you'll usually add the drawing code to the view doing the drawing. For example, you might create a subclass of UIView and add Quartz function calls to that class's drawRect: method. The drawRect: method is part of the UIView class definition and is called every time a view needs to redraw itself. If you insert your Quartz code in drawRect:, that code will be called, and then the view will redraw itself.

Quartz 2D's Graphics Contexts

In Quartz 2D, as in the rest of Core Graphics, drawing happens in a **graphics context**, usually just referred to as a **context**. Every view has an associated context. You retrieve the current context, use that context to make various Quartz drawing calls, and let the context worry about rendering your drawing onto the view.

This line of code retrieves the current context:

```
CGContextRef context = UIGraphicsGetCurrentContext();
```

> **NOTE:** Notice that we're using Core Graphics C functions, rather than Objective-C objects, to do our drawing. Both Core Graphics and OpenGL are C-based APIs, so most of the code we write in this part of the chapter will consist of C function calls.

Once you've defined your graphics context, you can draw into it by passing the context to a variety of Core Graphics drawing functions. For example, this sequence will create a **path**, consisting of a 4-pixel-wide line, in the context, and then draw that line:

```
CGContextSetLineWidth(context, 4.0);
CGContextSetStrokeColorWithColor(context, [UIColor redColor].CGColor);
CGContextMoveToPoint(context, 10.0f, 10.0f);
CGContextAddLineToPoint(context, 20.0f, 20.0f);
CGContextStrokePath(context);
```

The first call specifies that lines used to create the current path should be 4 pixels wide. We then specify that the stroke color should be red. In Core Graphics, two colors are associated with drawing actions:

- The **stroke color** is used in drawing lines and for the outline of shapes.

- The **fill color** is used to fill in shapes.

A context has a sort of invisible pen associated with it that does the line drawing. As drawing commands are executed, the movements of this pen form a **path**. When you call CGContextMoveToPoint(), you move the end point of the current path to that location, without actually drawing anything. Whatever operation comes next, it will do its work relative to the point to which you moved the pen. In the earlier example, for instance, we first moved the pen to (10, 10). The next function call drew a line from the current pen location (10, 10) to the specified location (20, 20), which became the new pen location.

When you draw in Core Graphics, you're not drawing anything you can actually see. You're creating a path, which can be a shape, a line, or some other object, but it contains no color or anything to make it visible. It's like writing in invisible ink. Until you do something to make it visible, your path can't be seen. So, the next step is to tell Quartz to draw the line using CGContextStrokePath(). This function will use the line width and the stroke color we set earlier to actually color (or "paint") the path and make it visible.

The Coordinate System

In the previous chunk of code, we passed a pair of floating-point numbers as parameters to `CGContextMoveToPoint()` and `CGContextLineToPoint()`. These numbers represent positions in the Core Graphics coordinate system. Locations in this coordinate system are denoted by their x and y coordinates, which we usually represent as (x, y). The upper-left corner of the context is (0, 0). As you move down, y increases. As you move to the right, x increases.

In the previous code snippet, we drew a diagonal line from (10, 10) to (20, 20), which would look like the one shown in Figure 14–1.

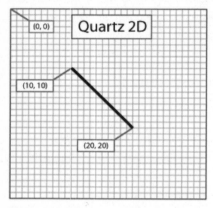

Figure 14–1. *Drawing a line using Quartz 2D's coordinate system*

The coordinate system is one of the gotchas in drawing with Quartz, because Quartz's coordinate system is flipped from what many graphics libraries use and from the traditional Cartesian coordinate system (introduced by René Descartes in the seventeenth century). In OpenGL ES, for example, (0, 0) is in the lower-left corner, and as the y coordinate increases, you move toward the top of the context or view, as shown in Figure 14–2. When working with OpenGL, you must translate the position from the view's coordinate system to OpenGL's coordinate system. That's easy enough to do, as you'll see when we work with OpenGL later in the chapter.

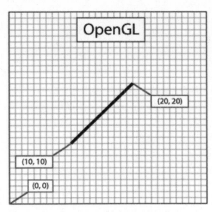

Figure 14–2. *In many graphics libraries, including OpenGL, drawing from (10, 10) to (20, 20) would produce a line that looks like this instead of the line in Figure 14–1.*

To specify a point in the coordinate system, some Quartz functions require two floating-point numbers as parameters. Other Quartz functions ask for the point to be embedded in a CGPoint, a struct that holds two floating-point values: x and y. To describe the size of a view or other object, Quartz uses CGSize, a struct that also holds two floating-point values: width and height. Quartz also declares a datatype called CGRect, which is used to define a rectangle in the coordinate system. A CGRect contains two elements: a CGPoint called origin, which identifies the top left of the rectangle, and a CGSize called size, which identifies the width and height of the rectangle.

Specifying Colors

An important part of drawing is color, so understanding the way colors work on iOS is critical. This is one of the areas where the UIKit does provide an Objective-C class: UIColor. You can't use a UIColor object directly in Core Graphic calls, but since UIColor is just a wrapper around CGColor (which is what the Core Graphic functions require), you can retrieve a CGColor reference from a UIColor instance by using its CGColor property, as we did earlier, in this code snippet:

```
CGContextSetStrokeColorWithColor(context, [UIColor redColor].CGColor);
```

We created a UIColor instance using a convenience method called redColor, and then retrieved its CGColor property and passed that into the function.

A Bit of Color Theory for Your iOS Device's Display

In modern computer graphics, a very common way to represent colors is to use four components: red, green, blue, and alpha. In Quartz 2D, each of these values is represented as CGFloat (which, on your iPhone and iPad, is a 4-byte floating-point value, the same as float) containing a value between 0.0 and 1.0.

NOTE: A floating-point value that is expected to be in the range 0.0 to 1.0 is often referred to as a **clamped floating-point variable**, or sometimes just a **clamp**.

The red, green, and blue components are fairly easy to understand, as they represent the **additive primary colors** or the **RGB color model** (see Figure 14–3). Combining these three colors in different proportions results in different colors. If you add together light of these three shades in equal proportions, the result will appear to the eye as either white or a shade of gray, depending on the intensity of the light mixed. Combining the three additive primaries in different proportions gives you range of different colors, referred to as a **gamut**.

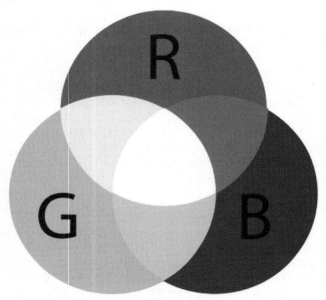

Figure 14–3. *A simple representation of the additive primary colors that make up the RGB color model*

In grade school, you probably learned that the primary colors are red, yellow, and blue. These primaries, which are known as the **historical subtractive primaries**, or the **RYB color model**, have little application in modern color theory and are almost never used in computer graphics. The color gamut of the RYB color model is extremely limited, and this model doesn't lend itself easily to mathematical definition. As much as we hate to tell you that your wonderful third-grade art teacher, Mrs. Smedlee, was wrong about anything, well, in the context of computer graphics, she was. For our purposes, the primary colors are red, green, and blue, not red, yellow, and blue.

In addition to red, green, and blue, both Quartz 2D and OpenGL ES use another color component, called **alpha**, which represents how transparent a color is. When drawing one color on top of another color, alpha is used to determine the final color that is drawn. With an alpha of 1.0, the drawn color is 100% opaque and obscures any colors beneath it. With any value less than 1.0, the colors below will show through and mix. When an alpha component is used, the color model is sometimes referred to as the **RGBA color model,** although technically speaking, the alpha isn't really part of the color; it just defines how the color will interact with other colors when it is drawn.

Other Color Models

Although the RGB model is the most commonly used in computer graphics, it is not the only color model. Several others are in use, including the following:

- Hue, saturation, value (HSV)

- Hue, saturation, lightness (HSL)

- Cyan, magenta, yellow, key (CMYK), which is used in four-color offset printing

- Grayscale

To make matters even more confusing, there are different versions of some of these models, including several variants of the RGB color space.

Fortunately, for most operations, we don't need to worry about the color model that is being used. We can just pass the CGColor from our UIColor object, and Core Graphics will handle any necessary conversions. If you use UIColor or CGColor when working with OpenGL ES, it's important to keep in mind that they support other color models, because OpenGL ES requires colors to be specified in RGBA.

Color Convenience Methods

UIColor has a large number of convenience methods that return UIColor objects initialized to a specific color. In our previous code sample, we used the redColor method to initialize a color to red.

Fortunately for us, the UIColor instances created by most of these convenience methods all use the RGBA color model. The only exceptions are the predefined UIColors that represent grayscale values, such as blackColor, whiteColor, and darkGrayColor, which are defined only in terms of white level and alpha. In our examples here, we're not using those, however. So, we can assume RGBA for now.

If you need more control over color, instead of using one of those convenience methods based on the name of the color, you can create a color by specifying all four of the components. Here's an example:

```
return [UIColor colorWithRed:1.0f green:0.0f blue:0.0f alpha:1.0f];
```

Drawing Images in Context

Quartz 2D allows you to draw images directly into a context. This is another example of an Objective-C class (UIImage) that you can use as an alternative to working with a Core

Graphics data structure (CGImage). The UIImage class contains methods to draw its image into the current context. You'll need to identify where the image should appear in the context using either of the following techniques:

- By specifying a CGPoint to identify the image's upper-left corner
- By specifying a CGRect to frame the image, resized to fit the frame, if necessary

You can draw a UIImage into the current context like so:

```
CGPoint drawPoint = CGPointMake(100.0f, 100.0f);
[image drawAtPoint:drawPoint];
```

Drawing Shapes: Polygons, Lines, and Curves

Quartz 2D provides a number of functions to make it easier to create complex shapes. To draw a rectangle or a polygon, you don't need to calculate angles, draw lines, or do any math at all, really. You can just call a Quartz function to do the work for you. For example, to draw an ellipse, you define the rectangle into which the ellipse needs to fit and let Core Graphics do the work:

```
CGRect theRect = CGMakeRect(0,0,100,100);
CGContextAddEllipseInRect(context, theRect);
CGContextDrawPath(context, kCGPathFillStroke);
```

You use similar methods for rectangles. There are also methods that let you create more complex shapes, such as arcs and Bezier paths.

> **NOTE:** We won't be working with complex shapes in this chapter's examples. To learn more about arcs and Bezier paths in Quartz, check out the *Quartz 2D Programming Guide* in the iOS Dev Center at
> `http://developer.apple.com/documentation/GraphicsImaging/Conceptua l/drawingwithquartz2d/` or in Xcode's online documentation.

Quartz 2D Tool Sampler: Patterns, Gradients, and Dash Patterns

Although not as expansive as OpenGL, Quartz 2D does offer quite an impressive array of tools. For example, Quartz 2D supports filling polygons with gradients, not just solid colors, and an assortment of dash patterns in addition to solid lines.

Take a look at the screenshots in Figure 14–4, which are from Apple's QuartzDemo sample code, to see a sampling of what Quartz 2D can do for you.

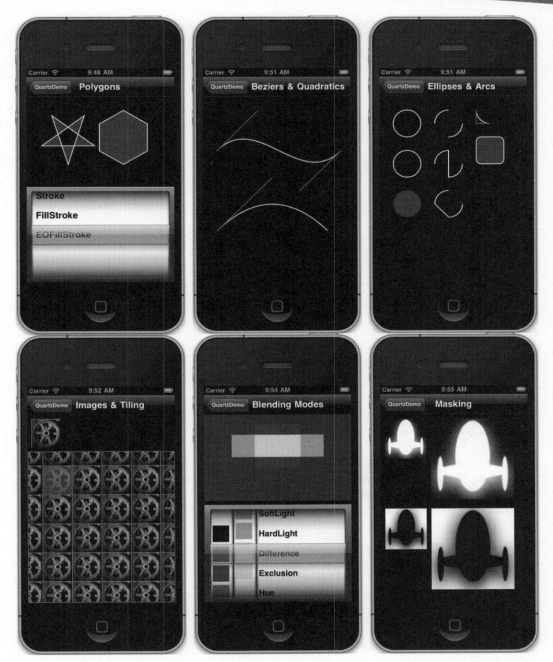

Figure 14–4. *Some examples of what Quartz 2D can do, from the QuartzDemo sample project provided by Apple*

Now that you have a basic understanding of how Quartz 2D works and what it is capable of doing, let's try it out.

The QuartzFun Application

Our next application is a simple drawing program (see Figure 14–5). We're going to build this application twice: now using Quartz 2D, and later using OpenGL ES, so you get a real feel for the difference between the two.

Figure 14–5. *Our chapter's simple drawing application in action*

The application features a bar across the top and one across the bottom, each with a segmented control. The control at the top lets you change the drawing color, and the one at the bottom lets you change the shape to be drawn. When you touch and drag, the selected shape will be drawn in the selected color. To minimize the application's complexity, only one shape will be drawn at a time.

Setting Up the QuartzFun Application

In Xcode, create a new iPhone project using the *View-based Application* template, and call it *QuartzFun*. Next, expand the *Classes* and *Resources* folders and select the *Classes* folder, where we'll add our classes.

The template already provided us with an application delegate and a view controller. We're going to be executing our custom drawing in a view, so we need to create a subclass of UIView where we'll do the drawing by overriding the drawRect: method.

With *Classes* selected, press ⌘N to bring up the new file assistant, and then select *Objective-C class* from the *Cocoa Touch Class* section. Then select *UIView* from the

Subclass of popup list. Just to repeat, use a *Subclass of UIView*, not *NSObject* as we've done in the past. Call the file *QuartzFunView.m,* and make sure you create the header file, too.

We're going to define some constants, as we've done in previous projects, but this time, our constants will be needed by more than one class. We'll create a header file just for the constants.

Select the *Classes* folder and press ⌘N to bring up the new file assistant. Select the *Header File* template from the *Mac OS X* section, *C and C++* heading, and name the file *Constants.h.*

We have two more files to go. If you look at Figure 14–5, you can see that we offer an option to select a random color. UIColor doesn't have a method to return a random color, so we'll need to write code to do that. We could put that code into our controller class, but because we're savvy Objective-C programmers, we're going to put it into a category on UIColor.

Again, select the *Classes* folder and press ⌘N to bring up the new file assistant. Select the *Objective-C class*, *Subclass of NSObject class* template from the *Cocoa Touch Class* heading, and name the file *UIColor-Random.m*. Be sure the header is created as well.

Creating a Random Color

Let's tackle the category first. Delete the contents of *UIColor-Random.h* and make it look like this:

```
#import <UIKit/UIKit.h>

@interface UIColor (UIColor_Random)
+ (UIColor *)randomColor;
@end
```

Note that since we're using UIColor, which is part of UIKit, we needed to import the UIKit framework instead of Foundation. Now, switch over to *UIColor-Random.m*, and replace the existing contents with this code:

```
#import "UIColor-Random.h"

@implementation UIColor (Random)
+ (UIColor *)randomColor {
    static BOOL seeded = NO;
    if (!seeded) {
        seeded = YES;
        srandom(time(NULL));
    }
    CGFloat red = (CGFloat)random()/(CGFloat)RAND_MAX;
    CGFloat blue = (CGFloat)random()/(CGFloat)RAND_MAX;
    CGFloat green = (CGFloat)random()/(CGFloat)RAND_MAX;
    return [UIColor colorWithRed:red green:green blue:blue alpha:1.0f];
}
@end
```

This is fairly straightforward. We declare a static variable that tells us if this is the first time through the method. The first time this method is called during an application's run, we will seed the random number generator. Doing this here means we don't need to rely on the application doing it somewhere else, and as a result, we can reuse this category in other iOS projects.

Once we've made sure the random number generator is seeded, we generate three random CGFloats with a value between 0.0 and 1.0, and use those three values to create a new color. We set alpha to 1.0 so that all generated colors will be opaque.

Defining Application Constants

Next, we'll define constants for each of the options that the user can select using the segmented controllers. Single-click *Constants.h*, and add the following:

```
typedef enum {
    kLineShape = 0,
    kRectShape,
    kEllipseShape,
    kImageShape
} ShapeType;

typedef enum {
    kRedColorTab = 0,
    kBlueColorTab,
    kYellowColorTab,
    kGreenColorTab,
    kRandomColorTab
} ColorTabIndex;

#define degreesToRadian(x) (M_PI * (x) / 180.0)
```

To make our code more readable, we've declared two enumeration types using typedef. One will represent the shape options available; the other will represent the various color options available. The values these constants hold will correspond to segments on the two segmented controllers we'll create in our application.

Implementing the QuartzFunView Skeleton

Since we're going to do our drawing in a subclass of UIView, let's set up that class with everything it needs except for the actual code to do the drawing, which we'll add later. Single-click *QuartzFunView.h*, and make the following changes:

```
#import <UIKit/UIKit.h>
#import "Constants.h"

@interface QuartzFunView : UIView {
    CGPoint firstTouch;
    CGPoint lastTouch;
    UIColor *currentColor;
    ShapeType shapeType;
```

```
        UIImage *drawImage;
        BOOL useRandomColor;
}
@property (nonatomic) CGPoint firstTouch;
@property (nonatomic) CGPoint lastTouch;
@property (nonatomic, retain) UIColor *currentColor;
@property (nonatomic) ShapeType shapeType;
@property (nonatomic, retain) UIImage *drawImage;
@property (nonatomic) BOOL useRandomColor;
@end
```

First, we import the *Constants.h* header we just created so we can make use of our enumerations. We then declare our instance variables. The first two will track the user's finger as it drags across the screen. We'll store the location where the user first touches the screen in firstTouch. We'll store the location of the user's finger while dragging and when the drag ends in lastTouch. Our drawing code will use these two variables to determine where to draw the requested shape.

Next, we define a color to hold the user's color selection and a ShapeType to keep track of the shape the user wants drawn. After that is a UIImage property that will hold the image to be drawn on the screen when the user selects the rightmost toolbar item on the bottom toolbar (see Figure 14–6). The last property is a Boolean that will be used to keep track of whether the user is requesting a random color.

Figure 14–6. *When drawing a UIImage to the screen, notice that the color control disappears. Can you tell which app is running on the tiny iPhone?*

Switch to *QuartzFunView.m*, and make the following changes:

```objc
#import "QuartzFunView.h"
#import "UIColor-Random.h"

@implementation QuartzFunView
@synthesize firstTouch;
@synthesize lastTouch;
@synthesize currentColor;
@synthesize shapeType;
@synthesize drawImage;
@synthesize useRandomColor;

- (id)initWithCoder:(NSCoder*)coder
{
    if (self = [super initWithCoder:coder]) {
        currentColor = [[UIColor redColor] retain];
        useRandomColor = NO;
        if (drawImage == nil) {
            drawImage = [[UIImage imageNamed:@"iphone.png"] retain];
        }
    }
    return self;
}

- (id)initWithFrame:(CGRect)frame {
    if ((self = [super initWithFrame:frame])) {
        // Initialization code
    }
    return self;
}

/*
// Only override drawRect: if you perform custom drawing.
// An empty implementation adversely affects performance during animation.
- (void)drawRect:(CGRect)rect {
    // Drawing code
}
*/

- (void)touchesBegan:(NSSet *)touches withEvent:(UIEvent *)event {
    if (useRandomColor) {
        self.currentColor = [UIColor randomColor];
    }
    UITouch *touch = [touches anyObject];
    firstTouch = [touch locationInView:self];
    lastTouch = [touch locationInView:self];
    [self setNeedsDisplay];
}

- (void)touchesEnded:(NSSet *)touches withEvent:(UIEvent *)event {
    UITouch *touch = [touches anyObject];
    lastTouch = [touch locationInView:self];

    [self setNeedsDisplay];
}
```

```
- (void)touchesMoved:(NSSet *)touches withEvent:(UIEvent *)event {
    UITouch *touch = [touches anyObject];
    lastTouch = [touch locationInView:self];

    [self setNeedsDisplay];
}

- (void)dealloc {
    [currentColor release];
    [drawImage release];
    [super dealloc];
}

@end
```

Because this view is being loaded from a nib, we first implement `initWithCoder:`. Keep in mind that object instances in nibs are stored as archived objects, which is the exact same mechanism we used in Chapter 12 to archive and load our objects to disk. As a result, when an object instance is loaded from a nib, neither `init` nor `initWithFrame:` is ever called. Instead, `initWithCoder:` is used, so this is where we need to add any initialization code. In our case, we set the initial color value to red, initialize `useRandomColor` to `NO`, and load the image file that we're going to draw.

The remaining methods, `touchesBegan:withEvent:`, `touchesMoved:withEvent:`, and `touchesEnded:withEvent:`, are inherited from `UIView` (but actually declared in `UIView`'s parent `UIResponder`). They can be overridden to find out where the user is touching the screen. They work as follows:

- `touchesBegan:withEvent:` is called when the user's finger first touches the screen. In that method, we change the color if the user has selected a random color using the new `randomColor` method we added to `UIColor` earlier. After that, we store the current location so that we know where the user first touched the screen, and we indicate that our view needs to be redrawn by calling `setNeedsDisplay` on `self`.

- `touchesMoved:withEvent:` is continuously called while the user is dragging a finger on the screen. All we do here is store the new location in `lastTouch` and indicate that the screen needs to be redrawn.

- `touchesEnded:withEvent:` is called when the user lifts that finger off the screen. Just as in the `touchesMoved:withEvent:` method, all we do is store the final location in the `lastTouch` variable and indicate that the view needs to be redrawn.

Don't worry if you don't fully grok the rest of the code here. We'll get into the details of working with touches and the specifics of the `touchesBegan:withEvent:`, `touchesMoved:withEvent:`, and `touchesEnded:withEvent:` methods in Chapter 15.

We'll come back to this class once we have our application skeleton up and running. That `drawRect:` method, which is currently commented out, is where we will do this application's real work, and we haven't written that yet. Let's finish setting up the application before we add our drawing code.

Adding Outlets and Actions to the View Controller

If you refer to Figure 14–5, you'll see that our interface includes two segmented controls: one at the top and one at the bottom of the screen. The one on top, which lets the user select a color, is applicable to only three of the four options on the bottom, so we're going to need an outlet to that top segmented controller, so we can hide it when it doesn't serve a purpose. We also need two methods: one that will be called when a new color is selected and another that will be called when a new shape is selected.

Select *QuartzFunViewController.h*, and make the following changes:

```
#import <UIKit/UIKit.h>

@interface QuartzFunViewController : UIViewController {
    UISegmentedControl *colorControl;
}
@property (nonatomic, retain) IBOutlet UISegmentedControl *colorControl;
- (IBAction)changeColor:(id)sender;
- (IBAction)changeShape:(id)sender;
@end
```

Nothing here should need explanation at this point, so switch over to *QuartzFunViewController.m*, and make these changes to the top of the file:

```
#import "QuartzFunViewController.h"
#import "QuartzFunView.h"
#import "Constants.h"

@implementation QuartzFunViewController
@synthesize colorControl;

- (IBAction)changeColor:(id)sender {
    UISegmentedControl *control = sender;
    NSInteger index = [control selectedSegmentIndex];

    QuartzFunView *quartzView = (QuartzFunView *)self.view;

    switch (index) {
        case kRedColorTab:
            quartzView.currentColor = [UIColor redColor];
            quartzView.useRandomColor = NO;
            break;
        case kBlueColorTab:
            quartzView.currentColor = [UIColor blueColor];
            quartzView.useRandomColor = NO;
            break;
        case kYellowColorTab:
            quartzView.currentColor = [UIColor yellowColor];
            quartzView.useRandomColor = NO;
            break;
        case kGreenColorTab:
```

```
            quartzView.currentColor = [UIColor greenColor];
            quartzView.useRandomColor = NO;
            break;
        case kRandomColorTab:
            quartzView.useRandomColor = YES;
            break;
        default:
            break;
    }
}

- (IBAction)changeShape:(id)sender {
    UISegmentedControl *control = sender;
    [(QuartzFunView *)self.view setShapeType:[control
        selectedSegmentIndex]];

    if ([control selectedSegmentIndex] == kImageShape)
        colorControl.hidden = YES;
    else
        colorControl.hidden = NO;
}
...
```

Let's also be good memory citizens by adding the following code to the existing
viewDidUnload and dealloc methods:

```
...
- (void)viewDidUnload {
    // Release any retained subviews of the main view.
    // e.g. self.myOutlet = nil;
    self.colorControl = nil;
    [super viewDidUnload];
}

- (void)dealloc {
    [colorControl release];
    [super dealloc];
}
...
```

Again, these code changes are pretty straightforward. In the changeColor: method, we
look at which segment was selected and create a new color based on that selection. We
cast view to QuartzFunView. Next, we set its currentColor property so that it knows
which color to use when drawing, except when a random color is selected. When a
random color is chosen, we just set the view's useRandomColor property to YES. Since all
the drawing code will be in the view itself, we don't need to do anything else in this
method.

In the changeShape: method, we do something similar. However, since we don't need to
create an object, we can just set the view's shapeType property to the segment index
from sender. Recall the ShapeType enum? The four elements of the enum correspond to
the four toolbar segments at the bottom of the application view. We set the shape to be
the same as the currently selected segment, and we hide and unhide the colorControl
based on whether the *Image* segment was selected.

Updating QuartzFunViewController.xib

Before we can start drawing, we need to add the segmented controls to our nib, and then hook up the actions and outlets. Double-click *QuartzFunViewController.xib* to edit the file in Interface Builder.

The first order of business is to change the class of the view, so single-click the *View* icon in the Interface Builder nib window titled *QuartzFunViewController.xib*, and open the identity inspector. Change the class from *UIView* to *QuartzFunView*.

Double-click the newly renamed *QuartzFunView* icon to open the *View* window. Next, look for a *Navigation Bar* in the library. Make sure you are grabbing a *Navigation Bar*—not a *Navigation Controller.* We just want the bar that goes at the top of the view. Place the *Navigation Bar* snugly against the top of the *View* window, just beneath the status bar.

Next, look for a *Segmented Control* in the library, and drag that directly on top of the *Navigation Bar*. Drop it in the center of the nav bar, not on the left or right side (see Figure 14–7).

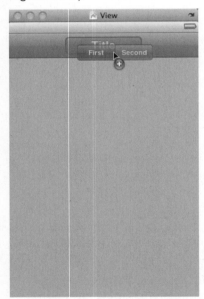

Figure 14–7. *Dragging out a segmented control, being sure to drop it on top of the navigation bar*

Once you drop the control, it should stay selected. Grab one of the resize dots on either side of the segmented control and resize it so that it takes up the entire width of the navigation bar. You won't get any blue guidelines, but Interface Builder won't let you make the bar any bigger than you want it in this case, so just drag until it won't expand any farther.

With the segmented control still selected, bring up the attributes inspector, and change the number of segments from *2* to *5*. Double-click each segment in turn, changing its label to (from left to right) *Red, Blue, Yellow, Green,* and *Random,* in that order. At this point, your *View* window should look like Figure 14–8.

Figure 14–8. *The completed navigation bar*

Control-drag from the *File's Owner* icon to the segmented control, and select the **colorControl** outlet. Make sure you are dragging to the segmented control and not the nav bar. Interface Builder will flash up a tool tip to let you know which item is the focus of the current drag, so this is actually not hard to do.

Next, make sure the segmented control is selected, and bring up the connections inspector. Drag from the *Value Changed* event to *File's Owner,* and select the **changeColor:** action.

Now look for a *Toolbar* in the library (*not* a *Navigation Bar*), and drag one of those over, snug to the bottom of the view window. The toolbar from the library has a button on it that we don't need, so select the button and press the delete key on your keyboard. The button should disappear, leaving a blank toolbar in its stead.

Next, grab another *Segmented Control,* and drop it onto the toolbar (see Figure 14–9).

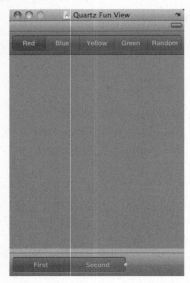

Figure 14–9. *The view, showing a toolbar at the bottom of the window with a segmented control dropped onto the toolbar*

As it turns out, segmented controls are a bit harder to center in a toolbar, so we'll bring in a little help. Drag a *Flexible Space Bar Button Item* from the library onto the toolbar, to the left of our segmented control. Next, drag a second *Flexible Space Bar Button Item* onto the toolbar, to the right of our segmented control (see Figure 14–10). These items will keep the segmented control centered in the toolbar as we resize it.

Figure 14–10. *The segmented control after we dropped the Flexible Space Bar Button Item on either side. Note that we have not yet resized the segmented control to fill the toolbar.*

Click the segmented control to select it, and resize it so it fills the toolbar, leaving just a bit of space to the left and right. Interface Builder won't give you guides or prevent you from making the segmented control wider than the toolbar, the way it did with the navigation bar, so you'll need to be a little careful to resize the segmented control to the right size.

Next, with the segmented control still selected, bring up the attributes inspector, and change the number of segments from *2* to *4*. Then double-click each segment and change the titles of the four segments to *Line, Rect, Ellipse, and Image*, in that order. Switch to the connections inspector, and connect the *Value Changed* event to *File's Owner's changeShape*: action method. Save and close the nib.

> **NOTE:** You may have wondered why we put a navigation bar at the top of the view and a toolbar at the bottom of the view. According to the *Human Interface Guidelines* published by Apple, navigation bars were specifically designed to be placed at the top of the screen and toolbars are designed for the bottom. If you read the descriptions of the *Toolbar* and *Navigation Bar* in Interface Builder's library window, you'll see this design intention spelled out.

Return to Xcode, and make sure that everything is in order by compiling and running your app. You won't be able to draw shapes on the screen yet, but the segmented controls should work, and when you tap the *Image* segment in the bottom control, the color controls should disappear.

Now that we have everything working, let's do some drawing.

Adding Quartz Drawing Code

We're ready to add the code that does the drawing. We'll draw a line, some shapes, and an image.

Drawing the Line

Back in Xcode, edit *QuartzFunView.m*, and replace the commented-out `drawRect`: method with this one:

```
- (void)drawRect:(CGRect)rect {
    CGContextRef context = UIGraphicsGetCurrentContext();

    CGContextSetLineWidth(context, 2.0);
    CGContextSetStrokeColorWithColor(context, currentColor.CGColor);

switch (shapeType) {
        case kLineShape:
            CGContextMoveToPoint(context, firstTouch.x, firstTouch.y);
            CGContextAddLineToPoint(context, lastTouch.x, lastTouch.y);
            CGContextStrokePath(context);
```

```
            break;
        case kRectShape:
            break;
        case kEllipseShape:
            break;
        case kImageShape:
            break;
        default:
            break;
    }
}
```

We start things off by retrieving a reference to the current context so we know where to draw.

```
CGContextRef context = UIGraphicsGetCurrentContext();
```

Next, we set the line width to 2.0, which means that any line that we stroke will be 2 pixels wide.

```
CGContextSetLineWidth(context, 2.0);
```

After that, we set the color for stroking lines. Since UIColor has a CGColor property, which is what this method needs, we use that property of our currentColor instance variable to pass the correct color onto this function.

```
CGContextSetStrokeColorWithColor(context, currentColor.CGColor);
```

We use a switch to jump to the appropriate code for each shape type. We'll start off with the code to handle kLineShape, get that working, and then we'll add code for each shape in turn as we make our way through this chapter.

```
switch (shapeType) {
    case kLineShape:
```

To draw a line, we tell the graphics context to create a path starting at the first place the user touched. Remember that we stored that value in the touchesBegan: method, so it will always reflect the start point of the most recent touch or drag.

```
CGContextMoveToPoint(context, firstTouch.x, firstTouch.y);
```

Next, we draw a line from that spot to the last spot the user touched. If the user's finger is still in contact with the screen, lastTouch contains Mr. Finger's current location. If the user is no longer touching the screen, lastTouch contains the location of the user's finger when it was lifted off the screen.

```
CGContextAddLineToPoint(context, lastTouch.x, lastTouch.y);
```

Then we just stroke the path. This function will stroke the line we just drew using the color and width we set earlier:

```
CGContextStrokePath(context);
```

After that, we finish the switch statement, and that's it for now.

```
            break;
        case kRectShape:
            break;
```

```
    case kEllipseShape:
        break;
    case kImageShape:
        break;
    default:
        break;
}
```

At this point, you should be able to compile and run once more. The *Rect, Ellipse,* and *Shape* options won't work, but you should be able to draw lines just fine using any of the color choices (see Figure 14–11).

Figure 14–11. *The line-drawing part of our application is now complete. Here, we are drawing using the color red.*

Drawing the Rectangle and Ellipse

Let's write the code to draw the rectangle and the ellipse at the same time, since Quartz 2D implements both of these objects in basically the same way. Make the following changes to your drawRect: method:

```
- (void)drawRect:(CGRect)rect {
    if (currentColor == nil)
        self.currentColor = [UIColor redColor];

    CGContextRef context = UIGraphicsGetCurrentContext();

    CGContextSetLineWidth(context, 2.0);
    CGContextSetStrokeColorWithColor(context, currentColor.CGColor);
```

```
        CGContextSetFillColorWithColor(context, currentColor.CGColor);
        CGRect currentRect = CGRectMake(firstTouch.x,
                                        firstTouch.y,
                                        lastTouch.x - firstTouch.x,
                                        lastTouch.y - firstTouch.y);

    switch (shapeType) {
        case kLineShape:
            CGContextMoveToPoint(context, firstTouch.x, firstTouch.y);
            CGContextAddLineToPoint(context, lastTouch.x, lastTouch.y);
            CGContextStrokePath(context);
            break;
        case kRectShape:
            CGContextAddRect(context, currentRect);
            CGContextDrawPath(context, kCGPathFillStroke);
            break;
        case kEllipseShape:
            CGContextAddEllipseInRect(context, currentRect);
            CGContextDrawPath(context, kCGPathFillStroke);
            break;
        case kImageShape:
            break;
        default:
            break;
    }
}
```

Because we want to paint both the ellipse and the rectangle in a solid color, we add a call to set the fill color using currentColor.

```
CGContextSetFillColorWithColor(context, currentColor.CGColor);
```

Next, we declare a CGRect variable. We'll use currentRect to hold the rectangle described by the user's drag. Remember that a CGRect has two members: size and origin. A function called CGRectMake() lets us create a CGRect by specifying the x, y, width, and height values, so we use that to make our rectangle. The code to make the rectangle is pretty straightforward. We use the point stored in firstTouch to create the origin. Then we figure out the size by getting the difference between the two x values and the two y values. Note that depending on the direction of the drag, one or both size values may end up with negative numbers, but that's OK. A CGRect with a negative size will simply be rendered in the opposite direction of its origin point (to the left for a negative width; upward for a negative height).

```
        CGRect currentRect = CGRectMake(firstTouch.x,
                                        firstTouch.y,
                                        lastTouch.x - firstTouch.x,
                                        lastTouch.y - firstTouch.y);
```

Once we have this rectangle defined, drawing either a rectangle or an ellipse is as easy as calling two functions: one to draw the rectangle or ellipse in the CGRect we defined, and the other to stroke and fill it.

```
        case kRectShape:
            CGContextAddRect(context, currentRect);
```

```
                CGContextDrawPath(context, kCGPathFillStroke);
                break;
            case kEllipseShape:
                CGContextAddEllipseInRect(context, currentRect);
                CGContextDrawPath(context, kCGPathFillStroke);
                break;
```

Compile and run your application and try out the *Rect* and *Ellipse* tools to see how you like them. Don't forget to change colors now and again and to try out the random color.

Drawing the Image

For our last trick, let's draw an image. There is an image in the *14 QuartzFun* folder called *iphone.png* that you can add to your *Resources* folder, or you can add any *.png* file you want to use, as long as you remember to change the file name in your code to point to that image.

Add the following code to your drawRect: method:

```
- (void)drawRect:(CGRect)rect {
    if (currentColor == nil)
        self.currentColor = [UIColor redColor];

    CGContextRef context = UIGraphicsGetCurrentContext();
    CGContextSetLineWidth(context, 2.0);
    CGContextSetStrokeColorWithColor(context, currentColor.CGColor);

    CGContextSetFillColorWithColor(context, currentColor.CGColor);
    CGRect currentRect = CGRectMake(firstTouch.x,
                                    firstTouch.y,
                                    lastTouch.x - firstTouch.x,
                                    lastTouch.y - firstTouch.y);

    switch (shapeType) {
        case kLineShape:
            CGContextMoveToPoint(context, firstTouch.x, firstTouch.y);
            CGContextAddLineToPoint(context, lastTouch.x, lastTouch.y);
            CGContextStrokePath(context);
            break;
        case kRectShape:
            CGContextAddRect(context, currentRect);
            CGContextDrawPath(context, kCGPathFillStroke);
            break;
        case kEllipseShape:
            CGContextAddEllipseInRect(context, currentRect);
            CGContextDrawPath(context, kCGPathFillStroke);
            break;
        case kImageShape: {
            CGFloat horizontalOffset = drawImage.size.width / 2;
            CGFloat verticalOffset = drawImage.size.height / 2;
            CGPoint drawPoint = CGPointMake(lastTouch.x - horizontalOffset,
                            lastTouch.y - verticalOffset);
            [drawImage drawAtPoint:drawPoint];
            break;
        }
```

```
        default:
            break;
    }
}
```

> **NOTE:** Notice that in the `switch` statement, we added curly braces around the code under `case kImageShape:`. The compiler has a problem with variables declared in the first line after a `case` statement. These curly braces are our way of telling the compiler to stop complaining. We could also have declared `horizontalOffset` before the `switch` statement, but this approach keeps the related code together.

First, we calculate the center of the image, since we want the image drawn centered on the point where the user last touched. Without this adjustment, the image would be drawn with the upper-left corner at the user's finger, also a valid option. We then make a new CGPoint by subtracting these offsets from the x and y values in `lastTouch`.

```
CGFloat horizontalOffset = drawImage.size.width / 2;
CGFloat verticalOffset = drawImage.size.height / 2;
CGPoint drawPoint = CGPointMake(lastTouch.x - horizontalOffset,
                                lastTouch.y - verticalOffset);
```

Now, we tell the image to draw itself. This line of code will do the trick:

```
[drawImage drawAtPoint:drawPoint];
```

Optimizing the QuartzFun Application

Our application does what we want, but we should consider a bit of optimization. In our little application, you won't notice a slowdown, but in a more complex application, running on a slower processor, you might see some lag.

The problem occurs in *QuartzFunView.m*, in the methods `touchesMoved:` and `touchesEnded:`. Both methods include this line of code:

```
[self setNeedsDisplay];
```

Obviously, this is how we tell our view that something has changed, and it needs to redraw itself. This code works, but it causes the entire view to be erased and redrawn, even if only a tiny bit changed. We do want to erase the screen when we get ready to drag out a new shape, but we don't want to clear the screen several times a second as we drag out our shape.

Rather than forcing the entire view to be redrawn many times during our drag, we can use `setNeedsDisplayInRect:` instead. `setNeedsDisplayInRect:` is an NSView method that marks just one rectangular portion of a view's region as needing redisplay. By using this, we can be more efficient by marking only the part of the view that is affected by the current drawing operation as needing to be redrawn.

We need to redraw not just the rectangle between `firstTouch` and `lastTouch`, but any part of the screen encompassed by the current drag. If the user touched the screen and then scribbled all over, but we redrew only the section between firstTouch and lastTouch, we would leave a lot of stuff drawn on the screen that we don't want.

The solution is to keep track of the entire area that has been affected by a particular drag in a CGRect instance variable. In touchesBegan:, we reset that instance variable to just the point where the user touched. Then in touchesMoved: and touchesEnded:, we use a Core Graphics function to get the union of the current rectangle and the stored rectangle, and we store the resulting rectangle. We also use it to specify which part of the view needs to be redrawn. This approach gives us a running total of the area impacted by the current drag.

Now, we'll calculate the current rectangle in the drawRect: method for use in drawing the ellipse and rectangle shapes. We'll move that calculation into a new method so that it can be used in all three places without repeating code. Ready? Let's do it. Make the following changes to *QuartzFunView.h*:

```
#import <UIKit/UIKit.h>
#import "Constants.h"

@interface QuartzFunView : UIView {
    CGPoint firstTouch;
    CGPoint lastTouch;
    UIColor *currentColor;
    ShapeType shapeType;
    UIImage *drawImage;
    BOOL useRandomColor;
    CGRect redrawRect;
}
@property CGPoint firstTouch;
@property CGPoint lastTouch;
@property (nonatomic, retain) UIColor *currentColor;
@property ShapeType shapeType;
@property (nonatomic, retain) UIImage *drawImage;
@property BOOL useRandomColor;
@property (readonly) CGRect currentRect;
@property CGRect redrawRect;
@end
```

We declare a CGRect called redrawRect that we will use to keep track of the area that needs to be redrawn. We also declare a read-only property called currentRect, which will return that rectangle that we were previously calculating in drawRect:. Notice that it is a property with no underlying instance variable, which is OK, as long as we implement the accessor rather than relying on @synthesize to do it for us.

Switch over to *QuartzFunView.m,* and insert the following code at the top of the file:

```
#import "QuartzFunView.h"

@implementation QuartzFunView
@synthesize firstTouch;
@synthesize lastTouch;
@synthesize currentColor;
```

```
@synthesize shapeType;
@synthesize drawImage;
@synthesize useRandomColor;
@synthesize redrawRect;


- (CGRect)currentRect {
    return CGRectMake (firstTouch.x,
                       firstTouch.y,
                       lastTouch.x - firstTouch.x,
                       lastTouch.y - firstTouch.y);
}
...
```

Now, in the drawRect: method, delete the lines of code where we calculated currentRect, and change all references to currentRect to self.currentRect so that the code uses that new accessor we just created:

```
...
- (void)drawRect:(CGRect)rect {
    CGContextRef context = UIGraphicsGetCurrentContext();

    CGContextSetLineWidth(context, 2.0);
    CGContextSetStrokeColorWithColor(context, currentColor.CGColor);

    CGContextSetFillColorWithColor(context, currentColor.CGColor);

    CGRect currentRect = CGRectMake(firstTouch.x,
            firstTouch.y,
            lastTouch.x - firstTouch.x,
            lastTouch.y - firstTouch.y);

    switch (shapeType) {
        case kLineShape:
            CGContextMoveToPoint(context, firstTouch.x, firstTouch.y);
            CGContextAddLineToPoint(context, lastTouch.x, lastTouch.y);
            CGContextStrokePath(context);
            break;
        case kRectShape:
            CGContextAddRect(context, self.currentRect);
            CGContextDrawPath(context, kCGPathFillStroke);
            break;
        case kEllipseShape:
            CGContextAddEllipseInRect(context, self.currentRect);
            CGContextDrawPath(context, kCGPathFillStroke);
            break;
        case kImageShape: {
            CGFloat horizontalOffset = drawImage.size.width / 2;
            CGFloat verticalOffset = drawImage.size.height / 2;
            CGPoint drawPoint = CGPointMake(lastTouch.x - horizontalOffset,
                            lastTouch.y - verticalOffset);
            [drawImage drawAtPoint:drawPoint];
            break;
        default:
            break;
    }
}
```

...

We also need to make some changes to in touchesEnded:withEvent: and touchesMoved:withEvent:. We need to recalculate the space impacted by the current operation and use that to indicate that only a portion of our view needs to be redrawn:

```
...
- (void)touchesEnded:(NSSet *)touches withEvent:(UIEvent *)event {
    UITouch *touch = [touches anyObject];
    lastTouch = [touch locationInView:self];

    [self setNeedsDisplay];
    if (shapeType == kImageShape) {
        CGFloat horizontalOffset = drawImage.size.width / 2;
        CGFloat verticalOffset = drawImage.size.height / 2;
        redrawRect = CGRectUnion(redrawRect,
            CGRectMake(lastTouch.x - horizontalOffset,
            lastTouch.y - verticalOffset, drawImage.size.width,
            drawImage.size.height));
    }
    else
        redrawRect = CGRectUnion(redrawRect, self.currentRect);
    redrawRect = CGRectInset(redrawRect, -2.0, -2.0);
    [self setNeedsDisplayInRect:redrawRect];
}

- (void)touchesMoved:(NSSet *)touches withEvent:(UIEvent *)event {
    UITouch *touch = [touches anyObject];
    lastTouch = [touch locationInView:self];

    [self setNeedsDisplay];
    if (shapeType == kImageShape) {
        CGFloat horizontalOffset = drawImage.size.width / 2;
        CGFloat verticalOffset = drawImage.size.height / 2;
        redrawRect = CGRectUnion(redrawRect,
            CGRectMake(lastTouch.x - horizontalOffset,
            lastTouch.y - verticalOffset, drawImage.size.width,
            drawImage.size.height));
    }
    redrawRect = CGRectUnion(redrawRect, self.currentRect);
    [self setNeedsDisplayInRect:redrawRect];
}
...
```

With only a few additional lines of code, we reduced the amount of work necessary to redraw our view by getting rid of the need to erase and redraw any portion of the view that wasn't been affected by the current drag. Being kind to your iOS device's precious processor cycles like this can make a big difference in the performance of your applications, especially as they get more complex.

> **NOTE:** If you're interested in a more in-depth exploration of Quartz 2D topics, you might want to take a look at *Beginning iPad Development for iPhone Developers: Mastering the iPad SDK* by Jack Nutting, Dave Wooldridge, and David Mark (Apress, 2010), which covers a lot of Quartz 2D drawing. All the drawing code and explanations in that book apply to the iPhone as well as the iPad.

The GLFun Application

As explained earlier in the chapter, OpenGL ES and Quartz 2D take fundamentally different approaches to drawing. A detailed introduction to OpenGL ES would be a book in and of itself, so we're not going to attempt that here. Instead, we're going to re-create our Quartz 2D application using OpenGL ES, just to give you a sense of the basics and some sample code you can use to kick-start your own OpenGL applications.

Let's get started with our application.

> **TIP:** If you want to create a full-screen OpenGL ES application, you don't need to build it manually. Xcode has a template you can use. It sets up the screen and the buffers for you, and even puts some sample drawing and animation code into the class, so you can see where to put your code. If you want to try this out after you finish up GLFun, create a new *iOS application*, and choose the *OpenGL ES Application* template.

Setting Up the GLFun Application

Create a new *View-based Application* in Xcode, and call it *GLFun*. To save time, copy the files *Constants.h*, *UIColor-Random.h*, *UIColor-Random.m*, and *iphone.png* from the *QuartzFun* project into the *Classes* and *Resources* folders of this new project.

Open GLFunViewController.h, and make the following changes. You should recognize them, as they're identical to the changes we made to *QuartzFunViewController.h*.

```
#import <UIKit/UIKit.h>

@interface GLFunViewController : UIViewController {
    UISegmentedControl *colorControl;
}
@property (nonatomic, retain) IBOutlet UISegmentedControl *colorControl;
- (IBAction)changeColor:(id)sender;
- (IBAction)changeShape:(id)sender;
@end
```

Switch over to *GLFunViewController.m*, and make the following changes at the beginning of the file. Again, these changes should look very familiar to you.

```
#import "GLFunViewController.h"
```

```
#import "GLFunView.h"
#import "Constants.h"

@implementation GLFunViewController
@synthesize colorControl;

- (IBAction)changeColor:(id)sender {
    UISegmentedControl *control = sender;
    NSInteger index = [control selectedSegmentIndex];

    GLFunView *glView = (GLFunView *)self.view;

    switch (index) {
        case kRedColorTab:
            glView.currentColor = [UIColor redColor];
            glView.useRandomColor = NO;
            break;
        case kBlueColorTab:
            glView.currentColor = [UIColor blueColor];
            glView.useRandomColor = NO;
            break;
        case kYellowColorTab:
            glView.currentColor = [UIColor yellowColor];
            glView.useRandomColor = NO;
            break;
        case kGreenColorTab:
            glView.currentColor = [UIColor greenColor];
            glView.useRandomColor = NO;
            break;
        case kRandomColorTab:
            glView.useRandomColor = YES;
            break;
        default:
            break;
    }
}

- (IBAction)changeShape:(id)sender {
    UISegmentedControl *control = sender;
    [(GLFunView *)self.view setShapeType:[control selectedSegmentIndex]];
    if ([control selectedSegmentIndex] == kImageShape)
        [colorControl setHidden:YES];
    else
        [colorControl setHidden:NO];
}
...
```

Let's not forget to deal with memory cleanup:

```
...
- (void)viewDidUnload {
    // Release any retained subviews of the main view.
    // e.g. self.myOutlet = nil;
    self.colorControl = nil;
```

```
    [super viewDidUnload];
}

- (void)dealloc {
    [colorControl release];
    [super dealloc];
}
...
```

The only difference between this and *QuartzFunController.m* is that we're referencing a view called GLFunView instead of one called QuartzFunView. The code that does our drawing is contained in a subclass of UIView. Since we're doing the drawing in a completely different way this time, it makes sense to use a new class to contain that drawing code.

Before we proceed, you'll need to add a few more files to your project. In the *14 GLFun* folder, you'll find four files named *Texture2D.h*, *Texture2D.m*, *OpenGLES2DView.h*, and *OpenGLES2DView.m*. The code in the first two files was written by Apple to make drawing images in OpenGL ES much easier than it otherwise would be. The second pair of files is a class we've provided based on sample code from Apple that configures OpenGL to do two-dimensional drawing (in other words, we've done the necessary configuration for you). You can feel free to use any of these files in your own programs if you wish.

Drawing with OpenGL

OpenGL ES doesn't have sprites or images, per se; it has one kind of image called a **texture**. Textures must be drawn onto a shape or object. The way you draw an image in OpenGL ES is to draw a square (technically speaking, it's two triangles), and then map a texture onto that square so that it exactly matches the square's size. Texture2D encapsulates that relatively complex process into a single, easy-to-use class.

OpenGLES2DView is a subclass of UIView that uses OpenGL to do its drawing. We set up this view so that the coordinate systems of OpenGL ES and the coordinate system of the view are mapped on a one-to-one basis. OpenGL ES is a three-dimensional system. OpenGLES2DView maps the OpenGL three-dimensional world to the pixels of our two-dimensional view.

Note that, despite the one-to-one relationship between the view and the OpenGL context, the y coordinates are still flipped. We need to translate the y coordinate from the view coordinate system, where increases in y represent moving down, to the OpenGL coordinate system, where increases in y represent moving up.

To use the OpenGLES2DView class, first subclass it, and then implement the draw method to do your actual drawing, just as we do in the following code. You can also implement any other methods you need in your view, such as the touch-related methods we used in the QuartzFun example.

Select the *Classes* folder, and then create a new file using the *Objective-C Class* template from the *Cocoa Touch Class* section. Select *NSObject* for *Subclass of*, and call it *GLFunView.m*. Be sure to create the header as well.

Single-click *GLFunView.h,* and make the following changes:

```
#import <Foundation/Foundation.h>
#import "Constants.h"
#import "OpenGLES2DView.h"

@class Texture2D;

@interface GLFunView : NSObject {
@interface GLFunView : OpenGLES2DView {
    CGPoint firstTouch;
    CGPoint lastTouch;
    UIColor *currentColor;
    BOOL useRandomColor;

    ShapeType shapeType;

    Texture2D *sprite;
}
@property CGPoint firstTouch;
@property CGPoint lastTouch;
@property (nonatomic, retain) UIColor *currentColor;
@property BOOL useRandomColor;
@property ShapeType shapeType;
@property (nonatomic, retain) Texture2D *sprite;
@end
```

This class is similar to *QuartzFunView.h*, but instead of using UIImage to hold our image, we use a Texture2D to simplify the process of drawing images into an OpenGL ES context. We also change the superclass from UIView to OpenGLES2DView so that our view becomes an OpenGL-backed view set up for doing two-dimensional drawing.

Switch over to *GLFunView.m*, and make the following changes:

```
#import "GLFunView.h"
#import "UIColor-Random.h"
#import "Texture2D.h"

@implementation GLFunView
@synthesize firstTouch;
@synthesize lastTouch;
@synthesize currentColor;
@synthesize useRandomColor;
@synthesize shapeType;
@synthesize sprite;

- (id)initWithCoder:(NSCoder*)coder {
    if (self = [super initWithCoder:coder]) {
        currentColor = [[UIColor redColor] retain];
        useRandomColor = NO;
        sprite = [[Texture2D alloc] initWithImage:[UIImage
```

```
                                        imageNamed:@"iphone.png"]];
        glBindTexture(GL_TEXTURE_2D, sprite.name);
    }
    return self;
}

- (void)draw  {
    glLoadIdentity();

    glClearColor(0.78f, 0.78f, 0.78f, 1.0f);
    glClear(GL_COLOR_BUFFER_BIT);

    CGColorRef color = currentColor.CGColor;
    const CGFloat *components = CGColorGetComponents(color);
    CGFloat red = components[0];
    CGFloat green = components[1];
    CGFloat blue = components[2];

    glColor4f(red,green, blue, 1.0);
    switch (shapeType) {
        case kLineShape: {
            glDisable(GL_TEXTURE_2D);
            GLfloat vertices[4];

            // Convert coordinates
            vertices[0] = firstTouch.x;
            vertices[1] = self.frame.size.height - firstTouch.y;
            vertices[2] = lastTouch.x;
            vertices[3] = self.frame.size.height - lastTouch.y;
            glLineWidth(2.0);
            glVertexPointer(2, GL_FLOAT, 0, vertices);
            glDrawArrays (GL_LINES, 0, 2);
            break;
        }
        case kRectShape: {
            glDisable(GL_TEXTURE_2D);
            // Calculate bounding rect and store in vertices
            GLfloat vertices[8];
            GLfloat minX = (firstTouch.x > lastTouch.x) ?
            lastTouch.x : firstTouch.x;
            GLfloat minY = (self.frame.size.height - firstTouch.y >
                            self.frame.size.height - lastTouch.y) ?
            self.frame.size.height - lastTouch.y :
            self.frame.size.height - firstTouch.y;
            GLfloat maxX = (firstTouch.x > lastTouch.x) ?
            firstTouch.x : lastTouch.x;
            GLfloat maxY = (self.frame.size.height - firstTouch.y >
                            self.frame.size.height - lastTouch.y) ?
            self.frame.size.height - firstTouch.y :
            self.frame.size.height - lastTouch.y;

            vertices[0] = maxX;
            vertices[1] = maxY;
            vertices[2] = minX;
```

```objc
                    vertices[3] = maxY;
                    vertices[4] = minX;
                    vertices[5] = minY;
                    vertices[6] = maxX;
                    vertices[7] = minY;

                    glVertexPointer (2, GL_FLOAT , 0, vertices);
                    glDrawArrays (GL_TRIANGLE_FAN, 0, 4);
                    break;
            }
            case kEllipseShape: {
                    glDisable(GL_TEXTURE_2D);
                    GLfloat vertices[720];

                    GLfloat xradius = fabsf((firstTouch.x - lastTouch.x) / 2);
                    GLfloat yradius = fabsf((firstTouch.y - lastTouch.y) / 2);
                    for (int i = 0; i <= 720; i += 2) {
                        GLfloat xOffset = (firstTouch.x > lastTouch.x) ?
                            lastTouch.x + xradius : firstTouch.x + xradius;
                        GLfloat yOffset = (firstTouch.y < lastTouch.y) ?
                            self.frame.size.height - lastTouch.y + yradius :
                            self.frame.size.height - firstTouch.y + yradius;
                        vertices[i] = (cos(degreesToRadian(i / 2))*xradius) + xOffset;
                        vertices[i+1] = (sin(degreesToRadian(i / 2))*yradius) +
                            yOffset;
                    }

                    glVertexPointer(2, GL_FLOAT , 0, vertices);
                    glDrawArrays (GL_TRIANGLE_FAN, 0, 360);
                    break;
            }
            case kImageShape:
                    glEnable(GL_TEXTURE_2D);
                    [sprite drawAtPoint:CGPointMake(lastTouch.x,
                                    self.frame.size.height - lastTouch.y)];
                    break;
            default:
                    break;
    }

    glBindRenderbufferOES(GL_RENDERBUFFER_OES, viewRenderbuffer);
    [context presentRenderbuffer:GL_RENDERBUFFER_OES];
}

- (void)dealloc {
    [currentColor release];
    [sprite release];
    [super dealloc];
}

- (void)touchesBegan:(NSSet *)touches withEvent:(UIEvent *)event {
    if (useRandomColor)
        self.currentColor = [UIColor randomColor];
```

```
        UITouch* touch = [[event touchesForView:self] anyObject];
        firstTouch = [touch locationInView:self];
        lastTouch = [touch locationInView:self];
        [self draw];
}

- (void)touchesMoved:(NSSet *)touches withEvent:(UIEvent *)event {
UITouch *touch = [touches anyObject];
        lastTouch = [touch locationInView:self];

        [self draw];
}

- (void)touchesEnded:(NSSet *)touches withEvent:(UIEvent *)event {
        UITouch *touch = [touches anyObject];
        lastTouch = [touch locationInView:self];

        [self draw];
}
@end
```

You can see that using OpenGL isn't by any means easier or more concise than using Quartz. Although OpenGL ES is more powerful than Quartz 2D, you're also closer to the metal, so to speak. OpenGL can be daunting at times.

Because this view is being loaded from a nib, we added an initWithCoder: method, and in it, we create and assign a UIColor to currentColor. We also defaulted useRandomColor to NO and created our Texture2D object.

After the initWithCoder: method, we have our draw method, which is where you can really see the difference between the two libraries.

Let's take a look at process of drawing a line. Here's how we drew the line in the Quartz version (we've removed the code that's not directly relevant to drawing):

```
        CGContextRef context = UIGraphicsGetCurrentContext();
        CGContextSetLineWidth(context, 2.0);
        CGContextSetStrokeColorWithColor(context, currentColor.CGColor);
        CGContextMoveToPoint(context, firstTouch.x, firstTouch.y);
        CGContextAddLineToPoint(context, lastTouch.x, lastTouch.y);
        CGContextStrokePath(context);
```

In OpenGL, we needed to take a few more steps to draw that same line. First, we reset the virtual world so that any rotations, translations, or other transforms that might have been applied to it are gone.

```
        glLoadIdentity();
```

Next, we clear the background to the same shade of gray that was used in the Quartz version of the application.

```
        glClearColor(0.78, 0.78f, 0.78f, 1.0f);
        glClear(GL_COLOR_BUFFER_BIT);
```

After that, we need to set the OpenGL drawing color by dissecting a UIColor and pulling the individual RGB components out of it. Fortunately, because we used the convenience class methods, we don't need to worry about which color model the UIColor uses. We can safely assume it will use the RGBA color space.

```
CGColorRef color = currentColor.CGColor;
const CGFloat *components = CGColorGetComponents(color);
CGFloat red = components[0];
CGFloat green = components[1];
CGFloat blue = components[2];
glColor4f(red,green, blue, 1.0);
```

Next, we turn off OpenGL ES's ability to map textures.

```
glDisable(GL_TEXTURE_2D);
```

Any drawing code that fires from the time we make this call until there's a call to glEnable(GL_TEXTURE_2D) will be drawn without a texture, which is what we want. If we allowed a texture to be used, the color we just set wouldn't show.

To draw a line, we need two vertices, which means we need an array with four elements. As we've discussed, a point in two-dimensional space is represented by two values: x and y. In Quartz, we used a CGPoint struct to hold these. In OpenGL, points are not embedded in structs. Instead, we pack an array with all the points that make up the shape we need to draw. So, to draw a line from point (100, 150) to point (200, 250) in OpenGL ES, we need to create a vertex array that looks like this:

```
vertex[0] = 100;
vertex[1] = 150;
vertex[2] = 200;
vertex[3] = 250;
```

Our array has the format {x1, y1, x2, y2, x3, y3}. The next code in this method converts two CGPoint structs into a vertex array.

```
GLfloat vertices[4];
vertices[0] = firstTouch.x;
vertices[1] = self.frame.size.height - firstTouch.y;
vertices[2] = lastTouch.x;
vertices[3] = self.frame.size.height - lastTouch.y;
```

Once we've defined the vertex array that describes what we want to draw (in this example, a line), we specify the line width, pass the array into OpenGL ES using the method glVertexPointer(), and tell OpenGL ES to draw the arrays.

```
glLineWidth(2.0);
glVertexPointer (2, GL_FLOAT , 0, vertices);
glDrawArrays (GL_LINES, 0, 2);
```

Whenever we finish drawing in OpenGL ES, we need to instruct it to render its buffer, and tell our view's context to show the newly rendered buffer.

```
glBindRenderbufferOES(GL_RENDERBUFFER_OES, viewRenderbuffer);
[context presentRenderbuffer:GL_RENDERBUFFER_OES];
```

To clarify, the process of drawing in OpenGL ES consists of three steps:

1. Draw in the context.

2. After all of your drawing is complete, render the context into the buffer.

3. Present your render buffer, which is when the pixels are actually drawn onto the screen.

As you can see, the OpenGL example is considerably longer.

The difference between Quartz 2D and OpenGL ES becomes even more dramatic when we look at the process of drawing an ellipse. OpenGL ES doesn't know how to draw an ellipse. OpenGL, the big brother and predecessor to OpenGL ES, has a number of convenience functions for generating common two- and three-dimensional shapes, but those convenience functions are some of the functionality that was stripped out of OpenGL ES to make it more streamlined and suitable for use in embedded devices like the iPhone. As a result, a lot more responsibility falls into the developer's lap.

As a reminder, here is how we drew the ellipse using Quartz 2D:

```
CGContextRef context = UIGraphicsGetCurrentContext();
CGContextSetLineWidth(context, 2.0);
CGContextSetStrokeColorWithColor(context, currentColor.CGColor);
CGContextSetFillColorWithColor(context, currentColor.CGColor);
CGRect currentRect;
CGContextAddEllipseInRect(context, self.currentRect);
CGContextDrawPath(context, kCGPathFillStroke);
```

For the OpenGL ES version, we start off with the same steps as before, resetting any movement or rotations, clearing the background to white, and setting the draw color based on currentColor.

```
glLoadIdentity();
glClearColor(1.0f, 1.0f, 1.0f, 1.0f);
glClear(GL_COLOR_BUFFER_BIT);
glDisable(GL_TEXTURE_2D);
CGColorRef color = currentColor.CGColor;
const CGFloat *components = CGColorGetComponents(color);
CGFloat red = components[0];
CGFloat green = components[1];
CGFloat blue = components[2];
glColor4f(red,green, blue, 1.0);
```

Since OpenGL ES doesn't know how to draw an ellipse, we need to roll our own, which means dredging up painful memories of Ms. Picklebaum's geometry class. We'll define a vertex array that holds 720 GLfloats, which will hold an x and a y position for 360 points, one for each degree around the circle. We could change the number of points to increase or decrease the smoothness of the circle. This approach looks good on any view that will fit on the iPhone screen, but probably does require more processing than strictly necessary if you're just drawing smaller circles.

```
GLfloat vertices[720];
```

Next, we'll figure out the horizontal and vertical radii of the ellipse based on the two points stored in firstTouch and lastTouch.

```
GLfloat xradius = fabsf((firstTouch.x - lastTouch.x)/2);
GLfloat yradius = fabsf((firstTouch.y - lastTouch.y)/2);
```

Then we'll loop around the circle, calculating the correct points around the circle.

```
for (int i = 0; i <= 720; i+=2) {
    GLfloat xOffset = (firstTouch.x > lastTouch.x) ?
        lastTouch.x + xradius : firstTouch.x + xradius;
    GLfloat yOffset = (firstTouch.y < lastTouch.y) ?
        self.frame.size.height - lastTouch.y + yradius :
        self.frame.size.height - firstTouch.y + yradius;
    vertices[i] = (cos(degreesToRadian(i / 2))*xradius) + xOffset;
    vertices[i+1] = (sin(degreesToRadian(i / 2))*yradius) +
        yOffset;
}
```

Finally, we'll feed the vertex array to OpenGL ES, tell it to draw it and render it, and then tell our context to present the newly rendered image.

```
glVertexPointer (2, GL_FLOAT , 0, vertices);
glDrawArrays (GL_TRIANGLE_FAN, 0, 360);
glBindRenderbufferOES(GL_RENDERBUFFER_OES, viewRenderbuffer);
[context presentRenderbuffer:GL_RENDERBUFFER_OES];
```

We won't review the rectangle method, because it uses the same basic technique. We define a vertex array with the four vertices to define the rectangle, and then we render and present it.

There's also not much to talk about with the image drawing, since that lovely Texture2D class from Apple makes drawing a sprite just as easy as it is in Quartz 2D. There is one important thing to notice there, though:

```
glEnable(GL_TEXTURE_2D);
```

Since it is possible that the ability to draw textures was previously disabled, we must make sure it's enabled before we attempt to use the Texture2D class.

After the draw method, we have the same touch-related methods as the previous version. The only difference is that instead of telling the view that it needs to be displayed, we just call the draw method. We don't need to tell OpenGL ES which parts of the screen will be updated; it will figure that out and leverage hardware acceleration to draw in the most efficient manner.

Finishing GLFun

Now, you can edit *GLFunViewController.xib* and design the interface. We're not going to walk you through it this time, but if you get stuck, you can refer to the "Updating QuartzFunViewController.xib" section earlier in this chapter for the specific steps. If you would rather not go through all the steps, just copy *QuartzFunViewController.xib* into the current project, rename it, and use that as a starting point. In either case, be sure to change the class of the main view to *GLFunView* instead of *QuartzFunView*.

Before you can compile and run this program, you'll need to link in two frameworks to your project. Follow the instructions in Chapter 7 for adding the Audio Toolbox framework (in the "Linking in the Audio Toolbox Framework" section), but instead of selecting *AudioToolbox.framework*, select *OpenGLES.framework* and *QuartzCore.framework*.

Frameworks added? Good. Go run your project. It should look just like the Quartz version. You've now seen enough OpenGL ES to get you started.

> **NOTE:** If you're interested in using OpenGL ES in your iPhone applications, you can find the OpenGL ES specification, along with links to books, documentation, and forums where OpenGL ES issues are discussed, at http://www.khronos.org/opengles/. Also, visit http://www.khronos.org/developers/resources/opengles/, and search for the word "tutorial." And be sure to check out the OpenGL tutorial in Jeff LaMarche's iPhone blog, at http://iphonedevelopment.blogspot.com/2009/05/opengl-es-from-ground-up-table-of.html.

Drawing to a Close

In this chapter, we've really just scratched the surface of the iOS drawing ability. You should feel pretty comfortable with Quartz 2D now, and with some occasional references to Apple's documentation, you can probably handle most any drawing requirement that comes your way. You should also have a basic understanding of what OpenGL ES is and how it integrates with iOS view system.

Next up? You're going to learn how to add gestural support to your applications.

Chapter 15

Taps, Touches, and Gestures

The screens of the iPhone, iPod touch, and iPad—with their crisp, bright, touch-sensitive display—are truly things of beauty and masterpieces of engineering. The multitouch screen common to all iOS devices is one of the key factors in the platform's tremendous usability. Because the screen can detect multiple touches at the same time and track them independently, applications are able to detect a wide range of gestures, giving the user power that goes beyond the interface.

As an example, suppose you're in the Mail application staring at a long list of junk e-mail that you want to delete. You have several options:

- You can tap each e-mail message individually, tap the trash icon to delete the message, and then wait for the next message to download, deleting each one in turn. This method is best if you want to read each e-mail message before you delete it.

- From the list of e-mail messages, you can tap the *Edit* button in the upper-right corner, tap each e-mail row to mark it, and then hit the *Delete* button to delete all marked messages. This method is best if you don't need to read each message before deleting it.

- Swipe an e-mail message in the list from side-to-side. This gesture produces a *Delete* button for that e-mail. Tap the *Delete* button, and the message is deleted.

These examples are just a few of the countless gestures that are made possible by the multitouch display. You can pinch your fingers together to zoom out while viewing a picture, or reverse-pinch to zoom in. You can long-press on an icon to turn on "jiggly mode," which allows you to delete applications from your iOS device.

In this chapter, we're going to look at the underlying architecture that lets you detect gestures. You'll learn how to detect the most common ones, and how to create and detect a completely new gesture.

Multitouch Terminology

Before we dive into the architecture, let's go over some basic vocabulary:

- **Event:** Generated when you interact with the device's multitouch screen. A gesture is passed through the system inside a series of events. Events contain information about the touch or touches that occurred. Events are passed through the responder chain, as discussed in the next section.

- **Gesture**: Any sequence of events that happens from the time you touch the screen with one or more fingers until you lift your fingers off the screen. No matter how long it takes, as long as one or more fingers are still against the screen, you are within a gesture (unless a system event, such as an incoming phone call, interrupts it). Note that Cocoa Touch doesn't expose any class or structure that represents a gesture. In a sense, a gesture is a verb, and a running app can watch the user input stream to see if one is happening.

- **Touch**: Refers to a finger being placed on the screen, dragging across the screen, or being lifted from the screen. The number of touches involved in a gesture is equal to the number of fingers on the screen at the same time. You can actually put all five fingers on the screen, and as long as they aren't too close to each other, iOS can recognize and track each of them. Now, there aren't many useful five-finger gestures, but it's nice to know the iOS can handle one if necessary.

> **NOTE:** In fact, experimentation has shown that the iPad can handle up to 11 simultaneous touches! This may seem excessive, but could be useful if you're working on a multiplayer game, where several players are interacting with the screen at the same time.

- **Tap**: Happens when the user touches the screen with a single finger and then immediately lifts the finger off the screen without moving it around. The iOS device keeps track of the number of taps and can tell you if the user double-tapped or triple-tapped, or even tapped 20 times. It handles all the timing and other work necessary to differentiate between two single-taps and a double-tap, for example.

- **Gesture recognizer**: An object that knows how to watch the stream of events generated by a user and recognize when the user is touching and dragging in a way that matches a predefined gesture. Included in iOS 3.2 and up, the `UIGestureRecognizer` class and its various subclasses can help take a lot of work off your hands when you want to watch for common gestures. It nicely encapsulates the work of looking for a gesture, and it can be easily applied to any view in your application.

The Responder Chain

Since gestures are passed through the system inside events, and events are passed through the **responder chain**, you need to understand how the responder chain works in order to handle gestures properly.

If you've worked with Cocoa for Mac OS X, you're probably familiar with the concept of a responder chain, as the same basic mechanism is used in both Cocoa and Cocoa Touch. If this is new material, don't worry; we'll explain how it works.

Several times in this book, we've mentioned the first responder, which is usually the object with which the user is currently interacting. The first responder is the start of the responder chain. There are other responders as well.

Any class that has UIResponder as one of its superclasses is a **responder**. UIView is a subclass of UIResponder, and UIControl is a subclass of UIView, so all views and all controls are responders. UIViewController is also a subclass of UIResponder, meaning that it is a responder, as are all of its subclasses like UINavigationController and UITabBarController. Responders, then, are so named because they respond to system-generated events, such as screen touches.

Up the Responder Chain

If the first responder doesn't handle a particular event, such as a gesture, it passes that event up the responder chain. If the next object in the chain responds to that particular event, it will usually consume the event, which stops the event's progression through the responder chain.

In some cases, if a responder only partially handles an event, that responder will take an action and forward the event to the next responder in the chain. That's not usually what happens, though. Normally, when an object responds to an event, that's the end of the line for the event. If the event goes through the entire responder chain and no object handles the event, the event is then discarded.

Let's take a more specific look at the responder chain. The first responder is almost always a view or control, and it gets the first shot at responding to an event. If the first responder doesn't handle the event, it passes the event to its view controller. If the view controller doesn't consume the event, the event is then passed to the first responder's parent view. If the parent view doesn't respond, the event will go to the parent view's controller, if it has one. The event will proceed up the view hierarchy, with each view and then that view's controller getting a chance to handle the event. If the event makes it all the way up through the view hierarchy, the event is passed to the application's window. If the window doesn't handle the event, it passes that event to the application's UIApplication object instance. If UIApplication doesn't respond to the event, it goes gently into that good night.

This process is important for a number of reasons. First, it controls the way gestures can be handled. Let's say a user is looking at a table and swipes a finger across a row of that table. Which object handles that gesture?

If the swipe is within a view or control that's a subview of the table view cell, that view or control will get a chance to respond. If it doesn't, the table view cell gets a chance. In an application like Mail, where a swipe can be used to delete a message, the table view cell probably needs to look at that event to see if it contains a swipe gesture. Most table view cells don't respond to gestures. In that case, the event proceeds up to the table view, and then up the rest of the responder chain, until something responds to that event or it reaches the end of the line.

Forwarding an Event: Keeping the Responder Chain Alive

Let's take a step back to that table view cell in the Mail application. We don't know the internal details of Apple's Mail application, but let's assume, for the nonce, that the table view cell handles the delete swipe, and only the delete swipe. That table view cell must implement the methods related to receiving touch events (which you'll see in the next section) so that it can check to see if that event contained a swipe gesture. If the event contains a swipe, then the table view cell takes an action, and that's that; the event goes no further.

If the event doesn't contain a swipe gesture, the table view cell is responsible for forwarding that event manually to the next object in the responder chain. If it doesn't do its forwarding job, the table and other objects up the chain will never get a chance to respond, and the application may not function as the user expects. That table view cell could prevent other views from recognizing a gesture.

Whenever you respond to a touch event, you need to keep in mind that your code doesn't work in a vacuum. If an object intercepts an event that it doesn't handle, it needs to pass it along manually, by calling the same method on the next responder. Here's a bit of fictional code:

```
-(void)respondToFictionalEvent:(UIEvent *)event {
    if (someCondition)
        [self handleEvent:event];
    else
        [self.nextResponder respondToFictionalEvent:event];
}
```

Notice how we call the same method on the next responder. That's how to be a good responder chain citizen. Fortunately, most of the time, methods that respond to an event also consume the event. But it's important to know that if that's not the case, you need to make sure the event gets pushed back into the responder chain.

The Multitouch Architecture

Now that you know a little about the responder chain, let's look at the process of handling gestures. As you've learned, gestures are passed along the responder chain, embedded in events. That means that the code to handle any kind of interaction with the multitouch screen needs to be contained in an object in the responder chain. Generally, that means you can either choose to embed that code in a subclass of UIView or embed the code in a UIViewController.

So does this code belong in the view or in the view controller?

Where to Put Touch Code

If the view needs to do something to itself based on the user's touches, the code probably belongs in the class that defines that view. For example, many control classes, such as UISwitch and UISlider, respond to touch-related events. A UISwitch might want to turn itself on or off based on a touch. The folks who created the UISwitch class embedded gesture-handling code in the class so the UISwitch can respond to a touch.

Often, however, when the gesture being processed affects more than the object being touched, the gesture code belongs in the view's controller class. For example, if the user makes a gesture touching one row that indicates that all rows should be deleted, the gesture should be handled by code in the view controller.

The way you respond to touches and gestures in both situations is exactly the same, regardless of the class to which the code belongs.

The Four Touch-Notification Methods

Four methods are used to notify a responder about touches: touchesBegan:withEvent:, touchesMoved:withEvent:, touchesEnded:withEvent:, and touchesCancelled:withEvent:.

When the user first touches the screen, the iOS device looks for a responder that has a method called touchesBegan:withEvent:. To find out when the user first begins a gesture or taps the screen, implement this method in your view or your view controller. Here's an example of what that method might look like:

```
- (void)touchesBegan:(NSSet *)touches withEvent:(UIEvent *)event {

    NSUInteger numTaps = [[touches anyObject] tapCount];
    NSUInteger numTouches = [touches count];

    // Do something here.
}
```

This method, and all of the touch-related methods, are passed an NSSet instance called touches and an instance of UIEvent. You can determine the number of fingers currently pressed against the screen by getting a count of the objects in touches. Every object in touches is a UITouch event that represents one finger touching the screen. If this touch is part of a series of taps, you can find out the tap count by asking any of the UITouch objects. If touches contains more than one object, you know the tap count must be one, because the system keeps tap counts only as long as just one finger is being used to tap the screen. In the preceding example, if numTouches is 2, you know the user tapped the screen with two fingers at once.

All of the objects in touches may not be relevant to the view or view controller where you've implemented this method. A table view cell, for example, probably doesn't care about touches that are in other rows or in the navigation bar. You can get a subset of touches that has only those touches that fall within a particular view from the event, like so:

```
NSSet *myTouches = [event touchesForView:self.view];
```

Every UITouch represents a different finger, and each finger is located at a different position on the screen. You can find out the position of a specific finger using the UITouch object. It will even translate the point into the view's local coordinate system if you ask it to, like this:

```
CGPoint point = [touch locationInView:self];
```

You can get notified while the user is moving fingers across the screen by implementing touchesMoved:withEvent:. This method is called multiple times during a long drag; each time it is called, you will get another set of touches and another event. In addition to being able to find out each finger's current position from the UITouch objects, you can also find out the previous location of that touch, which is the finger's position the last time either touchesMoved:withEvent: or touchesBegan:withEvent: was called.

When the user's fingers are removed from the screen, another event, touchesEnded:withEvent:, is invoked. When this method is called, you know that the user is finished with a gesture.

The final touch-related method that responders might implement is touchesCancelled:withEvent:. This method is called if the user is in the middle of a gesture when something happens to interrupt it, like the phone ringing. This is where you can do any cleanup you might need so you can start fresh with a new gesture. When this method is called, touchesEnded:withEvent: will not be called for the current gesture.

OK, enough theory—let's see some of this in action.

Detecting Touches

Our first example is a little application that will give you a better feel for when the four touch-related responder methods are called. In Xcode, create a new project using the *View-based Application* template. For *Product*, choose *iPhone*, and call the new project *TouchExplorer*.

Our TouchExplorer app will print messages to the screen containing the touch and tap count every time a touch-related method is called (see Figure 15–1).

Figure 15–1. *The TouchExplorer application*

> **NOTE:** Although the applications in this chapter will run on the simulator, you won't be able to see all of the available multitouch functionality unless you run them on an iPhone or iPod touch. If you've been accepted into the iOS Developer Program, you can run the programs you write on your device of choice. The Apple web site does a great job of walking you through the process of getting everything you need to prepare to connect Xcode to your device.

Building the TouchExplorer Application

We need three labels for this application: one to indicate which method was last called, another to report the current tap count, and a third to report the number of touches. Single-click *TouchExplorerViewController.h*, and add three outlets and a method declaration. The method will be used to update the labels from multiple places.

```
#import <UIKit/UIKit.h>

@interface TouchExplorerViewController : UIViewController {
    UILabel     *messageLabel;
    UILabel     *tapsLabel;
    UILabel     *touchesLabel;
}
@property (nonatomic, retain) IBOutlet UILabel *messageLabel;
@property (nonatomic, retain) IBOutlet UILabel *tapsLabel;
```

```
@property (nonatomic, retain) IBOutlet UILabel *touchesLabel;
- (void)updateLabelsFromTouches:(NSSet *)touches;
@end
```

Now, double-click *TouchExplorerViewController.xib* to edit the file. In Interface Builder, double-click the *View* icon in the dock to edit the view if the view editor is not already open. Drag three *Labels* from the library to the *View* window. Control-drag from the *File's Owner* icon to each of the three labels, connecting one to the *messageLabel* outlet, another to the *tapsLabel* outlet, and the last one to the *touchesLabel* outlet.

You should resize the labels so that they take up the full width of the view and also center the text, but the exact placement of the labels doesn't matter. You can also play with the fonts and colors if you're feeling a bit Picasso. When you're finished placing the labels, double-click each label and press the delete key to get rid of the text that's in them.

Finally, single-click the *View* icon in the main nib window and bring up the attributes inspector (see Figure 15–2). In the inspector, go to the bottom of the *View* section and make sure that both *User Interaction Enabled* and *Multiple Touch* are both checked. If *Multiple Touch* is not checked, your controller class's touch methods will always receive one, and only one, touch—no matter how many fingers are actually touching the screen.

Figure 15–2. *In the view's attributes, make sure both User Interaction Enabled and MultipleTouch are checked.*

When you're finished, save the nib. Then return to Xcode, select *TouchExplorerViewController.m*, and add the following code at the beginning of that file:

```
#import "TouchExplorerViewController.h"

@implementation TouchExplorerViewController
@synthesize messageLabel;
```

```
@synthesize tapsLabel;
@synthesize touchesLabel;

- (void)updateLabelsFromTouches:(NSSet *)touches {
    NSUInteger numTaps = [[touches anyObject] tapCount];
    NSString *tapsMessage = [[NSString alloc]
        initWithFormat:@"%d taps detected", numTaps];
    tapsLabel.text = tapsMessage;
    [tapsMessage release];

    NSUInteger numTouches = [touches count];
    NSString *touchMsg = [[NSString alloc] initWithFormat:
        @"%d touches detected", numTouches];
    touchesLabel.text = touchMsg;
    [touchMsg release];
}
...
```

Next, insert the following lines of code into the existing viewDidUnload and dealloc methods:

```
...
- (void)viewDidUnload {
    // Release any retained subviews of the main view.
    // e.g. self.myOutlet = nil;
    self.messageLabel = nil;
    self.tapsLabel = nil;
    self.touchesLabel = nil;
    [super viewDidUnload];
}
- (void)dealloc {
    [messageLabel release];
    [tapsLabel release];
    [touchesLabel release];
    [super dealloc];
}
...
```

And add the following new methods at the end of the file:

```
...
#pragma mark -
- (void)touchesBegan:(NSSet *)touches withEvent:(UIEvent *)event {
    messageLabel.text = @"Touches Began";
    [self updateLabelsFromTouches:touches];
}

- (void)touchesCancelled:(NSSet *)touches withEvent:(UIEvent *)event{
    messageLabel.text = @"Touches Cancelled";
    [self updateLabelsFromTouches:touches];
}

- (void)touchesEnded:(NSSet *)touches withEvent:(UIEvent *)event {
    messageLabel.text = @"Touches Ended.";
    [self updateLabelsFromTouches:touches];
}
```

```
- (void)touchesMoved:(NSSet *)touches withEvent:(UIEvent *)event {
    messageLabel.text = @"Drag Detected";
    [self updateLabelsFromTouches:touches];
}
@end
```

In this controller class, we implement all four of the touch-related methods discussed earlier. Each one sets messageLabel so the user can see when each method is called. Next, all four of them call updateLabelsFromTouches: to update the other two labels. The updateLabelsFromTouches: method gets the tap count from one of the touches, figures out the number of touches by looking at the count of the touches set, and updates the labels with that information.

Running TouchExplorer

Compile and run the application. If you're running in the simulator, try repeatedly clicking the screen to drive up the tap count, and try clicking and holding down the mouse button while dragging around the view to simulate a touch and drag. Note that a drag is not the same as a tap, so once you start your drag, the app will report zero taps.

You can emulate a two-finger pinch in the iPhone simulator by holding down the option key while you click with the mouse and drag. You can also simulate two-finger swipes by holding down the option key to simulate a pinch, moving the mouse so the two dots representing virtual fingers are next to each other, and then holding down the shift key (while still holding down the option key). Pressing the shift key will lock the position of the two fingers relative to each other, and you can do swipes and other two-finger gestures. You won't be able to do gestures that require three or more fingers, but you can do most two-finger gestures on the simulator using combinations of the option and shift keys.

If you're able to run this program on your iPhone or iPod touch, see how many touches you can get to register at the same time. Try dragging with one finger, then two fingers, and then three. Try double- and triple-tapping the screen, and see if you can get the tap count to go up by tapping with two fingers.

Play around with the TouchExplorer application until you feel comfortable with what's happening and with the way that the four touch methods work. When you're ready, move on to the next section, which demonstrates how to detect one of the most common gestures: the swipe.

Detecting Swipes

The application we're about to build, called Swipes, does nothing more than detect swipes, both horizontal and vertical (see Figure 15–3). If you swipe your finger across the screen from left to right, right to left, top to bottom, or bottom to top, Swipes will display a message across the top of the screen for a few seconds, informing you that a swipe was detected.

Figure 15–3. *The Swipes application will detect both vertical and horizontal swipes.*

Detecting swipes is relatively easy. We're going to define a minimum gesture length in pixels, which is how far the user must swipe before the gesture counts as a swipe. We'll also define a variance, which is how far from a straight line our user can veer and still have the gesture count as a horizontal or vertical swipe. A diagonal line generally won't count as a swipe, but one that's just a little off from horizontal or vertical will.

When the user touches the screen, we'll save the location of the first touch in a variable. Then we'll check as the user's finger moves across the screen to see if it reaches a point where it has gone far enough and straight enough to count as a swipe. Let's build it.

Building the Swipes Application

Create a new project in Xcode using the *View-based Application* template and a *Product* of *iPhone*. Name the project *Swipes*.

Click *SwipesViewController.h,* and add the following code:

```
#import <UIKit/UIKit.h>

@interface SwipesViewController : UIViewController {
    UILabel     *label;
    CGPoint     gestureStartPoint;
}
@property (nonatomic, retain) IBOutlet UILabel *label;
@property CGPoint gestureStartPoint;
- (void)eraseText;
@end
```

We start by declaring an outlet for our one label and a variable to hold the first spot the user touches. Then we declare a method that will be used to erase the text after a few seconds.

Double-click *SwipesViewController.xib* to open it for editing. In the attributes inspector, make sure that the view is set so *User Interaction Enabled* and *Multiple Touch* are both checked. Then drag a *Label* from the library and drop it on the *View* window. Set up the label so it takes the entire width of the view from blue line to blue line, and its alignment is centered. Feel free to play with the text attributes to make the label easier to read. Next, double-click the label and delete its text. Control-drag from the *File's Owner* icon to the label, and connect it to the *label* outlet.

Save your nib. Now return to Xcode, and select *SwipesViewController.m*. Add the following code at the top:

```
#import "SwipesViewController.h"

#define kMinimumGestureLength    25
#define kMaximumVariance         5

@implementation SwipesViewController
@synthesize label;
@synthesize gestureStartPoint;

- (void)eraseText {
    label.text = @"";
}
...
```

We start by defining a minimum gesture length of 25 pixels and a variance of 5. If the user is doing a horizontal swipe, the gesture could end up 5 pixels above or below the starting vertical position and still count as a swipe, as long as the user moves 25 pixels horizontally. In a real application, you will probably need to play with these numbers a bit to find what works best for that application.

Insert the following lines of code into the existing `viewDidUnload` and `dealloc` methods:

```
...
- (void)viewDidUnload {
    // Release any retained subviews of the main view.
    // e.g. self.myOutlet = nil;
    self.label = nil;
    [super viewDidUnload];
}

- (void)dealloc {
    [label release];
    [super dealloc];
}
...
```

And add the following methods at the bottom of the class:

```
#pragma mark -
- (void)touchesBegan:(NSSet *)touches withEvent:(UIEvent *)event {
```

```
        UITouch *touch = [touches anyObject];
        gestureStartPoint = [touch locationInView:self.view];
}

- (void)touchesMoved:(NSSet *)touches withEvent:(UIEvent *)event {
UITouch *touch = [touches anyObject];
        CGPoint currentPosition = [touch locationInView:self.view];

        CGFloat deltaX = fabsf(gestureStartPoint.x - currentPosition.x);
        CGFloat deltaY = fabsf(gestureStartPoint.y - currentPosition.y);

        if (deltaX >= kMinimumGestureLength && deltaY <= kMaximumVariance) {
            label.text = @"Horizontal swipe detected";
            [self performSelector:@selector(eraseText)
                withObject:nil afterDelay:2];
        }
        else if (deltaY >= kMinimumGestureLength &&
                deltaX <= kMaximumVariance){
            label.text = @"Vertical swipe detected";
            [self performSelector:@selector(eraseText) withObject:nil
                afterDelay:2];
        }
}
}

@end
```

Let's start with the touchesBegan:withEvent: method. All we do there is grab any touch from the touches set and store its point. We're primarily interested in single-finger swipes right now, so we don't worry about how many touches there are; we just grab one of them.

```
        UITouch *touch = [touches anyObject];
        gestureStartPoint = [touch locationInView:self.view];
```

In the next method, touchesMoved:withEvent:, we do the real work. First, we get the current position of the user's finger.

```
        UITouch *touch = [touches anyObject];
        CGPoint currentPosition = [touch locationInView:self.view];
```

After that, we calculate how far the user's finger has moved both horizontally and vertically from its starting position. The function fabsf() is from the standard C math library that returns the absolute value of a float. This allows us to subtract one from the other without needing to worry about which is the higher value.

```
        CGFloat deltaX = fabsf(gestureStartPoint.x - currentPosition.x);
        CGFloat deltaY = fabsf(gestureStartPoint.y - currentPosition.y);
```

Once we have the two deltas, we check to see if the user has moved far enough in one direction without having moved too far in the other to constitute a swipe. If they have, we set the label's text to indicate whether a horizontal or vertical swipe was detected. We also use performSelector:withObject:afterDelay:to erase the text after it has been on the screen for 2 seconds. That way, the user can practice multiple swipes without needing to worry whether the label is referring to an earlier attempt or the most recent one.

```
     if (deltaX >= kMinimumGestureLength && deltaY <= kMaximumVariance) {
       label.text = @"Horizontal swipe detected";
       [self performSelector:@selector(eraseText)
           withObject:nil afterDelay:2];
     }
   else if (deltaY >= kMinimumGestureLength &&
           deltaX <= kMaximumVariance){
       label.text = @"Vertical swipe detected";
       [self performSelector:@selector(eraseText)
           withObject:nil afterDelay:2];
   }
```

Go ahead and compile and run Swipes. If you find yourself clicking and dragging with no visible results, be patient. Click and drag straight down or straight across until you get the hang of swiping.

Using Automatic Gesture Recognition

The procedure we used for detecting a swipe isn't too bad. All the complexity is in the touchesMoved:withEvent: method, and even that isn't all that complicated. But there's an even easier way to do this. iOS now includes a class called UIGestureRecognizer, which eliminates the need for watching all the events to see how fingers are moving. You don't use UIGestureRecognizer directly, but instead create an instance of one of its subclasses, each of which is designed to look for a particular type of gesture, such as a swipe, pinch, double-tap, triple-tap, and so on.

Let's see how to modify the Swipes app to use a gesture recognizer instead of our hand-rolled procedure. As always, you might want to make a copy of your *Swipes* project folder and start from there.

Start off by selecting *SwipesViewController.m*, and deleting both the touchesBegan:withEvent: and touchesMoved:withEvent: methods. That's right, you won't be needing them. Then add a couple of new methods in their place:

```
- (void)reportHorizontalSwipe:(UIGestureRecognizer *)recognizer {
  label.text = @"Horizontal swipe detected";
  [self performSelector:@selector(eraseText) withObject:nil afterDelay:2];
}

- (void)reportVerticalSwipe:(UIGestureRecognizer *)recognizer {
  label.text = @"Vertical swipe detected";
  [self performSelector:@selector(eraseText) withObject:nil afterDelay:2];
}
```

Those methods implement the actual "functionality" (if you can call it that) that's brought about by the swipe gestures, just as the touchesMoved:withEvent: method did previously. Now, remove the comment markers around the viewDidLoad method, and add the new code shown here:

```
- (void)viewDidLoad {
    [super viewDidLoad];
    UISwipeGestureRecognizer *vertical = [[[UISwipeGestureRecognizer alloc]
        initWithTarget:self action:@selector(reportVerticalSwipe:)] autorelease];
    vertical.direction = UISwipeGestureRecognizerDirectionUp|
        UISwipeGestureRecognizerDirectionDown;
    [self.view addGestureRecognizer:vertical];

    UISwipeGestureRecognizer *horizontal = [[[UISwipeGestureRecognizer alloc]
        initWithTarget:self action:@selector(reportHorizontalSwipe:)] autorelease];
    horizontal.direction = UISwipeGestureRecognizerDirectionLeft|
        UISwipeGestureRecognizerDirectionRight;
    [self.view addGestureRecognizer:horizontal];
}
```

There you have it! To sanitize things even further, you can also delete the lines referring to gestureStartPoint from *SwipesViewController.h* (but leaving them there won't harm anything either).

Thanks to UIGestureRecognizer, all we needed to do here was create and configure some gesture recognizers, and add them to our view. When the user interacts with the screen in a way that one of the recognizers recognizes, the action method we specified is called.

In terms of total lines of code, there's not much difference between using gesture recognizers and the previous approach for a simple case like this. But the code that uses gesture recognizers is undeniably simpler to understand and easier to write. You don't need to give even a moment's thought to the issue of calculating a finger's movement over time, because that's already done for you by the UISwipeGestureRecognizer.

Implementing Multiple Swipes

In the Swipes application, we just grab any object out of the touches set to figure out where the user's finger is during the swipe. This approach is fine if we're interested in only single-finger swipes, the most common type of swipe used.

But what if we want to handle two- or three-finger swipes? In previous versions of this book, we dedicated about 50 lines of code, and a fair amount of explanation, to achieving this by tracking multiple UITouch instances across multiple touch events. Fortunately, now that we have gesture recognizers, this problem is solved.

A UISwipeGestureRecognizer can be configured to recognize any number of simultaneous touches. By default, each instance expects a single finger, but you can configure it to look for any number of fingers pressing the screen at once. Each instance responds to only the exact number of touches you specify. So, to update our app, we'll create a whole bunch of gesture recognizers in a loop.

Make yet another copy of your *Swipes* project folder. Edit *SwipesViewController.m* and modify the viewDidLoad method, replacing it with the one shown here:

```
- (void)viewDidLoad {
    [super viewDidLoad];
    UISwipeGestureRecognizer *vertical;

    for (NSUInteger touchCount = 1; touchCount <= 5; touchCount++) {
        vertical = [[[UISwipeGestureRecognizer alloc] initWithTarget:self
            action:@selector(reportVerticalSwipe:)] autorelease];
        vertical.direction = UISwipeGestureRecognizerDirectionUp|
            UISwipeGestureRecognizerDirectionDown;
        vertical.numberOfTouchesRequired = touchCount;
        [self.view addGestureRecognizer:vertical];

        UISwipeGestureRecognizer *horizontal;
        horizontal = [[[UISwipeGestureRecognizer alloc] initWithTarget:self
            action:@selector(reportHorizontalSwipe:)] autorelease];
        horizontal.direction = UISwipeGestureRecognizerDirectionLeft|
            UISwipeGestureRecognizerDirectionRight;
        horizontal.numberOfTouchesRequired = touchCount;
        [self.view addGestureRecognizer:horizontal];
    }
}
```

Note that in a real application, you might want different numbers of fingers swiping across the screen to trigger different behaviors. You can easily do that using gesture recognizers, simply by having each call a different action method.

Now, all we need to do is change the logging, by adding a method that gives us a handy description of the number of touches and using it in the "report" methods, as shown here. Add this method just below dealloc:

```
- (NSString *)descriptionForTouchCount:(NSUInteger)touchCount {
    if (touchCount == 2)
        return @"Double ";
    else if (touchCount == 3)
        return @"Triple ";
    else if (touchCount == 4)
        return @"Quadruple ";
    else if (touchCount == 5)
        return @"Quintuple ";
    else
        return @"";
}
```

Next, modify these two methods as shown:

```
- (void)reportHorizontalSwipe:(UIGestureRecognizer *)recognizer {
    label.text = @"Horizontal swipe detected";
    label.text = [NSString stringWithFormat:@"%@Horizontal swipe detected",
        [self descriptionForTouchCount:[recognizer numberOfTouches]]];
    [self performSelector:@selector(eraseText) withObject:nil afterDelay:2];
}

- (void)reportVerticalSwipe:(UIGestureRecognizer *)recognizer {
    label.text = @"Vertical swipe detected";
    label.text = [NSString stringWithFormat:@"%@Vertical swipe detected",
```

```
        [self descriptionForTouchCount:[recognizer numberOfTouches]]];;
    [self performSelector:@selector(eraseText) withObject:nil afterDelay:2];
}
```

Compile and run this version. You should be able to trigger double- and triple-swipes in both directions, and should still be able to trigger single-swipes. If you have small fingers, you might even be able to trigger a quadruple- or quintuple-swipe.

> **CAUTION:** With a multiple-finger swipe, be careful that your fingers aren't too close to each other. If two fingers are very close to each other, they may register as only a single touch. Because of this, you shouldn't rely on quadruple- or quintuple-swipes for any important gestures, because many people will have fingers that are too big to do those swipes effectively.

Detecting Multiple Taps

In the TouchExplorer application, we printed the tap count to the screen, so you've already seen how easy it is to detect multiple taps. However, in a real program, it's not quite as straightforward as it seems, because often you will want to take different actions based on the number of taps.

If the user triple-taps, you get notified three separate times: you get a single-tap, a double-tap, and finally a triple-tap. If you want to do something on a double-tap but something completely different on a triple-tap, having three separate notifications could cause a problem.

Fortunately, the engineers at Apple anticipated this situation, and provided a mechanism to let multiple gesture recognizers play nicely together, even when they're faced with ambiguous inputs that could seemingly trigger any of them. The basic idea is that you place a constraint on a gesture recognizer, telling it to not trigger its associated method unless some other gesture recognizer fails to do so itself.

That seems a bit abstract, so let's make it real. One commonly used gesture recognizer is represented by the UITapGestureRecognizer class. A tap gesture recognizer can be configured to do its thing when a particular number of taps occur. Imagine we have a view for which we want to define distinct actions that occur when the user taps once or double-taps. You might start off with something like the following:

```
UITapGestureRecognizer *singleTap = [[[UITapGestureRecognizer alloc] initWithTarget:
    self action:@selector(doSingleTap)] autorelease];
singleTap.numberOfTapsRequired = 1;
[self.view addGestureRecognizer:singleTap];

UITapGestureRecognizer *doubleTap = [[[UITapGestureRecognizer alloc] initWithTarget:
    self action:@selector(doDoubleTap)] autorelease];
doubleTap.numberOfTapsRequired = 2;
[self.view addGestureRecognizer:doubleTap];
```

The problem with this piece of code is that the two recognizers are unaware of each other, and they have no way of knowing that the user's actions may be better suited to another recognizer. With the preceding code, if the user double-taps the view, the doDoubleTap method will be called, but the doSingleMethod will also be called *twice*—once for each tap.

The way around this is to require failure. We tell singleTap that we want it to trigger its action only if doubleTap doesn't recognize and respond to the user input with this single line:

```
[singleTap requireGestureRecognizerToFail:doubleTap];
```

This means that when the user taps once, singleTap doesn't do its work immediately. Instead, singleTap waits until it knows that doubleTap has decided to stop paying attention to the current gesture (the user didn't tap twice). We're going to build on this further with our next project.

In Xcode, create a new project with the *View-based Application* template and a *Product* of *iPhone*. Call this new project *TapTaps*. This application will have four labels, to inform us when it has detected a single-tap, double-tap, triple-tap, or quadruple tap (see Figure 15–4).

Figure 15–4. *The TapTaps application detects up to four simultaneous taps.*

We need outlets for the four labels, and we also need separate methods for each tap scenario to simulate what you would have in a real application. We'll also include a method for erasing the text fields. Expand the *Classes* folder, single-click *TapTapsViewController.h*, and make the following changes:

```
#import <UIKit/UIKit.h>

@interface TapTapsViewController : UIViewController {
    UILabel *singleLabel;
    UILabel *doubleLabel;
    UILabel *tripleLabel;
    UILabel *quadrupleLabel;
}
@property (nonatomic, retain) IBOutlet UILabel *singleLabel;
@property (nonatomic, retain) IBOutlet UILabel *doubleLabel;
@property (nonatomic, retain) IBOutlet UILabel *tripleLabel;
@property (nonatomic, retain) IBOutlet UILabel *quadrupleLabel;
- (void)tap1;
- (void)tap2;
- (void)tap3;
- (void)tap4;
- (void)eraseMe:(UITextField *)textField ;
@end
```

Save the file.

Next, expand the *Resources* folder. Double-click *TapTapsViewController.xib* to edit the GUI. Once you're there, add four *Labels* to the view from the library. Make all four labels stretch from blue guideline to blue guideline, and then format them however you see fit. For example, feel free to make each label a different color. When you're finished, control-drag from the *File's Owner* icon to each label, and connect each one to *singleLabel*, *doubleLabel*, *tripleLabel*, and *quadrupleLabel*, respectively. Now, make sure you double-click each label and press the delete key to get rid of any text.

Save your changes and return to Xcode. Select *TapTapsViewController.m*, and add the following code at the top of the file:

```
#import "TapTapsViewController.h"

@implementation TapTapsViewController
@synthesize singleLabel;
@synthesize doubleLabel;
@synthesize tripleLabel;
@synthesize quadrupleLabel;

- (void)tap1 {
    singleLabel.text = @"Single Tap Detected";
    [self performSelector:@selector(eraseMe:)
        withObject:singleLabel afterDelay:1.6f];
}

- (void)tap2 {
    doubleLabel.text = @"Double Tap Detected";
    [self performSelector:@selector(eraseMe:)
        withObject:doubleLabel afterDelay:1.6f];
}

- (void)tap3 {
    tripleLabel.text = @"Triple Tap Detected";
```

```
        [self performSelector:@selector(eraseMe:)
            withObject:tripleLabel afterDelay:1.6f];
}

- (void)tap4 {
    quadrupleLabel.text = @"Quadruple Tap Detected";
    [self performSelector:@selector(eraseMe:)
        withObject:quadrupleLabel afterDelay:1.6f];
}

- (void)eraseMe:(UITextField *)textField {
    textField.text = @"";
}
...
```

Insert the following lines into the existing dealloc and viewDidUnload methods:

```
...
- (void)viewDidUnload {
        // Release any retained subviews of the main view.
    // e.g. self.myOutlet = nil;
    self.singleLabel = nil;
    self.doubleLabel = nil;
    self.tripleLabel = nil;
    self.quadrupleLabel = nil;
    [super viewDidUnload];
}

- (void)dealloc {
    [singleLabel release];
    [doubleLabel release];
    [tripleLabel release];
    [quadrupleLabel release];
    [super dealloc];
}
```

Now, uncomment viewDidLoad and add the following code:

```
- (void)viewDidLoad {
    [super viewDidLoad];

    UITapGestureRecognizer *singleTap =
        [[[UITapGestureRecognizer alloc] initWithTarget:self
                                        action:@selector(tap1)] autorelease];
    singleTap.numberOfTapsRequired = 1;
    singleTap.numberOfTouchesRequired = 1;
    [self.view addGestureRecognizer:singleTap];

    UITapGestureRecognizer *doubleTap =
        [[[UITapGestureRecognizer alloc] initWithTarget:self
                                        action:@selector(tap2)] autorelease];
    doubleTap.numberOfTapsRequired = 2;
    doubleTap.numberOfTouchesRequired = 1;
    [self.view addGestureRecognizer:doubleTap];
    [singleTap requireGestureRecognizerToFail:doubleTap];
```

```
UITapGestureRecognizer *tripleTap =
    [[[UITapGestureRecognizer alloc] initWithTarget:self
                                    action:@selector(tap3)] autorelease];
tripleTap.numberOfTapsRequired = 3;
tripleTap.numberOfTouchesRequired = 1;
[self.view addGestureRecognizer:tripleTap];
[doubleTap requireGestureRecognizerToFail:tripleTap];

UITapGestureRecognizer *quadrupleTap =
    [[[UITapGestureRecognizer alloc] initWithTarget:self
                                    action:@selector(tap4)] autorelease];
quadrupleTap.numberOfTapsRequired = 4;
quadrupleTap.numberOfTouchesRequired = 1;
[self.view addGestureRecognizer:quadrupleTap];
[tripleTap requireGestureRecognizerToFail:quadrupleTap];
}
```

The four tap methods do nothing more in this application than set one of the four labels and use `performSelector:withObject:afterDelay:` to erase that same label after 1.6 seconds. The `eraseMe:` method erases any label that is passed into it.

The interesting part of this is what occurs in the `viewDidLoad` method. We start off simply enough, by setting up a tap gesture recognizer and attaching it to our view.

```
UITapGestureRecognizer *singleTap =
    [[[UITapGestureRecognizer alloc] initWithTarget:self
                                    action:@selector(tap1)] autorelease];
singleTap.numberOfTapsRequired = 1;
singleTap.numberOfTouchesRequired = 1;
[self.view addGestureRecognizer:singleTap];
```

Note that we set both the number of *taps* (touches in the same position, one after another) required to trigger the action and *touches* (number of fingers touching the screen at the same time) to 1. After that, we set up another tap gesture recognizer to handle a double-tap.

```
UITapGestureRecognizer *doubleTap =
    [[[UITapGestureRecognizer alloc] initWithTarget:self
                                    action:@selector(tap2)] autorelease];
doubleTap.numberOfTapsRequired = 2;
doubleTap.numberOfTouchesRequired = 1;
[self.view addGestureRecognizer:doubleTap];
[singleTap requireGestureRecognizerToFail:doubleTap];
```

That's pretty similar to the previous recognizer, right up until that last line, in which we give `singleTap` some additional context. We are effectively telling `singleTap` that it should trigger its action only in case some other gesture recognizer—in this case, `doubleTap`—decides that the current user input isn't what it's looking for.

Let's think about what this means. With those two tap gesture recognizers in place, a single tap in the view will immediately make `singleTap` think, "Hey, this looks like it's for me." At the same time, `doubleTap` will think, "Hey, this looks like it *might* be for me, but I'll need to wait for one more tap." Because `singleTap` is set up to wait for `doubleTap`'s "failure," it doesn't send its action method right away; instead, it waits to see what happens with doubleTap.

After that first tap, if another tap occurs immediately, then doubleTap thinks, "Hey, that's mine all right," and fires its action. At that point, singleTap will realize what happened and give up on that gesture. On the other hand, if a particular amount of time goes by (the amount of time that the system considers to be the maximum length of time between taps in a double-tap), doubleTap will give up, and singleTap will see the failure and finally trigger its event.

The rest of the method goes on to define gesture recognizers for three and four taps, and at each point, configures one gesture to be dependent on the failure of the next.

```
UITapGestureRecognizer *tripleTap =
    [[[UITapGestureRecognizer alloc] initWithTarget:self
                                    action:@selector(tap3)] autorelease];
tripleTap.numberOfTapsRequired = 3;
tripleTap.numberOfTouchesRequired = 1;
[self.view addGestureRecognizer:tripleTap];
[doubleTap requireGestureRecognizerToFail:tripleTap];

UITapGestureRecognizer *quadrupleTap =
    [[[UITapGestureRecognizer alloc] initWithTarget:self
                                    action:@selector(tap4)] autorelease];
quadrupleTap.numberOfTapsRequired = 4;
quadrupleTap.numberOfTouchesRequired = 1;
[self.view addGestureRecognizer:quadrupleTap];
[tripleTap requireGestureRecognizerToFail:quadrupleTap];
```

Note that we don't need to explicitly configure every gesture to be dependent on the failure of each of the higher-tap-numbered gestures. That multiple dependency comes about naturally as a result of the chain of failure established in our code. Since singleTap requires the failure of doubleTap, doubleTap requires the failure of tripleTap, and tripleTap requires the failure of quadrupleTap, by extension, singleTap requires that all of the others fail.

Compile and run the app, and whether you single-, double-, triple-, or quadruple-tap, you should see only one label displayed.

Detecting Pinches

Another common gesture is the two-finger pinch. It's used in a number of applications—including Mobile Safari, Mail, and Photos—to let you zoom in (if you pinch apart) and zoom out (if you pinch together).

Detecting pinches is really easy, thanks to UIPinchGestureRecognizer. This one is referred to as a continuous gesture recognizer, because it calls its action method over and over again during the pinch.

While the gesture is underway, the pinch gesture recognizer goes through a number of states. The only one we want to watch for is UIGestureRecognizerStateBegan, which is the state that the recognizer is in when it first calls the action method after detecting that a pinch is happening.

At that moment, the pinch gesture recognizer's `scale` property is always set to `1.0`; for the rest of the gesture, that number goes up and down. We're going to use the `scale` value to resize the text in a label. We'll build the PinchMe app (see Figure 15–5), which will detect the pinch gesture for both zooming in and zooming out.

Figure 15–5. *The PinchMe application detects the pinch gesture, both for zooming in and zooming out.*

Create a new project in Xcode, again using the *View-based Application* template, and call this one *PinchMe*.

The PinchMe application is going to need only a single outlet for a label, but it also needs an instance variable to hold the size of the label's font at the start of the pinch. Expand the *Classes* folder, single-click *PinchMeViewController.h*, and make the following changes:

```
#import <UIKit/UIKit.h>

@interface PinchMeViewController : UIViewController {
    UILabel *label;
    CGFloat initialFontSize;
}
@property (nonatomic, retain) IBOutlet UILabel *label;
@property CGFloat initialFontSize;

@end
```

Now that we have our outlet, expand the *Resources* folder, and double-click *PinchMeViewController.xib*. In Interface Builder, make sure the view is displayed in its editing window, and drag a single label over to it. Resize the label to fill the entire view, and put a small word or just a letter or two into it. Be sure the label is resized blue guideline to blue guideline, from left to right and top to bottom. This text is what we'll be zooming in and out on. Set the label's alignment to centered. Next, control-drag from the *File's Owner* icon to the label, and connect it to the *label* outlet.

Save the nib, bounce back to Xcode to *PinchMeViewController.m*, and add the following code at the top of the file:

```
#import "PinchMeViewController.h"


@implementation PinchMeViewController
@synthesize label;
@synthesize initialFontSize;

...
```

Clean up our outlet in the `dealloc` and `viewDidUnload` methods:

```
...
- (void)viewDidUnload {
    // Release any retained subviews of the main view.
    // e.g. self.myOutlet = nil;
    self.label = nil;
    [super viewDidUnload];
}

- (void)dealloc {
    [label release];
    [super dealloc];
}
...
```

Then remove the comment marks around the `viewDidLoad` method, and add the following code to the method:

```
- (void)viewDidLoad {
    [super viewDidLoad];

    UIPinchGestureRecognizer *pinch = [[[UIPinchGestureRecognizer alloc]
        initWithTarget:self action:@selector(doPinch:)] autorelease];
    [self.view addGestureRecognizer:pinch];
}
```

And add the following method at the end of the file:

```
...
- (void)doPinch:(UIPinchGestureRecognizer *)pinch {
    if (pinch.state == UIGestureRecognizerStateBegan) {
        initialFontSize = label.font.pointSize;
    } else {
        label.font = [label.font fontWithSize:initialFontSize * pinch.scale];
    }
```

```
}
@end
```

In `viewDidLoad`, we set up a pinch gesture recognizer and tell it to notify us via the `doPinch:` method when pinching is occurring. Inside `doPinch:`, we look at the pinch's state to see if it's just starting; if so, we store the current font size for later use. Otherwise, if the pinch is already in progress, we use the stored initial font size and the current pinch scale to calculate a new font size.

And that's all there is to pinch detection. Compile and run the app to give it a try. As you do some pinching, you'll see the text change size in response. If you're on the simulator, remember that you can simulate a pinch by holding down the option key and clicking and dragging in the simulator window using your mouse.

Creating and Using Custom Gestures

You've now seen how to detect the most commonly used iPhone gestures. The real fun begins when you start defining your own, custom gestures! You've already seen how to use a few of `UIGestureRecognizer`'s subclasses, so now it's time to learn how to create your own gestures, which can be easily attached to any view you like.

Defining a custom gesture is tricky. You've already mastered the basic mechanism, and that wasn't too difficult. The tricky part is being flexible when defining what constitutes a gesture. Most people are not precise when they use gestures. Remember the variance we used when we implemented the swipe, so that even a swipe that wasn't perfectly horizontal or vertical still counted? That's a perfect example of the subtlety you need to add to your own gesture definitions. If you define your gesture too strictly, it will be useless. If you define it too generically, you'll get too many false positives, which will frustrate the user. In a sense, defining a custom gesture can be hard, because you need to be precise about a gesture's imprecision. If you try to capture a complex gesture like, say, a figure eight, the math behind detecting the gesture is also going to get quite complex.

When defining new gestures for your own applications, make sure you test them thoroughly, and if you can, have other people test them for you as well. You want to make sure that your gesture is easy for the user to do, but not so easy that it gets triggered unintentionally. You also need to make sure that you don't conflict with other gestures used in your application. A single gesture should not count, for example, as both a custom gesture and a pinch.

Defining the Check Mark Gesture

In our sample, we're going to define a gesture shaped like a check mark (see Figure 15–6).

Figure 15–6. *Our check mark gesture*

What are the defining properties of this check mark gesture? Well, the principal one is that sharp change in angle between the two lines. We also want to make sure that the user's finger has traveled a little distance in a straight line before it makes that sharp angle. In Figure 15–6, the legs of the checkmark meet at an acute angle, just under 90 degrees. A gesture that required exactly an 85-degree angle would be awfully hard to get right, so we'll define a range of acceptable angles.

Create a new project in Xcode using the *View-based Application* template, and call the project *CheckPlease*. In this project, we're going to need to do some fairly standard analytic geometry to calculate such things as the distance between two points and the angle between two lines. Don't worry if you don't remember much geometry; we've provided you with functions that will do the calculations for you.

Look in the *15 - CheckPlease* folder for the two files named *CGPointUtils.h* and *CGPointUtils.c*. Drag both of these to the *Other Sources* folder of your project. Feel free to use these utility functions in your own applications.

Control-click in the *Classes* folder, and add a new file to the project. Use the new file assistant to create a new Objective-C class (make it a subclass of NSObject for now, since the assistant doesn't give us a way to create a subclass of UIGestureRecognizer).

Call the file *CheckMarkRecognizer.m*, be sure to ask for the *.h* file, and save it in the project's *Classes* folder. Then select *CheckMarkRecognizer.h*, and make the following changes:

```
#import <Foundation/Foundation.h>

@interface CheckMarkRecognizer : NSObject {
@interface CheckMarkRecognizer : UIGestureRecognizer {
    CGPoint     lastPreviousPoint;
    CGPoint     lastCurrentPoint;
    CGFloat     lineLengthSoFar;
}
@end
```

Here we declare three variables: `lastPreviousPoint`, `lastCurrentPoint`, and `lineLengthSoFar`. Each time we're notified of a touch, we're given the previous touch point and the current touch point. Those two points define a line segment. The next touch adds another segment. We store the previous touch's previous and current points in `lastPreviousPoint` and `lastCurrentPoint`, which gives us the previous line segment. We can then compare that line segment to the current touch's line segment. Comparing these two line segments can tell us if we're still drawing a single line or if there's a sharp enough angle between the two segments that we're actually drawing a check mark.

Remember that every `UITouch` object knows its current position in the view as well as its previous position in the view. In order to compare angles, however, we need to know the line that the previous two points made, so we need to store the current and previous points from the last time the user touched the screen. We'll use these two variables to store those two values each time this method is called, so that we have the ability to compare the current line to the previous line and check the angle.

We also declare a variable to keep a running count of how far the user has dragged the finger. If the finger hasn't traveled at least 10 pixels (the value in `kMinimumCheckMarkLength`), whether the angle falls in the correct range doesn't matter. If we didn't require this distance, we would receive a lot of false positives.

Now, select *CheckMarkRecognizer.m*, and make the following changes:

```
#import "CheckMarkRecognizer.h"
#import "CGPointUtils.h"
#import <UIKit/UIGestureRecognizerSubclass.h>

#define kMinimumCheckMarkAngle     50
#define kMaximumCheckMarkAngle     135
#define kMinimumCheckMarkLength     10

@implementation CheckMarkRecognizer

- (void)touchesBegan:(NSSet *)touches withEvent:(UIEvent *)event {
    [super touchesBegan:touches withEvent:event];
    UITouch *touch = [touches anyObject];
    CGPoint point = [touch locationInView:self.view];
    lastPreviousPoint = point;
    lastCurrentPoint = point;
```

```
        lineLengthSoFar = 0.0f;
}

- (void)touchesMoved:(NSSet *)touches withEvent:(UIEvent *)event {
    [super touchesMoved:touches withEvent:event];
    UITouch *touch = [touches anyObject];
    CGPoint previousPoint = [touch previousLocationInView:self.view];
    CGPoint currentPoint = [touch locationInView:self.view];
    CGFloat angle = angleBetweenLines(lastPreviousPoint,
                                      lastCurrentPoint,
                                      previousPoint,
                                      currentPoint);
    if (angle >= kMinimumCheckMarkAngle && angle <= kMaximumCheckMarkAngle
        && lineLengthSoFar > kMinimumCheckMarkLength) {
        self.state = UIGestureRecognizerStateEnded;
    }
    lineLengthSoFar += distanceBetweenPoints(previousPoint, currentPoint);
    lastPreviousPoint = previousPoint;
    lastCurrentPoint = currentPoint;
}
@end
```

After importing *CGPointUtils.h*, the file we mentioned earlier, we import a special header file called *UIGestureRecognizerSubclass.h*, which contains declarations that are intended for use only by a subclass. The important thing this does for is to make the gesture recognizer's state property writable. That's the mechanism our subclass will use to affirm that the gesture we're watching for was completed successfully.

Then we define the parameters that we use to decide whether the user's finger-squiggling matches our definition of a check mark. You can see that we've defined a minimum angle of 50 degrees and a maximum angle of 135 degrees. This is a pretty broad range, and depending on your needs, you might decide to restrict the angle.

We experimented a bit with the angles and found that our practice check mark gestures fell into a fairly broad range, which is why we chose a relatively large tolerance here. We were somewhat sloppy with our check mark gestures, and so we expect that at least some of our users will be just as sloppy. As a wise man once said, "Be rigorous in what you produce and tolerant in what you accept."

Let's take a look at the touch methods. You'll notice that each of them first calls the superclass's implementation, something we've never done before. We need to do this in a UIGestureRecognizer subclass, so that our superclass can have the same amount of knowledge about the events as we do.

In touchesBegan:withEvent:, we determine the point that the user is currently touching and store that value in lastPreviousPoint and lastCurrentPoint. Since this method is called when a gesture begins, we know there is no previous point to worry about, so we store the current point in both. We also reset the running line length count to 0.

Then, in touchesMoved:withEvent:, we calculate the angle between the line from the current touch's previous position to its current position, and the line between the two points stored in the lastPreviousPoint and lastCurrentPoint instance variables. Once we have that angle, we check to see if it falls within our range of acceptable angles and check to make sure that the user's finger has traveled far enough before making that sharp turn. If both of those are true, we set the label to show that we've identified a check mark gesture. Next, we calculate the distance between the touch's position and its previous position, add that to `lineLengthSoFar`, and replace the values in `lastPreviousPoint` and `lastCurrentPoint` with the two points from the current touch so we'll have them the next time through this method.

Now that we have a gesture recognizer of our own to try out, it's time to connect it to a view, just as we've done with the others we've used.

Attaching the Check Mark Gesture to a View

Single-click *CheckPleaseViewController.h*, and make the following changes:

```
#import <UIKit/UIKit.h>

@interface CheckPleaseViewController : UIViewController {
    UILabel     *label;

}
@property (nonatomic, retain) IBOutlet UILabel *label;

@end
```

Here, we simply define an outlet to a label that we'll use to inform the user when we've detected a check mark gesture.

Expand the *Resources* folder, and double-click *CheckPleaseViewController.xib* to edit the GUI. Add a *Label* from the library and set it up the way you want it to look. Control-drag from the *File's Owner* icon to that label to connect it to the *label* outlet and double-click the label to delete its text. Save the nib file.

Now, return to Xcode, choose to edit *CheckPleaseViewController.m*, and add the following code to the top of the file:

```
#import "CheckPleaseViewController.h"
#import "CheckMarkRecognizer.h"

@implementation CheckPleaseViewController
@synthesize label;

- (void)doCheck:(CheckMarkRecognizer *)check {
    label.text = @"Checkmark";
    [self performSelector:@selector(eraseLabel)
               withObject:nil afterDelay:1.6];
}

- (void)eraseLabel {
    label.text = @"";
}
```

That gives us an action method to connect our recognizer to, which in turn triggers the familiar-looking eraseLabel method. Next, remove the comment markers around the viewDidLoad method, and add the following lines, which connect an instance of our new recognizer to the view:

```
- (void)viewDidLoad {
    [super viewDidLoad];
    CheckMarkRecognizer *check = [[[CheckMarkRecognizer alloc] initWithTarget:self
        action:@selector(doCheck:)] autorelease];
    [self.view addGestureRecognizer:check];
}
```

All that's left to do now is to add the following code to the existing viewDidUnload and dealloc methods:

```
- (void)viewDidUnload {
    // Release any retained subviews of the main view.
    // e.g. self.myOutlet = nil;
    self.label = nil;
    [super viewDidUnload];
}

- (void)dealloc {
    [label release];
    [super dealloc];
}
```

Compile and run the app, and try out the gesture.

Garçon? Check, Please!

You should now understand the mechanism iOS uses to tell your application about touches, taps, and gestures. You learned how to detect the most commonly used iOS gestures, and even got a taste of how you might go about defining your own custom gestures. The iOS interface relies on gestures for much of its ease of use, so you'll want to have these techniques at the ready for most of your iOS development.

When you're ready to move on, turn the page, and we'll tell you how to figure out where in the world you are using Core Location.

Chapter 16

Where Am I? Finding Your Way with Core Location

Every iOS device has the ability to determine where in the world it is using a framework called Core Location. There are actually three technologies that Core Location can leverage to do this: GPS, cell tower triangulation, and Wi-Fi Positioning Service (WPS). GPS is the most accurate of the three but is not available on first-generation iPhones, iPod touches, or Wi-Fi-only iPads; in short, any device with a 3G data connection also contains a GPS unit. GPS reads microwave signals from multiple satellites to determine the current location.

NOTE: Technically, Apple uses a version of GPS called Assisted GPS, also known as A-GPS. A-GPS uses network resources to help improve the performance of stand-alone GPS.

Cell tower triangulation determines the current location by doing a calculation based on the locations of the cell towers in the phone's range. Cell tower triangulation can be fairly accurate in cities and other areas with a high cell tower density but becomes less accurate in areas where there is a greater distance between towers. Triangulation requires a cell radio connection, so it works only on iPhone (all models, including the very first) and iPad with a 3G data connection. The last option, WPS, uses the MAC addresses from nearby Wi-Fi access points to make a guess at your location by referencing a large database of known service providers and the areas they service. WPS is imprecise and can be off by many miles.

All three methods put a noticeable drain on the battery, so keep that in mind when using Core Location. Your application shouldn't poll for location any more often than is absolutely necessary. When using Core Location, you have the option of specifying a desired accuracy. By carefully specifying the absolute minimum accuracy level you need, you can prevent unnecessary battery drain.

The technologies that Core Location depends on are hidden from your application. We don't tell Core Location whether to use GPS, triangulation, or WPS. We just tell it how accurate we would like it to be, and it will decide from the technologies available to it which is best for fulfilling your request.

The Location Manager

The Core Location API is actually fairly easy to work with. The main class we'll work with is `CLLocationManager`, usually referred to as the **location manager**. To interact with Core Location, we need to create an instance of the location manager, like this:

```
CLLocationManager *locationManager = [[CLLocationManager alloc] init];
```

This creates an instance of the location manager for us, but it doesn't actually start polling for our location. We have to create an object that conforms to the `CLLocationManagerDelegate` protocol and assign it as the location manager's delegate. The location manager will call delegate methods when location information becomes available or changes. The process of determining location may take some time, even a few seconds.

Setting the Desired Accuracy

After you set the delegate, you also want to set the requested accuracy. As we said before, don't specify a degree of accuracy any greater than you absolutely need. If you're writing an application that just needs to know which state or country the phone is in, don't specify a high level of precision. Remember, the more accuracy you demand of Core Location, the more juice you're likely to use. Also, keep in mind that there is no guarantee that you will get the level of accuracy you have requested.

Here's an example of setting the delegate and requesting a specific level of accuracy:

```
locationManager.delegate = self;
locationManager.desiredAccuracy = kCLLocationAccuracyBest;
```

The accuracy is set using a `CLLocationAccuracy` value, a type that's defined as a double. The value is in meters, so if you specify a `desiredAccuracy` of 10, you're telling Core Location that you want it to try to determine the current location within 10 meters, if possible. Specifying `kCLLocationAccuracyBest`, as we did previously, tells Core Location to use the most accurate method that's currently available. In addition to `kCLLocationAccuracyBest`, you can also use `kCLLocationAccuracyNearestTenMeters`, `kCLLocationAccuracyHundredMeters`, `kCLLocationAccuracyKilometer`, and `kCLLocationAccuracyThreeKilometers`.

Setting the Distance Filter

By default, the location manager will notify the delegate of any detected change in the device's location. By specifying a **distance filter**, you are telling the location manager not to notify you for every change and instead to notify you only when the location changes by more than a certain amount. Setting up a distance filter can reduce the amount of polling your application does. Distance filters are also set in meters.

Specifying a distance filter of 1000 tells the location manager not to notify its delegate until the iPhone has moved at least 1,000 meters from its previously reported position. Here's an example:

```
locationManager.distanceFilter = 1000.0f;
```

If you ever want to return the location manager to the default setting of no filter, you can use the constant kCLDistanceFilterNone, like this:

```
locationManager.distanceFilter = kCLDistanceFilterNone;
```

Just like when specifying the desired accuracy, you should take care to avoid getting updates any more frequently than you really need them, because otherwise you waste battery power. A speedometer app that's calculating the user's velocity based on their location will probably want to have updates as fast as possible, but an app that's going to show the nearest fast-food restaurant can get by with a lot less.

Starting the Location Manager

When you're ready to start polling for location, you tell the location manager to start, and it will then go off and do its thing and then call a delegate method when it has determined the current location. Until you tell it to stop, it will continue to call your delegate method whenever it senses a change that exceeds the current distance filter. Here's how you start the location manager:

```
[locationManager startUpdatingLocation];
```

Using the Location Manager Wisely

If you need to determine the current location only and have no need to continuously poll for location, you should have your location delegate stop the location manager as soon as it gets the information your application needs. If you need to continuously poll, make sure you stop polling as soon as you possibly can. Remember, as long as you are getting updates from the location manager, you are putting a strain on the user's battery. To tell the location manager to stop sending updates to its delegate, call stopUpdatingLocation, like this:

```
[locationManager stopUpdatingLocation];
```

The Location Manager Delegate

The location manager delegate must conform to the CLLocationManagerDelegate protocol, which defines two methods, both of which are optional. One of these methods is called by the location manager when it has determined the current location or when it detects a change in location. The other method is called when the location manager encounters an error.

Getting Location Updates

When the location manager wants to inform its delegate of the current location, it calls the locationManager:didUpdateToLocation:fromLocation: method. This method takes three parameters. The first parameter is the location manager that called the method. The second is a CLLocation object that defines the current location of the device, and the third is a CLLocation object that defines the previous location from the last update. The first time this method is called, the previous location object will be nil.

Getting Latitude and Longitude Using CLLocation

Location information is passed from the location manager using instances of the CLLocation class. This class has five properties that might be of interest to your application. The latitude and longitude are stored in a property called coordinate. To get the latitude and longitude in degrees, do this:

```
CLLocationDegrees latitude = theLocation.coordinate.latitude;
CLLocationDegrees longitude = theLocation.coordinate.longitude;
```

The CLLocation object can also tell you how confident the location manager is in its latitude and longitude calculations. The horizontalAccuracy property describes the radius of a circle with the coordinate as its center. The larger the value in horizontalAccuracy, the less certain Core Location is of the location. A very small radius indicates a high level of confidence in the determined location.

You can see a graphic representation of horizontalAccuracy in the Maps application (see Figure 16–1). The circle shown in Maps uses horizontalAccuracy for its radius when it detects your location. The location manager thinks you are at the center of that circle. If you're not, you're almost certainly somewhere inside the circle. A negative value in horizontalAccuracy is an indication that you cannot rely on the values in coordinate for some reason.

The CLLocation object also has a property called altitude that can tell you how many meters above or below sea level you are:

```
CLLocationDistance altitude = theLocation.altitude;
```

Each CLLocation object maintains a property called verticalAccuracy that is an indication of how confident Core Location is in its determination of altitude. The value in altitude could be off by as many meters as the value in verticalAccuracy, and if the verticalAccuracy value is negative, Core Location is telling you it could not determine a valid altitude.

CLLocation objects also have a timestamp that tells when the location manager made the location determination.

Figure 16–1. *The Maps application uses Core Location to determine your current location. The outer circle is a visual representation of the horizontal accuracy.*

In addition to these properties, CLLocation also has a useful instance method that will let you determine the distance between two CLLocation objects. The method is called distanceFromLocation:, and it works like this:

```
CLLocationDistance distance = [fromLocation distanceFromLocation:toLocation];
```

The preceding line of code will return the distance between two CLLocation objects, fromLocation and toLocation. This distance value returned will be the result of a great-circle distance calculation that ignores the altitude property and calculates the distance as if both points were at sea level. For most purposes, a great-circle calculation will be more than sufficient, but if you do need to take altitude into account when calculating distances, you'll have to write your own code to do it.

> **NOTE:** If you're not sure what's meant by "great-circle distance," you might want to think back to geography class and the notion of a "great-circle route." The idea is that the shortest distance between any two points on the earth's surface will be found along a route that goes the entire way around the earth: a "great circle." The calculation performed by the CLLocation calculates the distance between two points along such a route, taking the curvature of the earth into account. Without accounting for that curvature, you'd end up with the length of a straight line connecting the two points, which isn't much use since that line would invariable go straight through some amount of the earth itself!

Error Notifications

If Core Location is not able to determine your current location, it will call a second delegate method named `locationManager:didFailWithError:`. The most likely cause of an error is that the user denies access. The user has to authorize use of the location manager, so the first time your application goes to determine the location, an alert will pop up on the screen asking if it's OK for the current program to access your location (see Figure 16–2).

Figure 16–2. *The location manager access has to be approved by the user.*

If the user taps the *Don't Allow* button, your delegate will be notified of the fact by the location manager using the `locationManager:didFailWithError:` with an error code of `kCLErrorDenied`. At the time of this writing, the only other error code supported by the location manager is `kCLErrorLocationUnknown`, which indicates that Core Location was unable to determine the location but that it will keep trying. The `kCLErrorDenied` error generally indicates that your application will not be able to access Core Location any time during the remainder of the current session. On the other hand, `kCLErrorLocationUnknown` errors indicate a problem that may be temporary.

NOTE: When working in the simulator, a dialog will appear, outside of the simulator window, asking to use your current location. In that case, your location will be determined using a super-secret algorithm kept in a locked vault buried deep beneath Apple headquarters in Cupertino.

Trying Out Core Location

Let's build a small application to detect the iPhone's current location and the total distance traveled while the program has been running. You can see what our final application will look like in Figure 16–3.

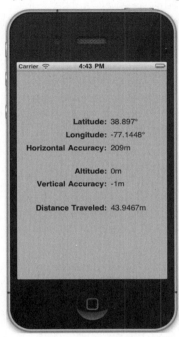

Figure 16–3. *The WhereAmI application in action. This screenshot was taken in the simulator. Notice that the vertical accuracy is a negative number, which tells us it couldn't determine the altitude.*

In Xcode, create a new project using the *View-based Application* template, use a *Product* of *iPhone*, and call the project WhereAmI. Expand the *Classes* and *Resources* folders, and select *WhereAmIViewController.h*. Make the following changes, which we'll discuss in a moment:

```
#import <UIKit/UIKit.h>
#import <CoreLocation/CoreLocation.h>

@interface WhereAmIViewController :
    UIViewController <CLLocationManagerDelegate> {

    CLLocationManager *locationManager;
    CLLocation        *startingPoint;

    UILabel *latitudeLabel;
    UILabel *longitudeLabel;
    UILabel *horizontalAccuracyLabel;
    UILabel *altitudeLabel;
    UILabel *verticalAccuracyLabel;
```

```
    UILabel *distanceTraveledLabel;
}
@property (nonatomic, retain) CLLocationManager *locationManager;
@property (nonatomic, retain) CLLocation *startingPoint;
@property (nonatomic, retain) IBOutlet UILabel *latitudeLabel;
@property (nonatomic, retain) IBOutlet UILabel *longitudeLabel;
@property (nonatomic, retain) IBOutlet UILabel *horizontalAccuracyLabel;
@property (nonatomic, retain) IBOutlet UILabel *altitudeLabel;
@property (nonatomic, retain) IBOutlet UILabel *verticalAccuracyLabel;
@property (nonatomic, retain) IBOutlet UILabel *distanceTraveledLabel;
@end
```

The first thing to notice is that we've included the Core Location header files. Core Location is not part of the UIKit, so we need to include the header files manually. Next, we conform this class to the CLLocationManagerDelegate method so that we can receive location information from the location manager.

After that, we declare a CLLocationManager pointer, which will be used to hold the instance of the Core Location we create. We also declare a pointer to a CLLocation, which we will set to the location we receive in the first update from the location manager. This way, if the user has our program running and moves far enough to trigger updates, we'll be able to calculate how far our user moved. Our delegate will be notified of the previous location with each call, but not the original starting location, which is why we store it.

The remaining instance variables are all outlets that will be used to update labels on the user interface.

Double-click *WhereAmIViewController.xib* to create the GUI. Using Figure 16–3 as your guide, drag 12 *Labels* from the library to the *View* window. Six of them should be placed on the left side of the screen, right justified, and made bold. Give the six bold labels the values *Latitude:, Longitude:, Horizontal Accuracy:, Altitude:, Vertical Accuracy:,* and *Distance Traveled:*. Since the *Horizontal Accuracy:* label is the longest, you might place that one first and then option-drag out copies of that label to create the other five left-side labels. The six right-side labels should be left justified and placed next to each of the bold labels.

Each of the labels on the right side should be connected to the appropriate outlet we defined in the header file earlier. Once you have all six attached to outlets, double-click each one in turn, and delete the text it holds.

Save your changes, return to Xcode, select *WhereAmIViewController.m,* and make the following changes at the top of the file:

```
#import "WhereAmIViewController.h"

@implementation WhereAmIViewController
@synthesize locationManager;
@synthesize startingPoint;
@synthesize latitudeLabel;
@synthesize longitudeLabel;
@synthesize horizontalAccuracyLabel;
@synthesize altitudeLabel;
```

```
@synthesize verticalAccuracyLabel;
@synthesize distanceTraveledLabel;

#pragma mark -
- (void)viewDidLoad {
    self.locationManager = [[CLLocationManager alloc] init];
    locationManager.delegate = self;
    locationManager.desiredAccuracy = kCLLocationAccuracyBest;
    [locationManager startUpdatingLocation];
}
...
```

Insert the following lines in viewDidUnload and dealloc to clean up our outlets:

```
...
- (void)viewDidUnload {
    // Release any retained subviews of the main view.
    // e.g. self.myOutlet = nil;
    self.locationManager = nil;
    self.latitudeLabel = nil;
    self.longitudeLabel = nil;
    self.horizontalAccuracyLabel = nil;
    self.altitudeLabel = nil;
    self.verticalAccuracyLabel = nil;
    self.distanceTraveledLabel= nil;
    [super viewDidUnload];
}

- (void)dealloc {
    [locationManager release];
    [startingPoint release];
    [latitudeLabel release];
    [longitudeLabel release];
    [horizontalAccuracyLabel release];
    [altitudeLabel release];
    [verticalAccuracyLabel release];
    [distanceTraveledLabel release];
    [super dealloc];
}
...
```

And insert the following new methods at the end of the file:

```
...
#pragma mark -
#pragma mark CLLocationManagerDelegate Methods
- (void)locationManager:(CLLocationManager *)manager
        didUpdateToLocation:(CLLocation *)newLocation
        fromLocation:(CLLocation *)oldLocation {

    if (startingPoint == nil)
        self.startingPoint = newLocation;

    NSString *latitudeString = [[NSString alloc] initWithFormat:@"%g\u00B0",
            newLocation.coordinate.latitude];
    latitudeLabel.text = latitudeString;
```

```
    [latitudeString release];

    NSString *longitudeString = [[NSString alloc] initWithFormat:@"%g\u00B0",
            newLocation.coordinate.longitude];
    longitudeLabel.text = longitudeString;
    [longitudeString release];

    NSString *horizontalAccuracyString = [[NSString alloc]
        initWithFormat:@"%gm",
        newLocation.horizontalAccuracy];
    horizontalAccuracyLabel.text = horizontalAccuracyString;
    [horizontalAccuracyString release];

    NSString *altitudeString = [[NSString alloc] initWithFormat:@"%gm",
            newLocation.altitude];
    altitudeLabel.text = altitudeString;
    [altitudeString release];

    NSString *verticalAccuracyString = [[NSString alloc]
        initWithFormat:@"%gm",
        newLocation.verticalAccuracy];
    verticalAccuracyLabel.text = verticalAccuracyString;
    [verticalAccuracyString release];

    CLLocationDistance distance = [newLocation
        distanceFromLocation:startingPoint];
    NSString *distanceString = [[NSString alloc]
        initWithFormat:@"%gm", distance];
    distanceTraveledLabel.text = distanceString;
    [distanceString release];
}

- (void)locationManager:(CLLocationManager *)manager
      didFailWithError:(NSError *)error {

    NSString *errorType = (error.code == kCLErrorDenied) ?
            @"Access Denied" : @"Unknown Error";
    UIAlertView *alert = [[UIAlertView alloc]
        initWithTitle:@"Error getting Location"
            message:errorType
            delegate:nil
    cancelButtonTitle:@"Okay"
    otherButtonTitles:nil];
    [alert show];
    [alert release];
}
@end
```

In the viewDidLoad method, we allocate and initialize a CLLocationManager instance, assign our controller class as the delegate, set the desired accuracy to the best available, and then tell our location manager instance to start giving us location updates:

```
- (void)viewDidLoad {
    self.locationManager = [[CLLocationManager alloc] init];
```

```
        locationManager.delegate = self;
        locationManager.desiredAccuracy = kCLLocationAccuracyBest;
        [locationManager startUpdatingLocation];
}
```

Updating Location Manager

Since this class designated itself as the location manager's delegate, we know that location updates will come into this class if we implement the delegate method `locationmanager:didUpdateToLocation:fromLocation:`, so let's look at our implementation of that method. The first thing we do in that method is check to see whether `startingPoint` is nil. If it is, then this update is the first one from the location manager, and we assign the current location to our `startingPoint` property.

```
    if (startingPoint == nil)
        self.startingPoint = newLocation;
```

After that, we update the first six labels with values from the `CLLocation` object passed in the `newLocation` argument:

```
        NSString *latitudeString = [[NSString alloc] initWithFormat:@"%g\u00B0",
            newLocation.coordinate.latitude];
        latitudeLabel.text = latitudeString;
        [latitudeString release];

        NSString *longitudeString = [[NSString alloc] initWithFormat:@"%g\u00B0",
            newLocation.coordinate.longitude];
        longitudeLabel.text = longitudeString;
        [longitudeString release];

        NSString *horizontalAccuracyString = [[NSString alloc]
            initWithFormat:@"%gm",
            newLocation.horizontalAccuracy];
        horizontalAccuracyLabel.text = horizontalAccuracyString;
        [horizontalAccuracyString release];

        NSString *altitudeString = [[NSString alloc] initWithFormat:@"%gm",
            newLocation.altitude];
        altitudeLabel.text = altitudeString;
        [altitudeString release];

        NSString *verticalAccuracyString = [[NSString alloc]
            initWithFormat:@"%gm",
            newLocation.verticalAccuracy];
        verticalAccuracyLabel.text = verticalAccuracyString;
        [verticalAccuracyString release];
```

NOTE: Both the longitude and latitude are displayed in formatting strings containing the cryptic-looking "\u00B0." This represents the Unicode representation of the degree symbol (°). It's never a good idea to put anything other than ASCII characters directly in a source code file, but including the hex value in a string is just fine, and that's what we've done here.

Determining Distance Traveled

Finally, we determine the distance between the current location and the location stored in startingPoint and display the distance. While this application runs, if the user moves far enough for the location manager to detect the change, the *Distance Traveled*: field will get continually updated with the distance away from where the users were when the application was started.

```
CLLocationDistance distance = [newLocation
    distanceFromLocation:startingPoint];
NSString *distanceString = [[NSString alloc]
    initWithFormat:@"%gm", distance];
distanceTraveledLabel.text = distanceString;
[distanceString release];
```

And there you have it. Core Location is fairly straightforward and easy to use.

Before you can compile this program, you have to add *CoreLocation.framework* to your project. You do this the same as you did in Chapter 7 when you added *AudioToolbox.framework*, except you choose *CoreLocation.framework* instead of *AudioToolbox.framework*. Compile and run the application, and try it. If you have the ability to run the application on your iPhone or iPad, try going for a drive with the application running and watch the values change as you drive. Um, actually, it's better have someone else do the driving!

Wherever You Go, There You Are

You've now seen pretty much all there is to Core Location. Although the underlying technology is quite complex, Apple has provided a simple interface that hides most of the complexity, making it quite easy to add location-related features to your applications so you can tell where the users are and identify when they move.

And speaking of moving, when you're ready, proceed directly to the next chapter so we can play with iPhone's built-in accelerometer and gyro.

Chapter 17

Whee! Gyro and Accelerometer!

One of the coolest features of the iPhone, iPad, and iPod touch is the built-in accelerometer—the tiny device that lets iOS know how the device is being held and if it's being moved. iOS uses the accelerometer to handle autorotation, and many games use it as a control mechanism. It can also be used to detect shakes and other sudden movement. This capability is extended even further with iPhone 4, which also includes a built-in gyroscope that lets you determine the angle at which the device is positioned around each axis. In this chapter, we're going to introduce you to the use of the Core Motion framework to access these values in your application.

Accelerometer Physics

An **accelerometer** measures both acceleration and gravity by sensing the amount of inertial force in a given direction. The accelerometer inside your iOS device is a three-axis accelerometer, meaning that it is capable of detecting either movement or the pull of gravity in three-dimensional space. As a result, you can use the accelerometer to discover not only how the device is currently being held (as autorotation does), but also if it's lying on a table, and even whether it's face down or face up.

Accelerometers give measurements in g-forces (g for gravity), so a value of 1.0 returned by the accelerometer means that 1 g is sensed in a particular direction, as in these examples:

- If the device is being held still with no movement, there will be approximately 1 g of force exerted on it by the pull of the earth.

- If the device is being held perfectly upright, in portrait orientation, it will detect and report about 1 g of force exerted on its y axis.

■   If the device is being held at an angle, that 1 g of force will be distributed along different axes depending on how it is being held. When held at a 45-degree angle, the 1 g of force will be split roughly equally between two of the axes.

Sudden movement can be detected by looking for accelerometer values considerably larger than 1 g. In normal usage, the accelerometer does not detect significantly more than 1 g on any axis. If you shake, drop, or throw your device, the accelerometer will detect a greater amount of force on one or more axes. Please do not drop or throw your own iOS device to test this theory.

Figure 17–1 shows a graphic representation of the three axes used by the accelerometer. Notice that the accelerometer uses the more standard convention for the y coordinate, with increases in y indicating upward force, which is the opposite of Quartz 2D's coordinate system discussed in Chapter 14. When you are using the accelerometer as a control mechanism with Quartz 2D, you need to translate the y coordinate. When working with OpenGL ES, which is more likely when you are using the accelerometer to control animation, no translation is required.

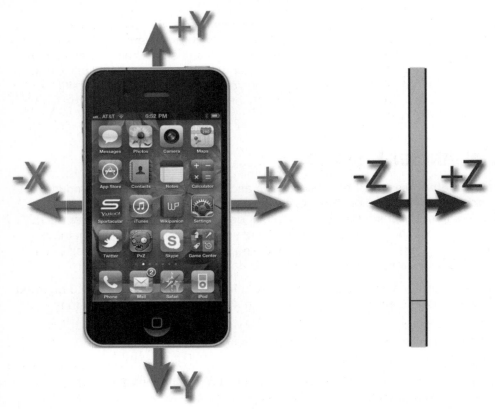

Figure 17–1. *The iPhone accelerometer's axes in three dimensions. The front view of an iPhone 4 on the left shows the x and y axes. The side view of an iPhone 4 on the right shows the z axis.*

Don't Forget Rotation

We mentioned earlier that iPhone 4 also includes a gyroscope sensor that lets you read values describing the device's rotation around its axes.

If the difference between this sensor and the accelerometer seems unclear, consider an iPhone lying flat on a table. If you begin to turn the phone around while it's lying flat, the accelerometer values won't change. That's because the forces bent on moving the phone—in this case, just the force of gravity pulling straight down the z-axis—aren't changing. (In reality, things are a bit fuzzier than that, and the action of your hand bumping the phone will surely trigger a small amount of accelerometer action.) During that same movement, however, the device's rotation values will change, in particular the z-axis rotation value. Turning the device clockwise will generate a negative value, and turning it counterclockwise gives a positive value. Stop turning, and the z-axis rotation value will go back to zero.

Rather than registering an absolute rotation value, the gyroscopes tell you about changes to the device's rotation as they happen. You'll see how this works in this chapter's first example, coming up shortly.

Core Motion and the Motion Manager

In iOS 4 and up, accelerometer and gyroscope values are accessed using the Core Motion framework. This framework provides, among other things, the CMMotionManager class, which acts as a gateway for all the values describing how the device is being moved by its user. Your application creates an instance of CMMotionManager, and then puts it to use in one of two modes:

- It can execute some code for you whenever motion occurs.
- It can hang on to a perpetually updated structure that lets you access the latest values at any time.

The latter method is ideal for games and other highly interactive applications that need to be able to poll the device's current state during each pass through the game loop. We'll show you how to implement both approaches.

Note that the CMMotionManager class isn't actually a singleton, but your application should treat it like one. You should create only one of these per app, using the normal alloc and init methods. So, if you need to access the motion manager from several places in your app, you should probably create it in your application delegate and provide access to it from there.

Besides the CMMotionManager class, Core Motion also provides a few other classes, such as CMAccelerometerData and CMGyroData, which are simple containers through which your application can access motion data. We'll touch on these classes as we get to them.

Event-Based Motion

We mentioned that the motion manager can operate in a mode where it executes some code for you each time the motion data changes. Most other Cocoa Touch classes offer this sort of functionality by letting you connect to a delegate that gets a message when the time comes, but Core Motion does things a little differently.

Since it's a new framework, available only in iOS 4 and up, Apple decided to let CMMotionManager use another new feature of the iOS 4 SDK: **blocks**. We've already used blocks a couple of times in this book, and now you're going to see another application of this technique.

Use Xcode to create a new *View-based Application* project named *MotionMonitor*. This will be a simple app that reads both accelerometer data and gyroscope data (if available) and displays them on the screen.

> **NOTE:** The applications in this chapter do not function on the simulator because the simulator has no accelerometer and no gyro. Aw, shucks.

First, we need to link Core Motion into our app. This is an optional system framework, so we must add it in. Follow the instructions from Chapter 7 for adding the Audio Toolbox framework (in the "Linking in the Audio Toolbox Framework" section), but instead of selecting *AudioToolbox.framework*, select the *CoreMotion.framework*. (In a nutshell, control-click the *Frameworks* folder and select **Add ➤ Existing Frameworks…** from the contextual menu that appears.)

Now select the *MotionMonitorViewController.h* file, and make the following changes:

```
#import <UIKit/UIKit.h>
#import <CoreMotion/CoreMotion.h>

@interface MotionMonitorViewController : UIViewController {
    CMMotionManager *motionManager;
    UILabel *accelerometerLabel;
    UILabel *gyroscopeLabel;
}

@property (nonatomic, retain) CMMotionManager *motionManager;
@property (nonatomic, retain) IBOutlet UILabel *accelerometerLabel;
@property (nonatomic, retain) IBOutlet UILabel *gyroscopeLabel;

@end
```

That provides us with a pointer for accessing the motion manager itself, along with outlets to a pair of labels where we'll display the information. Nothing much needs to be explained here, so just go ahead and save your changes.

Next, open *MotionMonitorViewController.xib* in Interface Builder.

Open the view by double-clicking its icon in the nib window, and then drag out a label from the library into the view. Resize the label to make it run from the left blue guideline to the right blue guideline, resize it to be about half the height of the entire view, and then align the top of the label to the top blue guideline.

Now open the attributes inspector and change the # *Lines* field from *1* to *0*. The # *Lines* attribute is used to specify just how many lines of text may appear in the label, and provides a hard upper limit. If you set it to 0, no limit is applied, and the label can contain as many lines as you like.

Next, option-drag the label to create a copy and align the copy with the blue guidelines in the bottom half of the view.

Finally, control-drag from the *File's Owner* icon to each of the labels, connecting *accelerometerLabel* to the upper one and *gyroscopeLabel* to the lower one.

This simple GUI is complete, so save your work and get ready for some coding.

Next, select *MotionMonitorViewController.m*, and add the property synthesizers to the top of the implementation block, and the memory management calls to the viewDidUnload and dealloc methods at the end:

```
#import "MotionMonitorViewController.h"

@implementation MotionMonitorViewController
@synthesize motionManager;
@synthesize accelerometerLabel;
@synthesize gyroscopeLabel;

...

- (void)viewDidUnload {
    // Release any retained subviews of the main view.
    // e.g. self.myOutlet = nil;
    self.motionManager = nil;
    self.accelerometerLabel = nil;
    self.gyroscopeLabel = nil;
    [super viewDidUnload];
}

- (void)dealloc {
    [motionManager release];
    [accelerometerLabel release];
    [gyroscopeLabel release];
    [super dealloc];
}
@end
```

Now comes the interesting part. Remove the comment marks around the viewDidLoad method, and give it the following content:

```
- (void)viewDidLoad {
    [super viewDidLoad];
    self.motionManager = [[[CMMotionManager alloc] init] autorelease];
    NSOperationQueue *queue = [[[NSOperationQueue alloc] init] autorelease];
    if (motionManager.accelerometerAvailable) {
        motionManager.accelerometerUpdateInterval = 1.0/10.0;
        [motionManager startAccelerometerUpdatesToQueue:queue withHandler:
```

```objc
        ^(CMAccelerometerData *accelerometerData, NSError *error){
            NSString *labelText;
            if (error) {
                [motionManager stopAccelerometerUpdates];
                labelText = [NSString stringWithFormat:
                            @"Accelerometer encountered error: %@", error];
            } else {
                labelText = [NSString stringWithFormat:
                        @"Accelerometer\n-----------\nx: %+.2f\ny: %+.2f\nz: %+.2f",
                        accelerometerData.acceleration.x,
                        accelerometerData.acceleration.y,
                        accelerometerData.acceleration.z];
            }
            [accelerometerLabel performSelectorOnMainThread:@selector(setText:)
                                            withObject:labelText
                                            waitUntilDone:YES];
        }];
    } else {
        accelerometerLabel.text = @"This device has no accelerometer.";
    }
    if (motionManager.gyroAvailable) {
        motionManager.gyroUpdateInterval = 1.0/10.0;
        [motionManager startGyroUpdatesToQueue:queue withHandler:
        ^(CMGyroData *gyroData, NSError *error) {
            NSString *labelText;
            if (error) {
                [motionManager stopGyroUpdates];
                labelText = [NSString stringWithFormat:
                            @"Gyroscope encountered error: %@", error];
            } else {
                labelText = [NSString stringWithFormat:
                            @"Gyroscope\n--------\nx: %+.2f\ny: %+.2f\nz: %+.2f",
                            gyroData.rotationRate.x,
                            gyroData.rotationRate.y,
                            gyroData.rotationRate.z];
            }
            [gyroscopeLabel performSelectorOnMainThread:@selector(setText:)
                                            withObject:labelText
                                            waitUntilDone:YES];
        }];
    } else {
        gyroscopeLabel.text = @"This device has no gyroscope";
    }
}
```

This method contains all the code we need to fire up the sensors, tell them to report to us every 1/10 second, and update the screen when they do so.

Thanks to the power of blocks, it's all really simple and cohesive. Instead of putting parts of the functionality in delegate methods, defining behaviors in blocks lets us see the behavior in the same method where it's being configured! Let's take this apart a bit. We start off with this:

```
self.motionManager = [[[CMMotionManager alloc] init] autorelease];
NSOperationQueue *queue = [[[NSOperationQueue alloc] init] autorelease];
```

That code first creates an instance of CMMotionManager, which we'll use to watch motion events. Then it creates an operation queue, which is simply a container for a pile of work that needs to be done, as you may recall from Chapter 13.

CAUTION: The motion manager wants to have a queue in which it will put the bits of work to be done, as specified by the blocks you will give it, each time an event occurs. It would be tempting to use the system's default queue for this purpose, but the documentation for CMMotionManager explicitly warns not to do this! The concern is that the default queue could end up chock full of these events and have a hard time processing other crucial system events as a result.

Then we go on to configure the accelerometer. We first check to make sure the device actually has an accelerometer. All handheld iOS devices released so far do have one, but it's worth checking in case some future device doesn't. Then we set the time interval we want between updates, specified in seconds. Here, we're asking for 1/10 second. Note that setting this doesn't guarantee that we'll receive updates at precisely that speed. In fact, that setting is really a cap, specifying the best rate the motion manager will be allowed to give us. In reality, it may update less frequently than that.

```
if (motionManager.accelerometerAvailable) {
    motionManager.accelerometerUpdateInterval = 1.0/10.0;
```

Next, we tell the motion manager to start reporting accelerometer updates. We pass in the queue where it will put its work and the block that defines the work that will be done each time an update occurs. Remember that a block always starts off with a carat (^), followed by a parentheses-wrapped list of arguments that the block expects to be populated when it's executed (in this case, the accelerometer data and potentially an error to alert us of trouble), and finishes with a curly brace section containing the code to be executed itself.

```
[motionManager startAccelerometerUpdatesToQueue:queue withHandler:
    ^(CMAccelerometerData *accelerometerData, NSError *error) {
```

And here's the content of the block. It creates a string based on the current accelerometer values, or it generates an error message if there's a problem. Then it pushes that string value into the accelerometerLabel. Here, we can't do that directly, since UIKit classes like UILabel usually work well only when accessed from the main thread. Due to the way this code will be executed, from within an NSOperationQueue, we simply don't know the specific thread in which we'll be executing. So, we use the performSelectorOnMainThread:withObject:waitUntilDone: method to make the main thread handle this.

Note that the accelerometer values are accessed through the acceleration property of the accelerometerData that was passed into it. The acceleration property is of type CMAcceleration, which is just a simple struct containing three float values.

accelerometerData itself is an instance of the CMAccelerometerData class, which is really just a wrapper for CMAcceleration! If you think this seems like an unnecessary profusion of classes for simply passing three floats around, well, you're not alone. Regardless, here's how to use it:

```
NSString *labelText;
if (error) {
    [motionManager stopAccelerometerUpdates];
    labelText = [NSString stringWithFormat:
                    @"Accelerometer encountered error: %@", error];
} else {
    labelText = [NSString stringWithFormat:
                    @"Accelerometer\n----------\nx: %+.2f\ny: %+.2f\nz: %+.2f",
                accelerometerData.acceleration.x,
                accelerometerData.acceleration.y,
                accelerometerData.acceleration.z];
}
[accelerometerLabel performSelectorOnMainThread:@selector(setText:)
        withObject:labelText
        waitUntilDone:YES];
```

Then we finish the block, and finish the square-bracketed method call where we were passing that block in the first place. Finally, we provide a different code path entirely, in case the device doesn't have an accelerometer. As mentioned earlier, all iOS devices so far have an accelerometer, but who knows what the future holds in store?

```
    }];
} else {
    accelerometerLabel.text = @"This device has no accelerometer.";
}
```

The code for the gyroscope is, as you surely noticed, structurally identical, differing only in the particulars of which methods are called and how reported values are accessed. It's similar enough that there's no need to walk you through it here.

Now, build and run your app on whatever iOS device you have, and try it out (see Figure 17–2). As you tilt your device around in different ways, you'll see how the accelerometer values adjust to each new position, and will hold steady as long as you hold the device steady.

Figure 17–2. *MotionMonitor running on an iPhone 4. Unfortunately, you'll get only a pair of error messages if you run this app in the simulator.*

If you have an iPhone 4 (or any future device containing the gyroscope), you'll see how those values change as well. Whenever the device is standing still, no matter which orientation it is in, the gyroscope values will hover around zero. As you rotate the device, however, you'll see that the gyroscope values change, depending on how you rotate it on its various axes. The values will always move back to zero when you stop moving the device.

Proactive Motion Access

You've seen how to access motion data by passing CMMotionManager blocks to be called as motion occurs. This kind of event-driven motion handling can work well enough for the average Cocoa app, but sometimes it doesn't quite fit an application's particular needs. Interactive games, for example, typically have a perpetually running loop that processes user input, updates the state of the game, and redraws the screen. In such a case, the event-driven approach isn't such a good fit, since you would need to implement an object that waits for motion events, remembers the latest positions from each sensor as they're reported, and is ready to report the data back to the main game loop when necessary.

Fortunately, CMMotionManager has a built-in solution. Instead of passing in blocks, we can just tell it to activate the sensors using the startAccelerometerUpdates and startGyroUpdates methods, after which we simply read the values any time we want, directly from the motion manager!

Let's change our MotionMonitor app to use this approach, just so you can see how it works. Start off by making a copy of your *MotionMonitor* project folder. Next, add a new instance variable and matching property to *MotionMonitorViewController.h*, a pointer to an NSTimer that will trigger all our display updates:

```
#import <UIKit/UIKit.h>
#import <CoreMotion/CoreMotion.h>

@interface MotionMonitorViewController : UIViewController {
    CMMotionManager *motionManager;
    UILabel *accelerometerLabel;
    UILabel *gyroscopeLabel;
    NSTimer *updateTimer;
}

@property (retain) CMMotionManager *motionManager;
@property (retain) IBOutlet UILabel *accelerometerLabel;
@property (retain) IBOutlet UILabel *gyroscopeLabel;
@property (retain) NSTimer *updateTimer;

@end
```

Now switch to *MotionMonitorViewController.m*, where you'll need to synthesize the new property, and release it in dealloc:

```
@implementation MotionMonitorViewController

@synthesize motionManager;
@synthesize accelerometerLabel;
@synthesize gyroscopeLabel;
@synthesize updateTimer;
...
- (void)dealloc {
    [motionManager release];
    [accelerometerLabel release];
    [gyroscopeLabel release];
    [updateTimer release];
    [super dealloc];
}
```

Get rid of the entire viewDidLoad method we had before, and replace it with this simpler version, which just sets up the motion manager and provides informational labels for devices lacking sensors:

```
- (void)viewDidLoad {
    [super viewDidLoad];
    self.motionManager = [[[CMMotionManager alloc] init] autorelease];

    if (motionManager.accelerometerAvailable) {
        motionManager.accelerometerUpdateInterval = 1.0/10.0;
        [motionManager startAccelerometerUpdates];
    } else {
        accelerometerLabel.text = @"This device has no accelerometer.";
```

```
    }
    if (motionManager.gyroAvailable) {
        motionManager.gyroUpdateInterval = 1.0/10.0;
        [motionManager startGyroUpdates];
    } else {
        gyroscopeLabel.text = @"This device has no gyroscope.";
    }
}
```

Normally, we use `viewDidLoad` and `viewDidUnload` to "bracket" the creation and destruction of properties related to the GUI display. In the case of our new timer, however, we want it to be active only during an even smaller window of time, when the view is actually being displayed. That way, we keep the usage of our main "game loop" to a bare minimum. We can accomplish this by implementing `viewWillAppear:` and `viewDidDisappear:` as follows. Add these two methods just after `viewDidLoad`:

```
- (void)viewWillAppear:(BOOL)animated {
    [super viewWillAppear:animated];
    self.updateTimer = [NSTimer scheduledTimerWithTimeInterval:1.0/10.0
                                                        target:self
                                                      selector:@selector(updateDisplay)
                                                      userInfo:nil
                                                       repeats:YES];
}


- (void)viewDidDisappear:(BOOL)animated {
    [super viewDidDisappear:animated];
    self.updateTimer = nil;
}
```

The code in `viewWillAppear:` creates a new timer and schedules it to fire once every 1/10 second, calling the `updateDisplay` method, which we haven't created yet. Add this method just below `ViewDidDisappear:`.

```
- (void)updateDisplay {
    if (motionManager.accelerometerAvailable) {
        CMAccelerometerData *accelerometerData = motionManager.accelerometerData;
        accelerometerLabel.text  = [NSString stringWithFormat:
                    @"Accelerometer\n-----------\nx: %+.2f\ny: %+.2f\nz: %+.2f",
                    accelerometerData.acceleration.x,
                    accelerometerData.acceleration.y,
                    accelerometerData.acceleration.z];
    }
    if (motionManager.gyroAvailable) {
        CMGyroData *gyroData = motionManager.gyroData;
        gyroscopeLabel.text = [NSString stringWithFormat:
                    @"Gyroscope\n--------\nx: %+.2f\ny: %+.2f\nz: %+.2f",
                    gyroData.rotationRate.x,
                    gyroData.rotationRate.y,
                    gyroData.rotationRate.z];
    }
}
```

Build and run the app on your device, and you should see that it behaves exactly like the first version. Now you've seen two ways of accessing motion data. Use whichever suits your applications best.

Accelerometer Results

We mentioned earlier that the iPhone's accelerometer detects acceleration along three axes, and it provides this information using the `CMAcceleration` struct. Each `CMAcceleration` has an x, y, and z field, each of which holds a floating-point value. A value of 0 means that the accelerometer detects no movement on that particular axis. A positive or negative value indicates force in one direction. For example, a negative value for y indicates that downward pull is sensed, which is probably an indication that the phone is being held upright in portrait orientation. A positive value for y indicates some force is being exerted in the opposite direction, which could mean the phone is being held upside down or that the phone is being moved in a downward direction.

Keeping the diagram in Figure 17–3 in mind, let's look at some accelerometer results. Note that, in real life, you will almost never get values this precise, as the accelerometer is sensitive enough to pick up even tiny amounts of motion, and you will usually pick up at least some tiny amount of force on all three axes. This is real-world physics, not high-school physics.

Probably the most common usage of the accelerometer in third-party applications is as a controller for games. We'll create a program that uses the accelerometer for input a little later in the chapter, but first, we'll look at another common accelerometer use: detecting shakes.

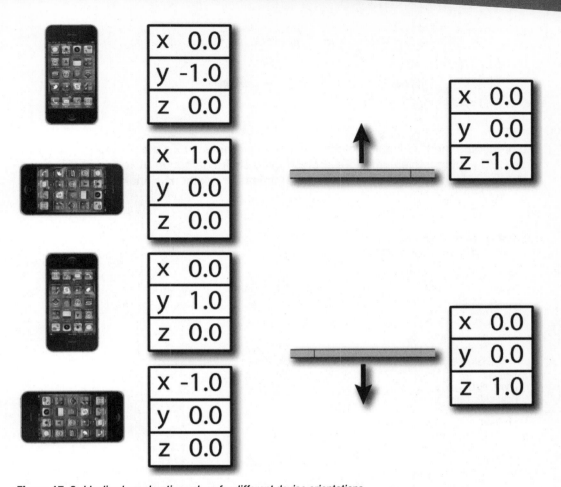

Figure 17–3. *Idealized acceleration values for different device orientations*

Detecting Shakes

Like a gesture, a shake can be used as a form of input to your application. For example, the drawing program GLPaint, which is one of the iOS sample code projects, lets the user erase drawings by shaking their iOS device, sort of like an Etch A Sketch.

Detecting shakes is relatively trivial. All it requires is checking for an absolute value on one of the axes that is greater than a set threshold. During normal usage, it's not uncommon for one of the three axes to register values up to around 1.3 g, but getting values much higher than that generally requires intentional force. The accelerometer seems to be unable to register values higher than around 2.3 g (at least in our experience), so you don't want to set your threshold any higher than that.

To detect a shake, you could check for an absolute value greater than 1.5 for a slight shake and 2.0 for a strong shake, like this:

```
- (void)accelerometer:(UIAccelerometer *)accelerometer
        didAccelerate:(UIAcceleration *)acceleration {

    if (fabsf(acceleration.x) > 2.0
        || fabsf(acceleration.y) > 2.0
        || fabsf(acceleration.z) > 2.0) {
        // Do something here...
    }
}
```

The preceding method would detect any movement on any axis that exceeded two g-forces. You could implement more sophisticated shake detection by requiring the user to shake back and forth a certain number of times to register as a shake, like so:

```
- (void)accelerometer:(UIAccelerometer *)accelerometer
        didAccelerate:(UIAcceleration *)acceleration {

    static NSInteger shakeCount = 0;
    static NSDate *shakeStart;

    NSDate *now = [[NSDate alloc] init];
    NSDate *checkDate = [[NSDate alloc] initWithTimeInterval:1.5f
        sinceDate:shakeStart];
    if ([now compare:checkDate] ==
        NSOrderedDescending || shakeStart == nil) {
        shakeCount = 0;
        [shakeStart release];
        shakeStart = [[NSDate alloc] init];
    }
    [now release];
    [checkDate release];

    if (fabsf(acceleration.x) > 2.0
        || fabsf(acceleration.y) > 2.0
        || fabsf(2.0.z) > 2.0) {
        shakeCount++;
        if (shakeCount > 4) {
            // Do something
            shakeCount = 0;
            [shakeStart release];
            shakeStart = [[NSDate alloc] init];
        }
    }
}
```

This method keeps track of the number of times the accelerometer reports a value above 2.0, and if it happens four times within a 1.5-second span of time, it registers as a shake.

Baked-In Shaking

There's actually another way to check for shakes—one that's baked right into the responder chain. Remember back in Chapter 15 how we implemented methods like touchesBegan:withEvent: to detect touches? Well, iOS also provides three similar responder methods for detecting motion:

- When motion begins, the `motionBegan:withEvent:` method is sent to the first responder and then on through the responder chain as discussed in Chapter 15.

- When the motion ends, the `motionEnded:withEvent:` method is sent to the first responder.

- If the phone rings, or some other interrupting action happens during the shake, the `motionCancelled:withEvent:` message is sent to the first responder.

This means that you can actually detect a shake without using `CMMotionManager` directly. All you have to do is override the appropriate motion-sensing methods in your view or view controller, and they will be called automatically when the user shakes their phone. Unless you specifically need more control over the shake gesture, you should use the baked-in motion detection rather than manual method in this chapter, but we thought we would show you the manual method in case you ever do need more control.

Now that you have the basic idea of how to detect shakes, we're going to break your phone.

Shake and Break

OK, we're not really going to break your phone, but we're going to write an application that detects shakes and then makes your phone look and sound like it broke as a result of the shake.

When you launch the application, the program will display a picture that looks like the iPhone home screen (see Figure 17–4).

Shake the phone hard enough, though, and your poor phone will make a sound that you never want to hear coming out of a consumer electronics device. What's more, your screen will look like the one shown in Figure 17–5. Why do we do these evil things?

Not to worry. You can reset the iPhone to its previously pristine state by touching the screen.

Figure 17–4. *The ShakeAndBreak application looks innocuous enough...*

Figure 17–5. *. . . but handle it too roughly and—oh no!*

NOTE: Just for completeness, we've included a modified version of ShakeAndBreak in the project archives based on the built-in shake-detection method. You'll find it in the project archive in a folder named *17 - ShakeAndBreak - Motion Methods*. The magic is in the `ShakeAndBreakViewController`'s `motionEnded:withEvent:` method.

Create a new project in Xcode using the *View-based Application* template. Call the new project *ShakeAndBreak*. In the *17 - ShakeAndBreak* folder of the project archive, we've provided you the two images and the sound file you need for this application. Drag *home.png*, *homebroken.png*, and *glass.wav* to the *Resources* folder of your project. There's also an *icon.png* in that folder. Add that to the *Resources* folder as well.

Next, expand the *Resources* folder, and select *ShakeAndBreak-Info.plist* to bring up the property list editor. We need to add an entry to the property list to tell our application not to use a status bar. Single-click any row in the property list, and click the plus sign icon at the right of the list to add a new row. Change the new row's *Key* to *UIStatusBarHidden* (see Figure 17–6). The *Value* of this row will default to NO (unchecked). Click the check box to check it. Finally, type *icon.png* in the *Value* column next to the *Icon file* key.

Key	Value
▼ Information Property List	(13 items)
Localization native development re	English
Bundle display name	${PRODUCT_NAME}
Executable file	${EXECUTABLE_NAME}
Icon file	icon.png
Bundle identifier	com.apress.${PRODUCT_NAME:rfc1034identifier}
InfoDictionary version	6.0
Bundle name	${PRODUCT_NAME}
Bundle OS Type code	APPL
Bundle creator OS Type code	????
Bundle version	1.0
Application requires iPhone enviror	☑
Main nib file base name	MainWindow
Status bar is initially hidden	☑

Figure 17–6. *Changing the Value Type for UIStatusBarHidden*

Now, expand the *Classes* folder. We're going to need to create an outlet to point to an image view so that we can change the displayed image. We'll also need a couple of `UIImage` instances to hold the two pictures, a sound ID to refer to the sound, and a Boolean to keep track of whether the screen needs to be reset. Single-click *ShakeAndBreakViewController.h*, and add the following code:

```
#import <UIKit/UIKit.h>
#import <CoreMotion/CoreMotion.h>
#import <AudioToolbox/AudioToolbox.h>

#define kAccelerationThreshold    1.7
```

```
#define kUpdateInterval            (1.0f/10.0f)

@interface ShakeAndBreakViewController :
    UIViewController <UIAccelerometerDelegate> {
    UIImageView *imageView;

    CMMotionManager *motionManager;
    BOOL brokenScreenShowing;
    SystemSoundID soundID;
    UIImage *fixed;
    UIImage *broken;
}
@property (nonatomic, retain) CMMotionManager *motionManager;
@property (nonatomic, retain) IBOutlet UIImageView *imageView;
@property (nonatomic, retain) UIImage *fixed;
@property (nonatomic, retain) UIImage *broken;
@end
```

Save the header file, and double-click *ShakeAndBreakViewController.xib* to edit the file in Interface Builder. Double-click the *View* icon to bring up the *View* window. In the attributes inspector, change the *Status Bar* popup under *Simulated Metrics Elements* from *Gray* to *Unspecified*. Now, drag an *Image View* over from the library to the window labeled *View*. The image view should automatically resize to take up the full window, so just place it so that it sits perfectly within the window.

Control-drag from the *File's Owner* icon to the image view, and select the *imageView* outlet. Then save the nib file.

Next, select the *ShakeAndBreakController.m* file, and add the following code near the top of the file:

```
#import "ShakeAndBreakViewController.h"

@implementation ShakeAndBreakViewController
@synthesize motionManager;
@synthesize imageView;
@synthesize fixed;
@synthesize broken;

- (void) viewDidLoad {
    NSString *path = [[NSBundle mainBundle] pathForResource:@"glass"
                                                ofType:@"wav"];
    AudioServicesCreateSystemSoundID((CFURLRef)[NSURL
                                    fileURLWithPath:path], &soundID);
    self.fixed = [UIImage imageNamed:@"home.png"];
    self.broken = [UIImage imageNamed:@"homebroken.png"];

    imageView.image = fixed;

    self.motionManager = [[[CMMotionManager alloc] init] autorelease];
    motionManager.accelerometerUpdateInterval = kUpdateInterval;
    NSOperationQueue *queue = [[[NSOperationQueue alloc] init] autorelease];
    [motionManager startAccelerometerUpdatesToQueue:queue
                                    withHandler:
```

```
        ^(CMAccelerometerData *accelerometerData, NSError *error){
            if (error) {
                [motionManager stopAccelerometerUpdates];
            } else {
                if (!brokenScreenShowing) {
                    CMAcceleration acceleration = accelerometerData.acceleration;
                    if (acceleration.x > kAccelerationThreshold
                        || acceleration.y > kAccelerationThreshold
                        || acceleration.z > kAccelerationThreshold) {
                        [imageView performSelectorOnMainThread:@selector(setImage:)
                                            withObject:broken
                                          waitUntilDone:NO];
                        AudioServicesPlaySystemSound(soundID);
                        brokenScreenShowing = YES;
                    }
                }
            }
        }];
    }
    ...
```

Insert the following lines of code into the existing `dealloc` and `viewDidUnload` methods:

```
...
- (void)viewDidUnload {
    // Release any retained subviews of the main view.
    // e.g. self.myOutlet = nil;
    self.motionManager = nil;
    self.imageView = nil;
    self.fixed = nil;
    self.broken = nil;
    [super viewDidUnload];
}

- (void)dealloc {
    [motionManager release];
    [imageView release];
    [fixed release];
    [broken release];
    [super dealloc];
}
...
```

And finally, add the following new method at the bottom of the file:

```
...
#pragma mark -
- (void)touchesBegan:(NSSet *)touches withEvent:(UIEvent *)event {
    imageView.image = fixed;
    brokenScreenShowing = NO;
}

@end
```

The first method we implement, and the one where most of the interesting things happen, is viewDidLoad. First, we load the glass sound file into memory and save the assigned identifier in the soundID instance variable.

```
NSString *path = [[NSBundle mainBundle] pathForResource:@"glass"
                                                ofType:@"wav"];
AudioServicesCreateSystemSoundID((CFURLRef)[NSURL
                                fileURLWithPath:path], &soundID);
```

We then load the two images into memory.

```
self.fixed = [UIImage imageNamed:@"home.png"];
self.broken = [UIImage imageNamed:@"homebroken.png"];
```

Finally, we set imageView to show the unbroken screenshot and set brokenScreenShowing to NO to indicate that the screen does not currently need to be reset.

```
imageView.image = fixed;
brokenScreenShowing = NO;
```

Then we create a CMMotionManager and an NSOperationQueue (just as we've done before), and start up the accelerometer, sending it a block to be run each time the accelerometer value changes.

```
self.motionManager = [[[CMMotionManager alloc] init] autorelease];
motionManager.accelerometerUpdateInterval = kUpdateInterval;
NSOperationQueue *queue = [[[NSOperationQueue alloc] init] autorelease];
[motionManager startAccelerometerUpdatesToQueue:queue
                        withHandler:
```

If the block finds accelerometer values high enough to trigger the "break," it makes imageView switch over to the broken image and starts playing the breaking sound. Note that imageView is a member of the UIImageView class, which, like most parts of UIKit, is meant to run only in the main thread. Since the block may be run in another thread, we force the imageView update to happen on the main thread.

```
^(CMAccelerometerData *accelerometerData, NSError *error){
    if (error) {
        [motionManager stopAccelerometerUpdates];
    } else {
        if (!brokenScreenShowing) {
            CMAcceleration acceleration = accelerometerData.acceleration;
            if (acceleration.x > kAccelerationThreshold
                || acceleration.y > kAccelerationThreshold
                || acceleration.z > kAccelerationThreshold) {
                [imageView performSelectorOnMainThread:@selector(setImage:)
                                    withObject:broken
                                    waitUntilDone:NO];
                AudioServicesPlaySystemSound(soundID);
                brokenScreenShowing = YES;
            }
        }
    }
}];
```

The last method is one you should be quite familiar with by now. It's called when the screen is touched. All we do in that method is to set the image back to the unbroken screen and set brokenScreenShowing back to NO.

```
imageView.image = fixed;
brokenScreenShowing = NO;
```

Finally, add the *CoreMotion.framework* as well as the *AudioToolbox.framework* so that we can play the sound file. You can link the frameworks into your application by following the instructions from earlier in the chapter.

Compile and run the application, and take it for a test drive. For those of you who don't have the ability to run this application on your iOS device, you might want to give the shake-event-based version a try. The simulator does not simulate the accelerometer hardware, but it does simulate the shake event, so the version of the application in *17 ShakeAndBreak - Motion Method* will work with the simulator.

Go have some fun with it. When you're finished, come on back, and you'll see how to use the accelerometer as a controller for games and other programs.

Accelerometer As Directional Controller

Commonly, instead of using buttons to control the movement of a character or object in a game, the accelerometer is used. In a car racing game, for example, twisting the iOS device like a steering wheel might steer your car, while tipping it forward might accelerate and tipping back might brake.

Exactly how you use the accelerometer as a controller will vary greatly depending on the specific mechanics of the game. In the simplest cases, you might just take the value from one of the axes, multiply it by a number, and tack that on to the coordinates of the controlled objects. In more complex games where physics are modeled more realistically, you would need to make adjustments to the velocity of the controlled object based on the values returned from the accelerometer.

The one tricky aspect of using the accelerometer as a controller is that the delegate method is not guaranteed to call back at the interval you specify. If you tell the motion manager to read the accelerometer 60 times a second, all that you can say for sure is that it won't update you more than 60 times a second. You're not guaranteed to get 60 evenly spaced updates every second. So, if you're doing animation based on input from the accelerometer, you must keep track of the time that passes between updates and factor that into your equations to determine how far objects have moved.

Rolling Marbles

For our next trick, we're going to let you move a sprite around iPhone's screen by tilting the phone. This is going to be a very simple example of using the accelerometer to receive input. We're going to use Quartz 2D to handle our animation.

> **NOTE:** As a general rule, when you're working with games and other programs that need smooth animation, you'll probably want to use OpenGL ES. We're using Quartz 2D in this application for the sake of simplicity and to reduce the amount of code that's unrelated to using the accelerometer. The animation won't be quite as smooth as if we were using OpenGL, but it will be a lot less work.

In this application, as you tilt your iPhone, the marble will roll around as if it were on the surface of a table (see Figure 17–6). Tip it to the left, and the ball will roll to the left. Tip it further, and it will move faster. Tip it back, and it will slow down and then start going in the other direction.

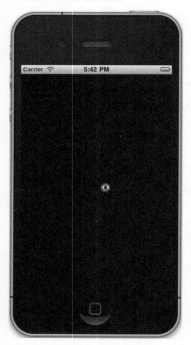

Figure 17–6. *The Rolling Marble application lets you do just that—roll a marble around the screen.*

In Xcode, create a new project using the *View-based Application* template, and call this one *Ball*. Expand the *Classes* and *Resource* folders, so you can see the files we will be working with. In the *17 - Ball* folder in the project archive, you'll find an image called *ball.png*. Drag that to the *Resources* folder of your project.

Now, single-click the *Classes* folder, and select **File ➤ New File….** Select *Objective-C class* from the *Cocoa Touch Class* category, and then select *UIView* in the *Subclass of* popup. Name the new file *BallView.m* and make sure a *.h* file is created. We'll get back to editing this class a little later.

Double-click *BallViewController.xib* to edit the file in Interface Builder. Single-click the *View* icon, and use the identity inspector to change the view's class from *UIView* to *BallView*. Next, switch to the attributes inspector, and change the view's *Background* to *Black Color*. Then save the nib.

Back in Xcode, select *BallViewController.h*. All we need to do here is prepare for Core Motion, so make the following changes:

```
#import <UIKit/UIKit.h>
#import <CoreMotion/CoreMotion.h>

#define kUpdateInterval    (1.0f/60.0f)

@interface BallViewController : UIViewController {
    CMMotionManager *motionManager;
}
@property (nonatomic, retain) CMMotionManager *motionManager;
@end
```

Next, switch to *BallViewController.m*, and add the following lines toward the top of the file:

```
#import "BallViewController.h"
#import "BallView.h"

@implementation BallViewController
@synthesize motionManager;
...
```

Next, replace the commented-out version of viewDidLoad with this version:

```
- (void)viewDidLoad {
    self.motionManager = [[[CMMotionManager alloc] init] autorelease];
    NSOperationQueue *queue = [[[NSOperationQueue alloc] init] autorelease];
    motionManager.accelerometerUpdateInterval = kUpdateInterval;
    [motionManager startAccelerometerUpdatesToQueue:queue withHandler:
     ^(CMAccelerometerData *accelerometerData, NSError *error) {
        [(BallView *)self.view setAcceleration:accelerometerData.acceleration];
        [(BallView *)self.view performSelectorOnMainThread:@selector(draw)
            withObject:nil waitUntilDone:NO];
    }];
    [super viewDidLoad];
}
```

The viewDidLoad method here is pretty similar to some of what we've done elsewhere in this chapter. The main difference is that we are declaring a much higher update interval of 60 times per second. In the block that we tell the motion manager to execute when there are accelerometer updates to report, we pass the acceleration object into our view, and then call a method named draw, which updates the position of the ball in the view based on acceleration and the amount of time that has passed since the last update. Since that block can be executed on any thread, and the methods belonging to UIKit objects (including UIView) can be safely used only from the main thread, we once again force the draw method to be called in the main thread.

Writing the Ball View

Since we're doing the bulk of our work in the `BallView` class, we had better write it, huh? Single-*click BallView.h*, and make the following changes:

```
#import <UIKit/UIKit.h>
#import <CoreMotion/CoreMotion.h>

@interface BallView : UIView {
    UIImage         *image;

    CGPoint         currentPoint;
    CGPoint         previousPoint;
    CMAcceleration  acceleration;
    CGFloat         ballXVelocity;
    CGFloat         ballYVelocity;
}
@property (nonatomic, retain) UIImage *image;
@property CGPoint currentPoint;
@property CGPoint previousPoint;
@property (nonatomic, assign) CMAcceleration acceleration;
@property CGFloat ballXVelocity;
@property CGFloat ballYVelocity;
- (void)draw;
@end
```

Let's look at the instance variables and talk about what we're doing with each of them. The first instance variable is a `UIImage` that will point to the sprite that we'll be moving around the screen.

```
    UIImage *image;
```

After that, we keep track of two `CGPoint` variables. The `currentPoint` variable will hold the current position of the ball. We'll also keep track of the last point where we drew the sprite. That way, we can build an update rectangle that encompasses both the new and old positions of the ball, so that it gets drawn at the new spot and erased at the old one.

```
    CGPoint     currentPoint;
    CGPoint     previousPoint;
```

Next is a pointer to an `acceleration` struct, which is how we will get the accelerometer information from our controller.

```
    CMAcceleration acceleration;
```

We also have two variables to keep track of the ball's current velocity in two dimensions. Although this isn't going to be a very complex simulation, we do want the ball to move in a manner similar to a real ball. We'll calculate the ball movement in the next section. We'll get acceleration from the accelerometer and keep track of velocity on two axes with these variables.

```
    CGFloat ballXVelocity;
    CGFloat ballYVelocity;
```

Let's switch over to *BallView.m* and write the code to draw and move the ball around the screen. First, make the following changes at the top of *BallView.m*:

```
#import "BallView.h"

@implementation BallView
@synthesize image;
@synthesize currentPoint;
@synthesize previousPoint;
@synthesize acceleration;
@synthesize ballXVelocity;
@synthesize ballYVelocity;

- (id)initWithCoder:(NSCoder *)coder {

    if (self = [super initWithCoder:coder]) {
        self.image = [UIImage imageNamed:@"ball.png"];
        self.currentPoint = CGPointMake((self.bounds.size.width / 2.0f) +
            (image.size.width / 2.0f),
            (self.bounds.size.height / 2.0f) + (image.size.height / 2.0f));

        ballXVelocity = 0.0f;
        ballYVelocity = 0.0f;
    }
    return self;
}
...
```

Now, replace the commented-out drawRect: method and add these lines to the dealloc method:

```
- (void)drawRect:(CGRect)rect {
    // Drawing code
    [image drawAtPoint:currentPoint];
}

- (void)dealloc {
    [image release];
    [super dealloc];
}
...
```

Then add these methods to the end of the class:

```
...
#pragma mark -
- (CGPoint)currentPoint {
    return currentPoint;
}

- (void)setCurrentPoint:(CGPoint)newPoint {
    previousPoint = currentPoint;
    currentPoint = newPoint;

    if (currentPoint.x < 0) {
        currentPoint.x = 0;
        ballXVelocity = 0;
    }
    if (currentPoint.y < 0){
```

```
            currentPoint.y = 0;
            ballYVelocity = 0;
        }
        if (currentPoint.x > self.bounds.size.width - image.size.width) {
            currentPoint.x = self.bounds.size.width - image.size.width;
            ballXVelocity = 0;
        }
        if (currentPoint.y > self.bounds.size.height - image.size.height) {
            currentPoint.y = self.bounds.size.height - image.size.height;
            ballYVelocity = 0;
        }

        CGRect currentImageRect = CGRectMake(currentPoint.x, currentPoint.y,
                currentPoint.x + image.size.width,
                currentPoint.y + image.size.height);
        CGRect previousImageRect = CGRectMake(previousPoint.x, previousPoint.y,
                previousPoint.x + image.size.width,
                currentPoint.y + image.size.width);
        [self setNeedsDisplayInRect:CGRectUnion(currentImageRect,
            previousImageRect)];
    }

- (void)draw {
    static NSDate *lastDrawTime;

    if (lastDrawTime != nil) {
        NSTimeInterval secondsSinceLastDraw =
            -([lastDrawTime timeIntervalSinceNow]);

        ballYVelocity = ballYVelocity + -(acceleration.y *
            secondsSinceLastDraw);
        ballXVelocity = ballXVelocity + acceleration.x *
            secondsSinceLastDraw;

        CGFloat xAcceleration = secondsSinceLastDraw * ballXVelocity * 500;
        CGFloat yAcceleration = secondsSinceLastDraw * ballYVelocity * 500;

        self.currentPoint = CGPointMake(self.currentPoint.x +
            xAcceleration, self.currentPoint.y + yAcceleration);
    }
    // Update last time with current time
    [lastDrawTime release];
    lastDrawTime = [[NSDate alloc] init];
}
@end
```

The first thing to notice is that one of our properties is declared as @synthesize, yet we have implemented the mutator method for that property in our code. That's OK. The @synthesize directive will not overwrite accessor or mutator methods that you write; it will just fill in the blanks and provide any that you do not.

Calculating Ball Movement

We are handling the `currentPoint` property manually, since, when the `currentPoint` changes, we need to do a bit of housekeeping, such as making sure that the ball hasn't rolled off of the screen. We'll look at that method in a moment. For now, let's look at the first method in the class, `initWithCoder:`. Recall that when you load a view from a nib, that class's `init` or `initWithFrame:` methods will never be called. Nib files contain archived objects, so any instances loaded from nib will be initialized using the `initWithCoder:` method. If we need to do any additional initialization, we must do it in that method.

In this view, we do have some additional initialization, so we've overridden `initWithCoder:`. First, we load the *ball.png* image. Second, we calculate the middle of the view and set that as our ball's starting point, and we set the velocity on both axes to 0.

```
self.image = [UIImage imageNamed:@"ball.png"];
self.currentPoint = CGPointMake((self.bounds.size.width / 2.0f) +
    (image.size.width / 2.0f), (self.bounds.size.height / 2.0f) +
    (image.size.height / 2.0f));

ballXVelocity = 0.0f;
ballYVelocity = 0.0f;
```

Our `drawRect:` method couldn't be much simpler. We just draw the image we loaded in `initWithCoder:` at the position stored in `currentPoint`. The `currentPoint` accessor is a standard accessor method. The `setCurrentPoint:` mutator is another story, however.

The first things we do in `setCurrentPoint:` is to store the old `currentPoint` value in `previousPoint` and assign the new value to `currentPoint`.

```
previousPoint = currentPoint;
currentPoint = newPoint;
```

Next, we do a boundary check. If either the x or y position of the ball is less than 0 or greater than the width or height of the screen (accounting for the width and height of the image), then the acceleration in that direction is stopped.

```
if (currentPoint.x < 0) {
    currentPoint.x = 0;
    ballXVelocity = 0;
}
if (currentPoint.y < 0){
    currentPoint.y = 0;
    ballYVelocity = 0;
}
if (currentPoint.x > self.bounds.size.width - image.size.width) {
    currentPoint.x = self.bounds.size.width - image.size.width;
    ballXVelocity = 0;
}
if (currentPoint.y > self.bounds.size.height - image.size.height) {
    currentPoint.y = self.bounds.size.height - image.size.height;
    ballYVelocity = 0;
}
```

TIP: Want to make the ball bounce off the walls more naturally, instead of just stopping? It's easy enough to do. Just change the two lines in setCurrentPoint: that currently read ballXVelocity = 0; to **ballXVelocity = - (ballXVelocity / 2.0);**. And change the two lines that currently read ballYVelocity = 0; to **ballYVelocity = - (ballYVelocity / 2.0);**. With these changes, instead of killing the ball's velocity, we reduce it in half and set it to the inverse. Now, the ball has half the velocity in the opposite direction.

After that, we calculate two CGRects based on the size of the image. One rectangle encompasses the area where the new image will be drawn, and the other encompasses the area where it was last drawn. We'll use these two rectangles to ensure that the old ball is erased at the same time the new one is drawn.

```
CGRect currentImageRect = CGRectMake(currentPoint.x, currentPoint.y,
        currentPoint.x + image.size.width,
        currentPoint.y + image.size.height);
CGRect previousImageRect = CGRectMake(previousPoint.x, previousPoint.y,
        previousPoint.x + image.size.width,
        currentPoint.y + image.size.width);
```

Finally, we create a new rectangle that is the union of the two rectangles we just calculated and feed that to setNeedsDisplayInRect: to indicate the part of our view that needs to be redrawn.

```
[self setNeedsDisplayInRect:CGRectUnion(currentImageRect,
    previousImageRect)];
```

The last substantive method in our class is draw, which is used to figure out the correct new location of the ball. This method is called in the accelerometer method of its controller class after it feeds the view the new acceleration object. The first thing this method does is declare a static NSDate variable that will be used to keep track of how long it has been since the last time the draw method was called. The first time through this method, when lastDrawTime is nil, we don't do anything because there's no point of reference. Because the updates are happening about 60 times a second, no one will ever notice a single missing frame.

```
static NSDate *lastDrawTime;
if (lastDrawTime != nil) {
```

Every other time through this method, we calculate how long it has been since the last time this method was called. We negate the value returned by timeIntervalSinceNow because lastDrawTime is in the past, so the value returned will be a negative number representing the number of seconds between the current time and lastDrawTime.

```
NSTimeInterval secondsSinceLastDraw =
        -([lastDrawTime timeIntervalSinceNow]);
```

Next, we calculate the new velocity in both directions by adding the current acceleration to the current velocity. We multiply acceleration by secondsSinceLastDraw so that our acceleration is consistent across time. Tipping the phone at the same angle will always cause the same amount of acceleration.

```
ballYVelocity = ballYVelocity + -(acceleration.y *
    secondsSinceLastDraw);
ballXVelocity = ballXVelocity + acceleration.x *
    secondsSinceLastDraw;
```

After that, we figure out the actual change in pixels since the last time the method was called based on the velocity. The product of velocity and elapsed time is multiplied by 500 to create movement that looks natural. If we didn't multiply it by some value, the acceleration would be extraordinarily slow, as if the ball were stuck in molasses.

```
CGFloat xAcceleration = secondsSinceLastDraw * ballXVelocity * 500;
CGFloat yAcceleration = secondsSinceLastDraw * ballYVelocity * 500;
```

Once we know the change in pixels, we create a new point by adding the current location to the calculated acceleration and assign that to currentPoint. By using self.currentPoint, we use that accessor method we wrote earlier, rather than assigning the value directly to the instance variable.

```
self.currentPoint = CGPointMake(self.currentPoint.x +
    xAcceleration, self.currentPoint.y + yAcceleration);
```

That ends our calculations, so all that's left is to update lastDrawTime with the current time.

```
[lastDrawTime release];
lastDrawTime = [[NSDate alloc] init];
```

Before you build the app, add the Core Motion framework using the technique mentioned earlier. Once it's added, go ahead and build and run.

> **NOTE:** Unfortunately, Ball just will not do much on the simulator. If you want to experience Ball in all its gravity-obeying grooviness, you'll need to join the for-pay iOS Developer Program and install it on your own device.

If all went well, the application will launch, and you should be able to control the movement of the ball by tilting the phone. When the ball gets to an edge of the screen, it should stop. Tip back the other way, and it should start rolling in the other direction. Whee!

Rolling On

Well, we've certainly had some fun in this chapter with physics and the amazing iOS accelerometer and gyro. We created a great April Fools' prank, and you got to see the basics of using the accelerometer as a control device. The possibilities for applications using the accelerometer and gyro are nearly as endless as the universe. So now that you have the basics down, go create something cool and surprise us!

When you feel up to it, we're going to get into using another bit of iOS hardware: the built-in camera.

iPhone Camera and Photo Library

By now, it should come as no surprise to you that the iPhone and iPod touch each have a built-in camera (which the current iPad unfortunately lacks) and a nifty application called Photos to help you manage all those awesome pictures and videos you've taken. What you may not know is that your programs can use the built-in camera to take pictures and that your programs can also allow the user to select from among the media already stored on the device.

Because of the way iOS applications are sandboxed, applications ordinarily can't get to photographs or other data that live outside of their own sandboxes. Fortunately, both the camera and the media library are made available to your application by way of an **image picker**. As the name implies, an image picker is a mechanism that lets you select an image from a specified source. At the time this class first appeared in iOS, it was only used for images. Nowadays you can use it to capture video just as well. Typically, an image picker will use a list of images and/or videos as its source (see the left of Figure 18–1). You can, however, specify that the picker use the camera as its source (see the right of Figure 18–1).

Figure 18–1. *An image picker in action. The user is presented with a list of images (left) and then, once an image is selected, they can move and scale the image (right).*

Using the Image Picker and UIImagePickerController

The image picker interface is implemented by way of a modal controller class called UIImagePickerController. You create an instance of this class, specify a delegate (as if you didn't see that coming), specify its image source and whether you want the user to pick an image or a video, and then launch it modally. The image picker will take control of the device to let the user either select a picture or video from the existing media library or take a new picture or video with the camera. Once the user makes their selection, you can give them an opportunity to do some basic editing, such as scaling or cropping an image or trimming away a bit of a video clip. All that behavior is implemented by the UIImagePickerController, so you really don't have to do much heavy lifting here. Assuming the user doesn't press cancel, the image or video the user takes or selects from the library will be delivered to your delegate.

Regardless of whether the user selects a media file or cancels, your delegate has the responsibility to dismiss the UIImagePickerController so that the user can return to your application.

Creating a UIImagePickerController is extremely straightforward. You just allocate and initialize an instance the way you would with most classes. There is one catch, however. Not every device that runs the iPhone OS has a camera. Older iPod touches were the first examples of this, and the first-generation iPad is currently the latest, but more such devices may roll off Apple's assembly lines in the future. Before you create an instance of UIImagePickerController, you need to check to see whether the device your program is currently running on supports the image source you want to use. For example, before letting the user take a picture with the camera, you should make sure the program is running on a device that has a camera. You can check that by using a class method on UIImagePickerController, like this:

```
if ([UIImagePickerController isSourceTypeAvailable:
    UIImagePickerControllerSourceTypeCamera]) {
```

In this example, we're passing UIImagePickerControllerSourceTypeCamera to indicate that we want to let the user take a picture or shoot a video using the built-in camera. The method isSourceTypeAvailable: will return YES if the specified source is currently available. There are two other values you can specify, in addition to UIImagePickerControllerSourceTypeCamera:

- UIImagePickerControllerSourceTypePhotoLibrary specifies that the user should pick an image or video out of the existing media library. That image will be returned to your delegate.

- UIImagePickerControllerSourceTypeSavedPhotosAlbum specifies that the user will select the image from the library of existing photographs but that the selection will be limited to the most recent camera roll. This option will run on a device without a camera but does not do anything useful.

After making sure that the device your program is running on supports the image source you want to use, launching the image picker is relatively easy:

```
UIImagePickerController *picker = [[UIImagePickerController alloc] init];
picker.delegate = self;
picker.sourceType = UIImagePickerControllerSourceTypeCamera;
[self presentModalViewController:picker animated:YES];
[picker release];
```

After we've created and configured the UIImagePickerController, we use a method that our class inherited from UIView called presentModalViewController:animated: to present the image picker to the user.

> **TIP:** The presentModalViewController:animated: method is not limited to just presenting image pickers; you can present any view controller to the user, modally, by calling this method on the view controller for a currently visible view.

Implementing the Image Picker Controller Delegate

The object that you want to be notified when the user has finished using the image picker interface needs to conform to the UIImagePickerControllerDelegate protocol, which defines two methods, imagePickerController:didFinishPickingMediaWithInfo: and imagePickerControllerDidCancel:.

The first of these methods, imagePickerController:didFinishPickingMediaWithInfo:, gets called when the user has successfully taken a photo or video or selected one from the media library. The first argument is a pointer to the UIImagePickerController that you created earlier. The second argument is an NSDictionary instance that will contain the chosen photo, or the URL of the chosen video, as well as optional editing info if you enabled editing and the user actually did some editing. That dictionary will also contain the original, unedited image stored under the key UIImagePickerControllerOriginalImage. Here's an example delegate method that retrieves the original image:

```
- (void)imagePickerController:(UIImagePickerController *)picker
  didFinishPickingMediaWithInfo:(NSDictionary *)info {

    UIImage *selectedImage = [info objectForKey:UIImagePickerControllerEditedImage];
    UIImage *originalImage = [info objectForKey:UIImagePickerControllerOriginalImage];

    // do something with selectedImage and originalImage

    [picker dismissModalViewControllerAnimated:YES];
}
```

The editingInfo dictionary will also tell you which portion of the entire image was chosen during editing by way of an NSValue object stored under the key UIImagePickerControllerCropRect. You can convert this string into a CGRect like so:

```
NSValue *cropRect = [editingInfo objectForKey:UIImagePickerControllerCropRect];
CGRect theRect = [cropRect CGRectValue];
```

After this conversion, theRect will specify the portion of the original image that was selected during the editing process. If you do not need this information, you can just ignore it.

> **CAUTION:** If the image returned to your delegate comes from the camera, that image will not get stored in the photo library. It is your application's responsibility to save the image if necessary.

The other delegate method, imagePickerControllerDidCancel:, gets called if the user decides to cancel the process without taking or selecting any media. When the image picker calls this delegate method, it's just notifying you that the user is finished with the picker and didn't choose anything.

Both of the methods in the UIImagePickerControllerDelegate protocol are marked as optional, but they really aren't, and here is why: Modal views like the image picker have to be told to dismiss themselves. As a result, even if you don't need to take any application-specific actions when the user cancels an image picker, you still need to dismiss the picker. At a bare minimum, your imagePickerControllerDidCancel: method will need to look like this in order for your program to function correctly:

```
- (void)imagePickerControllerDidCancel:(UIImagePickerController *)picker {

    [picker dismissModalViewControllerAnimated:YES];
}
```

Road Testing the Camera and Library

In this chapter, we're going to build an application that lets the user take a picture or shoot some video with the camera or select one from their photo library and then display the selection on the screen (see Figure 18–2). If the user is on a device without a camera, we will hide the *New Photo or Video* button and allow selection only from the photo library.

Figure 18–2. *The Camera application in action*

Create a new project in Xcode using the *View-based Application* template, naming the application *Camera*. Before working on the code itself, we need to add a couple of frameworks that our application will need to use. Using the techniques you've used in previous chapters, add the *MediaPlayer* and *MobileCoreServices* frameworks.

We'll need a couple of outlets in this application's view controller. We need one to point to the image view so that we can update it with the image returned from the image picker. We'll also need an outlet to point to the *New Photo or Video* button so we can hide the button if the device doesn't have a camera. Since we're going to allow users to choose themselves whether to grab a video or an image, we're also going to use the MPMoviePlayerController class to display the chosen video, so we need another instance variable for that. Two more instance variables keep track of the last selected image and video, along with a string to keep track of whether a video or image was the last thing chosen. Finally, we'll keep track of the size of the image view, for resizing the captured image to match our display size. We also need two action methods, one that will be used for both the *New Photo or Video* button and a separate one for letting the user select an existing picture from the photo library. Expand the *Classes* and *Resources* folders so that you can get to all the relevant files.

Select *CameraViewController.h* and make the following changes:

```
#import <UIKit/UIKit.h>
#import <MediaPlayer/MediaPlayer.h>

@interface CameraViewController : UIViewController
        <UIImagePickerControllerDelegate, UINavigationControllerDelegate> {
    UIImageView *imageView;
    UIButton *takePictureButton;
    MPMoviePlayerController *moviePlayerController;
    UIImage *image;
    NSURL *movieURL;
    NSString *lastChosenMediaType;
    CGRect imageFrame;
}
@property (nonatomic, retain) IBOutlet UIImageView *imageView;
@property (nonatomic, retain) IBOutlet UIButton *takePictureButton;
@property (nonatomic, retain) MPMoviePlayerController *moviePlayerController;
@property (nonatomic, retain) UIImage *image;
@property (nonatomic, retain) NSURL *movieURL;
@property (nonatomic, copy) NSString *lastChosenMediaType;

- (IBAction)shootPictureOrVideo:(id)sender;
- (IBAction)selectExistingPictureOrVideo:(id)sender;
@end
```

The first thing you might notice is that we've actually conformed our class to two different protocols: `UIImagePickerControllerDelegate` and `UINavigationControllerDelegate`. Because `UIImagePickerController` is a subclass of `UINavigationController`, we have to conform our class to both of these protocols. The methods in `UINavigationControllerDelegate` are both optional, and we don't need either of them to use the image picker, but we need to conform to the protocol or the compiler will give us a warning.

The other thing you might notice is that while we'll be dealing with an instance of `UIImageView` for displaying a chosen image, we don't have anything similar for displaying a chosen video. UIKit doesn't include any publicly available class like `UIImageView` that works for showing video content, so instead we'll use an instance of `MPMoviePlayerController`, grabbing its `view` property and inserting it into our view hierarchy. This is a highly unusual way of using any view controller, but this is actually the Apple-approved way to show video inside a view hierarchy.

Everything else here is pretty straightforward, so save it. Now, double-click *CameraViewController.xib* to edit the file in Interface Builder.

Designing the Interface

Drag two *Round Rect Buttons* from the library to the window labeled *View*. Place them one above the next, with the bottom button aligned with the bottom blue guideline. Double-click the top one, and give it a title of *New Photo or Video*. Then double-click the bottom button, and give it a title of *Pick from Library*. Next, drag an *Image View* from the library, and place it above the buttons. Expand it to take the entire space of the view above the buttons, as shown earlier in Figure 18–2.

Now, control-drag from the *File's Owner* icon to the image view, and select the *imageView* outlet. Drag again from *File's Owner* to the *New Photo or Video* button, and select the *takePictureButton* outlet.

Next, select the *New Photo or Video* button, and bring up the connections inspector. Drag from the *Touch Up Inside* event to *File's Owner*, and select the *shootPictureOrVideo:* action.

Next, click the *Pick from Library* button, drag from the *Touch Up Inside* event on the connections inspector to *File's Owner*, and select the *selectExistingPictureOrVideo:* action. Once you've made those connections, save your changes and return to Xcode.

Implementing the Camera View Controller

Select *CameraViewController.m,* and make the following changes at the beginning of the file:

```
#import "CameraViewController.h"
#import <MobileCoreServices/UTCoreTypes.h>

@interface CameraViewController ()
static UIImage *shrinkImage(UIImage *original, CGSize size);
- (void)updateDisplay;
- (void)getMediaFromSource:(UIImagePickerControllerSourceType)sourceType;
@end

@implementation CameraViewController
...
```

That interface declaration is a bit different from anything we've shown you earlier in this book. It's called an anonymous category and lets you declare a set of methods that will be implemented at some later point in your class definition. The methods we put here are utility methods, meant only for use within the class itself. Note that we also declared a normal C function in there. A category can really only contain methods, so this function doesn't actually belong to the category, technically speaking. However, in terms of structuring our code, it "belongs" to our class, so we'll list it here as well.

Now, move along to start defining the class. The viewDidLoad method will hide the takePictureButton if the device we're running on has no camera and also grabs the imageView's frame rect, since we're going to need that a little later. We also implement the viewDidAppear: method, having it call the updateDisplay method, which we haven't yet implemented. It's important to understand the distinction between the viewDidLoad and viewDidAppear: methods. The former is called only when the view has just been loaded into memory, while the latter is called every time the view is displayed, which happens both at launch and whenever we return to our controller after showing another full-screen view, such as the image picker.

Once you enter this code, you might want to delete the commented-out version of viewDidLoad to avoid later confusion.

```
...
@implementation CameraViewController
@synthesize imageView;
@synthesize takePictureButton;
@synthesize moviePlayerController;
@synthesize image;
@synthesize movieURL;
@synthesize lastChosenMediaType;

- (void)viewDidLoad {
    if (![UIImagePickerController isSourceTypeAvailable:
            UIImagePickerControllerSourceTypeCamera]) {
        takePictureButton.hidden = YES;
    }
    imageFrame = imageView.frame;
}

- (void)viewDidAppear:(BOOL)animated {
    [super viewDidAppear:animated];
    [self updateDisplay];
}
...
```

Next, insert the following lines of code into the existing viewDidUnload and dealloc methods. Normally, viewDidUnload only gets rid of views, but in this case we're also going to make it get rid of the moviePlayerController. Otherwise, we'd have that controller hanging around even when there are no views left to show it in.

```
...
- (void)viewDidUnload {
    // Release any retained subviews of the main view.
    // e.g. self.myOutlet = nil;
    self.imageView = nil;
    self.takePictureButton = nil;
    self.moviePlayerController = nil;
    [super viewDidUnload];
}

- (void)dealloc {
    [imageView release];
    [takePictureButton release];
    [moviePlayerController release];
    [image release];
    [movieURL release];
    [lastChosenMediaType release];
```

```
    [super dealloc];
}
...
```

Next, insert the following action methods that we declared in the header. Each of these simply calls out to one of the utility methods we declared earlier (but still haven't defined), passing in a value defined by UIImagePickerController to specify where the picture or video should come from.

```
- (IBAction)shootPictureOrVideo:(id)sender {
    [self getMediaFromSource:UIImagePickerControllerSourceTypeCamera];
}

- (IBAction)selectExistingPictureOrVideo:(id)sender {
    [self getMediaFromSource:UIImagePickerControllerSourceTypePhotoLibrary];
}
```

Next, let's implement the delegate methods for the picker view. The first one checks to see whether a picture or video was chosen, makes note of the selection (shrinking the chosen image, if any, to precisely fit the display size along the way), and then dismisses the modal image picker. The second one just dismisses the image picker.

```
#pragma mark UIImagePickerController delegate methods
- (void)imagePickerController:(UIImagePickerController *)picker
        didFinishPickingMediaWithInfo:(NSDictionary *)info {
    self.lastChosenMediaType = [info objectForKey:UIImagePickerControllerMediaType];
    if ([lastChosenMediaType isEqual:(NSString *)kUTTypeImage]) {
        UIImage *chosenImage = [info objectForKey:UIImagePickerControllerEditedImage];
        UIImage *shrunkenImage = shrinkImage(chosenImage, imageFrame.size);
        self.image = shrunkenImage;
    } else if ([lastChosenMediaType isEqual:(NSString *)kUTTypeMovie]) {
        self.movieURL = [info objectForKey:UIImagePickerControllerMediaURL];
    }
    [picker dismissModalViewControllerAnimated:YES];
}

- (void)imagePickerControllerDidCancel:(UIImagePickerController *)picker {
    [picker dismissModalViewControllerAnimated:YES];
}
```

Now let's move on to the function and methods we declared as a class extension early in the file. First up is the shrinkImage() function, which we use to shrink our image down to the size of the view we're going to show it in. Doing so reduces the size of the UIImage we're dealing with, as well as the amount of memory that imageView needs in order to display it. Add this code toward the end of the file:

```
#pragma mark -
static UIImage *shrinkImage(UIImage *original, CGSize size) {
    CGFloat scale = [UIScreen mainScreen].scale;
    CGColorSpaceRef colorSpace = CGColorSpaceCreateDeviceRGB();

    CGContextRef context = CGBitmapContextCreate(NULL, size.width * scale,
        size.height * scale, 8, 0, colorSpace, kCGImageAlphaPremultipliedFirst);
    CGContextDrawImage(context,
```

```
        CGRectMake(0, 0, size.width * scale, size.height * scale),
        original.CGImage);
    CGImageRef shrunken = CGBitmapContextCreateImage(context);
    UIImage *final = [UIImage imageWithCGImage:shrunken];

    CGContextRelease(context);
    CGImageRelease(shrunken);

    return final;
}
```

Don't worry about the details too much. What you're seeing there are a series of Core Graphics calls that create a new image based on the specified size and render the old image into the new one. Note that we get a value called scale from the device's main screen and use it as a multiplier when specifying the size of the new image we're creating. The scale is basically the number of physical screen pixels per unit point in all the calls we make. The iPhone 4 and the fourth-generation iPod touch have a scale of 2.0; all other previous devices will report 1.0. Using the scale this way lets us make an image that renders at the full resolution of the device on which we're running. Otherwise, the image would end up looking a bit jagged on the iPhone 4 (if you looked really closely, that is).

Next up is the updateDisplay method. Remember that this is being called from the viewDidAppear: method, which is called both when the view is first created and then again after the user picks an image or video and dismisses the image picker. Because of this dual usage, it has to make a few checks to see what's what and set up the GUI accordingly. The MPMoviePlayerController doesn't let us change the URL it reads from, so each time we want to display a movie we'll have to make a new controller. All of that is handled here. Add this code toward the bottom of the file:

```
- (void)updateDisplay {
    if ([lastChosenMediaType isEqual:(NSString *)kUTTypeImage]) {
        imageView.image = image;
        imageView.hidden = NO;
        moviePlayerController.view.hidden = YES;
    } else if ([lastChosenMediaType isEqual:(NSString *)kUTTypeMovie]) {
        [self.moviePlayerController.view removeFromSuperview];
        self.moviePlayerController = [[[MPMoviePlayerController alloc]
            initWithContentURL:movieURL] autorelease];
        moviePlayerController.view.frame = imageFrame;
        moviePlayerController.view.clipsToBounds = YES;
        [self.view addSubview:moviePlayerController.view];
        imageView.hidden = YES;
    }
}
```

The final new method is the one that both of our action methods call. It's pretty simple really; it just creates and configures an image picker, using the passed-in sourceType to determine whether to bring up the camera or the media library. Add this code toward the bottom of the file:

```
- (void)getMediaFromSource:(UIImagePickerControllerSourceType)sourceType {
    NSArray *mediaTypes = [UIImagePickerController
        availableMediaTypesForSourceType:sourceType];
    if ([UIImagePickerController isSourceTypeAvailable:
         sourceType] && [mediaTypes count] > 0) {
        NSArray *mediaTypes = [UIImagePickerController
            availableMediaTypesForSourceType:sourceType];
        UIImagePickerController *picker =
        [[UIImagePickerController alloc] init];
        picker.mediaTypes = mediaTypes;
        picker.delegate = self;
        picker.allowsEditing = YES;
        picker.sourceType = sourceType;
        [self presentModalViewController:picker animated:YES];
        [picker release];
    }
    else {
        UIAlertView *alert = [[UIAlertView alloc]
                              initWithTitle:@"Error accessing media"
                              message:@"Device doesn't support that media source."
                              delegate:nil
                              cancelButtonTitle:@"Drat!"
                              otherButtonTitles:nil];
        [alert show];
        [alert release];
    }
}
@end
```

That's all we need to do. Compile and run. If you're running on the simulator, you won't have the option to take a new picture. If you have the opportunity to run on a real device, go ahead and try it. You should be able to take a new picture and zoom in and out of the picture using the pinch gestures.

If you zoom in before hitting the *Use Photo* button, the image that gets returned to our application in the delegate method will be the cropped image.

It's a Snap!

Believe it or not, that's all there is to letting your users take pictures with the iPhone's camera so that the pictures can be used by your application. You can even let the user do a small amount of editing on that image if you so choose.

In the next chapter, we're going to look at reaching a larger audience for your iPhone applications by making them oh so easy to translate into other languages. *Êtes-vous prêt? Tournez la page et allez directement. Allez, allez!*

Chapter 19

Application Localization

At the time of this writing, the iPhone is available in more than 90 different countries, and that number will continue to increase over time. You can now buy and use an iPhone on every continent except Antarctica. The iPad is still being held back a bit, as Apple tries to satisfy demand in what it considers the most important countries first, but before long, it will surely be just as ubiquitous as the iPhone.

If you plan on releasing applications through the App Store, your potential market is considerably larger than just people in your own country who speak your own language. Fortunately, iOS has a robust **localization** architecture that lets you easily translate your application (or have it translated by others) into not only multiple languages, but even into multiple dialects of the same language. Want to provide different terminology to English speakers in the United Kingdom than you do to English speakers in the United States? No problem.

That is, localization is no problem if you've written your code correctly. Retrofitting an existing application to support localization is much harder than writing your application that way from the start. In this chapter, we'll show you how to write your code so it is easy to localize, and then we'll go about localizing a sample application.

Localization Architecture

When a nonlocalized application is run, all of the application's text will be presented in the developer's own language, also known as the **development base language**.

When developers decide to localize their application, they create a subdirectory in their application bundle for each supported language. Each language's subdirectory contains a subset of the application's resources that were translated into that language. Each subdirectory is called a **localization project**, or **localization folder**. Localization folder names always end with the extension *.lproj*.

In the Settings application, the user has the ability to set the language and region format. For example, if the user's language is English, available regions might be United States, Australia, or Hong Kong—all regions in which English is spoken.

When a localized application needs to load a resource—such as an image, property list, or nib—the application checks the user's language and region and looks for a localization folder that matches that setting. If it finds one, it will load the localized version of the resource instead of the base version.

For users who selected French as their iOS language and France as their region, the application will look first for a localization folder named *fr_FR.lproj*. The first two letters of the folder name are the ISO country code that represents the French language. The two letters following the underscore are the ISO two-digit code that represents France.

If the application cannot find a match using the two-digit code, it will look for a match using the language's three-digit ISO code. In our example, if the application is unable to find a folder named *fr_FR.lproj*, it will look for a localization folder named *fre_FR or fra_FR*.

All languages have at least one three-digit code. Some have two three-digit codes: one for the English spelling of the language and another for the native spelling. Only some languages have two-digit codes. When a language has both a two-digit code and a three-digit code, the two-digit code is preferred.

> **NOTE:** You can find a list of the current ISO country codes on the ISO web site. Both the two- and three-digit codes are part of the ISO 3166 standard (`http://www.iso.org/iso/country_codes.htm`).

If the application cannot find a folder that is an exact match, it will then look for a localization folder in the application bundle that matches just the language code without the region code. So, staying with our French-speaking person from France, the application next looks for a localization project called *fr.lproj*. If it doesn't find a language project with that name, it will look for *fre.lproj*, then *fra.lproj*. If none of those are found, it checks for *French.lproj*. The last construct exists to support legacy Mac OS X applications, and generally speaking, you should avoid it.

If the application doesn't find a language project that matches either the language/region combination or just the language, it will use the resources from the development base language. If it does find an appropriate localization project, it will always look there first for any resources that it needs. If you load a UIImage using `imageNamed:`, for example, the application will look first for an image with the specified name in the localization project. If it finds one, it will use that image. If it doesn't, it will fall back to the base language resource.

If an application has more than one localization project that matches—for example, a project called *fr_FR.lproj* and one called *fr.lproj*—it will look first in the more specific match; in this case, *fr_FR.lproj*. If it doesn't find the resource there, it will look in *fr.lproj*. This gives you the ability to provide resources common to all speakers of a language in one language project, localizing only those resources that are impacted by differences in dialect or geographic region.

You should choose to localize only those resources that are affected by language or country. For example, if an image in your application has no words and its meaning is universal, there's no need to localize that image.

Strings Files

What do you do about string literals and string constants in your source code? Consider this source code from the previous chapter:

```
UIAlertView *alert = [[UIAlertView alloc]
    initWithTitle:@"Error accessing photo library"
          message:@"Device does not support a photo library"
         delegate:nil
cancelButtonTitle:@"Drat!"
otherButtonTitles:nil];
[alert show];
[alert release];
```

If you've gone through the effort of localizing your application for a particular audience, you certainly don't want to be presenting alerts written in the development base language. The answer is to store these strings in special text files called **strings files**.

What's in a Strings File?

Strings files are nothing more than Unicode (UTF-16) text files that contain a list of string pairs, each identified by a comment. Here is an example of what a strings file might look like in your application:

```
/* Used to ask the user his/her first name */
"First Name" = "First Name";

/* Used to get the user's last name */
"Last Name" = "Last Name";

/* Used to ask the user's birth date */
"Birthday" = "Birthday";
```

The values between the /* and the */ characters are just comments for the translator. They are not used in the application, and you could skip adding them, though they're a good idea. The comments give context, showing how a particular string is being used in the application.

You'll notice that each line lists the same string twice. The string on the left side of the equal sign acts as a key, and it will always contain the same value, regardless of language. The value on the right side of the equal sign is the one that is translated to the local language. So, the preceding strings file, localized into French, might look like this:

```
/* Used to ask the user his/her first name */
"First Name " = "Prénom";

/* Used to get the user's last name */
"Last Name " = "Nom de famille";
```

```
/* Used to ask the user's birth date */
"Birthday" = "Anniversaire";
```

The Localized String Macro

You won't actually create the strings file by hand. Instead, you'll embed all localizable text strings in a special macro in your code. Once your source code is final and ready for localization, you'll run a command-line program, named genstrings, which will search all your code files for occurrences of the macro, pulling out all the unique strings and embedding them in a localizable strings file.

Let's see how the macro works. First, here's a traditional string declaration:

```
NSString *myString = @"First Name";
```

To make this string localizable, do this instead:

```
NSString *myString = NSLocalizedString(@"First Name",
    @"Used to ask the user his/her first name");
```

The NSLocalizedString macro takes two parameters:

- The first parameter is the string value in the base language. If there is no localization, the application will use this string.

- The second parameter is used as a comment in the strings file.

NSLocalizedString looks in the application bundle inside the appropriate localization project for a strings file named *localizable.strings*. If it does not find the file, it returns its first parameter, and the string will appear in the development base language. Strings are typically displayed only in the base language during development, since the application will not yet be localized.

If NSLocalizedString finds the strings file, it searches the file for a line that matches the first parameter. In the preceding example, NSLocalizedString will search the strings file for the string "First Name". If it doesn't find a match in the localization project that matches the user's language settings, it will then look for a strings file in the base language and use the value there. If there is no strings file, it will just use the first parameter you passed to the NSLocalizedString macro.

Now that you have an idea of how the localization architecture and the strings file work, let's take a look at localization in action.

Real-World iOS: Localizing Your Application

We're going to create a small application that displays the user's current **locale**. A locale (an instance of NSLocale) represents both the user's language and region. It is used by the system to determine which language to use when interacting with the user, as well as how to display dates, currency, and time information, among other things. After we create the application, we will then localize it into other languages. You'll learn how to localize nib files, strings files, images, and even your application's display name.

You can see what our application is going to look like in Figure 19–1. The name across the top comes from the user's locale. The words down the left side of the view are static labels that are set in the nib file. The words down the right side are set programmatically using outlets. The flag image at the bottom of the screen is a static `UIImageView`.

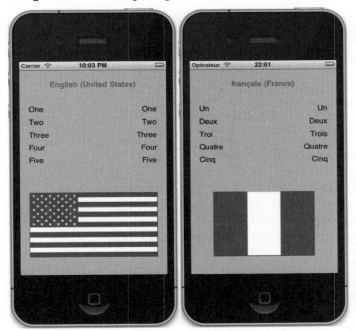

Figure 19–1. *The LocalizeMe application shown with two different language/region settings*

Let's hop right into it.

Setting Up LocalizeMe

Create a new project in Xcode using the *View-based Application* template, and call it *LocalizeMe*.

If you look in the source code archive, within the *19 - LocalizeMe* folder, you'll see a subfolder named *English.lproj*. Inside *English.lproj*, you'll find two images: *icon.png* and *flag.png*. Drag both of those to the *Resources* folder of your project, and be sure to enable the check box that copies the files to the project's directory.

Next, select *LocalizeMe-Info.plist*, and set the *Icon file* value to *icon.png* so that the icon image will be used as your application's icon.

We need to create outlets to a total of six labels: one for the blue label across the top of the view and five for the words down the right-hand side. Expand the *Classes* folder, select *LocalizeMeViewController.h*, and make the following changes:

```
#import <UIKit/UIKit.h>

@interface LocalizeMeViewController : UIViewController {
    UILabel *localeLabel;
    UILabel *label1;
    UILabel *label2;
    UILabel *label3;
    UILabel *label4;
    UILabel *label5;
}
@property (nonatomic, retain) IBOutlet UILabel *localeLabel;
@property (nonatomic, retain) IBOutlet UILabel *label1;
@property (nonatomic, retain) IBOutlet UILabel *label2;
@property (nonatomic, retain) IBOutlet UILabel *label3;
@property (nonatomic, retain) IBOutlet UILabel *label4;
@property (nonatomic, retain) IBOutlet UILabel *label5;
@end
```

Now double-click the *LocalizeMeViewController.xib* file to edit the GUI in Interface Builder. Make sure the *View* window is visible, and then drag a *Label* from the library, dropping it at the top of the view, aligned with the top blue guideline. Resize the label so that it takes the entire width of the view, from blue guideline to blue guideline. Press ⌘B (or select **Font ➤ Bold**) to make the text bold. With the label selected, open the attributes inspector. Set the text alignment to centered, and set the text color to a bright blue. You can also use the font selector to make the font size larger if you wish. As long as *Adjust to Fit* is selected in the object attributes inspector, the text will be resized if it gets too long to fit.

With your label in place, control-drag from the *File's Owner* icon to this new label, and select the *localeLabel* outlet.

Next, drag five more *Labels* from the library, and put them against the left margin using the blue guideline, one above the other (see Figure 19–1). Resize the labels so they go about halfway across the view, or a little less. Double-click the top one, and change it from *Label* to *One*. Repeat this procedure with the other four labels, changing the text to the numbers *Two* to *Five*.

Drag five more *Labels* from the library, this time placing them against the right margin. Change the text alignment using the object attributes inspector so that they are right-aligned, and increase the size of the label so that it stretches from the right blue guideline to about the middle of the view. Control-drag from *File's Owner* to each of the five new labels, connecting each one to a different numbered label outlet. Now, double-click each one of the new labels, and delete its text. We will be setting these values programmatically.

Finally, drag an *Image View* from the library over to the bottom part of the view. In the attributes inspector, select *flag.png* for the view's *Image* attribute, and resize the image to stretch from blue guideline to blue guideline. In the attributes inspector, change the

Mode attribute from its current value to *Aspect Fit*. Not all flags have the same aspect ratio, and we want to make sure the localized versions of the image look right. Selecting this option will cause the image view to resize any other images put in this image view so they fit, but it will maintain the correct aspect ratio (ratio of height to width). If you like, make the flag taller, until the sides of the flag touch the blue guidelines.

Save your changes and return to Xcode.

Back in Xcode, select *LocalizeMeViewController.m* and insert the following code at the top of the file:

```
#import "LocalizeMeViewController.h"

@implementation LocalizeMeViewController
@synthesize localeLabel;
@synthesize label1;
@synthesize label2;
@synthesize label3;
@synthesize label4;
@synthesize label5;

- (void)viewDidLoad {
    NSLocale *locale = [NSLocale currentLocale];
    NSString *displayNameString = [locale
        displayNameForKey:NSLocaleIdentifier
        value:[locale localeIdentifier]];
    localeLabel.text = displayNameString;

    label1.text = NSLocalizedString(@"One", @"The number 1");
    label2.text = NSLocalizedString(@"Two", @"The number 2");
    label3.text = NSLocalizedString(@"Three", @"The number 3");
    label4.text = NSLocalizedString(@"Four", @"The number 4");
    label5.text = NSLocalizedString(@"Five", @"The number 5");
    [super viewDidLoad];
}
...
```

Also, add the following code to the existing viewDidUnload and dealloc methods:

```
...
- (void)viewDidUnload {
    // Release any retained subviews of the main view.
    // e.g. self.myOutlet = nil;
    self.localeLabel = nil;
    self.label1 = nil;
    self.label2 = nil;
    self.label3 = nil;
    self.label4 = nil;
    self.label5 = nil;
    [super viewDidUnload];
}

- (void)dealloc {
    [localeLabel release];
    [label1 release];
```

```
    [label2 release];
    [label3 release];
    [label4 release];
    [label5 release];
    [super dealloc];
}
@end
```

The only item of note in this class is the viewDidLoad method. The first thing we do there is get an NSLocale instance that represents the users' current locale, which can tell us both their language and their region preferences, as set in their iPhone's Settings application.

```
    NSLocale *locale = [NSLocale currentLocale];
```

The next line of code might need a little bit of explanation. NSLocale works somewhat like a dictionary. It can give us a whole bunch of information about the current users' preferences, including the name of the currency they use and the date format they expect. You can find a complete list of the information that you can retrieve in the NSLocale API reference.

In this next line of code, we're retrieving the **locale identifier**, which is the name of the language and/or region that this locale represents. We're using a function called displayNameForKey:value:. The purpose of this method is to return the value of the item we've requested in a specific language.

The display name for the French language, for example, would be *Français* in French, but *French* in English. This method gives us the ability to retrieve data about any locale so that it can be displayed appropriately to any users. In this case, we're getting the display name for the locale in the language of that locale, which is why we pass [locale localeIdentifier] in the second argument. The localeIdentifier is a string in the format we used earlier to create our language projects. For an American English speaker, it would be *en_US*, and for a French speaker from France, it would be *fr_FR*.

```
    NSString *displayNameString = [locale
            displayNameForKey:NSLocaleIdentifier
            value:[locale localeIdentifier]];
```

Once we have the display name, we use it to set the top label in the view.

```
    localeLabel.text = displayNameString;
```

Next, we set the five other labels to the numbers one through five spelled out in our development base language. We also provide a comment telling what each word is. You can just pass an empty string if the words are obvious, as they are here, but any string you pass in the second argument will be turned into a comment in the strings file, so you can use this comment to communicate with the person doing your translations.

```
    label1.text = NSLocalizedString(@"One", @"The number 1");
    label2.text = NSLocalizedString(@"Two", @"The number 2");
    label3.text = NSLocalizedString(@"Three", @"The number 3");
    label4.text = NSLocalizedString(@"Four", @"The number 4");
    label5.text = NSLocalizedString(@"Five", @"The number 5");
```

Let's run our application now.

Trying Out LocalizeMe

You can use either the simulator or a device to test LocalizeMe. The simulator does seem to cache some language and region settings, so you may want to run the application on the device if you have that option. Once the application launches, it should look like Figure 19–2.

Figure 19–2. *The language running under the authors' base language. Our application is set up for localization but is not yet localized.*

By using the NSLocalizedString macros instead of static strings, we are ready for localization. But we are not localized yet. If you use the Settings application on the simulator or on your iPhone to change to another language or region, the results look essentially the same, except for the label at the top of the view (see Figure 19–3).

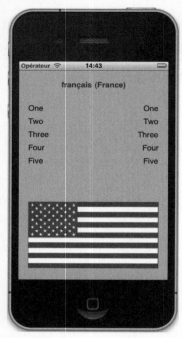

Figure 19–3. *The nonlocalized application run on an iPhone set to use the French language in France*

Localizing the Nib

Now, let's localize the nib file. The basic process for localizing any file is the same. In Xcode, single-click *LocalizeMeViewController.xib*, and then select **File ➤ Get Info** (or press ⌘I) to bring up the *Info* window for that file.

> **CAUTION:** Xcode will allow you to localize pretty much any file in the navigator. Just because you can, doesn't mean you should. Never localize a source code file. Doing so will cause compile errors, as multiple object files with the same name will be created.

When the *Info* window appears, select the *General* tab, and then click the button that says *Make File Localizable* in the lower left (see Figure 19–4).

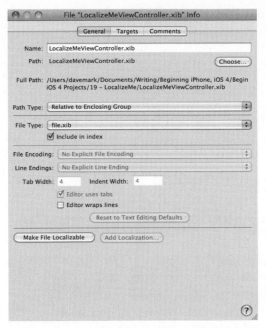

Figure 19–4. *The LocalizeMeViewController.xib Info window*

Close the *Info* window and look at the *Groups & Files* pane in Xcode. Notice that the *LocalizeMeViewController.xib* file now has a disclosure triangle next to it, as if it were a group or folder. Expand it, and take a look (see Figure 19–5).

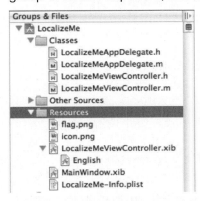

Figure 19–5. *Localizable files have a disclosure triangle and a child value for each language or region you add.*

In our project, *LocalizeMeViewController.xib* has one child: *English*. This child was created automatically, and it represents your development base language. Go to the Finder, and open your *LocalizeMe* project folder. You should see a new folder named *English.lproj* (see Figure 19–6).

Name
▶ ▦ build
▶ ▦ Classes
▶ ▦ English.lproj
▦ flag.png
▦ icon.png
ʰ LocalizeMe_Prefix.pch
🗋 LocalizeMe-Info.plist
🗋 LocalizeMe.xcodeproj
ᵐ main.m
🗋 MainWindow.xib

Figure 19–6. *From the outset, our Xcode project included a project folder for our base language. When we chose to make a file localizable, Xcode created a language project folder for the language we selected as well.*

NOTE: At the time of this writing, Xcode is still using the legacy project name for the development base language project, *English.lproj*, rather than following Apple's localization convention of using the ISO two-letter language code, which would have resulted in a folder called *en.lproj* instead. This is listed in the Xcode 3.*x* release notes as a known issue. You don't need to change this folder name, as it will work just fine, but use the ISO codes for any new localizations you add.

Single-click *LocalizeMeViewController.xib* in the *Groups & Files* pane again, and press ⌘I to bring up the *Info* window. Go back to the *General* tab if you're not on it, and click the *Add Localization* button. A sheet will drop down and ask you to enter the name of the new localization. Let's add localization for the French language, so type *fr*. Don't select **French** from the drop-down menu, as that will use the legacy name of *French*.

TIP: When dealing with locales, language codes are lowercase, but country codes are uppercase. So, the correct name for the French language project is *fr.lproj*, but the project for Parisian French (French as spoken by people in France) is *fr_FR.lproj*, not *fr_fr.lproj* or *FR_fr.lproj*. The iOS file system is case-sensitive, so it is important to match case correctly.

After you press return, Xcode will create a new localization project in your project folder called *fr.lproj* and make a copy of *LocalizeMeViewController.xib* in that folder. In the *Groups & Files* pane, *LocalizeMeViewController.xib* should now have two children: *English* and *fr*. Double-click *fr* to open the nib file that will be shown to French speakers.

The nib file that opens in Interface Builder will look exactly like the one you built earlier, because the nib file you just created is a copy of the earlier one. Any changes you make to this one will be shown to people who speak French. Double-click each of the labels on the left side and change them from *One, Two, Three, Four,* and *Five* to *Un, Deux,*

Trois, *Quatre*, and *Cinq*. Once you have changed them, save the nib, and go back to Xcode. Your nib is now localized in to French. Compile and run the program. After it launches, tap the home button.

The simulator caches settings, so if you were to just go ahead and run the application now, there's a very good chance you would see exactly what you saw before. In order to make sure you see the correct thing, you need to reset the simulator and do a clean build of your application (**Build ➤ Clean**, then rebuild).

The simulator has an option under the **iOS Simulator** menu to **Reset Content and Settings…**. Select that now. After you select it, you will be presented with the home screen. From there, go to the Settings application, and select the *General* row and then the row labeled *International*. From here, you'll be able to change your language and region preferences (see Figure 19–7).

Figure 19–7. *Changing the language and region—the two settings that affect the user's locale*

You want to change the *Region Format* first, because once you change the language, iOS will reset and return to the home screen. Change the *Region Format* from *United States* to *France* (which is under the row for *French*), and then change *Language* from *English* to *Français*. Click the *Done* button, and then quit the simulator. Now, your phone is set to use French.

Back in Xcode, run your app again. This time, the words down the left-hand side should show up in French (see Figure 19–8).

Figure 19–8. *The application is partially translated into French now.*

But the flag and right column of text are still wrong. We'll take care of the flag first.

Localizing an Image

We could have changed the flag image directly in the nib by just selecting a different image for the image view in the French localized nib file. Instead of doing that, we'll actually localize the flag image itself.

When an image or other resource used by a nib is localized, the nib will automatically show the correct version for the language (though not for the dialect, at the time of this writing). If we localize the *flag.png* file itself with a French version, the nib will automatically show the correct flag when appropriate.

First, quit the simulator and make sure your application is stopped. Back in Xcode, single-click *flag.png* in Xcode's *Groups & Files* pane. Next, press ⌘I to bring up the *Info* window for that file, and click the *Make File Localizable* button. Once you do that, Xcode will copy *flag.png* into the *English.lproj* folder (or from your base language folder, if it's different).

Switch back to the *General* tab, and then click the *Add Localization* button. When prompted for a language, type *fr* and click the *Add* button. You will now find another file in your *fr.lproj* folder inside your project folder. This new file, *flag.png*, is a copy of the *flag.png* file from the base language. Obviously, that's not the correct image. Since

Xcode doesn't let you edit image files, the easiest way get the correct image into the localization project is to just copy that image into the project using the Finder.

In the *Resources* folder of the *19 - LocalizeMe* folder, you'll find a folder called *fr*. In that subfolder, you'll find a *flag.png* file that contains the French flag, rather than the American one. Copy the *flag.png* file from there to your project's *fr.lproj* subfolder, overwriting the file that's there.

That's it. You're finished. If you are running in the simulator, reset the simulator, and then quit the simulator. Return to Xcode and select **Build ➤ Clean**, as you did earlier before rerunning the program. Once you rerun the app, you'll need to reset the region and language to get the French flag to appear.

If you're running on the device, your iPhone has probably cached the American flag from the last time you ran the application. Let's remove the old application from your iPhone using the *Organizer* window in Xcode.

Select **Window ➤ Organizer**, or press ^⌘0. Under the *Summary* tab (see Figure 19–9, you'll see three sections. The bottommost section is labeled *Applications*. In the list of applications, look for *LocalizeMe*. Select it, and click the minus button to remove the old version of that application and the caches associated with it.

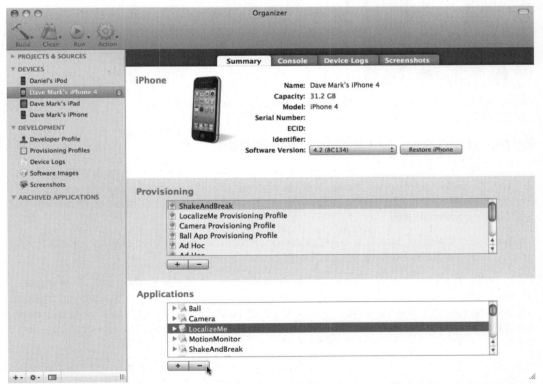

Figure 19–9. *If you are running your app on your iOS device, you'll use the Xcode Organizer window to delete the application.*

Now, select **Build ➤ Clean**, and build and run the application again. Once the application launches, you'll need to reset the region, then the language. The French flag should now come up in addition to the French words down the left-hand side (see Figure 19–10).

Figure 19–10. *The flag image and application nib are both localized to French now.*

Generating and Localizing a Strings File

In Figure 19–10, notice that the words on the right-hand side of the view are still in English. In order to translate those, we need to generate our base language strings file and then localize that. To accomplish this, we'll need to leave the comfy confines of Xcode for a few minutes.

Launch *Terminal.app*, which is in */Applications/Utilities/.* When the terminal window opens, type *cd* followed by a space. Don't press return.

Now, go to the Finder, and drag your *LocalizeMe* project folder to the terminal window. As soon as you drop the folder onto the terminal window, the path to the project folder should appear on the command line. Now, press return. The cd command is Unix-speak for "change directory," so what you've just done is steer your terminal session from its default directory over to your project directory.

Our next step is to run the program genstrings and tell it to find all the occurrences of NSLocalizedString in our *.m* files in the *Classes* folder. To do this, type the following command, and then press return:

```
genstrings ./Classes/*.m
```

When the command is finished executing (it just takes a second on a project this small), you'll be returned to the command line. In the Finder, look in the project folder for a new file called *Localizable.strings*. Drag that to the *Resources* folder in Xcode's project navigator, but when it prompts you, don't click the Add button just yet.

> **CAUTION:** You can rerun `genstrings` at any time to re-create your base language file, but once you have had your strings file localized into another language, it's important that you don't change the text used in any of the `NSLocalizedString()` macros. That base-language version of the string is used as a key to retrieve the translations, so if you change them, the translated version will no longer be found, and you will need to either update the localized strings file or have it retranslated.

Localizable.strings files are encoded in UTF-16, which is a 2-byte version of Unicode. Most of us are probably using UTF-8 or a language-local encoding scheme as our default encoding in Xcode. When we import the *Localizable.strings* file into our project, we need to take that into account. First, uncheck the box that says *Copy items into destination group's folder (if needed),* because the file is already in our project folder. More important, change the text encoding to *Unicode (UTF-16)*. If you don't do that, the file will look like gibberish when you try to edit it in Xcode.

Now, go ahead and click the *Add* button. Once the file is imported, single-click *Localizable.strings* in *Resources*, and take a look at it. It contains five entries, because we use `NSLocalizableString` five times with five distinct values. The values that we passed in as the second argument have become the comments for each of the strings.

The strings were generated in alphabetical order, which is a nice feature. In this case, since we're dealing with numbers, alphabetical order is not the most intuitive way to present them, but in most cases, having them in alphabetical order will be helpful.

```
/* The number 5 */
"Five" = "Five";

/* The number 4 */
"Four" = "Four";

/* The number 1 */
"One" = "One";

/* The number 3 */
"Three" = "Three";

/* The number 2 */
"Two" = "Two";
```

Let's localize this sucker.

Single-click *Localizable.strings*, and repeat the same steps we've performed for the other localizations:

- Open the info window if it's not already visible.

- Click the *Make File Localizable* button to make the file localizable.

- Switch to the *General* tab and click the *Add Localization* button. Enter *fr* for the name of the new localization, and then click *Add*.

Back in the *Groups & Files* pane, select the French localization of the file. In the editor, make the following changes:

```
/* The number 5 */
"Five" = "Cinq";

/* The number 4 */
"Four" = "Quatre";

/* The number 1 */
"One" = "Un";

/* The number 3 */
"Three" = "Trois";

/* The number 2 */
"Two" = "Deux";
```

In real life (unless you're multilingual), you would ordinarily send this file out to a translation service to translate the values to the right of the equal signs. In this simple example, armed with knowledge that came from years of watching *Sesame Street*, we can do the translation ourselves.

Now save, compile, and run the app. You should the relevant numbers translated into French.

Localizing the App Display Name

We want to show you one final piece of localization that is commonly used: localizing the app name that's visible on the home screen and elsewhere. Apple does this for several of the built-in apps, and you might want to do so as well.

The app name used for display is stored in your app's *Info.plist* file, which in our case is actually named *LocalizeMe-Info.plist*. Select this file for editing, and you'll see that one of the items it contains, *Bundle display name*, is currently set to ${PRODUCT_NAME}.

In the syntax used by *Info.plist* files, anything starting with a dollar sign is subject to variable substitution. In this case, this means that when Xcode compiles the app, the value of this item will be replaced with the name of the "product" in this Xcode project, which is the name of the app itself. This is where we want to do some localization, replacing ${PRODUCT_NAME} with the localized name for each language. However, as it turns out, this doesn't quite work out as simply as you might expect.

The *Info.plist* file is sort of a special case, and it isn't meant to be localized. Instead, if you want to localize the content of *Info.plist*, you need to make localized versions of a file named *InfoPlist.strings*. Let's create that file now.

Select the *Resources* folder and choose **File ➤ New File....** Select *Resource* under the *Mac OS X* heading, and choose *Strings File*. Click *Next*, and name the file *InfoPlist.strings*. Create a French localization using the same steps you did for the previous localizations.

Now, we want to add a line to define the display name for the app. In the *LocalizeMe-Info.plist* file, we were shown the display name associated with a dictionary key called *Bundle display name*, but that's not the real key name! It's merely an Xcode nicety, trying to give a more friendly and readable name. The real name is *CFBundleDisplayName*, which you can verify by selecting *LocalizeMe-Info.plist*, right-clicking anywhere in the view, and selecting **Show Raw Keys/Values**. This shows you the true names of the keys in use.

So, select the English localization of *InfoPlist.strings*, and add the following line:

```
CFBundleDisplayName = "Localize Me";
```

Now go ahead and make a new French localization of the *InfoPlist.strings* file, just as you've done with the others. Edit the file to give the app a proper French name:

```
CFBundleDisplayName = "Localisez Moi";
```

If you build and run in the simulator right now, you may not see the new name. iOS seems to cache this info when a new app is added, but doesn't necessarily change it when an existing app is replaced by a new version—at least not when Xcode is doing the replacing. So if you're running the simulator in French but you don't see the new name, don't worry. Just delete the app from the simulator, go back to Xcode, and build and run again.

Now, our application is fully localized for the French language.

> **TIP:** We've provided you with the information in the *Resources* subfolder of *19 LocalizeMe* to do the German and Canadian French localizations, if you want some more practice. You'll find two more copies of the *flag.png*, *Localizable.strings,* and *InfoPlist.strings* files that you can use if you want to try adding support for additional languages.

Auf Wiedersehen

If you want to maximize sales of your iOS application, localize it as much as possible. Fortunately, the iOS localization architecture makes easy work of supporting multiple languages, and even multiple dialects of the same language, within your application. As you saw in this chapter, nearly any type of file that you add to your application can be localized, as needed.

Even if you don't plan on localizing your application, get in the habit of using `NSLocalizedString` instead of just using static strings in your code. With Xcode's Code Sense feature, the difference in typing time is negligible, and should you ever want to translate your application, your life will be much, much easier.

At this point, our journey is nearly done. We're almost to the end of our travels together. After the next chapter, we'll be saying *sayonara, au revoir, auf wiedersehen, avtío, arrivederci,* and *adiós.* You now have a solid foundation you can use to build your own cool iOS applications. Stick around for the going-away party though, as we still have a few helpful bits of information for you.

Chapter 20

Where to Next?

Well, wow! You're still with us, huh? Great! It sure has been a long journey since that very first iOS application we built together. You've certainly come a long way. We would love to tell you that you now know it all. But when it comes to technology, and especially when it comes to programming, you never know it all.

The programming language and frameworks we've been working with for the past 19 chapters are the end result of more than 20 years of evolution. And Apple engineers are feverishly working round the clock, thinking of that next cool new thing. The iOS platform has just begun to blossom. There is so much more to come.

By making it through this book, you've built yourself a sturdy foundation. You have a solid knowledge of Objective-C, Cocoa Touch, and the tools that bring these technologies together to create incredible new iPhone, iPod touch, and iPad applications. You understand the iOS software architecture—the design patterns that make Cocoa Touch sing. In short, you're ready to chart your own course. We are so proud! So where to next?

Getting Unstuck

At its core, programming is about problem solving—figuring things out. It's fun, and it's rewarding. But, at times, you will run up against a puzzle that just seems insurmountable—a problem that appears to have no solution.

Sometimes, the answer will come to you if you just take a bit of time away from the problem. A good night's sleep or a few hours of doing something different can often be all that is needed to get you through it. Believe us—you can stare at the same problem for hours, overanalyzing and getting yourself so worked up that you miss an obvious solution.

And then there are times when even a change of scenery doesn't help. In those situations, it's good to have friends in high places. The following sections outline some resources you can turn to when you're in a bind.

Apple's Documentation

Become one with Xcode's documentation browser, grasshopper. The documentation browser is a front end to a wealth of incredibly valuable sample source code, concept guides, API references, video tutorials, and a whole lot more.

There are few areas of iOS that you won't be able to learn more about by making your way through Apple's documentation. And if you get comfortable with Apple's documentation, making your way through uncharted territories and new technologies as Apple rolls them out will be easier.

> **NOTE:** Xcode's documentation browser takes you to the same information you can get to by going to Apple's Developer Connection web site at `http://developer.apple.com`.

Mailing Lists

You might also want to sign up for these handy mailing lists:

Cocoa-dev: This moderately high-volume list run by Apple is primarily about Cocoa for Mac OS X. Because of the common heritage shared by Cocoa and Cocoa Touch, however, many of the people on this list may be able to help you. Make sure to search the list archives before asking your question, though.

`http://lists.apple.com/mailman/listinfo/cocoa-dev`

Xcode-users: Another list maintained by Apple, this one is specific to questions and problems related to Xcode.

`http://lists.apple.com/mailman/listinfo/xcode-users`

Quartz-dev: This is an Apple-maintained mailing list for discussion of the Quartz 2D and Core Graphics technologies.

`http://lists.apple.com/mailman/listinfo/quartz-dev`

Cocoa-unbound: This list, intended for discussion of both Mac and iOS development, appeared in 2010 in response to the sometimes heavy-handed moderation of some of the Apple-run lists, particularly Cocoa-dev. The posting volume is lower here, and topics can run a bit further afield.

`http://groups.google.com/group/cocoa-unbound`

IPhone SDK Development: Another third-party list, this one is focused entirely on iOS development. You'll find a medium-sized community here, with a nice cast of regulars.

`http://groups.google.com/group/iphonesdkdevelopment`

Discussion Forums

These discussion forums allow you to post your questions to a wide range of forum readers:

iphonedevbook.com: As the official forum for this book, this forum features an active, vibrant community, full of people with the wisdom and sensibility to buy our book, such as yourself.

`http://iphonedevbook.com/forum`

Apple Developer Forums: This is a web forum set up by Apple specifically for discussing iOS and Mac software development. Many iOS programmers, both new and experienced (including many of Apple's engineers and evangelists), contribute to these forums. It's also the only place you can legally discuss issues with prerelease versions of the SDK that are under nondisclosure agreements. You'll need to sign in with your Apple ID to access this forum.

`http://devforums.apple.com`

iPhone Dev SDK: On this web forum, iOS programmers, both new and experienced, help each other out with problems and advice.

`http://www.iphonedevsdk.com`

Apple Discussions, Developer Forums: This link connects you to Apple's community forums for Mac and iOS software developers.

`http://discussions.apple.com/category.jspa?categoryID=164`

Apple Discussions, iPhone: This link connects to Apple's community forums for discussing the iPhone.

`http://discussions.apple.com/category.jspa?categoryID=201`

Web Sites

Visit these web sites for helpful coding advice:

CocoaDev: The original and largest wiki focused on Cocoa development. A lot of what you'll find here predates iOS, but much of it applies equally well to both Mac and iOS.

`http://www.cocoadev.com`

Cocoa Dev Central: This portal contains links to a great many Cocoa-related web sites and tutorials.

`http://www.cocoadevcentral.com`

CocoaHeads: This is the site of a group dedicated to peer support and promotion of Cocoa. It focuses on local groups with regular meetings where Cocoa developers can get together, help each other out, and even socialize a bit. There's nothing better than knowing a real person who can help you out, so if there's a CocoaHeads group in your area, check it out. If there's not, why not start one?

http://cocoaheads.org

NSCoder Night: NSCoder Nights are weekly, organized meetings where Cocoa programmers get together to code and socialize. Like CocoaHeads meetings, NSCoder Nights are independently organized local events.

http://nscodernight.com

Stack Overflow: This is a community site targeted at programmers. Many experienced iOS programmers hang out here and answer questions.

http://stackoverflow.com

iDeveloper TV: This is a great resource for in-depth video training in iOS and Mac development, for a price. It also contains some nice, free video content, mostly from NSConference (listed in the "Conferences" section), which is run by the same people behind iDeveloper TV.

http://ideveloper.tv

Blogs

If you still haven't found a solution to your coding dilemma, you might want to read these blogs:

Wil Shipley's blog: Wil is one of the most experienced Objective-C programmers on the planet. His *Pimp My Code* series of blog postings should be required reading for any Objective-C programmer.

http://www.wilshipley.com/blog

Wolf Rentzsch's blog: Wolf is an experienced, independent Cocoa programmer and the founder of the C4 independent developers' conference.

http://rentzsch.tumblr.com

Chris Hanson's blog: Chris works at Apple on the Xcode team, and his blog is filled with great insight and information about Xcode and related topics.

http://eschatologist.net/blog

iDev Blog a Day: This is a multiauthor blog, whose authorship rotates daily among several indie developers of iOS and Mac software. Follow this blog, and you'll be exposed to new insights from different developers every day.

`http://idevblogaday.com`

CocoaCast: This (blogs, podcasts)has a blog and podcast about various Cocoa programming topics, available in both English and French.

`http://cocoacast.com/`

Mike Ash's blog: Mike is *just this guy*, you know. This RSS feed presents Mike's collection of his ongoing iOS Friday Q&A.

`http://www.mikeash.com/pyblog/`

Conferences

Sometimes, books and web sites aren't enough. Attending an iOS-focused conference can be a great way to get new insights and meet other developers. Here are a few:

WWDC: Apple's World Wide Developer Conference is the annual event where Apple typically unleashes the next great new things for its developer community.

`http://developer.apple.com/wwdc`

MacTech: This is a conference for Mac and iOS programmers and IT professionals.

`http://www.mactechcom/conference`

NSConference: This multiple-continent event has been held in both the United Kingdom and United States, so far. It's run and promoted by Steve "Scotty" Scott, perhaps the hardest working man in the Mac/iOS conference scene.

`http://nsconference.com`

360 iDev: This approximately once-a-year conference, which is hosted in a different city each time, seems to be gaining in popularity.

`http://www.360idev.com`

iPhone/iPad DevCon: This conferenceone is a newcomer. At the time of this writing, it has been held only once so far, but it's one to keep an eye on.

`http://www.iphonedevcon.com`

Follow the Authors

Dave, Jack, and Jeff are all active Twitter users. You can follow them via @davemark, @jacknutting, and @jeff_lamarche, respectively. They all have blogs, too:

- Jeff's iOS development blog contains a lot of great technical material. Be sure to check out the comprehensive series on OpenGL ES.

  http://iphonedevelopment.blogspot.com

- Dave's blog is his little slice of everything under the sun. There's some technical material, but mostly just stuff that catches his attention.

  http://www.davemark.com

- Jack's little corner of the Internet is so scarcely updated, it practically takes the "log" out of "blog." But he keeps promising to shape things up.

  http://www.nuthole.com

> **TIP:** Are you serious about diving more deeply into the iOS SDK, and especially interested in all the great new functionality introduced with the iOS 4 SDK (of which we only scratched the surface in this book)? If so, you should check out *More iPhone 4 Development: Further Explorations of the iOS SDK* (http://apress.com/book/view/1430232528), also by Dave Mark, Jack Nutting, and Jeff LaMarche (Apress, 2011).

And if all else fails, drop us an e-mail at begin4errata@iphonedevbook.com. This is the perfect place to send messages about typos in the book or bugs in *our* code. We can't promise to respond to every e-mail message, but we will read all of them. Be sure to read the errata on the Apress site and the forums on http://iphonedevbook.com/forum before clicking *Send*. And please do write and tell us about the cool applications you develop.

Farewell

We sure are glad you came along on this journey with us. We wish you the best of luck and hope that you enjoy programming iOS as much as we do.

Index

■D

K

L

You Need the Companion eBook

Your purchase of this book entitles you to buy the companion PDF-version eBook for only $10. Take the weightless companion with you anywhere.

We believe this Apress title will prove so indispensable that you'll want to carry it with you everywhere, which is why we are offering the companion eBook (in PDF format) for $10 to customers who purchase this book now. Convenient and fully searchable, the PDF version of any content-rich, page-heavy Apress book makes a valuable addition to your programming library. You can easily find and copy code—or perform examples by quickly toggling between instructions and the application. Even simultaneously tackling a donut, diet soda, and complex code becomes simplified with hands-free eBooks!

Once you purchase your book, getting the $10 companion eBook is simple:

1. Visit **www.apress.com/promo/tendollars/**.
2. Complete a basic registration form to receive a randomly generated question about this title.
3. Answer the question correctly in 60 seconds, and you will receive a promotional code to redeem for the $10.00 eBook.

THE EXPERT'S VOICE™

233 Spring Street, New York, NY 10013

Offer valid through 7/11.